LSAT Clarity

The First Complete LSAT Self-Study Guide

Copyright 2013 Outside LSAT. All rights Reserved.
Version 1.1

Published by Outside LSAT ~ www.OutsideLSAT.com
Comments & Questions ~ support@OutsideLSAT.com

ISBN -10: 0-9844569-2-9
ISBN-13: 978-0-9844569-2-5

All actual LSAT questions used within this work are used with the permission of Law School Admission Council, Inc., Box 2000, Newtown, PA 18940, the copyright owner. LSAC does not review or endorse specific test preparation materials or services, and inclusion of licensed LSAT questions within this work does not imply the review or endorsement of LSAC. LSAT is a registered trademark of LSAC.

Printed in the United States.

Contents

Using This Book

Welcome!

Thank you for purchasing *LSAT Clarity*. There are many LSAT guides available, and everyone at Outside LSAT appreciates you choosing this one. This book is special, and I would like to take a moment to explain how. That will require a bit of my story.

I self-studied for the LSAT during the summer of 2005. Being a strong test taker and low on cash, I decided to skip the expensive classes and learn about the LSAT from a self-study book. I checked out a Princeton Review LSAT guide from the library that had strategies for each section and three simulated tests. I read and took notes on the methods and then worked through the tests. This took me a week, and I assumed that it had given me a solid foundation to beat the LSAT. Accordingly, for the rest of my prep time, I took test after test and reviewed them. It was a grueling and monotonous process. Worse, my abilities peaked two weeks before my test date. Working as hard as ever, I watched my scores slowly decline from the high 170's to the low 170's. It was incredibly frustrating. Fortunately, I performed well on the official test (a 177), so I did not feel like my hundreds of hours of prep were wasted.

A year later, I founded Outside LSAT to help others succeed on the LSAT with efficient, focused preparation. Over the past five years, I have researched the LSAT and prep course design extensively. I have also tutored over 350 students through a full, custom-built prep course. Through these experiences, I learned an enormous amount about preparing for this difficult test. Almost immediately, I realized that I made many mistakes when I self studied, making my prep more stressful and time consuming than necessary. And, a few years ago, I realized that no complete LSAT self-study book was available to help students self-prep effectively.

Traditional guides, like the one I used when I prepped, have watered down methods that expect little from the student. Further, they rarely have targeted built in practice. Books that focus on a single section of the test (the Powerscore bibles being one popular series) have powerful methods and practice, but are overly long and expensive. More importantly, they do not provide guidance on creating a full prep course.

Great LSAT prep requires learning powerful methods, completing targeted practice, and working through a balanced and structured course. This book fulfills all three requirements. *LSAT Clarity* will give you the knowledge and tools to see your path to a high score clearly. I helped create this book because it is exactly what I needed when I self-studied.

If you find this book useful, please say so with a positive review on Amazon. This will help others to benefit from it. We welcome all feedback over email at support@outsidelsat.com. This is the first edition of many, so please help us to improve it.

Good luck with your LSAT prep!

Thomas Hall
CEO, Outside LSAT

Book Features

We want to help you score your highest on the LSAT with minimal effort and stress. To this end, we built unique features into this book that cannot be found in other LSAT Guides:

Perfect Amount of Depth

This book covers the theories underlying the Logical Reasoning, Reading Comprehension, and Games sections and the question types within those sections **in detail**. Learning "meaty" methods is important in scoring your highest. More advanced methods, while vital, take practice and **experimentation** to yield results. We will not teach you simple tricks, but new ways of approaching the LSAT that will allow you to make major progress. Learning complex methods is worth the time investment, because the LSAT is both difficult and difficult to improve on.

That being said, we have provided only the methods you really need. The LSAT requires some flexibility in approach, so we will not overload you with ultra-precise methods. The test is constantly evolving, but remains consistent in the skills tested. We have focused on the most useful skills. Much of the progress in LSAT prep comes from learning during practice what works best **for you**. These methods will give you a solid base for the practice you complete after working with this book.

Extensive Practice

Because the three section types test unfamiliar skills, practice is the core of good LSAT prep. To use an analogy, someone with a great understanding of how to surf will not become a great surfer until they take to the ocean, again and again. There is no substitute for lots of time riding waves. The same is true on the LSAT: you must **practice** the methods that you learn. Accordingly, most chapters have built-in practice questions and explanations. These should be completed immediately after reading the chapter. Additionally, problem sets in the *10 More Actual Official LSAT Book* (or 10 More book) are provided.

In Depth Prep Guidance

Effective prep requires experience with the LSAT. We have built our experience and knowledge into two detailed schedules that will help you work through the book. Prepping consistently is crucial, and following a day-by-day schedule will help you to do that. The schedules cover a range of different ability levels, allowing any student to effectively work through them. There is a "Key Concepts" schedule if you have limited prep time before your LSAT.

The final section of this chapter teaches you how to build an effective, full-length LSAT course using readily available and inexpensive materials. This is difficult as choosing which sections/tests to take and when to take them is complex. This guidance is based on years of teaching experience working one-on-one with hundreds of students. This chapter alone is worth the price of this book.

Outlines

The methods of each chapter and some sections are concluded by an outline of its core concepts. Read each outline after the methods to cement your learning. The outlines are also an easy way to refresh yourself on methods as you progress further into your prep. They will keep the key methods fresh in your mind.

Free Supplemental Packet

Your purchase of this book includes an electronic Supplemental Packet: LSAT Simulations MP3 files, a Comparative Reading Chapter, a Prep Journal, and a Test Day Guide. All four materials are valuable during your preparation.

Use our LSAT Simulations to have authentic test experiences before your official test. The audio tracks will walk you through the instructions and timing of the test. One track is silent and the other features realistic test noises and distractions. Load the tracks on an MP3 player or phone and use them whenever you take a practice LSAT to greatly increase the authenticity of the experience. This is as close as you can get to an official LSAT. The simulations will help you relax during your official test because you will be so familiar with the testing process. That will help your score.

The Comparative Reading chapter provides methods for the Comparative Reading passage set in the Reading Comprehension (or RC) section. These strategies are valuable when you are taking recent Tests (52 and up) that feature this unique passage set. We simply could not fit this chapter in this book!

Refine your techniques on the different question types and learn from your mistakes using the handy Prep Journal. Easily track your experiments with the methods during your prep. Also, track the errors you are making on different question types. Take notes on each full test you take. A must have. I recommend you print out this document.

Your Test Day Guide will ensure that you understand the rules and regulations of the test with a cleanly formatted packet on the procedures. Also, prepare smoothly the day before your test with an easy-to-use checklist.

Request Your Packet

To receive your Packet, please send an email to **packet@outsidelsat.com**.

Include in the email:

- Your First and Last Name
- Your expected LSAT date

We sincerely respect your privacy. Your information will be kept strictly confidential.

The Packet is free and extremely helpful. Please request it now!

Background Information

This chapter will give you foundational information helpful for using this book and preparing for the LSAT. Please read it in its entirety.

LSAT Facts

Because the LSAT is vitally important in the admissions process, you cannot treat your LSAT preparation too seriously. At most schools, your LSAT score is worth about 60% of your application. It is roughly **twice as important as your college GPA**. That is right: A test that takes a little over three hours is much more important to law schools than four years of academic work. This is because the LSAT is truly standardized and admissions committees can accurately use it to compare the aptitude of different applicants. That is not the case with GPAs from different schools and majors. Is a 3.4 GPA in engineering at the University of Texas more impressive than a 3.6 in English at Princeton University? Hard to say. But a 167 LSAT score is definitely superior to a 162.

Law school is extremely academic, featuring enormous amounts of reading and writing. Accordingly, admissions committees want students who can read and think logically at a high level. The LSAT is currently the best measure of these abilities. To admissions committees, the LSAT is the holy grail of applicant measures.

The Higher Your Score, The Better

Because admissions committees are obsessed with your LSAT score, you should be too. The quality of a law school has a large impact on your future career, so get accepted to the best schools you can. To do that, you have to earn the highest LSAT score possible. A great LSAT score will not only help you gain admission to better schools, it can save you money. When a school really wants you, it will offer you scholarships to entice you to enroll.

You Control Your Score

It would be rude to tell you how important your LSAT score is if it were not possible to greatly improve it. Fortunately, you can raise your score enormously with diligent prep. Our average full-course student improves 11 points from her diagnostic to **her official test**. A diagnostic score is inflated by at least two points because it is taken in a low stress environment different from the official test. This means that Outside LSAT students actually increase their score about 13 points. Going from a 151 (the average LSAT score of all takers) to a 164 opens all kinds of law school doors. We are not saying this to toot our own horn. Instead, we want to illustrate that with proper preparation, you can vastly increase your LSAT skills. The same methods and theories that help our full course students are encapsulated in this book.

Give it Your All

Unfortunately, the LSAT is a not an easy test to improve on. The test measures skills that take time to build. The timing pressures are intense, and the official test is very stressful, even for well prepared students. If you are serious about acquiring a JD, give your LSAT prep everything you can. Beyond giving yourself plenty of time to prepare (three and a half months is ideal for most students), focus on getting the most out of **each prep session**. Here are pieces of advice along these lines:

The Little Things Make a Big Difference

How much effort you put into **each prep session** will largely determine how much your score increases. The details are what LSAT prep is all about. We have found a direct correlation between how precise the emails are that we receive from a student and how much her score ultimately increases (our full courses use an Email tutoring format). Students who send regular, detailed emails increase their scores dramatically; students who email sparingly do not raise their scores as much. Emails are an indication of a student's attention to detail. How much you care about the little things in your prep will dictate how successful it is. For instance, you should read the methods presented here quite intently and review every question you miss thoroughly.

Employ the Methods

If you do not actively use the methods, you limit your progress. Using methods is **an active process**: you will often need to correct less efficient ways of tackling the questions that may initially feel more natural. Be conscious of how you approach each question early in your prep.

Practice Intensely

Attempt to answer **every** practice question correctly. Early on in your prep, take your time on the practice questions. This will help you explore the methods and learn how to get to the correct answer on different question types. Do not settle for careless errors in your prep.

Review the questions thoroughly and learn from your mistakes. Review is **crucial** for progress and will be discussed in detail.

Prep When You are Fresh

Prep at **an optimal time** each day, so that you are fresh and alert. For most students, the earlier the better. After a long day of work, you cannot deal as effectively with complex sentences and logic. Take advantage of days when you have more free time. If you are working full time, complete some prep before work or during your lunch break.

Quiet Environment

Prepare in a quiet, isolated environment where you will **not be distracted**. Because prep requires so much focus, distractions take a serious toll on efficiency. Noisy coffee shops are not a good place to prep. Libraries and your own home are.

Get Plenty of Sleep

Your brain consolidates learning when you sleep. Not sleeping enough will slow down your progress. Further, feeling rested for each prep session is crucial, as the LSAT requires an enormous amount of focus. Sleep more than you normally do during your prep.

Built in Practice

All official LSATs you use during your prep are tests that were administered in the past. There are two different groups of official LSAT questions provided throughout the book to supplement learning the methods:

Practice Questions

Practice questions are official LSAT questions built into the text after a chapter or section. They help you practice the methods you have just learned. For this reason, they should be completed immediately after reading the corresponding methods.

The practice questions are drawn almost exclusively from the 10 Actual book (Tests 7-18). These questions are all very difficult, ensuring that you practice the methods on questions that push you. The number of practice questions given roughly corresponds to how common that Logical Reasoning (or LR) question or game type is. Thorough explanations are provided immediately after each group of practice questions. To avoid accidentally looking at the answers as you work the questions, you may need to cover the explanations with a sheet of paper.

A group of LR practice questions will deal with a single LR question type. The same is true with game types. Reading Comprehension (or RC) practice questions are divided by the content of the passage: Humanities, Law, Social Sciences and Natural Sciences. Practice questions in the RC section are only provided after the final RC chapters. You need to build up all the skills in the previous chapters to approach a passage set.

Problem Sets

Problem sets are an Outside LSAT exclusive. Problem sets feature **groups of related question types**. For instance, the first LR problem sets have three types of Deduction questions: True Deduction, False Deduction and Core Deduction questions. A problem set tests you on question types that have been explained in the previous one or more chapters.

The problem sets provide practice on a group of similar skills. When you work the Flaw problem sets, you face two different question types (Flawed Parallel Structure and Flaw questions) that both test your ability to identify the flaw in a LR passage. Working related question types helps you simultaneously hone the underlying skills in the methods and get ready for full sections.

The problem sets are drawn from the 10 More Actual Official LSATs book (10 More book, Tests 19-28). You need to purchase that book to complete them. The book costs $19 on Amazon and is well worth it. If you plan on self-studying for your prep, we recommend doing one large Amazon order for prep supplies so that you can get all the extra books at once and utilize free shipping. More on which books to order at the end of the next chapter.

The problem sets are references to specific questions **within the 10 More book**. Provided question sheets tell you which questions to work. Two example questions:

19 / 2 # **17** Ⓐ Ⓑ Ⓒ Ⓓ Ⓔ
19 / 4 # **13** Ⓐ Ⓑ Ⓒ Ⓓ Ⓔ

The first question is from test 19, section 2. It is question number 17. To complete that question in the problem set, you would open the 10 More book, turn to test 19, flip to the second section and complete question #17. The next question in the problem set is test 19, section 4, question number 13. There are two LR sections in every full test. Answer keys are provided after the question sheets to help you quickly correct your work.

Each group of problem sets is divided into three difficulty levels: average, difficult and grueling. This division allows you to prep at an appropriate level for your skills. This will be discussed in detail in the section on using the book schedules.

Review Thoroughly

Throughout your prep, carefully review all questions that you answer incorrectly. Also review all questions that you **do not feel confident** about, but did answer correctly. Review may feel like a secondary step in the prep process, but it is absolutely crucial. During review you learn better ways to approach the questions. Review is also the perfect time to analyze challenging questions in depth. With no clock ticking and knowing the correct answer, you can truly pick apart a question. Here is our recommended approach for reviewing a question:

1. Determine why the correct answer is correct.

First, read the correct choice and question stem (the specific question asked) carefully to ensure that you understand both. Then, use all available information to help you understand **why the choice correctly answers the question**. On LR questions, read the passage and look for how the correct choice interacts with it. On RC questions, carefully refer to the passage to find the proof for the correct answer. On Games questions, use the setup, rules and your diagramming and inferences to understand the correct answer.

Be **crystal clear** on why the correct choice is correct before you move on to the next question to review. If you get stuck and cannot figure out why the choice is correct, carefully reread both the question and the choice to be sure you have not missed something. If you still do not understand why the correct choice is correct, reference an explanation for the question (this is typically the fourth step in review).

2. Determine why the answer you chose is incorrect.

Again, use all the available information to understand why the choice you selected is inferior to the correct answer. Compare your choice with the correct choice to find where they differ. Make sure you are clear on the meaning of the entire choice. Many incorrect choices have parts that are correct and other parts that cause them to be incorrect.

If you answered the question correctly, determine why **any tempting answer choices** are incorrect. In this case, you should skip step three.

3. Determine why you chose that incorrect choice.

This is not a difficult step, but it is one often overlooked. Articulate what went wrong when you solved the question the first time. Did you misread the choice? Did you miss an important inference on a game? Did you not understand part of an RC passage? Whatever the case may be, say in your own words why you missed the question. Be specific. Then, write down in your Prep Journal (from the Supplemental Packet) what you learned.

This step will help you to avoid a similar mistake in the future. Analyzing why you fell for an incorrect choice will help you see how you are approaching the question and how your approach needs to be adjusted for optimum performance.

4. Read an explanation to the question.

The final review step, reading a well thought-out explanation, will help you see how an LSAT professional views the question. This knowledge can help with the other reviewing steps. Using an explanation is the final review step because you should **complete the first three steps on your own**. Personally struggling with a question typically consolidates the learning more effectively than having someone else point out how the question works. So, only after step three, thoroughly use an explanation to be confident that you have a full grasp of the question. If you are stuck on step one, take another look at the question before you read an explanation.

Only the practice questions in this book have included explanations; the problem sets do not. A solid explanation to most LSAT questions can be found for free on the Manhattan LSAT website. Go to:

www.manhattanlsat.com/blog/index.php/tag/lsat-explanations

or google "Manhattan LSAT explanations" to find them.

Review Often During Practice

When working the practice questions and problem sets in the schedules provided in this book, review after **every four LR questions**, and **after every passage or game**. Reviewing often allows you to learn from your mistakes constantly as you practice. Also, the approach you took on the question is fresh in your mind when you review, which is helpful in analyzing mistakes made.

Take your review seriously and your LSAT skills will progress quickly. Only through refinement of your question approaches can you drastically improve your accuracy and speed.

Book Schedules & Diagnostic

Book Schedules

To help you effectively learn the methods in this book, we have provided two detailed daily schedules. The Complete Schedule covers every concept presented and includes prep sessions to work the problem sets. It is 33 sessions long. The Key Concepts Schedule is abbreviated: it does not include some of the less important chapters or the problem sets. This schedule does include the practice questions. Each of these schedules is for the first phase of your course, the Methods Phase.

You should work the Complete schedule unless you have less than a month and a half to devote to your preparation. In that case, work the Key Concept schedule. Further guidance on which schedule to use is provided in the next chapter.

LR Methods First

Each schedule begins with the LR methods. Because the two LR sections in every test are worth 50% of your score, it makes sense to learn that section all by itself. Then, you can tackle the methods of the remaining two sections. Your Methods Phase utilizes LR drills (taking half of an LR section) to keep those skills up as you learn about the RC and Games sections. You will need the Next 10 book (Tests 29-38) to complete those drills.

A Prep Session

A prep session is a group of assignments in your schedule designed to be completed in one sitting. The readings and/or practice are all of a related theme. For instance, one prep session might include reading the LR True Deduction question methods and then completing the True Deduction practice questions.

It is possible to complete two prep sessions in a single **calendar day**. If you do, separate the two sessions by at least two hours, so that you are fresh for the second session. For instance, on a Sunday, you might complete prep session 13 in the Complete schedule from 9 -11 AM. Then, from 5-7 PM you might complete session 14. So, in one calendar day (Sunday), you have completed two prep sessions (LR Methods Sessions 13 + 14). It is also possible to complete half of a prep session in a day. For instance, if you are strapped for time on a Monday night, you might complete the first half of prep session 15 from your LR schedule. You could then finish that session the next morning.

For a vast majority of students, each session will take between one and a half and two and a half hours. Each session is designed to be completed in one sitting, so try to do so. However, completing a full prep session can sometimes be difficult. If you plan to do some prep on a given day, doing less than a full session is better than completing no prep that day. The exception to this rule is when you are ill or extremely tired and the prep will be very low quality. On such days, you may wish to take an "off" day.

Off Days

Taking off days from prep is important to help you avoid burnout. We recommend taking at least one off day each week when you do not complete a prep session.

However, too many off days each week slow progress. So, once you begin preparing, **do not take more than two days off in a row**. Even an hour of prep on a given day will help you to keep your skills up. The example weekly prep schedules that follow shortly all have no more than one off day in a row.

Diagnostic

An important first step in using the book schedules is to take a diagnostic test. This baseline score will also help you track your progress during your prep.

A Recent LSAT Taken Under Official Timing

Your diagnostic needs to be similar to your upcoming LSAT to be a realistic baseline. LSAC, the company that administers the LSAT, offers a free LSAT that is perfect. It is the June 2007 LSAT, which we call test 51.5, because it was administered after Test 51 (The Dec. 2006 LSAT) and before Test 52 (Sept. 07). Go online and download and print the PDF file:

www.lsac.org/jd/pdfs/SamplePTJune.pdf

If that link is no longer valid, google "June 2007 LSAT." The first link referencing LSAC's site (www.LSAC.org) should be the correct one. If all else fails, check out www.LSAC.org and navigate to the "free prep materials."

Official Timing

The diagnostic needs to be taken under **official timing constraints**: a 35 minute time limit per section, with a 10 minute break after the third section. These time limits ensure that your performance is realistic. If you have taken a full official LSAT but you spent 40 minutes on each section or it was Test #37, then take another diagnostic. Or, if you are getting started again with the LSAT after a long break, take a diagnostic. You can also use tests 52 and up if you have already taken test 51.5 without official timing.

Take It

Once you download the file, **print it**. The LSAT is a paper and pencil test, so taking it on the computer is not ok. Next, figure out a time when you have two and a half hours free, the amount of time the test requires.

Take the test when you are rested and ready for it. Find a quiet, secluded place where you will not be distracted. A desk in your room is ideal, and libraries work well especially if they have quiet study rooms. Do your best on the test, but do not worry. The test will likely feel challenging, and the time restraints will be difficult. This will be the only time you take an LSAT without knowledge of the test.

Scaled Score

Use the answer key at the end of the test to score it, and add up the number of correct responses in the four sections. That is your raw score. Use it to find your scaled score in the table. Your scaled score is out of 180, and it is the one that counts. Any scaled score is directly comparable to any other scaled score. A 155 on the June 2000 test represents the same LSAT ability level as a 155 on the June 2011 test, even if the raw scores that earned those two scaled scores differ.

We designate three different ability levels based on your diagnostic scaled score:

Level	Score
High	155 +
Average	154 – 146
Low	145 -

A 150 is an average score, a 160 is a high score, and a 142 is a low score. For students at the extremes: a 161 or higher is a **very high** score, while a 139 or lower is a **very low** score. Remember, you can drastically improve your LSAT score, so if you start with a low score, realize you can improve it.

Using the Schedules

The Methods Phase Schedules in this book are designed for a student with an average diagnostic score. Each prep session will take such a student **about two hours** to complete. Likewise, the problem sets assigned (not the practice questions) are geared for average students. The distribution is centered around the difficult sets: some of the average sets, all of the difficult sets, and some of the grueling sets are assigned. If you are an average student, work the schedules just as they are, and expect each prep session to take about two hours. If you are a low or high student, then the schedules will work well for you too, but you should make some adjustments to them in terms of timing expectation and which problem sets are completed.

Low students: the readings and questions will likely take you longer than predicted in the schedules. So, each session might take you two and a half hours instead of two. If you are a very low student, each prep session might take you three hours. Ideally, work through each prep session in a single sitting. Or, you can sometimes take two days to finish a prep session as needed. On sessions devoted to the problem sets, you will need to stray from what is assigned. Your goal: complete **all of the average sets** and **some or all of the difficult sets**. It is probably not necessary to work any of the grueling problem sets.

High students: each prep session in the schedules will likely take you less than two hours. This is a good thing, because it means you can work through the schedules more quickly. When possible, complete two prep sessions in a single calendar day. Very high students should find this fairly easy to do. Regarding the problem sets: work all of the difficult and grueling problem sets. Skip the average sets as those questions will not be difficult for you.

Cut Them Out

Note that the schedules are designed to be cut out of this book so that they are easier to use. To do so, turn to the beginning of the schedules. Hold that page in your finger tips and then find the last page of the schedules. Use scissors to cut out the pages you are holding. Cut along the dashed line on the final page of the schedules.

Timing & Pacing

A two hour prep session is a comfortable stretch of time for most students to prepare. Any less time per session will build less mental endurance, a very important aspect of prep. Mental endurance is only built through long prep sessions. We use the term <u>pacing</u> to refer to how many prep sessions you complete each week. An ideal pacing is **six prep sessions a week**, assuming you have three months or more to prep.

If your LSAT date is far off (more than four months away) and you wish to spread out a schedule, you can take two or more off days each week. This is not necessarily recommended, as the more prep you complete the better. It is almost impossible to prepare too much. Most students should complete six prep sessions or more a week.

If you have more time available for prep (four hours on some days), you can complete **two prep sessions in a single day**. Separate those sessions by at least two hours, so that you are not mentally fatigued for the second prep session. Much more detail on planning your course schedule follows in the chapter on page 20, "LSAT Course Theory."

Building Your Weekly Prep Schedule

A good length LSAT course is about 72 prep sessions spread out over **three or more months**. If you have three or more months before your test, work the Complete Methods Phase Schedule, not the Key Concepts schedule. You can work through the schedule, and then plan the rest of your course with help from the LSAT Course Theory chapter. If you have less than three months to prepare, you may need to use the Key Concepts Methods Phase Schedule. If you are in this situation, you should read the LSAT Course Theory section **before beginning your Methods Phase**.

Regardless of course length, completing six prep sessions a week is ideal for most students. That will be ~12 hours of prep a week for average students, ~10 hours for high students, and ~15 hours for low. In general, the less off days you take each week, the better, and always avoid taking more than two days off in a row.

Below are three weekly plans with six, 2-hour prep sessions. These plans will work well for your entire course. We introduce them now so you can work through your Methods Phase without having to venture into the complexity of LSAT Course Theory. The time estimates given are for average students.

Balanced

In a Balanced schedule, prep is spread out evenly across the week. This is the ideal schedule. One prep session is completed each day, Sunday through Friday. There is one off day a week. Example schedule:

Day:	Mon	Tues	Wed	Thurs	Fri	Sat	Sun	Totals
Sessions:	1	1	1	1	1	0	1	**6**
Hours:	2	2	2	2	2	0	2	**12**

Weekend Focus

On a Weekend Focus schedule, the majority of prep is completed on the weekends. This schedule is effective for students busy during the work week. The student only prepares two week days. Ideally, that prep is completed before work or during her lunch break so that she is fresh for it. Two prep sessions are completed on Saturday and Sunday and one on Tuesday and Thursday. There are three off days a week in this example: Monday, Wednesday and Friday.

Day:	Mon	Tues	Wed	Thurs	Fri	Sat	Sun	Totals
Sessions:	0	1	0	1	0	2	2	**6**
Hours:	0	2	0	2	0	4	4	**12**

Weekday Focus

In a Weekday Focus schedule, a majority of prep is completed during the work week to free up the weekends. This is a great schedule for those who have time and wish to prep during the weekdays. Two prep sessions are conducted on Thursday and one on Monday, Tuesday, Wednesday and Friday. Saturday and Sunday are off each week.

Day:	Mon	Tues	Wed	Thurs	Fri	Sat	Sun	Totals
Sessions:	1	1	1	2	1	0	0	**6**
Hours:	2	2	2	4	2	0	0	**12**

LSAT Course Theory

This chapter will teach you how to design a full LSAT course for yourself. It will help you structure your prep successfully **after** you finish a Methods Phase schedule provided in this book. A highly effective, three phase, self-study course can be created fairly simply.

However, if this process feels overwhelming, or if you want to be positive that you use your prep time as efficiently as possible, we can help. Outside LSAT provides completely personalized prep courses with email support – visit **www.OutsideLSAT.com** to learn more. If you wish to design your own course, read on. We recommend reading this chapter now and again when you finish your Methods Phase.

A successful LSAT course needs to have balance: you must learn the right skills at the right times. You also need to use the available tests wisely; they are not all of equal value. Further, slowly adding to the complexity of your practice is vital. Dividing your prep into three distinct phases will accomplish all these requirements. Each phase has a specific goal for the skills you are building. It took us years to hone this knowledge, so implement the concepts in this chapter wisely, young padawan.

Methods Phase

Learning methods is the focus of the first phase of your course, the Methods Phase. The final two phases have you practice the methods you learn in this first phase. Without first solidly learning strategies, you cannot effectively build on them.

Planning your Methods Phase is made easy by the schedules in this book. How to use a schedule was covered in the previous chapter: take a diagnostic, learn how to modify the schedules for your ability level (if necessary), and then work through either the Complete or Keystone Methods Phase schedule. How quickly you should work through the schedule depends to some degree on the length of your course, which will be discussed at the end of this chapter. For most students, completing six prep sessions each week while working through the schedule is perfect.

The LSAT questions you complete during your Methods Phase are individual types (the practice questions) or questions grouped by the skill required (the problem sets). This narrow focus will help you to integrate the methods you read about. Recall that the practice questions in this book are drawn from the 10 Actual book (Tests 7-18) and the problem sets are drawn from the 10 More book (Tests 19-28).

The Most Important Phase

Give your Methods Phase ample time. The Complete Methods Phase schedule is 33 sessions. Contrast that with 20 sessions for the sample Practice Phase and 19 for the sample Tests Phase (you will see these shortly). Learning the methods comfortably takes time. For most students, about 40-50% of your prep time should be devoted to the Methods Phase. However, if your course is longer than three months, you might devote closer to a third of your time to your Methods Phase.

Tracking Your Progress

Great LSAT prep requires constant progress. During your Methods Phase, you should learn the methods steadily and become more comfortable with the practice questions you work. If you do not, slow down your reading of the methods and working of the questions. The Methods Phase is about **understanding**, not speed.

Practice Phase

The second phase of your course, your Practice Phase, has you hone the methods on **full sections**. This phase is the bridge between learning the methods and taking full tests during your Tests Phase (the final phase of your course). Your Practice Phase is the time to get comfortable with the sections and to hone the methods without the pressures associated with a full test. This phase is focused on practice, but you should also review the methods. The outlines of each chapter are a great resource when you want a refresher on specific methods but do not wish to reread a full chapter.

During this phase, **experiment with the methods**. You will know them fairly well, so tweak them to see what works best for you. For instance, try reading the RC (Reading Comprehension) passages more slowly than you normally do. See if that helps you to answer the questions more quickly. Or, try taking longer to envision a good answer on LR question types susceptible to envisioning. Take notes on your experiments in your Prep Journal.

Part One: Intermediate Timing

Divide your Practice Phase into two parts. Part One should take about half of the time allotted for your Practice Phase. Use the **Next 10 book** (Tests 29-38) as the source of practice sections during your Practice Phase. Use the first six tests (#'s 29-34) for Part One.

Same Section Practice

Part of the difficulty of the LSAT is that you have to deal with three different types of sections in each test. Remove that challenge in Part One by taking two of the same type of section during each prep session. This repetition will help you embrace the methods of the section more fully. Read chapter outlines of your choosing before your prep to build your skills in specific areas. For example, on a day when you take two RC sections, you might first read the outline for the chapter "Marking a Passage." Then, when you work those two RC sections, focus on marking the passages effectively. Review each section thoroughly **immediately after you complete it**. The sooner you review a section after taking it, the better you will remember the difficulties that you faced.

Reading several chapter outlines and then taking and reviewing two sections will require about two and half hours for most students. Getting in two full sections in a session is worth this time commitment.

Start with Untimed Practice

Initially, facing a full section where you must identify and attack a variety of question types is challenging. For this reason, practice during Part One will be untimed or within an Intermediate Time Limit. For the first few sessions, you should take the sections **with no time limit**. Work at a comfortable pace until you finish the section. Do time each section to see how long it takes you, so you can track how long you are spending. We recommend using a digital timer for this stage of your prep, although you will switch to an analog watch for timing in your Tests Phase.

Intermediate Time Limit

After that initial untimed period, complete your sections in an Intermediate Time Limit (ITL). Your ITL will force you to work with a time constraint but one that is more lax than 35 minutes per section. Calculate your Logical Reasoning ITL by timing yourself while you take a LR section at a **comfortable pace**. Push yourself slightly on speed, but do not rush. Take that number of minutes and **average it with 35**. That will yield your Logical Reasoning ITL.

For instance, if the LR section takes you 45 minutes, then your ITL is 40 minutes: 45 +35 = 80; 80/2 = 40. Calculate your RC and Games ITLs in the same way. High students: if the section you use to calculate your ITL takes you less than 35 minutes, use 35 minutes as your ITL. It is not helpful to practice finishing sections more quickly than the official timing.

When you take sections with your ITL, realize that you may need to guess on some questions if you do not have time to attempt them. Calculate your score including the questions you guessed on. Next, **before you review the section**, complete any questions that you did not have time to attempt initially. Finally, correct those questions, and then review the entire section.

Practice Phase: Part One - Sample Schedule (10 Sessions)

This sample schedule will give you an idea how to work through Part One of your Practice Phase. Note that the LR sections from Tests 29 + 30 were used during your Methods Phase.

Session 1

- Read two RC Chapter Outlines of your choice
- 29/2 (RC) – complete it untimed | review
- 30/3 (RC) – untimed | review

Session 2

- Read two Games Chapter Outlines
- 29/3 (G) – untimed | review
- 30/1 (G) – untimed | review

Session 3

- Read two LR Chapter Outlines
- 31/2 (LR) – untimed | review
- 31/4 (LR) – untimed | review

Session 4

- Read two RC Outlines
- 31/4 (RC) – time it | Calculate RC ITL | review
- 32/2 (RC) – complete in RC ITL | review

Session 5

- Read two Games Outlines
- 31/1 (G) – time it | Calculate G ITL | review
- 32/3 (G) – G ITL | review

Session 6

- Read two LR Outlines
- 32/1 (LR) – time it| Calculate LR ITL | review
- 32/3 (LR) – LR ITL | review

Session 7

- Read two RC Outlines
- 33/3 (RC) – RC ITL | review
- 34/1 (RC) – RC ITL | review

Session 8

- Read two LR Outlines
- 33/1 (LR) – LR ITL | review
- 33/3 (LR) – LR ITL | review

Session 9

- Read two Games Outlines
- 33/4 (G) – G ITL | review
- 34/4 (G) – G ITL | review

Session 10

- Read two LR Outlines
- 34/2 (LR) – LR ITL | review
- 34/3 (LR) – LR ITL | review

Tracking Your Progress

Your section scores should increase as you get accustomed to your ITLs. You should get faster and more accurate with more exposure to the questions. If you are not improving, more actively employ the methods. Also, make sure you are pacing yourself correctly: attempt less or more questions and see the results.

Part Two: 35 Minute Timing + Mixed Sections

Part Two of your Practice Phase will build your mental endurance: the ability to retain your skills when taking more than one section in a row. To do this, you will need to take two sections in a row **without pausing**. Review the two sections **after completing both**. Also, take off the timing training wheels: complete each section in Part Two in **35 minutes**. Learn to pace yourself to maximize your score. For most students, an appropriate pace feels quick but not rushed. You cannot rush the foundational work required by each section. During the LR sections, read the passage carefully. On Games, take time with the setup, and on RC, read the passage carefully.

During Part Two, shift to completing **two mixed sections** each session by working the sections in Tests 35-38 in order. For instance, in one session take 35/1 (a LR section) and 35/2 (a RC section). The next session, complete 35/3 (Games) and 35/4 (LR), and so on with Test 36 during the next prep session.

Test Every Five Days

Take a four section LSAT from the Next 10 book (Tests 52-61) about once **every five calendar days** during Part Two. Use an LSAT Simulation to time yourself. The test(s) will help the transition to your Tests Phase. Review each the day after you take it. If you work Part Two quickly, you will only take one test during it. If you take many off days during this part, you will take two tests.

Sample Part Two Schedule (10 sessions)

Session 1

- 35/1 + 35/2 | complete each in 35 minutes
- Review both sections

Session 2

- 35/3 + 35/4 | 35 minutes / section
- Review both sections

Session 3

- 36/1 + 36/2 |35 minutes / section
- Review both sections

Session 4

- 36/3 + 36/4 |35 minutes / section
- Review both sections

Session 5

- Test 52 | 35 minutes/section with a 10 minute break after section 3

Session 6

- Review Test 52; work any questions you did not attempt

Session 7

- 37/1 + 37/2 | 35 minutes / section
- Review both sections

Session 8

- 37/3 + 37/4 | 35 minutes / section
- Review both sections

Session 9

- 38/1 + 38/2 | 35 minutes / section
- Review both sections

Session 10

- 38/3 + 38/4 | 35 minutes / section
- Review both sections

Tracking Progress

If your ITL was 37 minutes or higher, your scores will probably dip when you switch to 35 minute timing. However, once you get into the swing of Part Two, you should see your scores steadily increase on all three sections. If you are not improving, be sure you are employing the methods and pacing yourself correctly. Also, increase the quality and time you spend reviewing each section. Learn from your mistakes.

Tests Phase

Your Tests Phase is when you put all your skills together on four- and five-section tests. Taking many tests is the best way to build your mental endurance so you can succeed on the final sections of your official test. On those, your skills will be compromised if you have not prepared to intensely focus for several hours in a row.

Scheduling: Three or Four Tests a Week

Taking **recent** official tests is crucial as they will be the most similar to your official test. Use the 10 New book (Tests 52-61) during your Tests Phase. Take **three or four** tests a week, with one of those as a five-section test. The day after you take a test, review it. On review sessions, you can reread the methods and/or work on specific question types giving you trouble. This schedule allows you to review carefully, and it is important that you **do not take a test daily**.

Try to take **at least nine** full tests during your Tests Phase to be ready for the real thing. If you have the time, purchase Tests 62 through the most recent available and add those to the end of this phase. Take the most recent tests immediately before your official test. Relax and rest the day before your official test; do not complete any prep.

Longer Sessions

Taking a test requires two and a half hours, which is a longer than most prep sessions in these schedules. This is balanced by the fact that reviewing the test the next day will likely take about an hour, even when you have to complete questions you did not attempt on the test. If you need more off days, take a test and review it on the same day so you can take the next day off.

Test Environment

Where you take the tests is important. Because the official test is uncomfortable and stressful, take every test in a quiet yet foreign environment, instead of in your room. Use a place where you will not be distracted and where you can work comfortably at a desk. Libraries are excellent; coffee shops tend to be too loud.

Use one of the **LSAT Simulations** to time each test. Having the timing out of your control is helpful because that mimics the official test. Primarily use the simulation without distractions, but mix in the track with distractions a few times. Note that the simulations are built for five section tests, so when you take a four section test, simply stop after the fourth section. Whenever time is called, put your pencil down, just as you will on the real exam. Always **guess on all questions** in a section before time runs out.

Speaking of timing, use an **analog wristwatch** to pace yourself on all sections during your Tests Phase. Digital watches are not allowed during the official test. If you do not have one, an analog watch is easily obtained at a large retailer. We recommend one with a bezel so that you can quickly track 35 minutes from any starting time.

Pretend that each test is the real thing: score your absolute highest on each one.

Five-Section Tests

The official test has five sections, but only four of them are scored (typically, one of the first three sections is the one not scored). You need to be able to tackle five sections effectively, and that means taking **several five-section tests**. We recommend primarily building your skills on four-section tests, because five-section tests are more difficult to fit in and are exhausting. You should not take more than four five-section tests.

One small issue is that all previously administered LSATs feature only the four scored sections. **Supplement** a four-section test with an additional section to "make" a five section test. Use a section from the June 2007 Test as the supplemental section. For example, Test 53 plus the section one of Test 51.5 will yield a five section test. Although you used the June 2007 test as your diagnostic, you have not seen it in a while and you never reviewed it. The timing for a five-section test is just like a four-section one: take a 10 minute break after section three. After the break, complete **two more sections**. Derive your scaled score from the four-section portion of the test, but remember to correct and review the supplemental section.

Additional Question Type Work

You can effectively add to your prep with work **focused on your weak areas.** Use challenging question sets like those found in our *Advanced LSAT Practice* book ($45 on Amazon, ALP for short). These questions are drawn from tests 1-28, so there will be some questions you saw early in your prep, but this should not be a problem because the questions were taken several months ago. Other question type workout books are available, but they focus on a single section and include easy and average questions. An hour of prep from this book targeting your weak areas can drastically increase your skills on specific LR types, Game types and RC passage types.

Sample Tests Schedule (19 sessions)

Session 1 - Test 53

Session 2 - Review the test + type work from ALP

Session 3 - Test 54

Session 4 - Review the test + type work

Session 5 - Test 55 + 51.5/1 (Five-Section Test)

Session 6 - Review the test + type work

Session 7 - Test 56

Session 8 - Review the test + type work

Session 9 - Test 57

Session 10 - Review the test + type work

Session 11 - Test 58 + 51.5/2 (Five-Section Test)

Session 12 - Review the test + type work

Session 13 - Test 59

Session 14 - Review the test + type work

Session 15 - Test 60 + 51.5/3 (Five-Section Test)

Session 16 - Review the test + type work

Session 17 - Test 61

Session 18 - Review the test + type work

Session 19 - Relax and Rest Day

Session 20 - Your Official Test Date

Tracking Progress

Your scaled scores should rise steadily throughout this phase, and you should be scoring at least 10 points higher than your diagnostic by the middle of the phase. If you are not, make sure you are getting enough sleep. Also, lower your stress with daily vigorous exercise, as stress can be a problem as you get closer to your test. As always, be sure that you are reviewing carefully and learning from your mistakes.

Adjusting the Schedules

Now that you have a general understanding of how to craft your LSAT prep course, we will teach you how to adjust the sample schedules for the length of time you have until your test. But first, a request: do not rush your LSAT prep. We strongly recommend preparing for **at least three months** or about 70 prep sessions. Even if you have a high diagnostic score or a great GPA, scoring extra points earned with more prep is well worth it. Recall that maximizing your LSAT score can not only get you into the best schools possible, it can also help you earn thousands of dollars in scholarships. If you have less than three months before your test, consider taking the next LSAT.

The Best Test Administrations

Applying late in the admissions cycle puts you at a disadvantage, so the best tests to take are the June and September/October tests. So, if you are rushing to prep for the June test, consider taking the September/October one instead. The December test is fine, if you earn the score you want on it. The problem there is that you cannot easily retake if the test does not go well. The February test is rarely ok unless you have already taken the test and use it to boost your score to gain acceptance to schools you have already applied to. If pushing your test back means taking the February LSAT instead of the December one, consider waiting another year to apply. Waiting can actually be helpful for your career: with more time to prep for the LSAT and prepare your applications, you will be accepted at better schools. Further, you can get more work experience before law school that can help you get more out of the experience.

That said, we will now teach you how to adjust the schedules to the specific **length of time you have to prepare**. You may not find an exact match for your needs, but you will be given enough guidance to craft an effective course. First decide how many prep sessions you can realistically complete each week, then read on.

Three to Three and a Half Months to Prep

The Complete Methods schedule and the sample Practice and Tests Phase schedules in this chapter add up to 72 prep sessions. If you complete six prep sessions a week, an ideal weekly pace, then the schedules will take you exactly **three months**. If you complete five prep sessions a week (also a fine pace), then the schedules will take you just over **three and a half months**. For most students, that will be a sufficient amount of prep. Because you will directly work the schedules provided, few adjustments need be made. Just balance your time well. It is crucial that you do not rush either your Methods or Tests Phase.

If you have the time and inclination, you can squeeze more prep in during this time period by completing **seven prep sessions** a week. In just over three months, you can complete 90 prep sessions at that weekly pace. When doing so, take an off day each week by doubling up on prep sessions another day of the week. You will need to add to the schedules if you complete more than 72 prep sessions during your course. Read the "More than 3.5 Months" section that follows to learn how to supplement the schedules.

Example 3 month schedule (6 sessions/wk x 12 weeks = 72 sessions)

- 32 session Complete Methods Phase
- 20 session Practice Phase (use the sample schedule)
- 19 session Tests Phase (use the sample schedule)

More than Three and a Half Months

If you have more than three and a half months to prep, you can choose to work through the schedules more slowly than six prep sessions each week. This choice makes sense if you cannot complete about 12 hours (or 10 hours for high students or 15 for low) of prep each week. If you complete an average of four and a half prep sessions a week, then you will need to prep for **four months** to finish the schedules. Alternatively, you can add to the schedules by supplementing one or more of the three phases:

Methods Phase: Your Methods Phase is a great phase to spend extra time on. To do so, take extra sessions to work **more of the problem sets** (this may not make sense for low students). And/or spend time **rereading chapters** and re-reviewing questions that gave you trouble.

Practice Phase: It is only necessary to supplement your Practice Phase if you have lots of extra time to prepare, as it is the least important of the three phases. To do so, **complete additional sections**, either with your ITL or with 35 minute timing. More ITL timed sections will help you get more comfortable with the question types and methods, while more 35 minute sections will help you work on your section pacing. Draw the sections from the *10 Actual book* ($19, Amazon) or from tests 39-47 ($8 each, Amazon). You will see some repeated questions in the *10 Actual book*, as the practice questions after each chapter are drawn from there. We do not recommend working with the *10 More book* if you complete the problem sets.

Tests Phase: A great phase to supplement. Test 62 and up can be purchased for $8 each on Amazon. These are the most recent tests available and are ideal practice for your official LSAT. Tests 48-51 ($8, Amazon) are also a good option, although these tests are older and will be a bit different than the newer tests.

Example 4 month schedule (6 sessions/wk x 16 weeks = 96 sessions)

- 36 session Methods Phase
    - 4 extra sessions: complete more of the problem sets and reread chapters of your choosing.
- 30 session Practice Phase
    - 10 extra sessions: complete 5 additional tests divided into sessions of two sections with review.
- 30 session Tests Phase
    - 10 extra sessions: at the end, take Tests 62-65 and review them the day after taking them.

Two to Three Months

If you have two to three months to prepare, you have several options. One is to complete the given schedules, at **a faster weekly pace**. If you average seven sessions a week, you can finish the schedules in **two and a half months**. If you use that pace, complete two prep sessions one day a week so that you can have an off day. Everyone needs a break from the LSAT.

If you do not have the time or inclination to complete seven prep sessions a week, skip **a small amount** of the prep provided in the schedules. The best phase to shorten dramatically is your Practice Phase.

Example 2.5 Month schedule (6 sessions/wk x 10 weeks = 60 sessions)

- 30 session Methods Phase - Skip two sessions devoted to problem sets you feel more comfortable with.
- 12 session Practice Phase - Work only the first six sessions of Part One and Two.
- 18 session Tests Phase - Cut 1 session by taking and reviewing a test in the same day one time.

Less than Two Months

It is possible to work the full schedules or only slightly abbreviated ones in this time period. If you work 8 sessions a week, you can complete 64 sessions (close to a full course) in two months. If you work 12 sessions a week, you can complete a full course in just a month and a half. Even if you have lots of time, do not complete more than 12 prep sessions a week. You can only absorb so much in a given time period.

If you must work an abbreviated course, use the Key Concepts Methods schedule and shorten the other phases.

Example 2 Month schedule (6 sessions/wk x 8 weeks = 48 sessions)

- 19 session Methods Phase - Use the Key Concepts schedule for your Methods Phase.
- 12 session Practice Phase - Work the first six sessions of Part One and Two.
- 17 session Tests Phase - Take eight tests, reviewing each the next day.

Example 1.5 Month schedule (6 sessions/wk x 6 weeks = 36 sessions)

- 19 session Methods Phase - Use the Key Concepts schedule for your Methods Phase.
- 8 session Practice Phase - Work the first four sessions of Part One and Two.
- 9 session Tests Phase - Use this schedule to get in six tests:
    - Session 1 – Test 56 + Review
    - Session 2 – Test 57
    - Session 3 – Review
    - Session 4 – Test 58 + Review
    - Session 5 – Test 59
    - Session 6 – Review
    - Session 7 – Test 60+ Review
    - Session 8 – Test 61
    - Session 9 – Review

Books Used in the Schedules

This table is a handy reference when buying books for your course. The prices are from Amazon.com; the costs are comparable on Amazon.ca:

Name + Tests	Tests	Cost	Phase	Priority
10 More Book	10	$19	Methods	Required
Next 10 Book	10	$19	Methods + Practice	Required
10 New book	10	$19	Tests	Required
Required Totals	***30***	***$57***		
Advanced LSAT Practice	9	$54	Tests	Recommended
Tests 62-65	4	$32	Tests	Recommended
Recommended Totals	***13***	***$86***		
10 Actual book	10	$19	Practice	Optional
Tests 47-51	5	$40	Tests	Optional
Tests 39-46	8	$64	Practice	Optional
Optional Totals	***23***	***$123***		

It is helpful to purchase all your books in a single Amazon order. The books are in order of usefulness. The required books are those that the sample schedules use. They are only $57, a great deal for 30 tests. All students should buy those books. For students who can afford them, the two recommended books are great additions to a course of any length. The optional books are useful for students with long courses and other serious students.

Schedule Compilation

To assist in your course creation, we present all the schedules covered and a few additional ones. All of these schedules use one of the Method Phase schedules and the sample Practice and Test Phase schedules provided earlier in this chapter.

Example 4 month schedule (6 sessions/wk x 16 weeks = 96 sessions)

- 36 session Methods Phase - Complete more of the problem sets and reread chapters of your choosing.
- 30 session Practice Phase - Complete 5 additional tests divided into sessions of two sections + review.
- 30 session Tests Phase - Take Tests 62-65 and review the next day at the end of phase.

Example 3.5 month schedule (6 sessions/wk x 14 weeks = 84 sessions)

- 34 session Methods Phase - Complete more of the problem sets and reread chapters of your choosing.
- 20 session Practice Phase – Use the sample schedule.
- 30 session Tests Phase

Example 3 month schedule (6 sessions/wk x 12 weeks = 72 sessions)

- 32 session Methods Phase – Use the Complete schedule.
- 20 session Practice Phase - Use the sample schedule.
- 19 session Tests Phase - Use the sample schedule.

Example 2.5 Month schedule (6 sessions/wk x 10 weeks = 60 sessions)

- 30 session Methods Phase - Skip two sessions devoted to problem sets you feel more comfortable with.
- 12 session Practice Phase - Work only the first six sessions of Part One and Two.
- 18 session Tests Phase - Cut 1 session by taking and reviewing a test in the same day one time.

Example 2 Month schedule (6 sessions/wk x 8 weeks = 48 sessions)

- 19 session Methods Phase - Use the Key Concepts schedule for your Methods Phase.
- 12 session Practice Phase - Work the first six sessions of Part One and Two.
- 17 session Tests Phase - Take eight tests, reviewing each the next day.

Example 1.5 Month schedule (6 sessions/wk x 6 weeks = 36 sessions)

- 19 session Methods Phase - Use the Key Concepts schedule for your Methods Phase.
- 8 session Practice Phase - Work the first four sessions of Part One and Part Two.
- 9 session Tests Phase - Take six recent tests with this pace: Test + Review, Test, Review.

Example 1 Month schedule (1 session/day for a month = 30 sessions)

- 15 session Methods Phase - Use the Key Concepts schedule for your Methods Phase.
- 6 session Practice Phase - Work the first three sessions of Part One and Part Two.
- 9 session Tests Phase - Take six recent tests with this pace: Test + Review, Test, Review.

Methods Phase Schedules

Methods Phase: Complete - 33 Sessions x 2 Hrs/Session

SESSION 1 - LR

☐ Read the **Introduction and Passages** Chapter (beginning of the LR Section)

- 22 pages, ~75 minutes
- Read Slowly and Carefully

☐ Read **Query and Choices** Chapter

- 14 pages, ~45 minutes
- Read Slowly and Carefully

SESSION 2 - LR

☐ Read **Conditionals**

- 16 pages, ~55 minutes
- Read Slowly and Carefully

☐ Read **Causal Reasoning + Metrics**

- 20 pages, ~65 minutes
- Read Slowly and Carefully

SESSION 3 - LR

☐ Read **Deduction**: True Deduction (only the first section of the chapter)

- 7 pages, ~25 minutes

☐ Work + Review the *True Deduction Practice Questions*

- 10 questions, ~45 minutes
- Employ the methods you learned
- Mark each question that you are unsure of
- 1B, 2D, 3C, 4D, 5E, 6B, 7B, 8E, 9E, 10A
- Review all questions you answered incorrectly or were unsure of
  - Review every four questions
  - First, reanalyze the question on your own, with the correct answer in mind
  - Next, read the explanation

☐ **Deduction**: False Deduction + *Practice Questions*

- 6 pages + 2 questions, ~30 minutes
- Work the questions carefully. Correct and review every four questions.
- 1C, 2B

SESSION 4 - LR

☐ Read **Deduction**: Core Deduction + *Practice Questions*

- 9 pages + 4 Questions, ~45 minutes
- 1A, 2C, 3D, 4A
- Read Slowly and Carefully

☐ <u>Deduction Problem Set</u>: Average, Part 2 (Start after the dividing line with question 25/2 #1)

- 14 questions, ~45 minutes (including review)
- Work the questions carefully. Correct and review every four questions.

SESSION 5 - LR

☐ <u>Deduction Problem Set</u>: Difficult

- 13 questions, ~50 minutes
- Work the questions carefully.
- Correct and review every four questions.

☐ <u>Deduction Problem Set</u>: Grueling, Part 1

- 13 questions, ~50 minutes
- Work the questions carefully.
- Correct and review every four questions.

☐ Read **Using this Book**: Review, Pgs. 13-14

- Read slowly and carefully.

SESSION 6 - LR

☐ Read **Assumption:** Introduction and Bridge Assumptions + *Justify Query Practice Questions*

- 12 pgs + 4 questions, ~55 minutes
- Read slowly and carefully.
- Then, complete the questions and review them.
- 1A, 2C, 3A, 4A

☐ Read **Assumption:** Keystone Assumptions + *Necessary Assumption Query Practice Questions*

- 6 pgs + 8 questions, ~55 minutes
- Read slowly and carefully. Next, complete the questions and review them.
- 1E, 2C, 3D, 4C, 5A, 6D, 7A, 8A

SESSION 7 - LR

- ☐ Assumption Problem Set: Average, Part 2
  - 14 questions, ~45 minutes
  - Work carefully, then correct + review.
- ☐ Assumption Problem Set: Difficult
  - 9 questions, ~35 minutes
  - Correct + review every 4 questions.
- ☐ Assumption Problem Set: Grueling, Part 1
  - 8 questions, ~40 minutes
  - Correct + review every 4 questions.

SESSION 8 - LR

- ☐ **Strengthen and Weaken:** Strengthen + *Practice Questions*
  - 5 pgs + 8 questions, ~50 minutes
  - Read slowly and carefully. Then, complete the questions and review them.
  - 1A, 2A, 3B, 4D, 5D, 6B, 7E, 8A
- ☐ **Strengthen and Weaken:** Weaken + *Practice Questions*
  - 7 pgs + 8 questions, ~60 minutes
  - Read slowly and carefully. Then, complete the questions and review them.
  - 1D, 2E, 3B, 4D, 5B, 6E, 7D, 8D
- ☐ **Using this Book**: Review section (Pgs. 13-14)
  - Read slowly and carefully.

SESSION 9 - LR

- ☐ **Support with Principle** + *Practice Questions*
  - 5 pgs + 8 questions, ~50 minutes
  - Read slowly and carefully. Then, complete the questions and review them.
  - 1E, 2A, 3E, 4B, 5D, 6D, 7C, 8D
- ☐ **Paradox Fix** + *Practice Questions*
  - 7 pgs + 8 questions, ~60 minutes
  - Read slowly and carefully. Then, complete the questions and review them.
  - 1D, 2E, 3E, 4B, 5D, 6A, 7C, 8B

SESSION 10 - LR

- ☐ Affect the Passage Set: Average, Part 2
  - 18 questions, ~50 minutes
  - Correct + review every 4 questions.
- ☐ Affect the Passage Set: Difficult, Part 1
  - 9 questions, ~35 minutes
  - Correct + review every 4 questions.
- ☐ Affect the Passage Set: Difficult, Part 2
  - 10 questions, ~40 minutes
  - Correct + review every 4 questions.

SESSION 11 - LR

- ☐ Affect the Passage Set: Grueling, Part 1
  - 10 questions, ~45 minutes
  - Work carefully, then correct + review.
- ☐ Affect the Passage Set: Grueling, Part 2
  - 11 questions, ~50 minutes
  - Work carefully, then correct + review.

SESSION 12 - LR

- ☐ **Argument Structure** (Stop at "Role" Section) + *Argument Structure Practice Questions*
  - 7 pgs + 4 questions, ~40 minutes
  - Read slowly and carefully. Work carefully and correct + review every 4 questions.
  - 1C, 2A, 3A, 4E
- ☐ **Argument Structure:** Role + *Practice Questions*
  - 4 pgs + 3 questions, ~30 minutes
  - Read slowly and carefully. Work carefully and correct + review every 4 questions.
  - 1C, 2C, 3B
- ☐ **Disagreement** + *Practice Questions*
  - 5 pgs + 4 questions, ~30 minutes
  - Read slowly and carefully. Work carefully and correct + review every 4 questions.
  - 1C, 2B, 3E, 4E

SESSION 13 - LR

☐ **Principle Match** + *Practice Questions*

- 6 pgs + 4 questions, ~35 minutes
- Read slowly and carefully. Work carefully and correct + review every 4 questions.
- 1B, 2E, 3B, 4D

☐ **Parallel Structure** + *Parallel Structure Practice Questions*

- 7 pgs + 8 questions, ~65 minutes
- Read slowly and carefully. Work carefully and correct + review every 4 questions.
- 1A, 2E, 3E, 4B, 5A, 6E, 7B, 8B

SESSION 14 - LR

☐ <u>Structure Problem Set</u>: Average, Part 2

- 15 questions, ~45 minutes
- Work carefully, then correct + review.

☐ <u>Structure Problem Set</u>: Difficult

- 7 questions, ~30 minutes
- Work carefully, then correct + review.

☐ <u>Structure Problem Set</u>: Grueling, Part 1

- 8 questions, ~35 minutes
- Work carefully, then correct + review.

SESSION 15 - LR

☐ Read **Flaw**

- 14 pgs, ~45 minutes
- Read slowly and carefully.

☐ *Flaw Practice Questions*

- 12 questions, ~45 minutes
- Complete the questions and review them.
- 1B, 2A, 3E, 4B, 5A, 6D, 7D, 8E, 9D, 10A, 11D, 12A

☐ *Flawed Parallel Structure Practice Questions*

- 8 questions, ~40 minutes
- Complete the questions and review them.
- 1C, 2D, 3E, 4E, 5C, 6B, 7D, 8D

SESSION 16 - LR

☐ <u>Flaw Problem Set</u>: Average, Part 2

- 9 questions, ~25 minutes
- Work carefully, then correct + review.

☐ <u>Flaw Problem Set</u>: Difficult, Part 1

- 10 questions, ~40 minutes
- Work carefully, then correct + review.

☐ <u>Flaw Problem Set</u>: Grueling, Part 1

- 12 questions, ~55 minutes
- Work carefully, then correct + review.

SESSION 17 - RC

☐ **Introduction and Reading a Passage** (first chapter of the RC Section)

- 21 pgs, ~75 minutes
- Read slowly and carefully.

☐ **More on Passages**

- 15 pgs, ~50 minutes
- Read slowly and carefully.

SESSION 18 - Games

☐ **Introduction** (Games Section)

- 13 pgs, ~40 minutes

☐ **Sequencing Games**

- 30 pgs, ~80 minutes
- Read slowly and carefully.

SESSION 19 - RC

☐ **Marking a Passage** (RC Section)

- 21 pgs, ~75 minutes
- Read slowly and carefully.

☐ <u>29/1 #1-12</u>

- 12 questions, ~35 minutes (including review)
- These interspersed LR drills will maintain your LR skills as you learn about the Games and RC sections.
- Complete the drill then review.

SESSION 20 - Games

☐ **Question Types** (Games Section)

- 17 pgs, ~45 minutes
- Read slowly and carefully.

☐ **Example Sequencing Games**

- 16 pgs, ~45 minutes

☐ *Sequencing Practice Games: #'s 1 + 2 Only*

- 12 questions, ~40 minutes
- Complete the questions and review after every game.

SESSION 21 - RC

☐ **The Questions** (RC Section)

- 10 pgs, ~35 minutes
- Read slowly and carefully.

☐ **Common Types** + *Humanities Practice Passages*

- 10 pgs + 15 questions, ~65 minutes
- Read slowly and carefully. Then practice on two RC passages. Review carefully after each passage.

☐ 29/1 #13-25

- 13 questions, ~40 minutes
- Complete the drill and then review.

SESSION 22 - Games

☐ *Sequencing Practice Games: #3 Only*

- 6 questions, ~15 minutes
- Complete the questions and review.

☐ **Relative Sequencing Games**

- 12 pgs, ~35 minutes
- Read slowly and carefully.

☐ *Relative Sequencing Practice Games*

- 11 questions, ~35 minutes
- Complete the questions and review after each game.

☐ 29/4 #1-12

- 12 questions, ~35 minutes
- Complete the drill and then review.

SESSION 23 - RC

☐ **More Common Types** (RC Section)

- 21 pgs, ~65 minutes
- Read slowly and carefully.

☐ *Law Practice Passages*

- 2 passages, ~40 minutes
- Review after each passage.

SESSION 24 - Games

☐ **Advanced Sequencing Games**

- ~50 minutes
- Read slowly and carefully.

☐ *Advanced Sequencing Practice Games*

- 12 questions, ~40 minutes
- Complete the questions and review after each game.

☐ 29/4 #13-25

- 13 questions, ~40 minutes
- Complete the drill and then review.

SESSION 25 - RC

☐ **Other Types**

- 24 pgs, ~75 minutes
- Read slowly and carefully.

☐ *Social Sciences Practice Passages*

- 2 passages, ~40 minutes
- Review after each passage.

SESSION 26 - Games

☐ Sequencing Sets: Average, Part 2

- 10 questions, ~30 minutes
- Complete the set and review.

☐ Sequencing Sets: Difficult, Part 1

- 17 questions, ~60 minutes
- Complete the set and review.

☐ 30/2 #1-12

- 12 questions, ~35 minutes
- This LR drill will keep up your skills.
- Complete the drill and review.

SESSION 27 - RC

- ☐ *Natural Sciences Practice Passages*
  - 2 passages, ~35 minutes
  - Complete the passages and review.
- ☐ Humanities & Law Sets: Average, Part 2
  - 2 passages, ~40 minutes
  - Complete the set and review.
- ☐ Humanities & Law Sets: Difficult
  - 2 passages, ~45 minutes
  - Complete the set and review.

SESSION 28 - Games

- ☐ Sequencing Sets: Difficult, Part 2
  - 11 questions, ~40 minutes
  - Complete the set and review.
- ☐ Sequencing Sets: Grueling, Part 1
  - 13 questions, ~50 minutes
  - Complete and review.
- ☐ 30/2 #13-25
  - 13 questions, ~40 minutes
  - This LR drill will keep up your skills.
  - Complete the drill and review.

SESSION 29 - RC

- ☐ Humanities & Law Sets: Grueling
  - 3 passages, ~65 minutes
  - Complete the set and review.
- ☐ Science Sets: Average, Part 2
  - 2 passages, ~35 minutes
  - Complete the set and review.

SESSION 30 - Games

- ☐ **Sort Games**
  - 24 pgs, ~50 minutes
  - Read slowly and carefully.
- ☐ *Sort Practice Games*
  - 18 questions, ~70 minutes
  - Complete the questions and review.

SESSION 31 - RC

- ☐ Science Sets: Difficult
  - 4 passages, ~60minutes
  - Complete the set and review.
- ☐ Science Sets: Grueling
  - 3 passages, ~55 minutes
  - Complete the set and review.
- ☐ 30/4 #1-12
  - 12 questions, ~30 minutes
  - This LR drill will keep up your skills.
  - Complete the drill and review.

SESSION 32 - Games

- ☐ **Select Games** + *Practice Game*
  - 16 pgs + 1 game, ~50 minutes
  - Read carefully then complete the practice game.
- ☐ **Combination Games** + *Practice Game*
  - 8 pgs + 1 game, ~35 minutes
  - Read carefully then complete the practice game.
- ☐ 30/4 #13-25
  - 13 questions, ~40 minutes
  - This LR drill will keep up your skills.
  - Complete the drill and review.

SESSION 33 - Games

- ☐ Grouping Sets: Difficult, Part 1
  - 12 questions, ~45 minutes
  - Complete and review.
- ☐ Grouping Sets: Difficult, Part 2
  - 20 questions, ~70 minutes
  - Complete and review.

Methods Phase: Key Concepts – 19 Sessions x 2 Hrs

SESSION 1 - LR

- [ ] Read the **Introduction and Passages** Chapter (beginning of the LR Section)
    - 22 pages, ~75 minutes
    - Read Slowly and Carefully
- [ ] Read **Query and Choices** Chapter
    - 14 pages, ~45 minutes
    - Read Slowly and Carefully

SESSION 2 - LR

- [ ] Read **Conditionals**
    - 16 pages, ~55 minutes
    - Read Slowly and Carefully
- [ ] Read **Deduction**: True Deduction (only the first section of the chapter)
    - 7 pages, ~20 minutes
- [ ] Work the *True Deduction Practice Questions*
    - 10 questions, ~30 minutes
    - Employ the methods you learned
    - Mark each question that you are unsure of
- [ ] Review the Questions
    - 10 questions, ~15 minutes
    - 1B, 2D, 3C, 4D, 5E, 6B, 7B, 8E, 9E, 10A
    - Review all questions you answered incorrectly or were unsure of
        - First, reanalyze the question on your own, with the correct answer in mind
        - Next, read the explanation

SESSION 3 - LR

- [ ] Read **Deduction**: Core Deduction + *Practice Questions*
    - 9 pages + 4 Questions, ~45 minutes
    - 1A, 2C, 3D, 4A
    - Read Slowly and Carefully
- [ ] Deduction Problem Set: Average, Part 2 (Start after the dividing line with question 25/2 #1)
    - 14 questions, ~45 minutes (including review)
    - Work the questions carefully. Then, correct and review them.

SESSION 4 - LR

- [ ] **Assumption:** Introduction and Bridge Assumptions + *Justify Query Practice Questions*
    - 12 pgs + 4 questions, ~55 minutes
    - Read slowly and carefully.
    - Then, complete the questions and review them.
    - 1A, 2C, 3A, 4A
- [ ] Read **Assumption:** Keystone Assumptions + *Necessary Assumption Query Practice Questions*
    - 6 pgs + 8 questions, ~55 minutes
    - Read slowly and carefully. Next, complete the questions and review them.
    - 1E, 2C, 3D, 4C, 5A, 6D, 7A, 8A

SESSION 5 - LR

☐ **Strengthen and Weaken:** Strengthen + *Practice Questions*

- 5 pgs + 8 questions, ~50 minutes
- Read slowly and carefully. Then, complete the questions and review them.
- 1A, 2A, 3B, 4D, 5D, 6B, 7E, 8A

☐ **Strengthen and Weaken:** Weaken + *Practice Questions*

- 7 pgs + 8 questions, ~60 minutes
- Read slowly and carefully. Then, complete the questions and review them.
- 1D, 2E, 3B, 4D, 5B, 6E, 7D, 8D

SESSION 6 - LR

☐ **Support with Principle** + *Practice Questions*

- 5 pgs + 8 questions, ~50 minutes
- Read slowly and carefully. Then, complete the questions and review them.
- 1E, 2A, 3E, 4B, 5D, 6D, 7C, 8D

☐ **Paradox Fix** + *Practice Questions*

- 7 pgs + 8 questions, ~60 minutes
- 1D, 2E, 3E, 4B, 5D, 6A, 7C, 8B

SESSION 7 - LR

☐ **Argument Structure** (Stop at "Role" Section) + *Argument Structure Practice Questions*

- 7 pgs + 4 questions, ~40 minutes
- Read slowly and carefully. Then, complete the questions and review them.
- 1C, 2A, 3A, 4E

☐ **Argument Structure:** Role + *Practice Questions*

- 4 pgs + 3 questions, ~30 minutes
- Read slowly and carefully. Then, complete the questions and review them.
- 1C, 2C, 3B

☐ **Disagreement** + *Practice Questions*

- 5 pgs + 4 questions, ~30 minutes
- Read slowly and carefully. Then, complete the questions and review them.
- 1C, 2B, 3E, 4E

SESSION 8 - LR

☐ **Principle Match** + *Practice Questions*

- 6 pgs + 4 questions, ~35 minutes
- Read slowly and carefully. Then, complete the questions and review them.
- 1B, 2E, 3B, 4D

☐ **Parallel Structure** + *Parallel Structure Practice Questions*

- 7 pgs + 8 questions, ~65 minutes
- Read slowly and carefully. Then, complete the questions and review them.
- 1A, 2E, 3E, 4B, 5A, 6E, 7B, 8B

SESSION 9 - LR

☐ Read **Flaw**

- 14 pgs, ~45 minutes
- Read slowly and carefully.

☐ *Flaw Practice Questions*

- 12 questions, ~45 minutes
- Complete the questions and review them.
- 1B, 2A, 3E, 4B, 5A, 6D, 7D, 8E, 9D, 10A, 11D, 12A

☐ *Flawed Parallel Structure Practice Questions*

- 8 questions, ~40 minutes
- Complete the questions and review them.
- 1C, 2D, 3E, 4E, 5C, 6B, 7D, 8D

SESSION 10 - RC

☐ **Introduction and Reading a Passage** (first chapter of the RC Section)

- 21 pgs, ~75 minutes
- Read slowly and carefully.

☐ **More on Passages**

- 15 pgs, ~50 minutes
- Read slowly and carefully.

SESSION 11 - Games

☐ **Introduction** (Games Section)

- 13 pgs, ~40 minutes

☐ **Sequencing Games**

- 30 pgs, ~80 minutes
- Read slowly and carefully.

SESSION 12 - RC

☐ **Marking a Passage** (RC Section)

- 21 pgs, ~75 minutes
- Read slowly and carefully.

☐ 29/1 #1-12

- 12 questions, ~35 minutes (including review)
- These interspersed LR drills will maintain your LR skills as you learn about the Games and RC sections.
- Complete the drill and review.

SESSION 13 - Games

☐ **Question Types** (Games Section)

- 17 pgs, ~45 minutes
- Read slowly and carefully.

☐ **Example Sequencing Games**

- 16 pgs, ~45 minutes

☐ *Sequencing Practice Games: #'s 1 + 2 Only*

- 12 questions, ~40 minutes
- Complete the questions and review.

SESSION 14 - RC

☐ **The Questions** (RC Section)

- 10 pgs, ~35 minutes
- Read slowly and carefully.

☐ **Common Types** + *Humanities Practice Passages*

- 10 pgs + 15 questions, ~65 minutes
- Read slowly and carefully. Then practice on two RC passages. Review carefully

☐ 29/1 #13-25

- 13 questions, ~40 minutes
- Complete the drill and review.

SESSION 15 - Games

☐ *Sequencing Practice Games: #3 Only*

- 6 questions, ~15 minutes
- Complete the questions and review.

☐ **Relative Sequencing Games**

- 12 pgs, ~35 minutes
- Read slowly and carefully.

☐ *Relative Sequencing Practice Games*

- 11 questions, ~35 minutes
- Complete the questions and review.

☐ 29/4 #1-12

- 12 questions, ~35 minutes
- Complete the drill and review.

SESSION 16 - RC

☐ **More Common Types** (RC Section)

- 21 pgs, ~65 minutes
- Read slowly and carefully.

☐ *Law Practice Passages*

- 2 passages, ~40 minutes
- Complete the passages and review.

SESSION 17 - Games

☐ **Advanced Sequencing Games**

- ~50 minutes
- Read slowly and carefully.

☐ *Advanced Sequencing Practice Games*

- 12 questions, ~40 minutes
- Complete the questions and review.

☐ 29/4 #13-25

- 13 questions, ~40 minutes
- Complete the drill and review.

SESSION 18 - RC

☐ **Other Types**

- 24 pgs, ~70 minutes
- Read slowly and carefully.

☐ *Social Sciences Practice Passages*

- 2 passages, ~35 minutes
- Complete the passages and review.

☐ *Natural Sciences Practice Passages*

- 2 passages, ~35 minutes
- Complete the passages and review.

SESSION 19 - Games

☐ **Sort Games**

- 24 pgs, ~50 minutes
- Read slowly and carefully.

☐ *Sort Practice Games*

- 18 questions, ~70 minutes
- Complete the questions and review.

Logical Reasoning

Introduction and Passages

This chapter will first give you a background on the Logical Reasoning (LR) section. Then, it will give you tools to interpret a Passage, a major step in every LR question.

Introduction

The Logical Reasoning section is extremely learnable. You will face two LR sections on the LSAT, accounting for 50% of your LSAT score, so prepare thoroughly for these sections.

Each LR section will feature 25 or 26 questions. You are given 35 minutes for each scored section on the LSAT. So, if you wish to answer every LR question in a section, you have 85 seconds, just under a minute and a half, for each one. It is quite possible that you will maximize your score on this section by not attempting every question, especially if that would cause you to rush. Regardless, you need to move quickly through an LR section, while trying to answer as many questions correctly as possible. The lessons featured here will help you to work with greater speed and accuracy.

The methods take time to master, so be patient. Some techniques force you to slow down and be self conscious of your actions when you first use them. Initially in your prep, focus on doing the questions with proper technique. With practice, you will be able to work LR questions more quickly.

Below is an official LR question that appeared in a past LSAT. The three parts of a LR question - the passage, the query and the answer choices - are separated. Please read each part:

The Passage:

(19/2 #24) The United States ranks far behind countries such as Sweden and Canada when it comes to workplace safety. In all three countries, joint labor-management committees that oversee workplace safety conditions have been very successful in reducing occupational injuries. In the United States, such committees are found only in the few companies that have voluntarily established them. However, in Sweden and several Canadian provinces, joint safety committees are required by law and exist in all medium-sized and large workplaces.

The Query:

Which one of the following is supported by the information above?

The Answer choices:

(A) The establishment of joint safety committees in all medium-sized and large workplaces in the United States would result in a reduction of occupational injuries.
(B) A joint safety committee that is required by law is more effective at reducing occupational injuries than is a joint safety committee that is voluntarily established.
(C) Workplace safety in Sweden and Canada was superior to that in the United States even prior to the passage of laws requiring joint safety committees in all medium-sized and large workplaces.
(D) Joint safety committees had been voluntarily established in most medium-sized and large workplaces in Sweden and several Canadian provinces prior to the passage of laws requiring such committees.
(E) The United States would surpass Sweden and Canada in workplace safety if joint safety committees were required in all medium-sized and large workplaces in the United States.

The passage (also called "the blurb") has one or two paragraphs with information or an argument. The query asks something related to the content of the passage. The answer choices (or choices) are the five statements labeled (A) through (E). The correct choice is the one that effectively answers the query. Each question is made up of all three parts. By the way, the correct answer to the question above is (A).

The Passage

When you read a passage, note the topic discussed. Avoid bringing in outside knowledge you know on the subject. The passages are their own worlds, and things in the LSAT world are different than you might expect. Facts can exist there that do not exist in the real world. If a passage says that pigs can fly, depending on the type of question, that information can be true. So, work with what the passage gives you. Please read this passage:

> (1/1 #1) It is difficult to keep deep wounds free of bacteria. Even strong antibiotics fail to kill the bacteria that live in such wounds. However, many physicians have succeeded in eliminating bacteria from deep wounds by packing the wound with a sweet substance like sugar.

Here, we must accept the fact that strong antibiotics do not kill the bacteria in deep wounds and that these bacteria **can** be killed by sweet substances. Accepting these ideas is required to answer the question correctly.

Of course, basic and widely-known facts do hold true. If a passage discusses a war, you should know that wars involve weapons and countries fighting one another, etc. But do not bring in your knowledge of World War II or specialized war tactics to that question.

When reading a passage, read for **details** because small phrasings or term shifts (from "environment" to "ecology" for instance) can be important. However, you are also under the clock and therefore must read quickly. Properly balancing these two competing goals is crucial to succeed on the LR section. The key is focus: give all your attention to the question at hand. That will allow you to read **quickly and thoroughly**. Practice is also vital: it takes time to get used to rapidly understanding a dense passage. Other than understanding the details of the passage, look at the argument structure, the pieces of the argument and how they fit together. This skill will be addressed in detail.

Topics

Passages feature topics from a multitude of sources: books or articles on everything from music to chemistry to economics. Get ready to read about a lot of different ideas. Note that the topic has no connection to the **logic** of the passage, the argument's parts. Logic works on a general level: many different facts could be plugged in for the same underlying argument structure. Of course, the details of the passage do matter; the information the argument uses makes a difference in that argument. But logic itself has no specific facts, only structures.

Speaking of facts, the LSAT will never assume you know advanced ideas from any field. A passage will explain all concepts it references that are not general knowledge. The LSAT is a test with no **content** to study. For instance, with regards to the passage about workplace safety, the passage will tell you everything you need to know about workplace safety to answer the question. Science-based or technical passages with esoteric terms are just like all others: read for the underlying logical structure while also soaking up the details. The topic is often only the background for the parts of the argument. The logical relationships contained within the passage are the most important aspect, but those do rely on the specifics of the situation.

Arguments & Fact-Groups

There are two kinds of LSAT passages: arguments and fact-groups. An argument consists of a group of statements where one statement, the conclusion, is supported by the other statements, the evidence (or premises).

> Everyone whose favorite color is red likes strawberries. Josh's favorite color is red. Therefore, Josh likes strawberries.

Here, the first two sentences serve as the evidence. They give the reasons for believing the final statement, the conclusion: "Josh likes strawberries." Josh falls under the category of those whose favorite color is red and all those people like strawberries. Therefore, it must be the case that Josh likes strawberries. The evidence provides the foundation that the conclusion rests on.

Fact-groups, on the other hand, do not have a conclusion. They are just a group of statements:

> Running backwards is a good workout for the hamstrings. Running sideways works the hip flexors, and running uphill focuses on the quadriceps.

Those statements could be evidence for a conclusion like this:

> Different types of running use different muscle groups.

Because no conclusion is present, the statements are only a fact-group. Reading a fact-group tends to feel anti-climatic, because no bigger point is made. The statements do not seem to "go" anywhere or build up to anything. Arguments have a different feel. The author of an argument is trying to make a point, trying to convince you of something. Because of this, arguments tend to cause a greater reaction when you read. About 75% of passages are arguments; only about a quarter are fact-groups.

Distinguishing Argument Parts

Understanding an argument, identifying its parts and how they work together, is the most fundamental skill you will learn for the LR section. Everything else builds upon it. Identifying the evidence and the conclusion quickly when reading an argument is equally crucial and this advice will help you do so.

A piece of evidence is a statement that supports, or helps to support, a conclusion. The evidence tells you why you should believe the conclusion. When trying to find the evidence of a passage, ask yourself:

- Does the author use this statement to support the conclusion?
- Is this statement more specific and concrete than others?

A conclusion is a statement based upon or inferred from premises. Conclusions rely on at least one premise or piece of evidence for support. Premises are the summary statements that build from the evidence in the passage. When trying to locate a conclusion, ask:

- Is this statement more general and controversial than the others?
- Is this statement based upon the others?
- What is the author trying to convince me of in big picture terms?
- Where does the passage lead?

Please take a few minutes and memorize the lists below. Knowing what part of an argument you are dealing with will help you do the more complex tasks required by the questions:

Premise signal words:

- Because
- Since
- For
- For instance
- In that
- Given that
- Due to
- For example

Conclusion signal words:

- Thus
- Therefore
- Hence
- So
- Accordingly
- Clearly
- Follows that
- Consequently

Signal words hint at what type of information (premise or conclusion) is coming next. Look at this short argument:

> Because they can keep each other company when their owner is not at home, it follows that raising two dogs is better than raising just one.

This sentence contains both a premise and a conclusion. "Because" signals that a premise is coming, and "follows that" signals that a conclusion is next. The information about dogs keeping each other company supports the idea that raising two dogs is better than raising one. The author wishes to express the second point and provides the first part of the sentence as the reason to believe the conclusion.

Both evidence and conclusions can be constructed without signal words:

> People who sleep more than 9 hours a night always have long life spans. I sleep 10 hours a night. I will probably live a long time.

The first two sentences are the premises and the final sentence is the conclusion, but no signal words are found in this paragraph. The premises and conclusion can also occur in any order, and their relationship will stay the same.

Interestingly, the conclusion can come before the premises that support it:

> Our company should acquire a shipping facility. The current facility is too small, and there are many facilities on the market at reasonable rates.

In the paragraph above, the conclusion comes first and the premises follow in the second sentence. The conclusion can also come in the middle of two premises:

> Beth cleaned both the house and the garage today. She had a productive Tuesday. She even weeded the garden.

Here, the conclusion is the second sentence: Beth had a productive day.

When analyzing a passage that is an argument, it is critical that you pinpoint the conclusion. Mark an "X" next to the conclusion when you find it. You can make as many marks in your test book (the one with the questions) as you wish, but your answer sheet (the one with the multiple choice bubbles to fill in) must be clean.

Knowing what the argument concludes will help you answer all questions with an argument as the passage. With fact-groups, there is no conclusion to point out, so your job is to understand each fact presented.

A Form Trick

The LSAT writers often use tricky tactics with the tougher passages. One such tactic is to place a signal word for a conclusion immediately in front of a signal word for a premise, with a comma separating the two. Example:

> Thus, since Dakota is a great artist, she will redefine drip painting.

The premise is contained within a clause: "since Dakota is a great artist." The premise clause is contained within commas and the conclusion follows the second comma. The conclusion's signal word is "thus." It is easy to see that this is the conclusion when the clause is taken away: "Thus, she will redefine drip painting."

Supplementary Premises

Authors often use supplementary premises to provide further support for a conclusion that already has evidence. Supplementary premise signals come before additional premises that may or may not be necessary for the conclusion. Other times, a supplementary premise will be more central to the argument. In order to tell the role these premises play, analyze the full argument. Supplementary Premise Signals:

- Moreover
- Besides
- Furthermore
- And
- In addition
- What's more

Example paragraph featuring a supplementary premise and signal word:

> Debbie decided to run for governor of Dallas, but she had no political experience and little campaign money. She had very little chance of compiling an effective campaign. Furthermore, she had an incompetent campaign manager.

The final line features the supplementary premise signal "furthermore," and what follows is indeed a supplementary premise. The conclusion that Debbie had little chance of putting together an effective campaign was already supported by the premises in the first sentence.

Anti Premises

Anti premises are information that goes against the conclusion. Initially it may seem strange to bring up a premise that that goes against the argument. However, this tactic makes the author's argument stronger by allowing the author to respond to potential critiques of the argument. One way to shore up weaknesses in the argument is for the author to address them himself within the argument. The author must first introduce the anti premise and then refute it.

Anti premise Signals:

- However
- On the other hand
- But
- Yet
- In contrast
- Although
- Even though
- Whereas
- Despite

Note that these signal words primarily indicate a change in direction of the argument, so they can be used in ways that that **do not** introduce an anti premise. Example argument with an anti premise:

> Abraham Lincoln was a fine president: he was instrumental in winning the civil war, and he brought a nation together. But some would argue that he did little to help the nation in terms of foreign policy. That is an unfounded criticism because in times of domestic stress, the president must focus all his attention at home.

The conclusion is that Lincoln was a fine president. That is supported by the evidence in the first sentence after the colon. The author uses an anti premise in the second sentence to introduce the idea that Lincoln may not have excelled as a president in relating to other countries. Then, the author explains why this critique does not weaken the conclusion: Lincoln should not have been expected to excel in foreign policy because the nation was in turmoil during his presidency.

Starting with an Anti Premise

A common argument technique involves starting out the argument by introducing the view that the argument will then disprove, i.e. starting with an anti premise. Example first sentence of an argument:

> Many critics state that Mozart's 40th symphony is his best.

The argument then goes on to argue against the view that was introduced:

> ... But this view is shown to be mistaken when one fully understands his 32nd symphony in a historical context. While the 40th may be Mozart's most beautiful and well constructed work, his 32nd was far more revolutionary and influential. Because every musician's work should be judged by the impact it had on other similar musicians, Mozart's 32nd symphony is his greatest.

These passages have a very specific first sentence. The format almost always involves a *percentage* of a *group* stating information. The percentage will be in general terms: "most, all, some, many, etc." The group can be any group of people: "trainers, mothers, lawyers, children, etc." Examples of this format:

> Most doctors believe...
>
> All car salesman state...
>
> No psychiatrists maintain...

Rarely, the number and/or the group will be dropped:

> Nutritionists hold that…" (No number)
>
> It has been claimed" (No number and No group)

Whenever the first sentence of a passage starts out with a specific claim in this format, you are likely dealing with a passage that starts with an anti premise and then refutes it.

Finding the Conclusion without Signal Words

On tougher LR questions, there may be no conclusion signals. The LSAT writers do this to make it harder to understand the argument:

> Doctors receive an extensive education, but it is one that can be lacking in important ways. In the typical medical school curriculum, there is an overemphasis on specific treatments through drug use and a lack of information on how to get patients involved in their own preventative health care. Medical students do not have the time to live a healthy, balanced lifestyle.

Not a single conclusion or premise indicator is featured. Fortunately, there are two effective ways of identifying the conclusion when no signal is present.

One way is to mentally arrange the statements in the passage in such a way that forces one of them to be the conclusion and the other(s) to be the premise(s). Adding the signal word "therefore" before the conclusion can be helpful. Once you have organized the statements, ask yourself if the argument makes sense. If it does, you have found the conclusion. If the ordering sounds illogical or confusing, rearrange the statements in another way and run the test again. Eventually, you will find a progression that sounds correct. You will know the conclusion because the other statements support it. With the argument above, we might try this initial ordering:

> Premise: Doctors receive an extensive but somewhat inadequate education.
>
> Premise: They learn about drug treatments but not preventative health care.
>
> Conclusion: Therefore, medical students do not have time for a healthy lifestyle.

This ordering of the argument does not make sense. Neither of the premises supports the conclusion by discussing why they do not have time for a healthy lifestyle: for instance, because they have exhausting schedules. So we try another ordering:

> Premise: They learn about drug treatments but not preventative health care.
>
> Premise: Medical students do not have time for a healthy lifestyle.
>
> Conclusion: Therefore, Doctors receive an extensive but somewhat inadequate education.

This ordering makes sense. The education is lacking because it does not sufficiently cover preventative health care, nor does it allow for the students to develop healthy lifestyles.

A better but more complex way to find the conclusion without signal words is to analyze the <u>scope</u> (or scale) of the information in each statement. The scope refers to how broad or specific a statement is. A conclusion relies upon evidence, so the information in a conclusion will be more general (less obvious and accepted) than the information in the premises. On the other hand, the premises will have a smaller scale; they will be narrower in scope and discuss a more specific topic. Example argument:

> Running is tough on one's body. The pounding that comes from your feet hitting pavement while running damages your knees and back.

"Running is tough on one's body" is the conclusion. This statement has a wide scope compared with the next sentence which discusses the effect one aspect of running, the impact, has on the knees and back. The premise is more specific than the conclusion. That is how a premise can serve as support; it can underlie the conclusion. In the argument above, the conclusion is backed up by the premise that running hurts your knees and back. That narrow information lends credence to the more general and controversial idea that running is tough on one's body.

Scope is determined in relation to the other statements in the argument.

> Running is tough on one's body. Some popular forms of exercise have negative impacts.

In this argument, "running is tough on one's body" is the premise for the next statement that is broader in scope. Notice the switch in subject matter from running to popular forms of exercise. The fact that running is itself one popular form of exercise, tells that the second statement is more general than the first. Likewise, being tough on the body is one example of a negative impact. All the information from the premise fits into and provides support for the information in the conclusion. The conclusion – "some popular forms of exercise have negative impacts" – relies on the specific information about running.

Complex Passages

Thus far, we have covered basic arguments, arguments that only have one conclusion. Passages can also feature multiple conclusions from one speaker; we call these advanced arguments. And two-speaker arguments are passages that feature two distinct speakers.

Advanced Arguments

Advanced Arguments use a premise to support a conclusion. Then, that conclusion becomes the premise for another, broader conclusion. A conclusion that serves as the premise for another conclusion is called a sub-conclusion. Here is an example of an Advanced Argument:

> Because Andrew works hard, his new business will be successful. So, we should buy stock in his company.

"Andrew works hard" is the evidence for the conclusion that his new business will be successful. And the fact that his business will be successful is the evidence for the final conclusion, that we should buy stock in his company. So, "his new business will be successful" is a sub-conclusion. The second statement is both a premise and a conclusion. The argument has three logical steps: a premise, a sub-conclusion and a conclusion. On the LSAT, there are very rarely more than three steps to an argument.

Sometimes, the LSAT writers use this confusing ordering for the pieces of an advanced argument:

> Conclusion → Premise → Sub-Conclusion

This ordering is challenging because students often do not pay as much attention to the first sentence of the passage as they should. And, after that first sentence, the argument appears to have a normal structure: a premise is introduced and followed by a conclusion. The problem with this interpretation is that the final part is actually a sub-conclusion that the primary conclusion (the first sentence) uses as evidence.

> Everyone who wants to be healthy should eat a salad daily. Fresh vegetables in salads are full of nutrients. Therefore, eating salads promotes good health.

Notice that the Sub-Conclusion - "eating salads promotes good health" - is preceded by the conclusion signal "therefore." This makes sense, because it **is a conclusion**, just not the main conclusion. Notice that the true conclusion has a broader scope than the sub-conclusion, which hints at its role in the argument, despite its coming first. Always be on the lookout for this ordering of argument parts.

Two-Speaker Arguments

Two-speaker arguments, another type of complex passage, feature two different authors discussing the same subject. Each author can put forth their own evidence and conclusion, but they do not always do so. For instance, one speaker might have a full argument (evidence and conclusion), while the other speaker only provides evidence, without a conclusion.

Two-speaker passages force you to follow how the two arguments interact with one another. When you read the second speaker's argument, actively figure out how it differs or agrees with the first speaker's argument. Example Two-Speaker Argument:

> Tim: Luxury cars should be taxed by the government. Those that can afford them can afford to pay a little more. And no one really needs a luxury car.
>
> Frank: I disagree. That would be a form of discrimination against a certain class of citizens, something our constitution stands against.

Here, Tim concludes that luxury cars should be taxed specially by the government. His evidence is twofold: those that can afford luxury cars can afford to pay the tax and luxury cars are also an unnecessary purchase.

Frank concludes that luxury cars should not be taxed by the government. We learn that conclusion from his first line: "I disagree." He is disagreeing with Tim's conclusion; this is the most logical way to interpret that line based on what Frank says after it. Frank's evidence is that a special luxury car tax would be a form of discrimination.

Analyzing Arguments

This section introduces new concepts to help you understand arguments in passages.

LSAT-Writers vs Authors

When you analyze arguments, keep in mind that the author of the argument is a different entity than the people who wrote the LSAT you are taking. The LSAT writers created the LR section to test your ability to understand arguments. On the other hand, the argument author, who is often given a name or title to the left of the passage such as Frank, Amy, Psychiatrist, Politician, etc., is simply trying to make a cohesive argument. Frank, the argument author, believes his argument to make sense, even if it does not. Example argument:

> Frank: Jumping down stairs is fun. So, everyone should jump down stairs.

Frank is not trying to trick us. He really is arguing that everyone should jump down stairs. He thinks that his premise fully supports his conclusion. So, accept the premises. The errors that authors make are usually in how they go about supporting their conclusion or in how they use their premises, not in the validity of the content of their premises.

Argument Scope

In analyzing an argument, you should be aware of the <u>scope</u> of the argument. We discussed the scope of individual statements to identify the conclusion when no signals are present. Now we are talking about scope on a bigger scale, that of the argument itself. Think of scope as the net that a particular argument casts. Example argument:

> Ken is very knowledgeable about nutrition. He has studied fruits and vegetables a great deal and the chemistry behind the digestive system.

This argument has a scope of Ken's knowledge of nutrition. Information about Ken's expertise in flying aircraft is outside the scope of the argument. The scope of this argument is fairly narrow. An argument with a broader scope has information that is more general; the information applies to more situations. Argument with a broader scope:

> Ken is very well educated. He knows a great deal about many things.

This argument casts a wider net because it describes a general trait about Ken. The previous argument zeroed in on one aspect of Ken's knowledge.

Scope is an important concept on the LR section because it helps you analyze the answer choices against the scope of the argument. An answer choice that has a scope that is too narrow contains information that is too specific to fit the passage. For instance, in the argument above, information about Ken's major in college would have too narrow a scope to match the argument. We only know that Ken is generally well educated; we know nothing about what he focused on studying in college. More on this to come when we discuss the individual questions.

Key Terms: Assumption and Inference

Two important concepts that you will run into repeatedly on the LR section are inferences and assumptions.

Inference

One of the most common question types on the LR section asks you to draw an inference from the passage. In real life, the term inference is used more loosely than on the LSAT. People typically think of an inference as something that is likely to be true based on other information. For instance, I might infer that a friend wants a bite of my spinach, almond and strawberry salad because she has commented on how delicious and crunchy it looks. But I do not know that to be true. On the LSAT, an inference is information that **must be true** based on the premises contained in the passage.

Information that, based on evidence, is **only likely to be true** is not an inference. Think of an inference as a strongly supported conclusion that is not stated. The evidence is there, but the inference is left unsaid in the passage. Example statements that can support an inference:

> Oak trees in Houston have green leaves. Oak leaves are only green if the tree gets a lot of rainfall.

Based on the two pieces of evidence above, we can make the inference that Houston receives a lot of rainfall. This must be the case because oak leaves are only green if the tree gets a lot of rainfall.

Assumption

Assumption is another important term on the LSAT. An assumption is an **unstated premise** that is required for a conclusion to be valid. Just like an inference, an assumption is not directly stated. Even so, it is a piece of evidence that an argument needs in order to function. Because that crucial information is not in the argument itself, we say that the author assumes the information to be true when she makes her conclusion. Example argument with an assumption:

> Tim ran a 3 minute mile. Therefore, Tim is the world record holder in the mile.

The author assumes that a 3 minute mile is the world record for the mile; it is the fastest mile ever run. This information is **required** to support his conclusion that Tim is the world record holder in the mile. Otherwise, without this assumption, if someone has run a 2 minute mile, then the conclusion is not valid. Tim is actually not the world record holder, because a 3 minute mile is not the fastest run.

Read Carefully

LR questions test your understanding of very small details in the passage. It is vital that you grasp the full meaning of what you read, not just the general ideas. The LSAT writers will trick you if you do not pay attention to the slight differences in meaning that specific phrasings or word choices create.

Amount

You must read passages carefully and note differences in amount, how many there are of a specific thing or trait. Example sentences with differences in amount:

> Every dog has a tail.
>
> Most dogs have a tail.

The first sentence talks about every single dog in existence, while the second only tells about most dogs, a majority of dogs. Let us say that an argument makes this conclusion:

> Because Max is a dog, he has a tail.

This conclusion is only logically valid if the first premise, the one about every dog, precedes it. Otherwise, if this conclusion follows the other premise, the one about **most** dogs, then the conclusion is not valid. In that situation, Max could be in the minority of dogs who do not have tails. That possibility means that the conclusion does not have to be true all the time. Therefore, it is not valid.

To do well on the logical Reasoning section, you must read carefully, and know exactly what the author said. Take a moment to read these amount signals several times:

Amount words:

- Every
- All
- Many
- Most
- A majority
- Some
- Several
- A few
- Only
- Not all
- None

Likelihood

Along with amount signals, you should also pay close attention to likelihood words which indicate the probability of an event occurring. Example of difference in likelihood:

> Tim may stop by the grocery store.
>
> Tim will stop by the grocery store.

Based on the first statement, we do not know whether Tim will stop by the grocery store. He may, or he may not. Using the second premise, we know for a fact that Tim is going to stop by the grocery store. "Will" in that statement indicates that there is a 100% probability of him doing so.

Likelihood words:

- Always
- Will
- Must
- Probably
- Likely
- Should
- May
- Sometimes
- Could
- Rarely
- Never

Pay attention to these signal words when you come across them.

In summary, likelihood signals give information about the probability of an event occurring, while amount signals tells the quantity of something. The LSAT writers use these signals against students who do not pay close attention to them. Ensure that you understand how they change the meaning of what they modify.

Passage Notes

Jotting a few notes as you read LR passages can help you follow them more fully. Use a pencil, not a highlighter, for your notes. It takes too long to switch back and forth between your highlighter and your pencil, which you need to fill in answer choices. Further, a pencil can make more precise marks than a highlighter.

X For Conclusion

One mark you should use is an "X" in the margin next to the conclusion. Pinpointing the conclusion is crucial for all passages that feature arguments and this practice will force you to do so. Fact-groups do not have conclusions, so you cannot use that notation with them.

Often, a concluding sentence will span multiple lines in the passage. Place the "X" on either side of the passage next to the sentence, wherever you feel is most appropriate. Conclusions often have a "core." Try to place the "X" as close to that core as possible.

Underlines (Optional)

Also, and this is optional, underline words that indicate a shift in viewpoint or subject. Transition words indicate a shift in the direction of the argument, for instance, that an anti-premise is coming up. Transition words include "however," "but," "yet," and "although." Amount and likelihood words, which have been covered thoroughly, should also be underlined. Often, the argument can hinge on just a few of those words. Underlining them forces you to make a note of their precise meaning. In summary, underline:

- Transition words or phrases
- Amount signals
- Likelihood signals

Do not underline premise or conclusion signals. With practice, you will pick up on these words without effort. Further, you will be marking the conclusion itself. Focus instead on becoming adept at identifying the argument parts as you read. Underline the information in that passage that helps to convey its meaning. Shifts in subject are more difficult to note than premise and conclusion signals, so they deserve a mark.

Important Phrases (Optional)

Finally, experiment with underlining important phrases in the passage. For some students, typically those who have a more difficult time on the LR section, this practice can help one follow the key ideas. Typically, underlining two to four phrases is all that is required to effectively highlight the crucial concepts in the passage. Example passage with important phrases underlined:

> A severe blow to the head can cause one to lose consciousness; from this some people infer that consciousness is a product of the brain and cannot survive bodily death. But a radio that becomes damaged may suddenly cease to broadcast the program it had been receiving, and we do not conclude from this that the program itself has ceased to exist. Similarly, more substantial evidence would be needed to conclude that consciousness does not survive bodily death.

The passage is about consciousness (we can tell this immediately because it is the first subject discussed and then the passage continues to explore the subject), so we underline "consciousness" in the first clause. That helps us to understand the rest of the passage. In the next clause, we underline "product of the brain" because that is the key topic in that clause. In the second sentence, "cease to broadcast the program" is a core idea, one that is a little slippery and elusive. Underlining it helps us to understand the comparison being drawn between the brain and a radio. In that sentence, we could just as easily have underlined "program itself has ceased to exist" as that gets at the same idea. Finally, in the last sentence, the conclusion, we underline "more substantial evidence" because that is the core of the conclusion.

It can be difficult to analyze the importance of ideas as you are reading a passage, and that is one reason why we do not emphasize underlining key phrases. Try underlining key phrases for a few LR sections and see how the practice works for you. Keep in mind that this notation will cause you to move more slowly, but hopefully grasp the passages more fully and therefore increase your accuracy.

Notations Summary

Overall, a few simple underlines can help you make much better sense of a passage. The act of visually identifying the words that have a large impact helps you understand the subtleties of the passage. Here is an example passage with transition, amount and likelihood phrases underlined; key phrases are not underlined:

> Bill: Cumulus clouds are typically gray or blue in color, although sometimes they can be a light green. The air temperature plays a major role in the coloration that can be seen. Only colder temperatures yield the rarer color in this type of cloud. Thus, the green cumulus clouds today are probably a result of the cold front that blew in yesterday. X

With practice, creating notes will require little extra time. Be consistent with your notes: always mark the same parts of the passage in the same way.

As you progress in your LR practice, you may find that you do not need to underline as many words and phrases as you see in the example passage above. Some students find only marking the conclusion helpful. In general, the higher you are scoring on the LR section, the less turning point, amount and likelihood signals you will need to underline because you are following the passages successfully. As you practice, experiment with less or more underlines to find the right balance for you. Note that all students should mark a conclusion with an "X".

*Introduction + Passages Review

Introduction Review

The chapters of this guide will be followed by an outline of the key points. Reading the outline immediately after the chapter will help you cement the knowledge just gained. Further, reread the outline of a chapter the day after you work through the chapter to further enforce the learning. You can also use the outlines to quickly refer to concepts as you progress in your prep.

- The two LR sections make up 50% of your LSAT score.
- To answer each of the 25 or 26 questions in 35 minutes, you will have 85 seconds per question. Many students will do best by not answering every question.
- The LR methods may initially cause you to slow down. With practice, you will speed up.
- Each question is made up of three parts: the passage, the query and the choices.
    - The passage has one or two paragraphs with information.
    - The query inquires something about the passage.
    - The choices attempt to answer that question.

Passages

- Introduction
    - Do not bring in specialized outside knowledge to a passage. Treat it as its own world.
        - Do realize that basic, well known facts hold true.
    - Read for details. Little differences in words can be quite important.
    - Learning how to read quickly and thoroughly is an important skill to develop.
- Topics
    - There are a wide variety of topics in the passages.
    - The topic is unconnected to the underlying logical structure of the passage.
    - A passage will explain all concepts used that are not general knowledge.
- Arguments and Fact-Groups
    - An argument has a conclusion supported by evidence.
        - Arguments tend to cause a reaction because a larger, more controversial point is made.
        - Arguments make up 75% of the passages.
    - Fact-groups are statements without a conclusion.
        - These tend to feel anti-climatic because no bigger point is made.

Distinguishing Argument Parts

- Identifying the parts of an argument is a vital skill.
    - To identify the evidence, ask yourself which statements are the most specific and concrete. Those are the premises used to support the conclusion.
    - To find the conclusion, ask yourself where the author is leading. Further ask which statement is the most general and/or controversial.
- Use signal words, words that tell which argument part is about to come, when they are available, but be aware that there are often none.
- The conclusion can come before the premises or in the middle of several premises.
- Supplementary premises provide extra support for a conclusion.
    - Signals: "moreover, besides, furthermore."
- Anti premises are information that goes against the author's conclusion.
    - The author will refute these premises to make his or her argument stronger.
    - Signals: however, on the other hand, but, yet.
- To locate the conclusion without signal words, analyze the scope of each statement.
    - The scope (how broad or specific the statement is) is determined by the statements around it.
    - The statement with the widest scope, the most general, is the conclusion.
    - The premises will have a narrower scope.

Complex Passages

- Advanced arguments have two conclusions.
    - The sub-conclusion is supported by other evidence.
        - The sub-conclusion supports the main conclusion.
    - Sometimes the ordering of the conclusions is counter intuitive.
- Two Speaker Arguments - two authors discussing the same topic from different angles.
    - Read them to see how the two authors' ideas interact.
    - The interaction between their points is often subtle.

Analyzing Arguments

- LSAT-Writers vs Authors
    - The authors of the passages believe in their arguments.
    - Generally, you can accept the statements in the passage as valid.
    - The LSAT-writers are trying to trick you, while the passage authors are not.
- An argument's scope is how broad or narrow the topic is.
    - Scope is a relative concept.
    - You need to compare various statements within a passage to identify the scope.
- Inferences and Assumptions
    - Inference - a statement that **must be true** based on evidence.
    - Assumption – an unstated premise that is required for a conclusion to be valid.
    - Both are concepts that are not directly stated but can be determined from the passage.

- Pay attention to differences in amount and likelihood.
  - Amount words give you quantity information.
    - every, all, many, most, a majority, some, several, a few, only, not all, none.
  - Likelihood words tell you probabilities.
    - always, will, must, probably, sometimes, likely, should, could, rarely, never, may.
- Passage Notes
  - Creating a select set of notes as you read a passage can help you understand it better.
    - Put an "X" next to the conclusion.
    - Underline turning-point signals, and amount and likelihood words
      - This is optional but recommended for lower scoring students.
    - Underline key phrases and terms (optional).
  - Experiment with marking as you practice to find what works for you.

*Drill - Identifying Argument Parts

Questions

Read and annotate the following passages. Then, where applicable, identify the premise(s) and conclusion. A paragraph may be a fact group. Check your work on the following page.

1) A course that helps a student think in a more quantitative way will serve them well later in life. Because all math courses help students think in more numerical, measurable ways, every student, regardless of their major, would be served well later in life by enrolling in a math course.

2) At the concert, I gave the bartender a $5 bill to pay for my drink. He gave me change as if I had given him ten dollars. I kept the extra five dollars. Since I did not threaten or deceive the bartender into giving me the extra five dollars, it was morally acceptable for me to keep the money.

3) The new iPad, a tablet computer released by Apple, will be a great financial success for the company. It is smaller and lighter than a laptop or netbook, and features both a beautiful screen and the ability to run all of the applications designed for the iPhone. Some critics warn that it lacks a niche and the computing power necessary to make a device that starts at $499 a must have for many people. However, its seamless design and fun factor should outweigh those critiques. Therefore, the iPad will be in high demand.

4) Almost all American men prefer to watch a basketball or football game rather than a cooking show. Most people in our society know far more about sporting events than they do about nutrition. Even though many women in our society are interested in preparing food, few know much about what vitamins and minerals various foods contain, or the best times to eat certain types of food. And women's interest in sports is growing rapidly, spurred on by advancements in the WNBA and the dominance of US women's softball globally.

Annotated Passages

Please use these annotated passages to check your work. For simplicity sake, we have often not underlined key phrases, and opted instead to underline only transition, amount and likelihood words.

> 1) A course that helps a student think in a more quantitative way will serve them well later in life. Because all math courses help students think in more numerical, measurable ways, every student, regardless of their X major, would be served well later in life by enrolling in a math course.

Premise 1 – "A course that helps a student think in a more quantitative way will serve them well later in life"

Premise 2 – "All math courses help students think in more numerical, measurable ways"

Conclusion – "Every student would be served well later in life by enrolling in a math course"

The first sentence is a premise that in conjunction with the second premise ("math courses help students think in more numerical, measurable ways"), makes the conclusion, which is marked with an "X," properly drawn. Note that we have to do a little translating here to see that "quantitative way" in the first sentence is synonymous with "numerical, measurable ways" in the second.

This argument has both a premise and a conclusion in its final sentence: the second premise is squeezed in just before the conclusion. This is a tricky format that the LSAT writers use, one to be aware of.

> 2) At the concert, I gave the bartender a five dollar bill to pay for my drink. He gave me change as if I had given him ten dollars. I kept the extra five dollars. Since I did not threaten or deceive the bartender into giving me the extra five dollars, it was morally acceptable for me to keep the money. X

Premise – "I did not threaten or deceive the bartender into giving me the extra five dollars"

Conclusion – "it was morally acceptable for me to keep the money"

This is a simple argument, with only one premise. The crucial parts of the last sentence – "threaten or deceive" and "morally acceptable" – are both underlined. These phrases are the core of the premise and conclusion.

When analyzing how well argued this passage is, we find it to be a weak argument because morals are typically based on honesty and being unselfish. The fact that the author did not threaten the bartender for the money does not make taking it morally acceptable. The premise here does not effectively support the conclusion.

X 3) The new iPad, a tablet computer released by Apple, will be a great financial success for the company. It is smaller and lighter than a laptop or netbook, and features both a beautiful screen and the ability to run all of the applications designed for the iPhone. Some critics warn that it lacks a niche and the computing power necessary to make a device that starts at $499 a must have for many people. However, its seamless design and fun factor should outweigh those critiques. Therefore, the iPad will be in high demand.

"Will" is a likelihood word, so we underline it. Still in the first sentence, we underline "great financial success" because it is general and controversial and therefore can be the conclusion; we have to read further into the passage to confirm that. The second sentence tells of iPad features that support the success idea, leading us to believe that the first sentence is the conclusion. The sentence that starts with "some critics" is an anti-premise that is disproved in the following sentence about the design and fun factor.

The final sentence has the conclusion signal "therefore" and then features a general statement that is a conclusion. However, the first sentence also featured a conclusion. Comparing the two, we see that the first sentence is the main conclusion and the final sentence is a sub conclusion. The iPad being in high demand is a statement that supports the even more general statement that the iPad will be a financial success for the company. High demand leads to financial success, i.e. profitability, not the other way around. This is an advanced argument.

4) Almost all American men prefer to watch a basketball or football game rather than a cooking show. Most people in our society know far more about sporting events than they do about nutrition. Even though many women in our society are interested in preparing food, few know much about what vitamins and minerals various foods contain, or the best times to eat certain types of food. And women's interest in sports is growing rapidly, spurred on by advancements in the WNBA and the dominance of US women's softball globally.

The final passage is a Fact-Group. All the facts discuss how in American society both men and women have more interest in sports than nutrition; nothing stands out as being supported by anything else, and the scope of all the statements is roughly the same.

Underlining all the amount words – "almost all," "many," etc. - is helpful. Knowing the thrust and scope of the passage will help you work the choices. The concepts discussed are simple, so underlining key phrases is probably unnecessary.

Query and Choices

The first thing you face in any Logical Reasoning question is the passage, as just discussed in detail. Directly after the passage, the query is the specific question asked **about** the passage. Example query:

> Which one of the following is supported by the information above?

The query tells you how to analyze the passage in order to correctly answer the entire question, which is made up of the passage, the query and the choices. The LSAT writers ask you to demonstrate your understanding of arguments in various ways through the different types of queries. There are eleven types of Logical Reasoning questions, so learning effective methods for all of them takes time.

The LSAT writers attempt to disguise the LR question type by using different words and phrasings in the queries for any given question type. By reading carefully for specific words and patterns, you will learn to identify each type. This helps in answering the question efficiently, because each type has its own qualities and specific methods.

Learn to quickly identify the various question types. This requires understanding generally what the types ask of you and typical phrasings that are used in different queries. If you misidentify a query then you are more likely to miss that question, so always read the query carefully.

Question Categories

Before explaining all eleven different question types in detail, it is helpful to divide the questions into two main categories: Identify Questions and Modify Questions. These categories relate to how you interact with the passage.

Identify Questions

Identify questions ask you to find the correct answer by directly using the information in the passage. The passage identifies the correct choice, so that answer choice will not contain any outside information, new information not featured in the passage. The correct answer will often be a synthesis or combination of information in the passage (such as an inference), but it will never be completely "outside" the information discussed by the passage. This fact helps you to eliminate answer choices on Identify questions that do feature new information.

For these reasons, the passage itself is a given: you should accept the statements within it without question. Assume a passage features this statement:

> Elephants always run sideways when happy.

For that question, believe that information to be true. If an elephant is said to be happy, you know it will be running sideways.

Further, the correct choice will never alter the meaning in the passage in any way or cause you to reconsider or doubt information in the passage. For example, Flaw questions are a question type in the Identify category. Flaw questions require you to identify the error in reasoning in the passage. The correct choice points out this flaw, and therefore contains no new concepts or discussion beyond the passage.

Identify Category Properties

- The passage identifies the correct choice.
- The passage is a given, so accept its information as true.
- The passage will not be modified by information in the choices.
- The correct choice will not feature new information not discussed in the passage.

Identify Question Types

The question types in both the Identify and Modify categories will be explained in detail later. These summaries of what the Identify question types ask you to do will give you a greater understanding of the properties of the category:

- Deduction - Make an inference from the information in the passage.
- Argument Structure - Describe the structure of the argument in general terms.
- Disagreement - Identify the point about which the two speakers disagree.
- Flaw - Pinpoint the flaw in reasoning in the argument.
- Principle - Identify the choice that works within the principle laid out in the passage.
- Parallel Structure - Match the structure of the argument with the arguments in the choices.

Modify Questions

Modify questions ask you to locate the choice that modifies (changes) the passage in a specific way. In order to do so, you must consider the passage to be malleable, able to be adjusted. Most Modify questions ask you to **support** the passage. You might be asked to use a principle that helps the conclusion make sense, to resolve a paradox in the passage, or to point out an unstated assumption of the passage. On the other hand, one Modify question type, Weaken questions, asks you to find the choice that successfully attacks the conclusion in the passage. But all the other types help the passage in some way.

Approach Modify questions from a different angle than you do Identify questions. Realize that the passage is not perfect; it lacks something that you will need to address. After all, you cannot help a solid argument or explain a fact-group that is logical. So, read the passage with a careful eye towards its potential fault. Identifying that will help you enormously when you work the choices.

Because you are asked to modify the passage, the correct choice on a question in the Modify category can bring in outside information. Therefore, accept the information in the choices, even outside information, as valid. Of course, only the correct choice will successfully modify the passage. This is another big difference between Modify and Identify questions.

Modify Question Properties

- The choice correctly modifies the passage.
- The passage is malleable and subject to change.
- The choices should be considered valid.
- The correct choice can feature outside information.

Modify Question Types

- Assumption - Fill in a gap in the logic of the argument by stating an assumption.
- Strengthen - Support the conclusion of the argument.
- Weaken - Attack the conclusion of the argument.
- Paradox Fix - Resolve the paradox in the Fact-Group.
- Support with Principle - Strengthen the argument by applying an appropriate Principle.

Query-Reversers

Even if you know the question type (and category) you are dealing with, a query-reverser can throw you a curve ball. Query-reversers are words that, when added to a query, change the meaning of a query to its logical opposite. There are two main query-reversers: "EXCEPT" and "LEAST." Because they have such a large impact, query-reversers always appear in capital letters. This makes it easier to spot one and adjust how you answer the question. Here is an example Deduction query with the query-reverser, "EXCEPT":

> "Each of the following is a valid inference of the passage EXCEPT…"

This Deduction query asks you which of the choices is **not** a valid inference of the passage. The four incorrect choices will be valid inferences from the passage. A typical Deduction query would ask you:

> "Which of the following is a valid inference of the passage?"

On this question, you are asked to find the single valid inference that fits the logic of the passage. The four incorrect choices will all be unsupported by the passage.

When a query-reverser is used, you are not always looking for a choice that is the opposite of what you would normally look for with that question type. You are instead looking for the logical opposite. This concept is evident with Strengthen and Weaken questions:

> "Which one of the following LEAST strengthens the argument?"

On this question, you are not necessarily weakening the conclusion, which would be the opposite of strengthening the argument (what you would do on a normal Strengthen question). Instead, you must find the choice that **does not** strengthen the argument. "Not strengthening" is the logical opposite of "strengthening." The correct choice may weaken the argument, or it may have no effect on the argument whatsoever. The other four choices on this question will strengthen the argument, which is why they are incorrect.

Put another way, a query-reverser asks you to find the choice that **does not** do what the other four (incorrect) choices do. Example query-reversed Weaken question:

> All of the following weakens the argument, EXCEPT..

The correct answer will not weaken the argument, while the other choices will. A simple rule of thumb for the correct choice on query-reversers: the correct choice does not satisfy the requirements of that question type. On Deduction questions normally your job is to find the choice that is a valid inference of the passage. On a query-reversed Deduction question, your job is find the choice that is not in line with the information in the passage. Likewise, the correct answer to a query-reversed Strengthen question will not support the conclusion, while the other four choices will support the conclusion.

Query-Reverser Summary

- The correct choice **does not** satisfy the normal requirements of the question type.
- Incorrect choices satisfy the normal requirements of the type.

Miscellaneous Question Type Information

Random Ordering

Within each LR section, you will face a jumble of the different question types. There is no specific ordering of the types of questions and rarely will you face two of the same question type in a row. This makes an LR section more challenging by forcing you to constantly change the skills you are using. Therefore, to do well on the LR section, you must stay light on your feet and take what the test throws at you. Expect the variation in question types. Realize that you will need to analyze arguments in different ways for each question.

One Correct Choice

Obviously, there is only one correct answer choice to each LR question. Do not be confused when a query includes the word "most."

> Which of the following choices most weakens the conclusion of the passage?

Just in case more than one choice does logically weaken the conclusion, there is still only has one answer: the choice that weakens it **the most**. Do not worry. One answer will always be superior when you understand the question.

The Answer Choices

Envision a Good Answer

Before discussing the answer choices more directly, we will introduce a crucial step in the approach to most LR questions: pausing to envision what a good answer looks like. To envision, take a few moments (5 – 10 seconds) to think about the elements (or properties) of the correct answer before even glancing at the choices.

If possible, state what you think the correct answer will be in your own words. If you have trouble getting at the correct answer or if the question is not conducive to envisioning, use the time to organize your understanding of the passage.

Helps You Work the Choices

Envisioning helps you condense your reading of the passage and transition to working the choices. This active thinking makes you less likely to fall for incorrect choices, many of which **sound** good. Even only knowing certain elements that will be in the correct choice can help in working through the choices, because you can eliminate choices that lack those elements. Envisioning helps you think of those features before you begin to take in the new information from the choices. On several question types, you should be able to envision the correct answer or a close approximation of it.

Save Time

Think of envisioning as an organizing step to use immediately after reading the passage. Envisioning is like reading the directions for a journey before you start driving the car. You have a good idea of what is going on when you hit the road because your thoughts are already collected and you have an understanding of the directions. Envisioning will help you get to your destination, the correct answer, faster. More on how to envision for different question types will be found in later chapters.

Choices Introduction

After the envision step, you will work the answer choices. Each LR question has five choices. The correct choice is superior to the other four, and is the only one that successfully answers the query. No questions have two equally correct answers but, rarely, a question will feature two choices that can both be said to answer the query, to different degrees. In those cases, one answer will answer the question more successfully. For instance, on a Weaken question, two choices could both weaken the argument, but the correct choice would weaken the argument more than the other choice. That question would be phrased such that the correct answer choice is the one that *most* weakens the argument. The other choice that only mildly weakens the argument does not fit the logical requirement of most weakening that the correct answer must have.

Incorrect Choices Do Not Answer the Query

A vast majority of the time, the incorrect choices do not come close to fulfilling the requirement of the query. For instance, on most Paradox questions, only the correct answer will resolve the paradox in the argument. The other four choices will not, in any way, settle the paradox. The incorrect choices may further the paradox (the opposite of what the query requests), or they may not affect the paradox. This is an important point: the incorrect choices will only "not fulfill" the query. That does not mean the incorrect choices do the **opposite** of what the query asks. For instance, incorrect choices on a Strengthen question do not necessarily weaken the conclusion. They often do not affect the conclusion one way or the other.

Read Every Choice

Speed/Accuracy Balance

The LR section requires you to move quickly in order to succeed. You have 35 minutes to answer 25 questions. So, if you wish to reach every question, you can spend an average of 84 seconds on each question. Of course, the reason to move quickly is to maximize the number of correct responses. Being accurate ("scoring" points) is all that matters for your score. You need to find the best balance between speed and accuracy. Striking that balance requires decisions. One big decision is whether to read each answer choice or to move on when you find a choice that you believe is correct.

Be Informed

We recommend that, a vast majority of the time, you read every answer choice. The LSAT writers are adept at creating incorrect choices that are quite appealing. Likewise, the correct answer choice will often be phrased in a strange way that makes it seem incorrect. For most questions, it is too costly to skip reading answer choices. The exceptions to this rule will be discussed in a moment. In general, reading every choice ensures that you are informed on all aspects of the question. If you do not read the correct choice, you cannot select it.

Duds & Hits

As you read the choices, sort them into two groups: duds and hits. We call this process working the choices.

Duds

Duds are choices that you **strongly** believe are incorrect; you need a good reason to label a choice as a dud. For instance, a choice on an Identify question may bring in outside information, or a choice may lack a crucial feature that you envisioned.

To designate a choice as a dud, cross out the letter (A, B, C, etc.) of the answer choice in the test booklet. Example:

> ~~A)~~ Paul is left handed.

By crossing off a dud, you are eliminating the choice, sending yourself a signal that the choice is incorrect. This helps you narrow your search for the correct answer. If you are unsure of whether a choice is incorrect, do not cross it off.

Hits

Hits are answer choices that seem like they could be correct. The envision step will hopefully help you identify elements in the correct answer, and your hits should have one or more of those elements with those. Or, you may simply identify a choice as a good match for the question.

To mark a hit, put a light dot next to the letter:

- D) Paul is a walrus.

As you progress through the choices, compare each new hit to previous ones (if any) and make a mental note of which choice is stronger. Actively evaluating the choices against one another as you progress through them helps you zero in on the correct choice. By the time you finish working the choices, you will often have a top candidate among the hits. In that case, circle that choice's letter:

- (D) Paul is a walrus.

That will be the answer you fill in on your answer sheet.

Note that you will not be able to evaluate some choices as either clear hits or duds. In those cases, just place no mark next to them.

Scenarios

After you finish working the choices, you will probably be in one of three scenarios:

1) You have a top candidate (its letter is circled).

- Your work is done. Fill in the appropriate bubble on your answer sheet, and move on to the next question.

2) You have two hits and cannot tell which one answers the question most effectively.

- If you feel that you may have misunderstood or misread one of the choices then carefully reread each of the two choices. Look for a subtle meaning you may have missed the first time. This is most likely to happen when the choices are long or complex.
- If you understand each choice, then return to the passage to find information that can help you distinguish between them. It might help to pick a single choice to eliminate or prove using the passage.
- After rereading the choices or returning to the passage, one choice should stand out. Select it and move on to the next question. Otherwise, if you are still stuck between the two choices, make your best guess and move on to the next question.

3) You have eliminated every choice as a Dud.

- If you feel that you may have misunderstood or misread one of the choices, reread all the choices carefully, looking for one or more that you may have eliminated without good reason. Remember that the logic for a choice may be tough to understand, so take your time during this reread of the choices.
- If you have a good grasp on the five choices, then return to the passage and reread it slowly for information that you missed the first time. You likely misread or misunderstood a key piece of the passage that caused you to eliminate a choice you should not have.
- When you find a choice that you believe is superior, select it and move on. Otherwise, if you still believe that no choice is correct, make a guess and move on to the next question.

Exceptions

The sorting process just described strikes the right balance between speed and accuracy because it helps you minimize rereading the passage and the choices. It also ensures that you do not miss a question because you selected an answer before reading the correct choice.

However, there are situations when you should not work through every choice, or even read some of the choices. The first is when you envision a full answer and find a choice that is very close or identical to your envisioned answer. If you feel confident on the question, select the choice and move on without reading the rest of the choices. This allows you to save time on easier questions, or questions where you effectively envisioned the answer. You should also forgo reading every choice when you are low on time at the end of a section and feel confident in an answer. This will save you time for the remaining questions.

Ignoring the "read every choice rule" should be done only in special situations, because it can lead to errors. Many students are better off **always** reading every choice. Use your practice to determine what works best for you.

Method for an LR Question

Below is a summary of the key steps to use in answering every Logical Reasoning question. Learning how to efficiently use these steps does take practice, but this is a balanced, effective way of approaching LR questions.

1) Read the Query

- Start out by reading the Query carefully. Pay attention to any Query Reversers.
- Identify the question type. Knowing this will help you work the passage more successfully.

2) Read the Passage

- Carefully read the Passage, keeping in mind the question type and the information it requires (more on this in the chapters on each particular question type). Use your knowledge of the Query to inform what you are looking for in the Passage.
- As you read, underline the important points and shifts in subject/viewpoint.
- If the Passage is an Argument, pinpoint the Conclusion and put an X next to it. If the Passage is a Fact-Group, simply read each premise carefully.
- Reading the passage slowly and carefully one time is often more efficient than reading it twice too quickly. Keep this in mind as you progress in your practice.

3) Envision

- Before looking at any of the choices, pause for a few seconds and think about the properties or elements the correct choice will have. If possible, state in your own words what the correct answer will be.
- If you have trouble envisioning elements of the answer or you are dealing with a question type that does not lend itself to envisioning, simply pause and organize your thoughts on the passage.

4) Sort the Choices

- Read each choice carefully, evaluating whether it is a Hit or a Dud. Cross out the letter of Duds and put a small dot next to the letter of each Hit.
- Compare each new Hit you see with your top Hit to that point.

5) Choose

- Use your markings to choose the best answer. Circle its letter.
- If necessary, reread answer choices or the Passage in a focused way, ideally to decide between two Hits.
- When you leave a problem, put it out of your mind.
- In most question explanations, steps 4 and 5 will be combined.

Skill Adjustment

Lower scoring students, those who have a diagnostic score below 150 or an average LR section diagnostic score under 14 correct, will likely benefit from reading the query after the passage. This method is straightforward. First, read the passage carefully, then read the query. This way, you can absorb the passage without trying to keep other information in mind at the same time. If this applies to you, experiment with reading the query before and after the passage to see which works best for you.

The major disadvantage of this approach is that you may need to return to the passage a second time to be able to answer the query. This extra step takes time, and is why we recommend that most students read the query first.

Questions 1-12 in an LR section are, on average, much less difficult than questions 13-25. So, if you are a lower scoring student, it may make sense for you to read the query before the passage on the first questions in the section, when the passages are less complex and you can keep the query in mind as you work it. Then, on question 13, switch to reading the passage first. Something to experiment with.

Bubbling Answers

Learning methods for the LR section will not help you unless you practice them. During practice, simulate the official testing experience as much as possible. One aspect of that is marking the answers on your answer sheet, the one with the bubbles:

Become proficient at filling in the answer sheet bubbles, as that is where you gain or lose points. When you complete a full LR section, fill in the bubbles after completing every *two pages* of LR questions, which will contain about six questions. This will save you valuable seconds over filling in the bubble after you complete each question. Practice this method thoroughly: it takes getting used to. After some time, it will be second nature and you will not make any mistakes while doing so.

Fill in only one bubble per question and leave no stray marks on your answer sheet. Otherwise, you run the risk of not getting credit for responses that the grading machine misread. Also, fill in each bubble darkly. Losing points by not filling in bubbles thoroughly or by having unnecessary marks on your answer sheet is silly.

Conclusion

You now have a foundation for understanding LR questions. It is understandable if some of the methods you read feel abstract. They will become clearer when they are illustrated through learning about the question types. This is like how traveling to a new city helps all the things you have heard about it come to life.

Everything covered in the rest of the LR methods will build upon the ideas presented. If you need to, return to these first few chapters for a refresher.

*Queries and Choices Review

Identify Question Category

- The correct choice is identified by the information in the passage.
    - It will not contain any outside information.
- Accept the statements in the passage.
    - The passage will not be affected by the correct choice.

Modify Question Category

- The correct choice changes the passage or changes how one sees the information in the passage.
    - A correct choice can contain new information.
- The passage should be considered malleable/flawed. Read it with this in mind.

Other Query Information

- Query-reversers change the meaning of the query to its logical opposite using the word "EXCEPT" or "LEAST."
    - For example, on a query-reversed Strengthen question, you are looking for the choice that **does not** strengthen the argument.
- Envisioning a good answer before looking at the choices is crucial because it helps you work through the choices successfully.

The Answer Choices

- Generally, read every answer choice. Exceptions include when you have found your envisioned answer or when you are strapped for time.
- Sort the choices into duds and hits.
    - A dud is a choice that you are confident is wrong: cross off the letter of that choice.
        - Avoid crossing off choices unless you are confident they are incorrect.
    - A hit is a choice that you believe is correct: mark it with a dot next to its letter.
- After you sort the five choices and you have at least one hit, select your top candidate among the hits.
    - If necessary, reread the hits and/or the passage to help you distinguish between two hits.
    - If you have five duds, reread either the passage or the choices, whichever you understood the least well.

Method for an LR question

1. Read the query.
    a. Identify the question category and type. Use this information when you read the passage.
2. Read the passage carefully.
    a. Caveat: if you are a lower scoring LR student, experiment with reading the passage before the query and do what works best for you.
3. Envision a good answer to the question (if applicable).
    a. At a minimum identify a few elements a good answer should have.
    b. If the type is not susceptible to envisioning, use this step to organize your thoughts on the passage.
4. Sort the choices.
    a. Mark duds and hits accordingly.
5. Choose the best hit.

Bubbling Answers

- Fill in answers on your answer sheet after completing two pages of LR questions, about 6 questions at a time.
- Be sure your answer sheet is clean. A stray mark could cost you a point.
- Fill in the bubbles darkly.

Conditionals

This chapter will cover conditionals, an underlying concept that can crop up on many different question types. A conditional is a statement created by combining two different conditions. Put another way, a conditional is a logical arrangement that features two or more conditions. Think of conditions as possibilities: states or events (occurrences) that can happen. A condition is often a state at a particular time. Example:

Jill is tired.

Being tired is a state. Someone can be tired or not tired; this state can change with time. Perhaps yesterday Jill was tired and today she is rested (not tired). This is the nature of a condition: it is either true or not true at any given time. We will also use the terms "met" or "not met" to signify this aspect of being true or false. When a condition is met, we say that the condition is true. If today Jill is tired, then she meets the condition of being tired. It is true that she is tired. Conditions can be more than states; they can also be events. Example of a condition that is an event:

to write a letter.

If Tom wrote a letter yesterday, then Tom met the condition of writing a letter. He completed that act.

Back to the larger picture, a conditional tells you how several conditions relate to one another. A conditional tells you how one condition is affected by another condition being true or false. Example conditional:

If someone swims often, *then* he or she will have a strong back.

Indicator & Requirement

Now to add some nuance: each conditional has two different types of conditions. The names of each part of a conditional tell you how that part relates to the other condition. It helps to focus on the name of the condition you have information about and refer to the other as "the other condition."

Every conditional has an indicator and a requirement. The indicator tells (indicates) when the other condition is true. In the example above, the first part of the conditional – "if someone swims often" – is the indicator because it tells when the other condition (having a strong back) will be true.

The requirement gives a prerequisite (or requirement) that must be fulfilled in order for the other condition to be true. "Then he or she will have a strong back" is the requirement because it tells one prerequisite of swimming often.

Indicator	**Requirement**
If someone swims often,	*then* he or she will have a strong back.

The Indicator

When the indicator is **true** (or met), when someone does swim often, it tells us that the other condition in the relationship (here, having a strong back) is also true. For example, if we know that Cathy swims often, then the indicator is true. That means that the other condition, having a strong back, must also be true. Because we know that Jane swims often we also know that she has a strong back. You can think of this as: when an indicator is activated (or true), it tells you the other condition occurs.

On the other hand, when the indicator is **false**, it does not tell us anything about the other condition. In that case, the other condition could be either true or false. For example, if we know that Phil does not swim often, that gives us no information about the strength of his back. Phil could have a strong back or he could have a weak one; we have no idea. The indicator only gives information about the other condition when it is true.

The Requirement

The requirement works in the opposite way that the indicator does. When the requirement is **false**, we know that the other condition (the indicator) is also false. The requirement is a prerequisite for the other condition to be true. Because of this, the requirement only gives us information about the other condition when it is not met. For instance, if we are told that Frank does not have a strong back, then that means the requirement is not met. Therefore, the other condition, swimming often, cannot be true. We know that Frank does not swim often. When a requirement is not met, the other condition cannot occur.

In contrast, if a requirement is true, that tells us nothing. The requirement being met does not prove that the other condition is met. This is because there may be **other requirements** for that condition besides the one requirement we know about, the one in the conditional. For example, having access to a pool may be another requirement for swimming often, on top of the prerequisite of having a strong back. For instance, if we know that Sam has a strong back, that means the requirement is met. It is possible that Sam swims often, but it is equally possible that he does not. Perhaps Sam lifts weights and that is why he has a strong back.

Summary

Here is a summary of the relationships between the indicator and the requirement:

We are told:	So we also know:
Indicator is True	Requirement is True
Indicator is False	Nothing about the requirement
Requirement is False	Indicator is False
Requirement is True	Nothing about the indicator

Diagramming Conditionals

It is usually easy to diagram a conditional and a symbolic representation makes them easier to understand. Creating a conditional diagram is a three step process. Let us continue with the same example:

If someone swims often, then they will have a strong back.

1) Figure out which part is the indicator and which part is the requirement.

With all "if/then" conditionals, the part after the "if" is the indicator. So, here, "someone swims often" is the indicator. Therefore, the other condition – "they will have a strong back" - is the requirement. Put another way, the condition after "then" is the requirement.

2) Condense the ideas from each condition into a one or two word symbol.

Choose a core idea of each condition to represent it:

If someone swims often	becomes	Swim
they will have a strong back	becomes	Strong

3) Plug the symbols into the conditional equation.

The conditional equation only has three parts: the two symbols that represent the conditions and an arrow placed in between them. The indicator symbol comes first and the requirement symbol comes after the arrow:

indicator --> requirement

Plug in "Swim" in the indicator spot and "Strong" in the requirement spot:

Swim -> *Strong*

If someone swims often, then they will have a strong back.

Information Flow

The diagram above tells us that if someone swims often, that person will have a strong back. When given information about one condition, the diagram helps you deduce specific information about the other condition.

The arrow in the diagram is useful. True information flows **with** the arrow, to the right. This is just a rephrasing of what we talked about earlier: when the indicator is true, so it the requirement. True information moves in that direction.

indicator = True --> requirement = True

When the indicator is false, that information does not flow with the arrow:

indicator = False --> requirement = ?

This shows that knowing that the indicator is false does not tell us anything about the requirement.

False information, information that a condition is not met, only moves from right to left. In other words, false information flows against the arrow. If we are told that the requirement in a conditional is false, then the indicator is also false:

indicator = False --> requirement = False

If someone does not have a strong back, then they must not swim regularly.

On the other hand, if we are given information that the requirement is true, that does not tell us anything about the indicator:

indicator = ? --> requirement = True

Even if Steve has a strong back, we do not know if he swims often.

Another Example

This conditional requires a more complicated diagram than the previous one:

If it does not snow tomorrow, then Eddie will play golf.

First, figure out which condition is the indicator and which is the requirement. Because this is an if/then conditional, the indicator follows "if" and the requirement comes after "then." The indicator is "does not snow," and the requirement is "Eddie will play golf."

The second step in diagramming a conditional is to pick symbols to represent each condition. "Does not snow tomorrow" has a negative meaning; it means the opposite of it does snow. So, use a negative sign before the symbol for "snow" to indicate that it does not snow. A negative sign before a symbol makes the meaning of that symbol the opposite of what it would be.

- Snow = does not snow

Use "Golf" as the symbol for the condition "Eddie will play golf."

To finish the diagram, put each symbol in its appropriate place in the diagram with the arrow:

- Snow -> Golf

We read this diagram: "if it does not snow tomorrow, Eddie will play golf."

Identifying Conditions

Now that you have a grasp on conditionals, we will give you tools to identify the two conditions in different situations. You see, not all conditionals are in the if/then format.

Indicator Phrased

An if/then conditional is an example of an indicator phrased conditional, a conditional that is worded in a way that emphasizes the role of the indicator. Below are indicator phrased conditionals that all express the meaning of the diagram:

Runs Fast -> Win

If Jane runs fast, **then** she will win the race.

Jane **always** wins the race **when** she runs fast.

Every time Jane runs fast, she wins the race.

Jane ran fast, **so** she must have won the race.

These conditionals all tell what happens when Jane runs fast. Their wording focuses on the outcome of a condition. Put another way, these conditionals tell you what a specific condition **indicates**. The key words in them are in bold. Common words that signal an indicator phrased conditional:

- if/then
- always/when
- every time
- so

Because we know which condition is the indicator we can easily diagram these conditionals. The "other condition" in these examples must be the requirement.

Requirement Phrased

As you can likely guess, a conditional is requirement phrased when its wording and meaning focus on the requirement. Put another way, it is a conditional that emphasizes the role of the requirement. Here are a few examples of requirement phrased conditionals:

Runs Fast -> Win

It is **necessary to** win in order to run fast.

Winning is **required for** Jane to run fast.

Jane **only** runs fast when she wins.

Signal words that you are dealing with a requirement phrased conditional:

- In order
- Necessary
- Required
- Only/ when

All of the examples tell us that Jane winning is a **requirement** for her to run fast. We know that winning is the requirement and running fast is the indicator.

Either condition can come first in a sentence, so pay attention to the underlying meaning of the conditions instead of their ordering.

The Contrapositive

Diagramming a conditional makes manipulating it easy. Why would you want to manipulate a conditional? Every conditional has two forms that are equally valid, two ways of expressing its information. Often, you need to "derive" the form you are not given in the passage in order to answer an LR question. You just learned how to diagram the traditional form for a conditional. The other form is called the contrapositive. From the traditional diagram of a conditional, you negate both conditions and reverse their order.

Negating a condition means making it its opposite. The condition, "Jane wins," becomes "Jane does not win" when it is negated. To negate a condition on the diagram, draw a negative sign before it:

Win becomes *-Win*

To negate a condition that is already negated, make that term positive (remove the negative sign before the term). When you negate a term that is already negated, the two negative signs cancel out. This is similar to how two negative numbers multiplied by each other yield a positive number. If we negate the condition "does not snow," we get "it does snow."

-Snow becomes *Snow*

Taking the Contrapositive

Let us walk through the steps for creating the contrapositive:

1) Negate BOTH of the terms in the usual diagram:

We start with the traditional diagram below, which reads: "if Jane runs fast, then she wins."

Fast -> Win

The traditional diagram above becomes:

-Fast -> -Win

We read that diagram, "if Jane does not run fast, she does not win." Both terms are negated.

2) Reverse the order of the terms:

-Fast -> -Win

Becomes:

-Win -> -Fast

We read this, "If Jane does not win, then she did not run fast." This is logically identical to what we started with: "if Jane runs fast, then she will win." We are saying the same thing in a different way. Because we know that Jane running fast indicates that she will win, we also know that if Jane does not win, then she did not run fast. The contrapositive is as valid as the original form, and that is why it can be useful. As you can see, once you have diagrammed the conditional, taking the contrapositive is not particularly difficult.

Taking the Contrapositive with Compound Conditionals

When a conditional has more than one indicator or requirement it is a compound conditional. Taking the contrapositive of compound conditionals requires some additional guidance. Look at this compound conditional:

If Alexis teaches a yoga class, then Tom and Stephanie will attend.

We diagram that conditional like this:

Alexis Teaches -> Tom + Stephanie

The plus sign means "and." The plus sign is crucial here. To derive the contrapositive of a compound conditional, negate the conditions and reverse them. Also, there is one new concept: change "and" to "or" and vice versa. So, the contrapositive of the conditional above is:

-Tom or -Stephanie -> -Alexis Teaches

"If Tom *or* Stephanie does not attend then Alexis did not teach a yoga class." We simply write out "or." There is no need to use a special symbol with it.

The switch from "and" to "or" when taking the contrapositive is intuitive because we know that if Alexis does teach, then both Tom **and** Stephanie will show up. If either Tom **or** Stephanie does not show up, then we know that Alexis did not teach a class.

Along these lines, exchange "or" for "and" when taking a contrapositive of a conditional that has "or" in the traditional diagram. Example conditional:

If Josh or Katy drive to the ranch, they will arrive before noon.

Diagram:

Josh or Katy -> Before Noon

To create the contrapositive, negate the terms, reverse them and insert an "and" where the "or" was:

-Before Noon -> -Josh + -Katy

If they do not get there before noon, then Josh did not drive **and** Katy did not drive. This contrapositive makes sense, because if they did not arrive before noon then neither of them drove. If either had driven, they would have arrived before noon.

More Conditionals

Now we will discuss a few of the subtle points of conditionals.

Conditional Errors

Beginning with a new example, we will look at two logical errors that crop up often in both LR passages and in the answer choices. Example conditional:

If the geese fly south, they will have plenty to eat this winter.

Our diagrams which are accurate:

South	->	Plenty	(Traditional Diagram)
-Plenty	->	-South	(Contrapositive)

If the birds do not have plenty to eat this winter, then they did not fly south.

Reversal Error

Now, we discuss some common errors that crop up when working with conditional diagrams. A reversal error occurs when one tries to diagram a conditional and accidentally puts the conditions in the wrong places:

If the geese fly south, they will have plenty to eat this winter.

Diagram that features a reversal error:

Plenty -> South

"If the birds have plenty to eat this winter, they flew south." This is the same as saying that when the requirement (plenty to eat this winter) is met, it means that the other condition is also met (flying south). This is not the case. The requirement can only tell when the indicator is **not valid**. The geese could have plenty to eat because a farmer gave them food, not because they flew south. Flying south guarantees that they get enough to eat, but it is not necessary that they fly south to get enough to eat.

Negation Error

A negation error occurs when one tries to diagram a conditional and puts the conditions in the correct order:

If the geese fly south, they will have plenty to eat this winter.

Diagram that features a negation error:

-South -> -Plenty

"If the birds do not fly south, then they will not have plenty to eat this winter." The indicator cannot tell when the requirement is not valid. The indicator can only signify when the requirement is met. It is faulty to say that because the geese did not fly south, they do not have enough to eat. The geese could have stayed put and still found enough food.

Reversal and negation errors will crop up often in the choices. When you see them, you can eliminate incorrect choices and identify flawed arguments.

Conditionals Do Not Signal Causation

Conditionals do not indicate causation, they do not tell you that one thing caused another. Conditional reasoning is about how conditions relate to each other, what they can tell us about each other. The indicator does not cause the requirement to happen. The indicator tells what also happens when the indicator condition is true.

There is no timing inherent in a conditional. The indicator can happen before, at the same time or after the requirement. A conditional is its own world and it does not have to make sense in reality:

> If I lift weights, I get weaker.

> *Lift -> Weaker*

People in the real world usually get stronger when they lift weights. However, each conditional is its own world and the logic holds together there. Judge the conditionals you see to be accurate. With the conditional above, we believe that the author gets weaker when she lifts weights. Maybe she needs more protein in her diet.

Lack Modifiers

These four words can make a conditional difficult to diagram:

- Unless
- Except
- Without
- Until

We call these words lack modifiers. Here is conditional with one:

> Unless Frank gets a job, he will have to foreclose on his house.

You can tease out the meaning of this conditional by carefully analyzing it. What makes it tough is that you need to negate one condition in order to form an accurate diagram. If Frank does not get a job, he will foreclose. So not getting a job is the indicator and foreclosing is the requirement.

> *-Job -> Foreclose*

These constructions do not tell you what a condition signifies like a normal conditional. Instead, they tell you what the **lack** of a condition signifies. This is why we call them Lack Modifiers. Above, the sentence tells us what Frank not getting a job signifies - that he foreclosed. You do not want to have to analyze every conditional to this degree because it leaves a lot of room for errors and confusion. And it takes more time than using a two step process.

Working with Lack Modifiers

Here is how you diagram a conditional that has a lack modifier:

1. Negate the condition modified by the lack modifier and make it the indicator. An easy way to remember this is that the lack modifier is **changing** (negating) the condition.
2. The other condition is the requirement.

In the previous example, Frank getting a job is modified by the term "unless," so we take getting a job and negate it and make that the indicator:

-Job ->

The other condition, "foreclosing on his house" is the requirement:

-Job -> Foreclose

If Frank does not get a job, he must foreclose on his house.

Here are more conditionals with the lack modifiers:

Humans cannot live without water.

"Without" modifies water. So, negate the symbol for water and place it as the indicator. Then, cannot live is the requirement:

-Water -> -Live

Final examples:

I will be tired until I get a nap.

-Nap -> Tired

Susan is happy except when she is working.

-Working -> Happy

Other Conditionals

We have discussed the common conditionals and also those that feature lack modifiers. There are two other types to note: "either/or" conditionals and "if and only if" conditionals.

Either/Or

Some conditionals feature an either/or relationship:

> Either Jane or Maria will go to the dance.

Either/or conditionals are not diagrammed in the usually way. This is because either/or conditionals signify that at least one will do the action in question. Either Jane will go to the dance or Maria will go to the dance. One of the two will definitely go. Unlike in real life, an either/or situation on the LSAT also means that it is possible that **both** go. With all this mind, diagram the conditional like this:

> -Jane -> Maria

If Jane does not go to the dance, then Maria will. The contrapositive:

> -Maria -> Jane

If Maria does not go to the dance, then Jane will. Notice that by diagramming the conditional this way, it is still possible that both Maria and Jane go. This is because we have no information about what happens one girl does go to the dance. Neither conditional above has an indicator that positively shows a girl going to the dance.

If and Only If

In if and only if conditionals, the two conditions only occur together:

> Bill will fly if, and only if, he has a business meeting.

If one of the conditions is not met, then the other does not occur. If one condition is met, then the other condition occurs as well.

Diagram if and only if conditionals by placing the two symbols for each condition together, right next to each other. This indicates that the conditions are an inseparable pair. Capitalize each symbol, as that will help you visually differentiate them. Also, keep each to a single word. The conditional above is diagrammed like this:

> FlyMeeting

If we are told that Bill does not have a business meeting then that also means that he does not fly, because this pair is inseparable. Or, if we know that Bill does fly tomorrow, then we know that he has a meeting.

Linking Conditionals

Now that you know all the different types of conditionals, we can introduce the concept of combining two conditionals. Linking conditionals together allows you to come up with new information and insights. Those insights may help you solve a LR question.

To link two conditionals, you need the conditionals to share a condition. One of the conditionals must have the condition as a requirement and the other as an indicator. Example conditionals that meet these criteria:

> If Phil studies hard, he will learn a great deal in school.
>
> Study -> Learn
>
> If he learns a lot in school, then he will have a stronger resume.
>
> Learn -> Resume

"Learn" is the shared condition. It is the requirement in the first conditional and the indicator in the second conditional, so it fits the prerequisite of linking. To link these two conditionals, we add another arrow after "learn" in the first conditional and place the requirement of the second conditional, "resume," after it:

> Study -> Learn -> Resume

You can visualize linkage as a process of addition:

	Study	->	Learn		
+			Learn	->	Resume
=	Study	->	Learn	->	Resume

Now we have one long chain of logic because we have multiple arrows. Because we know that "Study" indicates "Learn," and "Learn" indicates "Resume," we can drop the "Learn" in the middle and create this new conditional:

> Study -> Resume

If Phil studies hard, he will have a stronger resume. Its contrapositive:

> -Resume -> -Study

If Phil does not have a stronger resume, he did not study hard.

Linking conditionals will come in handy on many LR questions and on the Games section.

*Conditionals Review

Introduction

- A condition is a state at a particular time or an event.
- A conditional is a logical arrangement featuring multiple conditions.
- When the indicator is true, the other condition is as well. The indicator only gives information when true.
- The requirement is one prerequisite for the other condition to be true.
    - So, when the requirement is false, the other condition is as well.
    - The requirement only gives information when false.

Diagramming Conditionals

- 1) Figure out which condition is the indicator and which is the requirement.
- 2) Condense the core ideas from each condition into a one or two word symbol.
- 3) Plug the symbols into the appropriate spot in the conditional diagram:
    - indicator -> requirement
- A conditional is indicator phrased when it is worded in such a way that it emphasizes the role of the indicator.
    - Example: "Jane **always** wins the race **when** she runs fast."
    - Fast -> Win
- Requirement phrased is when a conditional focuses on the requirement, on what is necessary.
    - Example: "Jane **only** runs fast **when** she wins."

The Contrapositive

- To create the contrapositive:
    - 1) Negate both terms in the traditional diagram
        - Fast -> Win
        - becomes
        - -Fast -> -Win
        - When negating compound conditionals, change "and" to "or" and vice versa
    - 2) Reverse the negated conditions
        - -Fast -> -Win
        - becomes
        - -Win -> -Fast
- Negation error – negating both of the original conditions.
    - Example conditional: If the geese fly south, they will have plenty to eat this winter.
    - Correct Diagram: South -> Plenty
    - Negation Error: -South -> -Plenty

- Reversal error – reversing the order of the conditions from the proper diagram.
  - If the geese fly south, they will have plenty to eat this winter.
  - Correct Diagram: South --> Plenty
  - Reversal Error: Plenty --> South
- Both errors are equivalent to taking only one step towards creating the contrapositive. You must negate **and** reverse the original conditional diagram in order to create a correct diagram.

Dealing with Lack Modifiers (Unless, Except, Until, Without)

- 1) Negate the term modified by the lack modifier (unless, except, until, or without) and make it the indicator.
- 2) The other condition is the requirement.
- Example conditional: "Bill plays guitar well unless he has a cold."
  - Unless modifies "has a cold" so we negate that condition and place it as the indicator. "Plays guitar well" is therefore the requirement:
  - *-cold -> plays well*

Other Conditionals

- Either/Or
  - "Either Jane or Maria will go to the dance."
  - At least one of the conditions will be true, and possibly both will be true.
  - Diagrams (these say the same thing):
    - *-Jane -> Maria*
    - *-Maria -> Jane*
  - An alternative diagramming method is this: ***Jane/Maria***
- If and Only If
  - "Bill will fly if, and only if, he has a business meeting."
  - The two conditionals will either both be true or both be false.
  - Clump the terms together to show that they have the same outcome:
    - *FlyMeeting*

Amazon Review

- If you are finding this book helpful, please take five minutes now and post a review for it on Amazon.com. We really, really appreciate you doing so!

Causal Reasoning + Metrics

Causal reasoning and metrics are two more concepts that can underlie the logic of many different question types. In this way, they are similar to conditionals. We will cover how causal reasoning and metrics show up in LR questions and what to do when you see them.

Causal Reasoning

Being familiar with how the LSAT uses cause and effect (causal) reasoning gives you an advantage on many LR questions. Causal reasoning is when an author states that one thing caused another thing to occur. A cause is the event or situation responsible for an effect. Causal reasoning is easy to recognize because it involves one thing making another happen. Here are common terms used in causal reasoning:

- because of
- leads to
- induced by
- promoted by
- determined by
- is an effect of

Different than Conditional Reasoning

Causal reasoning is a different than conditional reasoning in a few ways. First, causality has a definite order: the cause occurs, then the effect occurs. With conditional reasoning, it is possible that the requirement occurs before the indicator. Next, causal reasoning features a direct connection between the two conditions: the cause makes the effect occur. Conditional reasoning is a less direct connection: the indicator does not cause the requirement, it just tells you when it is true.

The LR section will require you to do different things with each type of reasoning. With causal reasoning, you will be asked to show how the causality in an argument is incorrect. You have to do more complex things with conditionals, such as link them to form new deductions or identify the contrapositive in the choices.

Diagramming Causality

If necessary, diagram causal reasoning as you would a conditional, but use a wavy arrow to show that it is causality and not a conditional. Place the cause before the arrow (where the indicator goes in a conditional) and the effect after the arrow:

Becoming involved in a pyramid scheme will cause one to go bankrupt.

In this example, the effect follows the word "cause." This is typical. Diagram:

Pyramid Scheme ~> Bankrupt

Generally, it is not necessary to diagram causal reasoning. You only need to be aware that the question features causality to answer it correctly.

Location

Causal reasoning can appear either in the premises or conclusion of an argument; it rarely occurs in fact-groups. The placement is important because a conclusion with causal reasoning is always flawed, while causality in the premises should be accepted.

In the Premises

The premises in most arguments on the LR section should be accepted as valid. Even when you are finding a flaw in an argument, it will generally not come from a premise being faulty, it will come in the conclusion or in how the conclusion uses the premises. So, if causality is part of the evidence, believe that causality. Example argument that uses causal reasoning as evidence:

> Speeding causes fatal car accidents. Jim always speeds when he drives, so he is more likely to die in a car accident than Katy who never speeds.

The reasoning in the first sentence is one premise, and it should be accepted as accurate. We believe that speeding causes fatal car accidents. Because we accept that causality, the argument as a whole is logical.

In the Conclusion

A causal conclusion is when an author argues that one event caused another. These conclusions will often be based on one of two different situations in the premises.

The first situation is when a premise indicates that one event occurred before another event. Authors will often argue for causation in these situations; their conclusion will be based upon that. Here is an example argument of this type:

> The previews always come before the feature presentation when I go see a movie in a theatre. Therefore, the feature presentation is caused by the previews.

Obviously, the previews do not cause the feature to start, they just happen to come before the feature on the film reel. Assuming that because one thing came first it caused what followed it is a common causal reasoning error, and one you should be aware of. Note that we do not deny the premise here – the previews do start before the feature – we realize that the conclusion based on that premise is unfounded.

The second scenario where authors erroneously conclude that causality is involved is when two events occur at the same time in the premises. Example argument:

> George: I often see people wearing black clothing and crying at the same time. So, wearing black clothing must cause people to cry.

This argument argues that causation occurred when it is more likely that the two events are correlated (they occur together, but neither is responsible for the other). Or, it is possible that a third event or situation is causing both of the other two occurrences. For instance, people often wear all black and cry **at funerals**. Attending a funeral is likely the real cause of both of the two occurrences that occur together. Look out for causal conclusions where a third event is the true cause. A common way to weaken a causal conclusion is to point out the real cause.

The Only Possible Cause

On the LSAT, when a speaker makes a causal conclusion, that conclusion comes with the assumption that the stated cause is the **only cause** for that effect. This assumption, although extreme, is always present. Assume that the author analyzed all the other possible causes for the effect and decided that this is the real cause. This is not how we view causation in everyday life, so it is an instance of the LSAT being its own unique world. Example argument:

> The dam ruptured 12 hours after the testing crew finished their evaluation of its structural integrity. That means that the evaluation caused the dam to fail.

The conclusion is that the evaluation is what caused the dam to fail. The author says that none of these potential causes could have created the effect: dynamite set at the dam's weak spots, old age, a buildup of water pressure due to flooding, etc.

Knowing this always-present assumption regarding causation is helpful. Any choice with information about the assumption can weaken or strengthen the conclusion. For example, we can weaken the argument above by pointing out the fact that dynamite residue was found on debris of the dam. This implies that another potential cause is actually the correct cause. Or, the assumption that the stated cause is the only possible cause could be the gap in logic you must point out on a flaw question. There are different ways that knowing this central assumption in causal conclusions can come in handy: remember it when you deal with causality.

Metrics (Numbers and Percentages)

Metrics, the relationship between numbers and percentages, is sometimes featured in passages. Use this chapter to learn how the LSAT will try to use metrics to confuse you. Three ways of expressing numbers are used in passages: part percents, part numbers, and a total number.

Total Number (T)

A total number, represented with a "T," is the number of all of the parts in a whole. Adding together every part number will give you the total number. If there are 50 total dogs playing in the park, then 50 is the total number. Or, if there are four slices of pizza in a pizza then four is the total number. Common terms that signal that the total number is coming:

- sum
- total
- 100%
- whole

Part Metrics

Part Percent (%)

We represent part percents with a %. A part percent is a percentage, a proportion of a whole. We included the word "part" to force you to remember that there is a total. An example part percent is 25%. That is one quarter of a whole. If that whole includes four separate things, say slices of pizza, then 25% of the pizza would be one slice. Passages will refer to a part percent with these or similar terms:

- percent
- fraction
- ratio
- incidence
- segment
- share

Part Number (#)

A part number, represented by a #, tells the quantity of a specific part of a larger whole. If there are many dogs playing in a park, and George owns three of them, then three is the part number of George's dogs. Or, in an earlier example, one slice of pizza could be the part number. Passages will refer to a part number with terms like these:

- amount
- quantity
- count
- tally

While a part percent and a part number both describe a portion of a whole, they do so in different ways. A part percent tells you how much of the whole the part is responsible for. It is a **relative measure** because it tells you how big the part is in relation to the whole. On the other hand, a part number tells you the exact quantity of the part. It is an absolute measure, and it contains no information about the whole.

What you know

The previous discussion will help you see what information you can and cannot derive based on knowing only one of the three metrics (part percent, part number or total number). If you know any two metrics, then you can find out the third. But if you only have information on one metric, then you cannot find out either of the other two. For instance, if you know that a part number is 5, you have no way of finding out what the part percent is without knowing the total number. Or, if you only know that the part percent is 20%, then you cannot find out the part number.

The Total Number is Crucial

As you can see, the total number is required for you to translate from a part percent to a part number or vice versa. The LSAT-writers will try to trick you by asking you to go from a part metric (either % or #), to the other part metric, without knowing the total number. A passage will tell you about a change in one part metric, and then ask how the other part metric has changed. This would be easy to figure out, except you do not know how the total number changed when the part metric changed.

For instance, if I had 5 green apples in the basket yesterday and I have 10 green today, it is impossible to know whether the percentage of green apples (the part percent) went up without knowing how many total apples were in the basket on both days (the total numbers). If yesterday there were 10 total apples and today there are 30, then the part percent went down even though the part number went up:

	Part Number	Total Number	Part Percent
Yesterday	5 apples	10 apples	50%
Today	10 apples	30 apples	30%

Errors

Here are three possible errors you might make with metrics. These might show up in incorrect choices:

Part Percent Change = Part Number Change

This error involves believing that changing a part percentage leads to a number part changing in the same way. When the part percentage changes, it is possible that the total number also changes. That in turn might change the number part. Example argument that includes this error:

> On Monday, Fat Frank ate 25% of the cookies baked by a bakery. Then, on Tuesday, he ate 50% of the cookies baked by the bakery. <u>Therefore, he must have eaten more cookies on Tuesday</u>.

If the bakery baked fewer cookies on Tuesday that could offset the increasing percentage that Frank ate to the point where he actually ate **less cookies** on Tuesday. The part number could have decreased even though the part percent increased. Therefore, because we know nothing about the total number on both days, the argument above is unfounded. Remember that the total number is not a constant.

Part Number Change = Part Percent Change

This error is quite similar to the one previously discussed. It involves assuming that a change in the part number yields a corresponding change in the part percent. Example argument that makes this error:

> Aaron scored 2 more goals this game than last, so he must have accounted for a higher percentage of the team's goals this game than last game.

If the team scored 3 goals last game, and 10 goals this game, then the conclusion is faulty. If Aaron scored all 3 goals last game, making his part percent 100% that game, then this game he scored 5 goals and his part percent was 50% Without knowing how the total number changed from game to game, you cannot say how a change in the part number relates to a change in the part percent. To make these errors, one must assume that the total number stays the same. Do not make that unfounded assumption.

Part Magnitude = Percentage Magnitude

This error involves the belief that the size of a part number is an indicator of the percentage the part comprises of the whole. The size of a number does not tell you the size of a part percent, because you need information about the total number to make a judgment about the part percent. Even a huge number may be a tiny part percent; the US has 307 million people (as of 2011), but that is only 5% of the world population. Likewise, small part numbers can be a high percentage of their whole; a group of 30 presidents makes up over 50% of all the U.S. presidents. Do not equate a big or small part number with a big or small part percent.

A similar erroneous belief: the size of a part percent tells you something about the part number. Without knowing the total number, we cannot say that a high percentage means a big part number. Conversely, a low percent part can be a large part number. Less than 1% of the population of China is fluent in English, a very small part percent. Yet, that 1% comprises 10 million people, a massive part number.

Without Total Number

Again, most metrics errors stem from not knowing the total number. When part percentages are discussed, you are thinking about parts of a whole which could be changing. Therefore, one part metric cannot tell you about the other part metric without the total number. This knowledge can help you enormously when sorting the choices of questions that feature passages with metrics:

- If the passage only deals with part percents, choices that talk about part numbers are duds.
- If the passage only deals with part numbers, choices that deal with part percents are duds.
- If you are given any two metrics, then the choices can deal with any of the three metrics. When you know two, you can figure out the third metric.

Taking Notes

When you read a passage with metrics, write out the changes in the metrics using the symbol for the piece and an up or down arrow:

The Passage Says	Symbol to draw
Bill now owns 35% of the company, but last year he only owned 25%.	%↓
I lost three of the apples from my fruit basket.	#↓
The stock market grew from 10,000 to 11,000 in the last year.	T↑

Using Your Notes

These notations will help you quickly see how the information you have relates to other metrics. If you know that the part percent went up, you cannot say the part number went up:

%↑

does not mean

#↑

Unless:

T (T stays the same) *or* T↑

If the part percent went up and you know that total number stayed the same, then you can say the part number went up:

%↑ *and* T (T stays the same) *then we know that* #↑

Metrics often appear in True Deduction questions with fact-groups as their passages. They can also appear in Weaken or Flaw questions. On those question types, be aware of the metrics and how they change.

Other Metrics

Averages and market share are two other numerical concepts that are used by passages. These are less common than the metrics just covered, but they are still important.

Averages

As you likely know, an average combines information about many part numbers, by telling you the mean of the entire set. So, you cannot tell anything about individual part numbers from the average without additional information. For instance, if Jack and Jill have an average age of 40, Jack could be 1 and Jill could be 79. Or they could both be 40 and have the same part number.

Market Share

Market share is a number that references a specific part of the total market. The market is the total number in this situation and it is made up of all the companies in that market. A **share** of that market can be a part number or a part percent. For instance, in the 100 million dollar ketchup market (total number), a 10% market share (part percent) means that a company makes 10 million dollars a year in that market (the part number).

If a company gains market share, then the part percent for that company goes up: it owns a larger percentage of the market. If a company loses market share, then the part percent goes down. In these cases, you can only tell what is happening to the company's part number by knowing the total number as the part percent changes. For instance, if Heinz gained market share in the ketchup market from 2011-2012, but the market shrunk over that time period, it is possible that Heinz is actually making less total money (the part number) in 2012.

When you know how much money a company makes or the number of customers it has in a market (two different ways of expressing market share), you do not know the part percent unless you know the overall market size. A company could make more money from one year to the next and still lose market share because the market has grown enough to offset the increase. Or a company could lose customers and gain market share if the market shrinks enough (the total number decreases).

*Causal Reasoning + Metrics Review

Causal Reasoning

- Introduction
    - Causal Reasoning (or cause and effect reasoning, or causality) is where one event/situation caused another event/situation to occur
    - Signals – "because of, leads to, induced by, promoted by, determined by, is an effect of"
    - If necessary, diagram the causal relationship using the same format as conditional reasoning, except with a wavy arrow in between the two conditions:
        - *Cause ~> Effect*
- If causal reasoning occurs in the premises, accept the causal reasoning just as you accept the validity of most premises.
- If causal reasoning occurs in the conclusion, then the conclusion is likely flawed.
    - It could be the case that one event often comes before another event but does not cause it.
    - Or, it could be that two events simply occur together (correlation) and there may be a third event that causes both of the other two.
    - This is due to the central assumption of all causal reasoning that the named cause is the only possible cause of the effect.

Numbers and Percentages

- Total Number (*T*) – the amount of the whole.
    - Signal words: "sum, total, 100%, whole"
    - Example: there are 10 total apples in a basket
- Part Metrics
    - Part percent (symbol = **%**) – a percentage of a whole.
        - This is a relative measurement because it tells you how the part relates to the whole.
        - Signal words: "percent, fraction, ratio, incidence, segment, share"
        - Example: 25% of the apple basket
    - Part number (**#**) – the specific quantity of a part of the whole.
        - This is an absolute number: tells you nothing about the whole.
        - Signal words: "amount, quantity, count, tally"
    - If there is a change in one part metric (either percent or part) you cannot know how the other part metric changed unless you know how the total number changed.
- Other Metrics
    - An <u>average</u> combines information about many #'s, so they cannot tell you information about a specific # without knowing more.
    - Market Share is the amount of the total market that one company owns, usually in revenue.
- Avoid errors
    - Without knowing T, you cannot say what a change in % means for a change in #, and vice versa.
    - Taken alone, the size of % does not tell you anything about the size of #, and vice versa.

Deduction

Now that you have a firm grasp of several general concepts that are useful on the LR section, we will teach you about the specific question types. Each type has its own unique strategy and qualities; learning these will help you tackle the questions more quickly and effectively.

Deduction questions ask what must be true based on the passage. They are in the Identify question category, so use the passage to directly identify the correct answer. Being a member of this category also means that the correct answer will not feature new information not stated in the passage. There are three kinds of Deduction questions: True, False and Core.

True Deduction

True Deduction questions ask you to make an inference based on the information in the passage. Like many types in the Identify question family, True Deduction queries usually begin by telling you that the information in the passage should be considered accurate. Example phrase:

> "If the information above is correct..."

So, like all Identify questions, believe the passage. Not all True Deduction queries feature this information that the passage is valid, but most do. True Deduction queries always ask you which choice is a logical extension of the passage. Sample queries:

> "...which one of the following conclusions can be properly drawn on the basis of it?"
>
> "...it most strongly supports which one of the following?"
>
> "...which one of the following must also be true?"

An accurate inference will be one of two types:

- Restated information: restated information from the passage.
- Interaction information: the interaction or combination of information from the passage.

These are the two types of correct answers to a True Deduction question.

Restated Information

Restated information is a detail from the passage that a choice articulates in a new and different way. Correct choices do not repeat ideas verbatim; they use different wordings, stating the same idea from a different angle. Example True Deduction passage:

> Dogs' hind legs are typically far stronger than their front legs. This helps them in situations that require moving forward, but can hinder them when they move sideways or backwards.

Restated information in a correct choice:

> (A) Dogs' front legs are usually weaker than their hind legs.

This is a restatement of the first sentence of the passage. The choice focuses on the back legs, which are weaker than the front legs, so it says the same idea while focusing on the other subject in the front/back legs relationship. Correct answers to easy True Deduction questions are often simple rewordings of a part of the passage.

Interaction Information

The more difficult True Deduction questions generally feature interaction information in their correct choice. Again, this is "new" information formed by combining two or more details from the passage. Example True Deduction passage:

> Laura owns a flower shop and has thoughts on how the flowers smell in relation to their color. She thinks that yellow flowers smell better than pink ones. She also thinks that pink flowers smell better than red ones.

Example choice that features interaction information:

> (D) Yellow flowers smell better than red flowers.

This choice is a combination of the final two details in the passage. Pink flowers is the subject shared by both of those statements, and that subject connects yellow flowers to red ones. By looking at both statements, we see that choice (D) must be correct:

Yellow > Pink
\+ Pink > Red

= Yellow > Pink > Red

Because we know that yellow flowers smell better than pink ones (indicated with the greater than sign, >), and pink flowers smell better than red ones, it must be the case that yellow flowers smell better than red ones. We can see this by removing "> pink" in the final chain above:

Yellow > Red

Do Not Envision

True Deduction questions can have many possible correct answers based on the passage information, so do not waste any time envisioning an answer. Instead, move right to the choices and evaluate them carefully based on your knowledge of the passage.

Incorrect Choices

Because the correct answer to a True Deduction question is logically supported by the passage, all the incorrect choices are unsupported. This only means that the passage **does not prove** those choices to be true. Based on the passage, an incorrect choice could be true, or might likely be true. However, incorrect choices are never fully supported. Sometimes an incorrect choice will be the opposite of information in the passage; it will be proven false.

Incorrect answers can be appealing, especially if they are likely to be true. So, you must clearly understand what the passage states and does not state. True Deductions are the first question type covered because they test you on a skill required by all other LR question types, understanding the passage's meaning, which can often be subtle.

Common Incorrect Answers

Learning the categories of incorrect choices you will see on True Deduction questions will enable you to quickly label them as duds when you run across them. While it is generally more efficient to attempt to find the correct choice instead of using the process of elimination, eliminating incorrect choices does make it much easier to find the correct one. Note that some choices will fall into more than one of these categories.

Reasonable

Reasonable incorrect choices contain information that could be true or is probably true, but is not proven by the passage. Even though these are fair speculations, they are still speculations. A True Deduction question requires an answer that has written proof in the passage. Reasonable choices prey on your ability to think beyond the information stated, so stick with the facts.

Modified

The LSAT-writers will throw tricky answer choices at you, hoping that you will select them because they **sound good**. Modified answer choices are an example of this tactic. In these incorrect choices, information from the passage is changed or exaggerated to the point where it is no longer accurate. These choices often sound good because they feature ideas from the passage that you remember. That familiarity with the concepts discussed can make you feel comfortable that the choice matches the passage. For instance, if this is a sentence from a passage:

> Van Gough painted primarily in reds and blues in his early career.

This incorrect choice would be a modified choice:

> (B) Early in his career, Van Gough used only two colors.

Van Gough painted primarily, not **exclusively**, in reds and blues. (B) is an exaggeration of a detail from the passage. The LSAT-writers can often be more subtle when they modify details. For instance, they might switch out a word that changes the meaning of a concept but sounds the same. Look at this sentence from a passage:

> Journalists often nap in their cars when on stakeouts waiting for a story to break.

This choice features a tricky word swap:

> (D) When waiting for a lead, journalists will use their cars to sleep for the night.

Taking a nap and sleeping all night are not the same, but when you face choice (D) after reading a complex passage and three answer choices, you might overlook this fact. The most challenging modified choices count on you not seeing slight but important substitutions in ideas. Sometimes, a modified choice will switch the order of two parts of a detail.

Look at this passage:

> All cats take excellent care of most of their fur.

This is a modified choice where two words have been exchanged:

> (D) Most cats take excellent care of all of their fur.

Read the answer choices carefully to avoid falling for such choices. Now that you are aware they exist, you will be able to see how they change the meaning of the detail from the passage.

False

False choices state the opposite of information from the passage; they contradict information it contains. False choices can catch you off guard when you do not pay close attention to an amount or likelihood word (most, all, not, no, etc.). Because these incorrect choices feature the right concepts from the passage, only stated in the opposite way, they can sound familiar and correct.

19/2 #24

We will now demonstrate many of the True Deduction concepts discussed with a real LSAT question. As you can tell from the title, the question is from test 19, section 2, question 24 (abbreviated 19/2 #24).

> The United States ranks far behind countries such as Sweden and Canada when it comes to workplace safety. In all three countries, joint labor-management committees that oversee workplace safety conditions have been very successful in reducing occupational injuries. In the United States, such committees are found only in the few companies that have voluntarily established them. However, in Sweden and several Canadian provinces, joint safety committees are required by law and exist in all medium-sized and large workplaces.
>
> Which one of the following is supported by the information above?
>
> (A) The establishment of joint safety committees in all medium-sized and large workplaces in the United States would result in a reduction of occupational injuries.
>
> (B) A joint safety committee that is required by law is more effective at reducing occupational injuries than is a joint safety committee that is voluntarily established.
>
> (C) Workplace safety in Sweden and Canada was superior to that in the United States even prior to the passage of laws requiring joint safety committees in all medium-sized and large workplaces.
>
> (D) Joint safety committees had been voluntarily established in most medium-sized and large workplaces in Sweden and several Canadian provinces prior to the passage of laws requiring such committees.
>
> (E) The United States would surpass Sweden and Canada in workplace safety if joint safety committees were required in all medium-sized and large workplaces in the United States.

Here is how to complete the question using the five step method you learned for all LR questions:

1) Read the Query and Identify the Type

The query asks which choice is supported by the information above (the passage), which tells that it is a True Deduction question.

2) Read the Passage

Carefully read every True Deduction passage, attempting to fully understand each sentence. Your knowledge of the details is important, so avoid moving beyond a sentence you do not understand. Instead, reread the sentence. This strategy is less important on other question types.

Example notated passage:

> X The United States ranks far behind countries such as Sweden and Canada when it comes to workplace safety. In all three countries, joint labor-management committees that oversee workplace safety conditions have been very successful in reducing occupational injuries. In the United States, such committees are found only in the few companies that have voluntarily established them. However, in Sweden and several Canadian provinces, joint safety committees are required by law and exist in all medium-sized and large workplaces.

True Deduction passages are usually arguments, so be sure to draw an "X" next to the conclusion. In the passage above, the conclusion precedes the premises. The evidence for the first sentence is in the three sentences that follow it. Here is a paraphrasing of that information: the U.S. does not have mandatory joint safety committees and such committees are found only in a few companies in the US. With a good grasp of the passage, we move to the envision step.

3) Organize Your Thoughts

There are many possible correct answers to this question type because there are many inferences possible given a passage. So, **do not** envision an answer. The passage does not point to a single correct answer on True Deduction questions, something necessary to make envisioning useful.

Instead, take a moment to be sure you understand the passage. Think about what seems most important within it. This advice holds for all LR questions with many potential answers: use the "envision step" as mental organizing time.

4) Sort the Choices

The final step in working a True Deduction question is to sort or "work" the choices. Read them one by one, analyzing whether they match the information in the passage. Label the choices duds and hits as appropriate:

> (A) The establishment of joint safety committees in all medium-sized and large workplaces in the United States would result in a reduction of occupational injuries.

Choice (A) is a combination of the second and third lines of the passage:

> In all three countries, joint labor-management committees that oversee workplace safety conditions have been very successful in reducing occupational injuries. In the United States, such committees are found only in the few companies that have voluntarily established them.

If the committees reduce injuries **and** the US has few committees, then establishing the committees everywhere in the US will reduce the number of injuries. This is interaction information and answers the query correctly.

You may recall this information from your first reading of the passage, or you might need to quickly dip back into the passage to check this choice. It is acceptable to check for proof for a choice by rereading some of the passage, but avoid rereading the whole passage. If you find yourself often rereading the entire passage while working the choices, slow down your initial passage reading. Focus on understanding it more clearly. One slow passage reading generally takes less time than two quick readings.

Back to the question at hand. We have a very strong hit, which means we can read the rest of the choices a bit more quickly, primarily to see if any are superior to (A).

> (B) A joint safety committee that is required by law is more effective at reducing occupational injuries than is a joint safety committee that is voluntarily established.

This is an example of a reasonable choice. It is **likely** that safety committees required by law are more effective than those voluntarily established. This is because the government often has specific requirements that make the entity more effective than a similar one with less strict rules.

However, nowhere in the passage is the effectiveness of the committees compared, so we have no evidence one way or the other for this statement. We are only told that the committees have been successful in all three countries, and in the U.S. such committees are voluntary and in Sweden and Canada they are required by law. Nothing in the passage directly supports (B), so this choice is new information. New information is incorrect on a question in the Identify family. Therefore, this choice is clearly a dud. New information is also information that is out of the scope of the passage; it is not discussed by the passage.

> (C) Workplace safety in Sweden and Canada was superior to that in the United States even prior to the passage of laws requiring joint safety committees in all medium-sized and large workplaces.

The time **before the laws were passed** is not discussed and we need that information to prove (C). This information is out of the scope of the passage. (C) is a dud.

> (D) Joint safety committees had been voluntarily established in most medium-sized and large workplaces in Sweden and several Canadian provinces prior to the passage of laws requiring such committees.

Again, the time before the laws were passed is not discussed by the passage. This inference is pure speculation and is therefore a dud.

> (E) The United States would surpass Sweden and Canada in workplace safety if joint safety committees were required in all medium-sized and large workplaces in the United States.

The passage implies that if the U.S. required all medium and large workplaces to implement committees the workplace safety in the country would increase, and this is stated by (A). Nowhere does the passage support the idea that the U.S. would **surpass** Sweden and Canada in workplace safety with this measure. Therefore, (E) is beyond the scope of the passage. Dud.

*True Deductions Review

- Example query: "If the information above is correct it most strongly supports which one of the following?"
- True Deductions ask you to make a valid inference based on the passage.
- There are two types of inferences: Restated Information and Interaction Information.
    - Restated Information is a detail from the passage that a choice articulates in a new way.
        - The different wordings used can make these choices more challenging to identify.
    - Interaction Information is information found by combining details from the passage.
        - These choices are proven when you see how two details connect to form a new idea.
- Incorrect choices are not proven to be true by the passage.
    - They might sounds likely or probable, but they are not guaranteed true.
    - Reasonable choices sound good, but are only speculations based on information in the passage.
    - Modified choices are when information from the passage is twisted or exaggerated to the point where it is no longer accurate.
    - False choices feature the correct concepts from the passage, stated in the opposite way.

*True Deduction Practice Questions

1. The initial causes of serious accidents at nuclear power plants have not so far been flaws in the advanced-technology portion of the plants. Rather, the initial causes have been attributed to human error, as when a worker at the Browns Mills reactor in the United States dropped a candle and started a fire, or to flaws in the plumbing, exemplified in a recent incident in Japan. Such everyday events cannot be thought unlikely to occur over the long run.

   Which one of the following is most strongly supported by the statements above?

   (A) Now that nuclear power generation has become a part of everyday life, an ever-increasing yearly incidence of serious accidents at the plants can be expected.
   (B) If nuclear power plants continue in operation, a serious accident at such a plant is not improbable.
   (C) The likelihood of human error at the operating consoles of nuclear power generators cannot be lessened by thoughtful design of dials, switches, and displays.
   (D) The design of nuclear power plants attempts to compensate for possible failures of the materials used in their construction.
   (E) No serious accident will be caused in the future by some flaw in the advanced-technology portion of a nuclear power plant.

2. Criticism that the press panders to public sentiment neglects to consider that the press is a profit-making institution. Like other private enterprises, it has to make money to survive. If the press were not profit-making, who would support it? The only alternative is subsidy and, with it, outside control. It is easy to get subsidies for propaganda, but no one will subsidize honest journalism.

   It can be properly inferred from the passage that if the press is

   (A) not subsidized, it is in no danger of outside control
   (B) not subsidized, it will not produce propaganda
   (C) not to be subsidized, it cannot be a profit-making institution
   (D) to produce honest journalism, it must be a profit-making institution
   (E) to make a profit, it must produce honest journalism

3. Only if the electorate is moral and intelligent will a democracy function well.

   Which one of the following can be logically inferred from the claim above?

   (A) If the electorate is moral and intelligent, then a democracy will function well.
   (B) Either a democracy does not function well or else the electorate is not moral or not intelligent.
   (C) If the electorate is not moral or not intelligent, then a democracy will not function well.
   (D) If a democracy does not function well, then the electorate is not moral or not intelligent.
   (E) It cannot, at the same time, be true that the electorate is moral and intelligent and that a democracy will not function well.

4. The incidence in Japan of most types of cancer is remarkably low compared to that in North America, especially considering that Japan has a modern life-style, industrial pollution included. The cancer rates, however, for Japanese people who immigrate to North America and adopt the diet of North Americans approximate the higher cancer rates prevalent in North America.

   If the statements above are true, they provide the most support for which one of the following?

   (A) The greater the level of industrial pollution in a country, the higher that country's cancer rate will tend to be.
   (B) The stress of life in North America is greater than that of life in Japan and predisposes to cancer.
   (C) The staple foods of the Japanese diet contain elements that cure cancer.
   (D) The relatively low rate of cancer among people in Japan does not result from a high frequency of a protective genetic trait among Japanese people.
   (E) The higher cancer rates of Japanese immigrants to North America are caused by fats in the North American diet.

5. Farm animals have certain behavioral tendencies that result from the evolutionary history of these species. By imposing on these animals a type of organization that conflicts with their behavioral tendencies, current farm-management practices cause the animals more pain and distress than do practices that more closely conform to the animals' behavioral tendencies. Because the animals tend to resist this type of organization, current practices can also be less efficient than those other farm-management practices.

   If the statements above are true, which one of the following can be properly inferred from them?

   (A) Some of the behavioral tendencies of farm animals can be altered by efficient farm-management practices.
   (B) In order to implement efficient farm-management practices, it is necessary to be familiar with the evolutionary history of farm animals.
   (C) In order to create farm-management practices that cause less pain and distress to farm animals, a significant loss of efficiency will be required.
   (D) Farm-management practices that cause the least amount of pain and distress to farm animals are also the most efficient management practices.
   (E) Some changes in farm-management practices that lessen the pain and distress experienced by farm animals can result in gains in efficiency.

6. Comets do not give off their own light but reflect light from other sources, such as the Sun. Scientists estimate the mass of comets by their brightness: the greater a comet's mass, the more light that comet will reflect. A satellite probe, however, has revealed that the material of which Halley's comet is composed reflects 60 times less light per unit of mass than had been previously thought.

   The statements above, if true, give the most support to which one of the following?

   (A) Some comets are composed of material that reflects 60 times more light per unit of mass than the material of which Halley's comet is composed.
   (B) Previous estimates of the mass of Halley's comet which were based on its brightness were too low.
   (C) The total amount of light reflected from Halley's comet is less than scientists had previously thought.
   (D) The reflective properties of the material of which comets are composed vary considerably from comet to comet.
   (E) Scientists need more information before they can make a good estimate of the mass of Halley's comet.

7. It takes 365.25 days for the Earth to make one complete revolution around the Sun. Long-standing convention makes a year 365 days long, with an extra day added every fourth year, and the year is divided into 52 seven-day weeks. But since 52 times 7 is only 364, anniversaries do not fall on the same day of the week each year. Many scheduling problems could be avoided if the last day of each year and an additional day every fourth year belonged to no week, so that January 1 would be a Sunday every year.

   The proposal above, once put into effect, would be most likely to result in continued scheduling conflicts for which one of the following groups?

   (A) people who have birthdays or other anniversaries on December 30 or 31
   (B) employed people whose strict religious observances require that they refrain from working every seventh day
   (C) school systems that require students to attend classes a specific number of days each year
   (D) employed people who have three-day breaks from work when holidays are celebrated on Mondays or Fridays
   (E) people who have to plan events several years before those events occur

8. People cannot be morally responsible for things over which they have no control. Therefore, they should not be held morally responsible for any inevitable consequences of such things, either. Determining whether adults have any control over the treatment they are receiving can be difficult. Hence in some cases it can be difficult to know whether adults bear any moral responsibility for the way they are treated. Everyone, however, sometimes acts in ways that are an inevitable consequence of treatment received as an infant, and infants clearly cannot control, and so are not morally responsible for, the treatment they receive.

   Anyone making the claims above would be logically committed to which one of the following further claims?

   (A) An infant should never be held morally responsible for an action that infant has performed.
   (B) There are certain commonly performed actions for which no one performing those actions should ever be held morally responsible.
   (C) Adults who claim that they have no control over the treatment they are receiving should often be held at least partially responsible for being so treated.
   (D) If a given action is within a certain person's control that person should be held morally responsible for the consequences of that action.
   (E) No adult should be held morally responsible for every action he or she performs.

9. The body of anyone infected by virus X will, after a week, produce antibodies to fight the virus; the antibodies will increase in number for the next year or so. There is now a test that reliably indicates how many antibodies are present in a person's body. If positive, this test can be used during the first year of infection to estimate to within a month how long that person has had the virus.

Which one of the following conclusions is best supported by the statements above?

(A) Antibodies increase in number only until they have defeated the virus.
(B) Without the test for antibodies, there is no way of establishing whether a person has virus X.
(C) Antibodies are produced only for viral infections that cannot be fought by any other body defenses.
(D) If a person remains infected by virus X indefinitely, there is no limit to the number of antibodies that can be present in the person's body.
(E) Anyone infected by virus X will for a time fail to exhibit infection if tested by the antibody test.

10. Decision makers tend to have distinctive styles. One such style is for the decision maker to seek the widest possible input from advisers and to explore alternatives while making up his or her mind. In fact, decision makers of this sort will often argue vigorously for a particular idea, emphasizing its strong points and downplaying its weaknesses, not because they actually believe in the idea but because they want to see if their real reservations about it are idiosyncratic or are held independently by their advisers.

Which one of the following is most strongly supported by the statements above?

(A) If certain decision makers' statements are quoted accurately and at length, the content of the quote could nonetheless be greatly at variance with the decision eventually made.
(B) Certain decision makers do not know which ideas they do not really believe in until after they have presented a variety of ideas to their advisers.
(C) If certain decision makers dismiss an idea out of hand, it must be because its weaknesses are more pronounced than any strong points it may have.
(D) Certain decision makers proceed in a way that makes it likely that they will frequently decide in favor of ideas in which they do not believe.
(E) If certain decision makers' advisers know the actual beliefs of those they advise, those advisers will give better advice than they would if they did not know those beliefs.

*Explanations

1. (7/1 #21) ~ B

This passage builds up to the conclusion that serious accidents at nuclear power plants are not improbable. The evidence is that the initial causes of serious accidents have been caused by human error and that everyday events of human error cannot be thought unlikely to occur over the long run. This means that these events must be at least moderately likely to occur over the long run and an accident would come with them.

(A) is not a valid conclusion because it says ever-increasing incidence. That is not supported by the passage, which merely implies accidents are likely over the long run to occur.

(C) is not supported by the passage. This could very well be false.

(D) is not supported by the information in the passage.

(E) It is possible that in the future a serious accident could be caused by a flaw in the advanced-technology portion, it just has not happened in the past.

2. (9/2 #13) ~ D

The passage contains a lot of information, so work the choices carefully, seeing which is supported.

(A) The argument says that subsidy would bring outside control. That means subsidy is sufficient for outside control:

Subsidy -> Control

However, we cannot say that if it is not subsidized it is in no danger of Outside Control. In order to say that we need to know that subsidy is *necessary* for outside control.

(B) This is similar to Choice A. The argument never implies that if it is not subsidized, it will not produce propaganda.

(C) is not supported. The passage says that if it is not profit-making then it must be subsidized

Not Profit -> Subsidized

which is different than the statement in C.

(D) is supported by the passage. Here is the chain of logic:

Not Profit -> Subsidized

Subsidized -> Not Honest

substitute for the like term "Subsidized":

Not Profit -> Not Honest

If the firm is not for profit then it will not produce honest journalism. The contrapositive supports D:

Honest -> Profit

(E) This confuses the logic used in Choice D.

3. (9/4 #4) ~ C

This passage is a necessary statement:

function well -> electorate moral + intelligent

If a democracy is functioning well, then it has an electorate that is moral and intelligent. These qualities in the electorate are necessary for the democracy to function well, but not necessarily sufficient, meaning that we cannot say that when they are present the democracy will function well.

(A) This confuses the necessary condition of the passage with a sufficient one.

(B) This jumbles the logic.

(C) This is correct. If the necessary conditions are not met then the outcome of having the democracy function well will not be met either.

(D) There could be other reasons why the democracy does not function well besides lacking the two requirements outlined in the passage.

(E) This is the same as choice A: confuses necessary with sufficient.

4. (9/4 #7) ~ D

There is a lower cancer rate in Japan than in North America, even though Japan has a modern lifestyle with industrial pollution. However, when Japanese people move to North America and eat the diet of North Americans, their cancer rates become close to equal to those in North America.

(A) This may or may not be true. For all we know, industrial pollution may cause cancer rates to be lower.

(B) The argument does not mention stress and this is a big logical jump.

(C) Eating North American food seems to **increase cancer rates** for Japanese people, but we cannot say that Japanese food contains elements that **cure** cancer.

(D) This is a logical inference. If when Japanese people move to North America and adopt the diet their cancer rates go up, then they must not have a protective genetic trait that prevents cancer. If they had such a trait, then nothing would cause them to get cancer.

(E) This is a big jump. We cannot logically say this is true based on the passage.

5. (9/4 #23) ~ E

The argument says that some practices cause the animals more pain and distress than practices that match the behavioral tendencies of the animals. Next, it states that because the animals resist this type of organization, these practices can be less efficient than others. Combining these two tells that pain and distress cause inefficiency in farm practices.

(E) is correct: it is logical that lessening the pain and distress of the animals can result in efficiency gains.

(A) The argument never states that the behavioral tendencies can be altered.

(B) Tempting, but not logically supported. It would be possible to have practices aligned with the behavioral tendencies without being familiar with the animals' evolutionary history.

(C) The argument states the exact opposite: both efficiency gains and lessening of pain can be achieved with practices that are in line with the behavioral tendencies.

(D) This is not logically supported, because the argument says nothing about what is **most** efficient.

6. (7/1 #16) ~ B

This question can be answered by adding up the logic in the passage. Mass is estimated by brightness: the greater a comet's mass, the more light it reflects. Halley's Comet reflects much less light per unit of mass than originally thought.

When scientists first calculated the size of Halley's Comet they thought that it was a certain size because of how much light it was reflecting. But it turns out that the comet does not reflect as much light **per unit of mass** as originally thought. That means that, as was previously calculated, the total amount of light greatly **underestimated** the total mass of the comet. Think of it like this: instead of **one unit** of mass reflecting one unit of light, scientists realized that it took **60 units** of mass to reflect one unit of light. So, in that example, the size (as predicted from the total amount of light reflected) increases 60 times.

(A) We cannot say this for sure. Just because the scientists used that calculation originally does not mean that some comets actually are composed of a material like that.

(C) The total light reflected is the same.

(D) The information in the passage does not necessarily support this.

(E) The total light reflected and the amount of light per unit of mass might be all they need.

7. (7/4 #19) ~ B

Use the information in the passage to extrapolate to a group that would still have scheduling conflicts despite having one day each year belonging to no week. (B) is correct: at the end of the year, their one day would belong to **no week** which would shift the work week (Monday – Friday) one day forward. That would mean that these people would have a scheduling conflict between obeying their religious observance to not work and their duty to work for their job during the work week.

(A) These people would not necessarily have **scheduling conflicts**, their birthdays would simply belong to no week.

(C) There would still be the same number of days in each year.

(D) If the holiday is on Monday or Friday, then there would be no conflict.

(E) The calendar system proposed would allow long term planning.

8. (10/1 #18) ~ E

Read the passage carefully to understand the logic contained therein and see if it is building to any points. The passage says that people should not be held morally responsible for things over which they cannot control.

Cannot control -> not held responsible

Then it says that everyone sometimes acts in ways that are a consequence of treatment received as an infant. And infants cannot control the treatment they receive. Therefore, everyone sometimes does acts that are a consequence of treatment as an infant, over which they had no control.

Sometimes acts -> cannot control

Combining that with our earlier condensed logic, we see that everyone sometimes does acts which they should not be held morally responsible for:

Everyone some acts -> not held responsible

The contrapositive is:

held responsible -> no one all acts

We get this by negating everyone to get no one, and some to all and not held responsible to responsible. This is exactly what choice E states. No adult should be held morally responsible for every action, because everyone sometimes does acts that they cannot control.

(A) The argument never says that infants do not have control over **all** actions they perform, which is what would be required to say that they should never be held morally responsible for an action.

(B) The argument would have had to say that there are some actions over which no one ever has control of for this to be logically accurate.

(C) The argument never says one way or the other whether adults have control over the treatment they are receiving.

(D) The opening sentence only states that people cannot be held morally responsible for actions they have no control over. It does not say they can be held responsible for actions they do have control over.

Lots of formal logic here. Taking your time reviewing this question and seeing why the wrong answers are wrong is very valuable.

9. (10/1 #24) ~ E

Read the passage carefully and make sure you understand its logic. There is no obvious conclusion from the information, and it is not helpful to try and rehash it here. To answer this question, you simply have to work through each choice and see whether the logic in the passage supports it.

(A) The passage says nothing that indicates this. The line about the test being effective for the first year does not imply that the body only produces antibodies until the virus is defeated. It does state that the antibodies do increase in number for the first year.

(B) The passage says that the new test tells how many antibodies are in a person's body. This does not mean that there is not another test to tell if someone has virus X.

(C) This is not supported by the information in the passage.

(D) The passage states that after a year the antibodies will stop increasing, so this information cannot be true.

(E) The first line of the passage states that people only start producing antibodies after a week with the virus, so the antibody test would not detect infection for the first week.

10. (10/4 #10) ~ A

Read the passage carefully and make sure you understand the logic it contains. The passage states that one style of decision maker involves arguing vigorously for an idea, even though the maker may not actually believe in that idea. (A) is supported by the passage: a decision maker of the style discussed may be quoted as saying many things that imply that she supports an idea, when in fact she is actually arguing it to hear the response of her advisers. She could then make an entirely different decision after arguing for the one that was quoted.

(B) The passage does not talk specifically about decision makers not knowing which ideas they do not believe in.

(C) The passage does not support this.

(D) The passage never states that some decision makers act in a way in which they will decide in favor of ideas they do not believe in. They may argue for decisions they do not believe in.

(E) There is nothing in the passage to support this idea. In fact, the decision makers discussed in the passage, might rely on the fact that their advisors are unbiased by what the decision maker actually favors.

False Deduction

False Deductions are the second type of Deduction question. A False Deduction question asks you to locate the choice that **must be false** based on the passage. Therefore, the correct answers to these questions are the opposite of answers to True Deduction questions. On False Deductions, you use the passage to attack one of the answers, to find the choice that is logically disproven.

If a choice can be true or is true based on the passage, then it is a dud. Only the choice that must be false is the correct answer. This is counterintuitive, especially because you will see many more True Deduction than False Deduction questions. So, always proceed carefully when sorting the choices on this type.

False Deductions fall in the identify category. So, use the passage to prove one of the choices (to be false), and accept what the passage says. A correct choice cannot bring in outside information: the passage will show the correct answer to contain false information, and the passage cannot do so for information that it does not discuss. Of course, a correct choice can be proven false by an inference, which is not new information because it is based directly on the passage.

The exception to this rule of no new information is a variation of False Deduction questions that asks you for the choice least supported by the passage. On those questions, the correct choice **can** be new information because you are looking for the one choice that is not supported by the passage. Information not discussed is therefore a likely candidate. This sub-type will be discussed again in more detail.

Query

The LSAT-writers will introduce False Deduction queries in one of two ways. The first is when a query asks which information **cannot be true**. These queries are identical to a True Deduction query except for the word CANNOT or EXCEPT:

> "If the statements above are true, which one of the following CANNOT be true?"
>
> "If all of the claims made above are true, then each of the following could be true EXCEPT: "

Other queries for False Deduction questions will ask what must be **false**:

> "If the statements above are true, then which one of the following must be false?"
>
> "The statements above, if true, most seriously undermine which one of the following assertions?"

These two types of query both ask for the same thing. Remember: if a query looks like a True Deduction question but says "CANNOT" or "EXCEPT," or if a query asks what "must be false" then you are dealing with a False Deduction.

Always read the query carefully, as identifying the types allows you to implement the methods for it that you have learned. Further, on every question you must be looking for the right thing in the correct answer to find it. If you look for what must be true based on a False Deduction question, you will find a distracter (an incorrect choice).

Passage

False Deduction passages rarely have a conclusion; they are mostly fact-groups. So, you do not need to identify the argument's structure, because there is no argument. Instead, read each statement carefully and understand it. As you read, check the scope of each statement. The more general a statement is, the easier to go against it because it is more encompassing: many different types of information can undermine it. The more specific a statement is, the tougher it is to have information that contradicts it. This will help you work the choices because you can look out for a choice that contradicts a **general statement** from the passage.

Metrics

Numbers and percents appear in False Deduction passages. In these situations, the passage often allows you to make an inference, to figure out something new about a metric. The correct answer is shown to be false based on this deduction. Look at this short sample passage:

> This year, Jumbosoft's market share grew by 20%. The entire market contracted by 5%.

Notate the metrics like this:

%↑ T↓

The relative size of the arrows shows that the % (part percent) went up more than T (total number) went down. Recall that the total number (T) is the quantity of all the parts added together. T can also be thought of as 100% of the parts, meaning if the total number goes down by 5%, this makes each individual part decrease by 5% . The 20% growth in % outweighed the shrinking of T. Therefore, the part number (#), which is Jumbosoft's revenue, went up. Having made this deduction, look for information that goes against it in the choices. Example choice:

> (A) Jumbosoft's revenue went down this year.

Our inference is that Jumbosoft's revenue went **up**, so (A) is proven false by the passage and is therefore the correct choice. Generating inferences based on fact-groups in the right situations can save you time in working the choices.

Conditionals

Conditionals also appear in False Deductions passages. When they do, either diagram them or be sure you understand them. Then, look for any **obvious** inferences. There is no need to draw all inferences if there are many. Pick the low hanging fruit. Next, move to the choices and look for a conditional being violated. For instance, a choice that states that the indicator occurs, but the requirement does not, violates the conditional. On a False Deduction the correct choice will likely do just that. Example conditional:

> Every time that Bob talks to Jen, he puts his foot in his mouth.

Talks → *Foot*

The correct choice could be:

> (E) Bob talked to Jen and did not put his foot in his mouth.

(E) says that the indicator (Talks) occurred but the requirement (Foot) did not, which is faulty logic based on how the conditional works. Said differently: if the requirement of a conditional does not occur, then the indicator cannot occur either. Look for choices that violate this rule.

Envision

Most False Deduction questions have several possible correct answers, so normally, you should not envision an answer on this type. Instead of envisioning, pause and be sure you understood the passage and how its premises might lend to inferences. Find any **obvious** deductions. Do not spend more than about 10 seconds doing so, as there may be several different possible deductions and finding them all is not helpful.

As mentioned previously, there are situations when you can envision a good answer to a False Deduction question. If you face metrics in the passage, envision an answer that would go against an inference from those metrics. The same is true if there is conditional reasoning in the passage; look for an answer that says that the indicator occurs but the requirement does not. Or think of an answer that would be false based on an inference of the conditional reasoning.

Choices

Overall, your goal is to find information that must be false based on the passage. So, if a choice has information that **could be true**, then that choice is a dud. If you envisioned an answer, by all means look for it. Otherwise, sort the choices carefully. When doing so, you may need to prove choices as duds by referencing the passage to find information that shows they either can be true or are true. That can take time, but it will allow you to be confident in every answer you eliminate. Of course, you must learn to strike a balance between remembering the passage and using it when you need to eliminate or confirm a choice.

Finally, choices that bring in new information are incorrect, as a choice cannot be proven false if the passage does not talk about it. The exception to that rule is on questions with queries that look like this:

> Which of the following is least supported by the information above?

This is a rare question type that asks you for something a little different than information proven false by the passage. Instead, you must find a choice that is not proven correct. On this type, the correct answer can be new information, because obviously, that information is not well supported by the passage. All four incorrect choices will be proven by the passage, so using the process of elimination makes sense on this subtype.

19/4 #13

We will now work through an example False Deduction question:

> Some people think that in every barrel of politicians there are only a few rotten ones. But if deceit is a quality of rottenness, I believe all effective politicians are rotten. They must be deceitful in order to do the job properly. Someone who is scrupulously honest about obeying the rules of society will never be an effective politician.
>
> Assuming that the author's statements are accurate, which one of the following statements CANNOT be true?
>
> (A) Some people think all politicians are rotten.
> (B) Some politicians are scrupulously honest.
> (C) Some people define a politician's job as obeying the rules of society.
> (D) Some deceitful politicians are ineffective.
> (E) Some scrupulously honest politicians are effective.

1) Query

The phrase "CANNOT be true" in the query tells that we are dealing with a False Deduction question. We need to read the passage carefully, but not analyze the argument structure (see how the conclusion is supported by the premises). Read solely to understand the details discussed and how they fit together.

2) Passage

The passage as is a fact-group, which is common on this question type. We will analyze its sentences:

> Some people think that in every barrel of politicians there are only a few rotten ones.

This premise is straightforward and general in scope.

> If deceit is a quality of rottenness, I believe all effective politicians are rotten.

This sentence a conditional; we are clued into that due to the "if" that begins it. Here is how we diagram it:

deceit type of rottenness → *politicians rotten*

On to the next sentence:

> They must be deceitful in order to do the job properly.

This conditional is requirement phrased. Being deceitful is **necessary** for doing the job properly, so the first half of the sentence is the requirement:

job properly → *deceitful*

On to the final sentence:

> Someone who is scrupulously honest about obeying the rules of society will never be an effective politician.

This conditional is indicator phrased. If someone is honest about obeying the rules, then we are told what that indicates. Diagram:

Honest obeying → -effective politician

At the beginning of your LR prep, you should diagram all conditionals you run into. That will help you visualize how differently phrased conditionals work and how they can be combined or what their contrapositives are. Then, over time, you will be able to skip the diagramming step and simply read and understand the conditionals. Of course, with practice, you will get a feel for how much diagramming works best for you.

3) Envision

This passage is full of conditionals, so it makes sense to try and envision a good answer. We attempt to draw one or two deductions from the three conditional statements. There are no obvious ones, so we move to the choices.

4) Choices

Work the choices, looking for one that will go against a conditional by stating that the indicator of one of the conditionals is true, but its requirement is not.

(A) Some people think all politicians are rotten.

(A) could be true based on the first sentence, which only says that **some** people believe that only some politicians are rotten. Other people could believe that all politicians are rotten. Because this choice can be true, it is a dud.

(B) Some politicians are scrupulously honest.

(B) could be true based on the final sentence (*honest obeying -> -effective politician*). In this case, the honest politicians would not be effective politicians. Dud.

(C) Some people define a politician's job as obeying the rules of society.

Obeying the rules of society is mentioned only in the fourth sentence. The passage never suggests that some people define a politician's job as obeying the rules of society. Therefore, this is new information, so it cannot be the correct answer. The correct answer is directly proven false by the passage. Dud.

(D) Some deceitful politicians are ineffective.

The third sentence states that **effective politicians** are deceitful. We have no information about the group of **deceitful politicians**. This is new information that can be true, and is therefore a dud. We have now eliminated (A) through (D) as duds, so (E) must be correct.

(E) Some scrupulously honest politicians are effective.

(E) contradicts the fourth sentence, which states that if you are honest (which means the same thing as honestly obeying the laws of society), then you must be an **ineffective** politician. This choice says that the indicator occurs but the requirement does not, just what we were looking for. Because this is a hit and the other four choices are duds, we can be confident that this is the correct answer.

*False Deductions Review

- "If the statements above are true, which one of the following CANNOT be true?"
- Locate the choice that must be false based on the passage.
    - Use the passage to attack one of the answers. This is counterintuitive so be careful on the choices.
- These are Identify questions, so a correct choice cannot bring in new information. The choice will be proven false by the information in the blurb.
    - The exception is "least supported" questions, which can have new information in their choice..
- Most False Deduction passages are fact-groups.
    - Metrics appear in these passages.
        - If possible, make an inference by analyzing how two different numbers interact. Then find a choice that contradicts that inference.
    - Conditionals also appear in these passages; your job is to look for any obvious inferences.
        - Then, find a choice that contradicts your inference or one of the conditionals.
            - A classic instance is when a choice says the indicator occurs but the requirement does not.
- Envisioning
    - Only envision when you are dealing with metrics or conditionals, or have found an obvious inference you can contradict.
    - Otherwise, skip this step as there are many possible answers to these questions.
- Choices
    - Sort the choices carefully. Any choice that is supported by the passage is incorrect.
    - Strike a balance between remembering the passage and referencing the passage to prove a hit.

*False Deduction Practice Questions

1. When Alicia Green borrowed a neighbor's car without permission, the police merely gave her a warning. However, when Peter Foster did the same thing, he was charged with automobile theft. Peter came to the attention of the police because the car he was driving was hit by a speeding taxi. Alicia was stopped because the car she was driving had defective taillights. It is true that the car Peter took got damaged and the car Alicia took did not, but since it was the taxi that caused the damage this difference was not due to any difference in the blameworthiness of their behavior. Therefore Alicia should also have been charged with automobile theft.

   If all of the claims offered in support of the conclusion are accurate, each of the following could be true EXCEPT:

   (A) The interests of justice would have been better served if the police had released Peter Foster with a warning.
   (B) Alicia Green had never before driven a car belonging to someone else without first securing the owner's permission.
   (C) Peter Foster was hit by the taxi while he was running a red light, whereas Alicia Green drove with extra care to avoid drawing the attention of the police to the car she had taken.
   (D) Alicia Green barely missed hitting a pedestrian when she sped through a red light ten minutes before she was stopped by the police for driving a car that had defective taillights.
   (E) Peter Foster had been cited for speeding twice in the preceding month, whereas Alicia Green had never been cited for a traffic violation.

2. Certain instruments used in veterinary surgery can be made either of stainless steel or of nylon. In a study of such instruments, 50 complete sterilizations of a set of nylon instruments required 3.4 times the amount of energy used to manufacture that set of instruments, whereas 50 complete sterilizations of a set of stainless steel instruments required 2.1 times the amount of energy required to manufacture that set of instruments.

   If the statements above are true, each of the following could be true EXCEPT:

   (A) The 50 complete sterilizations of the nylon instruments used more energy than did the 50 complete sterilizations of the stainless steel instruments.
   (B) More energy was required for each complete sterilization of the nylon instruments than was required to manufacture the nylon instruments.
   (C) More nylon instruments than stainless steel instruments were sterilized in the study.
   (D) More energy was used to produce the stainless steel instruments than was used to produce the nylon instruments.
   (E) The total cost of 50 complete sterilizations of the stainless steel instruments was greater than the cost of manufacturing the stainless steel instruments.

*False Deduction Explanations

1. (7/1 #19) ~ C

Locate the information that is **not** supported by the passage. Choice C could be false because the argument says that the difference was not caused by a difference in blameworthiness. If Peter got hit running a red light, then he is certainly more to blame than Alicia, who broke no rules.

(A) is in line with the conclusion of the passage.

(B) is possible based on the information in the passage.

(D) is in line with the idea that the taxi caused the difference and there was no difference in blameworthiness **in how they were each caught**.

(E) could be true based on the passage; it does not conflict with the conclusion which is based on there being no difference in blameworthiness **in how they were each caught**. It doesn't really matter what happened before this incident.

2. (9/2 #17) ~ B

Find a statement that is false based on the passage. Work the choices carefully, looking for one that does not match the information in the passage. (B) stands out: the passage says that **50** sterilizations of the nylon instruments took 3.4 times as much energy as the manufacturing of that set. That means that it took much more energy to manufacture the set than to sterilize it once. So a single sterilization only takes a small fraction of the energy required for manufacturing.

(A) could be true. We do not know how much energy either material takes to sterilize.

(C) could be true: we do not know how many times each instrument was sterilized; we only have information about each instrument relative to its own manufacturing and sterilization energy requirements.

(D) & (E) can also be true: we do not have information about the **cost** of sterilizing the instruments.

Core Deduction

Core Deductions, the third kind of Deduction question, feature correct answers with more stringent requirements than the other two kinds. On a Core Deduction question, you are asked to infer the author's **main conclusion.** You must find the core, the heart of the passage. Just like on True Deduction questions, the correct answer is deduced from the passage. The difference is that a Core Deduction question requires a supported answer choice that is also the author's main point. This second requirement will help you distinguish between these two similar question types.

Like True and False Deduction questions, Core Deductions are members of the Identify question category. Accordingly, the passage's information should be accepted as accurate and that information points to the correct choice. The answer choice will not feature new information.

Query

Core Deduction queries ask you what the author's primary conclusion is. Examples:

> "Which one of the following most accurately expresses the main conclusion of the argument?"
>
> "The main point of the argument is that…"
>
> "Which one of the following most accurately restates the main point of the passage?"
>
> "Which one of the following most accurately expresses the conclusion of the politician's argument?"

Notice that these queries all include either "conclusion" or "main point." Likewise, all use some form of the verb "states" like "expresses," "restates" or "is." This verb helps you distinguish Core Deduction queries from True Deduction queries which feature more active verbs such as "drawn" or "supports."

Passage

The nature of a Core Deduction's passage indicates how you should approach the question. Most of the passages feature fact-groups. On these, determine what direction the author is **heading.** To do so, ask yourself these questions:

- Why did the author choose the evidence she did?
- Why did she finish with that sentence?
- What was she leading to?

Carefully follow the flow of the evidence. Think about how the premises work together to support a larger, unstated conclusion. The context clues in the passage are crucial: the author will give signals about what she is building up to. These include changes in subject or the direction of argumentation. Also, carefully follow the scale of each of the premises and how specific or general a claim is being made. The more general the claim, the more likely it is supporting the larger conclusion you are trying to identify.

Some Core Deduction questions feature a dash at the end of their passage, signaling that the passage is "unfinished." Example passage:

> Almost all foxes are difficult to track, but the tracking process becomes slightly easier when a fox is known to often be near a body of water. In these cases, the soil that the fox walks across will show more noticeable prints than if the fox was walking on drier ground. Therefore, those foxes that live next to rivers __.

This dash is a signal that you are dealing with a fact-group and will be asked to formulate the conclusion of the passage.

19/2 #17

Here is an example Core Deduction question with a fact-group passage:

> People cannot devote themselves to the study of natural processes unless they have leisure, and people have leisure when resources are plentiful, not when resources are scarce. Although some anthropologists claim that agriculture, the cultivation of crops, actually began under conditions of drought and hunger, the early societies that domesticated plants must first have discovered how the plants they cultivated reproduced themselves and grew to maturity. These complex discoveries were the result of the active study of natural processes.
>
> The argument is structured to lead to the conclusion that
>
> (A) whenever a society has plentiful resources, some members of that society devote themselves to the study of natural processes
> (B) plants cannot be cultivated by someone lacking theoretical knowledge of the principles of plant generation and growth
> (C) agriculture first began in societies that at some time in their history had plentiful resources
> (D) early agricultural societies knew more about the natural sciences than did early nonagricultural societies
> (E) early societies could have discovered by accident how the plants they cultivated reproduced and grew

1) Query

It can sometimes be challenging to differentiate True Deduction questions from Core Deductions based on their query. Here, "structured" is a clue that this is a Core Deduction. We are asked what the entire passage is organized to do, which is to express a conclusion. So, read the passage expecting a fact-group. Also, read the passage with an eye towards the direction the premises as a whole are leading.

2) Passage

As predicted, the passage is a fact-group. Each sentence has a narrow, focused scope; there are no statements that build upon any of the others and are therefore more general in scale. Example notes:

> People cannot devote themselves to the study of natural processes <u>unless</u> they have leisure, and people have leisure <u>when resources are plentiful</u>, not when resources are scarce. <u>Although</u> some anthropologists claim that agriculture, the cultivation of crops, actually began under conditions of drought and hunger, the early societies that domesticated plants must <u>first</u> have discovered how the plants they cultivated reproduced themselves and grew to maturity. These complex discoveries were the result of the active study of natural processes.

3) Envision

Core Deductions lend themselves well to envisioning, unlike True Deductions. The sentence that begins "Although some anthropologists..." is important because it introduces an idea that the argument **never finishes**. The use of "although" tells that the author thinks differently than the anthropologists. That is one way of introducing and rejecting an opposing view:

> Although anthropologists think X, I think Y.

In this passage, the author never finishes her train of thought. We never hear the Y, so that point will likely be the conclusion. This makes sense when we think about the first sentence: that people need leisure and plentiful resources to study natural processes. That premise is there for a reason, so it must connect with the anthropologist's view. The closing sentence about early societies learning about agriculture through an active study of natural processes is the connection to the beginning of the passage. Focus on these two ideas:

- People need leisure to study natural processes and plentiful resources to have leisure.
- Early societies that domesticated plants (and created agriculture) made those insights by studying natural processes.

These two ideas add up to the conclusion that early societies discovered agriculture at a time when they had leisure and plentiful resources (which are required for leisure). This is therefore interaction information. And, it is the Y from earlier, the idea that goes against the view that agriculture was born in times of **limited resources**. The author concludes that agriculture actually came about in times of plentiful resources without explicitly stating that.

4) Choices

We made major headway during the envision step. Note that sometimes the reading the passage and the envisioning steps are not entirely distinct. As you read the passage, you see how the statements work together. Likewise, when you envision, you might reference the passage.

Now, work the choices, keeping a close eye out for the envisioned conclusion:

> (A) whenever a society has plentiful resources, some members of that society devote themselves to the study of natural processes

(A) is not supported by the passage, but it sounds like it is. Here is the correct diagramming of the relevant parts of the passage:

> People cannot devote themselves to the study of natural processes unless they have leisure, and people have leisure when resources are plentiful.

Having plentiful resources is a **requirement** for leisure, and leisure is a requirement for people devoting themselves to the study of natural processes. So this single sentence has two conditionals. Diagrams:

Study Processes	->	*Leisure*
Leisure	->	*Plentiful Resources*

Because leisure appears in both, we can conclude:

Study Processes -> *Plentiful Resources*

By linking these two conditionals, we see that plentiful resources are a requirement for people devoting themselves to the study of natural resources. But that is not what (A) says. (A) states that whenever plentiful resources are around, some people **will** study natural processes. This is a reversal error: the terms in the conditional have been reversed. Something being necessary for something to occur is not at all the same as something being sufficient to cause that thing to occur. Dud.

> (B) plants cannot be cultivated by someone lacking theoretical knowledge of the principles of plant generation and growth

(B) is not the conclusion we envisioned, although it is a rephrasing of the final part of the second sentence. Even though this information is proven by the passage, we have the second requirement of a choice also being the main conclusion to worry about. This passage is a fact-group (which obviously does not have a conclusion), so a rephrasing of one of the statements cannot be the main point. We call this type of incorrect choice a premise repetition. Dud.

> (C) agriculture first began in societies that at some time in their history had plentiful resources

(C) matches what we envisioned, so it is a definite hit. It is probably the correct choice, but we read the final two answers to be positive (note that you would skip reading these last two answers if you were crunched for time):

> (D) early agricultural societies knew more about the natural sciences than did early nonagricultural societies

The passage does not discuss **early** nonagricultural societies, so this information is not supported. This is an example of a reasonable incorrect choice. The agricultural societies likely did know more about plants, but there is no proof in the passage that this is true. This fails the requirement of being supported by the passage. Dud.

> (E) early societies could have discovered by accident how the plants they cultivated reproduced and grew

This is an example of a false choice. The passage states that the early societies that domesticated plants must first have discovered how the plants they cultivated reproduced and grew to maturity. The last sentence of the passage also talks about agriculture as a complex discovery, not an accident. Dud.

Incorrect Answers

Choice (B), which we just analyzed, featured a rephrasing of a premise. This is a common kind of incorrect answer on Core Deduction questions: premise repetitions. On a **True Deduction** question, that could be the correct answer, because the information is proven by the Passage. However, on that question, it is a tricky incorrect choice. Remember that the correct answer must be both true and the main conclusion.

Another kind of incorrect answer is an accurate **inference** that is not the main conclusion. For instance, imagine this choice for that question:

(F) Plentiful resources are necessary for people to study natural processes.

This is an accurate inference, and one we covered when discussing (A), but it is not the author's main conclusion.

Argument Passages

Core Deduction questions with fact-group passages require a clear understanding of the passage. Answering a Core Deduction question with an argument passage is more straightforward. There, your job is to **find the choice that restates the passage's conclusion**. Unfortunately, it is not always easy to distinguish a fact-group from an argument. So, whenever you read a Core Deduction passage, see if you can pick out a conclusion. If you identify a definite conclusion, then you know you are dealing with an argument and you need only find the choice that restates the conclusion.

Conclusion Location

To make Core Deductions with argument passages more challenging, the LSAT-writers rarely put the conclusion at the end of the passage, where we tend to expect it. Instead, it may be at the beginning or in the middle of the passage. Be conscious of this possibility.

No Signals

On top of this, these arguments will rarely have conclusion or premise signal words, making the conclusion harder to identify. Recall that the key to finding a conclusion without signals is to pay close attention to the scale/scope of each statement. The **most general and controversial** statement is likely to be the conclusion. That is how an argument works: it proves a bigger, harder to believe statement by using focused, accepted premises. The premises will always be more specific and believably accepted. They will also have a smaller scale than the conclusion: they will address a more specific subject.

Finally, if the passage is a complex argument then identify the main conclusion, and do not be fooled by a sub-conclusion.

21/2 #1

Here is an example Core Deduction question with an **argument** for the passage:

> When politicians resort to personal attacks, many editorialists criticize these attacks but most voters pay them scant attention. Everyone knows such attacks will end after election day, and politicians can be excused for mudslinging. Political commentators, however, cannot be. Political commentators should be engaged in sustained and serious debate about ideas and policies. In such a context, personal attacks on opponents serve not to beat those opponents but to cut off the debate.
>
> Which one of the following most accurately states the main point of the argument?
>
> (A) Personal attacks on opponents serve a useful purpose for politicians.
> (B) Political commentators should not resort to personal attacks on their opponents.
> (C) Editorialists are right to criticize politicians who resort to personal attacks on their opponents.
> (D) The purpose of serious debate about ideas and policies is to counteract the effect of personal attacks by politicians.
> (E) Voters should be concerned about the personal attacks politicians make on each other.

1) Query

"States" and "main point" tell us that this is a Core Deduction question. So we know to read the passage looking for a conclusion.

2) Passage

Follow the premises and the direction of the passage carefully.

> When politicians resort to personal attacks, many editorialists criticize these attacks but most voters pay them scant attention. Everyone knows such attacks will end after election day, and politicians can be excused for mudslinging. X Political commentators, however, cannot be. Political commentators should be engaged in sustained and serious debate about ideas and policies. In such a context, personal attacks on opponents serve not to beat those opponents but to cut off the debate.

We underlined the subjects here because they play a crucial role. The third sentence - "Political commentators, however, cannot be" - is the conclusion and is marked with an X.

The structure of the argument:

- Introduce an action for one group: politicians giving personal attacks to opponents.
- Give a conclusion about that action in **another** group: political commentators giving personal attacks.
- Provide evidence for the conclusion: role of commentators should be serious debate and personal attacks cut off debate.

Arguments often introduce an idea and then either expand on it or reject it. In this argument, the author talks about editorialists criticizing politicians' use of personal attacks. The information about the editorialists is an anti-premise because the author disagrees with them. This is evident from the phrase "but most voters pay them scant attention" and the second sentence, which states that politicians can be excused for mudslinging. The first two sentences set up the bulk of the argument; the rest of the passage will expand on the subject of mudslinging.

The third sentence states that political commentators, unlike politicians, **cannot be excused** for mudslinging. The meaning of that sentence relies on the ending of the sentence before it: "can be excused for mudslinging." That the third sentence is the conclusion is hinted at in a few ways. First, the third sentences contains a statement that, up to that point in the passage, has no support. Second, the sentence is somewhat controversial: it would be possible to argue that political commentators can mudsling. Third, the sentences before it introduced the subject of personal attacks on politicians. Those sentences laid the ground work for the conclusion. Finally, the sentences directly after the conclusion provide direct support for it.

3) Envision

Simply find a rephrasing of the conclusion in the choices. The toughest part of Core Deduction questions with argument passages is finding the conclusion. Once that step is complete, the rest of the question takes care of itself.

4) Sort

With an envisioned answer in hand, you can work the choices more aggressively than normal:

(A) Personal attacks on opponents serve a useful purpose for politicians.

The conclusion in the passage deals with political commentators. Also, the passage supports the idea that politicians should not be criticized for mudslinging, which is not the same as saying that mudslinging serves a **useful purpose**. There is no support for (A), so it fails the first test of a Deduction question: being proven by the passage. Dud.

(B) Political commentators should not resort to personal attacks on their opponents.

This is a rephrasing of the third sentence: political commentators should not be excused for mudslinging, which is synonymous with personal attacks. We have found the restated conclusion, so we select it and move on to the next question, skipping the rest of the choices. This is one exception to the "read every choice" rule.

For illustrative purposes, we will walk through the final choices:

(C) Editorialists are right to criticize politicians who resort to personal attacks on their opponents.

(C) is a false choice. The second sentence says that politicians **can be** excused for mudslinging. That refutes the idea that editorialists are right to criticize the politicians who mudsling.

(D) The purpose of serious debate about ideas and policies is to counteract the effect of personal attacks by politicians.

The passage never says that serious debate counteracts the effect of personal attacks. The passage only states that the political commentator's role is to facilitate serious debate; **why** this is their role is not discussed. Dud.

(E) Voters should be concerned about the personal attacks politicians make on each other.

(E) is another false choice. The first sentence of the passage says that most voters pay personal attacks little attention. The second sentence gives evidence why this is acceptable: everyone knows the attacks will end after election day: the attacks are temporary. The author also says that politicians should not be held responsible for this action. So, according to the passage, there is no reason why voters should be concerned with these attacks.

Note that (E) and (C) are false choices that require you to fully understand the second sentence of the passage. When working the choices on Core Deduction questions, thinking about how each statement relates to what has come before pays off.

*Core Deductions Review

- "Which one of the following most accurately expresses <u>the main conclusion</u> of the argument?"
    - The queries will include the word "conclusion" or "main point."
- Locate the author's main conclusion
- The answer is deduced from the passage, but has the added requirement of being the primary point the author makes.
- The Passage
    - When you first read the passage, try to find a conclusion.
    - When there is no conclusion, when the passage is a fact-group, determine where the author is heading with the stated facts.
        - Think about how the evidence builds to a central idea.
        - Work each choice to see how well it summarizes that main point.
    - When the passage is an argument, find the choice that restates the conclusion.
        - Do not expect the conclusion to be at the end of the passage.
        - You will likely have to identify the conclusion without obvious signal words
            - Find the most general and controversial statement.
            - Do not get fooled into thinking a sub-conclusion is the main conclusion.
- Incorrect Answers
    - Premise repetition is a common type of incorrect answer.
        - These would be correct on a True Deduction question, but here they are traps because they are not the primary conclusion.
    - Other inferences from the passage that are not the main conclusion are also incorrect.

*Core Deduction Practice Questions

1. In clinical trials of new medicines, half of the subjects receive the drug being tested and half receive a physiologically inert substance - a placebo. Trials are designed with the intention that neither subjects nor experimenters will find out which subjects are actually being given the drug being tested. However, this intention is frequently frustrated because_______.

   Which one of the following, if true, most appropriately completes the explanation?

   (A) often the subjects who receive the drug being tested develop symptoms that the experimenters recognize as side effects of the physiologically active drug
   (B) subjects who believe they are receiving the drug being tested often display improvements in their conditions regardless of whether what is administered to them is physiologically active or not
   (C) in general, when the trial is intended to establish the experimental drug's safety rather than its effectiveness, all of the subjects are healthy volunteers
   (D) when a trial runs a long time, few of the experimenters will work on it from inception to conclusion
   (E) the people who are subjects for clinical trials must, by law, be volunteers and must be informed of the possibility that they will receive a placebo

2. Marcus: For most ethical dilemmas the journalist is likely to face, traditional journalistic ethics is clear, adequate, and essentially correct. For example, when journalists have uncovered newsworthy information, they should go to press with it as soon as possible. No delay motivated by the journalists' personal or professional interests is permissible.

   Anita: Well, Marcus, of course interesting and important information should be brought before the public —that is a journalist's job. But in the typical case, where a journalist has some information but is in a quandary about whether it is yet important or "newsworthy," this guidance is inadequate.

   The point made by Anita's statements is most accurately expressed by which one of the following?

   (A) Marcus' claim that traditional journalistic ethics is clear for most ethical dilemmas in journalism is incorrect.
   (B) A typical case illustrates that Marcus is wrong in claiming that traditional journalistic ethics is essentially correct for most ethical dilemmas in journalism.
   (C) The ethical principle that Marcus cites does not help the journalist in a typical kind of situation in which a decision needs to be made.
   (D) There are common situations in which a journalist must make a decision and in which no principle of journalistic ethics can be of help.
   (E) Traditional journalistic ethics amounts to no more than an unnecessarily convoluted description of the journalist's job.

3. Helen: It was wrong of my brother Mark to tell our mother that the reason he had missed her birthday party the evening before was that he had been in a traffic accident and that by the time he was released from the hospital emergency room the party was long over. Saying something that is false can never be other than morally wrong, and there had been no such accident--Mark had simply forgotten all about the party.

   The main conclusion drawn in Helen's argument is that

   (A) Mark did not tell his mother the truth
   (B) the real reason Mark missed his mother's birthday party was that he had forgotten all about it
   (C) it is wrong to attempt to avoid blame for one's failure to do something by claiming that one was prevented from doing that thing by events outside one's control
   (D) it was wrong of Mark to tell his mother that he had missed her birthday party as a result of having been in a traffic accident
   (E) it is always wrong not to tell the truth

4. Maria: Calling any state totalitarian is misleading: it implies total state control of all aspects of life. The real world contains no political entity exercising literally total control over even one such aspect. This is because any system of control is inefficient, and, therefore, its degree of control is partial.

   James: A one party state that has tried to exercise control over most aspects of a society and that has, broadly speaking, managed to do so is totalitarian. Such a system's practical inefficiencies do not limit the aptness of the term, which does not describe a state s actual degree of control as much as it describes the nature of a state's ambitions.

   Which one of the following most accurately expresses Maria's main conclusion?

   (A) No state can be called totalitarian without inviting a mistaken belief.
   (B) To be totalitarian, a state must totally control society.
   (C) The degree of control exercised by a state is necessarily partial.
   (D) No existing state currently has even one aspect of society under total control.
   (E) Systems of control are inevitably inefficient.

*Core Deduction Explanations

1. (7/4 #18) ~ A

The passage states that one of half of the subjects in trials receives the drug being tested and the other half receives a **physiologically inert substance**. The idea in the experiment is that the experimenters do not find out which subjects have the real drug. This fails frequently because the active drug causes signs or symptoms in the people that take it, while the placebo does not show these effects. This inference is an addition of the logic in the passage. The difference between the drug and the placebo (the placebo is inert, not active) leads to effects that are noticeable for the experimenters.

(B) The subjects taking the drug would also likely show improvements, so this would not be distinguishing for the experimenters.

(C) is irrelevant because it does not tell of a difference between the two groups, which is what the explanation must do.

(D) is irrelevant. It does not matter if the experimenters come or go.

(E) is irrelevant to the information being explained.

2. (9/4 #18) ~ C

Read both speakers argument's carefully, paying special attention to the thrust of Anita's argument. Marcus says that journalistic ethics make most **ethical dilemmas** easy to solve and gives the example of newsworthy information going to press as soon as possible. Anita says that **typical cases** are not at all easily decided by journalistic ethics. Notice this distinction between ethical dilemmas, which are **less common** cases, that Marcus is talking about and the **typical** cases that Anita talks about.

(A), (B) Anita never disagrees with his point about dilemmas.

(D) Anita does not say that **no principle** can be of help in these situations, only that Marcus's principle discussed does not help.

(E) Anita does not say that traditional ethics are unnecessarily convoluted, although she does imply that the ethic Marcus uses as an example is part of the job description of a journalist.

This question required a very close reading of the points of both speakers.

3. (23/3 #21) ~ D

Reading the passage, we see that the conclusion comes in the first sentence and the evidence comes afterward. It is unusual to be asked to identify a clearly stated conclusion, but this one is a bit harder to identify due to the fact that the conclusion comes first. (D) is correct: Helen's primary point is that Mark should not have lied to their mother in the way he did.

(A), (B), (C) and (E) are all evidence for the main conclusion.

4. (16/3 #19) ~ A

Read Maria's passage carefully, looking for the thrust of her argument. She begins by saying that calling a state totalitarian is misleading because the term implies complete control over all aspects of life. She then supports this claim with evidence on why no political entity can control even one aspect of life.

(A) This is correct. Maria's argument shows that the term totalitarian is misleading (leads to incorrect beliefs). These beliefs are that the state controls every aspect of life.

(B) Maria's point does not center on what it takes to be totalitarian. This is part of her evidence for her main point.

(C) Maria does imply this, but her argument is more interested in why the term totalitarian implies something that is not accurate.

(D) This, like (B), is part of her evidence.

(E) This is part of her evidence that no political entity can fully control even one aspect of life, which in turn is evidence for her main point that the term totalitarian is misleading.

*Deduction Problem Sets

Average (28)

Test / Section	#	Choices
19 / 2	# **17**	Ⓐ Ⓑ Ⓒ Ⓓ Ⓔ
19 / 4	# **13**	Ⓐ Ⓑ Ⓒ Ⓓ Ⓔ
20 / 4	# **6**	Ⓐ Ⓑ Ⓒ Ⓓ Ⓔ
21 / 2	# **10**	Ⓐ Ⓑ Ⓒ Ⓓ Ⓔ
21 / 3	# **1**	Ⓐ Ⓑ Ⓒ Ⓓ Ⓔ
22 / 2	# **17**	Ⓐ Ⓑ Ⓒ Ⓓ Ⓔ
22 / 4	# **4**	Ⓐ Ⓑ Ⓒ Ⓓ Ⓔ
22 / 4	# **14**	Ⓐ Ⓑ Ⓒ Ⓓ Ⓔ
23 / 2	# **2**	Ⓐ Ⓑ Ⓒ Ⓓ Ⓔ
23 / 2	# **7**	Ⓐ Ⓑ Ⓒ Ⓓ Ⓔ
23 / 3	# **4**	Ⓐ Ⓑ Ⓒ Ⓓ Ⓔ
24 / 2	# **2**	Ⓐ Ⓑ Ⓒ Ⓓ Ⓔ
24 / 2	# **12**	Ⓐ Ⓑ Ⓒ Ⓓ Ⓔ

Test / Section	#	Choices
25 / 2	# **1**	Ⓐ Ⓑ Ⓒ Ⓓ Ⓔ
25 / 2	# **7**	Ⓐ Ⓑ Ⓒ Ⓓ Ⓔ
26 / 2	# **8**	Ⓐ Ⓑ Ⓒ Ⓓ Ⓔ
26 / 2	# **9**	Ⓐ Ⓑ Ⓒ Ⓓ Ⓔ
26 / 3	# **12**	Ⓐ Ⓑ Ⓒ Ⓓ Ⓔ
26 / 3	# **15**	Ⓐ Ⓑ Ⓒ Ⓓ Ⓔ
27 / 1	# **3**	Ⓐ Ⓑ Ⓒ Ⓓ Ⓔ
27 / 1	# **12**	Ⓐ Ⓑ Ⓒ Ⓓ Ⓔ
27 / 1	# **22**	Ⓐ Ⓑ Ⓒ Ⓓ Ⓔ
27 / 4	# **14**	Ⓐ Ⓑ Ⓒ Ⓓ Ⓔ
27 / 4	# **17**	Ⓐ Ⓑ Ⓒ Ⓓ Ⓔ
27 / 4	# **23**	Ⓐ Ⓑ Ⓒ Ⓓ Ⓔ
28 / 1	# **14**	Ⓐ Ⓑ Ⓒ Ⓓ Ⓔ
28 / 1	# **16**	Ⓐ Ⓑ Ⓒ Ⓓ Ⓔ
28 / 3	# **12**	Ⓐ Ⓑ Ⓒ Ⓓ Ⓔ

Difficult (13)

Test / Section	#	Choices
19 / 2	# **24**	Ⓐ Ⓑ Ⓒ Ⓓ Ⓔ
20 / 1	# **23**	Ⓐ Ⓑ Ⓒ Ⓓ Ⓔ
20 / 4	# **13**	Ⓐ Ⓑ Ⓒ Ⓓ Ⓔ
21 / 3	# **16**	Ⓐ Ⓑ Ⓒ Ⓓ Ⓔ
22 / 2	# **2**	Ⓐ Ⓑ Ⓒ Ⓓ Ⓔ
23 / 2	# **10**	Ⓐ Ⓑ Ⓒ Ⓓ Ⓔ
24 / 3	# **11**	Ⓐ Ⓑ Ⓒ Ⓓ Ⓔ
24 / 3	# **15**	Ⓐ Ⓑ Ⓒ Ⓓ Ⓔ
25 / 2	# **8**	Ⓐ Ⓑ Ⓒ Ⓓ Ⓔ
25 / 2	# **19**	Ⓐ Ⓑ Ⓒ Ⓓ Ⓔ
25 / 4	# **15**	Ⓐ Ⓑ Ⓒ Ⓓ Ⓔ
28 / 1	# **18**	Ⓐ Ⓑ Ⓒ Ⓓ Ⓔ
28 / 1	# **22**	Ⓐ Ⓑ Ⓒ Ⓓ Ⓔ

Grueling (26)

Test / Section	#	Choices
19 / 4	# **12**	Ⓐ Ⓑ Ⓒ Ⓓ Ⓔ
20 / 1	# **24**	Ⓐ Ⓑ Ⓒ Ⓓ Ⓔ
20 / 4	# **10**	Ⓐ Ⓑ Ⓒ Ⓓ Ⓔ
20 / 4	# **19**	Ⓐ Ⓑ Ⓒ Ⓓ Ⓔ
21 / 2	# **8**	Ⓐ Ⓑ Ⓒ Ⓓ Ⓔ
21 / 3	# **24**	Ⓐ Ⓑ Ⓒ Ⓓ Ⓔ
22 / 2	# **15**	Ⓐ Ⓑ Ⓒ Ⓓ Ⓔ
22 / 2	# **22**	Ⓐ Ⓑ Ⓒ Ⓓ Ⓔ
23 / 2	# **24**	Ⓐ Ⓑ Ⓒ Ⓓ Ⓔ
23 / 3	# **20**	Ⓐ Ⓑ Ⓒ Ⓓ Ⓔ
23 / 3	# **21**	Ⓐ Ⓑ Ⓒ Ⓓ Ⓔ
23 / 3	# **25**	Ⓐ Ⓑ Ⓒ Ⓓ Ⓔ

Test / Section	#	Choices
25 / 2	# **13**	Ⓐ Ⓑ Ⓒ Ⓓ Ⓔ
25 / 2	# **21**	Ⓐ Ⓑ Ⓒ Ⓓ Ⓔ
25 / 4	# **16**	Ⓐ Ⓑ Ⓒ Ⓓ Ⓔ
25 / 4	# **26**	Ⓐ Ⓑ Ⓒ Ⓓ Ⓔ
26 / 2	# **19**	Ⓐ Ⓑ Ⓒ Ⓓ Ⓔ
26 / 3	# **20**	Ⓐ Ⓑ Ⓒ Ⓓ Ⓔ
26 / 3	# **22**	Ⓐ Ⓑ Ⓒ Ⓓ Ⓔ
27 / 1	# **19**	Ⓐ Ⓑ Ⓒ Ⓓ Ⓔ
27 / 1	# **20**	Ⓐ Ⓑ Ⓒ Ⓓ Ⓔ
28 / 1	# **11**	Ⓐ Ⓑ Ⓒ Ⓓ Ⓔ
28 / 1	# **20**	Ⓐ Ⓑ Ⓒ Ⓓ Ⓔ
28 / 1	# **25**	Ⓐ Ⓑ Ⓒ Ⓓ Ⓔ
28 / 3	# **8**	Ⓐ Ⓑ Ⓒ Ⓓ Ⓔ
28 / 3	# **14**	Ⓐ Ⓑ Ⓒ Ⓓ Ⓔ

*Deduction Problem Sets ~ Answers

Average

19 / 2 # **17** C
19 / 4 # **13** E
20 / 4 # **6** C
21 / 2 # **10** A
21 / 3 # **1** E
22 / 2 # **17** D
22 / 4 # **4** A
22 / 4 # **14** A
23 / 2 # **2** B
23 / 2 # **7** A
23 / 3 # **4** A
24 / 2 # **2** D
24 / 2 # **12** C

---

25 / 2 # **1** A
25 / 2 # **7** C
26 / 2 # **8** A
26 / 2 # **9** B
26 / 3 # **12** D
26 / 3 # **15** C
27 / 1 # **3** D
27 / 1 # **12** E
27 / 1 # **22** D
27 / 4 # **14** C
27 / 4 # **17** A
27 / 4 # **23** E
28 / 1 # **14** B
28 / 1 # **16** B
28 / 3 # **12** C

Difficult

19 / 2 # **24** A
20 / 1 # **23** E
20 / 4 # **13** A
21 / 3 # **16** C
22 / 2 # **2** B
23 / 2 # **10** C
24 / 3 # **11** B
24 / 3 # **15** E
25 / 2 # **8** A
25 / 2 # **19** B
25 / 4 # **15** E
28 / 1 # **18** E
28 / 1 # **22** B

Grueling

19 / 4 # **12** C
20 / 1 # **24** B
20 / 4 # **10** C
20 / 4 # **19** D
21 / 2 # **8** E
21 / 3 # **24** E
22 / 2 # **15** D
22 / 2 # **22** D
23 / 2 # **24** D
23 / 3 # **20** E
23 / 3 # **21** D
23 / 3 # **25** C

---

25 / 2 # **13** B
25 / 2 # **21** E
25 / 4 # **16** D
25 / 4 # **26** E
26 / 2 # **19** B
26 / 3 # **20** B
26 / 3 # **22** D
27 / 1 # **19** E
27 / 1 # **20** C
28 / 1 # **11** A
28 / 1 # **20** A
28 / 1 # **25** D
28 / 3 # **8** B
28 / 3 # **14** A

Assumption

Recall that an assumption on the LSAT is an **unstated** piece of information (a premise) that an argument relies upon. The author counts on an assumption to hold up the conclusion. Assumption questions ask you to identify an assumption in the passage.

Assumption questions fall into the Modify category: you are asked to support the passage by making an assumption explicit. Therefore, the correct choice can bring in outside information. The passage can be thought of as having a lacking, which you then modify by pointing out the assumption. Unlike Identify questions, the passage should not be taken at face value with Assumption questions.

Two Kinds of Assumption

There are two kinds of assumptions tested on the LSAT: Bridge Assumptions and Keystone Assumptions. Each has different characteristics.

Bridge Assumptions

Bridge assumptions link two pieces of an argument together, either a premise to the conclusion or a premise to another premise. Bridge assumptions create a bridge between two otherwise unconnected argument pieces. They fill in gaps. Consider this passage:

> On her date, Jamie will either go to the aquarium or the rodeo. Therefore, Jamie goes to the rodeo.

Notice a gap in logic? The conclusion is not supported by the single premise that Jamie will either go to the aquarium or the rodeo. An example bridge assumption is:

> On her date, Jamie does not go to the aquarium.

This unstated or missing premise makes the argument valid by connecting the premise to the conclusion. Without it, the conclusion has no support for why Jamie does not go to the aquarium.

Here is an example passage with an assumption that connects **two premises**:

> The study showed that meditation helps people clear their minds. Falling asleep quicker helps people get more done the next day at work. So, meditation can help people be more productive in their jobs.

There is no link between meditation (premise 1) and falling asleep quicker (premise 2), although there is a link between falling asleep quicker (premise 2) and being more productive (the conclusion). This assumption links premise 1 to premise 2:

> Having a clear mind helps people to fall asleep in less time.

This bridge assumption makes the conclusion valid.

Here is the logic diagrammed conditionally:

Mediation	->	*Clear Mind*	(Premise 1)
Clear Mind	->	*Asleep Quicker*	(Bridge Assumption)
Asleep Quicker	->	*Productive*	(Premise 2)

Therefore...

Mediation	->	*Productive*	(Conclusion)

Keystone Assumptions

In the real world, a keystone is a source of support and stability, usually for a structure.If a keystone fails, the structure it is supporting collapses. The same concept is true with a keystone assumption, an assumption required to hold up an argument as valid.

There are many keystone assumptions for every argument, but the LSAT will only ask you to point out the most obvious ones. Many of these assumptions simply dissolve **potential objections** to the argument. For instance, these are all keystone assumptions that eliminate threats to the conclusion that Jamie goes to the rodeo:

> Jamie is not incapacitated.
>
> The Rodeo is not canceled.
>
> Jamie does not go to the Aquarium.

The conclusion is built on these keystone assumptions (and many more). If any assumption is not the case, then she cannot go on her date. If the Rodeo is canceled, then she obviously cannot attend it. There are an infinite number of keystone assumptions supporting every conclusion, but again, the LSAT will test you on central and obvious ones.

Two Kinds of Query

The LR section has two different kinds of query for assumption questions.

Justify Queries

A justify query will ask you what additional piece of information will make the argument valid. These queries are based on sufficiency: the correct choice is enough to make the argument work, to support the conclusion fully. Examples justify queries:

> "Which one of the following is an assumption that would *justify* the conclusion above if added?"
>
> "The conclusion above *follows logically* if which one of the following is assumed?"
>
> "Which one of the following, if assumed, would allow the conclusion to be *properly drawn*?"

These queries usually feature the words "if assumed" or "if added" and something about the conclusion being valid: "follows logically" or "properly drawn." This makes sense due to the nature of these questions: if the assumption is added, then the conclusion is valid.

Necessary Assumption Queries

Necessary assumption queries ask you to locate an assumption that the argument needs. In this way, they are based on necessity: the correct choice is a requirement of the argument in order for the conclusion to work. However, that does not mean that with the assumption the argument is valid. These queries often feature words like "relies" or "depends." Examples:

> "The argument *assumes* which one of the following?"
>
> "The conclusion in the passage above *relies on* which one of the following assumptions?"
>
> "Which one of the following is an assumption upon which the argument *depends*?"

Necessary assumption queries do not feature words like "if added" or "if assumed," like justify queries do.

Type of Assumption Tested

You can tell, to some degree, which type of assumption you need to find in the passage by identifying the type of query. Each type of assumption should be handled differently. For instance, bridge assumptions are easy to envision while keystone assumptions are not.

Justify queries **only test you on bridge assumptions**. This is because a bridge assumption makes an argument valid, and that is what a justify query is looking for.

Necessary assumption queries test you on **both bridge and keystone assumptions**. About half of the necessary assumption queries will test you on bridge assumptions, the other half on keystone assumptions. You need to figure out which type of assumption the choices will be composed of. Do this by reading the passage. If the passage has a gap in reasoning, if premises do not directly connect to the conclusion, then you are looking for a bridge assumption. Otherwise, if the reasoning in the passage seems sound, then the choices will be keystone assumptions.

Bridge Assumptions

Again, when you read a Justify Query, you need to find a bridge assumption. And, about half the time when given a necessary assumption query, you need to locate a bridge assumption. There, your reading of the passage will tell you one way or the other.

Passage

When reading a passage on any assumption question, actively connect the argument parts together. On questions where you might need to find a bridge assumption, you do this to figure out if there is a gap in the logic, and where it is. Some sentences feature two premises or a premise and a conclusion, so you may need to pause in the middle of a sentence to do this mental matching. Make sure that you understand how each premise fits into the argument as a whole before moving on. Also, figure out how the conclusion is supported by the premises on a large scale.

Active reading is great for both types of assumptions tested. If you are dealing with a keystone assumption, reading actively will help you to figure out what obvious assumptions the choices might feature. This active reading will save you time on the question.

Identify the Argument Pieces

The pieces of the argument can come in any order, so watch for signal words and pay attention to the scale of the different statements. Paying attention to scale is a great way to identify a conclusion or sub-conclusion. Also, do not forget that bridge assumptions can link either a premise to the conclusion or one premise to another premise. Most of the time, however, they link a premise to the conclusion.

Conditionals and Metrics

Many questions with bridge assumptions have passages with conditional reasoning or metrics. This is something to look out for when reading the passage.

Envision

A bridge assumption will connect a premise to the conclusion:

Premise + *Bridge* = *Conclusion*

Bridge assumptions are ripe for envisioning, because the gap between the two argument pieces is possible to spot while reading the passage. You simply have to fill the gap and connect those two pieces. There are two methods for finding the gap. The first is straightforward: read the passage actively to find it. This one is ideal, because it is quick and requires no extra steps. The other, the unconnected element method, is explained below.

Unconnected Elements Method

Complex wording and topics can make it difficult to identify the gap while you are reading the passage. In these cases, use the Unconnected Elements Method of finding the gap, after you have read the passage thoroughly. The method is simple: find two subjects/topics that are only mentioned once in the passage (these are considered unconnected, or new). Then, connect those two pieces with an eye towards supporting the conclusion.

If you find an unconnected subject in the **conclusion**, then link that subject to one in the premises. The conclusion must be supported fully; it cannot use a new subject/element.

Example passage:

> Tom loves raccoons. Therefore, Tom owns a pair of binoculars.

We have three subjects/topics here: Tom, loving raccoons, and owning a pair of binoculars. Tom is featured in both of the sentences. "Loving raccoons" and "owning a pair of binoculars" are both unconnected because they are only mentioned once. So, here is the logical gap that we need to bridge:

> Tom loves raccoons. GAP Therefore, Tom owns a pair of binoculars.

We can connect these pieces **and** support the conclusion by showing that because Tom loves raccoons he must own a pair of binoculars:

> All raccoon lovers own a pair of binoculars.

Here is the full argument featuring our bridge assumption:

> Tom loves raccoons. *All raccoon lovers own a pair of binoculars.* Therefore, Tom owns a pair of binoculars.

Sometimes, both of the new subjects are in the premise, and you need to link those premises together:

> Cars with more than 90,000 miles are old. Jenny's car has traveled 100,000 miles. It therefore will break down soon, so she should sell it now.

"She should sell it now" is the conclusion. The fact that the car will break down soon is used to support the conclusion, but that premise itself is never supported. That subject is unconnected. Likewise, the subject "old cars" is not mentioned anywhere else in the argument.

After a little research, we have our two unconnected elements: "will break down soon" and "old cars." The bridge assumption:

> Old cars are likely to break down.

The complete argument, including the bridge assumption:

> Cars with more than 90,000 miles are old. *Old cars are likely to break down.* Jenny's car has traveled 100,000 miles and it therefore will break down soon, so she should sell it now.

Choices

You should be confident about the bridge assumption when moving to the choices. If you have little idea where the gap, many incorrect answers will be tempting. Return to the passage and find the gap.

Double Check the Conclusion

When you have an answer you are confident in, make sure that it **makes the conclusion valid**. If the conclusion is still left hanging, then you do not have the correct answer. With the correct bridge in place, the entire argument will be unified and the conclusion will be supported.

Conditional Errors

Incorrect choices are often reversal errors and negation errors, so look out for these. It is possible to find the gap but not bridge it successfully with these errors. For instance, a reversal error choice for the passage about Jenny's car would be:

> Cars about to break down are old.

This does not connect the premises in question, because it has the relationship backwards for what the conclusion requires. It does not support the idea that if a car is old, it will break down soon. It only supports the idea that if a car is about to break down, it must be old. That is a different concept.

19/4 #4

This question features a necessary assumption query and a passage that needs a bridge assumption.

> In order to increase production, ABC Company should implement a flextime schedule, which would allow individual employees some flexibility in deciding when to begin and end their workday. Studies have shown that working under flextime schedules is associated with increased employee morale.
>
> The argument depends on the assumption that
>
> (A) the employees who prefer a flextime schedule are the most productive employees at ABC Company
> (B) an increase in the morale of ABC Company's employees could lead to increased production
> (C) flextime schedules tend to be associated with reduced lateness and absenteeism
> (D) employees are most productive during the part of the day when all employees are present
> (E) companies that are in competition with ABC Company also use a flextime schedule

Query

The word "depends" is a requirement signal, and the query also features the word "assumption" so we know we are dealing with a necessary assumption query. That in turn means we could be looking for either type of assumption in the choices. So, when you read the passage, look for a gap to figure out if we are looking for a bridge or a keystone assumption in the choices.

Passage

The conclusion is couched in somewhat strange language: "The ABC Company should implement a flextime schedule to increase production." The premise: "Studies show that flextime schedules are associated with increased employee morale." The obvious gap in logic comes between these two, telling us that we need a bridge assumption. The new flextime schedule is supposed to **increase production**, but all we know about that schedule is that it improves morale.

Envision

We need to connect improved morale to increased production, so our envisioned bridge assumption is:

> *Increased morale leads to increased production.*

Move to the choices.

Sort

Work through the choices aggressively, looking for the envisioned assumption:

> (A) the employees who prefer a flextime schedule are the most productive employees at ABC Company

(A) tells us about employees who prefer flextime schedules. That does not give us information that the schedules lead to higher productivity. That type of information would use the schedules as the subject, not employees who prefer them. Also, this choice leaves out the unconnected premise about morale. Dud.

(B) an increase in the morale of ABC Company's employees could lead to increased production

Subset assumptions, assumptions that fit within a larger assumption, can still be valid assumptions. The fact that an increase in morale **could** lead to increased production is a subset assumption of "an increase in morale does lead to increased production."

(B) also passes the Opposite Weakens Test, which we will discuss in detail shortly. In brief, it involves negating an answer choice and seeing if that has an impact on the conclusion. If it does, then the choice is correct. So, if an increase in morale **does not** lead to increased production then the conclusion that the flextime schedules should be implemented falls apart. That conclusion rests on the premise that these schedules increase morale. If that is all they do, we have no evidence that the new schedules should be implemented **to increase productivity**.

(B) is a very strong hit, and it matches our envisioned answer. For teaching purposes we work (C) through (E):

(C) flextime schedules tend to be associated with reduced lateness and absenteeism

Reduced lateness and absenteeism are not the same as increased production. These qualities mean that employees are at work more often, not that they get more done when at work. (C) does not bridge the gap. Dud.

(D) employees are most productive during the part of the day when all employees are present

(D) **weakens** the conclusion, by showing that flextime schedules will not increase production because employees are most productive under a normal schedule, when everyone is in the office during set hours. Correct assumption answers strengthen the conclusion, so this is a clear dud. This choice is tempting because it mentions scheduling and productivity, two subjects we expect to see when supporting the conclusion.

(E) companies that are in competition with ABC Company also use a flextime schedule

(E) does not provide evidence that the schedules increase productivity. It is irrelevant information and therefore a dud.

21/2 #20

Our next example Assumption question features a justify query, so we know that we are looking for a bridge assumption in the choices:

> Ann will either take a leave of absence from Technocomp and return in a year or else she will quit her job there; but she would not do either one unless she were offered a one-year teaching fellowship at a prestigious university. Technocomp will allow her to take a leave of absence if it does not find out that she has been offered the fellowship, but not otherwise. Therefore, Ann will quit her job at Technocomp only if Technocomp finds out she has been offered the fellowship.
>
> Which one of the following, if assumed, allows the conclusion above to be properly drawn?
>
> (A) Technocomp will find out about Ann being offered the fellowship only if someone informs on her.
> (B) The reason Ann wants the fellowship is so she can quit her job at Technocomp.
> (C) Technocomp does not allow any of its employees to take a leave of absence in order to work for one of its competitors.
> (D) Ann will take a leave of absence if Technocomp allows her to take a leave of absence.
> (E) Ann would be offered the fellowship only if she quit her job at Technocomp.

Query

The phrases "if assumed" and "conclusion to be properly drawn" signal a justify assumption query, so we must find a bridge assumption.

Passage

There are lots of conditionals in the passage. We will work through each one and diagram them for teaching purposes. The most efficient way to approach this question is discussed later and does not involve this degree of analysis on each conditional. The first:

> Ann will either take a leave of absence from Technocomp and return in a year or else she will quit her job;

This is an Either/Or conditional, because Ann cannot take a leave of absence and quit her job. She must do one or the other. Diagram:

Absence /Quit

Next conditional:

> but she would not do either one unless she were offered a teaching fellowship at a prestigious university.

This conditional has a lack modifier, "unless." So, take that condition and negate it and place it as the indicator. The other conditionals, which the sentence refers to as "either one," are "not absence" and "not quit." Those are the requirements:

-Fellowship -> -Absence and -Quit

If Ann is not offered a fellowship, she will not take a leave of absence and she will not quit. This means that without the fellowship, she will stay at her job. We can take the contrapositive, which is easier to understand. The and changes to an "or."

Absence or Quit -> Fellowship

Next conditional from the passage:

> Technocomp will allow her to take a leave of absence if it does not find out that she has been offered the fellowship, but not otherwise.

This is an If And Only If conditional. Ann will be allowed an absence if, and only if, the company does not know about the fellowship. These conditionals are diagrammed by clumping the two conditions together. Here "Allowed Absence" is clumped next to "not find out" (represented by ~~FindOut~~):

AllowedAbsence~~FindOut~~

As a refresher, if either condition is true, then other is as well. The diagram above signifies that if we are told that she is allowed the absence, then the other condition that it is connected to, they did not find out, is also true. Likewise, if we are told that Technocomp did not find out, that means that she was allowed the absence.

On the other hand, if one condition in the pair is not true, the other is also not true. So if we are told that they do find out, then that means she is not allowed the absence and vice versa. Onto the next conditional:

> Therefore, Ann will quit her job at Technocomp only if Technocomp finds out she has been offered the fellowship.

This is the conclusion of the passage and it is requirement phrased: "find out" is the requirement to "quit."

Quit -> Find Out

Envision

When dealing with a passage full of conditionals, focus first on the conclusion. Then analyze the premises to see which is most relevant to the conclusion and where a gap may lie.

The either/or conditional from the beginning of this passage is applicable to the conclusion. We can sub in "not taking a leave of absence" for "quit" in the conclusion because according to the either/or conditional, if she quits then she does not take a leave of absence:

–Absence -> Find Out

The contrapositive may come in handy:

-Findout -> Absence

Sort the Choices

(A) Technocomp will find out about Ann being offered the fellowship only if someone informs on her.

(A) does not support the conclusion. The gap revolves around her making the choice to quit only if Technocomp finds out about the fellowship. Whether they will find out only if someone informs on her is irrelevant, because this does not tell us that they **have found out**. Dud.

(B) The reason Ann wants the fellowship is so she can quit her job at Technocomp.

The conclusion does not rely on her motivations for the fellowship, so (B) does not bridge the gap and is a dud.

(C) Technocomp does not allow any of its employees to take a leave of absence in order to work for one of its competitors.

It is unlikely that the university is a competitor of Technocomp, so this information is irrelevant. If we knew that the university offering Ann the fellowship was a competitor that would still not fill the gap, because we do not know that Technocomp has found out about the fellowship. Dud.

(D) Ann will take a leave of absence if Technocomp allows her to take a leave of absence.

Recall that one of the conditionals was if, and only if, Technocomp does not find out about the fellowship, then she will be allowed an absence (diagrammed AllowedAbsence~~FindOut~~). So we need one piece to bridge the contrapositive of the conclusion to the premises:

Allowed Absence -> Absence

If Ann is allowed an absence, then she will take it. This supports the conclusion because if she quits, it was because the company found out, and took away her option to take the absence. That is just what the conclusion says.

This is a strong hit, but with such a complex passage, make sure that (D) is the best choice by analyzing (E):

(E) Ann would be offered the fellowship only if she quit her job at Technocomp.

Diagram:

Offered Fellowship -> Quit

But we know that Ann will only quit or take a leave of absence if she is offered the fellowship. So information about the circumstances under which she will be offered the fellowship does not bridge the gap to the conclusion. Also, (E) has nothing to do with Technocomp finding out that she has been offered the fellowship, which is a big part of the conclusion. That is unaddressed here, making (E) a dud.

With such a complicated passage, working the choices was fairly easy. The small steps we took during the envisioning process to derive new forms of the conclusion came in handy.

*Assumption Review

- "The conclusion in the passage above relies on which one of the following assumptions?"
- Identify the unstated premise in the passage.
    - Support the passage by making an assumption explicit.
    - The correct choice must bring in new information.

Two Kinds of Assumption

- Bridge assumption – an assumption that links two pieces of information together.
    - Example argument with gap: "On her date, Jamie will either go to the aquarium or the rodeo. Therefore, Jamie goes to the rodeo."
        - Bridge assumption: "On her date, Jamie does not go to the aquarium."
    - Bridge assumptions make the argument valid.
- Keystone assumption – an assumption required for the argument to be valid.
    - There are thousands of keystone assumptions for any argument, but you are generally asked to point out the most obvious ones.
    - Example keystone assumption for the example above: "Jamie is not incapacitated."
        - If Jamie were incapacitated, she would not be able to go to the rodeo or the aquarium and the conclusion would fall apart.

Two Kinds of Query

- Justify query – this query asks you what additional information **will make the argument valid**.
    - "Which one of the following is an assumption that would justify the conclusion above if added?"
        - These queries imply that the conclusion will be logically drawn with the assumption.
    - The correct choices are always bridge assumptions.
- Necessary assumption query – locate the assumption that the argument **needs**.
    - "The conclusion in the passage above relies on which one of the following assumptions?"
    - The correct choice can be a bridge assumption or a keystone assumption. You can tell which it is by analyzing whether the passage has an obvious gap in logic.
        - If it does, you are looking for a bridge assumption.
        - Otherwise, if the argument is sound, you are looking for a keystone assumption.

Bridge Assumptions Approach

- When reading the passage of an assumption question, actively connect the argument parts.
    - Look for a gap between a premise and the conclusion.
- Always envision when you think you are dealing with a bridge assumption.
- Unconnected Elements method
    - Find two subjects that are only mentioned once in the passage.
    - Connect the two elements in a statement that supports the conclusion.
- Choices
    - Double check the correct choice to be sure that it makes the conclusion valid.
    - Watch out for conditional errors in the incorrect choices.

*Justify Query Practice Questions

1. Oil company representative: We spent more money on cleaning the otters affected by our recent oil spill than has been spent on any previous marine mammal rescue project. This shows our concern for the environment.

   Environmentalist: You have no such concern. Your real concern is evident in your admission to the press that news photographs of oil covered otters would be particularly damaging to your public image, which plays an important role in your level of sales.

   The environmentalist's conclusion would be properly drawn if it were true that the

   (A) oil company cannot have more than one motive for cleaning the otters affected by the oil spill
   (B) otter population in the area of the oil spill could not have survived without the cleaning project
   (C) oil company has always shown a high regard for its profits in choosing its courses of action
   (D) government would have spent the money to clean the otters if the oil company had not agreed to do it
   (E) oil company's efforts toward cleaning the affected otters have been more successful than have such efforts in previous projects to clean up oil spills

2. At the end of the year, Wilson's Department Store awards free merchandise to its top salespeople. When presented with the fact that the number of salespeople receiving these awards has declined markedly over the past fifteen years, the newly appointed president of the company responded, "In that case, since our award criterion at present is membership in the top third of our sales force, we can also say that the number of salespeople passed over for these awards has similarly declined."

   Which one of the following is an assumption that would allow the company president's conclusion to be properly drawn?

   (A) Policies at Wilson's with regard to hiring salespeople have not become more lax over the past fifteen years.
   (B) The number of salespeople at Wilson's has increased over the past fifteen years.
   (C) The criterion used by Wilson's for selecting its award recipients has remained the same for the past fifteen years.
   (D) The average total sales figures for Wilson's salespeople have been declining for fifteen years.
   (E) Wilson's calculates its salespeople's sales figures in the same way as it did fifteen years ago.

3. In experiments in which certain kinds of bacteria were placed in a generous supply of nutrients, the populations of bacteria grew rapidly, and genetic mutations occurred at random in the populations. These experiments show that all genetic mutation is random.

   Which one of the following, if true, enables the conclusion to be properly drawn?

   (A) Either all genetic mutations are random or none are random.
   (B) The bacteria tested in the experiments were of extremely common forms.
   (C) If all genetic mutations in bacteria are random, then all genetic mutations in every other life form are random also.
   (D) The kind of environment in which genetic mutation takes place has no effect on the way genetic mutation occurs.
   (E) The nutrients used were the same as those that nourish the bacteria in nature.

4. A poor farmer was fond of telling his children: "In this world, you are either rich or poor, and you are either honest or dishonest. All poor farmers are honest. Therefore, all rich farmers are dishonest."

   The farmer's conclusion is properly drawn if the argument assumes that

   (A) every honest farmer is poor
   (B) every honest person is a farmer
   (C) everyone who is dishonest is a rich farmer
   (D) everyone who is poor is honest
   (E) every poor person is a farmer

*Justify Query Explanations

1. (11/2 #22) ~ A

Assumptions help the conclusion to be properly drawn, so this stem tells us we are looking for an assumption in the environmentalist's argument. It is necessary to read both arguments here, to understand what the environmentalist is responding to. The environmentalist argues that the companies **only** concern is getting bad press. The evidence is that the company admitted that they were concerned about photos of otters damaging their public image. In order for the environmentalist's conclusion to be logical, we must assume that the oil company only has the single motive of protecting their public image here. Otherwise, it is possible that even though the company did say they were concerned about the photos, the company could **also** be concerned about the environment.

(B) This information about the otters does not support the environmentalist's conclusion in any way. It doesn't matter what would happen to the otters without the cleanup as long as the company is doing the cleanup only to protect their public image.

(C) Evidence about the oil company's past decisions does not support the argument about their current decision being **only** to protect their public image.

(D) This information about what would have happened had the company chose not to do the cleanup is irrelevant to the conclusion.

(E) How successful the cleanup efforts are is irrelevant to the conclusion about the company's motive for the cleanup.

2. (12/1 #22) ~ C

The stem tells us to find the assumption that allows the president's conclusion to be properly drawn. The president's conclusion is that the number of people passed over for the awards has decreased. This is in response to the statement that the number of people receiving the awards has decreased over the past fifteen years. The evidence for the president's conclusion is that **at present** the criterion of the award is being in the top third of the sales force. Notice "at present" in that statement. If this evidence is to support the conclusion, then we must assume that the criterion for the award, being in the top third, has stayed the same for the past fifteen years. Otherwise, if there was a different criterion in the past, for instance hitting a certain sales figure, then the number of people getting the award could have decreased while the number of people being passed over for it stayed the same. The president relies on the evidence that because the criterion is percentage based, as the number of people in the sales force decreases, so too do the total number of people getting the award and being passed over for the award. We must assume that the criterion of choosing a percentage covers the whole time period in question, or the evidence does not work.

(A) The argument hinges on getting the award or not getting it. Hiring policies do not directly effect this.

(B) This information weakens the conclusion, because the president is implying that the total number of people in the sales force has decreased over the past 15 years.

(D) The president talks about being in the top 33% percent of the sales force as the criterion (which is a **percentage**), so **total** sales figures do not matter.

(E) How the sales figures are calculated would not affect the total number of people selected when choosing a percentage of the sales force. It would perhaps shift some people from one group to another, selected for the award versus not selected, but this would not affect **total** numbers if a percentage criterion is used.

3. (15/3 #18) ~ A

The conclusion is the second and final sentence: the experiments show that all genetic mutation is random. The evidence is that experiments were conducted where bacteria grew quickly and genetic mutations occurred at random. We need to connect this evidence - about specific **bacteria** gene mutations being random - to all **genetic** mutation.

(A) This works because it means that all genetic mutations must be random, because the bacteria ones were. The evidence in the passage supports the conclusion because it shows which of the two possibilities the case is.

(B) This information does not fully support the conclusion about **all** genetic mutation. Just because common bacteria were the ones used, that does not mean that genetic mutation in animals or plants is not random.

(C) This is better than Choice B, but still not good enough. The passage does not show that all genetic mutations in bacteria are random which would be required to use this information to connect the evidence to the conclusion. The experiments only show that the bacteria in those experiments have random genetic mutations.

(D) This information does not help the conclusion, because although it makes the environment of the studies fit the universal conclusion, it does not show that mutations in these bacteria are the way that all mutations in all things work.

(E) This, like Choice B, does not fully support the conclusion. It strengthens the conclusion, but does not make it valid. Only Choice A does that.

4. (9/2 – 23) ~ A

Short passages can often be tricky, so read slowly and carefully. This one is doable if you break it into small chunks. The first sentence says that people are either rich or poor and either honest or dishonest:

Rich / Poor

Honest / Dishonest

People are one or the other on both of these traits. The passage then says that all poor farmers are honest. This information is irrelevant because it does not relate to the conclusion.

Conclusion: all rich farmers are dishonest:

Rich farmer -> dishonest

We need an assumption that proves this to be true. If we assume the contrapositive of this statement, then the statement must be true. Here is the contrapositive:

Not dishonest farmer -> not rich

If a farmer is not dishonest, then he must be honest. And if a farmer is not rich, then he must be poor. So the statement above also means this:

Honest farmer -> poor

This is what (A) states: every honest farmer is poor. This assumption makes sense: if every honest farmer is poor, then all rich farmers must be dishonest.

(B) This does not support the conclusion that all rich farmers are dishonest.

(C) This statement does not support the conclusion because there could still be honest people who are rich farmers.

(D) This still leaves open the possibility that rich people can be honest too.

(E) This does not support the conclusion.

Keystone Assumptions

When you read a necessary assumption query, you know that you **might be** looking for a keystone assumption. To figure that out, read the passage carefully to see if there are any major gaps in the logic. When you face an Assumption passage with no major gaps and no unconnected subjects, then you are probably looking for a keystone assumption in the choices. You will only know this after reading the passage.

Working the Passage

At that point, you can orient your approach to the question to this type. Make sure you understand the premises and conclusion and how they work together. As is the case for many question types, be positive that you know the conclusion.

Causal Reasoning

Some passages on keystone assumption questions use causal reasoning. The correct choice on these questions will usually support that reasoning in one of three ways. These are also discussed in more detail with Strengthen questions. We will use the conclusion "eating too much makes Jim gassy" for these examples:

Occurrences - Support the conclusion by showing that the effect occurs when the cause does:

(A) Every time that Jim eats too much, he gets gassy.

Or, show that the effect does not happen without the cause occurring.

(D) Jim only gets gassy when he eats too much.

One Cause – Eliminate other potential causes to support the causal relationship. Example:

(B) Jim does not get gas when he eats greasy foods in moderation.

Or, show that the effect does not give rise to the cause, eliminating the possibility that the argument has the causal relationship backwards.

(C) Being gassy does not make Jim eat more.

Evidence Reinforcement - Support the evidence underlying the causal relationship. Assume that the argument uses as evidence the fact that Jim's wife thinks he gets bad gas at night, post mealtime.

(B) Other people have commented on how bad Jim's gas is after dinner.

Conditional Reasoning

Paying attention to the type of reasoning in the passage also benefits you when the passage has conditional reasoning. In these cases, the correct choice will usually support the **requirement of the conclusion** or eliminate alternatives to it. If the conclusion is "If Sarah gets an MBA, she will be promoted," then a keystone assumption could be:

(B) The company has the liquidity to promote Sarah and pay her more.

This supports the requirement by showing that it is possible that she could be promoted. Or, the assumption could be:

(E) Sarah will not be fired if she goes back to school.

This eliminates another possibility that could occur instead of the requirement.

Envision

Often, keystone assumptions are somewhat obvious. They often dispel a noticeable weakness in the argument, or eliminate a possibility that would weaken the argument. As you progress in your practice on this type, you will be able to envision good answers to some of them. Early on in your practice, simply make sure that you marked the conclusion with an "X" and then work the choices carefully. Eventually, during the envisioning step, start actively analyzing the passage for some potential keystone assumptions. Overall, this is not the best type to envision on.

Choices

On both types of Assumption questions, the correct choice supports the argument, because the assumption is required by the conclusion. Therefore, any choice that weakens the conclusion is incorrect. Likewise, any information that is not absolutely necessary for the conclusion is also incorrect. So, a choice featuring information that could be true based on the passage, **but is not required** for the conclusion to be valid, is wrong.

With many choices on keystone assumption questions, you can tell that the choice does not affect the conclusion. Further, you will often find that because you have a good grasp of the passage, you can quickly identify a choice containing information that the conclusion rests opon.

Opposite Weakens Test

The Opposite Weakens Test can be used on a choice on an assumption question to find out if it is a required assumption. The test is simple:

- Negate the choice.
- Check if the negated choice weakens the argument.

If the negated choice weakens the argument, then you have a necessary assumption and the choice is correct. You can remember how the test works because if the choice matches the name of the test - the opposite of the choice weakens the conclusion - you have the correct answer. For instance, in the Jamie date argument, negating "Jamie is not incapacitated" yields "Jamie is incapacitated." That weakens the conclusion that she goes to the rodeo, because she cannot go anywhere. So that choice is a keystone assumption. If negating the choice does not weaken the argument, then you can eliminate that choice. If a choice for that same passage said "Jamie does not like the Rodeo" then the negated form would be "Jamie likes the rodeo." Her preferences do not come into play in the argument, so this choice does not weaken it. Therefore, it is not a required assumption.

Use this test after eliminating a few answer choices. That is the most efficient way to utilize it.

Negating a Choice

When negating a choice, take the **logical** opposite. This means either adding the word "not" or removing it:

Solving LSAT problems is easy.	becomes	Solving LSAT problems is **not** easy.
I worked all night.	becomes	I did **not** work all night.
Every monkey has a tail.	becomes	**Not** every monkey has a tail.

Notice that "I worked all night" **does not become** "I did not work at all last night" when it is negated. Likewise, "Every monkey has a tail" is not "No monkeys have a tail."

To negate, represent all the cases that are not the normal form. So if "every monkey has a tail" is the normal form, the negated form is "**not every** monkey has a tail." This negated form means that almost every monkey has a tail, or no monkeys do, or anything in between. Either way, it talks about monkeys having tails in all the ways that the original form does not.

To negate a conditional, just negate the requirement.

If Jerry talks loudly, people will laugh.			(original statement)
Loudly	->	*Laugh*	(diagram)
Loudly	->	*-Laugh*	(diagram for negated form)
If Jerry talks loudly, people will not laugh			(negated statement)

You need to know how to do this in case you wish to use the Opposite Weakens Test on an answer choice that happens to be a conditional. It is important to note that correct Keystone choices are often couched in negative terms: they tell what is not the case. This is logical because many Keystone Assumptions protect the argument by eliminating other possibilities. Do not be afraid of choices that use "not" or "never."

Final Tips

The scale of the subject plays a big role: it is much more likely that a choice that talks about "at least one" or "at least some" is the correct choice than a choice that talks about "many" or "all." Keystones need to disprove many possibilities that would threaten the conclusion and it is easier to protect a conclusion when dealing with small subjects. For instance, in the date example, it is a required assumption that "Jamie goes to the rodeo at least some of the time she goes on dates." Otherwise, if this were not true, if she **never** went to the rodeo on dates, then the conclusion that she is going to the rodeo on **this** date falls apart. However, we do not need to assume that "Jamie goes to the rodeo on many dates." That is not necessary. Because choices that feature "at least one" or "at least some" are required more often than more encompassing phrasings for assumptions, they are correct more often.

Avoid Extreme Choices

The strength of a choice's wording can make a big difference and choices with extreme wording are often wrong. These will often exaggerate the importance of one of the author's points or of the conclusion. For instance, in the date example, a choice that stated "Jamie's favorite activity is going to the rodeo" is totally unnecessary. Rarely are such strong, absolute assumptions required. In that example, keystone assumptions only need to support the idea that she is going to the rodeo that night. The LSAT-Writers know that students will fall for choices that sound crucial and very supporting. These choices are rarely necessary assumptions.

19/2 #2

This question features a necessary assumption query with a keystone assumption as the correct choice:

> A large number of drivers routinely violate highway speed limits. Since driving at speeds that exceed posted limits is a significant factor in most accidents, installing devices in all cars that prevent those cars from traveling faster than the speed limit would prevent most accidents.
>
> Which one of the following is an assumption on which the argument depends?
>
> (A) A person need not be a trained mechanic to install the device properly.
> (B) Most accidents are caused by inexperienced drivers.
> (C) A driver seldom needs to exceed the speed limit to avoid an accident when none of the other drivers involved are violating the speed limit.
> (D) Most drivers who exceed the speed limit do so unintentionally.
> (E) Even if the fines for speed-limit violations were increased, the number of such violations would still not be reduced.

Query

This is a classic necessary assumption query, so go into the passage looking for a gap to see if we need a bridge assumption or a keystone assumption.

Passage

This argument appears valid, there are no glaring gaps, so we are probably looking for a Keystone Assumption:

Premise - A large number of drivers routinely violate highway speed limits.

Premise - Driving at speeds that exceed posted limits is a significant factor is most accidents.

Conclusion - Installing devices in all cars that prevent them from traveling faster than the speed limit would prevent most accidents.

Envision

Because we have no gaps in the argument it is tough to envision an ideal choice. This is generally the case with keystone assumptions.

Choices

Take the choices one by one, looking for one that is required for the conclusion to be valid.

(A) A person need not be a trained mechanic to install the device properly.

The argument does not need (A) to be true because it would be easy to have mechanics install the devices in all cars. Or, they could be installed in new cars and maintained by trained mechanics. Mechanics work on cars all the time, so having this be a requirement does not hamper the conclusion. Dud.

(B) Most accidents are caused by inexperienced drivers.

(B) weakens the conclusion by stating that **inexperience** is the main cause of accidents, not speeding. This is a great example of an opposite choice because the correct choice will strengthen the argument.

(C) A driver seldom needs to exceed the speed limit to avoid an accident when none of the other drivers involved are violating the speed limit.

(C) works, although it is initially challenging to see how. The conclusion is that preventing cars from traveling faster than the speed limit would prevent most accidents. What about the possibility that if cars cannot go faster than the speed limit, they cannot **avoid** accidents? (C) eliminates that possibility by showing that that situation seldom occurs. Many keystone assumptions eliminate **unintended effects** of changes discussed in the passage. This is a very strong hit, and one you should choose and move on during a timed section. For teaching purposes:

(D) Most drivers who exceed the speed limit do so unintentionally.

(D) does not affect the conclusion, because the device prevents speeding whether drivers are speeding on purpose or not. Further, the argument shows that preventing cars from speeding should reduce accidents. Dud.

(E) Even if the fines for speed-limit violations were increased, the number of such violations would still not be reduced.

(E) is irrelevant because we are concerned with speeding, not speed-limit violations. These are not synonymous, but the choice treats them like they are. Also, even if this choice said that the fine increases would not reduce the amount of speeding that would not be a required assumption. The conclusion does not say that the device is the **only way** to reduce accidents. It only claims that it is **one way**. Dud.

*Keystone Assumptions Review

- With a necessary assumption query and no major gaps in the passage, you are likely looking for a keystone assumption in the choices.
- Causal Reasoning - when the passage uses this reasoning, the correct choice will often support the argument in one of these ways:
  - Occurrences - show that the effect occurs when the cause occurs or that the effect does not occur without the cause occurring.
  - One Cause – eliminate other potential causes.
  - Evidence Reinforcement – support the evidence underlying the causal relationship.
- Conditional Reasoning in the passage
  - The correct choice will often support the requirement of the conclusion.
  - This can be as simple as showing that what the requirement states is feasible for a specific reason.
- Envision
  - The keystone assumption will often be obvious: dispelling a weakness in the argument, etc.
  - However, this is not the best type to envision on
    - Just be sure you marked the conclusion with an "X" while reading the passage.
- Choices
  - Any choice that weakens the conclusion is incorrect.
  - Any choice that is not required by the conclusion to be valid is incorrect.
  - Opposite Weakens Test
    - Negate the choice, then check if the negated choice weakens the argument.
      - If the negated choice weakens the argument, then that assumption is required.
      - If it has no impact on the conclusion, then the choice is incorrect.
    - To negate a choice, take the logical opposite, which usually requires adding or removing the word "not."
    - To negate a conditional, negate the requirement.
- Avoid extreme choices
  - These choices often exaggerate the importance of one of the author's points.
  - Keystone assumptions can have relatively small scales; they can be quite specific in how they support the argument.

* Necessary Assumption Query Practice Questions

1. Marine biologists had hypothesized that lobsters kept together in lobster traps eat one another in response to hunger. Periodic checking of lobster traps, however, has revealed instances of lobsters sharing traps together for weeks. Eight lobsters even shared one trap together for two months without eating one another. The marine biologists' hypothesis, therefore, is clearly wrong.

   The argument against the marine biologists' hypothesis is based on which one of the following assumptions?

   (A) Lobsters not caught in lobster traps have been observed eating one another.
   (B) Two months is the longest known period during which eight or more lobsters have been trapped together.
   (C) It is unusual to find as many as eight lobsters caught together in one single trap.
   (D) Members of other marine species sometimes eat their own kind when no other food sources are available.
   (E) Any food that the eight lobsters in the trap might have obtained was not enough to ward off hunger.

2. The government provides insurance for individuals' bank deposits, but requires the banks to pay the premiums for this insurance. Since it is depositors who primarily benefit from the security this insurance provides, the government should take steps to ensure that depositors who want this security bear the cost of it and thus should make depositors pay the premiums for insuring their own accounts.

   Which one of the following is assumed by the argument?

   (A) Banks are not insured by the government against default on the loans the banks make.
   (B) Private insurance companies do not have the resources to provide banks or individuals with deposit insurance.
   (C) Banks do not always cover the cost of the deposit-insurance premiums by paying depositors lower interest rates on insured deposits than the banks would on uninsured deposits.
   (D) The government limits the insurance protection it provides by insuring accounts up to a certain legally defined amount only.
   (E) The government does not allow banks to offer some kinds of accounts in which deposits are not insured.

3. A university should not be entitled to patent the inventions of its faculty members. Universities, as guarantors of intellectual freedom, should encourage the free flow of ideas and the general dissemination of knowledge. Yet a university that retains the right to patent the inventions of its faculty members has a motive to suppress information about a potentially valuable discovery until the patent for it has been secured. Clearly, suppressing information concerning such discoveries is incompatible with the university's obligation to promote the free flow of ideas.

   Which one of the following is an assumption that the argument makes?

   (A) Universities are the only institutions that have an obligation to guarantee intellectual freedom.
   (B) Most inventions by university faculty members would be profitable if patented.
   (C) Publication of reports on research is the only practical way to disseminate information concerning new discoveries.
   (D) Universities that have a motive to suppress information concerning discoveries by their faculty members will occasionally act on that motive.
   (E) If the inventions of a university faculty member are not patented by that university, then they will be patented by the faculty member instead.

4. X: Since many chemicals useful for agriculture and medicine derive from rare or endangered plant species, it is likely that many plant species that are now extinct could have provided us with substances that would have been a boon to humanity. Therefore, if we want to ensure that chemicals from plants are available for use in the future, we must make more serious efforts to preserve for all time our natural resources.

   Y: But living things are not our "resources." Yours is a selfish approach to conservation. We should rather strive to preserve living species because they deserve to survive, not because of the good they can do us.

   X's argument relies on which one of the following assumptions?

   (A) Medicine would now be more advanced than it is if there had been a serious conservation policy in the past.
   (B) All living things exist to serve humankind.
   (C) The use of rare and endangered plant species as a source for chemicals will not itself render those species extinct.
   (D) The only way to persuade people to preserve natural resources is to convince them that it is in their interest to do so.
   (E) Few, if any, plant species have been saved from extinction through human efforts.

5. Many major scientific discoveries of the past were the product of serendipity, the chance discovery of valuable findings that investigators had not purposely sought. Now, however, scientific research tends to be so costly that investigators are heavily dependent on large grants to fund their research. Because such grants require investigators to provide the grant sponsors with clear projections of the outcome of the proposed research, investigators ignore anything that does not directly bear on the funded research. Therefore, under the prevailing circumstances, serendipity can no longer play a role in scientific discovery.

Which one of the following is an assumption on which the argument depends?

(A) Only findings that an investigator purposely seeks can directly bear on that investigator's research.
(B) In the past few scientific investigators attempted to make clear predictions of the outcome of their research.
(C) Dependence on large grants is preventing investigators from conducting the type of scientific research that those investigators would personally prefer.
(D) All scientific investigators who provide grant sponsors with clear projections of the outcome of their research receive at least some of the grants for which they apply.
(E) In general the most valuable scientific discoveries are the product of serendipity.

6. One sure way you can tell how quickly a new idea - for example, the idea of "privatization" - is taking hold among the population is to monitor how fast the word or words expressing that particular idea are passing into common usage. Professional opinions of whether or not words can indeed be said to have passed into common usage are available from dictionary editors, who are vitally concerned with this question.

The method described above for determining how quickly a new idea is taking hold relies on which one of the following assumptions?

(A) Dictionary editors are not professionally interested in words that are only rarely used.
(B) Dictionary editors have exact numerical criteria for telling when a word has passed into common usage.
(C) For a new idea to take hold, dictionary editors have to include the relevant word or words in their dictionaries.
(D) As a word passes into common usage, its meaning does not undergo any severe distortions in the process.
(E) Words denoting new ideas tend to be used before the ideas denoted are understood.

7. Medical research findings are customarily not made public prior to their publication in a medical journal that has had them reviewed by a panel of experts in a process called peer review. It is claimed that this practice delays public access to potentially beneficial information that, in extreme instances, could save lives. Yet prepublication peer review is the only way to prevent erroneous and therefore potentially harmful information from reaching a public that is ill equipped to evaluate medical claims on its own. Therefore, waiting until a medical journal has published the research findings that have passed peer review is the price that must be paid to protect the public from making decisions based on possibly substandard research.

The argument assumes that

(A) unless medical research findings are brought to peer review by a medical journal, peer review will not occur
(B) anyone who does not serve on a medical review panel does not have the necessary knowledge and expertise to evaluate medical research findings
(C) the general public does not have access to the medical journals in which research findings are published
(D) all medical research findings are subjected to prepublication peer review
(E) peer review panels are sometimes subject to political and professional pressures that can make their judgments less than impartial

8. Marcus: For most ethical dilemmas the journalist is likely to face, traditional journalistic ethics is clear, adequate, and essentially correct. For example, when journalists have uncovered newsworthy information, they should go to press with it as soon as possible. No delay motivated by the journalists' personal or professional interests is permissible.

Anita: Well, Marcus, of course interesting and important information should be brought before the public —that is a journalist's job. But in the typical case, where a journalist has some information but is in a quandary about whether it is yet important or "newsworthy," this guidance is inadequate.

In order to conclude properly from Anita's statements that Marcus' general claim about traditional journalistic ethics is incorrect, it would have to be assumed that

(A) whether a piece of information is or is not newsworthy can raise ethical dilemmas for journalists
(B) there are circumstances in which it would be ethically wrong for a journalist to go to press with legitimately acquired, newsworthy information
(C) the most serious professional dilemmas that a journalist is likely to face are not ethical dilemmas
(D) there are no ethical dilemmas that a journalist is likely to face that would not be conclusively resolved by an adequate system of journalistic ethics
(E) for a system of journalistic ethics to be adequate it must be able to provide guidance in every case in which a journalist must make a professional decision

* Explanations

1. (7/1 #14) ~ E

The stem asks you to find the assumption that the argument against the Marine Biologists hypothesis relies on, so when you read the passage focus on that argument and look for gaps in logic. The argument against the hypothesis is that lobsters can share traps for weeks and sometimes much longer without eating one another **out of hunger**. This assumes that the lobsters used as evidence were hungry but did not eat one another. (E) works. Without this assumption, those eight could not be used as evidence, because the argument needs to show that they were hungry and did not eat one another.

(A) The conclusion does not deal with lobsters out of traps, so this information is irrelevant.

(B) It does not matter if two months is a record for lobsters being kept together, it matters whether they are hungry and kept together.

(C) This information does not support the conclusion.

(D) provides support for the Biologists hypothesis and does not address a gap in the argument **against** the Biologists.

2. (7/4 #6) ~ C

The conclusion is that the government should take steps to ensure that depositors who want the insurance bear the cost of it. The argument must assume that the banks are **not already** making this happen in some way. (C) eliminates one way that the banks could force the depositors to bear the burden: getting lower interest rates. If you negate this information than the argument falls apart, because the government would not need to take steps for something that is already happening.

(A) is irrelevant because the conclusion regards deposits, not loans.

(B) Regardless of whether insurance companies can or cannot provide deposit insurance, the conclusion is that government needs to step in to ensure that depositors bear the burden of the insurance. Who can provide that insurance does not matter.

(D) is irrelevant.

(E) The fact is that depositors are receiving that insurance. Whether or not **some** accounts don't have insurance is irrelevant to the conclusion.

3. (9/2 #19) ~ D

Read the argument carefully looking for a gap in logic, while keeping in mind that because this is a late question in the section, it may be tough and the gap may be subtle.

Conclusion: a university should not be able to patent the inventions of its faculty.

Evidence: universities should guarantee intellectual freedom because if a university can patent inventions then it **has a motive** to suppress information about a potentially valuable discovery.

The argument assumes that University would *act* on this motive to suppress information, but this is never stated. For the argument to be logically correct, we must assume that universities would at least sometimes act on that motivation, otherwise universities would not suppress information and the conclusion falls apart with its evidence

(A) This information is irrelevant to the argument, which deals with universities.

(B) It is not required that most inventions would be profitable, only that information would be suppressed in anticipation of profit.

(C) How information is spread is not relevant. Whether it is suppressed or not is the issue.

(E) Irrelevant to the conclusion and evidence.

4. (10/4 #8) ~ C

For this question, we need only understand X's argument and identify the gap in logic there. X's conclusion is "if we want to ensure that chemicals from plants are available in the future, we must make more serious efforts to preserve for all time our natural resources." His evidence is that because many useful chemicals come from rare and endangered species, it is likely that extinct species could have provided valuable chemicals as well. This is implying that valuable plants pushed towards extinction through their use. Notice that his evidence talks about current useful plant species being rare and endangered. In order for his conclusion about plants being available in the future to be accurate, we must assume that any use of the current rare and endangered plants would not drive them extinct. They cannot be available for use in the future, if the act of using them drives them extinct, no matter what we do to conserve them.

(A) This information is not necessary to support X's argument.

(B) This assumption is not required to support the conclusion that if we want the plants to be available in the future we need to conserve them.

(D) The conclusion does not relate at all to convincing people, so this information is irrelevant.

(E) This information undermines the conclusion by implying that conservation will not help make more plants available in the future.

5. (7/1 #24) ~ A

This question comes at the end of the section and contains a long passage, so it will likely be a subtle assumption. Read carefully. The gap in logic comes in between the final two sentences. "Investigators ignore anything that does not directly bear on funded research." Ok. But then the conclusion is that "serendipity can no longer play a role in scientific discovery." We must assume that serendipity cannot directly bear on funded research. Otherwise scientists would pay attention to serendipity when it shows up there and it would play a role in scientific discovery.

(B) is not a necessary assumption, because if it is negated it does not affect the conclusion. The conclusion deals with the current state of serendipity.

(C) is irrelevant. It doesn't matter what the investigators prefer, because they still carry out the research.

(D) This is irrelevant. Investigators are still dependent on these grants and their criteria regardless of whether they all get grants or not.

(E) The conclusion is that serendipity will no longer play a **role**. Whether or not discoveries fueled by serendipity were **valuable** is irrelevant.

6. (7/4 #24) ~ D

Read the method very carefully, keeping in mind that this question is at the end of the passage and is therefore likely challenging. The method for telling how quickly a **new idea** is taking hold is to monitor how fast the **word(s)** that relate to that idea pass into common usage. Notice that the method requires one thing (the words) indicating the acceptance of something else (the idea). The method relies on the assumption that these two concepts retain their connection even after the word passes into common usage. Otherwise, if the word's meaning changes, then the word's popularity would not signal that the idea it was **originally** connected to is taking hold in the population, because that word could now express a different concept. This assumption is tricky and requires understanding that the relationship between the idea and the word leaves potential logical gaps.

(A) is irrelevant to the method.

(B) is irrelevant to the method. How the editors tell a word passed into common usage does not matter.

(C) is not necessary. The editors could say that the word passed into common usage and that would be enough to confirm that concept.

(E) is irrelevant. The method relies on a word entering **common usage**, not on a word simply being used.

7. (9/2 #25) ~ A

This is a long passage. Focus on understanding the conclusion and looking for gaps along the way. Conclusion: waiting until a **medical journal** has published the findings that passed peer review protects the public from making decisions based on potentially substandard research.

Evidence: prepublication peer review is the only way to prevent erroneous info from reaching the public. The evidence states that **peer review** is crucial for the studies being checked for errors. However, the conclusion says that the information **being published** in a medical journal is required to protect the public. We must assume that peer review will not occur outside of the medical journal setting, otherwise, the information could be checked by peer review elsewhere and safe information could be found outside of a medical journal.

(B) This is tempting, but not necessary for the conclusion to hold. It is ok if there are other people able to evaluate research, as long as the assumption in (A) is present.

(C) This is irrelevant.

(D) It only must be the case that all medical journal published findings are subject to peer review for the argument to hold.

(E) This information weakens the argument.

8. (9/4 #19) ~ A

The stem asks us to identify the assumption that helps Anita's statements show that Marcus claim is false. Marcus' claim: for most ethical dilemmas the journalist is likely to face, traditional journalistic ethics is clear.

Anita says that in the typical case where a journalist has some information but is unsure whether it is important or **newsworthy** the guidance is unclear about the ethics of the decision.

We must assume that knowing whether or not a piece of information **is newsworthy** can bring up an **ethical dilemma** for journalists. Otherwise, Anita's statement does not connect to Marcus' claim about ethics being clear. If not knowing whether info is newsworthy cannot raise an ethical dilemma, then the ethics are clear in the typical cases. The assumption here connects Anita's saying that the guidance is inadequate to Marcus' conclusion by showing that it is inadequate because it raises ethical dilemmas.

(B) Not a required assumption because Anita's statements deal with information that the journalist is not sure is newsworthy.

(C) is irrelevant information.

(D) supports Marcus' point of view.

(E) Anita shows that Marcus' statement that the ethics system works **most** of the time is incorrect.

*Assumption Problem Sets

Average (25)

19 / 2	#	**2**	Ⓐ Ⓑ Ⓒ Ⓓ Ⓔ
19 / 2	#	**9**	Ⓐ Ⓑ Ⓒ Ⓓ Ⓔ
19 / 2	#	**13**	Ⓐ Ⓑ Ⓒ Ⓓ Ⓔ
19 / 4	#	**8**	Ⓐ Ⓑ Ⓒ Ⓓ Ⓔ
19 / 4	#	**11**	Ⓐ Ⓑ Ⓒ Ⓓ Ⓔ
20 / 1	#	**11**	Ⓐ Ⓑ Ⓒ Ⓓ Ⓔ
20 / 1	#	**20**	Ⓐ Ⓑ Ⓒ Ⓓ Ⓔ
20 / 4	#	**16**	Ⓐ Ⓑ Ⓒ Ⓓ Ⓔ
21 / 3	#	**4**	Ⓐ Ⓑ Ⓒ Ⓓ Ⓔ
21 / 3	#	**6**	Ⓐ Ⓑ Ⓒ Ⓓ Ⓔ
22 / 4	#	**16**	Ⓐ Ⓑ Ⓒ Ⓓ Ⓔ
23 / 2	#	**9**	Ⓐ Ⓑ Ⓒ Ⓓ Ⓔ
23 / 3	#	**9**	Ⓐ Ⓑ Ⓒ Ⓓ Ⓔ
23 / 3	#	**11**	Ⓐ Ⓑ Ⓒ Ⓓ Ⓔ
24 / 2	#	**17**	Ⓐ Ⓑ Ⓒ Ⓓ Ⓔ
24 / 3	#	**10**	Ⓐ Ⓑ Ⓒ Ⓓ Ⓔ
24 / 3	#	**19**	Ⓐ Ⓑ Ⓒ Ⓓ Ⓔ
25 / 2	#	**12**	Ⓐ Ⓑ Ⓒ Ⓓ Ⓔ
25 / 4	#	**9**	Ⓐ Ⓑ Ⓒ Ⓓ Ⓔ
25 / 4	#	**18**	Ⓐ Ⓑ Ⓒ Ⓓ Ⓔ
26 / 2	#	**10**	Ⓐ Ⓑ Ⓒ Ⓓ Ⓔ
27 / 1	#	**16**	Ⓐ Ⓑ Ⓒ Ⓓ Ⓔ
28 / 1	#	**12**	Ⓐ Ⓑ Ⓒ Ⓓ Ⓔ
28 / 3	#	**19**	Ⓐ Ⓑ Ⓒ Ⓓ Ⓔ
28 / 3	#	**22**	Ⓐ Ⓑ Ⓒ Ⓓ Ⓔ

Difficult (9)

19 / 2	#	**15**	Ⓐ Ⓑ Ⓒ Ⓓ Ⓔ
20 / 4	#	**1**	Ⓐ Ⓑ Ⓒ Ⓓ Ⓔ
21 / 2	#	**11**	Ⓐ Ⓑ Ⓒ Ⓓ Ⓔ
21 / 2	#	**20**	Ⓐ Ⓑ Ⓒ Ⓓ Ⓔ
22 / 2	#	**14**	Ⓐ Ⓑ Ⓒ Ⓓ Ⓔ
25 / 2	#	**16**	Ⓐ Ⓑ Ⓒ Ⓓ Ⓔ
27 / 1	#	**21**	Ⓐ Ⓑ Ⓒ Ⓓ Ⓔ
27 / 4	#	**20**	Ⓐ Ⓑ Ⓒ Ⓓ Ⓔ
28 / 1	#	**21**	Ⓐ Ⓑ Ⓒ Ⓓ Ⓔ

Grueling (19)

19 / 2	#	**18**	Ⓐ Ⓑ Ⓒ Ⓓ Ⓔ
20 / 1	#	**16**	Ⓐ Ⓑ Ⓒ Ⓓ Ⓔ
21 / 2	#	**19**	Ⓐ Ⓑ Ⓒ Ⓓ Ⓔ
21 / 3	#	**8**	Ⓐ Ⓑ Ⓒ Ⓓ Ⓔ
22 / 2	#	**19**	Ⓐ Ⓑ Ⓒ Ⓓ Ⓔ
22 / 4	#	**13**	Ⓐ Ⓑ Ⓒ Ⓓ Ⓔ
22 / 4	#	**22**	Ⓐ Ⓑ Ⓒ Ⓓ Ⓔ
23 / 2	#	**17**	Ⓐ Ⓑ Ⓒ Ⓓ Ⓔ
24 / 2	#	**21**	Ⓐ Ⓑ Ⓒ Ⓓ Ⓔ
24 / 2	#	**24**	Ⓐ Ⓑ Ⓒ Ⓓ Ⓔ
24 / 3	#	**18**	Ⓐ Ⓑ Ⓒ Ⓓ Ⓔ
25 / 2	#	**24**	Ⓐ Ⓑ Ⓒ Ⓓ Ⓔ
25 / 4	#	**25**	Ⓐ Ⓑ Ⓒ Ⓓ Ⓔ
26 / 2	#	**22**	Ⓐ Ⓑ Ⓒ Ⓓ Ⓔ
26 / 2	#	**25**	Ⓐ Ⓑ Ⓒ Ⓓ Ⓔ
26 / 3	#	**21**	Ⓐ Ⓑ Ⓒ Ⓓ Ⓔ
27 / 4	#	**19**	Ⓐ Ⓑ Ⓒ Ⓓ Ⓔ
28 / 1	#	**24**	Ⓐ Ⓑ Ⓒ Ⓓ Ⓔ
28 / 3	#	**16**	Ⓐ Ⓑ Ⓒ Ⓓ Ⓔ

*Assumption Problem Sets ~ Answers

Average

19 / 2 # **2** C
19 / 2 # **9** B
19 / 2 # **13** A
19 / 4 # **8** E
19 / 4 # **11** B
20 / 1 # **11** D
20 / 1 # **20** C
20 / 4 # **16** D
21 / 3 # **4** A
21 / 3 # **6** C
22 / 4 # **16** E

---

23 / 2 # **9** E
23 / 3 # **9** E
23 / 3 # **11** B
24 / 2 # **17** B
24 / 3 # **10** D
24 / 3 # **19** D
25 / 2 # **12** A
25 / 4 # **9** B
25 / 4 # **18** D
26 / 2 # **10** C
27 / 1 # **16** D
28 / 1 # **12** B
28 / 3 # **19** A
28 / 3 # **22** B

Difficult

19 / 2 # **15** B
20 / 4 # **1** D
21 / 2 # **11** C
21 / 2 # **20** D
22 / 2 # **14** D
25 / 2 # **16** E
27 / 1 # **21** B
27 / 4 # **20** A
28 / 1 # **21** C

Very Difficult

19 / 2 # **18** E
20 / 1 # **16** A
21 / 2 # **19** C
21 / 3 # **8** C
22 / 2 # **19** A
22 / 4 # **13** D
22 / 4 # **22** D
23 / 2 # **17** D

---

24 / 2 # **21** A
24 / 2 # **24** E
24 / 3 # **18** A
25 / 2 # **24** E
25 / 4 # **25** E
26 / 2 # **22** C
26 / 2 # **25** E
26 / 3 # **21** C
27 / 4 # **19** A
28 / 1 # **24** A
28 / 3 # **16** B

Strengthen and Weaken

We group these two question types into a single chapter because they test very similar skills.

Strengthen

Strengthen questions ask you to support the conclusion with new information. The correct choice can help the argument enormously or just a little bit. Either way, it will be the only choice that helps it at all.

Strengthen questions are in the Modify question category. This means that you will modify, help in this case, the argument in the passage. Think of the passage as lacking in some way: relying on an assumption, etc. Because of this, the choices can bring in new information. Outside information is often needed to make an argument stronger. Examples of new information include: other evidence, explicitly stating an assumption, eliminating a possibility that weakens the argument, etc.

Query

The query will use the word "strengthen" or another word with the same meaning, like "helps" or "supports:."

> Which of the following, if true, most *strengthens* the argument?
>
> Which one of the following, if true, most helps to *support* the claim that...
>
> Which one of the following, if true, does the most to *justify* the position advanced by the passage?

Passage

To strengthen an argument, you must support its conclusion, so fully understanding the conclusion is a requirement on this type. Write an "X" next to the conclusion to force yourself to know exactly where it is. Many students miss strengthen questions because they do not have a good grasp of the conclusion.

Look for weaknesses

As you read the passage, look for weaknesses in the argument. Piece together the evidence and conclusion and see if there are any gaps in how they work. Think also about evidence that could potentially weaken the conclusion. Weak points can lead to correct answers because eliminating a weakness strengthens an argument.

It may help to pretend that someone is trying to convince you of the argument as you read. This helps you to think of gaps and weaknesses. This "place yourself in the argument" method is worth experimenting with in your active reading of the passage.

Envision

There are many ways to strengthen an argument, so you can envision a good answer to a strengthen question and that answer will not be among the choices. Other times, especially if there is a blatant weakness in the argument you can fill, you can envision the correct answer. Mentally say the weakness and then work the choices looking for one that shores it up.

If there is no obvious weakness, use your envisioning time to consolidate your understanding of how the argument works. Think about the conclusion and how it can be supported. Ensure you have a good grasp of the argument.

Eliminate Alternative Explanations

A common way to support an argument with causal reasoning is to eliminate alternative explanations for the situation in the conclusion. By narrowing the explanations, you strengthen the explanation that the argument pushes. If an argument concludes that snails are eating the cabbage leaves, then showing that rabbits are **not eating** those leaves helps the argument. This type of support works with the premises as well.

Sorting the Choices

The correct choice will support the argument, sometimes only marginally. If you are confident that a choice strengthens the argument, it is the correct answer. All of the other choices will not support the argument.

Look to actively strengthen the passage as you read the choices. One way to do so is to support the evidence. For instance, assume a doctor gives an expert opinion in a passage. There, a choice that tells **why** a doctor would be qualified to talk on that subject would strengthen the argument by assisting that premise.

Another way to actively support an argument is to **give an example** that illustrates a general or theoretical premise used in the argument. For example, if an argument features a parallel between cars and surfboards, stating another way that the two are similar would support the use of that analogy.

Incorrect Choices

Some incorrect choices **weaken** the argument. These can be tempting when they relate directly to the conclusion because you know the correct answer will do that as well. Obviously, the difference is that choices that weaken the conclusion affect it directly, but in the wrong way.

Other incorrect choices are irrelevant to the conclusion. They may come completely out of left field. Recall that on Modify questions, it is all right for the choices to bring in new information. Therefore, you can only eliminate these choices by the fact that **their new information** is not relevant to the conclusion.

Finally, some choices support a conclusion that is similar to, but not quite, the conclusion in the passage. These choice are tempting because they closely resemble the conclusion you are focusing on. They can be avoided by pinning down the conclusion after reading the passage. This point cannot be overemphasized: know the argument's conclusion, as that is what you are ultimately strengthening, even if you do so by supporting a premise. Every part of the argument supports the conclusion.

19/2 #21

Medieval Arabs had manuscripts of many ancient Greek texts, which were translated into Arabic when there was a demand for them. Medieval Arab philosophers were very interested in Aristotle's Poetics, an interest that evidently was not shared by medieval Arab poets, because a poet interested in the Poetics would certainly have wanted to read Homer, to whose epics Aristotle frequently refers. But Homer was not translated into Arabic until modem times.

Which one of the following, if true, most strongly supports the argument above?

(A) A number of medieval Arab translators possessed manuscripts of the Homeric epics in their original Greek.
(B) Medieval Arabic story cycles, such as the Arabian Nights, are in some ways similar to parts of the Homeric epics.
(C) In addition to translating from Greek, medieval Arab translators produced Arabic editions of many works originally written in Indian languages and in Persian.
(D) Aristotle's Poetics has frequently been cited and commented on by modem Arab poets.
(E) Aristotle's Poetics is largely concerned with drama, and dramatic works were written and performed by medieval Arabs.

Query

The phrase "most strongly supports" tells that this is a Strengthen question. Take note that most question types in the Modify category instruct you to take the answer choices as a given in their stem. Here, the words "if true" do that.

Passage

The argument begins with a premise: medieval Arabs had access to translations of Greek texts when there was a demand for them. Next comes the conclusion: Arab poets were not interested in Aristotle's Poetics. The conclusion is followed by two premises: poets interested in Poetics would have wanted to read Homer, and Homer was not translated into Arabic until modern times. The conclusion comes in the middle of the premises, but is fairly easy to spot because it is supported directly after it is made, and this is hinted at with "because." Further, all the premises are centered around supporting it.

Here is a more logical ordering of the argument parts:

1. Medieval Arabs had access to translations of Greek texts when there was a demand for them.
2. Poets interested in Poetics would have wanted Homer.
3. Homer was not translated into Arabic until modern times.
4. Therefore, Arab poets were not interested in Aristotle's Poetics.

Envision

The argument has no glaring weaknesses and it is not built on causal reasoning, so we have no big, obvious ways to strengthen it. Coming at it from another angle, we can think about how we would support a premise. For instance, we could support the premise "Homer was not translated into Arabic until modern times" by stating when the first translation into Arabic was made. That statement supports the conclusion by strengthening the idea that the Arab poets did not make any translations, which would have indicated demand and interest). We could also strengthen the first premise - "Arabs had access to translations of Greek texts when there was demand for them" - by showing that the translators could have made translations of Poetics if the Arab poets had wanted them.

You likely will not need to do this much analysis during the Envision step. We provide these details to help you see the type of analysis to use as you practice these questions.

Sort

Analyze each choice with an eye towards how it affects the conclusion.

(A) A number of medieval Arab translators possessed manuscripts of the Homeric epics in their original Greek.

(A) supports the premise that the Arab Poets could have had translations of Poetics if they had wanted them because it shows that the translators had the original documents to translate. (A) destroys a potential alternate explanation for the conclusion: that the Arab translators **could not make** translations of Poetics and that is why none existed until modern times. Because this choice strengthens the argument, it must be correct. We work the next four choices for teaching purposes:.

(B) Medieval Arabic story cycles, such as the Arabian Nights, are in some ways similar to parts of the Homeric epics.

(B) has no effect on the conclusion. Even if the story cycles are similar, that does not mean that Arab poets were interested or not interested in Poetics. This is irrelevant information. Dud.

(C) In addition to translating from Greek, medieval Arab translators produced Arabic editions of many works originally written in Indian languages and in Persian.

(C) relates to the first premise of the argument, but it does not bolster the conclusion. We already know that the translators produced Greek translations, that is what the conclusion relies on. This information is irrelevant. Dud.

(D) Aristotle's Poetics has frequently been cited and commented on by modern Arab poets.

The conclusion states that **medieval** Arab poets were not interested in Poetics. Therefore, information about **modern** ones does not matter. (D) could support a conclusion that modern Arab poets are interested in Poetics, but that is far from the conclusion we need to support. Knowing the exact conclusion helps us see that this is a dud.

(E) Aristotle's Poetics is largely concerned with drama, and dramatic works were written and performed by medieval Arabs.

(E) is similar to (B) because it seems to imply that because Poetics is concerned with drama and medieval Arabs were also interested in dramatic works, medieval Poets would have been interested in Poetics. But this is a stretch. Most world cultures have been interested in dramatic works, so it is not surprising that both Poetics and medieval Arabs were. Also, this choice does not reference medieval Arab **poets**, the subject of the conclusion.

*Strengthen Review

- Introduction
    - "Which of the following, if true, most strengthens the argument?"
    - Support the conclusion with new information.
        - The correct choice is the only choice that helps the conclusion in any way.
    - You will help the passage, so you should think of it as lacking in some way.
    - The choices can bring in new information to support the passage.
- Passage
    - You will support the conclusion, so you must fully understand it.
    - Actively look for weaknesses in the argument.
        - Piece together the evidence and the conclusion to find gaps or unconsidered possibilities.
- Envision
    - Only spend time envisioning if there is an obvious weakness in the argument.
        - If so, mentally articulate the weakness.
        - If not, just be sure you understand the passage.
    - If the passage has causal reasoning, think about alternative explanations for the situation in the conclusion.
- Choices
    - Look to support the passage by supporting the evidence or giving a relevant example.
    - Incorrect choices often weaken the conclusion or are irrelevant to it.
    - Other incorrect choices support a conclusion that is similar to, but not quite the conclusion.

*Strengthen Practice Questions

1. Eight years ago hunting was banned in Greenfield County on the grounds that hunting endangers public safety. Now the deer population in the county is six times what it was before the ban. Deer are invading residential areas, damaging property and causing motor vehicle accidents that result in serious injury to motorists. Since there were never any hunting - related injuries in the county, clearly the ban was not only unnecessary but has created a danger to public safety that would not otherwise exist.

   Which one of the following, if true, provides the strongest additional support for the conclusion above?

   (A) In surrounding counties, where hunting is permitted, the size of the deer population has not increased in the last eight years.
   (B) Motor vehicle accidents involving deer often result in damage to the vehicle, injury to the motorist, or both.
   (C) When deer populations increase beyond optimal size, disease and malnutrition become more widespread among the deer herds.
   (D) In residential areas in the county, many residents provide food and salt for deer.
   (E) Deer can cause extensive damage to ornamental shrubs and trees by chewing on twigs and saplings.

2. Teacher: Journalists who conceal the identity of the sources they quote stake their professional reputations on what may be called the logic of anecdotes. This is so because the statements reported by such journalists are dissociated from the precise circumstances in which they were made and thus will be accepted for publication only if the statements are high in plausibility or originality or interest to a given audience--precisely the properties of a good anecdote.

   Student: But what you are saying, then, is that the journalist need not bother with sources in the first place. Surely, any reasonably resourceful journalist can invent plausible, original, or interesting stories faster than they can be obtained from unidentified sources.

   Which one of the following, if true, most strengthens the teacher's argument?

   (A) A journalist undermines his or her own professional standing by submitting for publication statements that, not being attributed to a named source, are rejected for being implausible, unoriginal, or dull.
   (B) Statements that are attributed to a fully identified source make up the majority of reported statements included by journalists in stories submitted for publication.
   (C) Reported statements that are highly original will often seem implausible unless submitted by a journalist who is known for solid, reliable work.
   (D) Reputable journalists sometimes do not conceal the identity of their sources from their publishers but insist that the identity of those sources be concealed from the public.
   (E) Journalists who have special access to sources whose identity they must conceal are greatly valued by their publishers.

3. The use of automobile safety seats by children aged 4 and under has nearly doubled in the past 8 years. It is clear that this increase has prevented child fatalities that otherwise would have occurred, because although the number of children aged 4 and under who were killed while riding in cars involved in accidents rose 10 percent over the past 8 years, the total number of serious automobile accidents rose by 20 percent during that period.

   Which one of the following, if true, most strengthens the argument?

   (A) Some of the automobile safety seats purchased for children under 4 continue to be used after the child reaches the age of 5.
   (B) The proportion of serious automobile accidents involving child passengers has remained constant over the past 8 years.
   (C) Children are taking more trips in cars today than they were 8 years ago, but the average total time they spend in cars has remained constant.
   (D) The sharpest increase in the use of automobile safety seats over the past 8 years has been for children over the age of 2.
   (E) The number of fatalities among adults involved in automobile accidents rose by 10 percent over the past 8 years.

4. All zebras have stripes, and the most widespread subspecies has the best defined stripes. The stripes must therefore be of importance to the species. Since among these grassland grazers the stripes can hardly function as camouflage, they must serve as some sort of signal for other zebras.

   Which one of the following, if true, most strongly supports the conclusion regarding a signaling function?

   (A) The subspecies of zebras with the best defined stripes is also characterized by exceptional size and vigor.
   (B) In certain tall grasses zebras can be harder to spot than grazing animals with a coat of uniform color.
   (C) A visual signal transmitted among the members of a species can consist of a temporary change of color perceptible to other members of the species.
   (D) Zebras react much faster to moving shapes that have stripes than they do to moving shapes that are otherwise identical but lack stripes
   (E) Zebras have a richer repertoire of vocal signals than do similar species such as horses.

5. Defendants who can afford expensive private defense lawyers have a lower conviction rate than those who rely on court-appointed public defenders. This explains why criminals who commit lucrative crimes like embezzlement or insider trading are more successful at avoiding conviction than are street criminals.

The explanation offered above would be more persuasive if which one of the following were true?

(A) Many street crimes, such as drug dealing, are extremely lucrative and those committing them can afford expensive private lawyers.
(B) Most prosecutors are not competent to handle cases involving highly technical financial evidence and have more success in prosecuting cases of robbery or simple assault.
(C) The number of criminals convicted of street crimes is far greater than the number of criminals convicted of embezzlement or insider trading.
(D) The percentage of defendants who actually committed the crimes of which they are accused is no greater for publicly defended than for privately defended defendants.
(E) Juries, out of sympathy for the victims of crimes, are much more likely to convict defendants accused of violent crimes than they are to convict defendants accused of "victimless" crimes or crimes against property.

6. The number of aircraft collisions on the ground is increasing because of the substantial increase in the number of flights operated by the airlines. Many of the fatalities that occur in such collisions are caused not by the collision itself, but by an inherent flaw in the cabin design of most aircraft, in which seats, by restricting access to emergency exits, impede escape. Therefore, to reduce the total number of fatalities that result annually from such collisions, the airlines should be required to remove all seats that restrict access to emergency exits.

Which one of the following proposals, if implemented together with the proposal made in the passage, would improve the prospects for achieving the stated objective of reducing fatalities?

(A) The airlines should be required, when buying new planes, to buy only planes with unrestricted access to emergency exits.
(B) The airlines should not be permitted to increase further the number of flights in order to offset the decrease in the number of seats on each aircraft.
(C) Airport authorities should be required to streamline their passenger check-in procedures to accommodate the increased number of passengers served by the airlines.
(D) Airport authorities should be required to refine security precautions by making them less conspicuous without making them less effective.
(E) The airlines should not be allowed to increase the ticket price for each passenger to offset the decrease in the number of seats on each aircraft.

7. Asbestos, an almost indestructible mineral once installed as building insulation, poses no health risk unless the asbestos is disturbed and asbestos fibers are released into the environment. Since removing asbestos from buildings disturbs it, thereby releasing asbestos fibers, the government should not require removal of all asbestos insulation.

Which one of the following, if true, most strengthens the argument?

(A) Asbestos poses far less risk to health than does smoking, drug and alcohol abuse, improper diet, or lack of exercise.
(B) Asbestos can pose a health threat to workers who remove it without wearing required protective gear.
(C) Some kinds of asbestos, when disturbed, pose greater health risks than do other kinds.
(D) Asbestos is inevitably disturbed by building renovations or building demolition.
(E) Much of the time, removed asbestos is buried in landfills and forgotten, with no guarantee that it will not be disturbed again.

8. It is very difficult to prove today that a painting done two or three hundred years ago, especially one without a signature or with a questionably authentic signature, is indubitably the work of this or that particular artist. This fact gives the traditional attribution of a disputed painting special weight, since that attribution carries the presumption of historical continuity. Consequently, an art historian arguing for a deattribution will generally convince other art historians only if he or she can persuasively argue for a specific reattribution.

Which one of the following, if true, most strongly supports the position that the traditional attribution of a disputed painting should not have special weight?

(A) Art dealers have always been led by economic self-interest to attribute any unsigned paintings of merit to recognized masters rather than to obscure artists.
(B) When a painting is originally created, there are invariably at least some eyewitnesses who see the artist at work, and thus questions of correct attribution cannot arise at that time.
(C) There are not always clearly discernible differences between the occasional inferior work produced by a master and the very best work produced by a lesser talent.
(D) Attribution can shape perception inasmuch as certain features that would count as marks of greatness in a master's work would be counted as signs of inferior artistry if a work were attributed to a minor artist.
(E) Even though some masters had specialists assist them with certain detail work, such as depicting lace, the resulting works are properly attributed to the masters alone.

*Strengthen Explanations

1. (7/1 #15) ~ A

The conclusion is that the ban was not only unnecessary but **has created a danger** to public safety that would not otherwise exist. The evidence is that there were never any hunting-related accidents in the county and the increased deer population is causing public safety issues. (A) supports the idea that the **hunting ban** has increased the deer population, creating the danger to public safety in the conclusion. The choice does this by explaining that in other counties, where hunting is allowed, the deer population has stayed the same, which points directly to decreased hunting as the cause for population growth in Greenfield County.

(B) This does not support the conclusion because the passage already states that these accidents hurt motorists, which is all that is required to threaten public safety. Deer safety does not factor in there.

(C) is irrelevant to the conclusion because it does not address the ban having created a danger for public safety.

(D) is irrelevant.

(E) does not deal with public safety.

2. (11/4 #18) ~ A

The teacher's conclusion is that journalists who do not tell the identity of sources stake their reputations on what can be called the logic of anecdotes. The evidence is that the statements without identified sources are only accepted if they have qualities that anecdotes have.

(A) works because it shows that professional standing (reputation) is on the line based on what journalists submit, which is an unstated assumption of the argument. If this were not true, then the conclusion of the teacher's argument would not hold. Journalists would not be staking their reputation on the logic of anecdotes.

(B) The percentage of statements that do have sources is irrelevant to a conclusion about what happens when statements without sources are submitted.

(C) This information does not strengthen the argument because it does not distinguish between whether those statements have sources or not, so it cannot be directly relevant to the conclusion.

(D) Concealing the source's identify from the public is a different topic than that being discussed.

(E) This is neither here nor there regarding the conclusion of the argument, although it seems to be related because it talks about the publishers valuing the journalists who have unnamed sources. It doesn't directly support the conclusion that the journalists are staking their reputations on the logic of anecdotes.

3. (12/1 #19) ~ B

The conclusion is that the increase in child safety seats has prevented fatalities. The evidence is that even though the total number of serious accidents rose 20% during the time period in question, the amount of children killed during the period only increased by 10%. This evidence would be much stronger if we knew that the amount of serious accidents involving children remained fairly constant during this period. If the amount of children involved in serious accidents went down during this period, then it might mean that child fatalities only increasing by 10% is actually not an improvement, because the amount of serious accidents **involving children** might have increased by less than 10%. The information in choice B **connects** the two pieces of evidence.

(A) does not strengthen the argument. The evidence and conclusion deal with children under 4.

(C) potentially weakens the conclusion, by showing that children are spending the same amount of time in cars and yet dying 10% more during this period.

(D) is irrelevant to the conclusion that deals with the entire group of children under the age of 4.

(E) does not strengthen the conclusion because information about adult fatalities cannot be used to support the evidence about children. In fact, it potentially weakens the conclusion by showing that child fatalities have increased by the same percentage as adult fatalities, despite the increase in children's safety seat use.

4. (14/2 #7) ~ D

The conclusion is that the stripes serve some sort of signaling function for other zebras. One piece of evidence is that the most widespread sub species have the best defined stripes, so they must be important. Another piece of evidence is that stripes cannot function as camouflage. There is not a very obvious way to strengthen this argument, so we work the choices.

(A) The conclusion is that just having stripes serves as signals for other zebras. So A doesn't work, because we are not talking about having small vs big stripes.

(B) does nothing to support the conclusion about stripes signaling something to other zebras. In fact this works against the conclusion by supporting the idea that stripes serve a camouflage function.

(C) Zebras and their stripes do not change color, so this information is irrelevant to the argument.

(D) This supports the conclusion that the stripes signal to other zebras because it shows that effect in action through an experiment. Zebras react quicker to moving shapes that have stripes (like they would to each other), than the same shapes without stripes.

(E) The conclusion is concerned with visual signals, so this information about vocal signals does not support the argument.

5. (7/1 #23) ~ D

The conclusion is that expensive private defense attorneys are the reason why criminals who commit lucrative crimes are more successful at avoiding conviction than street criminals. This is a tough one to pre-phrase an answer for, so it is important to understand that information that will strengthen the argument will support the idea that the two groups (lucrative criminals vs. street criminals) are similar in all ways **except for** the quality of their attorneys. That will support the conclusion that it is the attorneys who are driving the lower conviction rates for lucrative criminals. (D) works because it shows that the two groups are **equally guilty** of committing the crimes they are convicted for.

(A) weakens the conclusion by stating that street criminals can also afford private defense attorneys.

(B) weakens the conclusion by showing a difference in the two groups: it is easier for prosecutors to convict the less complicated street crimes.

(C) The **total number** of the two types of criminals is irrelevant because the conclusion deals with **conviction rates**.

(E) weakens the explanation by explaining a **difference** between the two groups that explains the difference in conviction rates: juries favor lucrative criminals.

6. (9/2 #10) ~ B

Choose a proposal to go with the one in the passage (remove seats that impede escape) that would improve the prospects of reducing fatalities. The correct choice will relate to the proposal of removing seats in a way that makes it more effective.

(B) works. Increasing the number of flights would counteract the gains from making it easier to escape when planes crash. So preventing increases would save more lives. This proposal relates to the other because when the planes remove those seats that impede the exit rows, they lose seats to sell, the airlines would likely want to make up for the lost seats by running more flights.

(A) is incorrect because it does not address the current planes flying and it also does not relate to the proposal in the passage.

(C), (D) do not help reduce fatalities due to seats in the wrong place. Nor do they address the fact that the airlines will want to run more flights, due to there being less seats on each one.

(E) does not necessarily help reduce fatalities. With increased ticket prices, the airlines might sell just as many tickets as before, and/or increase the number of flights.

7. (15/3 #23) ~ E

The conclusion is that the government should not require the removal of all asbestos insulation. The evidence is that asbestos poses no risk unless it is disturbed and removal disturbs asbestos. We need outside information that will support the evidence and/or conclusion.

(A) Even if it poses less risk that does not support the idea that it should not be removed. This information does not support the internal logic of the passage.

(B) is wrong because the workers can just use safety equipment. That is not a good reason not to remove it.

(C) tells us that certain types more risk than others, but the conclusion is that the government should not require removal of all asbestos insulation. Therefore, this information does not strengthen the argument.

(D) weakens the conclusion. If asbestos can be disturbed at these times, that is a very good reason to require its removal.

(E) provides a great reason not to remove asbestos - it can cause problems later on when removed and stored in a dump.

8. (18/2 #21) ~ A

Support the position that the traditional attribution of a disputed painting should **not** have special weight. The passage says that it is especially difficult to correctly identify paintings that do not have a signature. The passage then states that this is why the traditional attribution has weight – "it carries the presumption of historical continuity." Work the choices looking for a reason that he traditional attribution should not have that weight – reasons why the historical continuity could have mislabeled the painting for instance.

(A) works perfectly. Art dealers would mislabel paintings to make them be worth more, so this means that the traditional attribution can be off, and should carry less weight.

(B) supports the attribution being correct historically – the exact opposite of what we want to do.

(C) does not directly weaken the idea that the historical attribution is off. In fact, it means that it is harder to correctly attribute the painting today.

(D) is irrelevant to the use of the historical attribution.

(E) somewhat supports the historical attribution as being valuable.

Weaken

The correct choice on a Weaken question attacks the passage's conclusion. To find that choice, as you read the passage, think about ways to attack the method the author uses to construct the argument. Weaken questions are common, so become familiar with their subtleties.

On a Weaken question you will be impacting the argument, so these are in the Modify category. That means that you should consider the argument to be weak in some way and actively search for vulnerability when you read it. Likewise, the correct choice can bring in new information, so do not eliminate a choice only because it mentions information not in the passage.

Query

Weaken questions are easy to identify because they feature "weaken," "undermines," "call into question" etc.. Example queries:

> Which one of the following, if true, most seriously weakens the argument?
>
> Which one of the following, if true, most undermines the politician's argument?
>
> Which one of the following, if true, most calls into question the claim above?
>
> Which one of the following, if true, would most call into question the lawyer's discussion of the trial?

Passage

The passages of Weaken questions are always arguments, because you cannot weaken a Fact-Group. Your main job is to understand the structure of the argument. Identifying the premises and conclusion is crucial here, as is seeing how the author uses them together to support the conclusion. These arguments often feature a specific vulnerability and your secondary job when reading the passage is to look for it.

Zero in on the Conclusion

You should always zero in on the conclusion and mark it with an "X" because most correct Weaken choices **directly** contradict it. Be sure that you identify the conclusion correctly. With an Advanced Argument, if you believe a sub-conclusion to be the main conclusion, you will probably miss that question. Read the conclusion very carefully and remember exactly what it says. For instance, this conclusion:

> Most politicians prefer to have a campaign manager with at least 15 years of experience.

Is not the same as:

> Politicians prefer to have a campaign manager with at least 15 years of experience.

If you do not know exactly what you are weakening, you may fall for incorrect choices designed to catch those who misread or generalize the conclusion.

Look for Weaknesses

Weaken questions rarely ask you to disprove a well crafted argument. Instead, you will generally use a fault in the passage to weaken it. As you analyze the passage, look for features that set it up to be attacked. It takes longer to read the passage this way, but it pays off because you will be more prepared to envision an answer and sort the choices. When you have little idea about how to weaken an argument, the choices take more time to analyze.

Think of the extra time spent on the passage as the time it takes to write a grocery list before shopping. You spend less time shopping when you know what you are buying. Likewise, you will be able to sort the choices more confidently. And, if you see a gap or think of a possibility that the passage overlooks, that could be the correct answer.

Common Areas to Attack

There are three common areas to attack in an argument: undue comparisons, incomplete information and questionable conclusions.

Undue Comparisons

You cannot logically compare apples to oranges, but some passages will try to. Usually, the two groups being compared will initially sound like they can be compared, but a closer look will reveal their differences. Whenever an argument relies on a comparison, watch out for this common fallacy. The correct choice in this situation will state **why** the two groups are not reasonable to compare. Look at this argument:

> James says that if we drive down to Michigan in his car we will use a lot of gas. But my car gets excellent mileage. So he must be mistaken.

Here, the comparison between the two cars is inappropriate. At the very least, we need more information that the two cars are similar in size or engine power or other factors that would influence fuel efficiency. For all we know, this argument relies on a comparison that has no grounding.

Incomplete Information

This error occurs when the passage misuses its evidence or fails to fully consider a certain element in its argument. By pointing out what is not addressed by the argument, you weaken it. Example passage with incomplete information:

> The dictator states that the major overhaul of the country's financial system will influence the banks to loan more money. That in turn will stimulate people to develop more new businesses. So the overhaul will help the country's economy.

The conclusion is that the country's economy will benefit from a financial system overhaul. The evidence is that banks will loan more money and that in turn will stimulate business development. This all sounds reasonable, but one might ask: "What other effects will the new financial system have on the economy?" If the interest rate skyrockets or if something else negative occurs, then perhaps the economy as a whole will not benefit. Any argument with a broad conclusion, such as "the economy will improve," may feature overlooked counter-points like these.

Questionable Conclusions

This error is when a passage has a conclusion that is only true in certain situations or under specific conditions. Example:

> Jim's business made a great profit last month. Therefore, the company is in the black.

We only know that Jim's company made money last month. It could have debt from before, so the conclusion is unsupported.

In general, to attack passages with questionable conclusions, show that the qualification given for the conclusion is unreasonable or that the premises do not support the conclusion because of the way the conclusion is confined.

Envision

Weaken questions can be good for envisioning. Thinking a little further about chinks in the armor of the argument might pay off. Keep in mind that in order for the author's argument to still be valid, the author would have to respond to the point. In general, do not spend much time envisioning on this question type, unless you spot an obvious flaw during your reading of the passage.

Weakening is not the same as demolishing. You do not need to destroy the argument and leave it with no shred of credibility. Correct choices simply call the conclusion into question.

Correct Choices

After the envisioning step, you should have a firm grasp on the argument's structure and the conclusion, and perhaps an idea how the argument is vulnerable. As you sort the choices, remember that the correct answer can bring in outside information. Pointing out relevant information that the passage overlooked weakens the conclusion. Questioning an assumption of the argument is another good example of outside information that can appear in the correct choice.

Reposition the Premises

Showing a premises to be false is almost never the correct way to weaken an argument. This is too simple and would not challenge enough test takers. Instead arguments are weakened **even though** the premises are true. The conclusion is usually attacked in an indirect way: by showing that **the way** the conclusion uses the premises is suspect, or that some aspect of the conclusion itself is suspect. "Attack the author's method of reasoning" should be your mantra when envisioning weaken answers. The author's assumptions or the relationships used by the author are the best areas to attack, not the validity of the premises.

The correct answer often makes you think about the premises differently, because it repositions them in relation to the conclusion. This is the nature of attacking an argument structurally: pointing out that **the way the premises are used** leads the conclusion to be invalid. Alternatively, the correct choice can show that the conclusion does not rest on the premises as it should.

Attack an argument with conditional reasoning by showing that the requirement does not occur when the indicator does. Example conclusion:

Therefore, the new bill led to the creation of thousands of jobs in the agricultural sector.

Here, a choice that says that the agricultural sector only had 500 new jobs created would weaken the argument. The indicator was true because the bill was passed, but the requirement was not. The conditional relationship does not work like the conclusion states, and therefore the conclusion is in serious doubt.

Incorrect Choices

To eliminate wrong choices, think of the author trying to sell you on the argument and your likely critical responses. If a choice does not sound like a rebuttal you would come up with, then that is a hint that the choice is incorrect. This method can be effective because it causes you to think about the argument in broader terms where you are more likely to spot vulnerabilities.

In general, answers that attack a premise are incorrect, for reasons discussed earlier. Also, choices that seem **overly** decisive in disproving the argument are likely incorrect. The LSAT-Writers use these as tempting wrong answers. While it is true that some of the easier Weaken questions have straightforward answers, usually the correct answers are subtle. Here are three more common types of incorrect answers:

Opposite answers

On Weaken questions, an opposite answer will strengthen the argument. These are often conclusion focused, as are correct answers, and that is what makes them tempting. Even though the right **kind** of information is featured by these choices, the information is used in the exact wrong way: they support the argument's conclusion.

Wrong Conclusion

Wrong conclusion choices attack a conclusion that is similar to the one in the argument and may, if read without a critical eye, sound the same. Your job is to weaken the exact conclusion in the passage, and a choice that does not do so is incorrect. Be sure that the answer you select does not only attack a closely related conclusion.

Irrelevant

These wrong answer choices are quite common. They talk to tangential issues in the argument, points that are not crucial for the conclusion. Or, they bring up information that sounds relevant, and may deal with a subject similar to that in the passage, but ultimately has no bearing on the conclusion. Always ask yourself how a choice relates to the argument at hand. If you cannot find a solid connection, you are likely dealing with an irrelevant choice.

19/4 #9

As you work this weaken question, keep focus on the conclusion in the passage.

> Measurements of the motion of the planet Uranus seem to show Uranus being tugged by a force pulling it away from the Sun and the inner planets. Neptune and Pluto, the two known planets whose orbits are farther from the Sun than is the orbit of Uranus, do not have enough mass to exert the force that the measurements indicate. Therefore, in addition to the known planets, there must be at least one planet in our solar system that we have yet to discover.
>
> Which one of the following, if true, most seriously weakens the argument?
>
> (A) Pluto was not discovered until 1930.
> (B) There is a belt of comets beyond the orbit of Pluto with powerful gravitational pull.
> (C) Neither Neptune nor Pluto is as massive as Uranus.
> (D) The force the Sun exerts on Uranus is weaker than the force it exerts on the inner planets.
> (E) Uranus' orbit is closer to Neptune's orbit than it is to Pluto's.

Query

"Most seriously weakens" tells that we are dealing with a weaken question. Beyond understanding the method of argumentation (something necessary on all LR questions), we enter the passage with these goals:

- Know **exactly** what the conclusion is.
- Look for inherent weaknesses in the argument. These are usually flaws in how the argument is put together or possibilities that it overlooks.

Passage

Let us break this passage down into pieces:

- Premise - The motion of Uranus indicates it is being pulled away from the Sun and inner planets.
- Premise - Neptune and Pluto, the two known planets whose orbits are farther from the Sun than that of Uranus, do not have enough mass to exert the force that the measurements indicate.
- Conclusion - There must be at least one planet in our solar system that we have yet to discover.

To analyze this argument's structure, let us discuss it in general terms. The premises say that there is a phenomenon occurring (Uranus being pulled away) and one explanation for the phenomenon can be ruled out (Neptune or Pluto pulling Uranus). The conclusion, in general terms, says that factor X (another planet) must be causing the phenomenon.

Envision

Whenever an argument says that one thing explains a situation, ask if it is possible that **something else** also explains that situation, perhaps more plausibly. Here, the argument is vulnerable because it argues that because two known planets cannot be pulling Uranus, a bigger unknown planet must be. This begs the question, why must a **planet** be pulling Uranus? It is reasonable to think that something else in space is causing the effect. After achieving this level of articulation regarding the argument's weak spot, move to the choices.

Choices

It is a good idea to remind yourself of the conclusion immediately before looking at the choices. Here it is: "There must be at least one planet in our solar system that we have yet to discover."

> (A) Pluto was not discovered until 1930.

(A) does not weaken the conclusion, because Pluto is not big enough to pull Uranus. Information about when Pluto was discovered does not help us attack the conclusion. In some ways this information **supports** the conclusion, because Pluto was not discovered until recently. Dud.

> (B) There is a belt of comets beyond the orbit of Pluto with powerful gravitational pull.

This is relevant new information. It is possible that this comet belt is pulling Uranus and that fact weakens the conclusion that an undiscovered planet is pulling Uranus. (B) weakens the argument by bringing in outside information that attacks an underlying premise of the argument. The argument assumes that a **planet** is pulling Uranus, but as we realized during the envision step, that does not have to be the case. This is a strong hit.

> (C) Neither Neptune nor Pluto is as massive as Uranus.

(C) is irrelevant information. The second premise already tells us that neither planet can be pulling Uranus because they do not have enough mass. (C) does not add anything new to the discussion. Dud.

> (D) The force the Sun exerts on Uranus is weaker than the force it exerts on the inner planets.

(D) does not relate to the conclusion. The fact that the sun pulls less hard on Uranus probably means that something with less gravitational force could more easily pull Uranus towards it than it could a planet closer to the sun. Showing this is unhelpful, because we are trying to weaken the idea that an **undiscovered planet** is pulling Uranus. Information on how Uranus's pull from the sun relates to the other planets does not factor in to this discussion. This irrelevant choice is a dud.

> (E) Uranus' orbit is closer to Neptune's orbit than it is to Pluto's.

Who cares? The argument tells us that neither Neptune nor Pluto is strong enough to be causing the phenomenon. Therefore it is irrelevant which one Uranus' orbit is closer to. This choice is a dud.

*Weaken Review

- Introduction
    - "Which one of the following, if true, most seriously weakens the argument?"
    - Weaken the author's conclusion.
    - Like Strengthen questions, read the passage looking for a vulnerability.
    - The correct choice must bring in new information.
- Passage
    - Read primarily to understand the argument structure.
        - Mark the conclusion with an "X".
        - Your secondary goal is to identify ways the argument is vulnerable.
- Common Areas to Attack
    - Undue comparisons – groups being compared that are too different to be compared.
        - The correct choice will say why they are not comparable.
    - Incomplete information – when the passage fails to consider a possibility.
        - The correct choice will point out that possibility.
    - Questionable conclusion – when the conclusion is only true in certain situations.
        - The correct choice will state situations when the conclusion is questionable.
- Envision
    - Do not spend much time envisioning on this type.
    - If there is an obvious weakness, think of a way to point it out.
- Correct choices
    - Evidence itself is rarely shown to be false as a way of weakening.
        - Instead, focus on how the evidence is **used**.
    - Attack arguments with conditional reasoning by showing that the requirement does not occur when the indicator does.
- Incorrect choices
    - Choices that seem to very strongly weaken the argument are often wrong.
    - Wrong conclusion – a choice that attacks a different conclusion.
    - Irrelevant – a choice that talks to tangential issues in the argument.

*Weaken Practice Questions

1. Waste management companies, which collect waste for disposal in landfills and incineration plants, report that disposable plastics make up an ever-increasing percentage of the waste they handle. It is clear that attempts to decrease the amount of plastic that people throw away in the garbage are failing.

   Which one of the following, if true, most seriously weakens the argument?

   (A) Because plastics create harmful pollutants when burned, an increasing percentage of the plastics handled by waste management companies are being disposed of in landfills.

   (B) Although many plastics are recyclable, most of the plastics disposed of by waste management companies are not.

   (C) People are more likely to save and reuse plastic containers than containers made of heavier materials like glass or metal.

   (D) An increasing proportion of the paper, glass, and metal cans that waste management companies used to handle is now being recycled.

   (E) While the percentage of products using plastic packaging is increasing, the total amount of plastic being manufactured has remained unchanged.

2. When butterfat was considered nutritious and healthful, a law was enacted requiring that manufacturers use the term “imitation butter” to indicate butter whose butterfat content had been diminished through the addition of water. Today, it is known that the high cholesterol content of butterfat makes it harmful to human health. Since the public should be encouraged to eat foods with lower rather than higher butterfat content and since the term “imitation” with its connotations of falsity deters many people from purchasing products so designated, manufacturers who wish to give reduced-butterfat butter the more appealing name of “lite butter” should be allowed to do so.

   Which one of the following, if true, most seriously undermines the argument?

   (A) The manufacturers who prefer to use the word “lite” instead of “imitation” are motivated principally by the financial interest of their stockholders.

   (B) The manufacturers who wish to call their product “lite butter” plan to change the composition of the product so that it contains more water than it now does.

   (C) Some individuals who need to reduce their intake of cholesterol are not deterred from using the reduced-butterfat product by the negative connotations of the term “imitation.”

   (D) Cholesterol is only one of many factors that contribute to the types of health problems with which the consumption of excessive amounts of cholesterol is often associated.

   (E) Most people deterred from eating “imitation butter” because of its name choose alternatives with a lower butterfat content than this product has.

3. The labeling of otherwise high calorie foods as "sugar free," based on the replacement of all sugar by artificial sweeteners, should be prohibited by law. Such a prohibition is indicated because many consumers who need to lose weight will interpret the label "sugar free" as synonymous with "low in calories" and harm themselves by building weight loss diets around foods labeled "sugar free." Manufacturers of sugar free foods are well aware of this tendency on the part of consumers.

   Which one of the following, if true, provides the strongest basis for challenging the conclusion in the passage?

   (A) Food manufacturers would respond to a ban on the label "sugar free" by reducing the calories in sugar free products by enough to be able to promote those products as diet foods.

   (B) Individuals who are diabetic need to be able to identify products that contain no sugar by reference to product labels that expressly state that the product contains no sugar.

   (C) Consumers are sometimes slow to notice changes in product labels unless those changes are themselves well advertised.

   (D) Consumers who have chosen a particular weight loss diet tend to persist with this diet if they have been warned not to expect very quick results.

   (E) Exactly what appears on a product label is less important to consumer behavior than is the relative visual prominence of the different pieces of information that the label contains.

4. There is relatively little room for growth in the overall carpet market, which is tied to the size of the population. Most who purchase carpet do so only once or twice, first in their twenties or thirties, and then perhaps again in their fifties or sixties. Thus as the population ages, companies producing carpet will be able to gain market share in the carpet market only through purchasing competitors, and not through more aggressive marketing.

   Which one of the following, if true, casts the most doubt on the conclusion above?

   (A) Most of the major carpet producers market other floor coverings as well.

   (B) Most established carpet producers market several different brand names and varieties, and there is no remaining niche in the market for new brands to fill.

   (C) Two of the three mergers in the industry's last ten years led to a decline in profits and revenues for the newly merged companies.

   (D) Price reductions, achieved by cost-cutting in production, by some of the dominant firms in the carpet market are causing other producers to leave the market altogether.

   (E) The carpet market is unlike most markets in that consumers are becoming increasingly resistant to new patterns and styles.

5. Logging industry official: Harvesting trees from old growth forests for use in manufacture can reduce the amount of carbon dioxide in the atmosphere, since when large old trees die in the forest they decompose, releasing their stored carbon dioxide. Harvesting old growth forests would, moreover, make room for rapidly growing young trees, which absorb more carbon dioxide from the atmosphere than do trees in old growth forests.

   Which one of the following, if true, most seriously weakens the official's argument?

   (A) Many old growth forests are the home of thousands of animal species that would be endangered if the forests were to be destroyed.
   (B) Much of the organic matter from old growth trees, unusable as lumber, is made into products that decompose rapidly.
   (C) A young tree contains less than half the amount of carbon dioxide that is stored in an old tree of the same species.
   (D) Much of the carbon dioxide present in forests is eventually released when wood and other organic debris found on the forest floor decompose.
   (E) It can take many years for the trees of a newly planted forest to reach the size of those found in existing old growth forests.

6. When the supply of a given resource dwindles, alternative technologies allowing the use of different resources develop, and demand for the resource that was in short supply naturally declines. Then the existing supplies of that resource satisfy whatever demand remains. Among the once dwindling resources that are now in more than adequate supply are flint for arrowheads, trees usable for schooner masts, and good mules. Because new technologies constantly replace old ones, we can never run out of important natural resources.

   Which one of the following, if true, most seriously undermines the conclusion?

   (A) The masts and hulls of some sailing ships built today are still made of wood.
   (B) There are considerably fewer mules today than there were 100 years ago.
   (C) The cost of some new technologies is often so high that the companies developing them might actually lose money at first.
   (D) Dwindling supplies of a natural resource often result in that resource's costing more to use.
   (E) The biological requirements for substances like clean air and clean water are unaffected by technological change.

7. Fares on the city-run public buses in Greenville are subsidized by city tax revenues, but among the beneficiaries of the low fares are many people who commute from outside the city to jobs in Greenville. Some city councilors argue that city taxes should be used primarily to benefit the people who pay them, and therefore that bus fares should be raised enough to cover the cost of the service.

   Each of the following, if true, would weaken the argument advanced by the city councilors EXCEPT:

   (A) Many businesses whose presence in the city is beneficial to the city's taxpayers would relocate outside the city if public-transit fares were more expensive.
   (B) By providing commuters with economic incentives to drive to work, higher transit fares would worsen air pollution in Greenville and increase the cost of maintaining the city's streets.
   (C) Increasing transit fares would disadvantage those residents of the city whose low incomes make them exempt from city taxes, and all city councilors agree that these residents should be able to take advantage of city-run services.
   (D) Voters in the city, many of whom benefit from the low transit fares, are strongly opposed to increasing local taxes.
   (E) People who work in Greenville and earn wages above the nationally mandated minimum all pay the city wage tax of 5 percent.

8. Between 1951 and 1963, it was illegal in the country of Geronia to manufacture, sell, or transport any alcoholic beverages. Despite this prohibition, however, the death rate from diseases related to excessive alcohol consumption was higher during the first five years of the period than it was during the five years prior to 1951. Therefore, the attempt to prevent alcohol use merely made people want and use alcohol more than they would have if it had not been forbidden.

   Each of the following, if true, weakens the argument EXCEPT:

   (A) Death from an alcohol related disease generally does not occur until five to ten years after the onset of excessive alcohol consumption.
   (B) The diseases that can be caused by excessive alcohol consumption can also be caused by other kinds of behavior that increased between 1951 and 1963.
   (C) The death rate resulting from alcohol related diseases increased just as sharply during the ten years before and the ten years after the prohibition of alcohol as it did during the years of prohibition.
   (D) Many who died of alcohol related diseases between 1951 and 1963 consumed illegally imported alcoholic beverages produced by the same methods as those used within Geronia.
   (E) Between 1951 and 1963, among the people with preexisting alcohol related diseases, the percentage who obtained lifesaving medical attention declined because of a social stigma attached to excessive alcohol consumption.

*Weaken Explanations

1. (9/2 #7) ~ D

Conclusion: attempts to decrease the **amount** of plastic that people throw away in the garbage are failing.

Evidence: waste management companies report that plastics make up an ever-increasing **percentage** of the waste they handle.

The conclusion states that the **total amount** of plastic that people throw away is increasing, but the evidence is based on the **percentage** that waste management companies deal with. (D) weakens the argument by telling that the percentage of plastics is going up because people are recycling more of the other types of waste that the companies used to deal with. This weakens the conclusion by showing that the efforts to decrease the total amount of plastic may be working, even though the percentage of plastic dealt with by the waste companies is going up. Different types of LR questions test your understanding of the difference between percentages and absolute numbers.

(A) does not affect the argument in any way. It only gives extra information on what the companies do with the plastic.

(B) is irrelevant because the conclusion involves decreasing the total amount of plastic thrown away. It does not matter if the plastic the companies deal with is recyclable or not.

(C) does not weaken the conclusion that the attempts to reduce plastic being thrown away are failing. It talks about consumer recycling behavior, but not how the behavior is being **affected**.

(E) is irrelevant because we are interested in plastic being thrown away, not manufactured.

2. (9/4 #22) ~ E

Conclusion: manufacturers should be allowed to use the term "lite butter" instead of "imitation butter." Evidence: the term imitation deters people and people should be induced to consume less butterfat content. (E) stands out. The argument uses as evidence for its argument that switching the term would lower butterfat consumption, but (E) contradicts that by pointing out that the term imitation butter deters people to **lower** butterfat content alternatives. So switching this term for a more appealing one, would switch those customers from the lower alternatives to the **higher** butterfat product. This is against the goal of lowering butterfat consumption.

(A) This information is irrelevant to the argument. It only matters what consumers are doing, not what the stockholders want.

(B) This **supports** the conclusion by showing that the "lite butter" labeled products would have even less butterfat.

(C) As long as **some** people are deterred by the term the argument still holds.

(D) This further supports the argument by showing just how dangerous the higher butterfat is.

3. (11/2 #11) ~ B

The words "strongest basis for challenging the conclusion" signal that this is a weaken question. Read the passage to fully understand its evidence and conclusion so we identify the type of information that will weaken it. The passage begins with the conclusion: high-calorie foods should not be allowed to label themselves sugar free when they replace all their sugar with artificial sweeteners. The evidence is that many consumers trying to lose weight misinterpret the label and harm themselves by eating many of those foods. Further, manufacturers are aware that consumers are doing this. So any information that implies that what the manufacturers should not be banned will weaken the conclusion. Understanding how the argument works, we move to the choices.

(A) This information supports the argument that banning the labels is a good idea.

(B) This weakens the conclusion by showing that banning the "sugar-free" labels would have undesired consequences: namely hurting diabetics' ability to identify which products have no sugar.

(C) This supports the argument by showing that clear labels do have an effect on purchasing decisions.

(D) This supports the argument by showing that people eating the foods they think are low in calories will continue to do so for a while because they believe results take time to surface.

(E) The argument does not discuss relative visual prominence, so this information is irrelevant.

4. (10/4 #9) ~ D

The conclusion is that as the population ages, carpet companies will only be able to gain market share by purchasing competitors, and not through marketing. The evidence is that most who purchase carpets only do so twice in their lives. We can weaken the conclusion by showing that there are other ways to gain market share besides buying competitors. Choice D gives just such information: customers must be sensitive to price if companies that lower their price are gaining market share and forcing other companies out of business.

(A) This is irrelevant to the conclusion about market share only being increased through buying other companies.

(B) This information supports the conclusion by showing that there are no open niches that would allow for gaining customers through different marketing and positioning.

(C) This information is irrelevant, because the conclusion only talks about market share – not profits or revenues.

(E) This information supports the conclusion, by showing that consumers are not open to new patterns or styles – ways to increase market share with different products.

5. (11/4 #11) ~ B

The conclusion is that harvesting old growth trees can reduce the amount of carbon dioxide in the atmosphere. The evidence is that using them in manufacture keeps these trees from decomposing when they die. We can weaken this argument with Choice B which states that using the trees in manufacturing also leads to their decomposing as products, which means that they are still releasing carbon dioxide. This weakens the conclusion that harvesting the trees limits the total amount of CO_2 in the air.

(A) This is irrelevant to the conclusion about carbon dioxide reduction in the atmosphere.

(C) This supports the argument that harvesting old trees makes sense because they have more carbon dioxide than young trees that would be released into the air if they were to decompose in the forest.

(D) This supports the argument by showing that the carbon dioxide in the trees would be released due to decomposition.

(E) This is irrelevant to whether harvesting old growth trees will lower carbon dioxide levels in the air.

6. (11/4 #21) ~ E

The conclusion is that we can never run out of important resources. The evidence is that new technologies constantly replace old ones. But technologies are not the same as resources are they? We work the choices keeping this in mind.

(A) This does not weaken the crux of the argument. The argument says that the remainder of the resource can fill whatever demand remains.

(B) This fits with the concept behind the argument of the resource dwindling but not running out.

(C) This does not weaken the conclusion. The companies can still make money in the long run and the resources will be used to substitute for others.

(D) This fits with the argument. A higher price makes substitutes more attractive and stops people consuming that resource.

(E) This weakens the argument by showing that we will always need certain resources – water and air – regardless of what technology can do. So the conclusion that we can never run out of important resources is not well supported by the evidence that technology can always be used to substitute for resources we need.

7. (10/1 #19) ~ D

Find the choice that **does not** weaken the argument. The conclusion of the councilors is that bus fares should be raised enough to cover the service. The evidence is that city taxes, which subsidize the public buses, should be used to primarily benefit the people who pay them.

Choice A – This shows how the lower bus fares do benefit the people who pay them by keeping businesses in the city.

Choice B – This weakens the argument by showing that the low fares help the tax payers by keeping other costs down.

Choice C – This weakens the argument by showing an unintended consequence that the proponents of the argument would not be happy with.

Choice D – This information is irrelevant to the argument at hand and does not weaken it. This choice is therefore correct.

Choice E – This weakens the argument by showing that everyone who **works** in Greenville pays the tax, not just the people who live there.

8. (14/2 #24) ~ D

Find the choice that does **not** weaken the argument. The conclusion is that the attempt to prevent alcohol use just made people want it more. The evidence is that the death rate related to excessive consumption of alcohol was higher during the first five years of the period than before the period.

(A) This weakens the argument by showing that the higher death rate in those first five years was due to the late onset of these type of deaths, not greater consumption during that period.

(B) This also explains another cause for the increased deaths: other causes increasing that lead to the same diseases.

(C) This weakens the conclusion by showing that the first five years of prohibition were too small a sample to look at and that the effect that was thought to have been there – increased deaths - was only there if looking at a short time scale.

(D) This **supports** the conclusion by showing that the attempt didn't work – people were still drinking during that period.

(E) This weakens the conclusion by showing that the higher deaths were due to something other than continued alcohol consumption: less medical attention.

Support With Principle

There are two distinct types of Principle questions. Both require a thorough understanding of the nature of a principle. A principle is a general rule or group of rules that tells what is appropriate in certain situations.

All good parents are actively involved in their child's education.

The sentence above is a principle because it tells how good parents (a specific group) should act regarding their child's education. "Parents can be ineffective or effective" is not a principle because it cannot be applied to any specific situations, nor does it contain any guidelines.

We call the situation a principle when it dictates behavior in a zone. Each principle only has implications in specific areas and/or for specific entities (people, things, etc.). The principle above only applies to parents. An aunt is not within this zone, so the principle does not apply to an aunt. Aunts therefore do not have to be actively involved in their nephew's education. If Zack is a father with a 10 year old son, he is within the zone, so the principle does apply to him. Principles have varying degrees of focus with their zones. "Parents in the San Diego area should be involved in their children's education" is a principle with a narrower zone than just "Parents."

Every principle has a certain rule or rules for its zone. We refer to these as standards. Any subject that fits within the zone must comply with the standards, or that subject violates the principle. In the principle above, parents with children are required to be actively involved in their children's education. They are held to this standard in order to be in line with the principle. If Zack has a son whose education he is not involved with, then Zack does not obey the principle.

When dealing with Principle questions, you must work on a more abstract level than most LSAT questions, just like on Argument Structure questions. A principle is by nature general: it can apply to many different situations.

Support with Principle

Support with Principle is the more common subtype of principle question. These questions ask you to support an argument with a relevant principle from the choices. Think of these as a type of strengthen question where you use a **broad rule** to help the argument. Often, the correct principle is assumed or relied on by the argument, but not stated. In this way, this type has elements of Assumption questions. Support with Principle questions require you to analyze up to five principles in the choices and that can make them time consuming.

Support with Principle questions fall in the Modify category because they ask you to actively help the argument in the passage. So you should read the argument with an eye towards what piece it needs to be complete. The correct choice will contain new information in the form of a principle.

Query

These queries are easy to spot because they have the word "principle" and they ask you to support an argument. "Conforms" is one way to say that an argument is in line with a principle, which means that the argument needs the principle.

> "Which one of the following *principles* most helps to *justify* the reasoning above?"

> "Which one of the following most accurately *expresses the principle* underlying the argumentation above?"

> "The information above most *closely conforms* to which one of the following principles?"

Passage

When reading the passage, get a feel for its structure and look for a gap between the premises and the conclusion. The correct choice will fill that gap with the appropriate principle. Read the passage like a justify assumption question: find the area where a logical piece is missing. One good way to do this is to look for new, unconnected subjects.

Envision

During the envision step, you should make sure you know the general type of information that the argument needs to be supported. If there is a gap in the logic, know where it is and what type of information could fill it. If the argument does not have an obvious gap, just know the conclusion well. It is impossible to predict the exact principle that will be used, so do not try to do so.

Choices

The correct choice will often be the broadest principle possible. The correct principle usually casts a zone wider than that used in the argument. A broad principle is as useful as a narrow one in supporting an argument. It just applies to more situations and is therefore harder to predict or envision. The correct principle will often not be geared directly at the argument because more general principles are more difficult to find in the choices and the LSAT-Writers try to keep you on your toes.

20/1 #5

As you work this Support with Principle question, find the gap in the passage and be clear on the conclusion.

> Archaeologist: A large corporation has recently offered to provide funding to restore an archaeological site and to construct facilities to make the site readily accessible to the general public. The restoration will conform to the best current theories about how the site appeared at the height of the ancient civilization that occupied it. This offer should be rejected, however, because many parts of the site contain unexamined evidence.
>
> Which one of the following principles, if valid, justifies the archaeologist's argument?
>
> (A) The ownership of archaeological sites should not be under the control of business interests.
> (B) Any restoration of an archaeological site should represent only the most ancient period of that site's history.
> (C) No one should make judgments about what constitutes the height of another civilization.
> (D) Only those with a true concern for an archaeological site's history should be involved in the restoration of that site.
> (E) The risk of losing evidence relevant to possible future theories should outweigh any advantages of displaying the results of theories already developed.

Query

> Which one of the following principles, if valid, justifies the archaeologist's argument?

We read "principle" and "justifies the ... argument" and know that this is a Support with Principle question. Read the passage looking for a weakness.

Passage

The archaeologist's conclusion is the last sentence: the offer to provide funding for restoration and facilities should be rejected. The support provided for that conclusion is that many parts of the site contain unexamined evidence. Further evidence is that the restoration will conform to the best of the current theories on how the site appeared at the height of the ancient civilization that occupied it.

Envision

The conclusion is not well supported by the premises. The first premise - that there is still evidence at the site that needs to be examined - does not connect to the conclusion. Even if there is unexamined evidence, perhaps the negatives related to losing that evidence through the restoration are outweighed by the positives of the restoration. The second premise tells that the restoration will conform to current theories on the civilization. Again, this does not support the conclusion. If anything, it seems to work against it, because the restoration would be the most accurate one possible.

Taking all this into consideration, we need a principle that explicitly connects the first premise about unexamined evidence to the conclusion. If the principle also addresses the premise about the accuracy of the restoration, then that is helpful, but probably unnecessary. This is enough to know to move to the choices.

Choices

(A) The ownership of archaeological sites should not be under the control of business interests.

(A) says nothing about the unexamined evidence. Further, we have no reason to believe that providing funding is the same as taking control of the site. Dud.

(B) Any restoration of an archaeological site should represent only the most ancient period of that site's history.

(B) could support the conclusion because the proposed restoration will not necessarily represent the most ancient period of the site's history. However, it is possible that the peak of that society was the most ancient period, in which case, this principle would not support the conclusion. Also, this does not talk about the unexamined evidence, which is the conclusion's primary support. (B) leaves that premise hanging, which is never a good thing. Label this a tentative hit and read the other choices.

(C) No one should make judgments about what constitutes the height of another civilization.

(C) does not support the conclusion. The passage talks about the best theories of how the civilization appeared at its height. Theories are similar to judgments but not quite the same. Regardless, (C) is peripheral to the argument, because saying the judgments should not have been made does not support the fact that it is inappropriate to **implement** those judgments in the restoration. Finally, (C) also neglects the unexamined evidence premise. Dud.

(D) Only those with a true concern for an archaeological site's history should be involved in the restoration of that site.

Who is to say that the large corporation does not have a true concern for the site's history? If they do, which the passage certainly allows, then the conclusion is still unsupported with this choice in place. There is also no mention of the unexamined evidence. Dud.

(E) The risk of losing evidence relevant to possible future theories should outweigh any advantages of displaying the results of theories already developed.

(E) is perfect. It shows that it is more important to preserve the unexamined evidence than it is to go through with the restoration and display the theories already developed. This ties the unexamined evidence premise to the conclusion, while also showing why the premise about the restoration method is not as important as the first premise. This principle directly supports the conclusion and is far superior to (B), the other hit.

*Support With Principle Review

- A principle is a general rule or group of rules that tells what is appropriate in certain situations.
    - Zone - the situation that the principle is relevant to.
    - Standards – the rules for those in the zone.
    - Principle - All good parents are actively involved in their child's education.
        - Zone – good parents.
        - Standards – being actively involved in their children's education.

Support with Principle Question Type

- Introduction
    - "Which one of the following principles most helps to justify the reasoning above?"
    - Support an argument with a relevant principle from the choices.
    - Often, the correct principle is relied on by the argument but not stated.
    - The correct choice must bring in new information.
- Passage – look for gaps in the argument.
    - Look for unconnected elements just as you would an assumption question.
- Envision
    - Know the gap and the conclusion.
    - Do not spend too much time on this step.
- Choices
    - The correct choice is often the broadest principle possible.

*Support With Principle Practice Questions

1. Cigarette smoking has been shown to be a health hazard; therefore, governments should ban all advertisements that promote smoking.

   Which one of the following principles, if established, most strongly supports the argument?

   (A) Advertisements should not be allowed to show people doing things that endanger their health.
   (B) Advertisers should not make misleading claims about the healthfulness of their products.
   (C) Advertisements should disclose the health hazards associated with the products they promote.
   (D) All products should conform to strict government health and safety standards.
   (E) Advertisements should promote only healthful products.

2. In a survey of consumers in an Eastern European nation, respondents were asked two questions about each of 400 famous Western brands: whether or not they recognized the brand name and whether or not they thought the products bearing that name were of high quality. The results of the survey were a rating and corresponding rank order for each brand based on recognition, and a second rating plus ranking based on approval. The brands ranked in the top 27 for recognition were those actually available in that nation. The approval ratings of these 27 brands often differed sharply from their recognition ratings. By contrast, most of the other brands had ratings, and thus rankings, that were essentially the same for recognition as for approval.

   Which one of the following, if each is a principle about consumer surveys, is violated by the survey described ?

   (A) Never ask all respondents a question if it cannot reasonably be answered by respondents who make a particular response to another question in the same survey.
   (B) Never ask a question that is likely to generate a large variety of responses that are difficult to group into a manageable number of categories.
   (C) Never ask all respondents a question that respondents cannot answer without giving up their anonymity.
   (D) It is better to ask the same question about ten different products than to ask ten different questions about a single product.
   (E) It is best to ask questions that a respondent can answer without fear of having gotten the answer wrong.

3. Pedigreed dogs, including those officially classified as working dogs, must conform to standards set by organizations that issue pedigrees. Those standards generally specify the physical appearance necessary for a dog to be recognized as belonging to a breed but stipulate nothing about other genetic traits, such as those that enable breeds originally developed as working dogs to perform the work for which they were developed. Since dog breeders try to maintain only those traits specified by pedigree organizations, and traits that breeders do not try to maintain risk being lost, certain traits like herding ability risk being lost among pedigreed dogs. Therefore, pedigree organizations should set standards requiring working ability in pedigreed dogs classified as working dogs.

   Which one of the following principles, if valid, justifies the argument's conclusion that pedigree organizations should set standards for working ability in dogs?

   (A) Organizations that set standards for products or activities should not set standards calling for a particular characteristic if such standards increase the risk of some other characteristic being lost.
   (B) Any standard currently in effect for a product or an activity should be rigorously enforced regardless of when the standard was first set.
   (C) Organizations that set standards for products or activities should be responsible for seeing to it that those products or activities conform to all the specifications called for by those standards.
   (D) Any standard that is set for a product or an activity should reflect the uses to which that product or activity will eventually be put.
   (E) Organizations that set standards for products or activities should attempt to ensure that those products or activities can serve the purposes for which they were originally developed.

4. There are rumors that the Premier will reshuffle the cabinet this week. However, every previous reshuffle that the Premier has made was preceded by meetings between me Premier and senior cabinet members. No such meetings have occurred or are planned. Therefore the rumors are most likely false.

Which one of the following most accurately expresses a principle of reasoning employed by the argument?

(A) When a conclusion follows logically from a set of premises, the probability that the conclusion is true cannot be any less than the probability that the premises are all true.
(B) A hypothesis is undermined when a state of affairs does not obtain that would be expected to obtain if the hypothesis were true.
(C) It is possible for a hypothesis to be false even though it is supported by all the available data.
(D) Even if in me past a phenomenon was caused by particular circumstances, it is erroneous to assume that the phenomenon will recur only under the circumstances in which it previously occurred.
(E) If two statements are known to be inconsistent with each other and if one of the statements is known to be false, it cannot be deduced from these known facts that the other statement is true.

5. Some critics claim that it is unfair that so many great works of art are housed in huge metropolitan museums, since the populations served by these museums already have access to a wide variety of important artwork. But this criticism is in principle unwarranted because the limited number of masterpieces makes wider distribution of them impractical. Besides, if a masterpiece is to be fully appreciated, it must be seen alongside other works that provide a social and historical context for it.

Which one of the following, if established, could most logically serve as the principle appealed to in the argument countering the critics' claim?

(A) In providing facilities to the public, the goal should be to ensure that as many as possible of those people who could benefit from the facilities are able to do so.
(B) In providing facilities to the public, the goal should be to ensure that the greatest possible number of people gain the greatest benefit possible from them.
(C) It is unreasonable to enforce a redistribution of social goods that involves depriving some members of society of these goods in order to supply others.
(D) For it to be reasonable to criticize an arrangement as unfair, there must be a more equitable arrangement that is practically attainable.
(E) A work of art should be displayed in conditions resembling as closely as possible those in which the work was originally intended to be displayed.

6. No one knows what purposes, if any, dreams serve, although there are a number of hypotheses. According to one hypothesis, dreams are produced when the brain is erasing “parasitic connections” (meaningless, accidental associations between ideas), which accumulate during the day and which would otherwise clog up our memories. Interestingly, the only mammal that does not have rapid eye movement sleep, in which we humans typically have our most vivid dreams, is the spiny anteater, which has been seen as anomalous in that it has a very large brain relative to the animal's size. This fact provides some confirmation for the parasitic-connection hypothesis, since the hypothesis predicts that for an animal that did not dream to have an effective memory that animal would need extra memory space for the parasitic connections.

The reasoning in the argument most closely conforms to which one of the following principles?

(A) Facts about one species of animal can provide confirmation for hypotheses about all species that are similar in all relevant respects to the particular species in question.
(B) A hypothesis from which several predictions can be drawn as logical conclusions is confirmed only when the majority of these predictions turn out to be true.
(C) A hypothesis about the purpose of an action or object is confirmed when it is shown that the hypothesized purpose is achieved with the help of the action or object and could not be achieved without that action or object.
(D) A hypothesis is partially confirmed whenever a prediction derived from that hypothesis provides an explanation for an otherwise unexplained set of facts.
(E) When several competing hypotheses exist, one of them is confirmed only when it makes a correct prediction that its rivals fail to make.

7. Police published a "wanted" poster for a criminal fugitive in a medical journal, because the fugitive was known to have a certain acute noninfectious skin problem that would eventually require a visit to a doctor. The poster asked for information about the whereabouts of the fugitive. A physician's responding to the poster's request for information would not violate medical ethics, since physicians are already subject to requirements to report gunshot wounds to police and certain infectious diseases to health authorities. These exceptions to confidentiality are clearly ethical

   Which one of the following principles, while remaining compatible with the requirements cited above, supports the view that a physician's responding to the request would violate medical ethics?

   (A) Since a physician acts both as a professional person and as a citizen, it is not ethical for a physician to conceal information about patients from duly constituted law enforcement agencies that have proper jurisdiction.
   (B) Since a patient comes to a physician with the expectation that the patient's visit and medical condition will remain confidential, it is not ethical for a physician to share this information with anyone except personnel within the physician's office.
   (C) Since the primary concern of medicine is individual and public health, it is not ethical for a physician, except in the case of gunshot wounds, to reduce patients' willingness to come for treatment by a policy of disclosing their identities to law enforcement agencies.
   (D) Except as required by the medical treatment of the patient, physicians cannot ethically disclose to others information about a patient's identity or medical condition without the patient's consent.
   (E) Except to other medical personnel working to preserve or restore the health of a patient or of other persons, physicians cannot ethically disclose information about the identity of patients or their medical condition.

8. Reporting on a civil war, a journalist encountered evidence that refugees were starving because the government would not permit food shipments to a rebel held area. Government censors deleted all mention of the government's role in the starvation from the journalist's report, which had not implicated either nature or the rebels in the starvation. The journalist concluded that it was ethically permissible to file the censored report, because the journalist's news agency would precede it with the notice "Cleared by government censors."

   Which one of the following ethical criteria, if valid, would serve to support the journalist's conclusion while placing the least constraint on the flow of reported information?

   (A) It is ethical in general to report known facts but unethical to do so while omitting other known facts if the omitted facts would substantially alter an impression of a person or institution that would be congruent with the reported facts.
   (B) In a situation of conflict, it is ethical to report known facts and unethical to fail to report known facts that would tend to exonerate one party to the conflict.
   (C) In a situation of censorship, it is unethical to make any report if the government represented by the censor deletes from the report material unfavorable to that government.
   (D) It is ethical in general to report known facts but unethical to make a report in a situation of censorship if relevant facts have been deleted by the censor, unless the recipient of the report is warned that censorship existed.
   (E) Although it is ethical in general to report known facts, it is unethical to make a report from which a censor has deleted relevant facts, unless the recipient of the report is warned that there was censorship and the reported facts do not by themselves give a misleading impression.

* Explanations

1. (11/2 #6) ~ E

The stem tells us to find the principle that supports the argument. This means we need to read the passage looking for areas it can be strengthened with a general principle that applies to the specific situation. The conclusion of the passage is that governments should ban **all advertisements** that promote smoking. The evidence is that smoking has been shown to be a health hazard. The principle we are looking for will bridge the gap between these two concepts. Taking a second to pre-phrase, we state the principle in our own words as **governments should ban the promotion of anything that has been shown to be dangerous to the population**. With this general principle filling the gap between the evidence and conclusion, the conclusion is justified.

(A) The conclusion talks about promoting smoking, so a principle that only discusses ads not being allowed to show people doing unhealthy things does not cover enough ground. There are potentially ads that promote smoking but do not show people smoking.

(B) There are probably ads that promote smoking but do not make any misleading claims, so this principle does not support the conclusion to ban **all** smoking ads.

(C) The conclusion we need to support says ban ads, not have ads disclose something new.

(D) This has nothing to do with banning ads, it has to do with the nature of products.

(E) works. With this principle in place, the government is right to ban all ads that promote smoking, because smoking has been shown to be unhealthy.

2. (13/4 #22) ~ A

Find the principle that is violated by the survey discussed in the passage. All but one of the choices will not be violated. Read the passage carefully and then work each of the choices. No need to pause and try to envision a good answer on a question that forces you to draw from the choices to find which one violates the passage.

(A) is violated by the passage, because many brands were included that were not available in that nation and the respondents were asked the quality of those brands. That question cannot reasonably be answered, while the question about recognition could be.

(B) The questions were Yes or No format ("whether they recognized the brand name") so this principle is not violated.

(C) No question here required giving up anonymity.

(D) Two questions were asked about many different products, so this works.

(E) These questions were about opinions: the respondents could not be wrong.

3. (15/2 #13) ~ E

The stem gives us a specific conclusion to support – that pedigree organizations should set standards for working ability in dogs. Read the passage carefully and see what the evidence is for this conclusion. The evidence is that the current standards do not try to maintain traits that the dogs were originally bred for – for instance herding ability. Without changing the standards, these traits risk being lost.

Work the choices, looking to support the conclusion while keeping in mind the evidence.

(A) does not support the conclusion because it only talks about eliminating standards that increase traits being lost, instead of supporting adding new standards which is the conclusion.

(B) does not support adding new standards. This principle only supports maintaining old ones.

(C) only supports the idea of enforcing standards.

(D) sounds good but doesn't work because the passage never says that the working dogs will actually be used for working. The conclusion is about conserving traits that were originally developed.

(E) is perfect because it supports working dogs having the ability they were bred for being maintained with new standards. This supports the conclusion and the evidence for it.

4. (19/2 #10) ~ B

State the principle. Read carefully and state generally what the passage is expressing. The passage says that because the event that normally happens before the event in question (meetings) did not happen, the event in question (reshuffle the cabinet) will probably not happen.

Read the choices carefully on Principle questions.

5. (9/4 #11) ~ D

Read the passage looking for the principle needed to support the argument in countering the critics' claim. The claim is that it is not fair to have so many great works of art housed in metropolitan museums because the populations who are served by that art already have access to a wide variety of important art work. The argument counters that claim by saying that wider distribution of the masterpieces is impractical. Find a principle that says a criticism is only reasonable if the situation has a practical solution.

(A) supports the critics.

(B) also supports the critics' stance.

(C) does not support the argument of the passage that the rearrangement is impractical.

(D) Works perfectly because it directly supports the evidence for the conclusion that the critics' suggestion is impractical.

(E) This supports the secondary point made by the argument, which is not the main counter to the critics.

6. (10/1 #23) ~ D

The argument says that the "parasitic connections" hypothesis is given some support with the example of the anteater. This animal does not have REM sleep and its brain is very large for its size. This is in line with the "parasitic connections" hypothesis because an animal that didn't clean out its extra connections would need a larger brain to have its memory work well. Note that the argument only says "this fact provides **some confirmation**." This will help us find a principle that matches. Now that you understand the passage, scan the choices.

(A) says "confirmation" and the passage says "some confirmation." Too strong.

(B) The passage never talks about a majority of predictions being true. It only discusses the single prediction of having a larger brain if an animal does not have REM.

(C) does not match the passage.

(D) matches perfectly. The hypothesis in the passage is confirmed because the prediction of a larger brain without REM fits the unexplained larger anteater brain.

(E) The passage does not discuss rival predictions.

7. (12/4 #13) ~ C

The principle must remain compatible with the requirements above **and** also support the view that a physician responding to the request would violate medical ethics. Work the choices with these two requirements in mind.

(A) does not support the view that a physician responding to the request would violate medical ethics (requirement from the stem).

(B) It would be a breach of confidentiality as stated in the passage for the physician to share the identity with personnel from the physician's office.

(C) works. It fits with the information in the passage (gunshot wounds are an exception to contacting the authorities) and it also supports the view that the physician would violate medical ethics by reporting the patient's identity.

(D) is not compatible with the information in the passage about confidentiality. It says gunshot wounds, and certain infectious diseases are the only exceptions there.

(E) is also not compatible with the information in the passage about confidentiality.

8. (16/3 #23) ~ D

"Ethical criteria" is another name for principle. The stem asks us to support the conclusion while impeding the flow of reported information as little as possible. Her conclusion is that it was ethically ok to file the report because it would be preceded by the notice that it was cleared by government censors. Relevant information in the passage is that the government censors deleted all information of the government's role in the starvation, and the report had not said that nature or the rebels were the source of the starvation. This implies that the article may have no explanation of where the starvation came from – if not the real cause, the government, or two other likely causes: nature and the opposing forces. Work the choices while keeping in mind the two things that the principle must accomplish.

(A) does not support the conclusion that it is ethically alright to file the censored report, because in that report, facts have been censored that would substantially alter how people view the government.

(B) does not support the conclusion, because the report does not exonerate the rebels in the starvation.

(C) does not support the reporter's conclusion because the censored information about the government causing the starvation would be unfavorable to the government.

(D) works. The conclusion that the filing is ethical works because although relevant facts have been censored, the recipient knows that censorship existed.

(E) The reported facts do give a misleading impression here because nature and the rebels were not discussed, so if the government is not implicated for the starvation, one of those two will be.

Paradox Fix

Paradox Fix questions ask you to resolve a paradox in the passage. In this situation, a paradox can be defined as a situation **that seems contradictory** based on two facts discussed in the passage. Those facts can be occurrences or concepts. Example paradox:

> Fido enjoys going for walks, but every time I take out his leash to go on one, he hides in the closet.

The fact that Fido enjoys going on walks does not match with him hiding in the closet when his leash is taken out. One would expect that when his leash is taken out, he would get excited. This is the nature of a paradox: one piece of information does not seem to meld with another piece.

Change how you see the information

Paradox questions are in the Modify question family, but the correct choice does not really modify the information in the passage, it only changes how one **understands** the information. To resolve a paradox on the LSAT, show that both facts are true, and provide additional information that explains how that is possible. In fact, outside information is required to answer Paradox questions correctly. So, consider each choice to be valid. For instance, look at this choice:

> (B) Fido is scared of his leash because aliens used the leash to pull him into their space ship last week

You should believe (B) to be true. In general, do not eliminate a choice because it seems implausible. Choices should only be eliminated because they do not actively help both pieces of information in the passage make sense together.

Note that (B) would be a correct answer to the question because it explains why Fido hides in the closet when he sees his leash, without contradicting the fact that he loves going on walks.

Query

The query for a Paradox Fix question will tell you that you are resolving a contradiction in terms. Accordingly, it always has two parts: **it asks you to explain** and **it says the passage is contradictory**. The queries ask you to explain by using action verbs such as "explain," "reconcile," "resolve." This is exactly what you are doing on these questions: explaining away the paradox. The query says the passage is contradictory using words like "paradox," "contradiction," "discrepancy," and "conflict." Paradox queries are easy to identify:

> "Which one of the following, if true, most helps to *resolve* the apparent *discrepancy* in the passage?"

> "Which one of the following, if true, would most effectively *explain* the apparent *paradox* above?"

Notice the "if true" part of the two queries above. This is a signal that appears in the queries for questions in the Modify family. It tells you to only question the choices effectiveness in answering the question, not their validity. Also, make note of the use of the word "apparent" in both of the example queries above. This is used because the information in the passage does not actually clash, it only appears to.

Passage

The passages for Paradox Fix questions are always Fact-Groups, never arguments. As you read, do not look for premises or a conclusion, simply identify the two facts that seem to contradict and understand why they create a paradox. When reading, it is often easy to spot the paradox, because these passages often feature opposing language: "however," "yet", "but," "surprisingly," "although." These words are signals that the information about to be presented clashes with information already discussed.

You must figure out what the paradox is. The incorrect choices are too well constructed to allow you to sort through them without a strong grasp on exactly why the two facts seem to clash.

Envision

Paradox Fix questions are somewhat susceptible to envisioning: once you know the paradox, you can brainstorm various ways to resolve it. It bears repeating; the correct answer must allow both facts to be true **at the same time**. It would be too easy to disprove or deny one side of the paradox, one of the facts. Show how both sides are true, even though they seem to contradict each other. Use outside/new information that shows how the situation in question came about or paints one of the elements of the paradox in a new light.

New light information frames one of the facts so that it fits with the other fact. Example paradox:

> Dexter is a serial killer who has killed 30 people. However, his friends all think he is a good man.

Serial killers are widely regarded as some of the worst people in society. They usually do not have a lot of friends, and rarely do people think well of them. Hence the paradox. But assume we are told:

> (A) Dexter only kills evil people that are a burden on society

This makes us look at the first fact - that Dexter is a serial killer - differently. Dexter is still technically a serial killer, but he kills people that deserve it, not innocent people. With that in place, we can see how most of his friends would believe that he is a good person, because his killings can be considered good deeds.

Or, we might be told:

> (D) None of Dexter's friends know that he is a killer because he hides his murders exceptionally well.

In this case, we see the second fact differently. Dexter's friends think he is a good man because they do not know about the people he has killed; **they do not know the real Dexter**.

In both cases, the outside information shows us how both facts can be true by changing how we see one fact so that it lines up with the other fact.

Correct Choices

Correct choices often show how two groups discussed by the passage, even though they seem the same, are actually different. Example passage:

> Ray's construction firm receives glowing reviews by clients and construction magazines. But, the houses he builds are less likely to last for 20 years than the average house built in the United States.

The houses built by Ray's firm are considered to be well built, but they do not last as long as the average house in the U.S. This is only strange when we assume that Ray's houses have **factors** in common with the average house that relate to the longevity of the house. Say we knew this:

> (E) Ray's houses are only built in areas plagued by Tornados

That explains why his houses do not last as long **even though** they are well built. Ray's houses have a much higher likelihood of getting destroyed by a tornado than the average house in the U.S., and that is an important factor. The two groups (Ray's houses and the average house built in the U.S.) are not truly comparable on longevity because of this difference. This passage shows a common paradox situation. Show that other factors exist for one of the groups to resolve a similar paradox with two groups.

Along these lines, on passages where two groups **seem different**, the correct choice will often show how they are actually the same in an important way.

Incorrect Choices

A common type of incorrect choice will discuss slightly different information than the passage. These choices are tricky because they seem to address the paradox, but they actually do not because they give information that is not applicable. In the previous example, a choice that says that Ray's firm builds inferior houses goes against the first information given by the passage: his company's work receives glowing reviews. But it does not disprove that information, because reviews are not the same thing as the quality of work. A review can and often does reflect the quality of work, but these concepts are not identical. Therefore, that information does not resolve the paradox because it does not tell us anything **new** about the situation.

Support only one side

Other incorrect choices will support one fact without addressing the paradox. The support given to that fact does not relate to the other fact. In general, if a paradox involves two things that seem like they are different because of the nature of the paradox, then incorrect answers will further show how they are **different**. This only makes the paradox worse. As mentioned earlier, the correct answer in this case will often show that the two groups only seem different, and are actually the same in important ways. Example passage:

> Michael goes to the gym daily and lifts weights, but Matthew never visits the gym. Surprisingly, both men are in excellent shape.

The paradox exists because we think that because the two men have different gym habits, they would not be in the same type of shape. They **seem different** in regards to workout habits. But perhaps Matthew runs and does pushups and pull-ups outside every day. In that case, it turns out that both men are in the same in terms of exercising daily.

An incorrect choice could be:

> (D) Matthew sits on his couch all day.

(D) promotes the idea that the men are different when it comes to exercising, and that makes the paradox more blatant.

Likewise, if a paradox involves two groups that look similar (but are actually different), then incorrect answers will show how they are the **same**. This too makes the paradox more prominent. In the house construction example, an incorrect choice could be:

> (B) Ray builds houses in parts of the country that never flood.

(B) shows that Ray's houses and the average house in the United States face similar threats of flooding, eliminating the possibility that they differ in that way. Another incorrect choice could be

> (C) The average house in the United States has the same chance of being infested with termites as Ray's houses.

This shows that the two groups of houses are equal in terms of the risk of termite damage. That eliminates the possibility that Ray's houses, even though well built, get eaten by termites more often than normal houses, which could explain the paradox.

Remember:

- If the two groups seem different, then information that furthers that difference will likely be incorrect.
- If the two groups seem similar, then information that furthers that similarity will likely be incorrect.

Paradox Sample Question (19/2 #5)

Be sure you identify the paradox, and the two facts that cause it, as you read the passage.

> Adults who work outside the home spend, on average, 100 minutes less time each week in preparing dinner than adults who do not work outside the home. But, contrary to expectation, comparisons show that the dinners eaten at home by the two groups of adults do not differ significantly with respect to nutritional value, variety of menus, or number of courses.
>
> Which one of the following, if true, most helps to resolve the apparent discrepancy in the information above?
>
> (A) The fat content of the dinners eaten at home by adults who do not work outside the home is 25 percent higher than national guidelines recommend.
> (B) Adults who do not work outside the home tend to prepare breakfast more often than adults who work outside the home.
> (C) Adults who work outside the home spend 2 hours less time per day on all household responsibilities, including dinner preparation, than do adults who do not work outside the home.
> (D) Adults who work outside the home eat dinner at home 20 percent less often than do adults who do not work outside the home.
> (E) Adults who work outside the home are less likely to plan dinner menus well in advance than are adults who do not work outside the home.

Query

> Which one of the following, if true, most helps to resolve the apparent discrepancy in the information above?

"Resolve the apparent discrepancy" tells that this is a Paradox Fix question.

Passage

Fact 1- Adults who work outside the home spend less time preparing dinner **each week** than adults who work from home.

Fact 2 – Dinners eaten by the two groups are comparable in quality.

These seem to conflict because one group spends less time cooking than the other, but the meals are comparable. Because we are crystal clear on each of the facts, we notice that the adults who work outside the home spend less **total time** each week cooking. Fact 2 talks about the quality of **each meal** cooked.

Envision

Fact 1 talks about total time spent cooking for the entire week, while Fact 2 talks about the quality of individual meals. We can explain the paradox by showing that the two groups spend the same amount of time cooking each individual meal. To do that, it would have to be the case that adults who work outside the home cook **less meals**. That way, they can spend less time cooking each week, but the same amount of time on any given meal. The paradox only exists because we assume the two groups are the same in the number of meals they cook each week.

Any choice that points out that the two groups are **different** in how many meals they cook will resolve the paradox by changing how we view Fact 1. Alternatively, any choice that shows that the two groups spend the same amount of time cooking each meal will also resolve the paradox, again by changing how we view Fact 1.

Choices

We have a good idea of what to look for in the choices, so we can work them aggressively.

> (A) The fat content of the dinners eaten at home by adults who do not work outside the home is 25 percent higher than national guidelines recommend.

(A) seems to show that adults who work outside the home prepare less healthy meals than adults who work from home. However, Fact 2 said that both groups produced meals of comparable nutritional quality. So if the adults who work outside the home are creating fattier meals than the national guidelines, then the adults who work from home must be doing so as well.

This information does not help explain the paradox because it does not address how the meals are comparable if one group spends less time each week making meals. This dud is a great example of irrelevant information about one fact in the passage.

> (B) Adults who do not work outside the home tend to prepare breakfast more often than adults who work outside the home.

(B) does not address the paradox. The passage only deals with dinner, so information about breakfast is irrelevant. This is a clear dud.

> (C) Adults who work outside the home spend 2 hours less time per day on all household responsibilities, including dinner preparation, than do adults who do not work outside the home.

This information **furthers** the paradox because it tells us that adults who work outside the home spend less time each day on tasks, including dinner preparation. We already know they spent less time cooking each week. The paradox is: how do they create comparable meals while spending less time per week at it? This choice does not answer that question. Dud.

> (D) Adults who work outside the home eat dinner at home 20 percent less often than do adults who do not work outside the home.

(D) is correct. Adults who work outside the home eat less dinners at home. This explains how they can spend 100 less minutes each week and still cook comparable meals: they are not cooking as many meals. They can spend the same amount of time cooking **each individual meal** as those who work from home.

For teaching purposes:

> (E) Adults who work outside the home are less likely to plan dinner menus well in advance than are adults who do not work outside the home.

Whether or not adults who work outside the home plan their dinner menus well in advance is irrelevant to the paradox, because this information does not tell us anything about time spent per meal or the number of meals cooked. Fact 2 tells us they somehow still cook comparable meals, so apparently the lack of planning does not affect the meal quality. Dud.

*Paradox Fix Review

- Introduction
  - o "Which one of the following, if true, most helps to resolve the apparent discrepancy in the passage?"
  - o Resolve the paradox - the situation that seems contradictory - in the passage.
  - o The correct choice changes how you understand the information, it does not refute either of the pieces of information.
  - o A correct choice brings in new information.
- Passage
  - o Passages on paradox questions are always fact-groups.
  - o As you read, identify the two facts that seem to contradict each other.
- Envision
  - o Once you know the paradox, you can think of ways to disprove it.
  - o Make sure the new information allows both facts to be true at the same time.
  - o The correct choice will have information that allows you to see one of the facts in a new light.
- Choices
  - o Correct choices often show how two groups that seem to be the same are actually different, or vice versa.
  - o Incorrect choices tend to support only one side of the paradox.

*Paradox Fix Practice Questions

1. Since the introduction of the Impanian National Health scheme, Impanians (or their private insurance companies) have had to pay only for the more unusual and sophisticated medical procedures. When the scheme was introduced, it was hoped that private insurance to pay for these procedures would be available at modest cost, since the insurers would no longer be paying for the bulk of health care costs, as they had done previously. Paradoxically, however, the cost of private health insurance did not decrease but has instead increased dramatically in the years since the scheme's introduction.

   Which one of the following, if true, does most to explain the apparently paradoxical outcome?

   (A) The National Health scheme has greatly reduced the number of medical claims handled annually by Impania's private insurers, enabling these firms to reduce overhead costs substantially.
   (B) Before the National Health scheme was introduced, more than 80 percent of all Impanian medical costs were associated with procedures that are now covered by the scheme.
   (C) Impanians who previously were unable to afford regular medical treatment now use the National Health scheme, but the number of Impanians with private health insurance has not increased.
   (D) Impanians now buy private medical insurance only at times when they expect that they will need care of kinds not available in the National Health scheme.
   (E) The proportion of total expenditures within Impania that is spent on health care has declined since the introduction of the National Health scheme.

2. Once consumers recognize that a period of inflation has begun, there is generally an increase in consumer spending. This increase can be readily explained by consumers' desire not to postpone purchases that will surely increase in price. But during protracted periods of inflation, consumers eventually begin to put off making even routine purchases, despite the fact that consumers continue to expect prices to rise and despite the fact that salaries also rise during inflationary periods.

   Which one of the following, if true, most helps to explain the apparent inconsistency in consumer behavior described?

   (A) During times of inflation consumers save more money than they do in noninflationary periods.
   (B) There is usually a lag between the leading economic indicators' first signaling the onset of an inflationary period and consumers' recognition of its onset.
   (C) No generalization that describes human behavior will be true of every type of human behavior.
   (D) If significant numbers of consumers are unable to make purchases, prices will eventually fall but salaries will not be directly affected.
   (E) Consumers' purchasing power decreases during periods of protracted inflation since salaries do not keep pace with prices.

3. The Gulches is an area of volcanic rock that is gashed by many channels that lead downhill from the site of a prehistoric glacier to a river. The channels clearly were cut by running water. It was once accepted as fact that the cutting occurred gradually, as the glacier melted. But one geologist theorized that the channels were cut in a short time by an enormous flood. The channels do show physical evidence of having been formed quickly, but the flood theory was originally rejected because scientists knew of no natural process that could melt so much ice so quickly. Paradoxically, today the scientific community accepts the flood theory even though scientists still do not know of a process that can melt so much ice so quickly.

   Which one of the following, if true, most helps to resolve the apparent paradox in the passage?

   (A) Ripples, which indicate that the channels were cut by water, have been discovered in the floors of the channels.
   (B) The Gulches is known to be similar in certain respects to many other volcanic rock formations.
   (C) More than one glacier was present in the area during prehistoric times.
   (D) Volcanic rock is more easily cut by water than are other forms of rock.
   (E) Scientists now believe that the prehistoric glacier dammed a source of water, created a huge lake in the process, and then retreated.

4. Calories consumed in excess of those with which the body needs to be provided to maintain its weight are normally stored as fat and the body gains weight. Alcoholic beverages are laden with calories. However, those people who regularly drink two or three alcoholic beverages a day and thereby exceed the caloric intake necessary to maintain their weight do not in general gain weight.

   Which one of the following, if true, most helps to resolve the apparent discrepancy?

   (A) Some people who regularly drink two or three alcoholic beverages a day avoid exceeding the caloric intake necessary to maintain their weight by decreasing caloric intake from other sources.
   (B) Excess calories consumed by people who regularly drink two or three alcoholic beverages a day tend to be dissipated as heat.
   (C) Some people who do not drink alcoholic beverages but who eat high-calorie foods do not gain weight.
   (D) Many people who regularly drink more than three alcoholic beverages a day do not gain weight.
   (E) Some people who take in fewer calories than are normally necessary to maintain their weight do not lose weight.

5. Throughout European history famines have generally been followed by periods of rising wages, because when a labor force is diminished, workers are more valuable in accordance with the law of supply and demand. The Irish potato famine of the 1840s is an exception; it resulted in the death or emigration of half of Ireland's population, but there was no significant rise in the average wages in Ireland in the following decade.

Which one of the following, if true, would LEAST contribute to an explanation of the exception to the generalization?

(A) Improved medical care reduced the mortality rate among able-bodied adults in the decade following the famine to below prefamine levels.

(B) Eviction policies of the landowners in Ireland were designed to force emigration of the elderly and infirm, who could not work, and to retain a high percentage of able-bodied workers.

(C) Advances in technology increased the efficiency of industry and agriculture, and so allowed maintenance of economic output with less demand for labor.

(D) The birth rate increased during the decade following the famine, and this compensated for much of the loss of population that was due to the famine.

(E) England, which had political control of Ireland, legislated artificially low wages to provide English-owned industry and agriculture in Ireland with cheap labor.

6. A group of scientists studying calcium metabolism in laboratory rats discovered that removing the rats' parathyroid glands resulted in the rats' having substantially lower than normal levels of calcium in their blood. This discovery led the scientists to hypothesize that the function of the parathyroid gland is to regulate the level of calcium in the blood by raising that level when it falls below the normal range. In a further experiment, the scientists removed not only the parathyroid gland but also the adrenal gland from rats. They made the surprising discovery that the level of calcium in the rats' blood decreased much less sharply than when the parathyroid gland alone was removed.

Which one of the following, if true, explains the surprising discovery in a way most consistent with the scientists' hypothesis?

(A) The adrenal gland acts to lower the level of calcium in the blood. (B) The adrenal gland and the parathyroid gland play the same role in regulating calcium blood levels.

(C) The absence of a parathyroid gland causes the adrenal gland to increase the level of calcium in the blood.

(D) If the adrenal gland, and no other gland, of a rat were removed, the rat's calcium level would remain stable.

(E) The only function of the parathyroid gland is to regulate the level of calcium in the blood.

7. A long term health study that followed a group of people who were age 35 in 1950 found that those whose weight increased by approximately half a kilogram or one pound per year after the age of 35 tended, on the whole, to live longer than those who maintained the weight they had at age 35. This finding seems at variance with other studies that have associated weight gain with a host of health problems that tend to lower life expectancy.

Which one of the following, if true, most helps to resolve the apparently conflicting findings?

(A) As people age, muscle and bone tissue tends to make up a smaller and smaller proportion of total body weight.

(B) Individuals who reduce their cholesterol levels by losing weight can thereby also reduce their risk of dying from heart attacks or strokes.

(C) Smokers, who tend to be leaner than nonsmokers, tend to have shorter life spans than nonsmokers.

(D) The normal deterioration of the human immune system with age can be slowed down by a reduction in the number of calories consumed.

(E) Diets that tend to lead to weight gain often contain not only excess fat but also unhealthful concentrations of sugar and sodium.

8. Oxygen-18 is a heavier-than-normal isotope of oxygen. In a rain cloud, water molecules containing oxygen-18 are rarer than water molecules containing normal oxygen. But in rainfall, a higher proportion of all water molecules containing oxygen 18 than of all water molecules containing ordinary oxygen descends to earth. Consequently, scientists were surprised when measurements along the entire route of rain clouds' passage from above the Atlantic Ocean, the site of their original formation, across the Amazon forests, where it rains almost daily, showed that the oxygen-18 content of each of the clouds remained fairly constant.

Which one of the following statements, if true, best helps to resolve the conflict between scientists' "expectations, based on the known behavior of oxygen-18, and the result of their measurements of the rain clouds' oxygen-18 content?

(A) Rain clouds above tropical forests are poorer in oxygen-18 than rain clouds above unforested regions.

(B) Like the oceans, tropical rain forests can create or replenish rain clouds in the atmosphere above them.

(C) The amount of rainfall over the Amazon rain forests is exactly the same as the amount of rain originally collected in the clouds formed above the Atlantic Ocean.

(D) The amount of rain recycled back into the atmosphere from the leaves of forest vegetation is exactly the same as the amount of rain in river runoffs that is not recycled into the atmosphere.

(E) Oxygen-18 is not a good indicator of the effect of tropical rain forests on the atmosphere above them.

*Paradox Fix Explanations

1. (7/4 #17) ~ D

The paradox is that when National health care was introduced and Impanians only had to pay for unusual and sophisticated medical procedures, private health insurance costs went up instead of down. We would typically expect private health costs to go down when national health care is introduced because it means less people have to use private health care. We need some way that the costs to private health insurance have **changed**. (D) works: Impanians are buying less private health care and only getting it when they need the unusual & sophisticated (more expensive) medical procedures. This means that the costs to provide private health insurance go up, because that type of insurance is covering only the expensive procedures.

(A) furthers the paradox by showing a way that the health insurance should have become cheaper.

(B) does not address the paradox because it does not talk about how those medical costs relate to health insurance costs.

(C) furthers the paradox by stating that the number of Impanians with private health insurance has not increased, which eliminates a possibility that could explain why costs could have gone up. More people using private insurance would allow the companies providing that insurance to charge more.

(E) does not address the increase in health insurance costs; it only gives relative information about total expenditures.

2. (10/1 #14) ~ E

The paradox is that at the beginning of an inflationary period consumers buy now because prices will be higher later, but as an inflationary period continues consumers begin to put of even routine purchases. There must be some specific reason related to a longer inflationary period that causes consumers not to make these purchases. Scanning the choices, we see that E works: consumers have less purchasing power during periods of protracted inflation and therefore cannot afford to buy those things that they are putting off.

(A) applies to both consumer situations described so it cannot help to resolve the paradox.

(B) The passage says that in both instances consumers are aware that they are in an inflationary period.

(C) The passage only discusses specific situations, so this information is totally irrelevant, although it sounds sort of good.

(D) We have no information about numbers of consumers not being able to make purchases.

3. (10/4 #17) ~ E

The paradox is that the flood theory for the channels is accepted even though the scientific community still does not know of a process that can melt ice so quickly. We can resolve the paradox with information that shows why the scientists would now approve of the theory despite their not understanding how the ice in the glacier could have melted so quickly. Choice E works perfectly: the scientists believed that a lake on the glacier flooded and created the channels instead of the glacier melting very quickly. This explains why they accept the flood theory: they believe the flood came from a source which has properties they understand, instead of from the glacier melting.

(A) no way explains why the scientists now believe the flood theory, which involves a lot of water moving quickly. The beginning of the passage states that the channels were clearly cut by water.

(B) does not explain the paradox.

(C) does not explain the paradox because it doesn't relate to why the scientists changed their minds.

(D) is irrelevant to the paradox at hand. It doesn't matter how easily volcanic rock is cut, what matters is why scientists believe the flood theory without knowing how the glacier could have melted so quickly.

4. (15/3 #20) ~ B

The paradox is that extra calories usually cause people to gain weight, but people who **drink** extra calories in alcoholic beverages typically do not gain weight. We need some way to explain why drinking the calories this way does not cause weight gain.

(A) The passage says that the two or three drinks **alone** exceed the caloric intake necessary to maintain their weight.

(B) works: people who drink in the calories this way get rid of some of the calories consumed as heat, so they are not actually getting extra calories, because they are burning some off.

(C) does not explain why the people who drink the extra calories do not gain weight. The first sentence contains information that leads to the conclusion that they would gain weight, and this new information does not contradict that.

(D) only furthers the paradox that is presented in the passage. If people who drink

(E) has the same problem as (C).

5. (10/4 #23) ~ D

The stem tells us that this is a paradox question (note the words "contribute an explanation of the exception") and that we are looking for the choice that **does not** resolve the paradox. The paradox is that normally wages rise after a famine, but they did not do so after the Irish potato famine. Anything that distinguishes this famine from others will help to resolve the paradox. Work each choice:

(A) If more able bodied people were kept alive due to the improved care, then that would explain why wages did not go up: the supply of workers rebounded after the famine which stabilized the wages.

(B) The passage says that the famine resulted in the death or **emigration** of half of the population. Because of the eviction policies: those that were emigrating were those that could not work. This means that the supply of workers was kept fairly constant.

(C) Less demand for labor means that even with less labor available wage prices could remain stable.

(D) Even if the birth rate goes up after the famine, those babies and children born that wouldn't have been with a lower birth rate are not working until after that decade so the labor force should still be shorthanded. This does not explain why wages did not go up.

(E) The English kept the wages down. This definitely explains the paradox.

6. (11/2 #23) ~ A

We are asked to explain the surprising discovery in a way consistent with the scientist's hypothesis. The paradox is that in the first experiment scientists removed the parathyroid gland and the blood levels of calcium went down, and in the second experiment, also removing the adrenal gland causes the calcium levels to not decrease as much. We need information that explains this, while still supporting the scientist's hypothesis that the parathyroid gland raises calcium levels when it needs to.

(A) works perfectly. The adrenal's job is to lower calcium, so when it is removed in the second experiment, the calcium levels are not being lowered by as much as when the adrenal is present in the first experiment.

(B) does not resolve the paradox. If the adrenal is supposed to raise calcium levels, then removing it too would cause the levels to be even lower in the second experiment.

(C) does not explain why removing the adrenal makes the calcium levels go up in experiment two.

(D) does not explain the paradox. We need information on why taking it out makes calcium levels increase.

(E) tells us nothing that resolves the paradox. We need information about the adrenal gland for that.

7. (12/4 #22) ~ C

The paradox is that the study found that those who gained about a pound a year after age 35 lived longer than those whose weight stayed the same. This seems to go against other studies that have found that weight gain is correlated with a host of other health problems that tend to lower life expectancy. Let's work the choices looking for a reason why the people who did not gain weight in the study would live less long than the people who did gain weight.

(A) The passage only talks about total body weight, so this doesn't explain why the two groups in the study are different, other than what we already know.

(B) does not resolve the paradox.

(C) can explain the paradox. The people who did not gain weight included more smokers than the group that did gain weight. And smokers die younger, so they lowered the average life span of the group that did not gain weight. Hence the paradoxical result of the study.

(D)only furthers the paradox.

(E) furthers the paradox, because it tells that those who gained weight were probably eating very bad diets.

8. (18/2 #19) ~ B

The Paradox is that more oxygen-18 falls out of rain clouds then normal oxygen, but clouds in different places (including over the Amazon where it rains daily) have the same amount of oxygen-18. It seems like Amazon clouds would have less, because they would lose it when it rains. Choice B explains how this can be so: the rain forests and oceans replenish the clouds above them, so the oxygen-18 is put back in to equal out the loss from rain.

(A) contradicts the information in the passage, so it cannot resolve the paradox.

(C) does not get at why the oxygen 18 levels stay constant; it is irrelevant to the paradox.

(D) does not get at why the oxygen 18 levels stay constant; it is irrelevant to the paradox.

(E) is also irrelevant. It doesn't matter if Oxygen-18 is a good indicator of the effect of rainforests on the atmosphere. We want information that explains why the Oxygen-18 levels stay the same despite rain taking more Oxygen-18 out than other oxygen.

*Affect the Passage Problem Sets

Average (36)

Test / Section	#	Question	Answer
19 / 4	#	**7**	Ⓐ Ⓑ Ⓒ Ⓓ Ⓔ
19 / 4	#	**20**	Ⓐ Ⓑ Ⓒ Ⓓ Ⓔ
20 / 1	#	**4**	Ⓐ Ⓑ Ⓒ Ⓓ Ⓔ
20 / 1	#	**12**	Ⓐ Ⓑ Ⓒ Ⓓ Ⓔ
21 / 2	#	**7**	Ⓐ Ⓑ Ⓒ Ⓓ Ⓔ
21 / 3	#	**9**	Ⓐ Ⓑ Ⓒ Ⓓ Ⓔ
22 / 2	#	**8**	Ⓐ Ⓑ Ⓒ Ⓓ Ⓔ
22 / 2	#	**9**	Ⓐ Ⓑ Ⓒ Ⓓ Ⓔ
22 / 2	#	**21**	Ⓐ Ⓑ Ⓒ Ⓓ Ⓔ
22 / 4	#	**8**	Ⓐ Ⓑ Ⓒ Ⓓ Ⓔ
22 / 4	#	**15**	Ⓐ Ⓑ Ⓒ Ⓓ Ⓔ
22 / 4	#	**17**	Ⓐ Ⓑ Ⓒ Ⓓ Ⓔ
22 / 4	#	**26**	Ⓐ Ⓑ Ⓒ Ⓓ Ⓔ
23 / 2	#	**13**	Ⓐ Ⓑ Ⓒ Ⓓ Ⓔ
23 / 2	#	**14**	Ⓐ Ⓑ Ⓒ Ⓓ Ⓔ
23 / 2	#	**18**	Ⓐ Ⓑ Ⓒ Ⓓ Ⓔ
23 / 3	#	**19**	Ⓐ Ⓑ Ⓒ Ⓓ Ⓔ
24 / 3	#	**9**	Ⓐ Ⓑ Ⓒ Ⓓ Ⓔ
25 / 2	#	**4**	Ⓐ Ⓑ Ⓒ Ⓓ Ⓔ
25 / 2	#	**10**	Ⓐ Ⓑ Ⓒ Ⓓ Ⓔ
25 / 2	#	**14**	Ⓐ Ⓑ Ⓒ Ⓓ Ⓔ
25 / 2	#	**15**	Ⓐ Ⓑ Ⓒ Ⓓ Ⓔ
25 / 2	#	**17**	Ⓐ Ⓑ Ⓒ Ⓓ Ⓔ
25 / 4	#	**14**	Ⓐ Ⓑ Ⓒ Ⓓ Ⓔ
26 / 2	#	**5**	Ⓐ Ⓑ Ⓒ Ⓓ Ⓔ
26 / 3	#	**18**	Ⓐ Ⓑ Ⓒ Ⓓ Ⓔ
27 / 1	#	**10**	Ⓐ Ⓑ Ⓒ Ⓓ Ⓔ
27 / 1	#	**18**	Ⓐ Ⓑ Ⓒ Ⓓ Ⓔ
27 / 4	#	**15**	Ⓐ Ⓑ Ⓒ Ⓓ Ⓔ
28 / 1	#	**8**	Ⓐ Ⓑ Ⓒ Ⓓ Ⓔ
28 / 1	#	**26**	Ⓐ Ⓑ Ⓒ Ⓓ Ⓔ
28 / 3	#	**11**	Ⓐ Ⓑ Ⓒ Ⓓ Ⓔ
28 / 3	#	**15**	Ⓐ Ⓑ Ⓒ Ⓓ Ⓔ
28 / 3	#	**17**	Ⓐ Ⓑ Ⓒ Ⓓ Ⓔ
28 / 3	#	**18**	Ⓐ Ⓑ Ⓒ Ⓓ Ⓔ
28 / 3	#	**24**	Ⓐ Ⓑ Ⓒ Ⓓ Ⓔ

Difficult (19)

Test / Section	#	Question	Answer
19 / 2	#	**5**	Ⓐ Ⓑ Ⓒ Ⓓ Ⓔ
19 / 2	#	**10**	Ⓐ Ⓑ Ⓒ Ⓓ Ⓔ
19 / 2	#	**21**	Ⓐ Ⓑ Ⓒ Ⓓ Ⓔ
20 / 1	#	**18**	Ⓐ Ⓑ Ⓒ Ⓓ Ⓔ
20 / 4	#	**17**	Ⓐ Ⓑ Ⓒ Ⓓ Ⓔ
20 / 4	#	**25**	Ⓐ Ⓑ Ⓒ Ⓓ Ⓔ
21 / 3	#	**3**	Ⓐ Ⓑ Ⓒ Ⓓ Ⓔ
21 / 3	#	**7**	Ⓐ Ⓑ Ⓒ Ⓓ Ⓔ
21 / 3	#	**23**	Ⓐ Ⓑ Ⓒ Ⓓ Ⓔ
23 / 3	#	**15**	Ⓐ Ⓑ Ⓒ Ⓓ Ⓔ
24 / 2	#	**25**	Ⓐ Ⓑ Ⓒ Ⓓ Ⓔ
24 / 3	#	**22**	Ⓐ Ⓑ Ⓒ Ⓓ Ⓔ
24 / 3	#	**26**	Ⓐ Ⓑ Ⓒ Ⓓ Ⓔ
25 / 4	#	**7**	Ⓐ Ⓑ Ⓒ Ⓓ Ⓔ
25 / 4	#	**13**	Ⓐ Ⓑ Ⓒ Ⓓ Ⓔ
25 / 4	#	**24**	Ⓐ Ⓑ Ⓒ Ⓓ Ⓔ
26 / 2	#	**18**	Ⓐ Ⓑ Ⓒ Ⓓ Ⓔ
27 / 4	#	**8**	Ⓐ Ⓑ Ⓒ Ⓓ Ⓔ
28 / 1	#	**17**	Ⓐ Ⓑ Ⓒ Ⓓ Ⓔ

Grueling (32)

Test / Section	#	Question	Choices
19 / 2	#	**4**	Ⓐ Ⓑ Ⓒ Ⓓ Ⓔ
19 / 4	#	**10**	Ⓐ Ⓑ Ⓒ Ⓓ Ⓔ
19 / 4	#	**23**	Ⓐ Ⓑ Ⓒ Ⓓ Ⓔ
19 / 4	#	**26**	Ⓐ Ⓑ Ⓒ Ⓓ Ⓔ
20 / 4	#	**26**	Ⓐ Ⓑ Ⓒ Ⓓ Ⓔ
21 / 2	#	**17**	Ⓐ Ⓑ Ⓒ Ⓓ Ⓔ
21 / 3	#	**15**	Ⓐ Ⓑ Ⓒ Ⓓ Ⓔ
21 / 3	#	**17**	Ⓐ Ⓑ Ⓒ Ⓓ Ⓔ
22 / 4	#	**19**	Ⓐ Ⓑ Ⓒ Ⓓ Ⓔ
22 / 4	#	**24**	Ⓐ Ⓑ Ⓒ Ⓓ Ⓔ
23 / 2	#	**8**	Ⓐ Ⓑ Ⓒ Ⓓ Ⓔ
23 / 2	#	**22**	Ⓐ Ⓑ Ⓒ Ⓓ Ⓔ
23 / 2	#	**26**	Ⓐ Ⓑ Ⓒ Ⓓ Ⓔ
23 / 3	#	**10**	Ⓐ Ⓑ Ⓒ Ⓓ Ⓔ
23 / 3	#	**13**	Ⓐ Ⓑ Ⓒ Ⓓ Ⓔ
24 / 2	#	**18**	Ⓐ Ⓑ Ⓒ Ⓓ Ⓔ
24 / 2	#	**19**	Ⓐ Ⓑ Ⓒ Ⓓ Ⓔ
24 / 2	#	**20**	Ⓐ Ⓑ Ⓒ Ⓓ Ⓔ
24 / 2	#	**22**	Ⓐ Ⓑ Ⓒ Ⓓ Ⓔ
24 / 3	#	**20**	Ⓐ Ⓑ Ⓒ Ⓓ Ⓔ
24 / 3	#	**23**	Ⓐ Ⓑ Ⓒ Ⓓ Ⓔ
25 / 2	#	**23**	Ⓐ Ⓑ Ⓒ Ⓓ Ⓔ
25 / 2	#	**25**	Ⓐ Ⓑ Ⓒ Ⓓ Ⓔ
25 / 4	#	**11**	Ⓐ Ⓑ Ⓒ Ⓓ Ⓔ
26 / 2	#	**12**	Ⓐ Ⓑ Ⓒ Ⓓ Ⓔ
26 / 2	#	**23**	Ⓐ Ⓑ Ⓒ Ⓓ Ⓔ
26 / 3	#	**14**	Ⓐ Ⓑ Ⓒ Ⓓ Ⓔ
26 / 3	#	**24**	Ⓐ Ⓑ Ⓒ Ⓓ Ⓔ
27 / 1	#	**24**	Ⓐ Ⓑ Ⓒ Ⓓ Ⓔ
27 / 4	#	**18**	Ⓐ Ⓑ Ⓒ Ⓓ Ⓔ
28 / 1	#	**23**	Ⓐ Ⓑ Ⓒ Ⓓ Ⓔ
28 / 3	#	**25**	Ⓐ Ⓑ Ⓒ Ⓓ Ⓔ

*Affect the Passage Problem Sets

Average

19 / 4 # **7** E
19 / 4 # **20** C
20 / 1 # **4** B
20 / 1 # **12** D
21 / 2 # **7** B
21 / 3 # **9** B
22 / 2 # **8** A
22 / 2 # **9** C
22 / 2 # **21** D
22 / 4 # **8** D
22 / 4 # **15** C
22 / 4 # **17** D
22 / 4 # **26** D
23 / 2 # **13** A
23 / 2 # **14** A
23 / 2 # **18** B
23 / 3 # **19** B

---

24 / 3 # **9** E
25 / 2 # **4** A
25 / 2 # **10** E
25 / 2 # **14** A
25 / 2 # **15** D
25 / 2 # **17** D
25 / 4 # **14** D
26 / 2 # **5** A
26 / 3 # **18** A
27 / 1 # **10** E
27 / 1 # **18** A
27 / 4 # **15** C
28 / 1 # **8** C
28 / 1 # **26** E
28 / 3 # **11** C
28 / 3 # **15** B
28 / 3 # **17** B
28 / 3 # **18** C
28 / 3 # **24** D

Difficult

19 / 2 # **5** D
19 / 2 # **10** B
19 / 2 # **21** A
20 / 1 # **18** C
20 / 4 # **17** E
20 / 4 # **25** D
21 / 3 # **3** E
21 / 3 # **7** D
21 / 3 # **23** C

---

23 / 3 # **15** B
24 / 2 # **25** A
24 / 3 # **22** C
24 / 3 # **26** B
25 / 4 # **7** A
25 / 4 # **13** B
25 / 4 # **24** D
26 / 2 # **18** C
27 / 4 # **8** B
28 / 1 # **17** D

Grueling

19 / 2 # **4** D
19 / 4 # **10** A
19 / 4 # **23** D
19 / 4 # **26** D
20 / 4 # **26** B
21 / 2 # **17** C
21 / 3 # **15** E
21 / 3 # **17** D
22 / 4 # **19** B
22 / 4 # **24** E

---

23 / 2 # **8** D
23 / 2 # **22** D
23 / 2 # **26** D
23 / 3 # **10** B
23 / 3 # **13** E
24 / 2 # **18** E
24 / 2 # **19** E
24 / 2 # **20** B
24 / 2 # **22** D
24 / 3 # **20** B
24 / 3 # **23** B

---

25 / 2 # **23** C
25 / 2 # **25** D
25 / 4 # **11** D
26 / 2 # **12** D
26 / 2 # **23** C
26 / 3 # **14** A
26 / 3 # **24** E
27 / 1 # **24** D
27 / 4 # **18** B
28 / 1 # **23** A
28 / 3 # **25** E

Argument Structure

Argument Structure questions ask you to describe the structure of an argument in general terms. A general structure can fit many different arguments. The specific details of the argument fit within the larger framework of its structure. It is that foundational, basic structure that you must locate in the choices.

Argument Structure questions are in the Identify category, so the correct choice will not bring in new information. This means that the correct choice must describe the structure of the passage, nothing more or less. Likewise, the passage should not be analyzed for weaknesses; accept it as given.

The Query

The queries of Argument Structure questions ask you about the "strategy" or "technique" that the author utilizes in the argument, or they ask you how the argument "proceeds" or "derives its conclusion:"

> "Frank uses which one of the following argumentative techniques…"
>
> "The argument employs which one of the following strategies?"
>
> "Which one of the following describes the technique of reasoning used above?"
>
> "The argument derives its conclusion by"
>
> "The woman's argument proceeds by…"

The Passage

To be successful on this type, you must be able to state how an argument works in abstract terms. You see, each argument works on two different levels: an information level and an abstract level. Deduction questions ask you to operate on the information level, to state what must be true based on the details in the passage. Argument Structure questions force you to see how the argument can be understood on the abstract level that works underneath the specific facts, that lies beneath the information level. Please read this passage:

> The United States fought the war in Vietnam over ideals. Some would argue that such wars cannot be won by either side. But World War II was a war fought over ideals, and the US was victorious. Therefore, the Vietnam War could have been won.

Here, we break the argument into its parts and arrange them in a logical order:

> Premise 1: The US fought the war in Vietnam over ideals.
>
> Premise 2: Some would argue that such wars cannot be won by either side.
>
> Premise 3: But World War II was a war fought over ideals, and the US was victorious.
>
> Conclusion: Therefore, the Vietnam War could have been won.

The statements above make up the information level of this argument. We laid out the pieces to help you see how they all work together. That understanding will allow us to grasp the argument as a whole on its abstract level. To get a feel for the abstract level, analyze the role each individual piece plays in the argument.

The argument begins with the **assertion** (or belief) that the United States fought the Vietnam War over ideals. When we label Premise 1 as an assertion, we state its role in a general way. There are other words we could choose in that situation; the key is to find a good match for the statements meaning.

Next, the argument introduces a **viewpoint** (a controversial belief) related to that assertion: wars over ideals cannot be won. This label describes how Premise 2 relates to Premise 1; it builds upon it.

Then, the argument gives an **example** that rejects the viewpoint just described: World War II was a war fought over ideals and the U.S. won that war. The third Premise is evidence that wars fought over ideals can be won.

Lastly, the argument combines its premises (Premise 1 and the combination of Premises 2 & 3) to arrive at its conclusion that the Vietnam war could have been won.

So, we can say that the argument, in general terms:

> *begins with an assertion and then uses an example to reject a viewpoint related to that assertion to support its conclusion.*

Many arguments could use this structure, and that is what makes this a description of the abstract level of the argument. Different facts or details can be plugged in to this format and the underlying structure remains the same while many specific arguments are created.

Form over Facts

Focusing on the form (underlying structure) over the facts (details) of the argument is a challenge. However, many argument structures that you will describe are less complex than the one in the previous example.

Pay attention to signal words for the evidence and conclusion. Break the argument down mentally into its parts as you read. After each sentence, pause for a moment and ask:

- What did that sentence do for the argument?
- How did that relate to what I have already read?

Understanding how the argument supports its conclusion helps you describe its structure.

Two Speakers

Argument Structure passages often feature two speakers, who each make a short argument. In these, the query usually asks you how the second speaker responds to the first argument. You must understand the first argument to see how the second relates to it. So, do not rush your reading of that argument. Then, **as you read** the second argument, ask yourself how it relates to the conclusion of the first argument.

Envisioning Answers

Ensure that you have a grasp of the structure **before you start envisioning.** If necessary, reread part or all of the argument. Because this type is very susceptible to envisioning, make sure you understand the passage well enough to take advantage of this step.

When you envision, think about how the parts of the argument work together. Next, say the structure in your own words. The phrasing you come up with will rarely match that in the correct choice, but that articulation process will still help you sort the choices. Even if you do not fully understand the argument, describing the parts you do understand in an abstract way will be quite helpful.

Start off on the right foot and practice envisioning every Argument Structure question you face. Envisioning will become easier with practice as you see how the correct choices tend to be worded.

The Choices

Argument Structure questions are challenging partly because articulating how an argument proceeds in abstract terms is a foreign skill for most students. This type is made more difficult by the **convoluted wording** often used to disguise the correct choice. Choices that describe things in an abstract way lend themselves to this: they can easily be phrased in unexpected ways. This can make it hard to find your envisioned answer. Therefore, go into the choices expecting to have your answer couched in different wording. Look for a **paraphrase** of your envisioned answer, one that expresses the same point in a different way. For instance, the argument structure above that we phrased like this:

> *The argument begins with an assertion and then uses an example to reject a viewpoint related to that assertion to support its conclusion.*

Could appear in a choice phrased like this:

(A) An example is used to support evidence that when combined with an earlier fact leads to the argument's main point.

All the elements of our envisioned answer are present in (A), but the phrasing is different. This is a crucial idea: all the big pieces of the argument must be in the correct choice.

Foreign Element Test

You can use this fact to eliminate incorrect choices. Simply find an element in a choice that does not appear in the passage. By element, we mean argument part, perhaps a description of how the evidence works or the conclusion. For instance, if a choice for the example question mentioned an **analogy**, then that choice could be eliminated because the passage does not feature an analogy (drawing a comparison in order to show a similarity in some respect). We call this process of eliminating choices on Argument Structure questions the <u>foreign element test.</u> You can use this method to check any choice on this question type. Most incorrect choices will feature an element that is not seen in the passage (other distracters may leave out crucial elements of the argument's structure).

More on the Distracters

Some incorrect choices start well by discussing elements that are definitely in the passage. Then, in their latter half, they mention elements not present in the passage. Be wary of these "half wrong" choices. They are common, and always incorrect. Other incorrect choices confuse parts of the passage, creating a jumble that does not correctly describe the underlying structure of the argument.

Remember: the foreign element test will eliminate all of the incorrect choices. Only the correct choice will feature **all** the elements of the argument in the correct relationship to one another.

Learn from Practice

Carefully review all the Argument Structure questions you face. Analyze not only the correct answer, but the incorrect ones as well. Looking closely at the incorrect choices will help you get a feel for how the LSAT-writers try to deceive you, and it will also help you learn new argument structures. An incorrect choice on one question could be the correct choice on a future question.

Keep a list of correct answers. After you write down a correct answer, reread the passage and mentally pair the description to the structure you are reading. You will learn many argument structures this way, and, more importantly, how the LSAT-writers phrase their choices. With time, this will help you dominate Argument Structure questions.

19/4 #18

Example Argument Structure question:

Politician: A government that taxes incomes at a rate of 100 percent will generate no revenue because all economic activity will cease. So it follows that the lower the rate of income tax, the more revenue the government will generate by that tax.

Economist: Your conclusion cannot be correct, since it would mean that an income tax of 0 percent would generate the maximum revenue.

Which one of the following argumentative strategies is used by the economist in responding to the politician?

(A) stating a general principle that is incompatible with the conclusion the politician derives
(B) providing evidence that where the politician's advice has been adopted, the results have been disappointing
(C) arguing that the principle derived by the politician, if applied in the limiting case, leads to an absurdly false conclusion
(D) undermining the credibility of the politician by openly questioning the politician's understanding of economics
(E) attacking the politician's argument by giving reason to doubt the truth of a premise

Query

"Argumentative strategies" tells us that we are dealing with an Argument Structure question. The query asks us how the **economist** responds, so focus on his argument.

Passage

Start by understanding the politician's argument. In order to understand how the second speaker responds, we must know what he is responding *to*. The politician's conclusion is his second sentence: the lower the income tax, the more tax revenue. This is easy to identify, thanks to the conclusion signal "so." This conclusion is a principle because it is applicable (it is relevant to any country with an income tax) and predictive (it tells them how high revenues will be based). That feature of the conclusion will be important. It is supported by the evidence that if the government taxes income at 100%, there would be no revenue. This is weak evidence for a large conclusion because it only talks about a single application of the principle: when taxes are at 100%.

With a grasp of the politician's argument, we move to the economist's response. The economist says the politician's conclusion cannot be correct. The evidence given by the economist is that the conclusion implies that an income tax of zero percent would yield maximum revenues.

Envision

First, describe the economist's response in general terms. Then, keep that in mind when moving to the choices:

The economist shows that a case that should be true based on the politician's conclusion – maximum revenue from a 0% rate of taxation - is ridiculous. We can say this in our own words as:

Showing a specific case supported by the conclusion to be impossible in reality

Recall that the correct choice likely will **sound** different from this envisioned answer. The key is that we understand the element (specific case that is impossible) that the correct choice must focus on.

Choices

Sort the choices quickly because our envisioning step gave us much direction.

(A) stating a general principle that is incompatible with the conclusion the politician derives

The economist uses a **specific** case, not a general principle, to respond. Also, the example cited is compatible with the conclusion, and that is the whole point. The politician's conclusion tells that example should be true, but is actually impossible. This choice fails the foreign element test in multiple ways. Dud.

(B) providing evidence that where the politician's advice has been adopted, the results have been disappointing

The politician does not provide **advice**; he tries to prove a point. Further, the economist does not talk about **disappointing results.** Little words can easily identify a distracter on this type. Clear dud.

(C) arguing that the principle derived by the politician, if applied in the limiting case, leads to an absurdly false conclusion

"Limiting case" means the extreme case in this instance: having an income tax rate of 0% or 100%. This choice is an obvious hit, even though it is worded differently from our envisioned answer. The economist does show that the conclusion (which is a principle) derived from the politician leads to a very false conclusion in the limiting case. If there is no income tax, then there are no revenues, not maximal revenues. With a hit this good, you can choose (C) and moving on without reading the last two choices. For teaching purposes:

(D) undermining the credibility of the politician by openly questioning the politician's understanding of economics

The economist never questions the politician's knowledge of economics, so this is a dud. This choice claims that the economist uses a <u>speaker attack</u>: attacking an argument by casting doubt on the person arguing it. Speaker attacks are a flawed way to attack a conclusion, and the economist is successful in weakening the politician's conclusion. Further proof that (D) is incorrect.

(E) attacking the politician's argument by giving reason to doubt the truth of a premise

The politician's premise is that a government that taxes at 100% will receive no revenue. Because the economist does not attack this premise, (E) is a dud. The economist goes straight for the jugular: he attacks the politician's conclusion, not his evidence.

*Argument Structure Review

- Introduction
    - "Frank uses which one of the following argumentative techniques…"
    - Argument Structure questions ask you to describe the underlying structure of an argument.
        - The choices are phrased in a general, abstract way.
    - This type is in the Identify category, so the correct choice cannot bring in new information.
        - The correct choice must describe the structure of the passage precisely.
- The Passage
    - Read for the argument structure – how the pieces fit together.
        - This is the abstract level of the argument: underneath the specific facts of the passage.
        - Understand each part of the argument and describe it in a general way.
    - When there are two speakers, read the second paragraph with an eye for how that speaker responds to the first speaker's argument.
- Envision
    - Always practice envisioning an answer to this type.
    - Make sure that you have a solid grasp of the structure.
        - If not, reread the passage.
    - Say the structure in your own words.
        - Even if you only understand a few parts, knowing those will be helpful.
- The Choices
    - They often have complex, confusing wording.
    - Look for a paraphrase of your envisioned answer, not an exact match.
    - Foreign Element test
        - If you find an element (argument part) in a choice that does not work, then that choice is incorrect.
    - Watch out for choices that start off well and then do not describe the passage.
- Keep a list of the correct answers to these questions to help you learn how the choices are phrased.

*Argument Structure Practice Questions

1. Coherent solutions for the problem of reducing health-care costs cannot be found within the current piecemeal system of paying these costs. The reason is that this system gives health-care providers and insurers every incentive to shift, wherever possible, the costs of treating illness onto each other or any other party, including the patient. That clearly is the lesson of the various reforms of the 1980s: push in on one part of this pliable spending balloon and an equally expensive bulge pops up elsewhere. For example, when the government health-care insurance program for the poor cut costs by disallowing payments for some visits to physicians, patients with advanced illness later presented themselves at hospital emergency rooms in increased numbers.

   The argument proceeds by

   (A) showing that shifting costs onto the patient contradicts the premise of health-care reimbursement
   (B) attributing without justification fraudulent intent to people
   (C) employing an analogy to characterize interrelationships
   (D) denying the possibility of a solution by disparaging each possible alternative system
   (E) demonstrating that cooperation is feasible by citing an instance

2. Historian: There is no direct evidence that timber was traded between the ancient nations of Poran and Nayal, but the fact that a law setting tariffs on timber imports from Poran was enacted during the third Nayalese dynasty does suggest that during that period a timber trade was conducted.

   Critic: Your reasoning is flawed. During its third dynasty, Nayal may well have imported timber from Poran, but certainly on today's statute books there remain many laws regulating activities that were once common but in which people no longer engage.

   The critic's response to the historian's reasoning does which one of the following?

   (A) It implies an analogy between the present and the past.
   (B) It identifies a general principle that the historian's reasoning violates.
   (C) It distinguishes between what has been established as a certainty and what has been established as a possibility.
   (D) It establishes explicit criteria that must be used in evaluating indirect evidence.
   (E) It points out the dissimilar roles that law plays in societies that are distinct from one another.

3. Graphologists claim that it is possible to detect permanent character traits by examining people's handwriting. For example, a strong cross on the "t" is supposed to denote enthusiasm. Obviously, however, with practice and perseverance people can alter their handwriting to include this feature. So it seems that graphologists must hold that permanent character traits can be changed.

   The argument against graphology proceeds by

   (A) citing apparently incontestable evidence that leads to absurd consequences when conjoined with the view in question
   (B) demonstrating that an apparently controversial and interesting claim is really just a platitude
   (C) arguing that a particular technique of analysis can never be effective when the people analyzed know that it is being used
   (D) showing that proponents of the view have no theoretical justification for the view
   (E) attacking a technique by arguing that what the technique is supposed to detect can be detected quite readily without it

4. Recently discovered fossil evidence casts doubt on the evolutionary theory that dinosaurs are more closely related to reptiles than to other classes of animals. Fossils show that some dinosaurs had hollow bones—a feature found today only in warm-blooded creatures, such as birds, that have a high metabolic rate. Dinosaurs had well developed senses of sight and hearing, which is not true of present day cold-blooded creatures like reptiles. The highly arched mouth roof of some dinosaurs would have permitted them to breathe while eating, as fast breathing animals, such as birds, need to do. Today, all fast breathing animals are warm-blooded. Finally, fossils reveal that many dinosaurs had a pattern of growth typical of warm-blooded animals.

   The argument in the passage proceeds by

   (A) attempting to justify one position by demonstrating that an opposing position is based on erroneous information
   (B) establishing a general principle that it then uses to draw a conclusion about a particular case
   (C) dismissing a claim made about the present on the basis of historical evidence
   (D) assuming that if all members of a category have a certain property then all things with that property belong to the category
   (E) presenting evidence that a past phenomenon is more similar to one rather than the other of two present-day phenomena

*Argument Structure Explanations

1. (7/1 #7) ~ C

The stem asks how the argument proceeds, which translates to "what is the argument's structure; how does it build up to its conclusion?" The argument begins with its conclusion: the solution to reducing healthcare costs cannot be found within the current system. The evidence: in this system, reducing costs in one area simply shifts those costs elsewhere. The evidence is illustrated with the analogy of a balloon. Reading the choices, (C) stands out: the argument does proceed by employing the balloon analogy to characterize the interrelationships of all the parties involved in the healthcare system.

(A) The argument does not discuss how shifting costs contradicts a premise of reimbursement.

(B) The argument does not attribute fraudulent intent to people.

(D) The argument never discusses alternative systems.

(E) The argument does not have "cooperation being feasible" as its conclusion.

2. (7/4 #21) ~ A

Read the critic's response carefully, keeping in mind how it relates to the historian's reasoning. The Critic says that the Historians reasoning is flawed, and implies an analogy (outdated laws on today's statute books) that helps to show why the laws on Nayal's books do not conclusively show that a timber trade occurred during the period. The analogy here is only implied. It is not made directly as that would require wording that more concretely ties the statement about today's laws and Nayal's laws together.

(B) The historian's reasoning does not violate a general principle.

(C) The critic argues against the historian's logic. Nothing has been established as a certainty.

(D) The critic does not establish any criteria for evaluating indirect evidence. Criteria would create a reference point for the evidence to be compared against. Instead, the critic unravels the historian's evidence with the analogy.

(E) This is the opposite of what the critic's response does. The critic uses a similarity between the roles that laws play between the two countries.

3. (7/4 #20) ~ A

Read the argument carefully keeping in mind how it proceeds in general terms. The argument first introduces the graphologist claim and an example of the claim being illustrated (strong cross on "t" denoting enthusiasm). Next it gives a fact that relates to the claim (people can alter their handwriting to include certain features). Finally, it combines the fact and the graphologist claim to create a surprising consequence (graphologists must hold that permanent character traits can be changed, this is indeed surprising). (A) matches.

(B) Platitude means "an obvious remark." The argument does not show that the interesting claim by the graphologists is obvious. It shows that it is absurd by its definition. Permanent traits cannot be changed because they are permanent.

(C) There is no discussion of the people analyzed knowing that the technique is being used.

(D) The argument does not show that the graphologists do not have theoretical justification for their claim.

(E) The argument never talks about ways that character traits can be detected.

4. (9/2 #11) ~ E

The argument begins by saying that recent fossil evidence casts doubt on the theory that dinosaurs are more closely related to reptiles than other animal classes. This is the introduction. Next, the argument lists many ways in which the fossils show that dinosaurs are more similar to warm-blooded creatures than reptiles: they have hollow bones, well-developed senses, etc. Overall, the argument presents evidence that a past phenomenon (dinosaurs) is more similar to one present day phenomenon (warm-blooded animals) than to another present day phenomenon (reptiles).

(A) is tempting but not accurate. The argument never says that the information that the reptile theory is based on is erroneous.

(B) The argument never establishes a general principle. A general principle is "a basic truth or law or assumption." Instead, the argument gives individual pieces of evidence.

(C) The claim is not about the present, it is about the past (what dinosaurs were like).

(D) The argument talks about **many** different properties of dinosaurs.

Role

Role questions are a variation of Argument Structure questions. They ask you to identify the role that a small part of the passage, usually a sentence, plays in the argument as a whole. Role questions are classified as Argument Structure questions because you must identify the **abstract role** that the part of passage fills. Just like with normal Argument Structure questions, you must work with the passage on the abstract level, not the information level. Role questions are identify questions, and, by now, you know what that entails.

Role questions are easy to identify because the query will almost always contain the word "role." Example queries:

> "Arnolds speech plays which of the following roles in the argument?"
>
> "Which of the following most accurately describes the role played in the passage by the information about whales?"

The query will tell you the part of the passage that you need to focus on. If you have difficulty keeping the part in mind as you read the passage, just learn from the query that it is a Role question. When you read the passage, get a good grasp of all of its parts. Then, quickly re-reference the query to refresh your memory on which part you need to identify the role of.

Passage

Role question passages are often challenging and complex. This makes it harder to identify the role of the part. The passages often feature multiple viewpoints or anti-premises. If you are not careful, these features can confuse you.

Advanced Arguments

Advanced arguments, those with both a sub-conclusion and a main conclusion, appear in Role passages. The LSAT-writers are aware that students can usually identify a conclusion when it appears **last** in a passage. They use this against you on Role questions when an advanced argument places the main conclusion first and the sub-conclusion last. To make these trickier, the sub-conclusion will often have a conclusion signal, likely a blatant one like "obviously" or "therefore."

Read the Entire Passage

On Role questions, a careful read through of the **full passage** is necessary for gathering context. Role passages are always arguments, never fact-groups. So, make sure that you identify the conclusion, and if applicable, the sub-conclusion.

After reading each sentence, you may wish to pause and ask how that information fits into what came before it. This tactic will slow you down, but it will also help you understand the passage's underlying structure by actively analyzing the parts.

The purpose of this careful reading is to identify the role of the part. If after reading the passage, you are still hazy on how the part fits into the argument, reread the sentences right before and after the part. Being more clear on that context will help you stand on firmer ground.

Envision

Just like on Argument Structure questions, use the envision step to articulate the ideal answer in your own words. Many Role questions ask you to point out a normal part of an argument, for instance, an assumption or a premise.

The choices may use convoluted wording, so keep your envisioned answer simple. On this question type, there is no excuse not to envision an answer because the role is readily identifiable in the passage and there is only one possible answer. Envisioning will help you locate the correct answer more quickly, even if it takes some practice to get good at articulating the Role.

Choices

Like all identify questions, the correct choice will be supported directly by the passage. The real work on Role questions comes when you read the passage and envision your answer. Avoid relying heavily on the choices to find the correct answer. In fact, do not start sorting the choices if you have little idea what the role is. That is a recipe for getting tripped up by a good-sounding distracter.

A common wrong answer choice will describe the role played by **another** part of the passage, not the part the query asks about. If you have not envisioned an answer, such choices might resonate because they match information in the passage. It is not the right information, so watch out for these.

23/2 #11

Please work this example role question and then check your approach by carefully reading the next few pages:

11. A severe blow to the head can cause one to lose consciousness; from this some people infer that consciousness is a product of the brain and cannot survive bodily death. But a radio that becomes damaged may suddenly cease to broadcast the program it had been receiving, and we do not conclude from this that the program itself has ceased to exist. Similarly, more substantial evidence would be needed to conclude that consciousness does not survive bodily death.

Which one of the following most accurately describes the role played in the argument by the example of the damaged radio?

(A) It is cited as evidence that consciousness does in fact survive bodily death.
(B) It is cited as a counterexample to a widely accepted belief about the nature of consciousness.
(C) It is cited as a case analogous to loss of consciousness in which people do not draw the same sort of conclusion that some people draw about consciousness.
(D) It is cited as the primary piece of evidence for the conclusion that the relationship of consciousness to the brain is analogous to that of a radio program to the radio that receives it.
(E) It is cited as an example of a case in which something consisting purely of energy depends on the existence of something material to provide evidence of its existence.

Query

The phrase "describes the role played in the argument" tells that we are dealing with a Role question. Understand how the entire argument works, and read each sentence with an eye towards how that sentence fits in.

Passage

It is up to you whether you try to remember that you are looking for the role played by the damaged radio. If you do, you can figure out the role **during** your reading of the passage and then state that role in your own words. Otherwise, if you wish to keep less in mind as you read the passage, simply get a good feel for the passage and then reference the query again afterward to pinpoint the specific part. Now, onto our analysis of the passage:

Breaking it into parts shows the thought process you should take on Role questions:

- *Premise 1:* A severe blow to the head can cause one to lose consciousness.
- *Premise 2:* From this, some people infer that consciousness is a product of the brain and cannot survive bodily death.
- *Premise 3:* A radio that becomes damaged may suddenly cease to broadcast the program it had been receiving. We do not conclude from this that the program itself has ceased to exist.
- *Conclusion:* More substantial evidence is needed to conclude that consciousness does not survive bodily death.

The argument contains two premises. Premise 1 is a general fact that will be used by the entire argument. Premise 2 is an anti-premise. Premise 3 rejects Premise 2 by providing a counter example. The conclusion relies on all three premises.

Envision

The first part of Premise 3 is the one we are interested in, so look at it closely in relation to the conclusion. The conclusion is supported by the analogy and implications of Premise 3, which is an analogy because it draws a comparison to the blow to the head and corresponding loss of consciousness (Premise 1). Unlike with that situation, no one would say that because a damaged radio is no longer playing a radio program that the radio program no longer exists (end of Premise 3). The analogy and what people would say based upon it support the conclusion. That last line can work as our envisioned answer:

> ***The example about the radio is an analogy and the fact that people would react differently in that situation supports the conclusion.***

Sort

Let us work the choices:

(A) It is cited as evidence that consciousness does in fact survive bodily death.

(A) initially sounds good but the argument's conclusion is not that consciousness **survives** bodily death. The passage's conclusion is that more evidence than the information about a blow to the head is needed to support the idea that consciousness **does not** survive bodily death. This is an important distinction, one that is easy to catch if you are clear on the conclusion.

(A) cites a conclusion that is too strong. Wrong choices on Role questions often exaggerate various parts of the argument. Another somewhat more subtle point: the information about the radio is only called "evidence." There is no mention of the fact that it is an analogy, nor that other evidence is based on it. While the piece is evidence, usually the correct choice is much more specific about the role played. Dud.

(B) It is cited as a counterexample to a widely accepted belief about the nature of consciousness.

There are two problems with (B). First, the passage does not imply that consciousness ending with death is a widely accepted belief. The passage says "some people" infer that. Second, the information about the radio is not an example, it is an analogy. In general, an example is a concrete occurrence that is typical of a class or group. Here, an example would be an instance of a person whose consciousness continued after their bodily death. The analogy is too abstract to be called an example. Dud.

(C) It is cited as a case analogous to loss of consciousness in which people do not draw the same sort of conclusion that some people draw about consciousness.

(C) matches our envisioned answer. The radio analogy is a case that parallels a loss of consciousness, and it is one in which people do not draw the same conclusion as the situation with consciousness. In this case, people still believe the radio program exists. Notice that the wording in this choice is challenging. The LSAT-Writers will almost always describe the role in a challenging way. This is why envisioning a correct answer is so important: it helps you look beyond the dense wording of a choice to its meaning.

On some question types when your envisioned answer is matched this neatly, you should select it and move on to the next question. On Role questions however, it is best to read all the choices.

(D) It is cited as the primary piece of evidence for the conclusion that the relationship of consciousness to the brain is analogous to that of a radio program to the radio that receives it.

(D) is a tricky incorrect choice because it mentions an analogy. However, the passage's conclusion is not "the relationship of consciousness to the brain is analogous to that of a radio program to the radio that receives it." This fact eliminates (D). Also, and we ran into this earlier, the information about the radio is not a primary piece of evidence. It **supports** a primary piece of evidence, but it itself is better described by (C). Clear Dud.

(E) It is cited as an example of a case in which something consisting purely of energy depends on the existence of something material to provide evidence of its existence.

This choice sounds alright until you realize that nowhere in the passage is it stated that "something consisting purely of energy depends on the existence of something material to provide evidence of its existence." This is new information, and it is not the focus of the passage. Dud.

*Role Questions Review

- "Which of the following most accurately describes the role played in the passage by…"
- Identify the role that a small part of the passage (usually a sentence) plays in the argument.
    - The correct choice will describe the role in an abstract way.
- Passage
    - Advanced arguments crop up here, so make sure you are clear on the conclusion.
    - Read the entire passage carefully to gain context on the specific part.
- Envision
    - Always envision on Role questions
    - Articulate the role in your own words.
- A common incorrect choice will describe the role of another part of the passage.

*Role Practice Questions

1. When Alicia Green borrowed a neighbor's car without permission, the police merely gave her a warning. However, when Peter Foster did the same thing, he was charged with automobile theft. Peter came to the attention of the police because the car he was driving was hit by a speeding taxi. Alicia was stopped because the car she was driving had defective taillights. It is true that the car Peter took got damaged and the car Alicia took did not, but since it was the taxi that caused the damage this difference was not due to any difference in the blameworthiness of their behavior. Therefore Alicia should also have been charged with automobile theft.

   The statement that the car Peter took got damaged and the car Alicia took did not plays which one of the following roles in the argument?

   (A) It presents a reason that directly supports the conclusion.
   (B) It justifies the difference in the actual outcome in the two cases.
   (C) It demonstrates awareness of a fact on which a possible objection might be based.
   (D) It illustrates a general principle on which the argument relies.
   (E) It summarizes a position against which the argument is directed.

2. Of every 100 burglar alarms police answer, 99 are false alarms. This situation causes an enormous and dangerous drain on increasingly scarce public resources. Each false alarm wastes an average of 45 minutes of police time. As a result police are consistently taken away from responding to other legitimate calls for service, and a disproportionate share of police service goes to alarm system users, who are mostly businesses and affluent homeowners. However, burglar alarm systems, unlike car alarm systems, are effective in deterring burglaries, so the only acceptable solution is to fine burglar alarm system owners the cost of 45 minutes of police time for each false alarm their systems generate.

   The statement that burglar alarm systems, unlike car alarm systems, are effective in deterring burglaries plays which one of the following roles in the argument?

   (A) It justifies placing more restrictions on owners of burglar alarms than on owners of car alarms.
   (B) It provides background information needed to make plausible the claim that the number of burglar alarms police are called on to answer is great enough to be a drain on public resources.
   (C) It provides a basis for excluding as unacceptable one obvious alternative to the proposal of fining owners of burglar alarm systems for false alarms.
   (D) It gives a reason why police might be more inclined to respond to burglar alarms than to car alarms.
   (E) It explains why a disproportionate number of the burglar alarms responded to by police come from alarm systems owned by businesses.

3. Pedigreed dogs, including those officially classified as working dogs, must conform to standards set by organizations that issue pedigrees. Those standards generally specify the physical appearance necessary for a dog to be recognized as belonging to a breed but stipulate nothing about other genetic traits, such as those that enable breeds originally developed as working dogs to perform the work for which they were developed. Since dog breeders try to maintain only those traits specified by pedigree organizations, and traits that breeders do not try to maintain risk being lost, certain traits like herding ability risk being lost among pedigreed dogs. Therefore, pedigree organizations should set standards requiring working ability in pedigreed dogs classified as working dogs.

   The phrase "certain traits like herding ability risk being lost among pedigreed dogs" serves which one of the following functions in the argument?

   (A) It is a claim on which the argument depends but for which no support is given.
   (B) It is a subsidiary conclusion used in support of the main conclusion.
   (C) It acknowledges a possible objection to the proposal put forth in the argument.
   (D) It summarizes the position that the argument as a whole is directed toward discrediting.
   (E) It provides evidence necessary to support a claim stated earlier in the argument.

*Role Practice Questions Explanations

1. (7/1 #18) ~ C

Read the passage with an eye towards the role the statement about Peter damaging and Alicia not damaging the car plays. Notice how that sentence starts with the phrase "It is true…" This is a fitting beginning because the statement demonstrates that the author acknowledges a difference in the two cases. However, the author still believes that there was no difference in the **blameworthiness** of the behavior of the two. That is the conclusion. So the statement shows an awareness on the author's part of a fact that an objection to the conclusion could be based on. That objection would be that he believes there is a difference in the two cases (damaging the car vs. not) yet no difference in blame.

(A) This statement does not support the conclusion. It is stated as being true even though it would seem to potentially weaken the conclusion.

(B) This is the opposite of the conclusion.

(D) The statement does not illustrate a general principle on which the argument relies. The argument relies on the principle of equal blameworthiness should lead to equal charges.

(E) is too strong, because that fact is not a full position against which the argument is directed. It's a potential objection, not an articulated position.

2. (9/4 #20) ~ C

Carefully read the parts surrounding the statement that burglar alarm systems, unlike car alarms, are effective in deterring burglaries. The passage states that false burglar alarms waste an enormous amount of policy time, because most alarms are false ones. The argument then says, "however," which shows that what comes next will be in contrast to what was talked about before. Even though burglar alarms waste a lot of police time, they are effective in preventing burglaries. This implies that their use should not be discontinued.

The argument then argues that fining owners is the best solution. The statement provides support that getting rid of the alarms is unacceptable. This is the alternative to fining the owners that the argument mentions.

(A) The statement does not do this and the argument does not deal with car alarms.

(B) The statement does not do this, nor is this necessary. The argument has already established that false alarms are a drain on public resources before the statement is used.

(D) The statement is used in the argument to support its conclusion and because the argument does not involve car alarms, we can eliminate this choice.

(E) The statement does not involve any distinction between systems owned by businesses versus those owned by individuals.

3. (15/2 #14) ~ B

Reread before and after the phrase in question in the passage. The main conclusion is that pedigree organizations should set standards requiring working ability in pedigree dogs classified as working dogs. The phrase in question is a subsidiary (supporting) conclusion to the main conclusion about what should be done about the standards for working dog traits. The supporting conclusion's evidence is that only those traits specified by breeders are kept, and this occurs right before the phrase. It is very important to be clear on the conclusion of the passage in order to realize that the information about herding ability being lost as a trait supports that conclusion.

(A) The support for this claim occurs right before the claim itself.

(C) There is no objection in the passage.

(D) The argument does not discredit this position.

(E) This does not serve as evidence for a claim earlier in the argument. The argument is very linear; the evidence builds to this subsidiary conclusion and this subsidiary conclusion supports the main conclusion.

Disagreement

Disagreement passages feature two speakers who argue about the same issue in different ways. The correct choice identifies the issue that they disagree over. These questions are similar to Core Deduction questions because on both types you must use specific statements to identify an **underlying** (think disguised or implied) conclusion. Disagreement questions generally require that you pinpoint the conclusion of each speaker.

Disagreement questions are in the Identify category, so you do not need to analyze the passages for weaknesses. Further, you can trust the information in the passages. One of the two speaker's arguments is often weak or flawed, but your goal is to understand how what each speaker is saying relates to what the other speaker said. Do not analyze these arguments like you would a modify question, looking for weaknesses. Any choice that involves new information is a dud. Only information in the passage, or hinted at by both speakers, can be correct.

Query

The query will ask you to describe how the two speakers disagree, where the crux of their disagreement lies. Queries often use the words "point at issue" or "disagree."

> "The dialogue above lends the most support to the statement that Nick and Bill *disagree* about which one of the following points?"
>
> "Which one of the following most accurately expresses *the point at issue* between James and Sherry?"
>
> "Based on their statements, Pedro and Jonathan are committed to *disagreeing* over whether"

Passage

The speakers often disagree over an issue involving ethics or a decision. The two speakers rarely disagree over facts, because this is a less complex disagreement and therefore a harder one for the LSAT-Writers to compose questions for. An ethical decision, on the other hand, asks what is "correct" in a certain situation, what people should or should not be allowed to do. When discussing such an issue, a factual statement with information about relevant situations cannot be the correct answer. The disagreement will center on a **subtle aspect** of the issue. The two speakers will often agree on various elements surrounding the point they disagree on. So, focus on the conclusion of each speaker as you read, as this will often help you see how they disagree.

Compare the Two Speakers

Read each argument carefully, one sentence at a time. When you read the first speaker's statements, get a feel for her main point, and how she goes about making it. Then, when you move to the second speaker's statements, look for the refinements, the differences from the first speaker's statements. The disagreement should become clear as you read the second speaker's argument.

The passages are made challenging because the conclusion of each speaker are usually implied, not directly stated. Look for where each speaker is **leading** with their words. Also, analyze how each argument is cumulative, how the different parts add up to imply something new.

Envision

When reading the passage, you will either catch the issue, or you will not. If you do catch it, say it in your own words, because these are great questions for envisioning. The choice will likely use wording similar to your own envisioned answer.

If you do not get a good idea of the issue from your first reading of the passage, return to it and find the issue. Most of the work on these questions is done when reading the passage, not in working the choices. The envisioning step is a time to articulate the disagreement, or realize that you did not find it.

The Fence Test

One speaker will agree with the correct issue and the other speaker will disagree with it. Each speaker will be on **one side** of the issue. The correct choice is a "fence" that splits the two speakers. So, when analyzing a choice, ask yourself if one speaker would have one take on the issue and the other speaker would have the opposite belief. Like other tests you have learned for specific question types, only use the fence test when you have already eliminated some choices.

Incorrect Choices

Understanding these common types of incorrect choices will help you eliminate them:

Off Sector Choices

Off sector choices do not match the nature of the argument. In arguments that have a moral consideration at their heart, fact based issues in the choices are incorrect. They are in a different sphere of discourse; they belong in a different discussion. For instance, in a discussion on whether terminal cancer patients should be allowed to die, a choice that talks about the worldwide number of such patients is incorrect. That is a factual issue, and the speakers are having a moral discussion. Off sector choices are usually easy to spot.

A Non Controversial Point

In any Disagreement question, the two speakers will agree on certain issues. Choices that feature these issues are incorrect. The real disagreement must be a divisive one: one speaker is on one side in how they see that issue and the other speaker is on the other side. Non controversial points are not at the heart of the conflict, but they may still be directly talked about by both speakers. This is what makes them tricky.

Non controversial points are a form of Opposite Answer. You are looking for how the two speakers disagree, not what they agree on. In the moral discussion about terminal cancer patients, both parties could agree that consent of the family must be given. That information in a choice would be a non controversial point.

Issues Addressed Once

The disagreement is what the two speakers are fighting over, so it must be mentioned by both parties. If a choice involves an issue that only one speaker commented on, then that choice must be a Dud. If you do not know how the other speaker feels about that issue, then you cannot know that the speaker disagrees about it. These are a subset of new information choices. Note that often how the speaker feels about an issue will be implied, not directly stated. Keep this in mind before eliminating a choice because you believe it is an issue only addressed once.

19/2 #16

Please work this example Disagreement question.

> Motorcoach driver: Professional drivers spend much more time driving, on average, than do other people and hence are more competent drivers than are other, less experienced drivers. Therefore, the speed limit on major highways should not be reduced, because that action would have the undesirable effect of forcing some people who are now both law-abiding and competent drivers to break the law.
>
> Police officer: All drivers can drive within the legal speed limit if they wish, so it is not true to say that reducing the speed limit would be the cause of such illegal behavior.
>
> The point at issue between the motorcoach driver and the police officer is whether
>
> (A) it would be desirable to reduce the speed limit on major highways
> (B) professional drivers will drive within the legal speed limit if that limit is reduced
> (C) reducing the speed limit on major highways would cause some professional drivers to break the law
> (D) professional drivers are more competent drivers than are other, less experienced drivers
> (E) all drivers wish to drive within the speed limit

Query

"Point at issue" in the query identifies the type. Enter the passage with a focus on the first speaker's conclusion. Then, read the second speaker's argument looking for how the two disagree.

Passage

The motorcoach driver concludes that the speed limit should not be reduced, because that would **force** some professional drivers to break the law. The police officer responds that any driver can obey the speed limit if they want to, so reducing it would not **cause** anyone to speed and break the law.

Envision

Like most Disagreement questions, this one is not based on the conclusion of the first author. The motorcoach driver does not say the speed limit should stay the same and the police officer says that it should be lowered. Such a disagreement would be easy to identify. This actual issue is more subtle.

The motorcoach driver says that the speed limit should not be lowered because, and here comes a premise, that action would cause professional drivers to break the law by speeding. He implies that professional drivers would have no choice but to speed.

This **premise** is what the officer disagrees with, and rightfully so. The officer replies that anyone can go the speed limit if they want to, so it is wrong to say that lowering the speed limit will force professional drivers to break the law. We want a short paraphrase of the issue to keep in mind when working the choices:

Lowering speed limits will force some people to break the law

Choices

(A) it would be desirable to reduce the speed limit on major highways

The two do not disagree over whether reducing the speed limit is desirable. Yes, the driver concludes that it is undesirable, but the police officer does not address this issue. Dud.

(B) professional drivers will drive within the legal speed limit if that limit is reduced

(B) is a tempting choice, but it is incorrect because the officer never mentions professional drivers. The real issue is breaking the law, not speeding. Also, whether or not these drivers **will** drive within the speed limit is not the issue. The disagreement is whether they can drive within the speed limit and be law abiding citizens. Dud.

(C) reducing the speed limit on major highways would cause some professional drivers to break the law

(C) is what we envisioned. The motorcoach driver argues that some professional drivers will be forced to break the law because they cannot help speeding. The officer argues that everyone can choose to not speed and therefore not break the law.

(D) professional drivers are more competent drivers than are other, less experienced drivers

(D) is a premise of the driver's argument, but the officer never mentions the competence of drivers. If one speaker does not address an issue, it cannot be the disagreement. This is an example of an issue addressed once. Dud.

(E) all drivers wish to drive within the speed limit

There is no discussion of **intentions** to speed by either person. The issue is instead whether drivers have control over speeding. Dud.

*Disagreement Review

- "Which one of the following most accurately expresses the point at issue between James and Sherry?"
  - The query will typically use the word "disagree" or "point at issue."
- Identify where the two speakers disagree.
  - Usually, you need to understand an **implied** conclusion.
  - You must understand how what each speaker is saying relates to what the other speaker said.
- Only information in the passage, or information hinted at by both speakers, can be correct.

The Passage

- The speakers often disagree on a specific decision or an ethical issue.
  - The disagreement will be on a subtle aspect of the decision or issue, not a fact.
- Analyze what each speaker is leading to with their ideas.
- As you read the second speaker's argument, ask yourself how it relates to what came before.

Additional Points

- Envision
  - This type is quite susceptible to envisioning, so be sure you envision.
  - Most of the work on this type is done before you reach the choices.
- The Fence Test
  - When you find the correct choice, the two speakers will have different views on the specific issue there.
    - One will be on each side of the issue (fence).
- Incorrect Choices
  - A <u>non controversial point</u> is one that the two speakers agree on.
  - Issues that are only addressed by a single speaker cannot be the point of disagreement.
    - Again, note that one of the speaker's stance on the correct issue might only be hinted at, not directly discussed.

*Disagreement Practice Questions

1. Henry: Some scientists explain the dance of honeybees as the means by which honeybees communicate the location of whatever food source they have just visited to other members of the hive. But honeybees do not need so complicated a mechanism to communicate that information. Forager honeybees returning to their hive simply leave a scent trail from the food source they have just visited. There must therefore be some other explanation for the honeybees' dance.

   Winifred: Not necessarily. Most animals have several ways of accomplishing critical tasks. Bees of some species can navigate using either the position of the Sun or the memory of landmarks. Similarly, for honeybees, scent trails are a supplementary not an exclusive means of communicating.

   The point at issue between Henry and Winifred is whether

   (A) theories of animal behavior can be established on the basis of evidence about only one species of animal
   (B) there is more than one valid explanation for the dance of the honeybees
   (C) honeybees communicate the location of food sources through their dance
   (D) the honeybee is the only species of bee that is capable of communicating navigational information to other hive members
   (E) the honeybee's sense of smell plays a role in its foraging strategies

2. Jones: Prehistoric wooden tools found in South America have been dated to 13,000 years ago. Although scientists attribute these tools to peoples whose ancestors first crossed into the Americas from Siberia to Alaska, this cannot be correct. In order to have reached a site so far south, these peoples must have been migrating southward well before 13,000 years ago. However, no such tools dating to before 13,000 years ago have been found anywhere between Alaska and South America.

   Smith: Your evidence is inconclusive. Those tools were found in peat bogs, which are rare in the Americas. Wooden tools in soils other than peat bogs usually decompose within only a few years.

   The point at issue between Jones and Smith is

   (A) whether all prehistoric tools that are 13,000 years or older were made of wood
   (B) whether the scientists' attribution of tools could be correct in light of Jones's evidence
   (C) whether the dating of the wooden tools by the scientists could be correct
   (D) how long ago the peoples who crossed into the Americas from Siberia to Alaska first did so
   (E) whether Smith's evidence entails that the wooden tools have been dated correctly

3. Conservative: Socialists begin their arguments with an analysis of history, from which they claim to derive certain trends leading inevitably to a socialist future. But in the day to day progress of history there are never such discernible trends. Only in retrospect does inevitability appear, for history occurs through accident, contingency, and individual struggle.

   Socialist: If we thought the outcome of history were inevitable, we would not work so hard to transform the institutions of capitalist society. But to transform them we must first understand them, and we can only understand them by an analysis of their history. This is why historical analysis is important in socialist argument.

   In the dispute the issue between the socialist and the conservative can most accurately be described as whether

   (A) a socialist society is the inevitable consequence of historical trends that can be identified by an analysis of history
   (B) the institutions of capitalist society stand in need of transformation
   (C) socialists' arguments for the inevitability of socialism are justified
   (D) it is possible for people by their own efforts to affect the course of history
   (E) socialists analyze history in order to support the view that socialism is inevitable

4. Monica: The sculpture commissioned for our town plaza has been scorned by the public ever since it went up. But since the people in our town do not know very much about contemporary art, the unpopularity of the work says nothing about its artistic merit and thus gives no reason for removing it.

   Hector: You may be right about what the sculpture's popularity means about its artistic merit. However, a work of art that was commissioned for a public space ought to benefit the public, and popular opinion is ultimately the only way of determining what the public feels is to its benefit. Thus, if public opinion of this sculpture is what you say, then it certainly ought to be removed.

   Monica's and Hector's statements commit them to disagreeing about which one of the following principles?

   (A) Public opinion of a work of art is an important consideration in determining the work's artistic merit.
   (B) Works of art commissioned for public spaces ought at least to have sufficient artistic merit to benefit the public.
   (C) The only reason for removing a work of art commissioned for a public space would be that the balance of public opinion is against the work.
   (D) The sculpture cannot benefit the public by remaining in the town plaza unless the sculpture has artistic merit.
   (E) In determining whether the sculpture should remain in the town plaza, the artistic merit of the sculpture should be a central consideration.

*Disagreement Explanations

1. (19/4 #16) ~ C

Henry states that honey bees can communicate the location of food with a scent trail, so they use their dance for something else. Winifred states that most animals have several methods of doing the same important thing and that scent trails are not the only way they communicate. The two disagree over the purpose of the dances, specifically whether the bees communicate the location of food through them. Winifred does not explicitly state that the bees dance to show where food is, but this is what she implies.

Note what the second speaker **implies**.

2. (8/1 #17) ~ B

Jones argues that the tools found in South America could not have belonged to people whose ancestors came from Siberia. His evidence is that no tools dating before 13,000 years ago have been found between Alaska and South America. And, to get from Siberia to South America, people would have needed to leave more than 13,000 years ago. So, the lack of tools "dropped along the way" supports the idea that the tools didn't come from migrating people.

Smith states that the evidence Jones puts forth is questionable, because tools dropped anywhere other than a peat bog would have decomposed quickly. So, the fact that other similar tools were not found in between Siberia and South America means little. If they were left, they already decomposed. So, the disagreement is over whether **Jones's evidence** can refute the scientist conclusion.

(A) is outside the scope of the discussion. They are discussing where these particular wooden tools came from, not all wooden tools.

(B) is a match. Skim the rest of the choices to be sure nothing is better.

(C) Both parties agree that the date of the tools is accurate. Jones states the date at the beginning of his discussion.

(D) is outside the scope of the discussion. The two are talking about the specific people that used these wooden tools. They are not arguing over when the first people migrated from Siberia.

(E) is tempting because it refers to evidence, but it is incorrect. Smith's evidence about peat bogs is used to refute Jones's evidence. Smith evidence has nothing to do with dating the tools; it has to do with how long they would last based on location (peat bog or not).

3. (14/4 #11) ~ E

The conservative says that socialists analyze history to show that a socialist future is inevitable, while the socialist says that socialists look to the past to analyze trends to enable them to better understand the current institutions. E is correct, the two disagree over why socialists analyze history.

(A) Neither the Socialist nor the Conservative agree with this statement.

(B) We do not know the Conservative's perspective on this one.

(C) Both agree that these arguments are not justified.

(D) Both agree with this.

4. (26/2 #24) ~ E

Monica says that even though the public does not like the statue, that implies nothing about its artistic merit, and it should not be removed. Hector agrees with her about the statue's artistic merit but says that it should be removed because it does not benefit the public. E describes the principle they disagree over: whether the sculpture's artistic merit should dictate whether it is removed or not. Monica thinks that artistic merit is paramount, while Hector says the artistic merit is less important than public benefit in determining whether to remove it.

Principle Match

On Principle Match questions, the passage is a principle, as opposed to all the choices being principles. You are asked to identify a specific situation in the choices that is in line with the principle. Four of the answer choices will not match the principle, only one will provide information that meets the principle's requirements.

Principle Match questions are in the **Identify** family of questions. As such, you should read the principle only to understand its zone and standards, not to look for weaknesses. The choices must match the principle, so any choice that does not is considered to be "new" and can be eliminated as a Dud. These questions are often long because you have to analyze each choice to see if it fulfills the principle's standards. However, with practice they become more straightforward. Principle Match questions are less common than Support with Principle questions, so you must attack them efficiently when you do face them or they will take a long time to complete.

Query

Principle Match queries ask you which answer choice the principle in the passage justifies. Words like "judgment," "argument," or "statement" are used to describe the choices. "Judgment" and its synonyms refer to an evaluation of a situation. Example queries:

> "Which one of the following *judgments* most closely conforms to the principle above?"

> "The principle above, if established, would justify which one of the following *arguments*?"

Passage

The principles in the passages are generally conditionals:

> Bartenders should not over serve their clients, unless the client is a dashing man or beautiful woman.

Your job is to understand both their zone and their standards. That knowledge will help you work the choices effectively. In the passage above, the zone is bartenders and the standard is that they should only over serve clients who are attractive.

When reading the passage, **circle** the zone the principle applies to, and **underline** the standards. This special notation is just for Principle Match questions. Example principle:

> To be an effective leader in emergency situations, it is necessary to stay calm and to speak in a commanding tone.

Here are the notations we would make on the principle:

> To be an effective leader in emergency situations, it is necessary to stay calm and to speak in a commanding tone.

The zone, those the principle applies to, is effective leaders in emergency situations. The standards, what those in the zone are held to, are staying calm and speaking in a commanding tone.

Envision

When facing a principle with conditionals, you can read it carefully to understand it, or, if you need to, you can diagram it. Let us review what we can know from conditionals. Remember that when the indicator is true, then the requirement is also true. Example conditional:

Jen walks three miles around the park only when she is happy.

3 miles -> Happy

Example choice:

(A) Jen walked three miles around the park so she must be happy.

(A) restates the conditional in its normal form, so this choice is valid according to the principle. Any answer choice that does so is obviously correct.

You are more likely to see a correct answer choice state that because the requirement did not occur, the indicator must not have occurred either. Example:

(C) Because Jen is not happy, she did not walk three miles around the park today.

This is the Contrapositive, and you are much more likely to see this than the standard form of the conditional because it is more challenging to identify among the choices.

A choice can also make a less definite statement based on the conditional. For instance, a choice could say that if the indicator is not met, then that means that the requirement could occur or could not occur. Example correct choice:

(D) Jen did not leave the house today, so she did not walk three miles around the park, and we do not know her emotional state.

When the indicator is not true, we have no information on the requirement. Another example correct choice with ambiguous information:

(B) Jen is happy today, and I do not know whether she walked around the park.

Recall that the requirement only gives information about the indicator when the requirement **is not** met. Here the requirement is met, so we have no clue on the state of the indicator.

If you cannot diagram the principle, do not worry. Not diagramming the principle saves time. As long as you know the zone and standards, you can see whether a choice fits the principle.

Choices

The correct choice agrees logically with the principle in the passage, meaning that is has specific information that is in line with the standards of the principle. Example principle:

> In order to be a good teacher, one must be selfless.
>
> *Good teacher -> Selfless*

Example correct answer that agrees with the principle:

> (A) Sam is not selfless, and she should not be considered a good teacher.

Because the requirement is not met, the indicator is not either. Another example correct answer:

> (B) Frank is a great gym teacher so he must be selfless.

A gym teacher is a type of teacher, so it is within the zone of the principle. Because the indicator is met, the requirement must be as well.

Incorrect Choices

Incorrect choices on Principle Match questions often have information irrelevant to the principle because the zone discussed is not the one used in the principle. For instance, this choice is incorrect because its zone does not match teachers:

> (E) Bill is a great fireman and because of that I would consider him to be selfless.

The principle does not give us any information about firemen. That profession is outside of its zone.

Other incorrect choices simply contradict the principle:

> (C) Jim is selfish and never thinks of anyone other than himself, but he is a superb math teacher.

(C) is an opposite answer, because it goes against the principle and we wish to locate the choice that is in line with the principle.

22/2 #18

As you work this Principle Match question, be sure you understand both the zone and the standards of the passage.

> To classify a work of art as truly great, it is necessary that the work have both originality and far-reaching influence upon the artistic community.
>
> The principle above, if valid, most strongly supports which one of the following arguments?
>
> (A) By breaking down traditional schemes of representation, Picasso redefined painting. It is this extreme originality that warrants his work being considered truly great.
>
> (B) Some of the most original art being produced today is found in isolated communities, but because of this isolation these works have only minor influence, and hence cannot be considered truly great.
>
> (C) Certain examples of the drumming practiced in parts of Africa's west coast employ a musical vocabulary that resists representation in Western notational schemes. This tremendous originality, coupled with the profound impact these pieces are having on musicians everywhere, is enough to consider these works to be truly great.
>
> (D) The piece of art in the lobby is clearly not classified as truly great, so it follows that it fails to be original.
>
> (E) Since Bach's music is truly great, it not only has both originality and a major influence on musicians, it has broad popular appeal as well.

Query

We are told the passage is a principle and asked which argument it supports, so we know we are dealing with a Principle Match question.

Passage

> To classify a work of art as truly great, it is necessary that the work have both originality and far-reaching influence upon the artistic community.

As you read, circle the zone (truly great art) and underline the standards (originality + far-reaching influence on the artistic community).

Envision

For teaching purposes, we diagram the principle and its conditional. This is a good step early in your practice, but one you may wish to discontinue as your LR skills build. This conditional features requirement phrasing:

Great Art -> originality + influence

Contrapositive ("and" converted to "or"):

–Originality or -Influence -> -Great Art

With a good understanding of the principle, move to the choices.

Choices

(A) By breaking down traditional schemes of representation, Picasso redefined painting. It is this extreme originality that warrants his work being considered truly great.

We know that originality is a **requirement** of a work being great, but it does not indicate that a work is great. Originality is not sufficient to say that a work is great. Therefore, this argument is not supported by the principle. Dud.

(B) Some of the most original art being produced today is found in isolated communities, but because of this isolation these works have only minor influence, and hence cannot be considered truly great.

(B) tells that because the works have only minor influence, they cannot be great. This is in line with the Contrapositive we covered during our envisioning step. With a hit that works this well on this question type, select it and move on.

For teaching purposes:

(C) Certain examples of the drumming practiced in parts of Africa's west coast employ a musical vocabulary that resists representation in Western notational schemes. This tremendous originality, coupled with the profound impact these pieces are having on musicians everywhere, is enough to consider these works to be truly great.

Originality and influence are necessary qualities to classify art as great, but the principle does not tell that they are **sufficient**. (C) suffers from a similar problem to (A). Looking at our two diagrams makes it clear that this choice is not in line with the principle. Dud.

(D) The piece of art in the lobby is clearly not classified as truly great, so it follows that it fails to be original.

The principle does not describes qualities of art that is **not great**, so (D) cannot be in line with the principle. It has the wrong zone. Dud.

(E) Since Bach's music is truly great, it not only has both originality and a major influence on musicians, it has broad popular appeal as well.

Broad popular appeal? The principle does not mention this quality of great art. So, (E) introduces a new aspect to the standard. Dud.

*Principle Match Review

- Introduction
  - "Which one of the following judgments most closely conforms to the principle above?"
  - Find the situation in the choices that is in line with the principle in the passage.
  - These questions often take a long time to complete.
- Passage
  - The principle in the passage often contains one or more conditionals.
    - You usually will not need to diagram them.
  - Understand their zone and standards.
    - Circle the zone and underline the principle in the passage to help you understand it.
- Envision
  - The correct answer can restate the conditional.
  - Or the correct answer can state the contrapositive: because the requirement did not occur, the indicator did not either.
- Choices
  - The correct choice must be in line with the standards of the principle.
  - If a choice is outside the zone of the principle it cannot be correct.

*Principle Match Practice Questions

1. Credit card companies justify charging cardholders additional fees for late payments by asserting the principle that those who expose other individuals, companies, or institutions to financial risk should pay for that risk, and by pointing out that late-paying cardholders present a greater risk of default than other cardholders. Without late fees, the companies argue, they would have to spread the cost of the risk over all cardholders.

   The principle invoked by the credit card companies would, if established, be most usefully invoked in which one of the following arguments?

   (A) School authorities should use student activity funds to pay for student-caused damages to school property since, even though only a few students cause any significant damage, authorities cannot in most instances determine which students caused the damage.

   (B) Insurance companies should demand higher insurance rates of drivers of sports cars than of other drivers, since sports car divers are more likely to cause accidents and thus are more likely to require the companies to pay out money in claims.

   (C) Libraries should charge high fines for overdue books, since if they did not do so some people would keep books out indefinitely, risking inconvenience to other library users who might want to use the books.

   (D) Cities should impose high fines for littering. The risk of being caught littering is quite low, so the fine for those who are caught must be correspondingly high in order to deter people from littering.

   (E) Municipalities should use tax money to pay for the maintenance of municipal roads, since if individuals paid for only those roads they used, some important roads in remote areas would be inadequately maintained.

2. Claim: Country X's government lowered tariff barriers because doing so served the interests of powerful foreign companies.

   Principle: In order for a change to be explained by the advantage some person or group gained from it, it must be shown how the interests of the person or group played a role in bringing about the change.

   Which one of the following, if true, can most logically serve as a premise for an argument that uses the principle to counter the claim?

   (A) Foreign companies did benefit when Country X lowered tariff barriers, but consumers in Country X benefited just as much.

   (B) In the period since tariff barriers were lowered, price competition among importers has severely limited importers' profits from selling foreign companies' products in Country X.

   (C) It was impossible to predict how Country X's economic reforms, which included lowering tariff barriers, would affect the economy in the short term.

   (D) Many of the foreign companies that benefited from Country X's lowering tariff barriers compete fiercely among themselves both in Country X and in other markets.

   (E) Although foreign companies benefited when Country X lowered tariff barriers, there is no other evidence that these foreign companies induced the change.

3. People who receive unsolicited advice from someone whose advantage would be served if that advice is taken should regard the proffered advice with skepticism unless there is good reason to think that their interests substantially coincide with those of the advice giver in the circumstance in question

This principle, if accepted, would justify which one of the following judgments?

(A) After learning by chance that Harriet is looking for a secure investment for her retirement savings, Floyd writes to her recommending the R&M Company as an especially secure investment. But since Floyd is the sole owner of R&M, Harriet should reject his advice out of hand and invest her savings elsewhere.

(B) While shopping for a refrigerator, Ramon is approached by a sales person who, on the basis of her personal experience, warns him against the least expensive model. However, the salesperson's commission increases with the price of the refrigerator sold, so Ramon should not reject the least expensive model on the salesperson's advice alone.

(C) Mario wants to bring pastry to Yvette's party, and when he consults her Yvette suggests that he bring his favorite chocolate fudge brownies from the local bakery. However, since Yvette also prefers those brownies to any other pastry, Mario would be wise to check with others before following her recommendation.

(D) Sara overhears Ron talking about a course he will be teaching and interrupts to recommend a textbook for his course. However, even though Sara and Ron each wrote a chapter of this textbook, since the book's editor is a personal friend of Sara's, Ron should investigate further before deciding whether it is the best textbook for his course.

(E) Mei is buying fish for soup. Joel, who owns the fish market where Mei is a regular and valued customer, suggests a much less expensive fish than the fish Mei herself prefers. Since if Mei follows Joel's advice, Joel will make less profit on the sale than he would have otherwise, Mei should follow his recommendation.

4. Ethicist: A society is just when, and only when, first, each person has an equal right to basic liberties, and second, inequalities in the distribution of income and wealth are not tolerated unless these inequalities are to everyone's advantage and are attached to jobs open to everyone.

Which one of the following judgments most closely conforms to the principle described above?

(A) Society S guarantees everyone an equal right to basic liberties, while allowing inequalities in the distribution of income and wealth that are to the advantage of everyone. Further, the jobs to which these inequalities are attached are open to most people. Thus, society S is just.

(B) Society S gives everyone an equal right to basic liberties, but at the expense of creating inequalities in the distribution of income and wealth. Thus, society S is not just.

(C) Society S allows inequalities in the distribution of income and wealth, although everyone benefits, and these inequalities are attached to jobs that are open to everyone. Thus, society S is just.

(D) Society S distributes income and wealth to everyone equally, but at the expense of creating inequalities in the right to basic liberties. Thus, society S is not just.

(E) Society S gives everyone an equal right to basic liberties, and although there is an inequality in the distribution of income and wealth, the jobs to which these inequalities are attached are open to all. Thus, society S is just.

*Principle Match Explanations

1. (26/3 #25) ~ B

The principle is that those who expose other individuals, companies or institutions to financial risk should pay for that risk. B fits – sports car drivers expose the company to risk and should pay for it in higher rates.

2. (15/2 #21) ~ E

This query is dense. We are asked to choose the answer that is evidence for an argument that uses the principle to counter the claim. Counter the conclusion that Country X's government lowered tariffs because this served powerful foreign companies. The principle dictates that we show that the foreign companies in question did not play a role in lowering the tariff. This will counter the claim that they did, while using the principle as a measure of whether or not it can be shown that change can be explained by it serving the foreign companies' interests. Choice E works perfectly: there is no evidence that the companies induced the change. According to the principle, if it cannot be shown how the interests brought about the change, then it cannot be concluded that the change is explained by those interests.

(A), (B), (C), (D) do not provide evidence that the foreign companies did not bring about the change.

3. (18/4 #19) ~ B

Read the principle carefully. To rephrase it: if you get advice from a person without asking, and that advice sounds like it will help that person, you should be skeptical, unless there is good reason to believe that the advice will also help you in the situation being discussed.

(A) does not match the principle, because the principle would recommend that Harriet invest her savings with Floyd because it helps them both.

(B) The principle supports this judgment. Ramon has no reason to believe that the advice will also help him, so he does not take it.

(C) This advice is gained from asking, so the principle does not apply.

(D) The principle would recommend that Ron buys the book because their interests coincide here, but he doesn't so this does not match the principle.

(E) This advice does not help Mel, so the principle does not justify the judgment.

4. (24/3 #24) ~ D

The two conditions given are sufficient **and** necessary for declaring a society just. We know this from the words "when and only when." "When" tells us that fulfilling the two conditions is sufficient because it causes the outcome. "Only when" lets us know that the two conditions are required. The conditions are: 1) Each person has an equal right to basic liberties. 2) Inequalities in the distribution of wealth are not tolerated **unless** these inequalities are to everyone's advantage and are attached to jobs open to everyone. The second condition is complicated so we need to watch out for it. We work the choices:

A) The jobs to which the inequalities attached are only open to **most** people, not everyone, so the second condition is not fulfilled.

B) The society could be just if the requirements relating to the inequalities are fulfilled, but we simply do not have this information. Proclaiming it unjust is not logically viable with the information given.

C) We hear nothing about the first condition, so we cannot declare the society just.

D) This is logically correct. The first condition is not met, so the society is **unjust**.

Parallel Structure

On a Parallel Structure question, you are asked to match the structure of the passage to the structure in the correct choice. Just like on Argument Structure questions, you will be dealing with the abstract level of reasoning. The major difference here is that you have to go one step further because the choices are each individual arguments, not abstract descriptions of a structure. That extra step can require extra time. Identifying the passage's structure is crucial, but only half the battle. Parallel Structure questions are somewhat notorious because they are challenging and time consuming. So, you may wish to skip them when running out of time on a section.

Parallel Structure questions are in the Identify category, so take the passage as a given. The correct choice will have no new features/elements not found in the passage's structure. All Parallel Structure questions are arguments; there are no Fact-Groups.

Query

These questions come in two flavors: normal and Flawed Parallel Structure questions. The difference is that Flawed Parallel Structure questions have an invalid argument in the passage. Both subtypes easy to recognize. Normal Parallel Structure queries will ask you to match the method of argument:

> Which one of the following arguments is *most similar in its reasoning* to the argument above?
>
> The *pattern of reasoning* in which of the following is most similar to that in the scientist's argument?

Flawed Parallel Structure queries state that the passage's argument has a flaw or "questionable reasoning:"

> The *questionable* pattern of reasoning in the argument is most similar to that in which one of the following?
>
> The *flawed* reasoning in which one of the following is most similar to the flawed reasoning in the argument above?

Search vs. Destroy

Your approach depends on whether you can clear identify the underlying structure of the passage. Many Parallel Structure questions have **classic** argument structures, such as linking conditionals or using an analogy to disprove a point. The lists of argument types you compile for Argument Structure questions will help you spot the structure on this type. Likewise, on Flawed Parallel Structure questions, you will often spot the flaw; your list of flaws compiled for Flaw questions will help you here. When you have a firm grasp on the passage's structure or flaw, your mission is simple: work the choices to find a match. As you do so, eliminate choices that do not fit the structure. In this scenario, you are primarily on a search mission.

When you cannot get a firm grasp on the passage's structure, you will need to use a different approach. The LSAT-Writers put together some confusing and rare argument structures for the passages, so this situation will not be uncommon. In this case, use your understanding of the passage to eliminate answer choices that are missing a key element **or** add in a new element. This is a destroy mission: eliminate incorrect choices to zero in on the correct one.

What Must Match

With both the approaches just discussed, your job is to see which choices do or do not match the argument's structure. You must match the **main elements** from the passage's argument: its structure and validity.

Structure

If you have a hard time articulating the general structure of the passage, describe in general terms how it proceeds. Removing the subjects helps enormously. Look at this example passage:

> Computers are like cities, they require a certain level of internal order to function. Cities also require major energy inputs. Therefore, computers require energy inputs.

Assuming you couldn't figure out the structure of this argument above, you could mentally describe it to yourself by replacing the subjects with subject holders (here thing 1 and thing 2):

> *"Thing 1 is like thing 2, which requires something to function. Thing 2 also requires something else to function. Therefore, Thing 1 requires that something else too."*

This degree of articulation of an argument can help you deal with tough argument structures.

Validity

The other element you must match in the correct choice is validity, whether the argument is valid or invalid. The **correct choice** on a Parallel Structure question will be valid: its conclusion will be well supported by its evidence. This makes sense because the passage too has no flaws. So, any choice with a flawed argument is incorrect.

Alternatively, on **Flawed** Parallel Structure questions, the correct choice must feature an invalid argument to match the flaw in the passage. Any answer choice with a valid argument or a flaw different from the passage is incorrect.

Argument Pieces

Finally, the argument pieces in the correct choice must match the pieces in the passage. The nature of the conclusion and the premises of the choices must match the corresponding piece from the passage. A match in the conclusion is often the easiest to check. Let us say that a passage's conclusion is:

> All goats are superior companions to cows.

The correct choice must fit that. The choice below is incorrect:

> (A) Some frogs will go down river.

(A) is off in two specific ways, on two specific elements of the conclusion. The passage's conclusion talks about all goats, while (A) talks only about some frogs. That is a major subject change. Secondly, the passage's conclusion has a comparison: goats are compared to cows as companions. (A) has an event that the frogs will undertake, which is a very different type of information.

The following could be the correct choice because it matches the passage's parts:

> (D) Fish are better swimmers than otters.

Although the word "all" is not featured, the subject is still an entire group. The comparison regarding certain features is present as well.

The correct choices' premises must also match the passage's premises. For instance, if the passage uses an analogy as a premise, the correct choice must have an analogy premise as well. Any choice that does not is incorrect. Or, if the passage contains a conditional premise, then so must the correct choice.

What Can Be Different

The topic and ordering of the elements in the correct choice need not match the passage.

Topic

The structure, validity and argument parts in the correct choice will all match those in the passage. However, the topic of the choice does not have to match the passage. In fact, it rarely will. Many **incorrect choices** feature the same or similar subject matter as the passage. The LSAT-Writers tempt you to select a choice with a similar subject to the passage, but a different structure. Do not be fooled: the answer choice will likely not have a similar subject. For instance, a passage argument about birds will likely have a correct choice about something other than birds.

Ordering

Just like the topic, the **ordering** of the elements in the answer does not have to match the ordering of the elements in the passage. Premises and conclusions can come in any sequence without changing the underlying structure. Take a look at these two arguments:

> Stain Sweeper is the best stain removal pen available. All of its competitors cost more. And Stain Sweeper is available in more stores than any other stain removal pen. Price and convenience of purchase are the only important characteristics of a stain pen.

> Store availability and price are the only important characteristics of a stain pen. Stain Sweeper is available in more stores than any other stain removal pen and costs less than all of its competitors. Therefore, Stain Sweeper is the best.

These arguments have the same structure:

> Availability Premise -> Cost Premise -> How to Judge Premise -> Conclusion

Often, the correct choice will feature a different ordering of its argument parts than the passage. This makes it even more helpful that you can compare the different argument parts as a way of evaluating choices. That is often easier than figuring out an argument's structure.

Unique Traits

Parallel Structure questions require you to go where the passage takes you. Each one is unique and there is no universal best way to approach every Parallel Structure question. However, there is a superior way to approach each individual question. These questions can take a lot of time so you need to work the choices in a way that gets you to the correct answer quickly. Flawed Parallel Structure questions are a bit different. The best way to way tackle them is to identify the flaw in the blurb and then find that flaw in one of the choices.

On normal Parallel Structure questions, analyze the passage for **unique traits** that will help you answer the question efficiently. Perhaps the passage has a discernable overall structure, or maybe it has a slightly unusual conclusion. Whatever it may be, use that trait to your advantage when you work the choices. If the conclusion is distinct because it features a Reversal Error based on the conditional reasoning of the premises, then use the conclusion of each choice as a potential elimination tool. Or if the argument relies on an expert witness as evidence, that might be the angle to focus on initially.

All at Once

No matter how you work the choices, you will need to do many different things simultaneously. As you look for a specific structure you identified in the passage, declare choices Duds that do not match the conclusion. Eliminate choices with missing features and hone in on the choice that works. Some general guidelines for Parallel Structure questions:

- With simpler passages, matching the conclusion is usually more effective than the premises. The opposite is the case for more complex passage arguments: analyze the premises of the choices first.
- Always eliminate choices that do not match the validity of the argument.
- It is usually best to read all the choices. Only move on before reading all the choices if you are running low on time for the section and feel you have a good grasp of the passage.
- The process of elimination should be fluid and flexible. With a firm understanding of the passage's structure, you can eliminate choices in a **variety of ways**.
- Searching for an argument structure you envisioned is ideal, but this usually still requires eliminating wrong choices. Always be on the lookout for parts that do not match **structurally**.

19/2 #20

Please work through this Parallel Structure question.

20. Anyone who insists that music videos are an art form should also agree that television gave rise to an art form, since television gave rise to music videos.

The pattern of reasoning displayed in the argument above most closely parallels that displayed in which one of the following?

(A) Anyone who claims that all vegetables are nutritious should also agree that some vegetables are harmful if eaten in large quantities.

(B) Anyone who holds that avocados are a fruit should also hold that pound cake is lower in fat than some fruit, since pound cake is lower in fat than avocados.

(C) Anyone who dislikes tomatoes should also agree that some people do like tomatoes, if that person agrees that no taste is universal.

(D) A person who eats a variety of vegetables is probably well nourished, since most people who eat a variety of vegetables generally eat well balanced meals.

(E) A person who claims to prefer fruit to vegetables should also prefer cake to bread, since fruit is sweeter than vegetables and cake is sweeter than bread.

1) Query

"Pattern of reasoning" tells that this is a Parallel Structure question. There is no mention of flawed reasoning, so we know the passage is a valid argument.

2) Passage

This is a short passage, so read it carefully and think about in abstract terms.

Premise: TV gave rise to music videos

Conclusion: Those who say that music videos are an art form should agree that TV gave rise to an art form.

The conclusion talks about a specific subject with a belief (those who say that music videos are an art form). The premise supports the conclusion that because of the first belief (music videos are an art form) that subject should also agree with a second statement (TV gave rise to an art form). The premise works with the introduction of the conclusion to support the heart of the conclusion:

TV gave rise to videos. Videos are an art form.

Therefore…

TV gave rise to an art form.

3) Envision

Never spend time visualizing a good answer to a Parallel Structure question. Instead, make sure you understand the structure of the passage to the best of your ability. Also, state something about the passage in your own words, in your head. For this question we might say:

> *Someone who believes this thing about a group X, must also believe this thing about group Y, because of information about groups X and Y.*

4) Sort

(A) Anyone who claims that all vegetables are nutritious should also agree that some vegetables are harmful if eaten in large quantities.

(A) lacks the connecting premise between X and Y that we found in the passage, making it a dud. We need information that all nutritious things are harmful if eaten in large quantities. We only have:

"All vegetables are nutritious" and "some vegetables are harmful if eaten in large quantities."

(B) Anyone who holds that avocados are a fruit should also hold that pound cake is lower in fat than some fruit, since pound cake is lower in fat than avocados.

(B) works perfectly. The premise connection is about fat and the conclusion features the "anyone who believes this should believe that" structure. Avocados are connected to pound cake by the fat information, just like TV is connected to an art form by the music video information in the passage.

(C) Anyone who dislikes tomatoes should also agree that some people do like tomatoes, if that person agrees that no taste is universal.

We are not dealing with the same conclusion in (C). The passage features "if you believe X, then you must believe Y" with Y being a **different statement** involving some information about X, not the **opposite** of X. Also, the premise that no taste is universal does not connect the two groups in the conclusion; it separates them. Dud.

(D) A person who eats a variety of vegetables is probably well nourished, since most people who eat a variety of vegetables generally eat well balanced meals.

(D) is missing the second premise, and it also does not feature the "anyone who believes x" idea in the conclusion. Dud.

(E) A person who claims to prefer fruit to vegetables should also prefer cake to bread, since fruit is sweeter than vegetables and cake is sweeter than bread.

The evidence works differently in (E) because it draws an analogy, not a direct connection. Fruit being sweeter than vegetables and cake being sweeter than bread makes a connection about why the person who claims to prefer fruit to vegetables does so. Such a person prefers the fruit **because of its sweetness**. But the passage has a direct connection: TV gave rise to videos. There is no double explanation in the premise of the passage. Dud.

*Parallel Structure Review

- "Which one of the following arguments is most similar in its reasoning to the argument above?"
- Match the structure of the passage to the argument structure in the correct choice.
    - The choices are all complete arguments that you must analyze the structure of.
    - You will be dealing with the abstract level of reasoning with the passage.
    - The correct choice will not have any new elements.
- These questions tend to be time consuming and challenging.
- Flawed Parallel Structure query – "The **questionable** pattern of reasoning in the argument is most similar to that in which one of the following?"
    - These will use a synonym of the word "flawed."

Search vs Destroy

- When you can get a firm grasp on the passage's structure (or flaw on the flawed variety), work the choices to find a match.
    - Many of the arguments have classic structures or flaws that you can quickly identify.
- When you do not have a firm grasp on the structure, work each choice, using what you do know about the passage's structure to **eliminate** incorrect choices.
    - For instance, if you know the passage uses an analogy as evidence, you can eliminate any choice that does not.

What must Match

- The correct choice must match the structure, validity and pieces of the passage.
- Structure - If you have a difficult time identifying the underlying structure, describe how the argument proceeds in general terms.
    - To do so, replace the subjects in the passage with subject holders.
- Validity - The correct choice must match the argument's validity.
    - Normal Parallel Structure questions will have a correct choice with a valid argument.
        - Eliminate choices with flaws.
    - Flawed Parallel Structure questions will have a choice with a flawed argument.
- Argument Pieces - The conclusion and the premises of the choice must match the same piece from the passage.
    - It is easiest to check the elements in the conclusion, so start there.
    - Match likelihood and amount words.

What can be Different

- Topic - The correct choice will rarely have a similar topic to the passage.
    - Many incorrect choices will have the same topic as the passage to trick you.
- Ordering - The ordering of the elements in the answer does not have to match that in the passage.
    - Premises and conclusions can come in any sequence without changing the underlying structure.
    - The correct choice often changes the ordering of the argument parts to confuse you.

Unique Traits

- Figure out the best way to attack each Parallel Structure question you face.
- Look for unique traits of the passage that will help you answer the question efficiently.
- Find an angle and use it on the choices.
    - For example, if the passage has a distinctive conclusion, check all the conclusions in the choices.

*Parallel Structure Practice Questions

1. Various mid fourteenth century European writers show an interest in games, but no writer of this period mentions the playing of cards. Nor do any of the mid fourteenth century statutes that proscribe or limit the play of games mention cards, though they do mention dice, chess, and other games. It is therefore likely that, contrary to what is sometimes claimed, at that time playing cards was not yet common in Europe.

   The pattern of reasoning in which one of the following is most similar to that in the argument above?

   (A) Neither today's newspapers nor this evening's television news mentioned a huge fire that was rumored to have happened in the port last night. Therefore, there probably was no such fire.

   (B) This evening's television news reported that the cruise ship was only damaged in the fire last night, whereas the newspaper reported that it was destroyed. The television news is based on more recent information, so probably the ship was not destroyed.

   (C) Among the buildings that are near the port is the newspaper's printing plant. Early editions of this morning's paper were very late. Therefore, the fire at the port probably affected areas beyond the port itself.

   (D) The newspaper does not explicitly say that the port reopened after the fire, but in its listing of newly arrived ships it mentions some arrival times after the fire. Therefore, the port was probably not closed for long.

   (E) The newspaper is generally more reliable than the television news, and the newspaper reported that the damage from last night's fire in the port was not severe. Therefore, the damage probably was not severe.

2. Zachary: One would have to be blind to the reality of moral obligation to deny that people who believe a course of action to be morally obligatory for them have both the right and the duty to pursue that action, and that no one else has any right to stop them from doing so.

   Cynthia: But imagine an artist who feels morally obliged to do whatever she can to prevent works of art from being destroyed confronting a morally committed antipornography demonstrator engaged in destroying artworks he deems pornographic. According to your principle that artist has, simultaneously, both the right and the duty to stop the destruction and no right whatsoever to stop it.

   Which one of the following, if substituted for the scenario invoked by Cynthia, would preserve the force of her argument?

   (A) a medical researcher who feels a moral obligation not to claim sole credit for work that was performed in part by someone else confronting another researcher who feels no such moral obligation

   (B) a manufacturer who feels a moral obligation to recall potentially dangerous products confronting a consumer advocate who feels morally obliged to expose product defects

   (C) an investment banker who believes that governments are morally obliged to regulate major industries confronting an investment banker who holds that governments have a moral obligation not to interfere with market forces

   (D) an architect who feels a moral obligation to design only energy efficient buildings confronting, as a potential client, a corporation that believes its primary moral obligation is to maximize shareholder profits

   (E) a health inspector who feels morally obliged to enforce restrictions on the number of cats a householder may keep confronting a householder who, feeling morally obliged to keep every stray that comes along, has over twice that number of cats

3. The fact that tobacco smoke inhaled by smokers harms the smokers does not prove that the much smaller amount of tobacco smoke inhaled by nonsmokers who share living space with smokers harms the nonsmokers to some degree. Many substances, such as vitamin A, are toxic in large quantities but beneficial in small quantities.

   In which one of the following is the pattern of reasoning most similar to that in the argument above?

   (A) The fact that a large concentration of bleach will make fabric very white does not prove that a small concentration of bleach will make fabric somewhat white. The effect of a small concentration of bleach may be too slight to change the color of the fabric.

   (B) Although a healthful diet should include a certain amount of fiber, it does not follow that a diet that includes large amounts of fiber is more healthful than one that includes smaller amounts of fiber. Too much fiber can interfere with proper digestion.

   (C) The fact that large amounts of chemical fertilizers can kill plants does not prove that chemical fertilizers are generally harmful to plants. It proves only that the quantity of chemical fertilizer used should be adjusted according to the needs of the plants and the nutrients already in the soil.

   (D) From the fact that five professional taste testers found a new cereal product tasty, it does not follow that everyone will like it. Many people find broccoli a tasty food, but other people have a strong dislike for the taste of broccoli.

   (E) Although watching television for half of every day would be a waste of time, watching television briefly every day is not necessarily even a small waste of time. After all, it would be a waste to sleep half of every day, but some sleep every day is necessary.

4. Everyone who is a gourmet cook enjoys a wide variety of foods and spices. Since no one who enjoys a wide variety of foods and spices prefers bland foods to all other foods, it follows that anyone who prefers bland foods to all other foods is not a gourmet cook.

   The pattern of reasoning displayed in the argument above is most similar to that displayed in which one of the following?

   (A) All of the paintings in the Huang Collection will be put up for auction next week. Since the paintings to be auctioned next week are by a wide variety of artists, it follows that the paintings in the Huang Collection are by a wide variety of artists.

   (B) All of the paintings in the Huang Collection are abstract. Since no abstract painting will be included in next week's art auction, nothing to be included in next week's art auction is a painting in the Huang Collection.

   (C) All of the paintings in the Huang Collection are superb works of art. Since none of the paintings in the Huang Collection is by Roue, it stands to reason that no painting by Roue is a superb work of art.

   (D) Every postimpressionist painting from the Huang Collection will be auctioned off next week. No pop art paintings from the Huang Collection will be auctioned off next week. Hence none of the pop art paintings to be auctioned off next week will be from the Huang Collection.

   (E) Every painting from the Huang Collection that is to be auctioned off next week is a major work of art. No price can adequately reflect the true value of a major work of art. Hence the prices that will be paid at next week's auction will not adequately reflect the true value of the paintings sold.

5. Last year the county park system failed to generate enough revenue to cover its costs. Any business should be closed if it is unprofitable, but county parks are not businesses. Therefore, the fact that county parks are unprofitable does not by itself justify closing them.

   The pattern of reasoning in the argument above is most closely paralleled in which one of the following?

   (A) A prime-time television series should be canceled if it fails to attract a large audience, but the small audience attracted by the documentary series is not sufficient reason to cancel it, since it does not air during prime time.

   (B) Although companies that manufacture and market automobiles in the United States must meet stringent air-quality standards, the OKESA company should be exempt from these standards since it manufactures bicycles in addition to automobiles.

   (C) Although the province did not specifically intend to prohibit betting on horse races when it passed a law prohibiting gambling, such betting should be regarded as being prohibited because it is a form of gambling.

   (D) Even though cockatiels are not, strictly speaking, members of the parrot family, they should be fed the same diet as most parrots since the cockatiel's dietary needs are so similar to those of parrots.

   (E) Since minors are not subject to the same criminal laws as are adults, they should not be subject to the same sorts of punishments as those that apply to adults.

6. Large inequalities in wealth always threaten the viability of true democracy, since wealth is the basis of political power, and true democracy depends on the equal distribution of political power among all citizens.

   The reasoning in which one of the following arguments most closely parallels the reasoning in the argument above?

   (A) Consumer culture and an emphasis on technological innovation are a dangerous combination, since together they are uncontrollable and lead to irrational excess.
   (B) If Sara went to the bookstore every time her pocket was full, Sara would never have enough money to cover her living expenses, since books are her love and they are getting very expensive.
   (C) It is very difficult to write a successful science fiction novel that is set in the past, since historical fiction depends on historical accuracy, whereas science fiction does not.
   (D) Honesty is important in maintaining friendships. But sometimes honesty can lead to arguments, so it is difficult to predict the effect a particular honest act will have on a friendship.
   (E) Repeated encroachments on one's leisure time by a demanding job interfere with the requirements of good health. The reason is that good health depends on regular moderate exercise, but adequate leisure time is essential to regular exercise.

7. Paulsville and Longtown cannot both be included in the candidate's itinerary of campaign stops. The candidate will make a stop in Paulsville unless Salisbury is made part of the itinerary. Unfortunately, a stop in Salisbury is out of the question. Clearly, then, a stop in Longtown can be ruled out.

   The reasoning in the argument above most closely parallels that in which one of the following arguments?

   (A) The chef never has both fresh radishes and fresh green peppers available for the chef's salad at the same time. If she uses fresh radishes, she also uses spinach. But currently there is no spinach to be had. It can be inferred, then, that she will not be using fresh green peppers.
   (B) Tom will definitely support Parker if Mendoza does not apply; and Tom will not support both Parker and Chung. Since, as it turns out, Mendoza will not apply, it follows that Chung will not get Tom's support.
   (C) The program committee never selects two plays by Shaw for a single season. But when they select a play by Coward, they do not select any play by Shaw at all. For this season, the committee has just selected a play by Shaw, so they will not select any play by Coward.
   (D) In agricultural pest control, either pesticides or the introduction of natural enemies of the pest, but not both, will work. Of course, neither will be needed if pest resistant crops are planted. So if pesticides are in fact needed, it must be that there are no natural enemies of the pest.
   (E) The city cannot afford to build both a new stadium and the new road that would be needed to get there. But neither of the two projects is worth doing without the other. Since the city will not undertake any but worthwhile projects, the new stadium will not be constructed at this time.

8. Further evidence bearing on Jamison's activities must have come to light. On the basis of previously available evidence alone, it would have been impossible to prove that Jamison was a party to the fraud, and Jamison's active involvement in the fraud has now been definitively established.

   The pattern of reasoning exhibited in the argument above most closely parallels that exhibited in which one of the following?

   (A) Smith must not have purchased his house within the last year. He is listed as the owner of that house on the old list of property owners, and anyone on the old list could not have purchased his or her property within the last year.
   (B) Turner must not have taken her usual train to Nantes today. Had she done so, she could not have been in Nantes until this afternoon, but she was seen having coffee in Nantes at 11 o'clock this morning.
   (C) Norris must have lied when she said that she had not authorized the investigation. There is no doubt that she did authorize it, and authorizing an investigation is not something anyone is likely to have forgotten.
   (D) Waugh must have known that last night's class was canceled. Waugh was in the library yesterday, and it would have been impossible for anyone in the library not to have seen the cancellation notices.
   (E) LaForte must have deeply resented being passed over for promotion. He maintains otherwise, but only someone who felt badly treated would have made the kind of remark LaForte made at yesterday's meeting.

*Parallel Structure Explanations

1. (13/2 #8) ~ A

The argument shows that no evidence is present in places where evidence for the existence of a phenomenon (playing cards in Europe the 14th century) would likely to be found. It therefore concludes that even though it has been claimed to be true, it is unlikely that cards were played in Europe in the 14th century. Choice A matches this exactly: if there was a huge fire, it is likely that the newspapers and TV news would mention it. Because they do not, there probably was no fire.

(B) involves two sources of information with contradictory evidence, while in the passage both the writers and the statues have the same evidence: no cards were being played.

(C) There is no discussion of the existence of a phenomenon and evidence against it here. The conclusion here that the fire affected other areas involves moving beyond evidence as opposed to weighing known evidence to see if a phenomenon happened at all.

(D)'s conclusion is that something did happen, while the passage regards something not happening.

(E) involves taking one source of evidence over another, rather than two sources that both lead to the same conclusion as the passage uses.

2. (14/2 #15) ~ E

We must understand Cynthia's underlying principle/message and find a substitute for the scenario about the artist. The scenario she depicts includes a single person (the artist) simultaneously having a moral obligation to both prevent the pornographic art from being destroyed and no right to do so. This is illustrating a situation where the principle that Zachary lays out is shown to be contradictory. Zachary's principle is that people have the right and obligation to pursue an action they believe to be morally obligatory, and no one else can stop that person from doing so.

(A) doesn't match because there is no contradiction shown. The medical researcher will not claim credit for the work, and the other researcher's lack of moral obligation to do so does not interfere with that.

(B) Same as A: the two moral obligations work together, and there is no conflict.

(C) Zachary talks about moral obligations for the **people** themselves. The bankers are talking about governments taking the actions. Notice the big change in scope and meaning. With the artist the moral obligation involves the artist herself.

(D) The architect and the corporation's moral obligations are not necessarily contradictory.

(E) matches perfectly. The health inspector is morally obligated to do something that would impinge on the householder doing something that she believes she is morally obligated to do. Just like in the artist example, based on Zachary's principle, the health inspector is at an impasse.

3. (11/2 #25) ~ E

The argument works by showing that even though inhaling smoke is bad, inhaling a much smaller amount may not be that bad. This is supported by the use of a further piece of evidence: many substances are toxic only in larger quantities, but beneficial in smaller ones and this is supported by the fact that vitamin a works this way.

(A) does not match, because it does not use evidence about an analogous situation (like vitamin a) and it also does not indicate that a small amount of bleach may do the opposite of a large amount.

(B) argues that if a small amount is good, a larger amount is not necessarily better. The passage, however, argues that if a large amount is bad, a small amount is not necessarily bad.

(C) does not argue that small amounts of fertilizer can be ok by reference to an analogous situation.

(D) has a format that talks about how it is hard to say whether people will like the new cereal, which is different than talking about consuming a small amount of cereal vs. consuming a large amount.

(E) matches the format of the passage. Big quantities of TV are bad, but small quantities may even be good. The evidence comes from the fact that sleeping is this way as well.

4. (15/2 #18) ~ B

This argument consists of two logic statements that have a shared subject that allows us to get to a logical conclusion:

1. gourmet -> enjoy spices

2. enjoy spices -> do not prefer bland

"No one who enjoys spices prefers bland foods" is another way of saying "All who enjoy spices do not prefer bland foods." Therefore:

gourmet -> don't prefer bland foods

We get this from substituting in "do not prefer bland" for "enjoy spices" in the logic statement 1.

The contrapositive:

Prefer bland foods -> not gourmet

(A) is flawed. We cannot say that because a wide variety of artists are included in the auction that the Huang collection is by a wide variety. The Huang collection is part of the group being auction, but it does not mean that it shares that trait of being by a wide variety of artists.

(B) matches.

huang -> abstract

abstract -> not in auction

Therefore

huang -> not in auction

(C) is flawed:

Huang -> superb

Huang -> no Roue

We cannot reason anything about Roue from these two logical statements because they have no connecting subject.

(D):

Postimpressionist from Huang -> auctioned

No pop art from Huang -> auctioned

No pop art auctioned -> Huang

This conclusion (the third statement) must be true, but it is based on the single logical statement, not the combination of them like in the passage.

(E):

Huang auctioned -> major

Major -> no price can reflect

Prices paid -> will not reflect value of the paintings

We cannot conclude this about all the painting sold – only the Huangs.

5. (18/4 #20) ~ A

This argument is composed of three parts:

1. Park system was unprofitable

2. Businesses should be closed if unprofitable, but parks are not businesses

3. Therefore, the fact that the park system is unprofitable does not justify closing it

Part three is a synthesis of parts 1 and 2. The basic argument is that because the specific case in question does not fit one requirement for a certain course of action, it does not matter that it fits another requirement for that course of action.

(A) matches the structure of the passage, although the ordering of the parts of the argument is different. The fact that the documentary didn't attract a large audience is not enough of a reason to cancel it because the documentary was not on prime time.

(B) doesn't match because the OKESA company fits the requirement of manufacturing automobiles. The passage includes an entity that does not fit a requirement.

(C) does not match the structure, because the entity in question is shown to fall into the category discussed.

(D) has a structure very different from the passage. One group is shown to be close enough to another to be prescribed the same directions.

(E) shows that minors are different from adults in one way so they should be treated differently in another way as well. This is not at all the same structure as the passage which tells that parks fit one requirement but not another to be given a certain outcome.

6. (10/1 #25) ~ E

The logic in the passage works like this:

No equal wealth -> threatens democracy

because

Wealth -> basis of political power

Democracy -> needs equal political power

Without equal wealth, there cannot be equal political power and without equal political power, there cannot be democracy. The argument uses a chain of logic to support its conclusion: wealth is connected to democracy through political power.

(A) talks about two things being a dangerous combination, while the passage talks about one thing being necessary for another thing, which is necessary for a third thing. Different logically structures here.

(B) The "if" at the beginning indicates that this is a different logical structure. The passage says that inequalities "always threaten" democracy. The passage establishes a constant relationship between inequalities in wealth and democracy, while this choice talks about a conditional (if/then) relationship.

(C) is not a chain of logic like the passage uses.

(D) shows that being honest does not always have a set outcome. The passage says that inequalities always threaten democracy.

(E) matches the passage: Leisure is connected to good health through regular exercise.

No leisure -> threatens good health

because

Leisure time -> essential to regular exercise

Good health -> needs regular exercise

7. (11/4 #22) ~ B

This is a formal chain of logic. The numbers below track the individual parts.

Never P and L (1)

P will be a stop unless S (2)

S is not a stop (3)

(So P must be a stop) and L cannot be (4)

The logic works by setting up two groups that cannot go together (1) and an unless statement (2). These combine with a factual statement about which of the pair is not selected (3) and that leads to the conclusion (4).

(A) is different and the conclusion is flawed. The argument tells us that radishes will not be used, because there is not spinach to use with them. This does not lead to the conclusion that peppers will be used. The argument would support that conclusion by showing that radishes will be used, but it does the opposite.

(B): **Support P if M does not apply.**

Not support both P and C.

M does not apply, so P is supported and C is not.

The order of the logic statements is different but the format remains the same.

(C) Not selecting any play at all is different than the passage, where an unless statement is used to show that one of the two will be selected.

(D) Again, the argument uses a possibility where neither of the two groups will be selected. This is different from one of the groups being selected unless a third condition is met.

(E) These two groups are tied together – one does not make sense without the other – and the argument is centered on this. Very different structure than the passage.

8. (16/3 #22) ~ B

The passage concludes that a specific event must have occurred (new evidence). The support for that conclusion is that a second event occurred (Jamison's active involvement was established) and that second event would have been impossible without the first event (new evidence). The first event was a **necessary requirement** of the second event.

(A) does not contain the concept of on event must have occurred because another event did occur.

(B) matches the passage. Specific event must have occurred (Turner did not take her usual train), because a second event occurred (Turner seen in Nantes at 11) and the second event would not have been possible without the first.

(C) uses a different type of evidence because there is no must have occurred event. The evidence is simply that "there is no doubt that she did authorize it."

(D)'s structure does not match. Where is the concept of the conclusion being a required event for a second event to have occurred that did occur?

(E) LaForte could have felt badly treated about something other than being passed over for the promotion. Therefore, the conclusion is not a necessary condition for him having made the remark he made.

*Structure Problem Sets

Average (30)

19 / 2 # **16** Ⓐ Ⓑ Ⓒ Ⓓ Ⓔ
19 / 2 # **20** Ⓐ Ⓑ Ⓒ Ⓓ Ⓔ
19 / 4 # **2** Ⓐ Ⓑ Ⓒ Ⓓ Ⓔ
19 / 4 # **17** Ⓐ Ⓑ Ⓒ Ⓓ Ⓔ
19 / 4 # **25** Ⓐ Ⓑ Ⓒ Ⓓ Ⓔ
20 / 1 # **8** Ⓐ Ⓑ Ⓒ Ⓓ Ⓔ
20 / 1 # **25** Ⓐ Ⓑ Ⓒ Ⓓ Ⓔ
20 / 4 # **9** Ⓐ Ⓑ Ⓒ Ⓓ Ⓔ
20 / 4 # **15** Ⓐ Ⓑ Ⓒ Ⓓ Ⓔ
20 / 4 # **21** Ⓐ Ⓑ Ⓒ Ⓓ Ⓔ
21 / 3 # **14** Ⓐ Ⓑ Ⓒ Ⓓ Ⓔ
22 / 2 # **11** Ⓐ Ⓑ Ⓒ Ⓓ Ⓔ
22 / 2 # **13** Ⓐ Ⓑ Ⓒ Ⓓ Ⓔ
22 / 2 # **16** Ⓐ Ⓑ Ⓒ Ⓓ Ⓔ
22 / 4 # **7** Ⓐ Ⓑ Ⓒ Ⓓ Ⓔ
22 / 4 # **10** Ⓐ Ⓑ Ⓒ Ⓓ Ⓔ

---

23 / 2 # **11** Ⓐ Ⓑ Ⓒ Ⓓ Ⓔ
24 / 2 # **13** Ⓐ Ⓑ Ⓒ Ⓓ Ⓔ
24 / 3 # **17** Ⓐ Ⓑ Ⓒ Ⓓ Ⓔ
24 / 3 # **21** Ⓐ Ⓑ Ⓒ Ⓓ Ⓔ
25 / 4 # **19** Ⓐ Ⓑ Ⓒ Ⓓ Ⓔ
25 / 4 # **21** Ⓐ Ⓑ Ⓒ Ⓓ Ⓔ
25 / 4 # **22** Ⓐ Ⓑ Ⓒ Ⓓ Ⓔ
26 / 2 # **16** Ⓐ Ⓑ Ⓒ Ⓓ Ⓔ
27 / 1 # **1** Ⓐ Ⓑ Ⓒ Ⓓ Ⓔ
27 / 1 # **14** Ⓐ Ⓑ Ⓒ Ⓓ Ⓔ
27 / 4 # **22** Ⓐ Ⓑ Ⓒ Ⓓ Ⓔ
28 / 1 # **10** Ⓐ Ⓑ Ⓒ Ⓓ Ⓔ
28 / 3 # **7** Ⓐ Ⓑ Ⓒ Ⓓ Ⓔ
28 / 3 # **23** Ⓐ Ⓑ Ⓒ Ⓓ Ⓔ

Difficult (7)

19 / 4 # **16** Ⓐ Ⓑ Ⓒ Ⓓ Ⓔ
24 / 2 # **14** Ⓐ Ⓑ Ⓒ Ⓓ Ⓔ
26 / 3 # **16** Ⓐ Ⓑ Ⓒ Ⓓ Ⓔ
26 / 3 # **25** Ⓐ Ⓑ Ⓒ Ⓓ Ⓔ
27 / 4 # **24** Ⓐ Ⓑ Ⓒ Ⓓ Ⓔ
28 / 1 # **7** Ⓐ Ⓑ Ⓒ Ⓓ Ⓔ
28 / 3 # **26** Ⓐ Ⓑ Ⓒ Ⓓ Ⓔ

Grueling (17)

19 / 4 # **24** Ⓐ Ⓑ Ⓒ Ⓓ Ⓔ
20 / 1 # **19** Ⓐ Ⓑ Ⓒ Ⓓ Ⓔ
20 / 1 # **21** Ⓐ Ⓑ Ⓒ Ⓓ Ⓔ
21 / 2 # **24** Ⓐ Ⓑ Ⓒ Ⓓ Ⓔ
21 / 3 # **22** Ⓐ Ⓑ Ⓒ Ⓓ Ⓔ
22 / 2 # **18** Ⓐ Ⓑ Ⓒ Ⓓ Ⓔ
22 / 4 # **20** Ⓐ Ⓑ Ⓒ Ⓓ Ⓔ
23 / 2 # **25** Ⓐ Ⓑ Ⓒ Ⓓ Ⓔ

---

23 / 3 # **18** Ⓐ Ⓑ Ⓒ Ⓓ Ⓔ
23 / 3 # **24** Ⓐ Ⓑ Ⓒ Ⓓ Ⓔ
24 / 3 # **24** Ⓐ Ⓑ Ⓒ Ⓓ Ⓔ
25 / 2 # **22** Ⓐ Ⓑ Ⓒ Ⓓ Ⓔ
26 / 2 # **24** Ⓐ Ⓑ Ⓒ Ⓓ Ⓔ
26 / 3 # **23** Ⓐ Ⓑ Ⓒ Ⓓ Ⓔ
27 / 1 # **17** Ⓐ Ⓑ Ⓒ Ⓓ Ⓔ
27 / 1 # **26** Ⓐ Ⓑ Ⓒ Ⓓ Ⓔ
27 / 4 # **21** Ⓐ Ⓑ Ⓒ Ⓓ Ⓔ

*Structure Problem Sets ~ Answers

Average

19 / 2 # **16** C
19 / 2 # **20** B
19 / 4 # **2** A
19 / 4 # **17** B
19 / 4 # **25** B
20 / 1 # **8** B
20 / 1 # **25** D
20 / 4 # **9** B
20 / 4 # **15** B
20 / 4 # **21** D
21 / 3 # **14** D
22 / 2 # **11** E
22 / 2 # **13** C
22 / 2 # **16** E
22 / 4 # **7** C
22 / 4 # **10** E

23 / 2 # **11** C
24 / 2 # **13** D
24 / 3 # **17** A
24 / 3 # **21** A
25 / 4 # **19** A
25 / 4 # **21** C
25 / 4 # **22** C
26 / 2 # **16** C
27 / 1 # **1** B
27 / 1 # **14** B
27 / 4 # **22** E
28 / 1 # **10** D
28 / 3 # **7** C
28 / 3 # **23** D

Difficult

19 / 4 # **16** C
24 / 2 # **14** A
26 / 3 # **16** D
26 / 3 # **25** B
27 / 4 # **24** C
28 / 1 # **7** E
28 / 3 # **26** D

Grueling

19 / 4 # **24** A
20 / 1 # **19** D
20 / 1 # **21** A
21 / 2 # **24** A
21 / 3 # **22** C
22 / 2 # **18** B
22 / 4 # **20** B
23 / 2 # **25** B

23 / 3 # **18** C
23 / 3 # **24** D
24 / 3 # **24** D
25 / 2 # **22** A
26 / 2 # **24** E
26 / 3 # **23** B
27 / 1 # **17** B
27 / 1 # **26** D
27 / 4 # **21** D

Flaw

Flaw questions ask you to identify the error in reasoning in an argument. Because the choices describe the flaw in abstract terms, these questions are similar to Argument Structure questions. However, Flaw questions are more focused because you must describe a specific logical error, not how the entire argument functions. Nonetheless, prepare yourself to think and operate on the abstract level when dealing with Flaw choices.

Flaws are in the Identify category: the choices cannot contain outside information. The correct choice is an abstract description of the flaw in the passage, so no new information can come into play. The correct choice is backed by the passage, which should be accepted at face value; there is no need to think about the implications of the argument. Simply find the flaw and describe it in abstract terms.

Flaw questions are foreign at first, but they are also very learnable. While this chapter is lengthy, learning many potential flaws will help you understand other flaws and the answer choices.

Query

Flaw queries are easy to identify. The query will state that the argument is flawed or vulnerable and then ask you how it is flawed:

> "Which one of the following most accurately describes a *flaw* in the argument's reasoning?"

> "The reasoning in the argument is most *vulnerable to criticism* on the ground that the argument…"

Example Flaws

This section covers common flaws that appear in the passages. Learning them will help you identify these and similar flaws quickly. As you know, moving rapidly is crucial on the LSAT.

Speaker Attack

These arguments attack the source of an idea and not the **content** of that idea. This is a faulty way to disprove an idea, because the merits of an idea are not connected to the speaker of that idea. Even if the speaker is biased, the idea could still be sound. Speaker attack arguments can attack the actions, motives, or character of a speaker. Here is an example of attacking a speaker based on motive:

> Frank hates romantic movies and he does not wish to see this one with us. That is the only reason why he says this movie is poorly directed. Therefore, Frank is wrong and the movie has great direction.

Attacking a speaker based on actions:

> Julian claims that Bill needs to get more exercise. But Julian never gets off the couch himself. So, he is mistaken about Bill needing to be more active.

Example wording to describe this type of flaw:

> The argument draws a conclusion about the merit of a position based on the position's source.

> It is directed against the proponent of a claim rather than against the claim itself.

Number Percent Confusion

We covered these errors during the discussion on metrics. With a number percent confusion flaw, the author acts as if a percentage is equal to a number. Example passage:

> Jenna ate 75% of the raisins in that bowl, therefore she ate a lot of raisins.

75% is a large percentage of the raisins in the bowl. However, that does not mean that the total number of raisins was large. There could have been 4 raisins in the bowl and Jenna ate 3. A high percentage does not signify a high number.

Alternatively, an author can assume that a number is the same thing as a percentage:

> San Antonio has 1.2 million people, so it must have a high percentage of the population of Texas.

Texas has 24 million people, so 1.2 million is only 5% of the state's population. Big numbers do not necessarily signify a high percentage. Example choice wording:

> The argument confuses the number of people with the percentage of the state's population.

Internal Contradiction

Sometimes an argument will contain two pieces of information that do not fit together. This internal contradiction undermines the argument's conclusion.

> The church will supply healthy dinners for every attendee. Fried chicken, potato chips and milkshakes will be served tonight. Therefore, those interested in eating a balanced, natural diet need not miss the meal.

The description of the food at the dinner indicates that the food will be unhealthy, instead of healthy as claimed. Example choice wording for this flaw:

> The conclusion is based on contradictory evidence.

> Assumes what it later denies, resulting in a disagreement in the argument.

History Support

Arguments with a history support flaw assume because a phenomenon was true in the past, it is true now.

> Humans have fought among one another since the dawn of human history. Therefore, world peace will not happen in my lifetime.

The conclusion above is not supported because even though there has not been world peace, that fact may have be a poor predictor of what will happen in the author's lifetime. Example choice wording:

> Treats a statement about what has been the case historically as if it were a statement about what is the case now.

Recasting (or Straw Man)

Recasting involves manipulating the elements in an argument to make that argument easier to weaken or contradict. Recasting arguments are often the second argument in passages with two speakers. This classic flaw is often called a Straw Man, because an argument is turned into something much easier to knock down than the original argument. Here is an example:

> Bill: I don't think that buying a bunch of goats is the best way to use our lottery winnings.
>
> Ted: 50 goats is not very many goats, so you are wrong.

Ted responds to Bill by altering Bill's conclusion. Bill thought there were better **things** to spend money on, but Ted pretends that Bill is most concerned with the **number of goats**. Ted's response is to that aspect of Bill's argument, not his real conclusion. Example choice wording:

> Portrays opponents' views as more extreme than they really are.
>
> The argument recasts the claim in such a way as to make it easier to disprove.

Term Manipulation

Term manipulation consists of using multiple definitions of a key term in an argument. This is unsound logically: a term must mean the same thing throughout the argument. Term manipulation are also common incorrect answer choices on Flaw questions. Example:

> Mary claims that it is my job to clean the kitchen every night. But my job is construction. So clearly she is mistaken.

Mary uses the term "job" to mean responsibility, but the author uses evidence about his **profession** to dispute her claim. Example wording for choices:

> Equivocates with respect to a central concept.
>
> Fails to define the term.

Circular Reasoning

With this flaw, the argument **assumes** its conclusion is valid, which creates a circular argument. When the conclusion supports the premise just as much as the premise supports the conclusion, the argument is unsound. Logical arguments feature conclusions that are supported by their premises. Example:

> Michael Jordan is the best basketball player ever. He won the MVP award three times, and that only happened because he is the best player in history.

There, the evidence is supported by the conclusion, and the conclusion is, in turn, supported by the evidence. It is a circle. Example wording for choices:

> Presupposes the truth of what it sets out to prove.
>
> It assumes what it seeks to establish.

Overgeneralization

A few instances cannot support large claims, but arguments that suffer from overgeneralization act like they can.

> Exxon has planted 100 trees in Haiti and also reduced its factory emissions by 10%. Therefore, it is an ecologically friendly company.

Showing that Exxon is ecologically friendly is a large conclusion that requires more than two small examples of the company being good to the environment. Example wording in choice:

> Bases a general claim on a few exceptional instances.

Poor Analogy

This flaw involves using an analogy (a comparison between two concepts) when one concept is not similar enough to the other concept for the analogy to work as evidence.

> Just like an acorn grows into a might oak, Bill's tiny company will eventually make the Fortune 500.

The way acorns develop is very different than how small companies grow. Any acorn given time and nutrients can grow into a big tree. The same is not true for every small company; it is very challenging for any company to make the Fortune 500. Example choice:

> Treats two kinds of things that differ in important respects as if they do not differ.

Part and Whole Errors

Some arguments claim that something true about a part of a whole is said to be true of the entire whole. However, parts are different than each other, and all the unique parts comprise the whole. Even if one part has a certain trait, that is no indication that the whole will have that trait.

> Houston is very humid and receives a great deal of rainfall. So, Texas, the state the city is in, is rainy.

Texas is a large state with many different climates. Even though the coast near Houston receives a lot of rain, most of the state is actually arid. Example choice wording:

> The climate of the state is extrapolated from a single portion of the state.

Along these lines, other arguments claim that something true about a whole (in general) is said to be true of one part of the whole. Parts often have different features than their wholes. For instance, the best soccer team in the league can have some of the worst individual players in the league.

> The NBA is a very tall group. Because Aaron Brooks is in the NBA, he must be very tall.

Aaron Brooks is 5'10" and is only average height. He is part of a whole (NBA players) that is tall, but he does not have that trait that the whole does. Example wordings:

> What is true of Republicans in general is said to hold true for a single Republican.
>
> Without supporting evidence, states that what is true of a whole must also be true of its parts.

Limited Options

This flaw assumes that **only two possibilities** exist in a situation where there are more. This is a faulty assumption that leads to an invalid conclusion. Example argument with limited options:

> Bill and Ted are traveling through time and have just reached a new time and place in history. Because they are not in medieval Europe, they must be in the Wild West.

Bill and Ted could also be in South America during the Mayan's time, or in France during the French Revolution. The argument never shows that there are only two options, but the conclusion assumes that. Example wording:

> More options for the travel plan exist, but are assumed not to exist.

Note that sometimes the author does effectively show that only two possibilities exist and arguments like that are valid. They often feature an either/or:

> Katy will either give away her cats or put them up for adoption. Because she is doubtful they will find a good home through adoption, she will give her cats away to a friend.

Conditional Reasoning Flaws

You already know that errors in understanding a conditional can result in a Reversal or Negation Error. These flaws can appear in the argument itself or in the answer choices as incorrect choices.

Reversal Error (The requirement is said to indicate)

Here is an example of conditional evidence that could be used in an argument:

> If David works hard, he will become a successful writer.

Diagrammed correctly:	*Works Hard*	->	*Successful Writer*
Reversal error:	*Successful Writer*	->	*Works Hard*

An argument that uses the reversal error as a premise might look like this:

> Because David is a successful writer, that means he works hard.

The argument above confuses a requirement for an indicator. Think of Reversal Errors as mixing up which condition is the requirement and which is the indicator. The choices that describe these flaws are not easy to understand, but focusing on how the sufficient and required phrasing words are used can help. Here are examples of wording in these choices:

> Arguing that something is sufficient for a condition when it is actually a requirement of that condition.
>
> Taking the nonexistence of something as proof that a requirement for that thing also did not occur
>
> Mistakes a necessary condition for a sufficient one.

Negation Error (Indicator is said to be a requirement)

This is another flaw that can come from a conditional reasoning error.

> If a David works hard, he will become a successful writer.

Correct diagram:	*Works Hard*	->	*Successful Writer*
Negation Error:	*-Works Hard*	->	*-Successful Writer*

This confuses the indicator for the requirement. David working hard is **sufficient** for him to be a successful writer, but not **required**. There are potentially other ways that he could become a successful writer. Example choices:

> Confuses being sufficient to secure the job as being required to secure it.
>
> Mistakes a sufficient condition for a required condition.

Again, the choices will use the words sufficient and necessary (or indicates, required ,etc.). When you see such phrasing in a choice, tease out exactly what the choice is saying: how the relationship in the conditional is confused. Then, check that against your knowledge of the error in the argument.

Cause and Effect Flaws

Arguments often misuse causal reasoning. When you read a passage that says one thing caused another thing look for these flaws:

Single Cause

Any conclusion that says that there is a single cause or explanation for a situation is flawed. This is because there can always be **another** explanation or cause. Arguments assume that there are no other causes because they cannot argue against all the other explanations. This flaw is common in causation based arguments, so be on the lookout for it. Example choice wording:

> Overlooks other potential explanations for how the event arose.
>
> Assumes without justification that the said cause is the correct and only one.

Sequence signals Cause

Because one thing occurred before another does not mean that the first event caused the other.

> Mistakes a temporal relationship for a causal relationship.

Further, two events occurring together (known as a correlation) does not signal causation. There may be an alternate cause for both the cause and effect, or the cause and effect may occur together for other reasons. Example argument:

> Billy gets bad acne every time he takes a test in school. Billy's acne is caused by test taking.

It could be that Billy becomes stressed before a test, and the stress gives him acne. If that is true, then the test taking is not giving him acne, the stress is. Example choice wording:

> Confusing the coincidence of two events with a causal relation between the two.

Relationship Confusion

Sometimes, an argument will get the cause and effect relationship backwards. The stated effect may actually be the cause in the situation.

> Jean is a going dancing a lot more than she used to. She has also lost weight. The dancing has probably helped her lose weight.

Perhaps Jean is going dancing because she has lost weight and feels more comfortable in public. So the weight loss could be causing the increase in dancing, not the other way around.

> The author confuses an effect for a cause.
>
> Concludes that one thing caused another, when it is just as possible that the reverse is true.

Fortunately, the choices generally use the words "cause" and/or "effect." Search the choices for these words when an argument has a causal conclusion. That can be shortcut to the correct answer.

Unfounded References

Arguments that make an appeal for support are often flawed. These often appear in advertisements. Here are the three general categories of references and their potential flaws:

Appeal to Authority

Support from an authority is only effective evidence if it is a relevant authority, an authority in the field in question.

> Salesman: Carl Lewis is an expert track runner and has won many Olympic gold medals. He says that this is the best Blue Ray player that money can buy. Therefore, you cannot go wrong by purchasing one of these players today.

Carl Lewis may be an expert on sprinting and the long jump, but he is not a relevant authority for electronics. The fact that he likes this Blue Ray player is not effective evidence. Example wording for an appeal to authority error:

> Attempts to support a claim by citing an irrelevant authority.

Appeal to Numbers

The fact that a lot people believe a statement cannot serve as evidence that the statement is accurate.

> Josh: Almost the entire high school class thinks that a new basketball gym would benefit the school. So, we should begin looking for funding for the gym.

The high school class can be wrong or biased. Therefore, the conclusion has no sound evidence to support it. Example choice wording:

> A claim is believed to be true merely because a large number of people believe it to be true.

Appeal to emotions

Language dominated by emotions does not create a successful argument.

> Agatha's puppy is very sick. The puppy is her only friend and companion. On top of that, Agatha recently had her purse stolen. Therefore her boss should give her the day off from work.

This argument appeals to the emotions of the reader, rather than reasoning why she should get the day off. Valid evidence could be the risk of her causing problems at work due to her emotional state. But instead the argument is geared towards making one feel sorry for Agatha. Example wording:

> The argument appeals to emotion rather than reason.

Survey Errors

Passages with surveys as evidence often use surveys that themselves have errors. Weak evidence makes for a weak argument.

Poor Sample

Surveys require good samples: ones that are large enough and not biased in a way that could influence the results. For example, if you ask 100 dog lovers what kind of pet they prefer, most will answer dogs. An argument that used that survey as evidence for the conclusion that most people prefer dogs would be invalid. Example wording:

> Generalizes from a sample that is unrepresentative of the population in the conclusion.

Biased Question

If a survey asks "which is your favorite food: chocolate or granola?" that is a biased question. There are only two possible answers, so if asparagus is your favorite food, you cannot give that information. A conclusion based on that survey could claim that most people's favorite food is chocolate. But the survey is flawed because the question dictates the answers that people can give. Example wording:

> The argument is based upon a sample with a limited range of responses.

Evidence Misuse

There are many ways that an argument can misuse evidence. This is at the heart of a flawed structure: evidence that itself is valid is used in a way that does not support the conclusion. Usually, the conclusion is too strong to be supported by the evidence.

Lack Equals False

Because evidence does not prove a statement **true**, that statement is considered to be false.

> Nick says that Patrick got engaged to his long-term girlfriend last week. But Patrick hasn't told me he got engaged, so Nick must be wrong.

The author has no information that Patrick did not get engaged. The lack of evidence that he did get engaged is used to support the idea that he did get engaged, but logically that does not work. Example wording:

> Taking a lack of evidence for an idea as evidence that undermines that idea.

Lack Equals True

An argument assumes that because there is no evidence against a claim, the claim must be true. Again, a lack of evidence cannot serve as evidence itself.

> I have no reason to believe that the surprise party was not a success, so it was a great party.

Example wording:

> Treating the failure to establish that a claim is false as equal to a demonstration that it is true.

Partial Support

Some arguments misuse their evidence by having conclusions that are too strong based on the premises. Just because there is **some evidence** that a claim is true, that does not mean that the claim is true. It takes strong evidence to prove or disprove a claim. Strengthening a claim is not the same as proving it. All that applies for disproving a claim as well. Example argument:

> Joey is the best basketball player on his high school team. So, he will get a scholarship to Duke.

This passage uses evidence that supports the idea that Joey could get a scholarship to prove that he will get it.

> Uses evidence showing merely that its point may be true as support that the conclusion is true.

Irrelevant Evidence

Making a conclusion that is not supported by the evidence; the evidence is irrelevant to the conclusion.

> Mark Twain was an expert in dialect. He knew 37 different versions of the Mississippi dialect and even more dialects from Tennessee. Therefore, he was a great author.

Twain's dialect expertise does not relate to the conclusion that he was a great author. Example wording:

> It fails to give any reason for the judgment it reaches.

Working Flaw Questions

In general, to find a flaw in the passage, analyze how the premises are used to support the conclusion. The structure of the argument is generally where the flaw resides, not in the validity of a premise. Consider the information in the premises to be valid, but the way they are used to be suspect.

Compile a List

As you now know, there are many flaws that can appear in the passages. We recommend compiling a list of all the flaws in the correct answers that you face during the beginning of your practice (the first several weeks you face Flaw questions). To do so, write down the flaw in your own words based on the answer choice. Example:

Answer choice: "is directed toward disproving a claim that Marcia did not make."

Write down in your Flaw list: *disproves the wrong conclusion*

This list will help you identify flaws more quickly and also understand the wording used in the choices.

Envisioning

Flaw questions are ripe for envisioning; the flaw is right there in front of you. However, do not expect your wording of the flaw to match the correct choice. The LSAT-Writers love to obscure the meaning of Flaw choices with convoluted writing. So, do not spend much time articulating the flaw perfectly. Say the flaw in your own words, and describe it abstractly. The flaw should not feature any of the **specifics** of the argument. Your envisioned answer must describe generally how the argument is invalid and be applicable to a variety of arguments.

Be confident that you understand the flaw before moving to the choices. If you have no clue of the flaw at the envisioning stage, quickly return to the passage for another look at the argument.

Sorting the Choices

By the time you reach the choices, most of the work required by the question will be done. Read carefully to understand each choice. Flaw choices will likely take you longer to read than other types because the abstract description of an argument can lead to some strangely worded choices. Consciously slow yourself down, and be sure you understood a choice before you label it as a dud or hit.

The correct choice will often sound strange, not at all like you envisioned it. As you practice, you will find yourself grasping the meaning more quickly. The first few words of the correct choice often sound "off," so be sure you read and piece together the **entirety** of each choice.

Incorrect Choices are Other Flaws

Incorrect choices will reference a different flaw, not the one featured in the passage. The previous discussion of all the flaw types under the passage section is useful for understanding incorrect flaw choices.

Sometimes, an incorrect choice will discuss a different part of the passage (in abstract terms, of course) that is not the flaw. Remember: if it is not the flaw that the conclusion makes, then the choice is not correct. Do not select a choice merely because it rings true with something you read in the passage.

19/2 #1

Example Flaw question:

> Director of Ace Manufacturing Company: Our management consultant proposes that we reassign staff so that all employees are doing both what they like to do and what they do well. This, she says, will "increase productivity by fully exploiting our available resources." But Ace Manufacturing has a long-standing commitment not to exploit its workers. Therefore, implementing her recommendations would cause us to violate our own policy.
>
> The director's argument for rejecting the management consultant's proposal is most vulnerable to criticism on which one of the following grounds?
>
> (A) failing to distinguish two distinct senses of a key term
> (B) attempting to defend an action on the ground that it is frequently carried out
> (C) defining a term by pointing to an atypical example of something to which the term applies
> (D) drawing a conclusion that simply restates one of the premises of the argument
> (E) calling something by a less offensive term than the term that is usually used to name that thing

Query

"Most vulnerable to criticism" tells that we are dealing with a Flaw question. Read the passage first to identify the conclusion, and then pinpoint how the argument supports it.

Passage

The conclusion is that implementing the management consultant's proposal (reassigning staff) would cause the company to violate its own policy of not exploiting its workers. One premise is that the consultant said that the reassignment will increase productivity by fully exploiting the workers. The other premise is that the company has a policy of not exploiting its workers. The consultant used "exploit" as **get a lot of value out of**, and the company policy uses exploit to mean **abuse or mistreat**.

Envision

The argument features term manipulation. The term "exploit" is used in two different ways, and this double use is illogical.

Choices

With a good envisioned answer, we can quickly skim the choices for it:

> (A) failing to distinguish two distinct senses of a key term

(A) works. The argument does not distinguish the two uses of the term "exploit." The consultant uses the term one way, and the author another. During a section, you should select a match this strong and move on.

> (B) attempting to defend an action on the ground that it is frequently carried out

The argument never attempts to defend any action. Dud.

(C) defining a term by pointing to an atypical example of something to which the term applies

This is a tempting incorrect choice, because it mentions the misuse of a term. However, the argument does not define the term by pointing to an atypical example of something to which the term applies. An example of that would be saying that exploit means to mine resources from the ground. That is not the typical way that term is used. Dud.

(D) drawing a conclusion that simply restates one of the premises of the argument

(D) says that the argument uses circular reasoning. The argument does not: the premises are distinct from the conclusion. Dud.

(E) calling something by a less offensive term than the term that is usually used to name that thing

The argument does not call something by a less offensive term than is usually used to name that thing. An example of this would be calling a robbery a "borrowing expedition." (E) is a dud.

*Flaw Review

- "Which one of the following most accurately describes a flaw in the argument's reasoning?"
- Identify the error in reasoning in an argument.
    - You will be asked to describe the flaw in general terms.

Example Flaws

- Speaker attack – the author attacks the proponent of an idea, not the idea itself.
    - Example choice: "The argument draws a conclusion about the merit of a position based on the position's source."
- Number percent confusion - the author acts as if a percentage is equal to a number.
    - Example passage - "Jenna ate 75% of the raisins in that bowl, therefore she ate a lot of raisins."
- Internal contradiction – an argument contains two pieces of information that do not fit together.
    - Example choice - "The argument assumes what it later denies, resulting in a disagreement in the argument."
- History support – the author thinks that because a phenomenon was true in the past, it is true now.
    - Example choice - "Treats a statement about what has been the case historically as if it were a statement about what is the case now."
- Recasting - manipulating an argument to make that argument easier to weaken.
    - "Bill: I don't think that buying a bunch of goats is the best way to use our lottery winnings."

      "Ted: 50 goats is not very many goats, so you are wrong."
    - Example choice – "The argument recasts the claim in such a way as to make it easier to disprove."
- Term manipulation – using multiple definitions of a key term in an argument.
    - "Emo claims that it is my job to clean the kitchen every night. But my job is construction. So clearly she is mistaken."
    - Example choice – "Equivocates with respect to a central concept."
- Circular reasoning - the argument **assumes** its conclusion is valid, which creates a circular argument
    - "Michael Jordan is the best basketball player in history. He won the MVP award three times, and that only happened because he is the best player in history."
    - Example choice – "Presupposes the truth of what it sets out to prove."
- Overgeneralization – acting like a few instances of a phenomenon can support a large claim.
    - "Exxon has planted 100 trees in Haiti and reduced its factory emissions by 10%. Therefore, it is an ecologically friendly company."
    - Example choice - "Bases a general claim on a few exceptional instances."
- Poor analogy - using an analogy when one concept is not similar enough to the other concept.
    - "Just like an acorn grows into a might oak, Bill's tiny company will make the Fortune 500."
    - Example choice – "Treats two things that differ in important respects as if they do not differ."
- Part and whole - something true about a part is said to be true of the whole.
    - "Houston is humid and receives a great deal of rainfall. So, Texas, the state the city is in, is rainy."
    - Example choice – "The climate of the state is extrapolated from a single portion of the state."

- Limited options – the author assumes that only two possibilities exist when there are more.
  - "Bill and Ted are traveling through time and have just reached a new time and place in history. Because they are not in medieval Europe, they must be in the Wild West."
  - Example choice – "More options for the travel plan exist, but are assumed not to exist."

Conditional Flaws

- Reversal error – when an argument confuses a requirement for an indicator.
  - Assume the argument uses this conditional as evidence:
    - "If David works hard, he will become a successful writer."
  - The argument would then say that because David is a successful writer, he works hard.
    - This is not necessarily true.
    - When the requirement is true, we do not know if the indicator is true or not.
  - Example choices:
    - "Mistakes a necessary condition for a sufficient one."
- Negation error – confusing the indicator for the requirement.
  - Using the example above, the argument could say that because David does not work hard, he will not be a successful writer.
    - This is an error because working hard is sufficient to be a successful writer, not necessary (a requirement) for it.
  - Example choice – "Mistakes a sufficient condition for a required condition."

Cause and Effect Flaws

- Single cause - a conclusion that says that there is a single cause for a situation is flawed, because there can always be another explanation or cause.
  - Example choice – "Assumes without justification that the said cause is the only one."
- Sequence signals cause - assuming that because one thing occurred **before** another, the first event caused the second.
    - Example choice – "Mistakes a temporal relationship for a causal relationship."
  - An author can also assume that because two events **occurred together**, one caused the other.
    - It is possible that both were caused by a third event.
    - Example choice – "Confusing the coincidence of two events with a causal relation between the two."
- Relationship confusion - the author thinks that the effect is actually the cause.
  - Example choice – "Concludes that one thing caused another, when it is just as possible that the reverse is true."

Unfounded References Flaws

- Appeal to authority – this is only effective it the authority is relevant.
  - Example choice – "Attempts to support a claim by citing an irrelevant authority."
- Appeal to numbers – the fact that a lot of people believe a statement is used as evidence that the statement is true.
  - Example choice – "A claim is believed to be true merely because a large number of people believe it to be true."

Survey Flaws

- Poor sample – the sample in a survey is biased or too small.
    - Example choice – "Generalizes from a sample that is unrepresentative of the population in the conclusion."
- Biased question – the question asked in a survey partly dictates the answer.
    - Example choice – "The argument is based upon a sample with a limited range of responses."

Evidence Flaws

- Lack equals false – because evidence does not prove a statement true, that statement is thought to be proven false.
    - Example choice – "Taking a lack of evidence for an idea as evidence that undermines that idea."
- Lack equals true - because there is no evidence against a claim, the claim is assumed to be true.
    - Example choice – "Treating the failure to establish that a claim is false as equal to a demonstration that it is true."
- Partial support – the conclusion is too strong to be supported by the evidence given.
    - Example choice – "Uses evidence showing merely that its point may be true as support that the conclusion is true."
- Irrelevant evidence – the evidence is irrelevant to the conclusion.
    - Example choice – "It fails to give any reason for the judgment it reaches."

Working Flaw Questions

- Analyze how the premises are used to support the conclusion.
    - The premises are likely valid, it is how they are used that is in doubt.
- Compile a list of all the flaws in the correct answers during the beginning of your practice.
    - This will help you understand the wording used in the choices of these questions.
- Envisioning
    - **Always** envision on this type.
    - Say the flaw in your own words without mentioning any of the specifics of the argument.
        - Try to find a paraphrase of the flaw in the choices as your envisioned answer will probably not be an exact match.
        - The wordings used by the choices are often strange, so be ready for that.
- The Choices
    - Take your time reading the choices.
    - Make sure you understand each choice before labeling a dud or a hit.
        - Read the entirety of each choice to ensure that you are not thrown off by the first words.
    - Incorrect choices are often other flaws or describe another part of the passage.

*Flaw Practice Questions

1. Office manager: I will not order recycled paper for this office. Our letters to clients must make a good impression, so we cannot print them on inferior paper.

   Stationery supplier: Recycled paper is not necessarily inferior. In fact, from the beginning, the finest paper has been made of recycled material. it was only in the 1850s that paper began to be made from wood fiber, and then only because there were no longer enough rags to meet the demand for paper.

   In which one of the following ways does the stationer's response fail to address the office manager's objection to recycled paper?

   (A) It does not recognize that the office manager's prejudice against recycled paper stems from ignorance.
   (B) It uses irrelevant facts to justify a claim about the quality of the disputed product.
   (C) It assumes that the office manager is concerned about environmental issues.
   (D) It presupposes that the office manager understands the basic technology of paper manufacturing.
   (E) It ignores the office manager's legitimate concern about quality.

2. Scientific research at a certain university was supported in part by an annual grant from a major foundation. When the university's physics department embarked on weapons-related research, the foundation, which has a purely humanitarian mission, threatened to cancel its grant. The university then promised that none of the foundation's money would be used for the weapons research, whereupon the foundation withdrew its threat, concluding that the weapons research would not benefit from the foundation's grant.

   Which one of the following describes a flaw in the reasoning underlying the foundation's conclusion?

   (A) It overlooks the possibility that the availability of the foundation's money for humanitarian uses will allow the university to redirect other funds from humanitarian uses to weapons research.
   (B) It overlooks the possibility that the physics department's weapons research is not the only one of the university's research activities with other than purely humanitarian purposes.
   (C) It overlooks the possibility that the university made its promise specifically in order to induce the foundation to withdraw its threat.
   (D) It confuses the intention of not using a sum of money for a particular purpose with the intention of not using that sum of money at all.
   (E) It assumes that if the means to achieve an objective are humanitarian in character, then the objective is also humanitarian in character.

3. Of 2,500 people who survived a first heart attack, those who did not smoke had their first heart attack at a median age of 62. However, of those 2,500, people who smoked two packs of cigarettes a day had their first heart attack at a median age of 51. On the basis of this information, it can be concluded that nonsmokers tend to have a first heart attack eleven years later than do people who smoke two packs of cigarettes a day.

   The conclusion is incorrectly drawn from the information given because this information does not include

   (A) the relative severity of heart attacks suffered by smokers and nonsmokers
   (B) the nature of the different medical treatments that smokers and nonsmokers received after they had survived their first heart attack
   (C) how many of the 2,500 people studied suffered a second heart attack
   (D) the earliest age at which a person who smoked two packs a day had his or her first heart attack
   (E) data on people who did not survive a first heart attack

4. Editorial: In rejecting the plan proposed by parliament to reform the electoral process, the president clearly acted in the best interests of the nation. Anyone who thinks otherwise should remember that the president made this decision knowing it would be met with fierce opposition at home and widespread disapproval abroad. All citizens who place the nation's well-being above narrow partisan interests will applaud this courageous action.

   The reasoning in the editorial is in error because

   (A) it confuses a quality that is merely desirable in a political leader with a quality that is essential to effective political decision-making
   (B) it fails to distinguish between evidence concerning the courage required to make a certain decision and evidence concerning the wisdom of making that decision
   (C) it ignores the likelihood that many citizens have no narrow partisan interest in the proposed election reform plan
   (D) it overlooks the possibility that there was strong opposition to the parliament's plan among members of the president's own party
   (E) it depends on the unwarranted assumption that any plan proposed by a parliament will necessarily serve only narrow partisan interests

5. Many people change their wills on their own every few years, in response to significant changes in their personal or financial circumstances. This practice can create a problem for the executor when these people are careless and do not date their wills: the executor will then often know neither which one of several undated wills is the most recent, nor whether the will drawn up last has ever been found. Therefore, people should not only date their wills but also state in any new will which will it supersedes, for then there would not be a problem to begin with.

The reasoning in the argument is flawed because the argument

(A) treats a partial solution to the stated problem as though it were a complete solution
(B) fails to distinguish between prevention of a problem and successful containment of the adverse effects that the problem might cause
(C) proposes a solution to the stated problem that does not actually solve the problem but merely makes someone else responsible for solving the problem
(D) claims that a certain action would be a change for the better without explicitly considering what negative consequences the action might have
(E) proposes that a certain action be based on information that would be unavailable at the time proposed for that action

6. Historian: There is no direct evidence that timber was traded between the ancient nations of Poran and Nayal, but the fact that a law setting tariffs on timber imports from Poran was enacted during the third Nayalese dynasty does suggest that during that period a timber trade was conducted.

Critic: Your reasoning is flawed. During its third dynasty, Nayal may well have imported timber from Poran, but certainly on today's statute books there remain many laws regulating activities that were once common but in which people no longer engage.

The critic's response to the historian is flawed because it

(A) produces evidence that is consistent with there not having been any timber trade between Poran and Nayal during the third Nayalese dynasty
(B) cites current laws without indicating whether the laws cited are relevant to the timber trade
(C) fails to recognize that the historian's conclusion was based on indirect evidence rather than direct evidence
(D) takes no account of the difference between a law's enactment at a particular time and a law's existence as part of a legal code at a particular time
(E) accepts without question the assumption about the purpose of laws that underlies the historian's argument

7. Politician: From the time our party took office almost four years ago the number of people unemployed city-wide increased by less than 20 percent. The opposition party controlled city government during the four preceding years, and the number of unemployed city residents rose by over 20 percent. Thus, due to our leadership, fewer people now find themselves among the ranks of the unemployed, whatever the opposition may claim.

The reasoning in the politician's argument is most vulnerable to the criticism that

(A) the claims made by the opposition are simply dismissed without being specified
(B) no evidence has been offered to show that any decline in unemployment over the past four years was uniform throughout all areas of the city
(C) the issue of how much unemployment in the city is affected by seasonal fluctuations is ignored
(D) the evidence cited in support of the conclusion actually provides more support for the denial of the conclusion
(E) the possibility has not been addressed that any increase in the number of people employed is due to programs supported by the opposition party

8. The proper way to plan a scientific project is first to decide its goal and then to plan the best way to accomplish that goal. The United States space station project does not conform to this ideal. When the Cold War ended, the project lost its original purpose, so another purpose was quickly grafted onto the project, that of conducting limited-gravity experiments, even though such experiments can be done in an alternative way. It is, therefore, abundantly clear that the space station should not be built.

The reasoning in the argument is flawed because the argument

(A) attacks the proponents of a claim rather than arguing against the claim itself
(B) presupposes what it sets out to prove
(C) faults planners for not foreseeing a certain event, when in fact that event was not foreseeable
(D) contains statements that lead to a self-contradiction
(E) concludes that a shortcoming is fatal, having produced evidence only of the existence of that shortcoming

9. A standard problem for computer security is that passwords that have to be typed on a computer keyboard are comparatively easy for unauthorized users to steal or guess. A new system that relies on recognizing the voices of authorized users apparently avoids this problem. In a small initial trial, the system never incorrectly accepted someone seeking access to the computer's data. Clearly, if this result can be repeated in an operational setting, then there will be a way of giving access to those people who are entitled to access and to no one else.

The reasoning above is flawed because it

(A) makes a faulty comparison, in that a security system based on voice recognition would not be expected to suffer from the same problems as one that relied on passwords entered from a keyboard
(B) bases a general conclusion on a small amount of data
(C) fails to recognize that a security system based on voice recognition could easily have applications other than computer security
(D) ignores the possibility that the system sometimes denies access to people who are entitled to access
(E) states its conclusion in a heavily qualified way

10. The proposal to extend clinical trials, which are routinely used as systematic tests of pharmaceutical innovations, to new surgical procedures should not be implemented. The point is that surgical procedures differ in one important respect from medicinal drugs: a correctly prescribed drug depends for its effectiveness only on the drug's composition, whereas the effectiveness of even the most appropriate surgical procedure is transparently related to the skills of the surgeon who uses it.

The reasoning in the argument is flawed because the argument

(A) does not consider that new surgical procedures might be found to be intrinsically more harmful than the best treatment previously available
(B) ignores the possibility that the challenged proposal is deliberately crude in a way designed to elicit criticism to be used in refining the proposal
(C) assumes that a surgeon's skills remain unchanged throughout the surgeon's professional life
(D) describes a dissimilarity without citing any scientific evidence for the existence of that dissimilarity
(E) rejects a proposal presumably advanced in good faith without acknowledging any such good faith

11. Since anyone who supports the new tax plan has no chance of being elected, and anyone who truly understands economics would not support the tax plan, only someone who truly understands economics would have any chance of being elected.

The reasoning in the argument is flawed because the argument ignores the possibility that some people who

(A) truly understand economics do not support the tax plan
(B) truly understand economics have no chance of being elected
(C) do not support the tax plan have no chance of being elected
(D) do not support the tax plan do not truly understand economics
(E) have no chance of being elected do not truly understand economics

12. Without information that could only have come from someone present at the secret meeting between the finance minister and the leader of the opposition party, the newspaper story that forced the finance minister to resign could not have been written. No one witnessed the meeting, however, except the minister's aide. It is clear, therefore, that the finance minister was ultimately brought down, not by any of his powerful political enemies, but by his own trusted aide.

The argument commits which one of the following errors of reasoning?

(A) drawing a conclusion on the basis of evidence that provides equally strong support for a competing conclusion
(B) assuming without warrant that if one thing cannot occur without another thing's already having occurred, then the earlier thing cannot occur without bringing about the later thing
(C) confusing evidence that a given outcome on one occasion was brought about in a certain way with evidence that the same outcome on a different occasion was brought about in that way
(D) basing its conclusion on evidence that is almost entirely irrelevant to the point at issue
(E) treating evidence that a given action contributed to bringing about a certain effect as though that evidence established that the given action by itself was sufficient to bring about that effect

*Flaw Explanations

1. (7/1 #17) ~ B

Read both viewpoints and keep your eye on how the supplier does not respond to the manager's objection. The manager says that recycled paper is unacceptable because it is inferior. The supplier says that it is not inferior and then says that the finest paper long ago was made of recycled materials. Then the supplier talks about why paper was made of wood in the 1850s. None of this information **actually supports** the claim that recycled paper is not inferior. The points the supplier makes are irrelevant.

(A) There is no indication that the manager's viewpoint stems from ignorance.

(C) The supplier never talks about the environmental issues.

(D) The supplier never talks about technology of paper manufacturing.

(E) The supplier does address the concern about quality, but doesn't support his argument that it is of equal quality, which is what Choice B states.

2. (7/4 #11) ~ A

The foundation's conclusion, found in the final line, is that the weapon's research would not **benefit** from the foundation's grant. The evidence is that the university promised that none of the foundation's money would be used for weapons research. The flaw is evident here: the conclusion says that the research will not **benefit** weapons research, while the university promised that the foundation's **money** would not go **directly** to the weapon's research. The foundation's money is going somewhere in the university though, and it is very possible that wherever it goes will free up money that can be used on the weapon's research. That means that the research can benefit even if the foundation's money does not go directly to it.

(B) The conclusion does not overlook this; it deals only with the weapon's research.

(C) It is very unlikely that a university would do this, and is also not a flaw in the conclusion.

(D) The conclusion does not confuse these two things. It allows for the possibility that the money be used, but overlooks what is stated explicitly in Choice A.

(E) The conclusion does not make this assumption.

3. (10/1 #8) ~ E

We are asked what the argument leaves out that makes the conclusion incorrectly drawn from the evidence. The conclusion deals with people who **have** their first heart attack, but all the evidence is about people who **survive** their first heart attack. In order to draw the conclusion about non smokers have their first heart attack later than smokers, we need information about the people who **did not** survive their first heart attack. This information, combined with the information about people who did survive, will allow the conclusion to perhaps be properly drawn. The evidence will match the conclusion in discussing all first heart attack people, not just those people who survive.

On flaw questions, be on the lookout for changes in subject between the evidence and the conclusion.

(A) Severity does not matter.

(B), (C) Irrelevant to the conclusion about when people have their first heart attack.

(D) The conclusion is about averages, so the earliest age does not matter.

4. (10/1 #13) ~ B

Read the argument carefully and look for how the evidence does not add up to the conclusion. The conclusion is that the president acted in the best interests of the nation in rejecting the plan. The evidence is that the president knew that the decision would be met with fierce opposition. Obviously, the evidence does not support the conclusion. Just because the president knew it would not be a popular decision does not mean it is in the best interests of the nation. (B) is correct: the evidence supports the decision being courageous, but does not show it to be wise.

(A) Being brave may be a desirable quality, but the argument says it is **sufficient** for good decision making, while this choice says it is only **necessary**.

(C) The argument does not address this, but it is not necessary for the conclusion to be accurate.

(D) Again, it is not necessary for the argument to deal with this possibility. It is irrelevant to the conclusion that the decision was a good one.

(E) The argument does not depend on this assumption.

5. (10/4 #19) ~ A

The argument says that the practice of updating wills and not dating them can cause two problems: the execution not knowing which of several wills is the most recent and also not knowing whether the most recent will has been found. The argument then states that if people just dated their wills then the problem would be solved. But that would only solve the first problem created – knowing which will is the most recent out of several that are known. But the second problem – knowing whether the most recent will has been found – is not resolved by dating the wills and saying which will is superseded by which. Choice A states this clearly: the argument only gives a partial solution, but claims that it is a full solution to both problems.

(B) There is no need to make this distinction. The argument does not have to deal with the containment of the adverse effects – that is outside the scope of the argument, which only discusses preventing the problem.

(C) The proposed solution does not suggest making someone else responsible for the problem – it suggests a partial solution.

(D) This is not the flaw in the argument and there do not seem to be any obvious negative consequences to dating wills.

(E) The person writing the will would certainly have access to the current date.

6. (7/4 #22) ~ D

The flaw here is subtle. The Historian says that a law setting tariffs on timber imports from Poran was **enacted** during the third dynasty and that this supports the idea that timber trade occurred during this time. Next, the critic gives an analogy about how today there **remain** many laws that regulate activities in which people no longer engage. The critic does not understand the difference between a law being **enacted** at a certain time (which implies it is relevant because people are just putting it into place right then) and a law **remaining** in place (which **could** mean that it is no longer relevant, because it was enacted in the past). Always look for subtle verb changes in flaw questions.

(A) The critic's evidence is consistent with there having been a timber trade.

(B) This choice is tempting. The critic does not cite current laws, she instead brings up a general point about laws being outdated, which is relevant to the discussion at hand.

(C) This distinction between direct and indirect evidence is not relevant.

(E) The critic rejects the assumption in the historian's argument that the purpose of laws is sometimes to regulate certain activities.

7. (9/2 #22) ~ D

Conclusion: fewer people are now unemployed (last line of the passage). Notice that this is a paraphrasing of the longer conclusion.

Evidence: unemployment **increased** by less than 20% over the last four years when the party has been in office.

The evidence actually shows that **more** people are unemployed now than when the party took office, because unemployment increased. (D) is correct: the evidence goes against the conclusion, rather than for it.

(A) The conclusion does not deal with the claims made by the opposition.

(B) The conclusion says nothing about the decline being uniform.

(C) This is ignored, but that is alright because it is irrelevant to the conclusion.

(E) There is no increase in the number of people employed.

8. (10/4 #21) ~ E

The argument's conclusion is that the space station should not be built. The evidence is that the space station does not conform to the ideal for projects of first deciding a goal and then planning the best way to accomplish a goal. The passage states that limited-gravity experiments can be done in an alternative way, but never states that the alternative way is superior to the space station. Choice E is correct – the argument gives evidence that there is an alternative way to accomplish the goal, but never shows it to be fatal by saying that the alternative is superior to the path chosen.

(A) The argument never attacks the proponents of the space station.

(B) The argument does not assume that the space station is the wrong choice. It builds up an argument that simply does not hold together.

(C) It does not fault the planners for not seeing the end of the Cold War.

(D) There is no self-contradiction in the argument.

9. (11/2 #15) ~ D

Read the passage carefully looking for an error in the logic. The passage says that in the small trial, the system never incorrectly accepted someone seeking entrance to the data. That is really important, but that doesn't give us the full story on how well the system works, because it doesn't tell us how well it allowed the correct people access. The conclusion on the final line says that if the trial could be replicated on a bigger scale, then this would be a way of giving access to those people who are entitled. But we have absolutely no proof that it would give that access to those who are entitled. Reading the conclusion very carefully and seeing that the evidence only supports half of it is crucial on this question.

(A) The argument does not make this assumption. The evidence shows that the voice recognition system is potentially more secure than a password system.

(B) The argument says that if the result of the small experiment is replicated on a bigger scale, then the conclusion would be justified.

(C) It is ok if the system has other applications. That in no way is a flaw of the argument.

(D) This is just what we pre-phrased.

(E) Qualified here means in a limited way. The argument does do this: it qualifies the conclusion by saying that the experimental results need to be confirmed. This, however, is not a flaw, qualifying the conclusion in this way is appropriate in this argument.

10. (11/4 #19) ~ A

The argument is that clinical trials should not be done for surgical procedures because the effectiveness of surgical procedures depends on how good the surgeon is. This is in contrast to pharmaceutical drugs that are constant every time they are given. This argument is centered on the idea that clinical trials do not make sense when there is variability in the effectiveness of what is administered. The main flaw here is that the intrinsic differences in different surgeries may make trials very worthwhile. If a surgery is more dangerous than another no matter who is doing it, then surgical trials could discover that.

(B) The proposal is not deliberately crude and designed to elicit criticism. It is a reasonable proposal.

(C) The argument does not assume this. It only assumes that different surgeons have different levels of ability.

(D) This dissimilarity is indisputable and does not require scientific evidence. Some surgeons are better than others.

(E) The proposal is not a sensitive one that would require its advancement in good faith to be recognized.

11. (14/4 #9) ~ D

The conclusion is that only someone who understands economics would have a chance of being elected. The evidence is that **anyone** who truly understands economics would oppose the tax plan (and in order to have a chance of being elected, one must not support the tax plan). This is a **sufficient** condition: understanding economics is sufficient for not supporting the tax plan. The conclusion is based on understanding economics as being **necessary** to not supporting the tax plan. In reality, people who do not know anything about economics could be against the new tax plan, and the argument ignores this possibility.

(A) The middle statement in the passage directly contradicts this.

(B) The conclusion states the opposite of this.

(C) The argument does not overlook this possibility. The conclusion only states that someone must understand economics to have a chance of being elected.

(E) The argument does not ignore this possibility.

12. (15/2 #19) ~ A

The conclusion is that the finance minister was brought down by his aide. The evidence is that information that came from someone at the secret meeting between the finance minister and the leader of the opposition party allowed the article to be written that brought down the minister. The only person at the meeting, besides the **opposition party leader**, was the ministers aide. Clearly, the leader of the party that was running against the finance minister could have leaked the information to the newspaper just as easily as the aide. (A) is correct: the evidence that the aide was the only person at the meeting except for the two having the meeting provides strong support that the opposition leader leaked the info.

(B) The argument does not make this error. It does not assume that the leaked information would force the article, it only assumes that because the article could not have been written without the info and the article was written, the information must have been leaked.

(C) The argument does not make this error. In order for that article to be written, the information must have been leaked. There is no discussion of past articles.

(D) The evidence about who was present at the meeting is relevant because only someone who was there could have leaked the information for the article.

(E) We do know that the action was sufficient: he resigned because of the article.

*Flawed Parallel Structure Practice Questions

1. Biographer: Arnold's belief that every offer of assistance on the part of his colleagues was a disguised attempt to make him look inadequate and that no expression of congratulations on his promotion should be taken at face value may seem irrational. In fact, this belief was a consequence of his early experiences with an admired older sister who always made fun of his ambitions and achievements. In light of this explanation, therefore, Arnold's stubborn belief that his colleagues were duplicitous emerges as clearly justified.

   The flawed reasoning in the biographer's argument is most similar to that in which one of the following?

   (A) The fact that top executives generally have much larger vocabularies than do their subordinates explains why Sheldon's belief, instilled in him during his childhood, that developing a large vocabulary is the way to get to the top in the world of business is completely justified.

   (B) Emily suspected that apples are unhealthy ever since she almost choked to death while eating an apple when she was a child. Now, evidence that apples treated with certain pesticides can be health hazards shows that Emily's long held belief is fully justified.

   (C) As a child, Joan was severely punished whenever she played with her father's prize Siamese cat. Therefore, since this information makes her present belief that cats are not good pets completely understandable, that belief is justified.

   (D) Studies show that when usually well-behaved children become irritable, they often exhibit symptoms of viral infections the next day. The suspicion, still held by many adults, that misbehavior must always be paid for is thus both explained and justified.

   (E) Sumayia's father and mother were both concert pianists, and as a child, Sumayia knew several other people trying to make careers as musicians. Thus Sumayia's opinion that her friend Anthony lacks the drive to be a successful pianist is undoubtedly justified.

2. Advertisement: HomeGlo Paints, Inc., has won the prestigious Golden Paintbrush Award given to the one paint manufacturer in the country that has increased the environmental safety of its product most over the past three years for HomeGlo Exterior Enamel. The Golden Paintbrush is awarded only on the basis of thorough tests by independent testing laboratories. So when you choose HomeGlo Exterior Enamel, you will know that you have chosen the most environmentally safe brand of paint manufactured in this country today.

   The flawed reasoning in the advertisement most closely parallels that in which one of the following?

   (A) The ZXC audio system received the overall top ranking for looks, performance, durability, and value in Listeners' Report magazine's ratings of currently produced systems. Therefore, the ZXC must have better sound quality than any other currently produced sound system.

   (B) Morning Sunshine breakfast cereal contains, ounce for ounce, more of the nutrients needed for a healthy diet than any other breakfast cereal on the market today. Thus, when you cat Morning Sunshine, you will know you are eating the most nutritious food now on the market.

   (C) The number of consumer visits increased more at Countryside Market last year than at any other market in the region. Therefore, Countryside's profits must also have increased more last year than those of any other market in the region.

   (D) Jerrold's teachers recognize him as the student who has shown more academic improvement than any other student in the junior class this year. Therefore, if Jerrold and his classmates are ranked according to their current academic performance, Jerrold must hold the highest ranking.

   (E) Margaret Durring's short story "The Power Lunch" won three separate awards for best short fiction of the year. Therefore, any of Margaret Durring's earlier stories certainly has enough literary merit to be included in an anthology of the best recent short fiction.

3. Of the two proposals for solving the traffic problems on Main Street, Chen's plan is better for the city as a whole, as is clear from the fact that the principal supporter of Ripley's plan is Smith Stores. Smith Stores, with its highly paid consultants, knows where its own interest lies and, moreover, has supported its own interests in the past, even to the detriment of the city as a whole.

   The faulty reasoning in which one of the following is most parallel to that in the argument above?

   (A) Surely Centreville should oppose adoption of the regional planning commission's new plan since it is not in Centreville's interest, even though it might be in the interest of some towns in the region.

   (B) The school board should support the plan for the new high school since this plan was recommended by the well qualified consultants whom the school board hired at great expense.

   (C) Of the two budget proposals, the mayor's is clearly preferable to the city council's, since the mayor's budget addresses the needs of the city as a whole, whereas the city council is protecting special interests.

   (D) Nomura is clearly a better candidate for college president than Miller, since Nomura has the support of the three deans who best understand the president's job and with whom the president will have to work most closely.

   (E) The planned light rail system will clearly serve suburban areas well, since its main opponent is the city government, which has always ignored the needs of the suburbs and sought only to protect the interests of the city.

4. A letter submitted to the editor of a national newsmagazine was written and signed by a Dr. Shirley Martin who, in the text of the letter, mentions being a professor at a major North American medical school. Knowing that fewer than 5 percent of the professors at such schools are women, the editor reasons that the chances are better than 19 to 1 that the letter was written by a man.

   Which one of the following involves flawed reasoning most like that used by the editor?

   (A) Since 19 out of 20 home computers are purchased primarily for use with computer games, and the first computer sold today was purchased solely for word processing, the next 19 computers sold will almost certainly be used primarily for computer games.

   (B) Fewer than 1 in 20 of the manuscripts submitted to Argon Publishing Co. are accepted for publication. Since only 15 manuscripts were submitted last week, there is almost no chance that any of them will be accepted for publication.

   (C) Fewer than 5 percent of last year's graduating class took Latin in secondary school. Howard took Latin in secondary school, so if he had graduated last year, it is likely that one of the other Latin scholars would not have graduated.

   (D) More than 95 percent of the planes built by UBC last year met government standards for large airliners. Since small planes account for just under 5 percent of UBC's output last year, it is almost certain that all their large planes met government standards.

   (E) Since more than 19 out of every 20 animals in the wildlife preserve are mammals and fewer than 1 out of 20 are birds, there is a greater than 95 percent chance that the animal Emily saw flying between two trees in the wildlife refuge yesterday morning was a mammal.

5. In Sheldon most bicyclists aged 18 and over have lights on their bicycles, whereas most bicyclists under the age of 18 do not. It follows that in Sheldon most bicyclists who have lights on their bicycles are at least 18 years old.

Which one of the following exhibits a pattern of flawed reasoning most similar to that in the argument above?

(A) Most of the people in Sheldon buy gasoline on Mondays only. But almost everyone in Sheldon buys groceries on Tuesdays only. It follows that fewer than half of the people in Sheldon buy gasoline on the same day on which they buy groceries.
(B) The Sheldon Library lent more books during the week after it began lending videos than it had in the entire preceding month. It follows that the availability of videos was responsible for the increase in the number of books lent.
(C) Most of the residents of Sheldon who voted in the last election are on the Conservative party's mailing list, whereas most of Sheldon's residents who did not vote are not on the list. It follows that most of the residents of Sheldon on the Conservative party's mailing list voted in the last election.
(D) In the county where Sheldon is located, every town that has two or more fire trucks has a town pool, whereas most towns that have fewer than two fire trucks do not have a town pool. It follows that Sheldon, which has a town pool, must have at least two fire trucks.
(E) In Sheldon everyone over the age of 60 who knits also sews, but not everyone over the age of 60 who sews also knits. It follows that among people over the age of 60 in Sheldon there are more who sew than there are who knit.

6. According to sources who can be expected to know, Dr. Maria Esposito is going to run in the mayoral election. But if Dr. Esposito runs, Jerome Krasman will certainly not run against her. Therefore Dr. Esposito will be the only candidate in the election.

The flawed reasoning in the argument above most closely parallels that in which one of the following?

(A) According to its management, Brown's Stores will move next year. Without Brown's being present, no new large store can be attracted to the downtown area. Therefore the downtown area will no longer be viable as a shopping district.
(B) The press release says that the rock group Rollercoaster is playing a concert on Saturday. It won't be playing on Friday if it plays on Saturday. So Saturday will be the only day this week on which Rollercoaster will perform.
(C) Joshua says the interviewing panel was impressed by Marilyn. But if they were impressed by Marilyn, they probably thought less of Sven. Joshua is probably right, and so Sven will probably not get the job.
(D) An informant says that Rustimann was involved in the bank robbery. If Rustimann was involved, Jones was certainly not involved. Since these two are the only people who could have been involved, Rustimann is the only person the police need to arrest.
(E) The review said that this book is the best one for beginners at programming. If this book is the best, that other one can't be as good. So this one is the book we should buy.

7. Government official: Clearly, censorship exists if we, as citizens, are not allowed to communicate what we are ready to communicate at our own expense or if other citizens are not permitted access to our communications at their own expense. Public unwillingness to provide funds for certain kinds of scientific, scholarly, or artistic activities cannot, therefore, be described as censorship.

The flawed reasoning in the government official's argument is most parallel to that in which one of the following?

(A) All actions that cause unnecessary harm to others are unjust; so if a just action causes harm to others, that action must be necessary.
(B) Since there is more to good manners than simply using polite forms of address, it is not possible to say on first meeting a person whether or not that person has good manners.
(C) Acrophobia, usually defined as a morbid fear of heights, can also mean a morbid fear of sharp objects. Since both fears have the same name, they undoubtedly have the same origin.
(D) There is no doubt that a deed is heroic if the doer risks his or her own life to benefit another person. Thus an action is not heroic if the only thing it endangers is the reputation of the doer.
(E) Perception of beauty in an object is determined by past and present influences on the mind of the beholder. Thus no object can be called beautiful, since not everyone will see beauty in it.

8. If the majority of the residents of the apartment complex complain that their apartments are infested with ants, then the management of the complex will have to engage the services of an exterminator. But the majority of the residents of the complex indicate that their apartments are virtually free of ants. Therefore, the management of the complex will not have to engage the services of an exterminator.

Which one of the following arguments contains a flawed pattern of reasoning parallel to that contained in the argument above?

(A) A theater will be constructed in the fall if funds collected are at least sufficient to cover its cost. To date, the funds collected exceed the theater's cost, so the theater will be constructed in the fall.
(B) The number of flights operated by the airlines cannot be reduced unless the airlines can collect higher airfares. But people will not pay higher airfares, so it is not the case that the number of flights will be reduced.
(C) In order for the company to start the proposed building project, both the town council and the mayor must approve. Since the mayor has already approved, the building project will be started soon.
(D) Most employees will attend the company picnic if the entertainment committee is successful in getting a certain band to play at the picnic. But that band will be out of the country on the day of the picnic, so it is not true that most employees will attend.
(E) Either the school's principal or two thirds of the parent council must approve a change in the school dress code in order for the code to be changed. Since the principal will not approve a change in the dress code, the code will not be changed.

*Flawed Parallel Structure Explanations

1. (18/2 #17) ~ C

The flaw in the passage is that it explains the origin in a belief and then says that because in the original situation that belief was justified that it is justified in the current situation. However, just because Arnold's older sister always made fun of his achievements, that does not mean that Arnold's belief about his colleagues now "is justified." Just because there is an understandable reason for why Arnold feels that way, does not mean that his belief makes sense in the current situation.

(A) does not match the passage flaw, because Sheldon's belief is actually supported by the current example.

(B) is the same as A. Emily's belief formed long ago is justified by current data.

(C) matches the flawed passage exactly. Joan's early experience is said to be understandable and to justify her present belief that cats are not good pets, when in fact that old evidence she has does not support her current conclusion.

(D) does not match the structure of the passage because it is not about a single person's bias.

(E) does not match the passage, because it shows that Sumayia has experience that supports her belief.

2. (7/4 #14) ~ D ~ Parallel Structure (4)

Read the passage and state the reasoning flaw in your own words. The conclusion is that the Exterior Enamel is the most environmentally safe brand of paint manufactured in this country today. The evidence is that its environmental safety has **increased** the most over the last three years of any paint in the country. The flaw is that the conclusion is an absolute statement (Exterior Enamel is the most environmentally safe brand of paint, meaning no paint is safer), while the evidence is relative information: Exterior Enamel has **increased** in safety the most over three years. The evidence only means that Exterior Enamel has **improved** more than other paints. An absolute judgment involves a rating of something comparing it to other things in its class, whereas a relative judgment compares something to itself. Because of this mismatch, the evidence does not support the conclusion. For all the argument tells us, the Enamel could have gone from having horrible environmental safety to ok safety, which makes it the biggest **improver**. It could still not be even close to the environmentally safest brand available. (D) matches: Jerrod has shown the most academic improvement (relative judgment) but that does not mean that he is necessary ranked the highest (absolute judgment).

(A) deals with absolute evidence and an absolute conclusion.

(B) deals with absolute evidence and an absolute conclusion.

(C) deals with relative evidence and a relative conclusion.

(E) contains a different kind of conclusion, where the quality of one story is used to support the quality of earlier, other stories by the same author. This is a different structure than the passage.

3. (11/2 #17) ~ E

The stem tells us that the passage has faulty reasoning. So identify the flaw and understand it before moving to the choices. The conclusion of the argument is that Chen's plan is better for the city. The evidence is that the other plan is supported by Smith Stores who has supported its own interest in the past. The flaw here is that even though Ripley's plan is supported by biased parties, that does not mean that the plan itself is biased and not superior to Chen's plan. The argument does not come up with a valid reason in its conclusion of which plan is superior.

(A)'s argument makes sense. If the new plan is not in Centreville's interest, then Centreville should oppose the plan.

(B) does not have the flaw of the passage. If the consultants are well qualified then their recommendation is valid to use in supporting the plan.

(C) The mayor's budget has legitimate reasons why it is superior to the city council's budget.

(D) Nomura has valid reasons for being a better candidate.

(E) matches the flaw of the passage. Just because the main opponent is the city government and in the past the government ignored the suburbs, that does not mean that this plan is good for the suburbs. The evidence does not support the conclusion.

4. (14/2 #25) ~ E

In the passage, Shirley is probably a woman (due to the obvious evidence of her name), and the editor chooses to ignore that evidence and instead look at a general statistic that only explains the percentages of the large group of which Shirley is a part. Same with E, Emily saw an animal flying in between the trees so it was probably a bird (because it was flying), but she chooses to use statistics instead to come to a different conclusion.

(A) This argument confuses how statistics work, but it doesn't ignore better evidence in reaching its conclusion.

(B) confuses how statistics work, but just like A, doesn't ignore better evidence.

(C) Same as A.

(D) This argument assumes that the 5% of the small planes account for the 5% of large planes that did not meet the government standards. This is confusing the two groups (small planes and big planes) to be in the same group. But this not the same flaw as the passage.

5. (15/3 #22) ~ C

It could be that many more bicyclists are age 18 and younger, meaning that even though a smaller **percentage** of them have lights, the total **number** of them that have lights on their bikes could be higher than the number of bicyclists who are older than 18 and have lights on their bikes. This is a percentages and total number confusion. The percentage of bicyclists age 18 and older with lights on their bikes is higher than the percentage of bicyclists with lights under 18, but we do not know the total size of either of the two groups. Anytime you are dealing with a flaw in an argument, be aware that the argument may be comparing two groups in a way that is not appropriate because they groups are different.

(A) has no flaw.

(B) has a very different structure than the passage.

(C) matches. The two groups are residents who voted and residents who did not. Just because a higher percentage of the residents who voted are on the Conservative parties mailing list than not on it, that does not mean that most of the people on the list did vote. Perhaps there were tons of people who did not vote, so even though most of them were not on the list,

(D) misunderstands how percentages work, but it does not confuse percentages with total numbers like the passage.

(E) has no flaw. Everyone over the age of 60 who knits also sews, but the reverse is not true. So there must be more people who sew.

6. (7/1 #20) ~ B

The stem tells we are dealing with flawed reasoning, so read the passage looking for the flaw. The argument says that Dr. Esposito is going to run in the election and if she runs then Jerome will not run against her. The flaw is that the conclusion assumes that Dr. Esposito will be the **only** candidate in the election. Another candidate besides Jerome could run against her. In general terms, the flawed reasoning is assuming that there are limited options when there may or may not be. (B) matches the form and flaw: Rollercoaster could play on any other day of the week besides Friday.

(A) does not contain the flaw because the argument says that without Brown's being there, **no new large store** will be attracted to the downtown area. This means the conclusion can be correct.

(C) contains accurate logic because the conclusion is based directly off the evidence. If they were impressed by Marilyn and therefore thought less of Sven, then Sven probably will not get the job.

(D) limits the options with the line "since these are the only two people that could have been involved." That limitation makes the conclusion work.

(E) also contains a limitation – "the best." If that book is the best, then it is accurate to say that others cannot be as good.

7. (10/1 #20) ~ D

The argument describes two examples of censorship, and then states that a third situation must not be censorship. It confuses sufficient conditions for censorship with necessary ones. It may not be necessary to have the second scenario (that other citizens are not permitted access to our communications at their own expense to have censorship), but this is what the argument says. Work the choices looking for a match.

(A)'s logic adds up correctly. Unnecessary harm in an action makes it unjust, so if a just action causes harm, then it must be unnecessary harm, otherwise the action would be unjust.

(B) also has sound logic. The argument says that polite manners requires more than polite address, so it would take more than just seeing whether someone has a polite address to determine whether they have good manners.

(C) has a form clearly different than that in the passage. The argument says that because two different things have the same name, they both stem from the same cause. This is faulty, but not from a sufficient/necessary confusion.

(D) matches the form of the passage exactly. A deed risking the life of one for another is sufficient to be heroic. Then the argument implies that quality is necessary by saying that an action is not heroic if the only thing it endangers is the reputation of the doer.

(E) The conclusion here is that no object can be called beautiful since not everyone will see beauty in it. There is a gap in logic that an assumption could fill, but no necessary/sufficient error.

8. (11/4 #20) ~ D

The argument confuses a sufficient condition with a necessary one. If most of the residents complain, then that will be **sufficient** for the apartment to get an exterminator. The argument acts like this is this is **necessary** for the apartment to get an exterminator when it says that because most of the residents are not going to complain, the apartment will not get an exterminator. The apartment could still hire an exterminator regardless of how many people complain.

(A) has no flaw. Having enough funds is a sufficient condition that is met, so the theatre will be built.

(B) too has no flaw. It is necessary that the airlines collect higher fares if they want to reduce the number of flights. This condition cannot be met, so the airlines cannot reduce the number of flights.

(C) has a flaw, but not the right kind. The flaw here is that only one sufficient condition is met out of two, but the argument concludes like both have been met.

(D) matches because the argument confuses the committee being successful as necessary for getting most of the employees to attend, when it is actually sufficient.

(E)'s flaw is that only one of two conditions is required to get an outcome and the argument assumes because one of the conditions has not been met the outcome will not be reached. It is possible that two thirds of the parent council will approve the change and the code will be changed, but the argument acts like this is not possible, like both conditions are necessary.

*Flaw Problem Sets

Average (19)

PrepTest / Section	#	Question	Answer
19 / 2	#	**7**	Ⓐ Ⓑ Ⓒ Ⓓ Ⓔ
19 / 2	#	**23**	Ⓐ Ⓑ Ⓒ Ⓓ Ⓔ
20 / 1	#	**17**	Ⓐ Ⓑ Ⓒ Ⓓ Ⓔ
20 / 4	#	**14**	Ⓐ Ⓑ Ⓒ Ⓓ Ⓔ
20 / 4	#	**22**	Ⓐ Ⓑ Ⓒ Ⓓ Ⓔ
22 / 2	#	**7**	Ⓐ Ⓑ Ⓒ Ⓓ Ⓔ
22 / 2	#	**20**	Ⓐ Ⓑ Ⓒ Ⓓ Ⓔ
22 / 4	#	**21**	Ⓐ Ⓑ Ⓒ Ⓓ Ⓔ
24 / 3	#	**4**	Ⓐ Ⓑ Ⓒ Ⓓ Ⓔ
24 / 3	#	**12**	Ⓐ Ⓑ Ⓒ Ⓓ Ⓔ
25 / 2	#	**18**	Ⓐ Ⓑ Ⓒ Ⓓ Ⓔ
25 / 4	#	**8**	Ⓐ Ⓑ Ⓒ Ⓓ Ⓔ
25 / 4	#	**12**	Ⓐ Ⓑ Ⓒ Ⓓ Ⓔ
26 / 3	#	**13**	Ⓐ Ⓑ Ⓒ Ⓓ Ⓔ
26 / 3	#	**19**	Ⓐ Ⓑ Ⓒ Ⓓ Ⓔ
27 / 4	#	**7**	Ⓐ Ⓑ Ⓒ Ⓓ Ⓔ
28 / 1	#	**3**	Ⓐ Ⓑ Ⓒ Ⓓ Ⓔ
28 / 1	#	**19**	Ⓐ Ⓑ Ⓒ Ⓓ Ⓔ
28 / 3	#	**2**	Ⓐ Ⓑ Ⓒ Ⓓ Ⓔ

Difficult (18)

PrepTest / Section	#	Question	Answer
20 / 1	#	**14**	Ⓐ Ⓑ Ⓒ Ⓓ Ⓔ
21 / 2	#	**21**	Ⓐ Ⓑ Ⓒ Ⓓ Ⓔ
21 / 2	#	**22**	Ⓐ Ⓑ Ⓒ Ⓓ Ⓔ
21 / 3	#	**19**	Ⓐ Ⓑ Ⓒ Ⓓ Ⓔ
22 / 2	#	**12**	Ⓐ Ⓑ Ⓒ Ⓓ Ⓔ
22 / 2	#	**24**	Ⓐ Ⓑ Ⓒ Ⓓ Ⓔ
23 / 2	#	**23**	Ⓐ Ⓑ Ⓒ Ⓓ Ⓔ
23 / 3	#	**22**	Ⓐ Ⓑ Ⓒ Ⓓ Ⓔ
24 / 2	#	**1**	Ⓐ Ⓑ Ⓒ Ⓓ Ⓔ
24 / 3	#	**25**	Ⓐ Ⓑ Ⓒ Ⓓ Ⓔ
26 / 2	#	**15**	Ⓐ Ⓑ Ⓒ Ⓓ Ⓔ
26 / 2	#	**17**	Ⓐ Ⓑ Ⓒ Ⓓ Ⓔ
26 / 2	#	**20**	Ⓐ Ⓑ Ⓒ Ⓓ Ⓔ
26 / 2	#	**21**	Ⓐ Ⓑ Ⓒ Ⓓ Ⓔ
26 / 3	#	**10**	Ⓐ Ⓑ Ⓒ Ⓓ Ⓔ
26 / 3	#	**17**	Ⓐ Ⓑ Ⓒ Ⓓ Ⓔ
27 / 1	#	**25**	Ⓐ Ⓑ Ⓒ Ⓓ Ⓔ
28 / 3	#	**20**	Ⓐ Ⓑ Ⓒ Ⓓ Ⓔ

Grueling (24)

PrepTest / Section	#	Question	Answer
19 / 2	#	**22**	Ⓐ Ⓑ Ⓒ Ⓓ Ⓔ
19 / 4	#	**21**	Ⓐ Ⓑ Ⓒ Ⓓ Ⓔ
20 / 1	#	**22**	Ⓐ Ⓑ Ⓒ Ⓓ Ⓔ
20 / 4	#	**18**	Ⓐ Ⓑ Ⓒ Ⓓ Ⓔ
20 / 4	#	**20**	Ⓐ Ⓑ Ⓒ Ⓓ Ⓔ
21 / 2	#	**15**	Ⓐ Ⓑ Ⓒ Ⓓ Ⓔ
21 / 2	#	**25**	Ⓐ Ⓑ Ⓒ Ⓓ Ⓔ
21 / 3	#	**25**	Ⓐ Ⓑ Ⓒ Ⓓ Ⓔ
22 / 2	#	**10**	Ⓐ Ⓑ Ⓒ Ⓓ Ⓔ
22 / 2	#	**23**	Ⓐ Ⓑ Ⓒ Ⓓ Ⓔ
22 / 2	#	**25**	Ⓐ Ⓑ Ⓒ Ⓓ Ⓔ
22 / 4	#	**18**	Ⓐ Ⓑ Ⓒ Ⓓ Ⓔ
23 / 2	#	**19**	Ⓐ Ⓑ Ⓒ Ⓓ Ⓔ
23 / 2	#	**21**	Ⓐ Ⓑ Ⓒ Ⓓ Ⓔ
23 / 3	#	**16**	Ⓐ Ⓑ Ⓒ Ⓓ Ⓔ
23 / 3	#	**23**	Ⓐ Ⓑ Ⓒ Ⓓ Ⓔ
24 / 2	#	**23**	Ⓐ Ⓑ Ⓒ Ⓓ Ⓔ
25 / 2	#	**20**	Ⓐ Ⓑ Ⓒ Ⓓ Ⓔ
25 / 4	#	**17**	Ⓐ Ⓑ Ⓒ Ⓓ Ⓔ
25 / 4	#	**23**	Ⓐ Ⓑ Ⓒ Ⓓ Ⓔ
27 / 1	#	**23**	Ⓐ Ⓑ Ⓒ Ⓓ Ⓔ
27 / 4	#	**13**	Ⓐ Ⓑ Ⓒ Ⓓ Ⓔ
27 / 4	#	**25**	Ⓐ Ⓑ Ⓒ Ⓓ Ⓔ
28 / 3	#	**21**	Ⓐ Ⓑ Ⓒ Ⓓ Ⓔ

*Flaw Problem Sets ~ Answers

Average

Test / Section	#	Question	Answer
19 / 2	#	**7**	B
19 / 2	#	**23**	E
20 / 1	#	**17**	D
20 / 4	#	**14**	C
20 / 4	#	**22**	A
22 / 2	#	**7**	E
22 / 2	#	**20**	E
22 / 4	#	**21**	D
24 / 3	#	**4**	E
24 / 3	#	**12**	D
25 / 2	#	**18**	E
25 / 4	#	**8**	A
25 / 4	#	**12**	D
26 / 3	#	**13**	E
26 / 3	#	**19**	D
27 / 4	#	**7**	D
28 / 1	#	**3**	A
28 / 1	#	**19**	A
28 / 3	#	**2**	E

Difficult

Test / Section	#	Question	Answer
20 / 1	#	**14**	C
21 / 2	#	**21**	A
21 / 2	#	**22**	E
21 / 3	#	**19**	B
22 / 2	#	**12**	B
22 / 2	#	**24**	C
23 / 2	#	**23**	E
23 / 3	#	**22**	E
24 / 2	#	**1**	B
24 / 3	#	**25**	D
26 / 2	#	**15**	C
26 / 2	#	**17**	B
26 / 2	#	**20**	C
26 / 2	#	**21**	E
26 / 3	#	**10**	D
26 / 3	#	**17**	D
27 / 1	#	**25**	B
28 / 3	#	**20**	B

Grueling

Test / Section	#	Question	Answer
19 / 2	#	**22**	D
19 / 4	#	**21**	C
20 / 1	#	**22**	E
20 / 4	#	**18**	A
20 / 4	#	**20**	E
21 / 2	#	**15**	A
21 / 2	#	**25**	E
21 / 3	#	**25**	E
22 / 2	#	**10**	B
22 / 2	#	**23**	E
22 / 2	#	**25**	B
22 / 4	#	**18**	B
23 / 2	#	**19**	B
23 / 2	#	**21**	E
23 / 3	#	**16**	C
23 / 3	#	**23**	B
24 / 2	#	**23**	A
25 / 2	#	**20**	D
25 / 4	#	**17**	B
25 / 4	#	**23**	B
27 / 1	#	**23**	C
27 / 4	#	**13**	D
27 / 4	#	**25**	E
28 / 3	#	**21**	D

Reading Comprehension

Introduction and Reading a Passage

The Reading Comprehension (or RC) section asks you to efficiently read challenging passages and then answer questions regarding them. You have not seen many of these question types elsewhere, so we will break them down in detail. We will also show you how to effectively read and make notations on a passage, called "marking" the passage. Whether you consider yourself a strong or mediocre reader, studying the particular twists of the RC section will help you earn the most points you can. Of course, the more you practice RC questions, the better and faster you will become on them, but you will get much more out of your practice with a solid theoretical understanding on how to tackle the passages.

Section Structure

The LSAT has a single scored Reading Comprehension section that comprises 27% of your total LSAT score, making it the single most important section on the test. If you encounter two Reading Comprehension sections on your official LSAT, one will be experimental and not count towards your score, while the other will be scored. It is difficult to know which section counts toward your score during your official test.

A Reading Comprehension section has four passage sets, each made up of one or two passages followed by 5 to 8 questions. Three of the passage sets will have a single long passage of approximately 500 words. One passage set, called the Comparative Reading set or Dual Passage set, has two shorter passages that relate to the same topic. This type of passage set was introduced on the June 2007 LSAT (the free LSAT test available on LSAC). To practice on this passage set type, you must take Preptests numbered 52 and higher. The Comparative Reading set can appear anywhere among the other three passage sets.

An example layout for an RC section:

Passage Set	Questions
One Long Passage	6
Two Short Passages (Comparative Reading)	8
One Long Passage	7
One Long Passage	6

You will have 35 minutes to complete the 27 questions in this section. This averages out to 8 minutes and 45 seconds per passage set. **On average**, you have less than nine minutes to read the passage or passages and to answer all the questions. However, some passage sets are designed to take longer than others. How long you spend on a passage set will vary according to the number and difficulty of the questions in that set. For instance, in the example layout above, the Comparative Reading set with eight questions might take the average student eleven minutes, while the first passage set with only six questions might take only seven minutes. Through practice, you will learn how to appropriately pace yourself on this section.

The time limit is one of the major challenges of the RC section. Much of this guide will focus on teaching you how to work more efficiently – how to answer more questions correctly in less time. Yet initially many of the techniques will slow you down. With practice you will find they help you work more quickly through the section.

Official Directions

Read through the RC directions now so that you feel comfortable with them. Do not waste time looking at them on your test day:

> Each passage in this section is followed by a group of questions to be answered on the basis of what is stated or implied in the passage. For some of the questions, more than one of the choices could conceivably answer the question. However, you are to *choose the best answer*; that is, the response that most accurately and completely answers the question, and blacken the corresponding space on your answer sheet.

You are asked to find the "best" answer among those given. There may be no absolutely "correct" or perfect answer; several answer choices may have parts of them that work. Some answers may be correct but too narrow in scope (the range of information they cover). Other answers may be generally correct but too broad to be supported by the passage. Some answers will contain phrases from the passage that make that answer sound good, but the order of the wording has been distorted or a piece has been added that makes the choice incorrect. We will highlight these and similar faults when we talk about the types of incorrect answers.

Read through All the Choices

For now, just remember that because the incorrect choices sound quite appealing, you should read through **all** of the answer choices to make sure you have chosen the best one. The exception to this rule is when you are **extremely** confident you have found the correct choice. Wouldn't it be quicker to move on as soon as you find a correct answer? The test makers realize these are typical instincts and may deliberately place an attractive but incorrect answer just before the right answer, leading impatient test takers to choose the wrong answer and move on. We will discuss better ways to maximize your time throughout this guide.

Common Knowledge Required

The test makers claim that no extra/outside knowledge is required to answer the questions beyond common knowledge that any college graduate could be expected to know. What does common knowledge mean? The test makers will expect you to have **some** understanding of complex systems and ideas from various academic fields (economics, history, etc.) but no in depth knowledge. Some of the vocabulary and concepts used are on the edge of common knowledge, and you will find that technical terms used in the passages are usually defined in the passage or surrounded by context that alert readers will be able to use. Sometimes a Reading Comprehension passage will force you to learn new ideas. But in general, all the information you need to answer the questions is right there in the passage.

Why RC Matters

As this section has the most questions of any section on the test, it matters a great deal for your LSAT score. It is on the test because you will be doing so much of this type of in-depth reading as a law student and lawyer. While your practice now is motivated by excelling on the LSAT, the skills of reading for detail, logical consequences, and comprehensive understanding will serve you well as you continue in your law career.

The Passages

The passage subjects break down into these general categories: natural sciences, social sciences, humanities and law. While it is impossible to predict what specific topics you will see on your test day, the typical passage will include one science passage, one humanities passage, one law passage, and a history or economics passage. The passages are often excerpted from scholarly journals and have a dense, academic feel to them.

Difficulty is Hard to Predict

The content of the passage is largely unconnected to its difficulty level. Some students are less comfortable with natural science passages (biology, chemistry, physics topics), but these typically do not contain harder questions. However, students do perform a little better on passages that feature topics they are more comfortable with. We will discuss how to use this to your advantage later on.

Complexity

One characteristic that most passages share is complexity: they rarely allow a simple understanding. Some descriptive or informative passages may not explicitly include the author's opinion; other passages will include not only the author's opinion, but the argument and counterargument of different groups as well. We will discuss the best way to keep track of these different speakers.

Although the content and style will vary, you are always asked for the same type of information from the passage, such as the main conclusion, specific details, the function and interaction of certain details (inferences), what statements the author would agree with, etc. You will likely find the Reading Comprehension passages full of challenging language, complex details, and possibly many subtle switches in perspective. Get ready to read closely.

Open Book

The Reading Comprehension section is an open book test: the passage is front of you, and you may refer back to it as much as you want as you complete the questions. Still, you must use the passage as quickly and wisely as possible due to the tight time constraint. We recommend that you read, not skim, the passage, and then move to the questions. The time pressure means your initial reading of the passage must be a fairly thorough one because the complexity of the passages makes quicker readings ineffective.

Approaching a Passage Set

The best way to attack each passage set is comprised of two steps:

1. Do a **thorough** reading of the passage (or passages) to form a solid understanding of it. Do not skim the passage. Mark the passage as you read.
2. Answer the questions. Refer back to the passage to answer individual questions as necessary.

Skimming Does Not Work

You may have heard of other strategies for approaching a passage set, such as pre-reading the questions before reading the passage, or skimming the first and last paragraphs of the passage. Reading the questions before the passage is ineffective because that forces you to hold extra information in mind as you work the passage. The passages are complex enough; you do not need to add to your cognitive load as you work through them. And skimming the passage then working the questions does not work well. The passages are no cake-walk. You need to read every sentence of the passage somewhat carefully to understand the complexities of the passage. Skimming does not give you the clarity needed to work the questions. Skimming is especially dangerous because then you will recognize certain phrases in the answers, but not have the proper understanding to tell you if the test makers have distorted or misused them.

The "passage first, questions second" strategy we recommend will help you answer the questions correctly and quickly. With one thorough reading and marking of the passage, you will make sense of it. As you read the passage, you may **very rarely** find yourself looking back at part of a paragraph you have already read for clarification. That is fine. But once you have finished reading the passage, you will have a solid understanding of the author's points. After that, you will only need to dip back into the passage here and there to get specific information you need to answer questions.

Reading Carefully Is Crucial

LSAT passages are dense and complicated. You must take some time to decipher them. The questions and answers are designed to confuse you if you do not understand the subtleties of the passage. Skipping over parts of the passage you do not understand will only force you to return later and spend time re-reading, so get it all on the first go. In order to unravel all the twists and turns in the questions and answers, you must have a basic mental map of the passage and a good grasp of the big and medium ideas it contains.

General Reading Tips

The RC section is unlike any Reading Comprehension test you have seen. The RC section is substantially more difficult than the Reading Comprehension section on the SAT (or ACT) because the **questions** are more demanding. Of course, how well you do on the questions is largely determined by how well you read the passage. Clearly understanding the topic and how the author chose to discuss it enables you to answer challenging questions. Many RC questions ask you to first understand an idea in the passage and then to go a step further and apply that understanding to another situation. Here is an example question that asks you to do this:

> The approach to poetry taken by a modern-day Italian immigrant in America would be most analogous to Phillis Wheatley's approach, as it is described in the passage, if the immigrant...

Here is the paragraph in the passage that describes Wheatley's approach to poetry. Take a moment to read this, looking for an understanding of that approach:

> (1.1) The standards of eighteenth-century English poetry, which itself reflected little of the American language, led Wheatley to develop a notion of poetry as a closed system, derived from imitation of earlier written works. No place existed for the rough-and-ready Americanized English she heard in the streets, for the English spoken by Black people, or for Africanisms. The conventions of eighteenth-century neoclassical poetry ruled out casual talk; her voice and feelings had to be generalized according to rules of poetic diction and characterization; the particulars of her African past, if they were to be dealt with at all, had to be subordinated to the reigning conventions. African poetry did not count as poetry in her new situation, and African aesthetic canons were irrelevant to the new context because no linguistic or social framework existed to reinforce them. Wheatley adopted a foreign language and a foreign literary tradition; they were not extensions of her past experience, but replacements.

The final sentence of that paragraph describes her approach. One might sum it up like this: "Wheatley worked within the confines of English poetry to such a degree that her perspective and voice played a small role in her poetry." With that understanding in place, we can approach the question. The correct answer is:

> (E) adopted the language and forms of modern American poetry

A knowledge of Wheatley's approach to poetry was required to answer this, but that knowledge alone was not enough. We had to move beyond it and be able to apply that knowledge to a similar situation: an Italian immigrant writing poetry. It is this process of moving *beyond* the information in the passage that makes many of the RC questions so difficult. What follows are techniques for reading the passages that will help you reach a level of comprehension that allows you to correctly answer hard questions like this.

Focus Steadily

First of all, you must give 100% of your attention when you read a passage. It is easy to "zone out" while reading. We have all done this, read a paragraph or two in a book or magazine and then realized our mind was elsewhere. Letting your thoughts wander while reading is a recipe for disaster on the LSAT.

Most of what you read in normal life is designed to entertain you and be easy to absorb. Magazine articles and novels are written to be palatable and smooth reading, because this makes them enjoyable. RC Passages, on the other hand, due to their academic nature, are written to convey **complex** information and to express intricate, balanced viewpoints. You must focus on each sentence you read to get the most out of it. Anything less, and you may miss a nuanced point or a crucial detail.

Every time you begin reading a passage, take a moment to zero in. Clear your head of all other thoughts and prepare to absorb the passage. Most students only need a maximum of four minutes to read a passage; this is not a long stretch to stay focused. If you catch yourself thinking about something beyond the sentence at hand, pause, close your eyes and take a deep breath. Return to the passage with your full attention. This will likely be difficult at first during your practice on the RC section, but it gets much easier with time. Be patient with yourself and constantly hone your ability to focus when reading the passages.

One Sentence at a Time

You cannot rush through the dense, complex sentences in the RC passages. Take each sentence one at a time and follow the ideas. At least early on, when you practice reading passages, constantly check that you are engaging with what you are reading. Reading is fairly unconscious because you have done it a great deal. It is therefore possible to plow through a sentence without actually taking it in.

If it helps, **early in your practice** get in the habit of incorporating a very slight pause in between each sentence to make sure that understood it. If you did not, reread that sentence with better focus.

Because the big and medium points that the author is making are what is important, as you progress in your preparation, do not return to the sentence you did not fully understand. Instead, pick up the flow of ideas in the next sentence and save that time you would spend rereading. There is a natural reading pace that you will shift into when you focus on the content of each sentence. Find that pace and closely follow the content: the author's ideas and thoughts.

Punctuation is A Guide

As you read each sentence, use the punctuation within it to guide you. Because the passages are written in an academic style, the sentence structures used are often quite complex. Look at this sentence from the paragraph we summarized earlier:

> The conventions of eighteenth-century neoclassical poetry ruled out casual talk; her voice and feelings had to be generalized according to rules of poetic diction and characterization; the particulars of her African past, if they were to be dealt with at all, had to be subordinated to the reigning conventions.

This one sentence contains **three** independent clauses. Each could be its own complete sentence:

> The conventions of eighteenth-century neoclassical poetry ruled out casual talk.
>
> Her voice and feelings had to be generalized according to rules of poetic diction and characterization.
>
> The particulars of her African past, if they were to be dealt with at all, had to be subordinated to the reigning conventions.

The two semi-colons join these related statements within this one sentence. They dictate the rhythm your reading should have through the sentence. You should absorb the point contained in each clause, and see the semi-colon as only a partial barrier, not as hard as a period. Ideas separated by semi-colons should be considered more interrelated than those separated by a period. As you absorb each statement, realize that they are interconnected. When reading a very long sentence like the one above, your comprehension will increase if you take it in chunks. The author has dictated where to naturally divide your reading with the semi-colons, so use them.

Be sure to use commas as well. Look at this sentence:

> The standards of eighteenth-century English poetry, which itself reflected little of the American language, led Wheatley to develop a notion of poetry as a closed system, derived from imitation of earlier written works.

There are two dependent clauses here, and each expands on the information given, although in slightly different ways. The first clause – "which itself reflected little of the American language" – gives us **additional** information about eighteenth-century English poetry. We learn that this poetry does not reflect much of the American language. This is a relevant point because the paragraph the sentence is in discusses how Wheatley was restrained by the rules of this type of poetry and therefore did not use it to express uniquely American or Black versions of English.

The second clause – "derived from imitation of earlier works" – defines the term that it precedes: "a closed system." That clause tells us what "poetry as a closed system" meant to Wheatley. She viewed poetry as derivative, and felt she had to work with the rules laid out by earlier poems. Without this clause, describing poetry as a closed system is ambiguous. The second clause of this sentence is explanatory while the first clause is expansionary in nature. The first clause is set off in the middle of the sentence and starts with "which;" these are clues that the information given will be supplementary. The second clause is a classic definition dependent clause and contains no preposition to start it.

Get ready to read sentences full of clauses like these, as the passages use them liberally. Be sure that you understand the type of information they provide. As you read, pause just slightly before each clause and then absorb it. Clauses add details and flesh out ideas that help you follow the author's thinking. Do not race through a sentence full of clauses. Reading long, complex sentences that way will confuse you.

Signal Words

Heeding signal words, words that indicate what is coming next, helps you understand and follow a passage. Signal words are like guideposts; using them allows you to track the flow of information more easily. We have already discussed the use of signal words in LR passages, but you should review this information. After all, an RC passage contains argumentation just like a blurb, only it is much more detailed and drawn out.

Right now, turn and reread the section on signal words on page 45.

Pay Attention to Your Reactions

As you read, you should note the reactions you have to the content. If you are surprised by a fact or an idea, make a mental note of what you were surprised by. This will not only help you stay engaged with the reading, it can also help you answer questions. Content that surprises you might be controversial or important: content that the questions will deal with.

To illustrate that idea, recall the paragraph about Wheatley's views on poetry that we have been discussing so much. That paragraph was the third in the passage. The paragraph immediately before it talks about how Wheatley was at the center of a meeting between the African **oral** tradition and the English **literary** tradition. She could write English poetry well yet her roots were in Africa (she was brought over to the U.S. as a slave). This combination of skills and background put her in a unique position.

The second paragraph ends with this sentence:

> Given her African heritage and her facility with English and the conventions of English poetry, Wheatley's work had the potential to apply the ideas of a written literature to an oral literary tradition in the creation of an African American literary language.

After reading the sentence above, the first sentence of the **third** paragraph, the one about her views on poetry, might surprise you. Here is its ending: "...led Wheatley to develop a notion of poetry as a closed system, derived from imitation of earlier written works." One might expect Wheatley to have created the African American **literary** language that she was capable of bringing into the world by combining her writing skills with her knowledge of African oral tradition. The fact that she did not do so, that she instead worked within the confines of English poetry, is striking. Paying attention to this contrast that the passage sets up is important. In fact, it is one of the big ideas that the author wants to convey. So, if you notice that you are surprised by what you learn in the third paragraph, you have zeroed in on an important point. Noticing your surprise and the information it is centered on would directly help you to answer one of the questions.

Also pay attention to when you **agree** or **disagree** with something you read. This often happens when you read an opinion, and noting opinions can be quite important. Rarely will you disagree with something factual, a scientific theory or something along those lines. Usually students react more strongly to less concrete, more opinionated content. Make a mental note when this happens.

Read for the Message, Not the Details

Understand and try to remember the big and medium points the author is making. Do not attempt to **memorize** the small details, as that would slow your reading down too much, but do try and note most of them. The more challenging questions tend to test you on whether you followed the **larger** message given by the author. This is not always easy, because the author will likely be making points that are complicated and not easily reduced to simple explanations.

Follow the gist of what the passage says. If you need to, rephrase complex sentences or ideas into your own words, before moving on with the passage. Stopping the flow of your reading is not ideal, but it is worth it to be sure you are **understanding** the big ideas and not just reading the details. For instance, look at this part of the Wheatley paragraph:

> The conventions of eighteenth-century neoclassical poetry ruled out casual talk; her voice and feelings had to be generalized according to rules of poetic diction and characterization; the particulars of her African past, if they were to be dealt with at all, had to be subordinated to the reigning conventions. African poetry did not count as poetry in her new situation, and African aesthetic canons were irrelevant to the new context because no linguistic or social framework existed to reinforce them. Wheatley adopted a foreign language and a foreign literary tradition; they were not extensions of her past experience, but replacements.

We can sum these sentences up as: "Wheatley was limited in how much she could express her heritage and its unique voice by the conventions of 18th century poetry."

This is the main idea. This is the kind of understanding you should focus on taking away from what you read in the passage. Should you face a detail question regarding this paragraph, because you know the general content, you would know where to look in the passage to answer it. In this way, reading for the larger points helps you with the smaller details by giving you a general understanding of how the passage is organized and how it progresses with its ideas. We call this a mental map and will discuss this in detail later on.

This advice may seem to contrast with the idea of reading every sentence carefully that we exposed earlier. This is not the case. Only by reading every sentence carefully will you be able to grasp these bigger points. They are typically too subtle to catch with a more cursory reading. So, focus closely but do not obsess over the details. The details are there to support the conclusions, and the conclusions are what you need to know.

Name the Subject of Each Paragraph

To help you remember the big ideas of the passage, pause for about five seconds after reading each paragraph and **mentally** state the topic of the paragraph. Writing the topic takes too long; it is best to say your topic in your head. Or, if it comes easily, state a brief, one sentence summary of that paragraph in your own words. Do not try and articulate a well crafted and detailed summary.

This practice will assist you in a few ways. Primarily, it will help you **digest** the complex content. Stating the main subject of a paragraph forces you to interpret it. That helps you follow the passage as a whole because you will be clear on the main idea(s) of each paragraph before you move on to the next. This practice will also help you remember what you are reading when you move to the questions. Sifting through the details looking for the underlying point fixes the main ideas in your mind. Yes, it takes a little extra time, about 5 seconds for each paragraph, or about 20 seconds for the entire passage, but that is time well spent.

Split Long Paragraphs

Some long paragraphs have more than one main subject – try to state both of them. These long paragraphs usually appear in passages that have only three paragraphs. About half of the long passage sets have three paragraphs, the rest have four paragraphs. Note that Comparative Reading Passages sets typically have four to six paragraphs in their two passages. Look at this paragraph:

> (1.4) Outside the medical profession, there are various efforts to cut medicine down to size: not only widespread malpractice litigation and massive governmental regulation, but also attempts by consumer groups and others to redefine medicine as a trade rather than as a profession, and the physician as merely a technician for hire under contract. Why should physicians (or indeed all sensible people) resist such efforts to give the practice of medicine a new meaning? We can gain some illumination from etymology. "Trade," from Germanic and Anglo Saxon roots meaning "a course or pathway," has come to mean derivatively a habitual occupation and has been related to certain skills and crafts. On the other hand, while "profession" today also entails a habit of work, the word "profession" itself traces to an act of self-conscious and public---even confessional-speech. "To profess" preserves the meaning of its Latin source, "to declare publicly; to announce, affirm, avow." A profession is an activity or occupation to which its practitioner publicly professes, that is, confesses, devotion. But public announcement seems insufficient; publicly declaring devotion to plumbing or auto repair would not turn these trades into professions.

This long paragraph appears in a single passage set with four paragraphs. Like many long paragraphs, it has two main ideas. The first is found in the first two sentences:

> Outside the medical profession, there are various efforts to cut medicine down to size: not only widespread malpractice litigation and massive governmental regulation, but also attempts by consumer groups and others to redefine medicine as a trade rather than as a profession, and the physician as merely a technician for hire under contract. Why should physicians (or indeed all sensible people) resist such efforts to give the practice of medicine a new meaning?

We can state this core idea as: "Medical profession criticized, renamed as trade." As you can see, paragraph subjects can be described simply.

Or, if you have the time and inclination, articulate a full summary: "Efforts being made to criticize or hamper the medical profession including labeling medicine as a trade instead of a profession, are resisted by physicians."

In general, the ideas at the beginning of the first paragraph in a passage introduce the overall subject of the passage, setting the stage for the discussion to come. The second major part of **this** paragraph, with its own main idea, is this:

> We can gain some illumination from etymology. "Trade," from Germanic and Anglo Saxon roots meaning "a course or pathway," has come to mean derivatively a habitual occupation and has been related to certain skills and crafts. On the other hand, while "profession" today also entails a habit of work, the word "profession" itself traces to an act of self-conscious and public---even confessional-speech. "To profess" preserves the meaning of its Latin source, "to declare publicly; to announce, affirm, avow." A profession is an activity or occupation to which its practitioner publicly professes, that is, confesses, devotion. But public announcement seems insufficient; publicly declaring devotion to plumbing or auto repair would not turn these trades into professions.

The main idea of this section is that professions differ from trades in that a profession requires a public devotion to the occupation. However, this is only one distinguishing feature. This idea is distinct from the first core idea in the paragraph and should be thought of as such. We can describe this topic as: "Roots of trade vs profession."

When you are reading a long paragraph and notice a subject change, draw a dark, vertical line where it occurs. This splits the large paragraph into two, making it more manageable, both as you read, and if you need to return to that paragraph when working the questions. Here is how we would draw a line in this paragraph:

> (1.4) Outside the medical profession, there are various efforts to cut medicine down to size: not only widespread malpractice litigation and massive governmental regulation, but also attempts by consumer groups and others to redefine medicine as a trade rather than as a profession, and the physician as merely a technician for hire under contract. Why should physicians (or indeed all sensible people) resist such efforts to give the practice of medicine a new meaning?|We can gain some illumination from etymology. "Trade," from Germanic and Anglo Saxon roots meaning "a course or pathway," has come to mean derivatively a habitual occupation and has been related to certain skills and crafts. On the other hand, while "profession" today also entails a habit of work, the word "profession" itself traces to an act of self-conscious and public---even confessional-speech. "To profess" preserves the meaning of its Latin source, "to declare publicly; to announce, affirm, avow." A profession is an activity or occupation to which its practitioner publicly professes, that is, confesses, devotion. But public announcement seems insufficient; publicly declaring devotion to plumbing or auto repair would not turn these trades into professions.

This is an example of marking the passage; more on marking to come in a later chapter.

Unfamiliar Terms

Some passages will contain a word or phrase you are not familiar with. **Make your best guess** as to the meaning of the word or phrase. Your guess should fit smoothly into the sentence. Then, continue reading. Context from sentences **after** the word may help you figure out whether your guess was right or wrong. Many unfamiliar terms are defined directly or through context a sentence or more after first being used.

Force yourself to make a guess, because that guess will act as a placeholder for that word. Difficult vocabulary from the passage is often the basis of a question; by making a guess as to the meaning, you are able to test your guess out over your reading of the rest of the passage.

Attitude Matters

If you actively enjoy the passages, you will perform much better on the RC section. People focus more fully on those things that they enjoy. The passages are actually full of interesting information and ideas if you give them a chance. This is not to say that the test makers do not try and intimidate you with subjects that seem tough and foreign. They do. But, if you stay calm and take the passage one sentence at a time, you will find that you are given all the information you need to understand that intimidating topic. Try to enjoy what you are learning; think of the information as a mini-lecture on a subject you would otherwise know little about. It may take some exposure to the passages to reach this point, but it is well worth it when you do. Embracing the content helps you follow the author's ideas, something crucial to scoring your highest.

A Fully Analyzed Passage

To illustrate the reading techniques covered so far, we will now walk through an entire new passage, paragraph by paragraph. Recall that before you start reading a passage, you should take a moment to zero in. Give it 100% of your attention and follow each sentence carefully.

Note that from now on when discussing multiple paragraphs in a passage, we will label paragraphs with a "P" and the number of the paragraph. So, the third paragraph in a passage would be "P3." Here we go with P1:

> (1.3) There are two major systems of criminal procedure in the modem world-the adversarial and the inquisitorial. Both systems were historically preceded by the system of private vengeance in which the victim of a crime fashioned a remedy and administered it privately, either personally or through an agent.

This introductory paragraph introduces the main subject of the passage: a comparison of the adversarial and inquisitorial systems of criminal procedure. A specific topic, the system of private vengeance, is said to precede these two systems. The system of private vengeance is defined as a victim dealing with the remedy of the crime **privately**. We can mentally summarize this paragraph: "the adversarial and inquisitorial systems of dealing with crimes came after the system of private vengeance."

From an organization standpoint, this paragraph acquaints us with the subject that the rest of the passage will discuss in depth. We do not know the main point of the passage yet, the author's primary point, and this is not uncommon after reading the first paragraph. Next paragraph:

> The modern adversarial system is only one historical step removed from the private vengeance system and still retains some of its characteristic features. For example, even though the right to initiate legal action against a criminal has now been extended to all members of society (as represented by the office of the public prosecutor), and even though the police department has effectively assumed the pretrial investigative functions on behalf of the prosecution, the adversarial system still leaves the defendant to conduct his or her own pretrial investigation. The trial is viewed as a forensic duel between two adversaries, presided over by a judge who, at the start, has no knowledge of the investigative background of the case. In the final analysis the adversarial system of criminal procedure symbolizes and regularizes punitive combat.

The second paragraph tells how the adversarial system has aspects in common with the private vengeance system. That is the conclusion argued in the paragraph, and the second sentence signals that **evidence** is coming with the phrase "for example." That sentence begins with two clauses that start with "even though." This tells us that the information in the clause ahead runs counter to a later point. These two clauses give us information on how the adversarial system is **different** from the private vengeance system: right to legal action is available for all members of society (this is therefore not the case in the private vengeance system) and the police department does all the pretrial investigative functions for the prosecution. This is a form of balanced information: the author explains exceptions to the rule that she is trying to prove, that the adversarial system still has characteristic features from the system of private vengeance. After the two clauses, we learn that the defendant has to conduct his own pretrial investigation in the adversarial system. This is similar to the defendant fully representing himself in the private vengeance system. The final two sentences of the paragraph name other features that these two systems have in common.

We can summarize this paragraph as: "The adversarial system has many features in common with the private vengeance system, although it does have some modern features." And the condensed topic is simply: "Overlap between the adversarial and private."

Because this paragraph delved into the details of one of the two main systems, we expect the third paragraph to elaborate on the other system, the inquisitorial.

> By contrast, the inquisitorial system begins historically where the adversarial system stopped its development. It is two historical steps removed from the system of private vengeance. From the standpoint of legal anthropology, then, it is historically superior to the adversarial system. Under the inquisitorial system, the public prosecutor has the duty to investigate not just on behalf of society but also on behalf of the defendant. Additionally, the public prosecutor has the duty to present the court not only evidence that would convict the defendant, but also evidence that could prove the defendant's innocence. The system mandates that both parties permit full pretrial discovery of the evidence in their possession. Finally, an aspect of the system that makes the trial less like a duel between two adversarial parties is that the inquisitorial system mandates that the judge take an active part in the conduct of the trial, with a role that is both directive and protective.

This paragraph starts with the term "by contrast" meaning that follows is different than what came before. The inquisitorial system **began** its development with the adversarial system, meaning that the inquisitorial system is further evolved. This is the conclusion of the paragraph. The next two sentences only refine and clarify this idea: because the inquisitorial system used the adversarial system as a starting point and then built upon and (likely) improved it, it can be considered "historically superior." We get our first real evidence for this conclusion with the fourth sentence: under this system, the public prosecutor investigates on behalf of the defendant. That is certainly an evolution from the adversarial system and its predecessor, where the defendant had to fend for himself.

The next sentence starts with the signal word "additionally," which indicates that the information coming is along the same lines as what came before. So, we expect more evidence on how the inquisitorial system is more evolved than the adversarial. That is what we get: the prosecutor not only has to collect evidence that can help the **defendant**, he also has to present that evidence to the court. Next, we learn that both parties have to make their evidence open before the trial, a sort of cooperation not seen in the other two criminal systems. The last sentence gives another contrast: the judge plays an active role in the trial, serving as a sort of mediator. That contrasts with the adversarial system where the judge is less involved and knows nothing about the trial before it starts.

The summary for this paragraph could be: "the inquisitorial system is more evolved than the adversarial and focuses on the facts." Mental summaries do not have to be very detailed; simply trying to compile the information into a sentence is quite helpful. And the condensed, mental topic is simply: "Inquisitorial more evolved."

We have now seen a detailed analysis of both the adversarial and inquisitorial systems. From here, the passage could either compare and contrast them further, or go into detail on one of them. Moving on:

> Fact-finding is at the heart of the inquisitorial system. This system operates on the philosophical premise that in a criminal action the crucial factor is the body of facts, not the legal rule (in contrast to the adversarial system), and the goal of the entire procedure is to attempt to recreate, in the mind of the court, the commission of the alleged crime.

The first line of this paragraph, as is generally the case, tells us what the paragraph will discuss: more information about the inquisitorial system. This system is focused on finding out the facts of the case. That can serve as the mental summary. Another contrast to the adversarial system is drawn, as the adversarial system is centered less on the body of facts and more on the legality of the situation.

There are no real signal words in this short paragraph, but following the content is not hard. We are given more information that distinguishes our two main subjects.

The final paragraph:

> Because of the inquisitorial system's thoroughness in conducting its pretrial investigation, it can be concluded that, if given the choice, a defendant who is innocent would prefer to be tried under the inquisitorial system, whereas a defendant who is guilty would prefer to be tried under the adversarial system.

This passage is drawn from an older LSAT: the new long passages feature only three or four paragraphs, as opposed to the five paragraphs here. In a way, that makes this one easier, because we faced no long passages that required that we split them in two.

Often, the last paragraph of a passage will provide some sort of closure or summary, and this one is no different. Note the words "it can be concluded." This implies that a summation of ideas is coming. We have learned a great deal about the two systems, and author draws a fascinating conclusion from it: innocent defendants are more likely to be proven innocent in the inquisitorial system, which makes sense because of the focus in that system on getting at the facts of the crime and the support given from the prosecutor to the defendant. Guilty defendants, however, would prefer to be tried under the adversarial system because they can provide their own defense and the lessened focus on the facts of the case can work in the defendants favor. A summary of this paragraph could consist of "Innocent defendants prefer inquisitorial, guilty prefer adversarial."

This is a novel idea to end the passage, but note that passages are often drawn from select parts of larger works, meaning that we may only be getting a snapshot of the author's full thrust.

Having read the entire passage and summarized each paragraph, we can now use the summaries to "map" the passage:

- the adversarial and inquisitorial systems came after the system of private vengeance
- the adversarial system has many features in common with the private vengeance system, although it does have some modern features
- the inquisitorial system is more evolved than the adversarial and focuses on the facts
- the goal of inquisitorial system is to have an accurate account of the nature of the crime
- innocent defendants prefer inquisitorial, guilty prefer adversarial

To clarify our analysis, we have laid the summaries. The organization: two systems of dealing with crimes are introduced, the focus of each system and its origins are discussed, and an analysis of the impacts of each on a defendant is given.

Passage organization questions no longer appear on the RC section, although they did up until about 5 years ago (stopping with PT 51). However, tracking the organization through making mental summaries is a useful exercise; it gives you a map for how to reference specific parts of the passage. For instance, if we want details on the nature of the inquisitorial system, we need to go to paragraph 3.

Basic Elements

As you utilize the general reading tips, there are specific elements, parts of each passage, which you should pay attention to as you read. Being aware of these distinct elements helps you follow the passage so that you can attack the questions. In your initial passage reading, you want to learn the composition of the passage, creating a "mental map" of where different topics are located and identifying these elements will help you do so.

Subject

The overall subject of the passage is the big topic discussed by the author. For instance, an earlier passage we analyzed was about Wheatley's poetry, that is the subject. The previous passage had a subject of two legal systems. Passages can have more abstract subjects, for example "the philosophical differences between humanists and scientists." Every passage has a readily identifiable subject, one usually introduced at the end of the first paragraph. Sometimes more complex and theoretical (less concrete) subjects are introduced in the second paragraph. One of your main jobs when you **begin** reading a passage is to identify the subject.

Main Point

The main point (or main idea) of the passage is what the author argues about the subject. In the Wheatley passage, the main point was "Phillis Wheatley's poetry did not fulfill the potential inherent in her experience but did represent a significant accomplishment." The main point centers on the subject and goes beyond it by making a specific argument about the subject. The main idea in the legal system passage would be something along the lines of: "The inquisitorial system is more modern, and based on fact-finding than the adversarial system of criminal procedure."

This is a crucial element for a few reasons, but primarily because main idea questions are a very common type and appear in almost every passage set. Further, understanding the main point will help you answer other questions because you know the core of the passage, and correct answers generally reflect that central message. For instance, in a question about the author's attitude on a certain subject, the correct answer will not contradict the main point. Knowing what that core idea is will help you work the choices, because you can eliminate those that go against it. This is why we could eliminate "perfunctory dismissal" in the question above: it contradicted the authors main point that Wheatley was overall a success as a poet. Finally, you must understand the author's main point in order to have a good grasp on the passage itself.

The author's main point is rarely **directly** stated in the passage. To identify it, track the author's smaller conclusions, just like you do with LR blurbs. The **largest** conclusion with the most support is the main point. The passage as a whole supports the main point, so it cannot be unique to one paragraph. We will discuss how to identify the main point in further detail when we discuss specific question types. For now, realize that it is an important element to look for in your initial reading.

Topics

Make special note of the topics, the concepts and ideas discussed by the author in explaining the subject. The topics are what the passage uses to make its argument, so identify these groups and understand their role played in the discussion. To help you understand the distinction between the subject and the topics, think about this example. In a passage that discusses the ramifications of drug legalization (the subject), the topics might include the legal status of specific drugs, such as marijuana, cocaine and ecstasy, and policy makers who have opinions about the subject. The topics are used as **tools** in discussing the more general and encompassing subject.

New topics are usually introduced throughout the entire passage, even in the last paragraph. Sometimes most of the topics are introduced early on in the passage and then discussed for the next paragraph or two. Either way, note only the more important subjects – those that are mentioned repeatedly or carry more weight in the passage. Take a look at this paragraph:

> (1.2) The relationship of cytology (cell biology) to biochemistry in the late nineteenth century, when both disciplines were growing at a rapid pace, exemplifies such a pattern. Researchers in cell biology found mounting evidence of an intricate cell architecture. They also deduced the mysterious choreography of the chromosomes during cell division. Many biochemists, on the other hand, remained skeptical of the idea that so much structure existed, arguing that the chemical reactions that occur in cytological preparations might create the appearance of such structures. Also, they stood apart from the debate then raging over whether protoplasm, the complex of living material within a cell, is homogeneous, network like, granular, or foam like. Their interest lay in the more "fundamental" issues of the chemical nature of protoplasm, especially the newly formulated enzyme theory of life.

This passage uses the differences between cytology and biochemistry to illustrate a phenomenon about closely-related disciplines in the sciences. This subject is an abstract one: closely related disciplines in the sciences. The main topics here are cytology and biochemistry, two scientific disciplines, and the researchers in these fields, cell biology researchers and biochemists. Some smaller, less important topics discussed are protoplasm and the enzyme theory of life.

To grasp the passage's more subtle points, you need to be clear on what properties are being attributed to which scientific discipline. To do that, you need to note the fact that cytology and biochemistry are the main disciplines. Many natural science passages will throw tricky terms at you, and the main topics are important to follow throughout the passage because the new terms will often center around the bigger topics. Just like in the passage above, protoplasm and the enzyme theory of life are relevant only in relation to biochemists' interest in them.

Speakers

An author will often attribute an opinion, a stance or belief about a topic, to a specific person or group. We call people or groups with opinions <u>speakers</u>. Because speakers are entities used by the author in discussing the subject, they themselves are a specific type of topic in the passage, a specific type.

Tracking the speakers in the passage will help you notice their opinions, and those are often tested by the questions. The **complexity** that opinions offer makes them quite appealing to the test-makers. Look at this paragraph, drawn from the same passage as the previous example:

> In general, ***biochemists*** judged cytologists to be too ignorant of chemistry to grasp the basic processes, whereas ***cytologists*** considered the methods of biochemists inadequate to characterize the structures of the living cell. The renewal of Mendelian genetics and, later, progress in chromosome mapping did little at first to effect a synthesis.

We are given two opinions and a statement in these sentences. The first sentence contains the two opinions. The first of these is a view attributed to biochemists: they think that cytologists are too ignorant of chemistry to grasp the basic processes of the living cell. So, biochemists are a speaker in the passage; they have an opinion.

Next, cytologists state that the **methods** used by biochemists are incapable of characterizing the structures of the living cell. So, cytologists are another speaker with an opinion.

Note that the opinion of the cytologists is centered on the methods of the biochemists, not the biochemists themselves. On the other hand, the opinion of the biochemists is about the cytologists directly. This is a subtle distinction, but one that a difficult question could test. You would not be expected to remember such a tiny detail for your first reading of the passage, but you should remember which paragraph features the two types of scientist giving opinions of each other.

The final sentence of the paragraph is information from the author: "The renewal of Mendelian genetics and, later, progress in chromosome mapping did little at first to effect a synthesis." The lack of a person or group attributed with giving this idea indicates that it is coming from the author. The author has opinions too and often gives them.

Delving deeper, this statement regarding Mendelian genetics is hard to identify as either an opinion or a fact **because** it comes from the author. The author controls the flow of information in the passage, meaning it is not always easy to distinguish the more concrete and verifiable information (facts) from something more controversial that the author believes (opinions). The language the author uses will likely be stronger and less academic for opinions. Opinions are much less common because in academic style articles the author's goal is to have a well reasoned and supported argument that contains few easily identifiable opinions.

Here is the final paragraph in that same science passage. As you read it, identify the speakers:

> This interaction between paired disciplines can have important results. In the case of late nineteenth-century cell research, progress was fueled by competition among the various attitudes and issues derived from cell biology and biochemistry. Joseph Fruton, a biochemist, has suggested that such competition and the resulting tensions among researchers are a principal source of vitality and "are likely to lead to unexpected and exciting novelties in the future, as they have in the past."

The first two sentences are attributable to the author because they have no other speaker. The final sentence gives the viewpoint of Fruton, a new speaker, who says that the competition among researchers is positive and will lead to further advances in science. That is his opinion on the overall subject of the passage.

The Author's Tone

The fifth element to read for is the author's <u>tone</u>. This is a much more subtle element than an opinion. The author's tone refers to how the author views something, the degree to which the author feels positively or negatively about the overall subject, or sometimes a topic. Because the passages are written in an academic style, rarely is the author's tone or language **extreme**. For instance, you will likely never hear an author describe an idea she likes as "exceptional" or "brilliant." There is no room for such powerful words in a passage that is written to be fair to the treatment of its subject. Instead, words like "successful," "well-reasoned," and "accurate" would be used to indicate that the author approves of an idea or topic.

Obviously, the author does not have an attitude toward every subject in the passage. Generally, only the primary subject of the passage is given an opinion by the author. In some passages, the author does not express a tone towards anything.

Look at this sentence from the Wheatley passage:

> (1.1) Thus limited by the eighteenth-century English literary code, Wheatley's poetry contributed little to the development of a distinctive African American literary language. Yet by the standards of the literary conventions in which she chose to work, Wheatley's poetry is undeniably accomplished, and she is justly celebrated as the first Black American poet.

The first sentence talks about how because Wheatley never pushed the boundaries of English poetry. She was never able to utilize her skills to create a form of expression for her unique background. This is a lacking in her poetry that the author discussed thoroughly. However, the phrases "undeniably accomplished" and "justly celebrated" in the second sentence above tell us that the author respects the work Wheatley did **within** her boundaries and that the author has a positive attitude towards her poetry. These are as positive as any words an author will use in a passage. Taking these two sentences together, we get a good feel for the author's overall view of Wheatley's poetry: generally positive, but with some reservations. And that is exactly what we need to know to answer this question, which tests us on our knowledge of the author's tone:

8. Which one of the following most accurately characterizes the author's attitude with respect to Phillis Wheatley's literary accomplishments?

   (A) enthusiastic advocacy
   (B) qualified admiration
   (C) dispassionate impartiality
   (D) detached ambivalence
   (E) perfunctory dismissal

The correct answer is (B).

(A) and (E) are both extreme attitudes for the author to take. "Enthusiastic advocacy" is a strong stance and rarely is the author purely positive on a subject. Almost never will an author dismiss something in a perfunctory way, like in (E), as this means without much reflection. Generally, the authors reflect at least a little bit on everything they hold opinions on. The strong attitudes in (A) and (E) **can** be correct, but they rarely are and they are not correct on this question.

Keep in mind that the author's tone on the subject is developed over the **entire** passage and will therefore match the passage as a whole. Take **all** the language used by the author regarding the subject into account. One negative statement does not make a negative tone, as we saw in this question and corresponding passage. Even though the author spends a whole paragraph discussing how Wheatley was unable to realize her full potential as a writer, in other parts of the passage, Wheatley's writing skills are praised. That combination gives us the balanced attitude of "qualified admiration."

Passage Organization

As you read a passage, follow its general structure. This helps you to refer back to the correct part of the passage when answering questions, something you will do regularly.

We already discussed describing in your own words the main idea/subject of each paragraph. You want those ideas to be condensed enough so that you can remember them. To know how the passage proceeds, all you need to do is track how those subjects relate to one another as you read. All of them together give you a mental map for where different types of content can be found in the passage. To illustrate this idea, read the entire Wheatley passage:

> For the poet Phillis Wheatley, who was brought to colonial New England as a slave in 1761, the formal literary code of eighteenth-century English was thrice removed: by the initial barrier of the unfamiliar English language, by the discrepancy between spoken and literary forms of English, and by the African tradition of oral rather than written verbal art. Wheatley transcended these barriers - she learned the English language and English literary forms so quickly and well that she was composing good poetry in English within a few years of her arrival in New England.
>
> Wheatley's experience exemplifies the meeting of oral and written literary cultures. The aesthetic principles of the African oral tradition were preserved in America by folk artists in work songs, dancing, field hollers, religious music, the use of the drum, and, after the drum was forbidden, in the perpetuation of drum effects in song. African languages and the functions of language in African societies not only contributed to the emergence of a distinctive Black English but also exerted demonstrable effects on the manner in which other Americans spoke English. Given her African heritage and her facility with English and the conventions of English poetry, Wheatley's work had the potential to apply the ideas of a written literature to an oral literary tradition in the creation of an African American literary language.
>
> But this was a potential that her poetry unfortunately did not exploit. The standards of eighteenth-century English poetry, which itself reflected little of the American language, led Wheatley to develop a notion of poetry as a closed system, derived from imitation of earlier written works. No place existed for the rough-and-ready Americanized English she beard in the streets, for the English spoken by Black people, or for Africanisms. The conventions of eighteenth-century neoclassical poetry ruled out casual talk; her voice and feelings had to be generalized according to rules of poetic diction and characterization; the particulars of her African past, if they were to be dealt with at all, had to be subordinated to the reigning conventions. African poetry did not count as poetry in her new situation, and African aesthetic canons were irrelevant to the. new context because no linguistic or social framework existed to reinforce them. Wheatley adopted a foreign language and a foreign literary tradition; they were not extensions of her past experience, but replacements.
>
> Thus limited by the eighteenth-century English literary code, Wheatley's poetry contributed little to the development of a distinctive African American literary language. Yet by the standards of the literary conventions in which she chose to work, Wheatley's poetry is undeniably accomplished, and she is justly celebrated as the first Black American poet.

We can describe this organization in some depth by stating the subject/main idea of each paragraph, in order:

"The barriers a poet had to overcome are described, a unique potential the artist had is outlined, why the poet did not achieve that potential is described and then the passage is concluded."

*Introduction and Reading a Passage Review

Introduction

- Get the most out of your RC preparation by gaining a solid theoretical understanding on how to tackle the passage sets.
- The RC section is the single most important section on the test.
    - It is worth 27% of your LSAT score.
- Each RC section has 4 passages sets: 3 long passages and 1 comparative reading set.
- If you wish to answer every question, you have an average of 8 minutes and 45 seconds per passage set.
    - Different passage sets take differing amounts of time based on their difficulty and number of questions.

Passage Introduction

- The general categories that the topics are drawn from: Natural Sciences, Social Sciences, Humanities, Law.
- The category of the passage is largely unconnected to its difficulty level.
- The passages are complex and do not allow a simple understanding.
    - You must read slowly and carefully to be able to effectively answer the questions.
- You must use the passage efficiently to succeed on a passage set.
- Approach:
    - Read the passage thoroughly and carefully.
    - Next, answer the questions, referencing the passage as necessary.

General Reading Tips

- Before you begin reading a passage, pause and zero in.
    - Give it 100% of your attention.
- Use the punctuation (commas, semi-colons, etc.) as a guide.
- Watch the signal words the author uses.
- Watch your reactions: when something surprises you, make a mental note of it.
- Read for the message and details, but do not try to memorize the details.
- Name the subject of each paragraph after you finish it. (Optional)
- Split longer paragraphs in two where the main idea changes.
    - Use a vertical dash.
- Use the context to make your best guess on unfamiliar terms and keep reading.

Basic Elements

- Read for these with each passage:
    - Subject – the overall topic discussed by the author, the primary discussion.
    - Main Point – the author's core conclusion.
    - Topics – people, concepts or ideas discussed by the author in exploring the subject.
    - Speakers – people that give opinions in the passage.
    - Tone - the degree to which the author feels positively or negatively about the subject or a topic.

More on Passages

We will now delve deeper into how to read the passages by discussing pacing, elements tested by the questions, and elements that add difficulty.

Pacing Guidelines

How fast should you read each passage? You might think that slowing down your reading speed will help you retain more of the passage. Comprehension actually has more to do with how **focused** you are on the passage. It is possible to read a passage slowly while your mind is drifting and retain very little of it. If your full attention is on the passage, then you will get much more out of it. Try to read somewhat quickly, while still understanding and assimilating all of what you are reading. If you find yourself slowing down, then your attention may be waning. Shake yourself awake (at least mentally) and speed up slightly. This advice is only there to help you focus: do not speed up if you are focused and moving at a normal pace.

Your ideal pace will allow you to remember the medium and big points of the passage and create a mental map of the location of **details**. If you are trying to commit every small detail to memory, you are going too slowly. You cannot be expected to memorize every small detail, but the test makers will expect you to have a good idea on where to look up a specific point. Locating the right paragraph that contains the detail is enough. The balance between reading quickly and understanding what you are reading takes practice.

Time Per Passage

As a guideline, great readers tend to read the passage in about two and half minutes; slower readers around four to five minutes. If you take much longer than about four minutes to read the passages, you will likely not be able to finish all questions in the section. For many students, not finishing the section is ok, as that is not the goal. Getting the most points out of each section is the goal. Depending on your skills, that can require attempting only two or three passage sets and guessing in an educated way on the rest of the questions. More discussion on time management is at the end of the RC section.

Learn to Read Effectively

The strategies discussed here will not teach you to be a faster reader. Your reading speed is somewhat set, having been developed over many, many years of practice. We will teach you how to be a more **effective** reader, by showing you what to look for in the passage and how to understand some of the more elusive ideas the authors of the passage use. That being said, through steady LSAT practice, your reading speed on the passages will increase. Even working on your Logical Reasoning skills requires focused reading, and that spills over to the RC section.

Time Yourself

Take a moment now and time yourself on these two passages. Read quickly and with purpose (like you are working a section with a time limit), but slowly enough so that you can look for the Basic Passage Elements you just learned about: subject, Main Idea, Topics, Speakers, Author's Tone, and Passage Organization. Use a digital watch or timer and write down how long each passage takes you.

(2.1) There is substantial evidence that by 1926, with the publication of *The Weary Blues,* Langston Hughes had broken with two well established traditions in African American literature. In *The Weary Blues,* Hughes chose to modify the traditions that decreed that African American literature must promote racial acceptance and integration, and that, in order to do so, it must reflect an understanding and mastery of Western European literary techniques and styles. Necessarily excluded by this decree, linguistically and thematically, was the vast amount of secular folk material in the oral tradition that had been created by Black people in the years of slavery and after. It might be pointed out that even the spirituals or "sorrow songs" of the slaves as distinct from their secular songs and stories had been Europeanized to make them acceptable within these African American traditions after the Civil War. In 1862 northern White writers had commented favorably on the unique and provocative melodies of these "sorrow songs" when they first heard them sung by slaves in the Carolina sea islands. But by 1916, ten years before the publication *of The Weary Blues,* Harry T. Burleigh, the Black baritone soloist at New York's ultrafashionable Saint George's Episcopal Church, had published *Jubilee Songs of the United States,* with every spiritual arranged so that a concert singer could sing it "in the manner of an art song." Clearly, the artistic work of Black people could be used to promote racial acceptance and integration only on the condition that it became Europeanized.

Even more than his rebellion against this restrictive tradition in African American art, Hughes's expression of the vibrant folk culture of Black people established his writing as a landmark in the history of African American literature. Most of his folk poems have the distinctive marks of this folk culture's oral tradition: they contain many instances of naming and enumeration, considerable hyperbole and understatement, and a strong infusion of street talk rhyming. There is a deceptive veil of artlessness in these poems. Hughes prided himself on being an impromptu and impressionistic writer of poetry. His, he insisted, was not an artfully constructed poetry. Yet an analysis of his dramatic monologues and other poems reveals that his poetry was carefully and artfully crafted. In his folk poetry we find features common to all folk literature, such as dramatic ellipsis, narrative compression, rhythmic repetition, and monosyllabic emphasis. The peculiar mixture of irony and humor we find in his writing is a distinguishing feature of his folk poetry. Together, these aspects of Hughes's writing helped to modify the previous restrictions on the techniques and subject matter of Black writers and consequently to broaden the linguistic and thematic range of African American literature.

Time (Minutes and Seconds): ________

(2.2) Historians generally agree that, of the great modern innovations, the railroad had the most far reaching impact on major events in the United States in the nineteenth and early twentieth centuries, particularly on the Industrial Revolution. There is, however, considerable disagreement among cultural historians regarding public attitudes toward the railroad, both at its inception in the 1830s and during the half century between 1880 and 1930, when the national rail system was completed and reached the zenith of its popularity in the United States. In a recent book, John Stilgoe has addressed this issue by arguing that the "romantic-era distrust" of the railroad that he claims was present during the 1830s vanished in the decades after 1880. But the argument he provides in support of this position is unconvincing.

What Stilgoe calls "romantic-era distrust" was in fact the reaction of a minority of writers, artists, and intellectuals who distrusted the railroad not so much for what it was as for what it signified. Thoreau and Hawthorne appreciated, even admired, an improved means of moving things and people from one place to another. What these writers and others were concerned about was not the new machinery as such, but the new kind of economy, social order, and culture that it prefigured. In addition, Stilgoe is wrong to imply that the critical attitude of these writers was typical of the period; their distrust was largely a reaction against the prevailing attitude in the 1830s that the railroad was an unqualified improvement.

Stilgoe's assertion that the ambivalence toward the railroad exhibited by writers like Hawthorne and Thoreau disappeared after the 1880s is also misleading. In support of this thesis, Stilgoe has unearthed an impressive volume of material, the work of hitherto unknown illustrators, journalists, and novelists, all devotees of the railroad; but it is not clear what this new material proves except perhaps that the works of popular culture greatly expanded at the time. The volume of the material proves nothing if Stilgoe's point is that the earlier distrust of a minority of intellectuals did not endure beyond the 1880s, and, oddly, much of Stilgoe's other evidence indicates that it did. When he glances at the treatment of railroads by writers like Henry James, Sinclair Lewis, or F. Scott Fitzgerald, what comes through in spite of Stilgoe's analysis is remarkably like Thoreau's feeling of contrariety and ambivalence. (Had he looked at the work of Frank Norris, Eugene O'Neill, or Henry Adams, Stilgoe's case would have been much stronger.) The point is that the sharp contrast between the enthusiastic supporters of the railroad in the 1830s and the minority of intellectual dissenters during that period extended into the 1880s and beyond.

Time (Minutes and Seconds): ________

Reading Speed Analysis

Now, average the two times and look at the table below:

< 2 minutes → Reading too quickly

2-3 minutes → Faster than Average LSAT Reader

3-4.5 minutes → Average LSAT Reader

> 4.5 minutes → Slower than Average LSAT Reader

With an average of under nine minutes for each passage set, if you spent an average of four minutes or less reading these passages (Average LSAT reader or above), you will likely be able to finish the questions in this section after building up your skills using this guide.

If it took you less than two minutes to read a passage, that pace is unnecessarily fast for the RC section. Taking 3-4.5 minutes is ideal for most students. Slowing down and reading more carefully will likely help your performance.

If you are a slower than average LSAT reader, do not be discouraged. It helps to be a fast reader on the RC section, but it is not required. You can greatly improve your ability to work the passage and answer the questions through learning techniques and applying them in practice. It is possible to build your reading skills to some degree in a short period of time. To do so, complete reading speed workouts during your LSAT prep. These are outlined in the final RC chapter.

Question-Specific Elements

Although we have stressed the importance of reading for content, there are passage elements that come **directly** from the text that are asked about in the questions. To grasp them, you do not need to look beyond the words for their meaning. You need only remember the details you read. Learn the following elements well because when you are aware of them, they can often award you easy points.

First and Last Lines

The test makers often test your knowledge of details of the passage that were presented at the very beginning or very ending. These are ripe targets because students often forget details from the beginning of the passage because they were getting a feel for topic when they read those lines and did not focus intently on the details. Further, by the time you face the questions, the first lines of the passage will have been read several minutes before. For slightly different reasons, students are more likely to forget information from the end of the passage. This is due partly to students looking for a sort of summation of the ideas at the end, and this can cause one to pay less attention to the details. Also, many students get excited about finishing a passage and moving to the questions, so they rush the reading of the very last lines.

Our advice is two-fold. First, do not rush your reading of the final sentences of a passage. Progress smoothly at the pace you have been reading through the end of the passage. If anything, focus more on the first and last lines of the passage. The introduction orients you to the subject and the ending often contains important summary points or the author's overall conclusion. Secondly, when you cannot find an answer to a question in the passage, realize that the information you need might be at the very beginning or ending. Reference those spots accordingly.

Examples

Authors often use examples to clarify and/or support points. An example is a type of evidence that helps the reader relate to the passage or understand more complex ideas. Noting the examples in the passage also helps you with the questions, which can test your knowledge of how the examples are used.

As you likely know, examples are introduced with "for example," "for instance," and "as shown by." Learn to spot these terms and pay special attention to the example that follows. Here is an paragraph that utilizes examples:

> (1.4) Their titles and the respect they are shown superficially signify and acknowledge something deeper, that physicians are persons of the professional sort, knowingly and freely devoting themselves to a way of life worthy of such devotion. ***Just as lawyers devote themselves to rectifying injustices, looking up to what is lawful and right; just as teachers devote themselves to the education of the young, looking up to truth and wisdom***; so physicians heal the sick, looking up to health and wholesomeness.

These examples help you understand the concept of devoting oneself to a life with a beneficial focus. When the details about physicians are given, they are easier to understand because of the examples with lawyers and teachers. The length of examples varies, but they are often short and support a single point. Example paragraph:

> (2.3) Developmental responses, however, are usually permanent and irreversible; they become fixed in the course of the individual's development in response to environmental conditions at the time the response occurs. ***One such response occurs in many kinds of water bugs. Most water-bug species inhabiting small lakes and ponds have two generations per year.***

The example about water bugs supports the first sentence, and it does so concisely.

Sometimes, examples are long. Here is a thoroughly elaborated example:

> (3.3) Antitrust laws do not attempt to counter the mere existence of monopoly power, or even the use of monopoly power to extract extraordinarily high profits. For example, a firm enjoying economies of scale-that is, low unit production costs due to high volume does not violate the antitrust laws when it obtains a large market share by charging prices that are profitable but so low that its smaller rivals cannot survive. If the antitrust laws posed disincentives to the existence and growth of such firms, the laws could impair consumers' welfare. Even if the firm, upon acquiring monopoly power, chose to raise prices in order to increase profits, it would not be in violation of the antitrust laws.

The example in this paragraph regarding a firm enjoying economies of scale requires three sentences to develop. Be aware that examples can take many forms and be of varying lengths.

Remember that examples are not the conclusion; they are the evidence. Above, the point being made is that anti-trust laws "do not attempt to counter the mere existence of monopoly power, or even the use of monopoly power to extract extraordinarily high profits." The example supports that point. The details about the firm with economies of scale are not the point the author is making. You may be tested on this concept.

Definitions

Definitions given in the text can be tested. Usually the terms defined are important. The test makers may challenge your understanding of the word and how it is used. So, when you read a definition, make a mental note and ensure that you understood why that word was important.

Definitions can appear in a variety of forms, and this part of a paragraph features a definition **through context**:

> (2.3) Their wings are absolutely necessary for this seasonal dispersal. The summer (early) generation, in contrast, is usually dimorphic - ***some individuals have normal functional (macropterous) wings; others have much-reduced (micropterous) wings of no use for flight. The summer generation's dimorphism is a compromise strategy, for these individuals usually do not leave the ponds and thus generally have no use for fully developed wings. But small ponds occasionally dry up during the summer, forcing the water bugs to search for new habitats, an eventuality that macropterous individuals are well adapted to meet.***

Dimorphic is defined by explaining its implications in this situation. The summer generation is said to be dimorphic and in this generation, some of the bugs have functional wings, others have smaller wings that do not work. This gives us context for what dimorphic means: two different forms for a given quality in offspring (here wing functionality). Dimorphic is defined entirely through context; we must read the information that follows the dash carefully to understand it.

This next paragraph features a word being defined after a **comma**:

> (2.4) The Constitution of the United States does not explicitly define the extent of the President's authority to involve United States troops in conflicts with other nations in the absence of a declaration of war. Instead, the question of the President's authority in this matter falls in the hazy area of concurrent power, ***where authority is not expressly allocated to either the President or the Congress.***

"Concurrent power" is a term that most of us are not familiar with, but could perhaps deduce based on the meaning of concurrent (operating at the same time). However, the paragraph defines this term as a situation where the President and Congress share power. This definition helps you work with a new term quickly and in a specific context.

These next sentences feature a direct definition:

> (3.3) One type of violation of the antitrust laws is the abuse of monopoly power. Monopoly power is the ability of a firm to raise its prices above the competitive level - that is, above the level that would exist naturally if several firms had to compete - without driving away so many customers as to make the price increase unprofitable.

Monopoly power is explicitly defined. This is important, because the ins and outs of what constitutes monopoly power are a focus of the passage that contains that excerpt. Whenever you see a **direct, lengthy** definition, that term will play a major role in the passage.

A last note on examples: if you see a strange term that is not defined right away, be patient. Some terms are defined a sentence or two after they first appear. In these cases, make your best guess at the meaning of the word and keep reading.

Lists

Authors will often elucidate points using lists. Make a mental note when you encounter a list as the information it contains can be tested. Lists are usually a series of examples that support a conclusion or reasons why something happened. Some lists are extremely short, like this one that appears at the end of a sentence:

> For the poet Phillis Wheatley, who was brought to colonial New England as a slave in 1761, the formal literary code of eighteenth-century English was thrice removed: ***by the initial barrier of the unfamiliar English language, by the discrepancy between spoken and literary forms of English, and by the African tradition of oral rather than written verbal art.***

Other lists have longer individual elements. Some lists features a paragraph for each point. These big lists are structured with specific wording like "First, Second, Third" or "One possibility... the second possibility... and the final possibility." Sometimes lists do not have such convenient identifiers, so you must be aware that the author is organizing her ideas into a list. To spot that situation, notice that the content all relates to a larger point.

Here is a two element list that takes place over two paragraphs and uses the signal words "first" and "second" to start each paragraph. This example starts with the last sentence from a paragraph, the sentence that introduces the big list:

> (5.1) However, their argument is flawed on at least two counts.
>
> ***First***, in French law not all government contracts are treated as administrative contracts. Some contracts are designated as administrative by specific statute, in which case the contractor is made aware of the applicable legal rules upon entering into agreement with the government. Alternatively, the contracting government agency can itself designate a contract as administrative by including certain terms not found in private civil contracts. Moreover, even in the case of administrative contracts, French law requires that in the event that the government unilaterally modifies the terms of the contract, it must compensate the contractor for any increased burden resulting from the government's action. In effect, the government is thus prevented from modifying those contractual terms that define the financial balance of the contract.
>
> ***Second***, the French law of administrative contracts, although adopted by several countries, is not so universally accepted that it can be embraced as a general principle of law. In both the United States and the United Kingdom, government contracts are governed by the ordinary law of contracts, with the result that the government can reserve the power to modify or terminate a contract unilaterally only by writing such power into the contract as a specific provision. Indeed, the very fact that termination and modification clauses are commonly found in government contracts suggests that a government's capacity to modify or terminate agreements unilaterally derives from specific contract provisions, not from inherent state power.

This next paragraph includes a list where the elements are identified by these terms: "One," "Moreover," and "Finally."

> (3.2) Why were the contributions of these technicians not recognized by their employers? ***One reason*** is the historical tendency, which has persisted into the twentieth century, to view scientific discovery as resulting from momentary flashes of individual insight rather than from extended periods of cooperative work by individuals with varying levels of knowledge and skill. ***Moreover***, despite the clamor of seventeenth-century scientific rhetoric commending a hands-on approach, science was still overwhelmingly an activity of the English upper class, and the traditional contempt that genteel society maintained for manual labor was pervasive and deeply rooted. ***Finally***, all of Boyle's technicians were "servants," which in seventeenth-century usage meant anyone who worked for pay. To seventeenth-century sensibilities, the wage relationship was charged with political significance. Servants, meaning wage earners were excluded from the franchise because they were perceived as ultimately dependent on their wages and thus controlled by the will of their employers.

The list explains the three reasons why the contributions of the techs were not recognized.

Dates

Note when a passage features a specific <u>date</u>. Dates can help you understand the content of a passage because they give you a reference for when certain events occurred. Dates sometimes do not matter much in a passage when they are used in a discussion of a topic but are not **integral** to that discussion. On the other hand, dates can be important in a passage. The more dates you see, the more important they likely are. This is because a passage with a lot of dates may use a chronological structure, an organization with time as its backbone. When you notice a lot of dates, pay attention to them and understand the importance of the ordering of the events they refer to. If you want to draw a timeline in such a situation, you can, but it is likely not necessary. Below is an example of important dates:

> (2.2) There is, however, considerable disagreement among cultural historians regarding public attitudes toward the railroad, both at its inception in the ***1830s*** and during the half century between ***1880*** and ***1930***, when the national rail system was completed and reached the zenith of its popularity in the United States. In a recent book, John Stilgoe has addressed this issue by arguing that the "romantic-era distrust" of the railroad that he claims was present during the 1830s vanished in the decades after 1880. But the argument he provides in support of this position is unconvincing.

The dates tell when the railroad was created and when it was popular. This context is used in the second sentence to explain other aspects of the railroad. Understanding why the dates are used is required for understanding other points in the passage.

Numbers

<u>Numbers</u> is the next element to be aware of. Numbers are less common than dates, but are used similarly, to give context to other concepts. When an author discusses or compares numbers, they can be important, so pay attention. The example below consists of two snippets from a passage, the first from the beginning of the passage (but not the very beginning) and the next from the end.

> (3.1) ...If a bowling ball were orbiting about the Sun in the asteroid belt, it could have a pebble orbiting it as far away as a few hundred radii (or about 50 meters) without losing the pebble to the Sun's gravitational pull.
>
> ...The presence of a secondary body near Herculina thus seemed strongly indicated. To cause the secondary occultation, an unseen satellite would have to be about ***45 kilometers*** in diameter, a quarter of

the size of Herculina, and at a distance of ***990 kilometers*** from the asteroid at the time. These values are within theoretical bounds, and such an asteroid-satellite pair could be stable.

This passage is about whether comets can have objects orbiting them. The author uses numbers to show that specific arrangements are possible.

Questions (Asked or Answered)

Rarely, authors pose a question in the passage. A question is a unique tool in an author's arsenal and it often signals importance for the topic asked about. Instead of making a statement, the author **emphasizes** the answer using the question format. Note the question and its answer (wherever it may be in the passage). They are likely to show up in the questions. Look at these two paragraphs. The first paragraph starts the passage, the second ends the passage:

> (1.4) Outside the medical profession, there are various efforts to cut medicine down to size: not only widespread malpractice litigation and massive governmental regulation, but also attempts by consumer groups and others to redefine medicine as a trade rather than as a profession, and the physician as merely a technician for hire under contract. ***Why should physicians (or indeed all sensible people) resist such efforts to give the practice of medicine a new meaning?*** We can gain some illumination from etymology. "Trade," from Germanic and Anglo Saxon roots meaning "a course or pathway," has come to mean derivatively a habitual occupation and has been related to certain skills and crafts. On the other hand, while "profession" today also entails a habit of work, the word "profession" itself traces to an act of self-conscious and public - even confessional - speech. "To profess" preserves the meaning of its Latin source, "to declare publicly; to announce, affirm, avow." A profession is an activity or occupation to which its practitioner publicly professes, that is, confesses, devotion. But public announcement seems insufficient; publicly declaring devotion to plumbing or auto repair would not turn these trades into professions.
>
> ...Professing oneself a professional is an ethical act because it is not a silent and private act, but an articulated and public one; because it promises continuing devotion to a way of life, not merely announces a present preference or a way to a livelihood; because it is an activity in service to some high good that insists on devotion; because it is difficult and demanding. A profession engages one's character and heart, not merely one's mind and hands.

The question of why a doctor would be against changing the title of "profession" is the focus of the entire passage. The question is introduced in the first paragraph and then answered over the next **three** paragraphs. If you noticed the question when you first read it, that would have helped you follow the author's discussion for the entire passage. What luck!

Other times, questions are **answered** in the passage without being explicitly asked. For instance, a psychologist may say that exposure to a specific drug explains a phenomenon. The question of what underlies the phenomenon is implied. This concept is a little abstract, but you will likely see when a speaker in the passage (likely the author) provides the answer to a question not directly stated. Note that answer!

Cause and Effect

You remember this concept from the LR methods. Causal reasoning is not uncommon in passages because whenever an author attempts to explain **why** something occurred, she must use causal reasoning to do so. Unlike in an LR blurb, an RC author has time and space to develop the explanation. This is one of the reasons why causality should be accepted as correct, along with the rest of the author's points in a passage. This is a stark contrast to causality in an LR blurb, which always has the weakness that the author considers the cause to be the *only* possible cause. You do not need to be critical when reading a passage, as you are reading to absorb and understand, not critique.

Look at this example of causality, drawn from the end of one paragraph and the beginning of the next:

> (6.1) ...Specifically, Carroll indicates that while right-to-work laws may not "destroy" unions by reducing the absolute number of unionized workers, they do impede the spread of unions and thereby reduce wages within right-to-work states. Because the countervailing power of unions is weakened in right-to-work states, manufacturers and their suppliers can act collusively in competitive labor markets, thus lowering wages in the affected industries.
>
> Such a finding has important implications regarding the demographics of employment and wages in right-to-work states. Specifically, if right-to-work laws lower wages by weakening union power, minority workers can be expected to suffer a relatively greater economic disadvantage in right-to-work states than in union shop states...

Carroll, a speaker, thinks that right-to-work laws have an effect of impeding the spread of unions and weakening a union's power. This effect is developed over several paragraphs, so this is a good example of the complexity that you will find in causality in passages.

Expect the causality to be developed over a longer period of writing, perhaps up to three or more sentences. "X caused Y," explained in a single sentence does not occur often.

Elements that Add Difficulty

Now that you know general reading tips and basic elements to keep an eye out for, we will discuss some of the ways that the test makers make the passages challenging to read. Being aware of these tactics will help you to overcome them successfully.

Challenging Subject

It may surprise you to learn that your familiarity with the subject of the passage generally does not correlate highly with how difficult the passage is. **On average**, the different types of passages – Humanities, Law, Social Sciences and Natural Sciences - vary little in the average difficulty of their questions. On average, Humanities passages tend to be the easiest and Natural Sciences the most difficult, but the difference between these two is miniscule. So, the topic of a passage should not be a cause for concern. The information you need is always in the passage. Remain calm even if the subject seems challenging or very foreign, for instance, cytology compared with cell biology. Read the passage carefully and you will learn all you must know. Read this paragraph:

> (3.3) Three basic adaptive responses - regulatory, acclimatory, and developmental - may occur in organisms as they react to changing environmental conditions. In all three, adjustment of biological features (morphological adjustment) or of their use (functional adjustment) may occur. Regulatory responses involve rapid changes in the organism's use of its physiological apparatus-increasing or decreasing the rates of various processes, for example. Acclimation involves morphological change-thickening of fur or red blood cell proliferation-which alters physiology itself. Such structural changes require more time than regulatory response changes. Regulatory and acclamatory responses are both reversible.

The paragraph looks like it begins a passage with an intimidating topic, but in actuality the passage set is only moderately difficult.

Foreign Terms

Along these lines, foreign terms do not add much difficulty to a passage. Recall that such terms will either be defined directly in the passage or through the context they are placed in. Topic specific terms such as a type of legal rule or a chemistry term, will often be given definitions. Acronyms (a word formed from the initial letters of the several words in the name, for instance: A.K.A. = Also Known As) are usually clearly defined, so do not stress over them.

Tough Vocabulary Words

On the other hand, difficult and rare vocabulary words (words in common usage) can make a passage more challenging, especially if they are central to a major theme of the passage. Usually, if you do not know the meaning of a challenging word you can figure it out through context. Do not panic when you read the word in the sentence and do not know what it means. As mentioned earlier, simply continue reading into the next sentence, looking for clues. If it does not become clear, make your best guess and move on. Often these challenging vocabulary words will be important to a question or **will be featured in the incorrect choices** to trip up students who did not understand them and think they are important. Be wary of this situation.

Writing Style

Unlike the subject of a passage, the complexity of the writing in a passage **is** a good indicator of how difficult that passage set will be. Even passages with simple subjects can be challenging when written about with difficult vocabulary and long, intricate sentences. Likewise, abstract, demanding topics can be easy to understand when written in direct language.

It is not always easy to tell how difficult the writing style of the passage will be from its beginning. The test makers know that some students want to attempt the easier passages first, so they often make the first paragraph of a passage unrepresentative of the overall writing style. This certainly does not happen all the time, so you can generally make an educated guess as to the difficulty of a passage based on its first couple of sentences. Then, assuming you know that you will not be able to finish all the passages in the section, you can skip that particular passage. More on time management is in the final RC chapter.

To illustrate this point about wording and themes, look at this introductory paragraph of a passage:

> (1.2) One scientific discipline, during its early stages of development, is often related to another as an antithesis to its thesis. The thesis discipline tends to concern itself with discovery and classification of phenomena, to offer holistic explanations emphasizing pattern and form, and to use existing theory to explain the widest possible range of phenomena. The paired or antidiscipline, on the other hand, can be characterized by a more focused approach, concentrating on the units of construction, and by a belief that the discipline can be reformulated in terms of the issues and explanations of the anti discipline.

The passage set this paragraph begins is very difficult, and a large part of that difficulty comes from the complex language of the passage and the abstract nature of its central ideas.

We have no special advice when dealing with difficultly written passages. As always, bring your full attention to each sentence you read and be sure to implement the reading tips and look for the important passage elements. Realize that the passage will require more time to absorb and consider skipping it if you feel that you are, or will be, short on time.

Many Speakers

The test makers can also include many speakers with different opinions to add difficulty. It is easier to get confused with many viewpoints to sort through. The opinions might only be subtly different from one another regarding the topic and that will add further difficulty. Be sure to track each speaker carefully as you read, and sort through the viewpoints as you can, keeping in mind that understanding how the passage is organized may be more important than remembering or understanding every detail. You can always refer back to the passage to answer specific questions.

Rapid Fire Opinions

A similar technique that test-makers use to add difficulty involves introducing two or more opinions from different speakers in a row, making it difficult to follow which speaker thinks what. When this occurs, consciously slow down your reading and pay close attention to each viewpoint. Because it is hard to follow several different speakers' opinions in a single paragraph, there is a good chance a question will require that you do.

Combining Two Topics

Often an author will combine a discussion of two people or things into a single paragraph, making that paragraph confusing. Usually, these discussions are a comparison between the two topics, and it can be hard to track the features or attributes that are being discussed. It is easier to follow an explanation about one entity at a time. Look at this paragraph:

> (5.4) Anthropologist David Mandelbaum makes a distinction between life-passage studies and life-history studies which emerged primarily out of research concerning Native Americans. Life-passage studies, he says, "emphasize the requirements of society, showing how groups socialize and enculturate their young in order to make them into viable members of society." Life histories, however, "emphasize the experiences and requirements of the individual, how the person copes with society rather than how society copes with the stream of individuals." Life-passage studies bring out the general cultural characteristics and commonalities that broadly define a culture, but are unconcerned with an individual's choices or how the individual perceives and responds to the demands and expectations imposed by the constraints of his or her culture. This distinction can clearly be seen in the autobiographies of Native American women.

This is a fairly tame example of this phenomenon, but it shows a back and forth treatment of two different topics in a single paragraph. The discussion alternates between describing life-passage studies and life-history studies. This makes the attributes assigned to the studies harder to remember.

If, in a paragraph like this, you have difficulty following the content, do not worry. Make a mental or physical note to yourself that the paragraph involves a comparison of two subjects and move on. If you need to find a detail about one of those topics to answer a question, you can refer back to that paragraph. This situation occurs often, so be ready.

Split Content

When the test writers separate information about a topic, we call this <u>split content</u>. Generally, the discussion of the topic is divided by information that expands on one aspect of the topic. This is a natural way to write, but it can make following the overall discussion on the topic difficult. Questions often test your ability to follow the discussion of the topic as a whole despite the distraction in the middle. These paragraphs feature split content (the distracting content in italics):

> (3.2) Historians attempting to explain how scientific work was done in the laboratory of the seventeenth century chemist and natural philosopher Robert Boyle must address a fundamental discrepancy between how such experimentation was actually performed and the seventeenth-century rhetoric describing it. ***Leaders of the new Royal Society of London in the 1660s insisted that authentic science depended upon actual experiments performed, observed, and recorded by the scientists themselves. Rejecting the traditional contempt for manual operations, these scientists, all members of the English upper class, were not to think themselves demeaned by the mucking about with chemicals, furnaces, and pumps; rather, the willingness of each of them to become, as Boyle himself said, a mere "drudge" and "under-builder" in the search for God's truth in nature was taken as a sign of their nobility and Christian piety.***
>
> This rhetoric has been so effective that one modern historian assures us that Boyle himself actually performed all of the thousand or more experiments he reported. In fact, due to poor eyesight, fragile health, and frequent absences from his laboratory, Boyle turned over much of the labor of obtaining and recording experimental results to paid technicians, although published accounts of the experiments rarely, if ever, acknowledged the technicians' contributions. Nor was Boyle unique in relying on technicians without publicly crediting their work.

The fundamental discrepancy that is mentioned in the first sentence is developed in the middle of the **second** paragraph. The first paragraph is devoted to opinions on how experiments were supposed to be performed. The second paragraph describes how Boyle's experiments were actually performed. To follow this discussion, you need to keep in mind that there is a discrepancy while reading the remainder of the first paragraph. Then, you eventually find the information to understand the discrepancy in the second paragraph. That process takes more mental work than if the topic were explained normally, in a single paragraph.

Deceptive Line References

Rarely, a question will ask you about the topic and give you a line reference that only starts the topic. Because there is a separation in the middle of the discussion of that topic, the information you need to answer the question might be in a different part of the passage than that line reference. This means you have to know how the topic is discussed throughout the passage to find the correct information about it, and that can be difficult. Of course, now that you are conscious of the Split Content trick, this may not fool you. Although this situation is not common, you should be aware of it.

*More on Passages Review

Pacing Guidelines

- Comprehension has more to do with focus than reading speed.
- Read somewhat quickly, but do not rush.
- Taking 3 - 4.5 minutes to read each passage is a good goal.

Question-Specific Elements

- All of the Following passage elements can be asked about by the questions:
    - The First and Last lines of the passage
    - Examples - Recall that these are evidence, not the conclusion.
    - Definitions - These can be long or in depth.
    - Lists - These are a series of items that support or illustrate a point.
    - Dates - Either important in a passage (many are used) or not.
    - Numbers - Similar to dates.
    - Questions either asked or answered.
        - Authors use this tactic to emphasize importance.
    - Cause and Effect.
        - Usually developed thoroughly in the passage.
        - Used when explaining why something happened.

Elements that Do Not Add Difficulty

- The subject matter usually **does not** determine the difficulty of the passage .
- Nor do foreign terms, as these are generally defined in the passage.

Elements that Add Difficulty

- Tough vocabulary words
    - These are words in common usage that are not defined.
    - Use context and make your best guess of the meaning.
    - Sometimes tough words are featured in the incorrect choices to confuse students
- Challenging writing style
    - makes a huge difference in how hard the passage is.
    - Can tell this early on in the passage to some degree.
- Many speakers.
    - The more opinions and different Speakers, the harder it is to keep track of them.
    - Circle the different speakers to keep track of their opinions.
- Paragraphs with two topics.
    - The discussion of the attributes of two topics is combined into a single paragraph.
    - You can make a note in the margin and move on without having to sort through it all.
- Split Content
    - This is when the author divides a discussion on a topic with related information.
    - You must track the discussion across the distraction.
    - Split content is often tested by the questions.

Marking a Passage

As you read a passage, use your **pencil** to create specific marks on it. You are allowed to bring a highlighter into the official test, but we do not recommend you use it to mark a passage because you cannot make precise marks with it; a highlighter is only good for highlighting, not circling or writing or underlining. If you are accustomed to using a highlighter to mark your reading materials, please make the switch now.

Marking the passage helps you to follow it, and you know how important it is to stay engaged with the passage. Perhaps more importantly, your markings will help you refer back to specific parts of the passage when you work the questions. At least a couple of questions in each passage set will require you to refer back to the passage, but will not tell you where to look. On those questions, your markings will support your mental map of the passage and help you find the right part in the passage to use. That saves you time and energy searching the passage, and time is precious on the question-rich RC section.

Minimal Marking

The most important thing to do when reading a passage is to stay with the content, to follow the flow of the author's ideas. Any marking forces you to pause your reading and do some writing, so it must be quite worthwhile in order to justify that departure from the passage's content. For this reason, we recommend marking only a few different elements, ones that confer great benefit when you pay them extra attention as you read. These elements are: topics, speakers, author's opinions and lists.

Try working at least **six** passages while only marking these few elements and see how this works for you. As with many powerful LSAT methods, it takes practice to become proficient with these marking guidelines.

Basic Marks

These are the most necessary marks. You will use most of them on every passage.

Underline Topics

Underline the main topics, those few topics that the passage revolves around. This will help you follow the discussion because it calls your attention to the big ideas, concepts, and people being discussed. And when you reference the passage after your first read, you have a visual map of the topics that helps you see what each paragraph is about. Underlining is the quickest way to draw attention to a part of the text. The fact that you are working in the text itself - as opposed to writing something in the margin - means that you can stay connected to the ideas and flow of the passage as you underline each main topic.

We have a separate marking system for speakers (people who voice opinions on topics) that we will cover shortly.

Main vs Secondary Topics

Passages contain many secondary topics that are not as important as the main topics. It is not always easy to tell which topics are important and which are not during the first read through. Here is one way: the main topics are those most directly connected to the overall subject. Main topics are also most important in any given paragraph. Secondary topics support the discussion of the main topics by serving as examples or by illustrating points made about the main topics.

Evaluate the importance and role of the different topic as you read. Underline those topics that are the most central to the points being made. As a guide, the first and second paragraphs of most passages have two to four main topics, while later paragraphs usually have fewer. This is a rough guide; some longer body paragraphs might have 2 or more main topics, or a short first paragraph might have only one or two main topics.

Example Paragraph Marked

Look at this paragraph, the first from the Wheatley passage:

> For the poet Phillis Wheatley, who was brought to colonial New England as a slave in 1761, the formal literary code of eighteenth-century English was thrice removed: by the initial barrier of the unfamiliar English language, by the discrepancy between spoken and literary forms of English, and by the African tradition of oral rather than written verbal art. Wheatley transcended these barriers - she learned the English language and English literary forms so quickly and well that she was composing good poetry in English within a few years of her arrival in New England.

In most introductory paragraphs, at least one main topic is introduced. The passages are short (450 words), so the author must jump right into talking about the subject. An author needs the main topics to develop the discussion of the subject. In the intro paragraph above, Wheatley is presented immediately. After reading the first sentence, we suspect that she will be a main topic; we do not know for sure. After reading the second sentence, all about her poetry, we confirm that she is central to the subject and a main topic.

The second sentence of the paragraph talks about her transcending the barriers to her writing English and poetry. Because these barriers are mentioned in both the first and second sentences, they can be considered main topic. Any topic mentioned that often early in a passage is likely to be a main topic.

There are several secondary topics in the first sentence: New England, the formal literary code of 18th-century English, the African tradition of oral art, etc. We know think these are Secondary Topics, because they are all mentioned in reference to Wheatley. They are details about **her**.

Here is how we would mark this paragraph, underlining each main topic:

> For the poet Phillis <u>Wheatley</u>, who was brought to colonial New England as a slave in 1761, the formal literary code of eighteenth-century English was thrice removed: by the initial barrier of the unfamiliar English language, by the discrepancy between spoken and literary forms of English, and by the African tradition of oral rather than written verbal art. Wheatley transcended these <u>barriers</u> - she learned the English language and English literary forms so quickly and well that she was composing good poetry in English within a few years of her arrival in New England.

Keep your underlining to a minimum to help you to see the main topics when referring. The less that is underlined, the easier it is to find a specific topic. When dealing with a topic that is a person, underline only her last name, because after first presenting the full name, the passage will use only the last name to refer to her.

Sometimes underlining adjectives next to topics can be quite helpful, but it is unnecessary if you can easily remember the associated information when you see only the topic itself underlined. For instance, if we considered "poetry" a Main Topic, then we could underline "good" along with it:

> ...and English literary forms so quickly and well that she was composing <u>good poetry</u> in English within a few years of her arrival in New England.

Paragraph Subjects

Recall that you should pause after reading each paragraph to quickly state its subject (this distinct from the overall subject of the passage). Underlining the main topics in each paragraph will help you do. As you read the paragraph you will give extra attention to the most important topics. That helps you remember those topics. Also, as you are pinpointing the subject of the paragraph, you can use the topics you underlined as a reference. The paragraph subject will involve those Topics; all you need to do is supply the verbs that connect or describe them. For instance, with the two topics above (Wheatley, barriers) we can state the subject: "Wheatley overcame the barriers to writing poetry."

Another Example

After reading the first paragraph, we had a feel for the subject of the passage: it involves Wheatley's poetry. We take that knowledge into the paragraph, which does not directly deal with her poetry until the final line. Identify and underline the main topics from the second paragraph from the Wheatley passage:

> Wheatley's experience exemplifies the meeting of oral and written literary cultures. The aesthetic principles of the African oral tradition were preserved in America by folk artists in work songs, dancing, field hollers, religious music, the use of the drum, and, after the drum was forbidden, in the perpetuation of drum effects in song. African languages and the functions of language in African societies not only contributed to the emergence of a distinctive Black English but also exerted demonstrable effects on the manner in which other Americans spoke English. Given her African heritage and her facility with English and the conventions of English poetry, Wheatley's work had the potential to apply the ideas of a written literature to an oral literary tradition in the creation of an African American literary language.

Generally, the first line of a paragraph gives an idea of the paragraph's subject. In the paragraph above, we are told that Wheatley's experience is characteristic of the meeting of two different kinds of culture: literary and oral.

We can presume that the passage will discuss how this is so, especially along the lines of the **oral** culture, because the first paragraph dealt with the written culture Wheatley experienced. Underline "oral and written cultures," as that is certainly a main topic. This is **not a crucial** topic to underline, but certainly a helpful one. It is not always clear which are the best Topics to underline. That is fine, as long as you underline at least one topic in every paragraph, and you judge the importance of the topics you read.

The second and third sentences talk about African oral tradition and how it was preserved in America. We do not need to underline this because we already captured that essence with "oral... cultures." The third sentence goes into more depth on how the African oral culture played a part in American culture. No big topics to underline there. "Black English" is a secondary topic that supports the effects of the African oral tradition. The final sentence of the paragraph contains an abstract, but useful topic: "potential." That is what the entire paragraph has been leading up to. Wheatley's unique experiences gave her this potential. Here is the paragraph with the recommended underlines:

> Wheatley's experience exemplifies the meeting of oral and written literary cultures. The aesthetic principles of the African oral tradition were preserved in America by folk artists in work songs, dancing, field hollers, religious music, the use of the drum, and, after the drum was forbidden, in the perpetuation of drum effects in song. African languages and the functions of language in African societies not only contributed to the emergence of a distinctive Black English but also exerted demonstrable effects on the manner in which other Americans spoke English. Given her African heritage and her facility with English and the conventions of English poetry, Wheatley's work had the potential to apply the ideas of a written literature to an oral literary tradition in the creation of an African American literary language.

We can summarize this paragraph using the topics we underlined: "Wheatley had the potential to unite the African oral tradition with the English written culture in her writing." The subject can be as simple as "her potential."

As you can see, underlining the main topics is powerful. It forces you to understand the relevance of different topics, and it helps you pinpoint the subject and summarize each paragraph. It is the core marking technique, so embrace it.

Oval Speakers

Even though speakers are a type of topic, they deserve a unique mark. So, draw an **oval** around the name of each person or group that expresses an opinion. speakers and the viewpoints that they express are so important it is worth distinguishing them visually from normal topics. An oval allows you to easily see where all the speakers are when you reference the passage. Not every passage features a speaker, only a little more than half do. Those passages that do not feature a speaker will likely contain the author's opinion at least once. More on marking that in a moment.

Use Verbs to Identify Speakers

A speaker has an opinion and to express that opinion, the author will use a verb that is a synonym of "thinks" or "believes." These words are signals that you are about to read an opinion. Example:

> In general, biochemists ***judged*** cytologists to be too ignorant of chemistry to grasp the basic processes, whereas cytologists ***considered*** the methods of biochemists inadequate to characterize the structures of the living cell. The renewal of Mendelian genetics and, later, progress in chromosome mapping did little at first to effect a synthesis.

The biochemists **judged** the cytologists to be ignorant of chemistry. The cytologists **considered** the biochemists methods to be inadequate. "Judge" and "consider" are both synonyms of "think."

Other terms you will see used are:

- Argue
- Contend
- Advocate
- Believe
- Prefer
- Add

Take a moment and reread those verbs. The verb is your signal, and it tells you to oval the speaker. As we began reading the first sentence of the above paragraph, we know that biochemists are a group that can hold an opinion (because they are not an inanimate object or idea) and the word "judge" tells us that we are about to read the opinion that they hold.

Here is how we circle the speakers in that paragraph:

> In general, biochemists judged cytologists to be too ignorant of chemistry to grasp the basic processes, whereas cytologists considered the methods of biochemists inadequate to characterize the structures of the living cell. The renewal of Mendelian genetics and, later, progress in chromosome mapping did little at first to effect a synthesis.

Read this paragraph and identify the speakers within:

> Because of the inquisitorial system's thoroughness in conducting its pretrial investigation, it can be concluded that, if given the choice, a defendant who is innocent would *prefer* to be tried under the inquisitorial system, whereas a defendant who is guilty would *prefer* to be tried under the adversarial system.

The signal word for the opinions is "prefer." The first speaker is an innocent defendant. This is an abstract category of person; anyone could be that, given the right circumstances. The viewpoint is to rather be tried under the inquisitorial system. The next speaker is a guilty defendant who is guilty and their view is obvious.

The circles we would draw:

> Because of the inquisitorial system's thoroughness in conducting its pretrial investigation, it can be concluded that, if given the choice, a defendant who is innocent would prefer to be tried under the inquisitorial system, whereas a defendant who is guilty would prefer to be tried under the adversarial system.

Multiple Opinions

Sometimes a single person or group will give multiple opinions in the passage. These will almost always be accompanied by the name of the person or group. So, if the opinions are spread out in the passage, you can easily circle the speaker in all those spots.

When a speaker has multiple opinions in a row, circle the first mention of the Speakers name. Some paragraphs will be occupied by the views of one or more speakers, and often the views of one of them will be elaborated over two or more sentences. No need to circle the speakers over again within a few sentences.

People are Often Just Topics

Of course, the author will often mention a person or group that does not have any opinion (without using a "think" synonym). In that situation, the person or group is a topic, not a speaker, because only speakers have specific viewpoints.

The Author's Opinion

In most passages, the author remains fairly impartial, giving information in a balanced and reasoned way. This is especially true at the beginning of a passage, when an author introduces and explains the main topics. In some passages, the author never gives his opinion(s). In others, that author does. It can be challenging to identify author opinions, but with practice, you will become proficient at it. An author's opinion will often involve taking a side on an issue that has been discussed by the passage in depth. To illustrate this, reread this introductory paragraph:

> (1.4) Outside the medical profession, there are various efforts to cut medicine down to size: not only widespread malpractice litigation and massive governmental regulation, but also attempts by consumer groups and others to redefine medicine as a trade rather than as a profession, and the physician as merely a technician for hire under contract. Why should physicians ***(or indeed all sensible people)*** resist such efforts to give the practice of medicine a new meaning? We can gain some illumination from etymology. "Trade," from Germanic and Anglo Saxon roots meaning "a course or pathway," has come to mean derivatively a habitual occupation and has been related to certain skills and crafts. On the other hand, while "profession" today also entails a habit of work, the word "profession" itself traces to an act of self-conscious and public---even confessional-speech. "To profess" preserves the meaning of its Latin source, "to declare publicly; to announce, affirm, avow." A profession is an activity or occupation to which its practitioner publicly professes, that is, confesses, devotion. But public announcement seems insufficient; publicly declaring devotion to plumbing or auto repair would not turn these trades into professions.

This is mostly a fact-based discussion, one that presents the main topics. We learn that efforts are being made to hamper the field of medicine, including redefining it as a trade. Next is a discussion on the origins of the words "trade" and "profession."

Other parts of this paragraph are the author's opinion. The words in parenthesis (italicized by us for emphasis) tell us that the author believes that all sensible people, people who think clearly, should resist these relabeling efforts. This contrasts the view of consumer groups and others who think that medicine **should be** relabeled, and contrasting a view in the passage is a clue that we have the author's opinion on our hands. The words used are striking: **all** people who show sound judgment should agree with physicians and the author on this point. That is strong language for an RC passage.

The final sentence of the paragraph is also an opinion, but a less notable one. The author states that publicly announcing devotion to a job is not enough to make that job a profession. This is a lead in for the next paragraph. The fact that we do not know if anyone would argue against this view is a good indication that it does not need to be marked. Only mark the author's opinions that are important, centered on a main topic. This opinion could go either way.

Mark with an "A"

Because the author's opinion is given rarely and it gives insight into the author's thoughts on a topic, it is tested by the questions. Therefore, it is crucial to mark author opinions. Unlike a speaker, the name of the author is not identified in the passage right before the opinion is given, so there is nothing to circle. Instead, write an "A" on the right side of the passage (the side without the line numbering) next to an author opinion. To mark the author's opinion in the previous paragraph, we would place an "A" alongside the line with the parenthesis comment. We choose the right side of the text because it is free of line numbers and is thus easier to spot. If you prefer marking on the left, no problem.

Word Selection

An author can express a viewpoint using a **single**, well chosen word. Often, the word passes judgment on the viewpoint of someone else. This example includes the ending of one paragraph and the beginning of another:

> ...The knowledge involved makes the profession one of the learned variety, but its professional quality is rooted in something else.
>
> Some ***mistakenly*** seek to locate that something else in the prestige and honor accorded professionals by society, evidenced in their special titles and the special deference and privileges they receive. But externalities do not constitute medicine a profession. Physicians are not professionals because they are honored; rather, they are honored because of their profession...

The key word here is "mistakenly" at the beginning of the second paragraph. With this word, the author indicates that those who seek the professional quality in the prestige given to professionals are looking in the wrong place. The next sentence supports this point: the externalities (or effects) of medicine being a profession are not what makes medicine a profession. Prestige is an externality. "Mistakenly" hints at an idea that is elaborated later. "Mistakenly" is a clue that helps us follow the author's point throughout the paragraph.

This is not a notable opinion because it is a stepping stone in the author's argument. It is another example of an aspect that does not make a job a profession. Eventually the author will describe what qualities *do* make a profession. That is the larger conclusion that intermediary points, like this opinion, are building to. Any information that serves as evidence for larger conclusion is usually not crucial to note as an attitude. Regardless, here is how we would mark this passage assuming it was an important author opinion:

> Some mistakenly seek to locate that something else in the prestige and honor accorded professionals by society, evidenced in their special titles and the special deference and privileges they receive. But externalities do not constitute medicine a profession. Physicians are not professionals because they are honored; rather, they are honored because of their profession. A

Authors often give opinions in the **final** paragraph of the passage, when topics previously elaborated can be evaluated by the author. So, when you read the final paragraph, look for opinions. About half of the passages feature important author opinions.

Main Point

As you read a passage, keep an eye out for its main point as knowing the overall conclusion is incredibly helpful. Not surprisingly, some passages have a sentence or two that directly expresses the main point. We call these <u>main point declarations</u>, or <u>MPDs</u>. Note that an MPD is a type of opinion from the author, but it is a special one, so it gets its own mark.

No passages feature the main point perfectly stated - identical to the correct answer choice on a main point question. MPDs occur in less than a third of RC passages, as most passages develop their conclusion over the entire passage or at least several paragraphs. And passages almost never feature a concluding paragraph that ties everything together. Digesting the passage is **your** job, done through careful reading.

MPDs in the First Paragraph

When the passage includes a MPD, you can spot it by paying attention to the scope of the conclusions. Sometimes, the MPD is in the first paragraph. The trouble there is that you know little about the subject at that point. If you run across a sentence or two in the first paragraph that is general in scope and supported by the other sentences in that paragraph, then it could be a MPD. As you read on, you will know.

Write a "MP" for "main point" next to the line that the MPD **begins** on. Example MPD in an introductory paragraph:

> (2.4) The Constitution of the United States does not explicitly define the extent of the President's authority to involve United States troops in conflicts with other nations in the absence of a declaration of war. Instead, the question of the President's authority in this matter falls in the hazy area of concurrent power, where authority is not expressly allocated to either the President or the Congress. The Constitution gives Congress the basic power to declare war, as well as the authority to raise and support armies and a navy, enact regulations for the control of the military, and provide for the common defense. The President, on the other hand, in addition to being obligated to execute the laws of the land, including commitments negotiated by defense treaties, is named commander in chief of the armed forces and is empowered to appoint envoys and make treaties with the consent of the Senate. Although this allocation of powers does not expressly address the use of armed forces short of a declared war, the spirit of the Constitution at least MP requires that Congress should be involved in the decision to deploy troops, and in passing the War Powers Resolution of 1973, Congress has at last reclaimed a role in such decisions.

The main point is described at the end of the final sentence: "in passing the War Powers Resolution of 1973, Congress has at last reclaimed a role in such decisions." The sentences before this one give background information on the President and Congress's powers to declare war. The final sentence is the culmination of this introductory discussion and it is weighty: it gives a strong statement that the rest of the passage will develop.

When the MPD is in the first paragraph, it is often at the **end**. This allows the second paragraph to immediately begin supporting and/or exploring the conclusion.

In the Last Paragraph

When the main point is stated at the end, it is easier to spot because you have read most of the passage and understand what the author is trying to say. You can then recognize when the author articulates her primary conclusion. Everything you have read up until that point will have, in some way, contributed to the MPD.

Look at the final paragraph from the Wheatley passage:

> (1.1) Thus limited by the eighteenth-century English literary code, Wheatley's poetry contributed little to the development of a distinctive African American literary language. Yet by the standards of the literary conventions in which she chose to work, Wheatley's poetry is undeniably accomplished, and she is justly celebrated as the first Black American poet. MP

This short paragraph articulates the author's main point. You should notice the importance of those sentences as you read, and draw a "MP" next to them. The exact location is not crucial – right in the middle of the paragraph makes sense because the entire paragraph is the main point. That quick mark makes this question especially easy.

Below is the correct answer choice to a question which asks for the main idea:

> (C) Phillis Wheatley's poetry did not fulfill the potential inherent in her experience but did represent a significant accomplishment.

(C) is a rewording of the two final sentences. Here is another MPD that appears in the **last** paragraph of the passage. This paragraph is drawn from the passage about scientific disciplines:

> (1.2) This interaction between paired disciplines can have important results. MP In the case of late nineteenth-century cell research, progress was fueled by competition among the various attitudes and issues derived from cell biology and biochemistry. Joseph Fruton, a biochemist, has suggested that such competition and the resulting tensions among researchers are a principal source of vitality and "are likely to lead to unexpected and exciting novelties in the future, as they have in the past."

The first sentence here – "This interaction between paired disciplines can have important results" – is the MPD. Organization wise, the passage fits the MPD: The first paragraph of the passage describes the concept of two competing scientific disciplines, the second paragraph builds on this concept with the examples of cytology and biochemistry, and then the third and fourth paragraphs talk about how the competition between these two forces both disciplines to grow. Here is the correct answer to the main point question in this passage set:

> Antithetical scientific disciplines often interact with one another in ways that can be highly useful.

You can see the similarity between this and the short introduction to the final paragraph.

Divide Paragraphs

Split up long paragraphs that contain two main ideas. Draw a vertical line in between two sentences where the paragraph shifts from one idea to another. This will help you visually distinguish between the two ideas the author is developing within that one paragraph.

> The problem is that, as an Elizabethan playwright, Webster has become a prisoner of our critical presuppositions. We have, in recent years, been dazzled by the way the earlier Renaissance and medieval theater, particularly the morality play, illuminates Elizabethan drama. We now understand how the habit of mind that saw the world as a battleground between good and evil produced the morality play. Morality plays allegorized that conflict by presenting characters whose actions were defined as the embodiment of good or evil. This model of reality lived on, overlaid by different conventions, in the more sophisticated Elizabethan works of the following age. | Yet Webster seems not to have been as heavily influenced by the morality play's model of reality as were his Elizabethan contemporaries; he was apparently more sensitive to the more morally complicated Italian drama than to these English sources. Consequently, his characters cannot be evaluated according to reductive formulas of good and evil, which is precisely what modern critics have tried to do. They choose what seem to be the most promising of the contradictory values that are dramatized in the play, and treat those values as if they were the only basis for analyzing the moral development of the play's major characters, attributing the inconsistencies in a character's behavior to artistic incompetence on Webster's part. The lack of consistency in Webster's characters can be better understood if we recognize that the ambiguity at the heart of his tragic vision lies not in the external world but in the duality of human nature. Webster establishes tension in his plays by setting up conflicting systems of value that appear immoral only when one value system is viewed exclusively from the perspective of the other. He presents us not only with characters that we condemn…

Notice how the focus on the paragraph shifts with the sentence "Yet Webster…" We mark that shift with a vertical line. This helps you follow the flow of the what would otherwise be a dauntingly long paragraph.

Optional Marks

Every LSAT student is different and some benefit from marking a passage to a greater degree. The following are additional passage elements that you can mark: lists, examples, definitions, dates and questions. We do not condone these marks, as keeping the passage relatively clean helps you use the marks you have more effectively. Further, the less marking you do, the more easily you can follow the content and details of the passage.

For most students, these optional marks are far less helpful than the ones already covered and somewhat counterproductive. This is not to say that these **elements** are not important; they are. If you find that marking them is helpful for you noting them, then by all means, use these markings. These are in order of usefulness to mark:

Lists

We prefer that you take the time to mark lists over examples (discussed momentarily). Lists give more structure to a passage, mostly because they are usually longer. Lists are also more likely to tested on than information in an Example.

The advantage of marking a list is that you can easily return to it and its specific parts, because you have markers for them. Write the numbers of each item on the right side of the passage. Example list numbered:

1 First, in French law not all government contracts are treated as administrative contracts. Some contracts are designated as administrative by specific statute, in which case the contractor is made aware of the applicable legal rules upon entering into agreement with the government. Alternatively, the contracting government....

2 Second, the French law of administrative contracts, although adopted by several countries, is not so universally accepted that it can be embraced as a general principle of law. In both the United States and the United...

When you deal with lists that do not use numbers, ones that designate item parts with terms like "primarily," "next" and "finally," the numbering helps you see where each item starts. Another example marking of a list:

1 (3.2) Why were the contributions of these technicians not recognized by their employers? One reason
is the historical tendency, which has persisted into the twentieth century, to view scientific discovery as
resulting from momentary flashes of individual insight rather than from extended periods of cooperative
2 work by individuals with varying levels of knowledge and skill. Moreover, despite the clamor of
seventeenth-century scientific rhetoric commending a hands-on approach, science was still overwhelmingly
an activity of the English upper class, and the traditional contempt that genteel society maintained for
3 manual labor was pervasive and deeply rooted. Finally, all of Boyle's technicians were "servants," which in
seventeenth-century usage meant anyone who worked for pay. To seventeenth-century sensibilities, the
wage relationship was charged with political significance. Servants, meaning wage earners were excluded
from the franchise because they were perceived as ultimately dependent on their wages and thus controlled
by the will of their employers.

Examples

Examples are generally not tested enough in the questions to warrant a specific mark. That being said, if you find that you have trouble identifying examples as you read, or are missing questions that test the information within examples, then perhaps marking them will help. To do so, write an "E" next to the start of the example.

> (1.4) Their titles and the respect they are shown superficially signify and acknowledge something deeper, that physicians are persons of the professional sort, knowingly and freely devoting themselves to a *E*
> way of life worthy of such devotion. Just as lawyers devote themselves to rectifying injustices, looking up to what is lawful and right; just as teachers devote themselves to the education of the young, looking up to truth and wisdom; so physicians heal the sick, looking up to health and wholesomeness.

With the "E" in place, you can easily refer back to these examples if necessary.

Dates

In passages that feature a lot of dates (two or more), feel free to **underline** or **oval** them. They are likely important topics when that many appear, and it may be helpful to be able to locate them quickly.

Definitions

When the author teaches you a new term with a definition, that term is probably important. We recommend that you make a mental instead of physical note when you encounter a definition. However, if you prefer to use a mark, perhaps because you find yourself breezing over definitions and want to force yourself to remember them, use a "D" on the line the definition begins on. Here is an example:

> (2.3) Three basic adaptive responses-regulatory, acclimatory, and developmental-may occur in
> organisms as they react to changing environmental conditions. In all three, adjustment of biological *D*
> features (morphological adjustment) or of their use (functional adjustment) may occur. Regulatory *D*
> responses involve rapid changes in the organism's use of its physiological apparatus-increasing or decreasing the rates of various processes, for example. Acclimation involves morphological change-thickening of fur or red blood cell proliferation-which alters physiology itself. Such structural changes require more time than regulatory response changes. Regulatory and acclimatory responses are both reversible.

The author defines "regulatory responses" and "acclimation." These are good definitions to notice because they are key terms. They are more **explained** than defined. This format is not the normal way you see definitions given, so it is easier to miss. The definition of key terms of a passage is more likely to be tested on than other definitions, so definitely pay attention to those.

Questions

Recall that whenever an author poses a question or answers one, that information is important. Questions are used for emphasis. Like definitions, you will probably not need to refer back to a question when working the questions, so we do not believe that it is very helpful to mark them. That being said, if you want to, mark them with a "Q" alongside the passage. Questions posed and answered in passages are fairly rare, so whether or not you mark them is not a big deal.

Unhelpful Marks

Two marks that are recommended by many LSAT prep books and companies that we are actively against: writing paragraph summaries in the margins and underlining words that are not topics. Neither helps you when referring back to the passage, and both take time to create.

Paragraph Summaries

Stating the subject of each paragraph you read ensures that you understood the paragraph and helps you remember what you just learned. The extra step of writing out a short summary in the margin takes time, breaks the flow of your reading, and does not serve any real purpose. Writing down even a few words switches you from reading mode into writing mode, something that can cause you to lose focus.

The main topics and speakers in each paragraph will be underlined. When you refer back to the passage to find something, those marks will guide you to the location you need. No need to add a summary for each paragraph in the margin.

Words that are Not Topics

Students often want to mark non-topic words that they feel are important, especially signal words that the author uses to direct the flow of the passage. These might be amount words – "some, many, most, all" – or transition words – "however, except, along these lines, but." As long as you read the passage carefully, you do not need to mark signal words. Only underlining the topics keeps those easy to see, and they are quite useful in referencing.

Use the amount and transition words, because they are important. Those words will help you follow the flow of the discussion. But save **marking** for other passage elements.

Example Marked Passages

To add authenticity to these examples, we will use the two column format found on the LSAT.

Read and mark each passage. Then, look at our markings on the next page and read the explanations.

(1.3) There are two major systems of criminal procedure in the modem world-the adversarial and the inquisitorial. Both systems were historically preceded by the system of private vengeance in which the victim of a crime fashioned a remedy and administered it privately, either personally or through an agent.

The modern adversarial system is only one historical step removed from the private vengeance system and still retains some of its characteristic features. For example, even though the right to initiate legal action against a criminal has now been extended to all members of society (as represented by the office of the public prosecutor), and even though the police department has effectively assumed the pretrial investigative functions on behalf of the prosecution, the adversarial system still leaves the defendant to conduct his or her own pretrial investigation. The trial is viewed as a forensic duel between two adversaries, presided over by a judge who, at the start, has no knowledge of the investigative background of the case. In the final analysis the adversarial system of criminal procedure symbolizes and regularizes punitive combat.

By contrast, the inquisitorial system begins historically where the adversarial system stopped its development. It is two historical steps removed from the system of private vengeance. From the standpoint of legal anthropology, then, it is historically superior to the adversarial system. Under the inquisitorial system, the public prosecutor has the duty to investigate not just on behalf of society but also on behalf of the defendant. Additionally, the public prosecutor has the duty to present the court not only, evidence that would convict the defendant, but also evidence that could prove the defendant's innocence. The system mandates that both parties permit full pretrial discovery of the evidence in their possession. Finally, an aspect of the system that makes the trial less like a duel between two adversarial parties is that the inquisitorial system mandates that the judge take an active part in the conduct of the trial, with a role that is both directive and protective.

Fact-finding is at the heart of the inquisitorial system. This system operates on the philosophical premise that in a criminal action the crucial factor is the body of facts, not the legal rule (in contrast to the adversarial system), and the goal of the entire procedure is to attempt to recreate, in the mind of the court, the commission of the alleged crime.

Because of the inquisitorial system's thoroughness in conducting its pretrial investigation, it can be concluded that, if given the choice, a defendant who is innocent would prefer to be tried under the inquisitorial system, whereas a defendant who is guilty would prefer to be tried under the adversarial system.

There are two major systems of criminal procedure in the modem world-the adversarial and the inquisitorial. Both systems were historically preceded by the system of private vengeance in which the victim of a crime fashioned a remedy and administered it privately, either personally or through an agent.

The modern adversarial system is only one historical step removed from the private vengeance system and still retains some of its characteristic features. For example, even though the right to initiate legal action against a criminal has now been extended to all members of society (as represented by the office of the public prosecutor), and even though the police department has effectively assumed the pretrial investigative functions on behalf of the prosecution, the adversarial system still leaves the defendant to conduct his or her own pretrial investigation. The trial is viewed as a forensic duel between two adversaries, presided over by a judge who, at the start, has no knowledge of the investigative background of the case. In the final analysis the adversarial system of criminal procedure symbolizes and regularizes punitive combat.

By contrast, the inquisitorial system begins historically where the adversarial system stopped its development. It is two historical steps removed from the system of private vengeance. From the standpoint of legal anthropology, then, it is historically superior to the adversarial system. Under the inquisitorial system, the public prosecutor has the duty to investigate not just on behalf of society but also on behalf of the defendant. Additionally, the public prosecutor has the duty to present the court not only, evidence that would convict the defendant, but also evidence that could prove the defendant's innocence. The system mandates that both parties permit full pretrial discovery of the evidence in their possession. Finally, an aspect of the system that makes the trial less like a duel between two adversarial parties is that the inquisitorial system mandates that the judge take an active part in the conduct of the trial, with a role that is both directive and protective.

Fact-finding is at the heart of the inquisitorial system. This system operates on the philosophical premise that in a criminal action the crucial factor is the body of facts, not the legal rule (in contrast to the adversarial system), and the goal of the entire procedure is to attempt to recreate, in the mind of the court, the commission of the alleged crime.

Because of the inquisitorial system's thoroughness in conducting its pretrial investigation, it can be concluded that, if given the choice, a defendant who is innocent would prefer to be tried under the inquisitorial system, whereas a defendant who is guilty would prefer to be tried under the adversarial system.

This passage is informative, not argumentative. The differences between the two systems of criminal procedure are thoroughly analyzed. Because of its nature, there are a lot of different topics discussed, but no important opinions. The field of legal anthropology referenced in paragraph 3, might be considered a speaker, the opinion being that inquisitorial is superior. So, we circle that.

The author states that the inquisitorial system is newer; the inquisitorial system started developing where the adversarial system left off. The author never expresses any notable opinions. The closest is the information in the last paragraph. The author describes how innocent defendants would prefer to be tried under the inquisitorial system. This is because that system is focused on fact-finding and getting to the truth of whether the alleged crime was committed. Likewise, the author says that a guilty defendant would prefer the adversarial system, and we assume this is because the defendant can defend himself in that case and the judge is less active. This makes the trial less open and more likely that a guilty defendant could be acquitted. Both of these statements by the author are closer to conclusions than opinions, but we mark them with an "A" anyway.

As far as the main topics underlined, the emphasis is obviously on the most important of each paragraph. For instance, paragraph two focuses on the adversarial system, so that topic is underlined. The fact that the defendant must conduct his own pretrial investigation is notable, so "defendant" is underlined. And "forensic duel" is a notable and expressive term, so it too is underlined.

There is no MPD. We have marked the definition of private vengeance in the first paragraph – this is optional.

This passage has five paragraphs; the newer passages typically have 3-4. This might mean that we underline fewer topics in each paragraph than normal, but the fact-filled nature of the passage balances out the fact that the content is divided over more paragraphs.

Do not worry if you made different choices in your markings. Analyze the choices you made and how helpful they were in understanding the passage.

Now, read and mark this passage:

(2.2) Historians generally agree that, of the great modern innovations, the railroad had the most far-reaching impact on major events in the United States in the nineteenth and early twentieth centuries, particularly on the Industrial Revolution. There is, however, considerable disagreement among cultural historians regarding public attitudes toward the railroad, both at its inception in the 1830s and during the half century between 1880 and 1930, when the national rail system was completed and reached the zenith of its popularity in the United States. In a recent book, John Stilgoe has addressed this issue by arguing that the "romantic-era distrust" of the railroad that he claims was present during the 1830s vanished in the decades after 1880. But the argument he provides in support of this position is unconvincing.

What Stilgoe calls "romantic-era distrust" was in fact the reaction of a minority of writers, artists, and intellectuals who distrusted the railroad not so much for what it was as for what it signified. Thoreau and Hawthorne appreciated, even admired, an improved means of moving things and people from one place to another. What these writers and others were concerned about was not the new machinery as such, but the new kind of economy, social order, and culture that it prefigured. In addition, Stilgoe is wrong to imply that the critical attitude of these writers was typical of the period; their distrust was largely a reaction against the prevailing attitude in the 1830s that the railroad was an unqualified improvement.

Stilgoe's assertion that the ambivalence toward the railroad exhibited by writers like Hawthorne and Thoreau disappeared after the 1880s is also misleading. In support of this thesis, Stilgoe has unearthed an impressive volume of material, the work of hitherto unknown illustrators, journalists, and novelists, all devotees of the railroad; but it is not clear what this new material proves except perhaps that the works of popular culture greatly expanded at the time. The volume of the material proves nothing if Stilgoe's point is that the earlier distrust of a minority of intellectuals did not endure beyond the 1880s, and, oddly, much of Stilgoe's other evidence indicates that it did. When he glances at the treatment of railroads by writers like Henry James, Sinclair Lewis, or F. Scott Fitzgerald, what comes through in spite of Stilgoe's analysis is remarkably like Thoreau's feeling of contrariety and ambivalence. (Had he looked at the work of Frank Norris, Eugene O'Neill, or Henry Adams, Stilgoe's case would have been much stronger.) The point is that the sharp contrast between the enthusiastic supporters of the railroad in the 1830s and the minority of intellectual dissenters during that period extended into the 1880s and beyond.

Historians generally agree that, of the great modern innovations, the railroad had the most far-reaching impact on major events in the United States in the nineteenth and early twentieth centuries, particularly on the Industrial Revolution. There is, however, considerable disagreement among cultural historians regarding public attitudes toward the railroad, both at its inception in the 1830s and during the half century between 1880 and 1930, when the national rail system was completed and reached the zenith of its popularity in the United States. In a recent book, John Stilgoe has addressed this issue by arguing that the "romantic-era distrust" of the railroad that he claims was present during the 1830s vanished in the decades after 1880. But the argument he provides in support of this position is unconvincing.

What Stilgoe calls "romantic-era distrust" was in fact the reaction of a minority of writers, artists, and intellectuals who distrusted the railroad not so much for what it was as for what it signified. Thoreau and Hawthorne appreciated, even admired, an improved means of moving things and people from one place to another. What these writers and others were concerned about was not the new machinery as such, but the new kind of economy, social order, and culture that it prefigured. In addition, Stilgoe is wrong to imply that the critical attitude of these writers was typical of the period; their distrust was largely a reaction against the prevailing attitude in the 1830s that the railroad was an unqualified improvement.

Stilgoe's assertion that the ambivalence toward the railroad exhibited by writers like Hawthorne and Thoreau disappeared after the 1880s is also misleading. In support of this thesis, Stilgoe has unearthed an impressive volume of material, the work of hitherto unknown illustrators, journalists, and novelists, all devotees of the railroad; but it is not clear what this new material proves except perhaps that the works of popular culture greatly expanded at the time. The volume of the material proves nothing if Stilgoe's point is that the earlier distrust of a minority of intellectuals did not endure beyond the 1880s, and, oddly, much of Stilgoe's other evidence indicates that it did. When he glances at the treatment of railroads by writers like Henry James, Sinclair Lewis, or F. Scott Fitzgerald, what comes through in spite of Stilgoe's analysis is remarkably like Thoreau's feeling of contrariety and ambivalence. (Had he looked at the work of Frank Norris, Eugene O'Neill, or Henry Adams, Stilgoe's case would have been much stronger.) The point is that the sharp contrast between the enthusiastic supporters of the railroad in the 1830s and the minority of intellectual dissenters during that period extended into the 1880s and beyond.

This passage analyzes Stigloe's ideas, and the author does not agree with them. There are two different types of information given: Stigloe's ideas and support for them, and the author's response to those ideas and support for the author's view. Therefore, much of the passage contains the author's opinions. We know they are opinions, because they are in **reaction** to Stilgoe's ideas. Only two important author opinions in the passage are marked: the one at the beginning of P1, and the one at the beginning of P3. In a passage that is full of author viewpoints, it is not necessary to mark every one. We could have also marked the last sentence of P1, and parts of the end of P3. The important thing is to be aware that the author is **steadily** rejecting Stilgoe's views on public attitudes towards the railroads.

We circled "Stigloe" towards the end of P1, because he gives a view about romantic-era distrust there and is a speaker. The words "arguing" and "claims" are clear signals that this is a viewpoint. Note that you might have to backtrack a little to circle Stigloe after reading part or all of that sentence. P1 also begins with a view of historians regarding the impact of the railroad, so we circled "Historians."

The last sentence of P3, starts with "the point," a signal that summary information is coming. Also, after having read the passage, you will note that this sentence is a MPD. P2 introduces the author's idea that there was a contrast between popular views on the railroad and the views of a small and vocal minority. Then, P3 argues that these views for each group were steady from the 1830s through the 1880s. The final sentence of P3 captures many of the author's points. But, the passage is about how Stilgoe's beliefs are wrong, so the main point must mention that.

There are quite a few main topics, so discretion is required. Reading P1 is straight-forward: "railroad, public attitudes and romantic-era distrust" are the main topics. The dates in that paragraph deserve a special mention. It is important to understand their meaning. They distinguish two time periods: when the railroads were first blossoming in the 1830's and the height of the railroads from 1880 to 1930. As long as you grasp that point, there is no reason to mark the dates.

In P2, we underline "reaction of a minority" which is an abstract but important topic because the author argues that a minority of intellectuals were the only ones who were against the railroad. They were concerned about the "new kind of economy, social order and culture" brought about by the RR. Reading for the author's ideas in this paragraph leads to discovering and underlining some fairly **elusive**, subtle concepts. Those markings are powerful as they relate to the author's opinions.

P3 also features a concept (not person, place, etc.) as a topic: the ambivalence toward the railroad exhibited by writers. Stigloe believed this ambivalence disappeared at the height of the railroads popularity, but the author disagrees and uses the rest of the paragraph to prove that point. Two other main topics are the "impressive volume of material" that Stigloe collects and the "other evidence" that the author believes is more relevant. The final two underlines are groups of writers that support a side on the issue. Evidence of the sort that supports each side could easily be tested by the questions.

Practice Makes Perfect

Ultimately, you need to work many RC sections and analyze how well your markings assisted you. Evaluate them in three different ways:

- How focused they kept you as you read each paragraph.
- How much they helped you reference the passage for specific questions.
- How applicable your markings were to the questions you faced.

That analysis, over time, will truly help you to find the right methods of the marking the passage to maximize your RC score.

*Marking A Passage Review

- Use a pencil for all markings.
- Marking helps you reference the passage effectively.
- This system is designed to be lean.
    - Strike the right balance between reading and marking.

Underline Topics

- Underline the main topics - the more important ideas, people, concepts discussed.
- There are usually 2-4 important topics in the first two paragraphs, and then 1-3 in the later paragraphs.
- Use your underlined topics to help you state the subject of each paragraph after you finish reading it.

Oval Speakers

- Speakers are people with opinion.
    - Draw an oval around them.
- A little over half the passages will have at least one speaker.
- Use the "believe" type verbs to identify speakers.
    - These verbs are signals that an opinion is about to be given: "state" and "argue."

The Author's Opinion

- Write an "A" next to the author's opinion, on the right side of the column away from the line numberings.
- Authors often comment on an issue from the passage.

Main Point

- Main point declarations (or MPDs) are when the author directly states the main point.
    - Mark these with an "MP" in the margin.
- These occur in about a third of passages.
- Normally the main point is developed over more than a few sentences.
    - Or it is not explicitly stated.
- The main point can be in the first paragraph.
    - It will be supported by the other statements in that paragraph.

Divide Paragraphs

- Split long paragraphs which contain two ideas in half with a vertical bar where the focus shifts.

Optional Marks

- Lists – Number the different elements in the margin.
    - These are likely to be tested.
    - The numbering helps you easily see where they are.
- Examples – mark with an "E."
    - Not a very important mark.
- Dates – when a passage features a lot of them, underline the dates in the passage.
- Definitions – mark terms that are defined with a "D" in the margin.
- Questions – mark with a "Q" in the margin.

Practice Makes Perfect

- Practice marking many full passages and be patient with your progress.
- Work the questions and see how much the marks helped you refer back and how applicable they were to the questions you faced.
    - Use that analysis to refine how you mark over time.

The Questions

Understanding a passage and marking it appropriately are two of the hardest parts of a passage set. When you do those well, you make the questions much easier to tackle. Just as you will see with the Games section, the work done before attacking the questions is arguably the most important work.

With that emphasized, it is time to learn about the different types of questions that the RC section will throw at you. In order to help you approach the questions, we categorize them in two ways, by reference and type. The reference refers to where the query directs you to find the information needed to answer that question in the passage. Unsurprisingly, the type refers to the kind of information the question asks for, what the question asks you to do. You are familiar with types from the divisions used in the LR methods.

The queries tell you both the reference and the type. To a large degree, the types are tied to the kind of reference they provide. For instance, main point questions **always** have a Global reference, which means that no specific reference is given by the query. So, we will first explain the three kinds of references and then walk through the various types, relating the two divisions as we go.

References

The questions can ask you about any part of the passage. Because of this, the test makers usually provide you with guidance on what part of the passage to refer to in order to find the information to answer the question. We call this information a reference. About 60% of the RC questions from recent LSATs (#s 56-61) contained references in their queries. References often determine how you approach the question: whether you should refer back to the passage and where to look. We will explain the two types of references, topic and exact, before delving into the question types.

Noting the references in the query allows you to use the relevant parts of the passage **before** looking at the choices. That means you walk into the choices informed, which allows you to evaluate the choices more quickly and effectively. This prevents tempting incorrect ones from seducing you.

Exact References

About one fourth of queries contain an exact reference. These are precise references that tell you the exact part of the passage that the question is concerned with. An exact reference may give you line numbers:

> By a "closed system" of poetry (lines 34-35), the author most probably means poetry that

This query asks the meaning of a phrase, "closed system," and tells you the location of that phrase. You can very quickly find the sentence where "closed system" is used. A majority of exact references use line numbers, but some will direct you by mentioning a specific paragraph:

> The passage suggests that which one of the following has been established by the case discussed in the ***third paragraph***?

This question asks you the impact of the case discussed in P3. If you need to refresh your memory of this case, you would refer back to P3 and do so.

Exact References do not require you to use your mental map that you created during your first reading of the passage; they take the guess work out of referencing.

Read the Relevant Parts

Only a few question types provide exact references and these will be discussed in detail later. Any question featuring an exact reference is best approached by reading the parts referenced. Generally, you should start reading a bit before the exact reference, ideally at a **logical starting point**, like the beginning of a paragraph. This question for instance, references lines 25-29:

> It can be inferred from the passage that in the late nineteenth century the debate over the structural nature of protoplasm (lines 25-29) was most likely carried on…

To answer this question it is necessary to begin reading on line 21:

> choreography of the chromosomes during cell division. Many biochemists, on the other hand, remained skeptical of the idea that so much structure existed, arguing that the chemical reactions that occur in cytological preparations might create the appearance of such structures. Also, they stood apart from the debate then raging over whether protoplasm, the complex of living material within a cell, is homogeneous, network like, granular, or foam like.

Line 21 tells us that **biochemists** are the ones who stood apart from the debate on protoplasm. This means that the debate was carried on among cytologists, the other main group. If we had only read the lines of the reference (25-29), then we would not have been able to answer the question. For exact references with line numbers, begin your reading on the sentence before the reference so you have context. And if you need to, read the sentence **after** the reference. If the exact reference tells a paragraph, start reading at the beginning of the paragraph until you find the information you need. The reference tells you the location of a central aspect of the relevant information, but often those lines are not enough to answer the question.

Topic References

<u>Topic references</u> give less specific guidance than exact references. A topic reference tells you the topic (recall that this means the subject matter) that the question deals with. The topic could be a secondary or main one. Usually, that topic will only appear in a few places in the passage, allowing you to zero in on the information you need. Here is an example query with a topic reference. Note how the reference is built into the query, because it is the topic asked about:

> According to the passage, the ***standards of eighteenth century English poetry*** permitted Wheatley to include which one of the following in her poetry?

This query asks us about "standards of eighteenth century English poetry" so that is our topic reference. When we refer back to the passage, we want to find out what those standards allowed Wheatley to include in her poetry. P3 of that passage contains the information we need. We found that topic using our underlining.

Most of that paragraph:

> The standards of eighteenth-century English poetry, which itself reflected little of the American language, led Wheatley to develop a notion of poetry as a closed system, derived from imitation of earlier written works. No place existed for the rough-and-ready Americanized English she heard in the streets, for the English spoken by Black people, or for Africanisms. The conventions of eighteenth-century neoclassical poetry ruled out casual talk; her voice and feelings had to be generalized according to rules of poetic diction and characterization; the particulars of her African past, if they were to be dealt with at all, had to be subordinated to the reigning conventions.

The answer is contained in the third sentence: "her voice and feelings had to be generalized according to the rules of poetic diction and characterization." The correct answer is "generalized feelings."

Sometimes, a query will ask about a main topic in the passage which occurs frequently, or is even the overall subject. In these cases, it is difficult to know where to refer back to in the passage and that makes the reference less helpful. Questions with such a widely discussed topic should be considered global questions (questions with no reference).

Use your Markings

Finding the correct paragraph in the question above was doable because we had already read and marked the passage. We underlined "standards of eighteenth-century English poetry" because it is the Main Topic of that paragraph. That marking made it much easier and quicker to find the right part of the passage.

About one third of RC questions feature topic references, substantially more than the number of questions that feature an exact reference. So, get ready to use your mental map and underlines often as you reference the passage.

Topics can Be Abstract

Here is another query that features a topic reference:

> Which one of the following most accurately characterizes the author's attitude with respect to Phillis Wheatley's literary accomplishments?

This question asks you about the author's **attitude** towards Wheatley's literary accomplishments. Topic references sometimes give you better guidance than others. "Wheatley's literary accomplishments" is a fairly abstract, encompassing concept; it is the subject. The whole passage is about Wheatley's literary accomplishments. However, we are looking for the author's opinion on those accomplishments, which is a narrower topic. The author's opinion on the subject of the passage can often be found near the **end** of the passage. This question is no exception, and the last paragraph features the information we need:

> Thus limited by the eighteenth-century English literary code, Wheatley's poetry contributed little to the development of a distinctive African American literary language. Yet by the standards of the literary conventions in which she chose to work, Wheatley's poetry is undeniably accomplished, and she is justly celebrated as the first Black American poet.

The author is impressed with Wheatley's poetry, with certain caveats: the lack of development of a distinctively African American literary language. The correct answer to this question is: "qualified admiration."

Regardless of whether the topic reference is concrete or abstract, it will help you use the passage.

Skipping Referring

As your passage reading skills progress, you will find yourself remembering the relevant parts of the passage enough to answer questions with topic references **without referencing the passage**. In these cases, the query and its topic tell you only the information you are looking for in the answer choices. The reference aspect of the query is irrelevant. In contrast, for a majority of exact reference questions, you will benefit from rereading the area of the passage that is referenced.

No Reference (Global Questions)

A little over 40% of questions feature no reference; they provide no information about where to find the answer in the passage. We call these <u>global questions</u>. Here is an example of a global query:

> Which one of the following statements is affirmed by the passage?

We are asked which choice is proven in the passage, but there is no reference. You cannot refer back to the passage before working the choices, because you would not know where to look. Of course, you can always look to the passage to prove or disprove a choice. By their nature, global queries test how effective your first reading was. For this reason, most global questions are centered on the big ideas from the passage. A question without a reference cannot reasonably test your knowledge of smaller details in the passage because it is very difficult to remember all those from your first read through.

Identify References Drill

Identify the following queries as containing either an exact or topic reference, or no reference (a global question). Write an "E," "T" or "G" as appropriate next to the question number. Explanations are on the next page.

1. According to the author, which one of the following is required in order that one be a professional?
2. Which one of the following best expresses the main point made by the author in the passage?
3. The question posed by the author in lines 7-10 of the passage introduces which one of the following?
4. In the passage, the author mentions or suggests all of the following EXCEPT...
5. The author's attitude towards professionals is best described as...
6. Based on the information in the passage, it can be inferred that which one of the following would most logically begin a paragraph immediately following the passage?
7. Which one of the following best describes the author's purpose in lines 18-42 of the passage?
8. The author mentions which one of the following as an example of the influence of Black folk culture on Hughes's poetry?
9. The author suggests that the "deceptive veil" (line 42) in Hughes's poetry obscures...
10. With which one of the following statements regarding *Jubilee Songs of the United States* would the author be most likely to agree?
11. The author most probably mentions the reactions of northern White writers to non - Europeanized "sorrow songs" in order to...
12. The passage suggests that the author would be most likely to agree with which one of the following statements about the requirement that Black writers employ Western European literary techniques?
13. Which one of the following aspects of Hughes's poetry does the author appear to value most highly?

*Answers

1. According to the author, which one of the following is required in order that one be a professional?

T

2. Which one of the following best expresses the main point made by the author in the passage?

G

3. The question posed by the author in lines 7-10 of the passage introduces which one of the following?

E

4. In the passage, the author mentions or suggests all of the following EXCEPT...

G

5. The author's attitude towards professionals is best described as...

T

6. Based on the information in the passage, it can be inferred that which one of the following would most logically begin a paragraph immediately following the passage?

E/G

7. Which one of the following best describes the author's purpose in lines 18-42 of the passage?

E

8. The author mentions which one of the following as an example of the influence of Black folk culture on Hughes's poetry?

T

9. The author suggests that the "deceptive veil" (line 42) in Hughes's poetry obscures...

E

10. With which one of the following statements regarding *Jubilee Songs of the United States* would the author be most likely to agree?

T

11. The author most probably mentions the reactions of northern White writers to non - Europeanized "sorrow songs" in order to...

T

12. The passage suggests that the author would be most likely to agree with which one of the following statements about the requirement that Black writers employ Western European literary techniques?

T

13. Which one of the following aspects of Hughes's poetry does the author appear to value most highly?

T

The Question Types

Now that you have a good grasp of references, you can learn specific strategies for attacking each different type of RC question. Like the LR questions, you can identify the type of RC question, and its unique requirements and features, by analyzing its query. You cannot apply the strategies specific to a question type unless you know what type it is. Understanding the ins and outs of the different types takes time and practice, but this effort helps you work the questions quickly **and** accurately. Most students have room for improvement in both these areas. Because the RC section has the most questions of any section on the LSAT, it also has the greatest time pressure. Learn the types well and attack the questions efficiently.

The comparative reading passage set has unique question types that are similar to the basic types seen in the long passages. All information on the comparative reading set will be in a later chapter.

The Proof is in the Passage

All questions are answered based on the passage, but questions vary in how **directly** you can use the passage. Some questions ask you to move beyond the content in a specific way, to read between the lines. For instance, a Weaken question may ask you to attack the conclusion of a speaker in the passage. There, you would first need to know the speaker's conclusion, and then you would move a step forward using that understanding to identify the choice that weakens the conclusion. The correct choice will not contain direct or summated information from the passage, unlike the correct choices in many question types. This means that an extra step of thinking is involved in solving that question.

Fortunately, only about 15% of RC questions ask you to move beyond the content of the passage (they tend to be quite difficult). 85% of the RC questions only ask you to identify what is in the passage or what is implied in the passage, a deduction. So, for the vast majority of questions, you simply need to find the right part of the passage or to interpret parts of the passage correctly. While this task is often harder than it sounds, the point is that the passage is your guide for answering the questions. Follow it closely and you cannot go wrong.

General Question Approach

While different types of questions demand different approaches, it is helpful to layout a general formula for answering any question. One key aspect: do any possible work on a question **before** working the choices. The choices are worded to confuse you and to tempt you into choosing the wrong one. The more research you can do before working the choices, the less likely you are to fall for a distracter. This is not to say that you **must** refer to the passage to answer every question, or even most questions, but at the least, you should analyze the question and organize your thoughts before jumping to the choices.

Here is the four step approach we recommend. Not every step of this approach should be applied on every question.

1) Read the Query

The first step on any question is a careful reading of the query to learn both the kind of reference (exact, topic, or global) and the question type. The reference in a question dictates how you approach the question. For instance, you should always read the sentence or paragraph featuring an exact reference. On the other hand, if you are comfortable with the topic given from your first reading of the passage, you do not need to use a topic reference to reference the passage. Figuring out the question type is equally important as different types have quite different approaches.

2) Use the Reference (If applicable)

On global questions, you cannot refer back to the passage before working the choices, the second step of the approach. Yet, when given an exact reference, you should reread the relevant parts of the passage. Questions that feature such references demand a comprehensive knowledge of that part of the passage, one that you are unlikely to have from your initial reading.

With a topic reference, you can decide whether you need to refer to the passage before working the choices. If you feel comfortable with that topic in reference to the question, then you can work the choices immediately. If you are not comfortable, or simply want to use the passage first, do so. Because the reference is inexact, use your memory of the passage and your markings (mostly topic underlines) to find the appropriate part.

3) Envision (If applicable)

Depending on the type, you may be able to envision what a good answer to the question will look like, before you evaluate any choices. Even articulating some aspects of what the correct answer will feature before looking at the choices can work wonders. Whether envisioning is possible depends on the nature of the question type. Main point questions can always be envisioned. The same is not true for deduction questions, which can feature many different possible correct answers given the question.

We will outline which question types are ripe for envisioning shortly. For now, one tip that tells you to envision an answer is when the query gives you enough information to point to only *one* possible correct answer. If it does, think about what you know about the question and what answer would fit. If the query is not specific enough to limit the number of possibilities, then skip the envision step.

4) Work the Choices

Work through the choices one by one, eliminating duds (choices that you believe to be incorrect) by crossing off their letters. Example:

1. Which one of the following best expresses the main idea of the passage?

   ~~(A)~~ Folk artists employed more principles of African oral tradition in their works than did Phillis Wheatley in her poetry.

   ~~(B)~~ Although Phillis Wheatley had to overcome significant barriers in learning English, she mastered the literary conventions of eighteenth-century English as well as African aesthetic canons.

   (C) Phillis Wheatley's poetry did not fulfill the potential inherent in her experience but did represent a significant accomplishment.

   (D) The evolution of a distinctive African American literary language can be traced from the creations of African American folk artists to the poetry of Phillis Wheatley.

   ~~(E)~~ Phillis Wheatley joined with African American folk artists in preserving the principles of the African oral tradition.

Choices (A), (B) and (C) have been eliminated as duds. (C) and (D) are remaining choices after this first evaluation and are therefore hits. They will be considered further.

Unless you are extremely confident of an answer, or are running out of time on the section, we strongly recommend you read every choice through one time. Even if, on that particular question, (B) seems likely, it is possible that you will find (E) to be a better answer. The RC choices are challenging to interpret due to their wording, so read every one before deciding on an answer. This will help your overall accuracy rate; you cannot select what you do not see.

This tactic will slow you down a touch, so when time is getting short, you can select good answers and move on without reading the rest of the choices.

*The Questions Review

- We categorize questions based on both reference and type.
    - The two are generally connected.
- The reference refers to where the query directs you to find the information needed to answer that question in the passage.

Exact References

- These are precise references that tell you exactly where in the passage (either line or paragraph number) to look for the information you need.
    - Use these to refer to that part of the passage.
- You often need to begin reading before the reference and perhaps read past it to gain context for the question.
- If you remember the detail, you can answer these questions from your memory.

Topic References

- This reference tells you the topic (the subject matter) that the question deals with.
- Use your underlines of main topics in the passage to locate the information you need.
- You will often be able to answer these questions from memory.

Global Questions

- No reference of any kind is given.
    - It is not possible to reference the passage before working the choices.
- These make up ~40% of the RC questions in a section.
- You will often be able to answer these questions from memory.

The Question Types

- Identifying the specific type of question allows you to use methods in tackling it.
- All questions are answered based on the passage.
    - Having evidence (either remembered or referred) is crucial.
- Questions vary in how directly you can use the passage.

General Question Approach

1. Read the query.
    a. Note the reference and type.
2. Use the Reference (if applicable).
    a. If you need to, reference the passage to get background to answer the question
3. Envision (if applicable).
    a. Think of a good answer to the question before looking at the choices.
    b. This is not always possible, depending on the specifics of the question.
        i. Many RC questions simply require you to effectively work the choices.
4. Work the Choices.
    a. Walk through each choice, labeling them duds or hits.
    b. You can use the passage to confirm or deny your hits.

Common Types

We will now teach you detailed methods for tackling the different RC question types. The first six are the most common question types – they make up about three quarters of each RC section. Learn their particulars well, and you will improve your RC scores drastically. Onto the most common question types:

Main Point

Main point questions ask you for the author's Main Point, the central argument of the passage. You can think of the main point as a **weighted summary** of the passage: it summarizes the passage, but focuses on the most important paragraphs. You are not looking to sum up every paragraph in the passage. The main point is more concentrated than that.

These are a good type to begin with because the main point is such an important element to read for during your first reading of the passage. Building those skills now will help you with most other types, because no correct answer contradicts the author's main point.

Query, References and Frequency

Main point are easy questions to identify by their queries because they feature the words "main point" or "main idea" etc. These queries will also use a phrase like "best expresses" or "most accurately states," right before "main point." Example main point queries:

> Which one of the following best expresses the ***main idea*** of the passage?
>
> Which one of the following ***most accurately expresses the main point*** of the passage?
>
> Which one of the following ***best states the central idea*** of the passage?

Main point questions are almost always first in the questions. You will not have any trouble identifying them. These questions are common: 11% of the RC questions in PTs #56-61 were main point questions.

Main point questions are always global questions. They ask about the core conclusion of the **entire** passage, so no reference can be given. Despite the lack of a reference, you should still envision a good answer to them.

Approach

One of your primary tasks while reading a passage is to identify the author's main point, so this question type will often require little more than envisioning and working the choices. Usually, you will only know the main point after reading the whole passage. The ideal approach on this type depends on whether you identified the main point during your initial read through and whether the author included a main point declaration (MPD).

MPD

The author **may** state the main conclusion explicitly; in that case, you will have written a "MP" next to that MPD. In that situation, you can simply reread that sentence or two before moving onto the choices. No need to spend time envisioning – the passage spelled out the main point for you.

No MPD

Only about 30% of recent passages featured MPDs. More often, the main point requires a synthesis of several parts of the passage. This is not easy, but identifying **the most important paragraphs** can help. As you read the passage, you can track which paragraphs hold the most crucial ideas by seeing which ideas have the most support. If the author explains a scientific concept in P1 and then uses examples to illustrate that concept in P2 and P3, you know that P1 is more important than the other two paragraphs. The example paragraphs are there to support the concept.

Different Structures

The organization of a passage dictates when and how the author expresses the main point. In some passages, the author slowly builds to her main point through a detailed examination of the subject. There, the last few paragraphs may be the most important because they articulate the argument, while the earlier paragraphs serve as an introduction and give background information on the subject. Other times, the author examines the different viewpoints of several speakers throughout the whole passage. In that case, each paragraph may be of equal importance. The main point is a synthesis of the discussion on the different viewpoints. Another possibility is that the author articulates her main point over the first two paragraphs and then uses the rest of the passage to support it. Each passage is different, and the main point can be expressed in many different ways and in many different places.

Envision

Main point questions are well suited for envisioning. Pause before working the choices and form the main point in your own words. The answer choices often feature complex or unexpected wording; knowing what you are looking for will help. Much of the work on these questions is the process of elimination, and you can reject choices that are missing elements from your envisioned answer.

All Paragraphs Support the Main Point

When working the choices, keep in mind that every paragraph must support the main point. Stated another way, the main point will not contradict any paragraphs. So, if you see an answer choice that doesn't meld with an important choice, you know that it cannot be correct.

This is not to say that the correct answer will touch on something from every paragraph. Some paragraphs support the main point but are not important enough to be part of the description of the main point. This is the case with background or introductory paragraphs, and paragraphs that feature extended examples. Those paragraphs help the author give context or support her ideas, but they may not be mentioned in the description of the main point.

Incorrect Choices

Being aware of these common forms for incorrect choices will help you identify and avoid them.

True but Not the Main Point

Watch out for choices that state information from the passage but do not encapsulate the main point. The correct choice will definitely be supported by the passage, but this is not enough; it must also state the author's core conclusion. For example, in the Wheatley passage, an incorrect choice could be:

> C) Wheatley overcame many barriers to be able to write English poetry.

This information is certainly true, but it is not the author's main point. It is a much smaller conclusion than the actual main point – that Wheatley was quite an accomplished poet despite not actualizing her potential. You may recall this "true but not correct" concept from the discussion on Core Deduction LR questions.

Misleading choices of this nature generally have a scope that is too narrow. They might focus too much on a few paragraphs, while missing the bigger argument. Especially tricky versions regurgitate parts of the passage. Those can be tempting because they sound quite familiar. Again, envisioning will help you avoid *incomplete* choices like that because you will have an idea of what the main point is. Proven information from the passage will not tempt you if it does not match your envisioned answer.

Extreme Choices

The way a choice **phrases** the main point can be important. A common type of incorrect answer is one that involves extreme wording. For instance, if a passage argues that a new weight loss drug appears to be effective but is untested, then an extreme choice would say that the weight loss drug is highly effective. That is not accurate, because it skews the author's meaning to the positive extreme. That choice is incorrect but tempting, because it is close to the main point.

New Information

It may sound obvious, but any choice that brings in information not in the passage must be incorrect. The main point is a specialized summation of the passage (if it is not featured directly), so new information can never be part of it.

Example Questions

Read and mark this passage, while thinking about its main point. Markings, the main question, and its explanation are on the next page.

(1.4) Outside the medical profession, there are various efforts to cut medicine down to size: not only widespread malpractice litigation and massive governmental regulation, but also attempts by consumer groups and others to redefine medicine as a trade rather than as a profession, and the physician as merely a technician for hire under contract. Why should physicians (or indeed all sensible people) resist such efforts to give the practice of medicine a new meaning? We can gain some illumination from etymology. "Trade," from Germanic and Anglo Saxon roots meaning "a course or pathway," has come to mean derivatively a habitual occupation and has been related to certain skills and crafts. On the other hand, while "profession" today also entails a habit of work, the word "profession" itself traces to an act of self-conscious and public---even confessional-speech. "To profess" preserves the meaning of its Latin source, "to declare publicly; to announce, affirm, avow." A profession is an activity or occupation to which its practitioner publicly professes, that is, confesses, devotion. But public announcement seems insufficient; publicly declaring devotion to plumbing or auto repair would not turn these trades into professions.

Some believe that learning and knowledge are the diagnostic signs of a profession. For reasons probably linked to the medieval university, the term "profession" has been applied to the so-called learned professions-medicine, law, and theology-the practices of which are founded upon inquiry and knowledge rather than mere "knowhow." Yet it is not only the pursuit and acquisition of knowledge that makes one a professional. The knowledge involved makes the profession one of the learned variety, but its professional quality is rooted in something else.

Some mistakenly seek to locate that something else in the prestige and honor accorded professionals by society, evidenced in their special titles and the special deference and privileges they receive. But externalities do not constitute medicine a profession. Physicians are not professionals because they are honored; rather, they are honored because of their profession. Their titles and the respect they are shown superficially signify and acknowledge something deeper, that physicians are persons of the professional sort, knowingly and freely devoting themselves to a way of life worthy of such devotion. Just as lawyers devote themselves to rectifying injustices, looking up to what is lawful and right; just as teachers devote themselves to the education of the young, looking up to truth and wisdom; so physicians heal the sick, looking up to health and wholesomeness. Being a professional is thus rooted in our moral nature and in that which warrants and impels making a public confession to a way of life.

Professing oneself a professional is an ethical act because it is not a silent and private act, but an articulated and public one; because it promises continuing devotion to a way of life, not merely announces a present preference or a way to a livelihood; because it is an activity in service to some high good that insists on devotion; because it is difficult and demanding. A profession engages one's character and heart, not merely one's mind and hands.

Outside the medical profession, there are various efforts to cut medicine down to size: not only widespread malpractice litigation and massive governmental regulation, but also attempts by consumer groups and others to redefine medicine as a trade rather than as a profession, and the physician as merely a technician for hire under contract. Why should physicians (or indeed all sensible people) resist such efforts to give the practice of medicine a new meaning? We can gain some illumination from etymology. "Trade," from Germanic and Anglo Saxon roots meaning "a course or pathway," has come to mean derivatively a habitual occupation and has been related to certain skills and crafts. On the other hand, while "profession" today also entails a habit of work, the word "profession" itself traces to an act of self-conscious and public---even confessional-speech. "To profess" preserves the meaning of its Latin source, "to declare publicly; to announce, affirm, avow." A profession is an activity or occupation to which its practitioner publicly professes, that is, confesses, devotion. But public announcement seems insufficient; publicly declaring devotion to plumbing or auto repair would not turn these trades into professions.

Some believe that learning and knowledge are the diagnostic signs of a profession. For reasons probably linked to the medieval university, the term "profession" has been applied to the so-called learned professions-medicine, law, and theology-the practices of which are founded upon inquiry and knowledge rather than mere "knowhow." Yet it is not only the pursuit and acquisition of knowledge that makes one a professional. The knowledge involved makes the profession one of the learned variety, but its professional quality is rooted in something else.

Some mistakenly seek to locate that something else in the prestige and honor accorded professionals by society, evidenced in their special titles and the special deference and privileges they receive. But externalities do not constitute medicine a profession. Physicians are not professionals because they are honored; rather, they are honored because of their profession. Their titles and the respect they are shown superficially signify and acknowledge something deeper, that physicians are persons of the professional sort, knowingly and freely devoting themselves to a way of life worthy of such devotion. Just as lawyers devote themselves to rectifying injustices, looking up to what is lawful and right; just as teachers devote themselves to the education of the young, looking up to truth and wisdom; so physicians heal the sick, looking up to health and wholesomeness. Being a professional is thus rooted in our moral nature and in that which warrants and impels making a public confession to a way of life.

Professing oneself a professional is an ethical act because it is not a silent and private act, but an articulated and public one; because it promises continuing devotion to a way of life, not merely announces a present preference or a way to a livelihood; because it is an activity in service to some high good that insists on devotion; because it is difficult and demanding. A profession engages one's character and heart, not merely one's mind and hands.

This passage discusses the definition of a "professional" as it applies to the medical profession. The first paragraph is introductory: we learn that **some** think that medicine should be called a "trade" rather than a "profession" and the author dives into the etymology of both words. P2 and P3 disprove popular notions about what makes a job a profession: it is not the learning associated or the prestige and honor given. P4 gives us the real reason that a doctor is a professional: because physicians make a public commitment to the greater good with their work. The entire last paragraph articulates the main point of the passage, so the placement of the "MP" does not matter much. That is a two sentence MPD.

Now onto the main point question in the passage set:

> Which one of the following best expresses the main point made by the author in the passage?

This is clearly a Main Point query. Because we have a good grasp of the author's main point, we can envision a good answer: "Physicians are professionals because they have publicly devoted themselves to helping others through their work." Anything along those lines is fine. If you could not envision a good answer easily, then you would simply return to the "MP" in the passage and reread the final paragraph. That would give you the guidance to articulate the main point.

Some crucial elements the correct choice should include are **physicians**, **professional**, **public devotion**, and **helping in their work.** If a choice does not mention being a professional, it cannot be correct because a central part of the passage is exploration of what a professional really is. Our envisioning work done, we attack the choices, one by one:

> (A) Medicine is defined as a profession because of the etymology of the word "profession."

This choice misstates the main point. The etymology of the word profession, as discussed in the second half of P1, is important because it introduces the idea of a profession being a public commitment. But that is *only part* of the story, and the author goes on to explain the other requirements of a profession. The last sentence of P1 says that publicly professing devotion to a line of work is not enough to make something a profession.

> (B) It is a mistake to pay special honor to the knowledge and skills of physicians.

This choice confuses information that appears in P2 and P3. The author says that the knowledge and skills of physicians are not what make them professionals. Never does the author say that it is a mistake to pay special honor to the knowledge and skills of the physicians. Beyond this, this choice entirely misses the main point.

> (C) The work of physicians is under attack only because it is widely misunderstood.

This choice focuses on information at the very beginning of the passage that talks about those attacking medicine and physicians. Because it does not mention why physicians should be considered professionals (due to their devotion to the public good) it cannot be correct. Also, the author never explains why the work of physicians is under attack, so this is **new information**, a common type of incorrect choice.

> (D) The correct reason that physicians are professionals is that their work involves public commitment to a high good.

This choice is correct; it states the author's main ideas as featured in P2 and P3 and the MPD in P4. It also matches all the elements of our envisioned answer, which gives us confidence in the choice.

> (E) Physicians have been encouraged to think of themselves as technicians and need to reorient themselves toward ethical concerns.

"Physicians have been encouraged to think of themselves as technicians" is new information; the passage never says this. The rest of the choice is false information. The author emphasizes that physicians **are ethical**. The final sentence of the passage is: "A profession engages one's character and heart, not merely one's mind and hands." So, this choice is half new information and half false information. It is 100% incorrect.

Detail

Detail questions are quite different than main point questions because they focus on a small part of the passage. These are some of the most straight forward questions: they simply ask you to identify a specific piece of information from the passage. You do not need to interpret the information, or analyze how the author used it. You only need to find the correct detail, and you can refer back to the passage to do so.

Query, References and Frequency

Query

The distinguishing characteristic of Detail queries is that they ask you for information directly from the passage. Phrases used are: "according to the passage," "the passage provides information," "mentioned in the passage," or "the passage indicates." You do not need to move beyond the content of the passage in any way. The queries will usually ask you for information regarding a certain topic. Below are example queries:

> The ***passage indicates*** that using radiocarbon dating to date past earthquakes may be unreliable due to...
>
> Which one of the following is ***mentioned in the passage*** as evidence tending to support the view regarding the relationship between dental caries and carbohydrate consumption?
>
> The ***passage states*** that a role of medical experts in relation to custom-made medical illustrations in the courtroom is to...

Those are the standard queries seen for detail questions. Recently, a new form has appeared, one that asks you which **question** in the choices is best answered by the passage. Accordingly, the choices for this variation of Detail question are all questions themselves. Here is an example Detail question with this unique form:

> The passage most helps to answer which one of the following questions?
>
> (A) Did any men write domestic novels in the 1850s?
> (B) Were any widely read domestic novel written after the 1860s?
> (C) How did migration to urban areas affect the development of domestic fiction in the 1850s?

We call these Passage Answer Detail questions. Over the four most recent tests, Detail questions of this form made up about a third of all Detail questions, so it is important to know how to tackle them. The approach will be covered shortly.

References

With the previous type there were no references in the query. Detail questions are different: most give you a topic reference. The first example query above asks why radiocarbon dating may be unreliable to date earthquakes. That is a specific topic you can find in the passage and use to answer the question effectively.

Only about 30% of Detail questions do not contain a reference. Example query for a global Detail question:

> According to the passage, which of the following is true?

Passage Answer Detail questions are all global as well; their queries look like this: "The passage most helps to answer which one of the following questions?" On global Detail questions, you must thoroughly work the choices because you cannot envision the answer, nor can you reference the passage. The choices are all you have to go on.

No Detail questions give you an exact reference. This would take a lot of the difficulty out of the question because you would know exactly where to look for the information you need to answer the question. Topic references, on the other hand, force you to use your mental map and markings to find the correct area of the passage to reference.

Detail are the most common question type on the RC section: they made up 17% of all questions on PTs 56-61. Carefully learning their methods is well worth your time.

Approach

You must tailor your approach based on whether or not the query has a reference.

Detail Questions with Topic References

First, read the query. If it is long or dense, you can rephrase into your own words. Example wordy Detail query:

> Which one of the following is mentioned in the passage as evidence tending to support the view regarding the relationship between dental caries and carbohydrate consumption?

We can rephrase this to make it easier to understand:

> What supports the connection between caries and carbohydrate consumption?

Evaluate how well you remember the topic from your first reading. If you feel confident in your knowledge of it, then you can save time by not referring back to the passage. If you are unsure of the topic, then refer back to the passage. Use your mental map and your underlined topics to find the appropriate part of the passage. Carefully reread the relevant text to find the **exact** detail you need. If you are not precise enough during this research step, then you may find only enough information to lead you to a distracter. Locating the **right** fact within the passage is often the most challenging part of answering a Detail question, so do not rush it.

Use the results of your referencing (or your memory of the passage) to envision a good answer. Then, work the choices with that answer in mind. Because the question tells you exactly what information you need, once you have your answer, you can **attack** the choices.

Be Prepared to Translate

One subtlety here: the correct choice will often match only the **meaning** of the detail you found (or remembered), not the exact form from the passage. So, you may need to do some translation to see that the correct choice has the right information. The test makers add difficulty to many Detail questions by changing the wording of the concept from that in the passage. Eliminate any choices that do match the passage. Using process of elimination is often helpful on Detail questions where you cannot find the correct answer in the passage. Alternatively, if you work the choices without referring back, then process of elimination will help you zero in on the right choice that you might not **quite** remember by eliminating other choices that you know are false.

Global Detail Questions

All global Detail questions, whether they are the normal form or the Passage Answer variety, need to be approached in the same way. With no topic to reference or recall, you must look through the choices for the only choice that features information that accurately matches the passage. The other four choices will provide details that were not given by the passage, although they may sound like they were. For this reason, you must work the choices more carefully than on Detail questions with a reference and use the process of elimination more heavily.

Many of the choices will blatantly contradict what you have read in the passage. Those are easy to eliminate. On others, it will be more difficult to tell whether they are supported by the passage. Regardless, you are in "sort and eliminate" mode when you face a global Detail question. When you have a topic reference, you simply search for the ideal answer, and eliminate choices as you go by comparing them with your envisioned answer. On global Detail questions, you must eliminate choices based not on your knowledge of a specific topic, but instead based on your knowledge of the **entire** passage. Take more time for the choices and work through them especially carefully, keeping in mind the main idea of the passage.

Work through **all** the choices before referring back to the passage. Even if you are struggling, you will likely eliminate at least two choices. This saves time because it gives you a feel for all the choices before you start examining the passage. For example, you might want to use the passage to check on (B), but then find that (E) is a great answer, so you save that referring time.

After sorting the choices into duds and hits, you can thoroughly analyze those remaining. During that analysis, you can refer back to the passage to check the best choice. At this stage, you can also reference the passage to eliminate a choice. That process is less useful than referencing to confirm a choice unless you are down to two choices. In that situation, you can eliminate a choice by referencing the passage and then be left with the correct answer.

Passage Answer Questions (Subtype)

You may see several Passage Answer Detail questions on your official LSAT, or you may see none. In case they play a prominent role in your RC section, it is important to know their unique qualities. They are always global questions, so the guidance you just read applies: use process of elimination and only reference the passage after working all the choices.

The difference with this subtype is that the choices are in question format. You think about whether the *answer* to that question was provided in the passage and can require some translation. This is not too challenging, because reading the choice will tell you the topic that the question is concerned with. Try and remember whether the passage addressed that topic. For instance, if this is a choice:

(A) Did any men write domestic novels in the 1850s?

Ask yourself if the passage talked about men writing domestic novels in the 1850s. Perhaps, the passage mentioned a specific male poet. Conversely, it might have stated that **only** women wrote domestic novels in the 1850s. Generally, the correct choice will be a question on a topic that is fairly important in the passage. Read through every choice, eliminating those you know were not addressed. Then, if necessary, use the passage to confirm or disprove the remaining hits.

EXCEPT Detail Questions (Subtype)

You may face a few EXCEPT Detail questions. These questions ask you to find the choice that contains a detail **not found** in the passage. You can think of them as the **opposite** of Passage Answer questions, which ask you to find the only choice that is featured in the passage. Because EXCEPT questions ask you for information that is not in the passage, they take some getting used to. At first, you may feel that you have to think backwards on the question, and that is what makes them challenging.

Example EXCEPT Detail query:

> Each of the following is supported by the passage EXCEPT...

EXCEPT Detail questions are global questions, so no referencing can be done before the choices. Work through the choices and label them as duds or hits. As you do so, find the choice that contradicts something you remember from the passage. The correct answer can also be irrelevant or not covered by the passage, but those varieties are both less common and more difficult to spot.

Focus also on eliminating those choices that feature information you definitely remember from the passage. A good first reading of the passage will illustrate the type of information covered, and that should take you far in spotting duds. The correct choice might feature information that sounds similar to an idea in the passage, but has a different meaning (making the choice not supported by the passage and therefore the correct answer). Those choices are easy to label as duds if you are not reading carefully.

Incorrect Choices

Now you have a feel for how to approach all the varieties of Detail question (topic reference, global reference, Passage Answer, and EXCEPT). Below, we describe some of the common types of incorrect choices, to help you avoid duds when working the choices.

Similar Sounding

The trickiest wrong answer choices sound similar to the information in the correct answer, but are slightly different, in a way that makes them incorrect. We call these similar sounding choices. Look at these two choices to a Passage Answer question:

(D) How do scientists measure lichen growth rates under the varying conditions that lichens may encounter?

(E) What are some of the conditions that encourage lichens to grow at a more rapid rate than normal?

The second choice here is correct, but the first sounds a lot like it. Both discuss lichen growth rates, but (D) is incorrect because the passage never talks about how **scientists** measure lichen growth rates under different conditions. So, that choice is not featured in the passage; it is also a new information wrong choice, which we will discuss in a moment. The similarity to (E) can be confusing. Detail questions will often have one similar sounding choice, so be sure that you read the **entirety** of each choice and are clear on its meaning. These are the easiest distracters to fall for because they match up at least partly with the passage *and* the correct choice.

Wrong Part

These are incredibly common on Detail questions. Wrong part incorrect choices have information from the passage that does not answer the question. For instance, if a question asks you what obstacles Wheatley overcame to write effective poetry, a wrong part choice might be:

(B) Despite her background, she failed to develop a uniquely African literary language.

That information is true based on the passage, but does not answer the question. It does not tell us anything about obstacles. Avoid selecting wrong part choices by sticking to the question. Just because a choice is supported by the passage, that does not mean a choice is correct. Being proven by the passage is one requirement; correctly answering the specific question asked is more important.

False

Some distracters are the opposite of a detail in the passage. False choices may sound familiar because they are closely related to information in the passage. For instance, if a passage says that substitute teachers are not supposed to handle disciplinary issues by themselves, a false choice could be:

(D) Substitute teachers assist the primary teacher by handling disciplinary issues when the primary teacher is out of the room.

This choice is tempting because **exact** words from the passage are there: "handle disciplinary issues." If you did not read the passage carefully enough, you might recall those words but not their **context**. You could feel comfortable with this choice, even though it contradicts the passage.

You should be able to eliminate False choices because they contradict your understanding of the subject, or because you remember the point that they misstate. The correct answers to Detail questions are often a rephrasing of something from the passage, so be wary of choices that sound too familiar. If necessary, refer back to the passage to confirm the context of the statement.

New Information

These choices relate to topics from the passage, but the specific information they hold is not discussed. For instance, a passage might talk about railroad construction, and then a new information choice will talk about railroad construction **companies**. If the passage focused on railroad construction **technologies** and never mentioned companies, that choice would be incorrect but might be tempting because it sounds right because the topic is so close to those discussed in the passage.

If your first reading of the passage is a careful one, you will be able to spot and eliminate most new information choices. You can identify them because they sound a little "off" because they bring up something specific that you did not read about. When you need to, reference the passage to disprove one of these choices; you will be unable to find the detail.

Example Detail Question

This Detail question comes from the Wheatley passage, which is provided below for reference. First, try the question on your own and then read the explanation on the next page:

For the poet Phillis Wheatley, who was brought to colonial New England as a slave in 1761, the formal literary code of eighteenth-century English was thrice removed: by the initial barrier of the unfamiliar English language, by the discrepancy between spoken and literary forms of English, and by the African tradition of oral rather than written verbal art. Wheatley transcended these barriers-she learned the English language and English literary forms so quickly and well that she was composing good poetry in English within a few years of her arrival in New England.

Wheatley's experience exemplifies the meeting of oral and written literary cultures. The aesthetic principles of the African oral tradition were preserved in America by folk artists in work songs, dancing, field hollers, religious music, the use of the drum, and, after the drum was forbidden, in the perpetuation of drum effects in song. African languages and the functions of language in African societies not only contributed to the emergence of a distinctive Black English but also exerted demonstrable effects on the manner in which other Americans spoke English. Given her African heritage and her facility with English and the conventions of English poetry, Wheatley's work had the potential to apply the ideas of a written literature to an oral literary tradition in the creation of an African American literary language.

But this was a potential that her poetry unfortunately did not exploit. The standards of eighteenth-century English poetry, which itself reflected little of the American language, led Wheatley to develop a notion of poetry as a closed system, derived from imitation of earlier written works. No place existed for the rough-and-ready Americanized English she heard in the streets, for the English spoken by Black people, or for Africanisms. The conventions of eighteenth-century neoclassical poetry ruled out casual talk; her voice and feelings had to be generalized according to rules of poetic diction and characterization; the particulars of her African past, if they were to be dealt with at all, had to be subordinated to the reigning conventions. African poetry did not count as poetry in her new situation, and African aesthetic canons were irrelevant to the new context because no linguistic or social framework existed to reinforce them. Wheatley adopted a foreign language and a foreign literary tradition; they were not extensions of her past experience, but replacements.

Thus limited by the eighteenth-century English literary code, Wheatley's poetry contributed little to the development of a distinctive African American literary language. Yet by the standards of the literary conventions in which she chose to work, Wheatley's poetry is undeniably accomplished, and she is justly celebrated as the first Black American poet.

3. According to the passage, African languages had a notable influence on…

(A) the religious music of colonists in New England
(B) the folk art of colonists in New England
(C) formal written English
(D) American speech patterns
(E) eighteenth-century aesthetic principles

3. According to the passage, African languages had a notable influence on

This is a classic Detail query. We are given a topic reference: African languages. We need to know what they had an notable influence on. Assuming you cannot remember that detail from your first reading, you can refer back to the passage. Using your mental map and underlined topics, you should find that P3 has the information we need:

> languages and the functions of language in African societies not only contributed to the emergence of a distinctive Black English ***but also exerted*** demonstrable effects on the manner in which other Americans spoke English.

Rereading those lines, we can envision our answer as "the manner in which other Americans spoke English." The hard work is done, so we move to the choices in attack mode. Any choice that does not match our envisioned answer is likely a dud. Onto the choices:

(A) the religious music of colonists in New England

(A) is incorrect, it is not even close to our envisioned answer.

(B) the folk art of colonists in New England

The same paragraph we found the answer in also featured discussion on the folk art of colonists, which makes this a tricky wrong choice. We can label it a wrong part choice, even though it is close to the correct part of the passage. Do not expect the distracters on Detail questions to come out of left field; they will very often be drawn from the passage.

(C) formal written English

This choice is a bit tempting because the passage mentions formal written English as a barrier that Wheatley overcomes. It is another wrong part incorrect choice.

(D) American speech patterns

This is our envisioned answer. Only a little translation is required to go from "the manner in which Americans speck English" to "American speech patterns." When you have an answer that fits this well, you can select it and move on.

(E) eighteenth-century aesthetic principles

Another wrong part distracter – these principles were mentioned early in the passage in reference. We easily label this a dud due to our careful referencing of the passage.

Deduction

Deduction (or Inference) questions are quite similar to LR Deduction questions. On the RC section, a Deduction question asks you to deduce valid information from the passage. Usually, the information that you will infer is straightforward and simply requires understanding a concept in the passage or combining two related pieces of information. For example, if a passage tells you that gold is primarily mined along rivers, the correct choice to a Deduction question may be:

> (A) Desert towns rarely feature gold mining operations.

This choice is logically proven because desert towns do not have rivers and gold is mostly mined next to rivers. This is not a complicated concept, but to correctly answer the question, you are forced to interpret the passage. Deduction questions require you to **understand** what you read and to connect concepts to the answer choices. This distinguishes Deduction questions from Detail. Deduction questions test you on the **meaning of** the passage, while Detail questions test you on the literal information **in** the passage.

Query, References and Frequency

Deduction queries may at first glance seem similar to Detail queries. They often ask you what "inference" the passage "supports":

> Which one of the following ***inferences*** about gold mining does the passage ***support***?

> The passage most strongly ***supports*** which one of the following ***inferences***?

Although sometimes the word inference is swapped out for "statement":

> Which one of the following ***statements*** is most strongly supported by Franklin's research, as reported in the passage?

Or, Deduction queries will ask what the passage "implies" or "suggests" as these are terms that ask you to deduce information from the passage:

> The passage ***implies*** that the Big Bang theory is

> The passage most strongly ***suggests***

The key idea here is that you are asked about what is **implied** by the passage, not what is stated directly in it.

References and Frequency

Deduction queries often feature a topic reference, and sometimes they give you no reference. Quite rarely, they have an Exact reference. A reference narrows the nature of the inference you are looking for. Look at this query:

> Which one of the following statements is most strongly supported by Franklin's research, as reported in the passage?

You need to find the choice supported by Franklin's research, instead of supported by the passage as a whole. A topic reference gives you a smaller amount of information from the passage to draw a deduction from. Deduction questions are quite common: you will see 2-4 of them on your official LSAT.

Approach

There are two different ways of drawing an inference: through understanding a concept or by rephrasing passage information. Seeing how these work will help you grasp correct choices on Deduction questions more quickly.

Extension of a Concept

Deduction questions often test your knowledge of the concepts (think ideas or topics) in the passage. On this variation, the correct choice is an extension of a concept from the passage, called a concept inference. The information in the choice must be true based on how that concept works. For instance, suppose a passage tells you that a painting should be considered a forgery if it copies an original vision or idea of another artist. This concept supports the idea that a painting can be a forgery even if it does not copy a specific piece of art by another artist. That deduction follows logically from the concept of a forgery as the passage explains it.

Over half of all Deduction questions feature a correct answer that is an extension of a concept from the passage; many of these are global questions. Understanding ideas explained in the passage is not always easy. A careful first reading will help you grasp the key concepts and answer many deduction questions without having to refer back to the passage.

Rephrased Information

Other Deduction questions require you to summarize several sentences from the passage or to rephrase the information from one sentence. Look at this example paragraph:

> Rachel found that she lacked butter to make the biscuits for the parade, but baked them anyway. The year before her biscuits had been one of the most popular items on the buffet spread, but not this year. A few of her friends complained that the biscuits "lacked a richness" or "were not the same." Out of her batch of 50, only 30 were eaten this year; last year every biscuit was consumed.

A rephrasing of this paragraph could be:

> (A) The lack of butter in this year's batch of biscuits had an impact on their popularity.

The passage implies this by establishing that this year the biscuits lacked butter and they were less popular. We infer the connection that the lack of butter lowered their popularity. Seeing a rephrased information inference often requires you to see how a few closely related ideas can be linked together. Rephrased Information deductions are more likely to be the correct answer on questions with a topic reference. This is because such questions are focused on a specific portion of the passage that can be rephrased. Usually, a rephrasing deduction will express the implications of **several** sentences, not just one.

It is not always clear whether a Deduction is an extension of a concept or rephrased information. You need to be aware of these two general types of deductions so you can spot them, but you *do not need* to label the type of deduction as you work the question. However, it is helpful to identify the inference type during review of questions you missed.

Using References

On global Deduction questions, work the choices after reading the query. Your knowledge of the passage will take you far, and you will likely know the correct answer when you run across it without referring back to the passage.

When you are given a reference, unless you feel quite confident about the topic, reread the relevant area of the passage. Not all topics referenced are in a single location. Some Main Topics span the passage, and on these you are often best served by working the choices without referring to the passage first. This is partly because there may be no obvious place to first reference and also because important topics often have deductions that can be located using the knowledge gained during your initial passage reading. You will recognize the main topics when they are referenced because they were featured prominently in the passage.

Do Not Envision

Deduction questions are not conducive to envisioning. The questions, even those with topic references, are generally not specific enough to help you zero in on what a single good answer would look like. So, read the query, reference if you need to, and then work the choices.

Incorrect Choices

You are familiar with these incorrect choice variations; we will explain how they are used in Deduction questions.

New Information

Incorrect choices on Deduction questions very often feature new information, a statement not supported by the passage. Students not focused on finding information that is **logically proven** in the passage, often feel comfortable with choices that seem like they should be true. Just because an answer sounds reasonable based on the passage, that does not mean it is a logical deduction.

You will often spot new information choices right away on Deduction questions. They will have information relevant to a topic that is not an extension of a concept or a rephrasing of several lines. For instance, in a passage that discusses custom drawn medical illustrations and medical text book illustrations, a new information choice might state that the same illustrators are likely to draw both types of images. This is quite reasonable, but unless this is implied by the passage directly, the choice is incorrect. You should remember the information that supports a choice as being correct. If a choice feels "fresh" or not quite proven in the passage, then it is likely incorrect. Refer back to the passage to either prove or disprove a choice as necessary. Do so when you are unsure of whether a choice is truly supported.

False

The next most common type of incorrect choice is one which contradicts the meaning of the passage. Often, these choices are the opposite of an **inference** from the passage. For instance, if the passage on medical illustrations implies that the illustrations in text books use more color and detail than custom made illustrations, then a false choice will say that custom illustrations tend to rely more on the use of color.

Example Questions

We will work two Deduction questions, one an extension of a concept inference and another that is a rephrased information inference. See if you can figure out which comes first! Begin by reading and marking this passage:

One scientific discipline, during its early stages of development, is often related to another as an antithesis to its thesis. The thesis discipline tends to concern itself with discovery and classification of phenomena, to offer holistic explanations emphasizing pattern and form, and to use existing theory to explain the widest possible range of phenomena. The paired or antidiscipline, on the other hand, can be characterized by a more focused approach, concentrating on the units of construction, and by a belief that the discipline can be reformulated in terms of the issues and explanations of the anti discipline.

The relationship of cytology (cell biology) to biochemistry in the late nineteenth century, when both disciplines were growing at a rapid pace, exemplifies such a pattern. Researchers in cell biology found mounting evidence of an intricate cell architecture. They also deduced the mysterious choreography of the chromosomes during cell division. Many biochemists, on the other hand, remained skeptical of the idea that so much structure existed, arguing that the chemical reactions that occur in cytological preparations might create the appearance of such structures. Also, they stood apart from the debate then raging over whether protoplasm, the complex of living material within a cell, is homogeneous, network like, granular, or foam like. Their interest lay in the more "fundamental" issues of the chemical nature of protoplasm, especially the newly formulated enzyme theory of life.

In general, biochemists judged cytologists to be too ignorant of chemistry to grasp the basic processes, whereas cytologists considered the methods of biochemists inadequate to characterize the structures of the living cell. The renewal of Mendelian genetics and, later, progress in chromosome mapping did little at first to effect a synthesis.

Both sides were essentially correct. Biochemistry has more than justified its extravagant early claims by explaining so much of the cellular machinery. But in achieving this feat (mostly since 1950) it has been partially transformed into the new discipline of molecular biology-biochemistry that deals with spatial arrangements and movements of large molecules. At the same time cytology has metamorphosed into modern cellular biology. Aided by electron microscopy, it has become more similar in language and outlook to molecular biology. The interaction of a discipline and its antidiscipline has moved both sciences toward a synthesis, namely molecular genetics.

This interaction between paired disciplines can have important results. In the case of late nineteenth-century cell research, progress was fueled by competition among the various attitudes and issues derived from cell biology and biochemistry. Joseph Fruton, a biochemist, has suggested that such competition and the resulting tensions among researchers are a principal source of vitality and "are likely to lead to unexpected and exciting novelties in the future, as they have in the past."

14. Which one of the following inferences about when the enzyme theory of life was formulated can be drawn from the passage?

One scientific discipline, during its early stages of development, is often related to another as an antithesis to its thesis. The thesis discipline tends to concern itself with discovery and classification of phenomena, to offer holistic explanations emphasizing pattern and form, and to use existing theory to explain the widest possible range of phenomena. The paired or antidiscipline, on the other hand, can be characterized by a more focused approach, concentrating on the units of construction, and by a belief that the discipline can be reformulated in terms of the issues and explanations of the anti discipline.

The relationship of cytology (cell biology) to biochemistry in the late nineteenth century, when both disciplines were growing at a rapid pace, exemplifies such a pattern. Researchers in cell biology found mounting evidence of an intricate cell architecture. They also deduced the mysterious choreography of the chromosomes during cell division. Many biochemists, on the other hand, remained skeptical of the idea that so much structure existed, arguing that the chemical reactions that occur in cytological preparations might create the appearance of such structures. Also, they stood apart from the debate then raging over whether protoplasm, the complex of living material within a cell, is homogeneous, network like, granular, or foam like. Their interest lay in the more "fundamental" issues of the chemical nature of protoplasm, especially the newly formulated enzyme theory of life.

In general, biochemists judged cytologists to be too ignorant of chemistry to grasp the basic processes, whereas cytologists considered the methods of biochemists inadequate to characterize the structures of the living cell. The renewal of Mendelian genetics and, later, progress in chromosome mapping did little at first to effect a synthesis.

Both sides were essentially correct. Biochemistry has more than justified its extravagant early claims by explaining so much of the cellular machinery. But in achieving this feat (mostly since 1950) it has been partially transformed into the new discipline of molecular biology - biochemistry that deals with spatial arrangements and movements of large molecules. At the same time cytology has metamorphosed into modern cellular biology. Aided by electron microscopy, it has become more similar in language and outlook to molecular biology. The interaction of a discipline and its antidiscipline has moved both sciences toward a synthesis, namely molecular genetics.

This interaction between paired disciplines can have important results. In the case of late nineteenth-century cell research, progress was fueled by competition among the various attitudes and issues derived from cell biology and biochemistry. Joseph Fruton, a biochemist, has suggested that such competition and the resulting tensions among researchers are a principal source of vitality and "are likely to lead to unexpected and exciting novelties in the future, as they have in the past."

This is a dense scientific passage with many different terms. As always, following the author's **ideas**, as opposed to the smaller details, is the most important thing to do while reading. For instance, in P1, we hear some challenging terms (antithesis, antidiscipline), but the ideas are not too tricky. The author says that two competing disciplines in science will take different approaches to understand the same field of study. Likewise, in P2 has many "science sounding" terms. There, the author illustrates how cytology took a different approach to the study of the study of a cell than biochemistry.

Underlining the topics that seem important helps you to refer back to the passage later, but do not get so caught up in doing so that you lose focus of the ideas. Following the main idea of each paragraph is more important than marking.

There are a couple of viewpoints in P3, and the author's opinion is given at both the beginning of P4 and P5. Those opinions are important because they express some of the big ideas of the passage: that the competition between paired disciplines is **beneficial** for science as a whole. In a passage that explains so many scientific concepts, keep your eye on what the author believes.

Now onto the Deduction questions from this passage:

Example Deduction Question

14. Which one of the following inferences about when the enzyme theory of life was formulated can be drawn from the passage?

The word "inferences" tells us that we are dealing with a deduction question.

There is a topic reference: when the enzyme theory of life was formulated. We underlined this topic, so it is easy to find at the end of P2. It helps to start reading a couple of sentences before the topic is mentioned. Biochemists are the ones that were so interested in the enzyme theory of life, and the theory was newly formulated in the late nineteenth century, when the debate between biochemists and researchers in cell biology was raging. That is all we need to answer the question, so we work the choices:

(A) The theory was formulated before the appearance of molecular biology.

Apparently, the choices will not have specific dates, like the later 1800's, the early 1900's, etc. Instead, we are given references to **other events** mentioned in the passage. This is challenging, because it forces us to understand the formation of the theory in relation to another event. To analyze this choice, we need to know when molecular biology appeared and see if the theory was formulated before it. If you do not remember this information, it is given in P4. Molecular biology is what biochemistry evolved into in the 1950s. This choice is correct because the enzyme theory of life was formulated in the late 1800's and molecular biology appeared in the 1950s. The theory was formulated before the molecular biology originated.

This is a concept inference. Because biochemists were fascinated with the enzyme theory of life and biochemistry morphs into molecular biology, we know that the enzyme theory predated the origin of molecular biology. This concept of biochemistry being a precursor to molecular biology is the crux of the question.

When you find a Deduction answer that is logically proven in the passage, select it and move on. For teaching purposes we will explain the rest of the choices:

(B) The theory was formulated before the initial discovery of cell architecture.

When the initial discovery of cell architecture was can be found at the beginning of P2, close to the Topic reference. Cell biology researchers found evidence of cell architecture in the **late nineteenth century**. This is also the rough time when the enzyme theory of life was originated. Without more concrete information, we cannot say which of these two events came first.

(C) The theory was formulated after the completion of chromosome mapping.

The **completion** of chromosome mapping is never mentioned in the passage. At the end of P3, we learn that there was progress in chromosome mapping. This progress occurred at some time **after** the enzyme theory of life was formed. So, this choice must be incorrect. Chromosome mapping **only started** after the theory originated. This is a false choice because it contradicts the passage.

(D) The theory was formulated after a synthesis of the ideas of cytologists and biochemists had occurred.

We learned in P2 that cytologists and biochemists were in disagreement when the enzyme theory of life originated. Therefore, this is another false choice. The synthesis of ideas between the two disciplines is referenced by the passage as occurring around 1950 (the end of P4).

(E) The theory was formulated at the same time as the beginning of the debate over the nature of protoplasm.

We do not know when the debate over the nature of protoplasm **began**. The debate is mentioned in P2 as "already raging" at around the same time that the enzyme theory of life was coming into being. Like (B), we cannot confirm or deny this choice, making it incorrect.

Example Deduction Question 2

Another Deduction question from this passage:

11. It can be inferred from the passage that in the late nineteenth century the debate over the structural nature of protoplasm (lines 25-29) was most likely carried on

There is an exact reference, something uncommon in Deduction questions. For clarity, a quick glance at the choices tells us the type of inference we need: who the debate over the structural nature of protoplasm was carried on between (which groups were involved). Like many references, it helps to start reading a bit before the reference to gain context:

> "Also, they stood apart from the debate then raging over whether protoplasm, the complex of living material within a cell, is homogeneous, network like, granular, or foam like."

This does not tell us **who** was debating the nature of protoplasm. "They" stood apart from the debate, but, without reading earlier lines, we do not know who "they" is. This illustrates the principle that the exact reference you are given is rarely enough to answer the question. We need to backtrack and figure out who "they" is. If we start at line 17, **three sentences** before the reference, we get all the information we need:

> Researchers in cell biology found mounting evidence of an intricate cell architecture. They also deduced the mysterious choreography of the chromosomes during cell division. Many biochemists, on the other hand, remained skeptical of the idea that so much structure existed, arguing that the chemical reactions that occur in cytological preparations might create the appearance of such structures. Also, they stood apart from the debate then raging over whether protoplasm, the complex of living material within a cell, is homogeneous, network like, granular, or foam like.

This paragraph illustrates the differences between cytologists and biochemists. It starts by talking about cytologists and then switches to biochemists. Biochemists are the ones who stay out of the debate. We know that if biochemists stood apart from the debate over protoplasm, then it must have been raging among cytologists, the only other party discussed. This is a rephrasing inference. The passage tells us that cytologists and biochemists could be involved in the debate, and then says that biochemists are not involved.

Deduction questions are often not susceptible to envisioning. This one, however, happens to be so specific that it is. Envisioned answer – Cytologists - in hand, we move to the choices.

(A) among cytologists

(A) is just what we envisioned. Select this choice and move on. For teaching purposes:

(B) among biochemists

We know that biochemists stay out of the debate, so this is a false choice.

(C) between cytologists and biochemists

This cannot be true for the same reason that (B) is incorrect.

(D) between cytologists and geneticists

(E) between biochemists and geneticists

The last two choices are both duds because geneticists are never mentioned in the paragraph and we have no reason to believe that they were involved in the debate. These are new information choices.

*Common Types Review

Main Point

- "Which one of the following best expresses the main idea of the passage?"
- Identify the author's primary conclusion.
- The main point is a weighted summary: it focuses on the most important passages.
- Approach
    - If there is MPD in the passage, reread it.
        - Main Point questions of this type are well suited for envisioning.
    - Keep in mind that, all paragraphs support the main point.
- Incorrect choices
    - These may be true based on the passage, but are never the author's big conclusion.
    - Watch extreme choices that exaggerate the conclusion.

Detail

- "The **passage indicates** that using radiocarbon dating to date earthquakes may be unreliable due to…"
- Identify a specific piece of information from the passage.
- Most Detail questions give you a topic reference.
- Approach
    - If there is a reference, use it if you need to.
    - Be ready to do some translating from the passage to the choice.
    - If the question is global, work the choices.
        - Realize that many incorrect choices will contradict the passage.
    - Passage Answer subtype - Think about whether the Topic was present or not.
    - EXCEPT subtype – Find the choice that contradicts the passage.
- Incorrect Choices
    - Similar sounding - these sound like the correct choice but skew a part of it.
    - Wrong Part – detail from another area of the passage.
    - False – opposite of a detail in the passage.
    - New Information – not in the passage but perhaps sound like it, similar topic, etc.

Deduction

- "Which one of the following **inferences** about gold mining does the passage **support**?"
- Deduce valid information from the passage.
- Usually topic references, sometimes these questions are global.
- Approach
    - Extension of a concept deduction – information must be true based on how the concept works.
    - Rephrased information deduction – summarize one or more sentences from the passage.
    - Use the topic reference.
    - Do not envision on this type.
- Incorrect choices
    - New information – the choice sounds like it should be in the passage but it is not.
    - False – the choice contradicts the passage.

*Humanities Practice Passages

A fake can be defined as an artwork intended to deceive. The motives of its creator are decisive, and the merit of the object itself is a separate issue. The question mark in the title of Mark Jones' s *Fake? The Art of Deception* reveals the study's broader concerns. Indeed, it might equally be entitled Original?, and the text begins by noting a variety of possibilities somewhere between the two extremes. These include works by an artist's followers in the style of the master, deliberate archaism, copying for pedagogical purposes, and the production of commercial facsimiles.

The greater part of *Fake?* is devoted to a chronological survey suggesting that faking feeds on the many different motives people have for collecting art, and that, on the whole, the faking of art flourishes whenever art collecting nourishes. In imperial Rome there was a widespread interest in collecting earlier Greek art, and therefore in faking it. No doubt many of the sculptures now exhibited as "Roman copies" were originally passed off as Greek. In medieval Europe, because art was celebrated more for its devotional uses than for its provenance or the ingenuity of its creators, the faking of art was virtually nonexistent. The modern age of faking began in the Italian Renaissance, with two linked developments: a passionate identification with the world of antiquity and a growing sense of individual artistic identity. A patron of the young Michelangelo prevailed upon the artist to make his sculpture *Sleeping Cupid* look as though it had been buried in the earth so that "it will be taken for antique, and you will sell it much better." Within a few years, however, beginning with his first masterpiece, the Bacchus, Michelangelo had shown his contemporaries that great art can assimilate and transcend what came before, resulting in a wholly original work. Soon his genius made him the object of imitators.

Fake? also reminds us that in certain cultures authenticity is a foreign concept. This is true of much African art, where the authenticity of an object is considered by collectors to depend on its function. As an illustration, the study compares two versions of a chi wara mask made by the Bambara people of Mali. One has pegs allowing it to be attached to a cap for its intended ceremonial purpose. The second, otherwise identical, lacks the pegs and is a replica made for sale. African carving is notoriously difficult to date, but even if the ritual mask is recent, made perhaps to replace a damaged predecessor, and the replica much older, only the ritual mask should be seen as authentic, for it is tied to the form's original function. That, at least, is the consensus of the so-called experts. One wonders whether the Bambaran artists would agree.

1. The passage can best be described as doing which one of the following?
   - (A) reconciling varied points of view
   - (B) chronicling the evolution of a phenomenon
   - (C) exploring a complex question
   - (D) advocating a new approach
   - (E) rejecting an inadequate explanation

2. Which one of the following best expresses the author's main point?
   - (A) The faking of art has occurred throughout history and in virtually every culture.
   - (B) Whether a work of art is fake or not is less important than whether it has artistic merit.
   - (C) It is possible to show that a work of art is fake, but the authenticity of a work cannot be proved conclusively.
   - (D) A variety of circumstances make it difficult to determine whether a work of art can appropriately be called a fake.
   - (E) Without an international market to support it, the faking of art would cease.

3. According to the passage, an artwork can be definitively classified as a fake if the person who created it
   - (A) consciously adopted the artistic style of an influential mentor
   - (B) deliberately imitated a famous work of art as a learning exercise
   - (C) wanted other people to be fooled by its appearance
   - (D) made multiple, identical copies of the work available for sale
   - (E) made the work resemble the art of an earlier era

4. The author provides a least one example of each of the following EXCEPT:

   (A) categories of art that are neither wholly fake nor wholly original
   (B) cultures in which the faking or art flourished
   (C) qualities that art collectors have prized in their acquisitions
   (D) cultures in which the categories "fake" and "original" do not apply
   (E) contemporary artists whose works have inspired fakes.

5. The author implies which one of the following about the artistic merits of fakes?

   (A) Because of the circumstances of its production, a fake cannot be said to have true artistic merit.
   (B) A fake can be said to have artistic merit only if the attempted deception is successful.
   (C) A fake may or may not have artistic merit in its own right, regardless of the circumstances of its production.
   (D) Whether a fake has artistic merit depends on whether its creator is accomplished as an artist.
   (E) The artistic merit of a fake depends on the merit of the original work that inspired the fake.

6. By the standard described in the last paragraph of the passage, which one of the following would be considered authentic?

   (A) an ancient Roman copy of an ancient Greek sculpture
   (B) a painting begun by a Renaissance master and finished by his assistants after his death
   (C) a print of a painting signed by the artist who painted the original
   (D) a faithful replica of a ceremonial crown that preserves all the details of, and is indistinguishable from, the original
   (E) a modern reconstruction of a medieval altarpiece designed to serve its traditional role in a service of worship

7. Which one of the following best describes how the last paragraph functions in the context of the passage?

   (A) It offers a tentative answer to a question posed by the author in the opening paragraph.
   (B) It summarizes an account provided in detail in the preceding paragraph.
   (C) It provides additional support for an argument advanced by the author in the preceding paragraph.
   (D) It examines another facet of a distinction developed in the preceding paragraphs.
   (E) It affirms the general principle enunciated at the beginning of the passage.

James Porter (1905-1970) was the first scholar to identify the African influence on visual art in the Americas, and much of what is known about the cultural legacy that African-American artists inherited from their African forebears has come to us by way of his work. Porter, a painter and art historian, began by studying African-American crafts of the eighteenth and nineteenth centuries. This research revealed that many of the household items created by African-American men and women-walking sticks, jugs, and textiles displayed characteristics that linked them iconographically to artifacts of West Africa. Porter then went on to establish clearly the range of the cultural territory inherited by later African-American artists.

An example of this aspect of Porter's research occurs in his essay "Robert S. Duncanson, Midwestern Romantic-Realist." The work of Duncanson, a nineteenth-century painter of the Hudson River school, like that of his predecessor in the movement, Joshua Johnston, was commonly thought to have been created by a Euro-American artist. Porter proved definitively that both Duncanson and Johnston were of African ancestry. Porter published this finding and thousands of others in a comprehensive volume tracing the history of African-American art. At the time of its first printing in 1943, only two other books devoted exclusively to the accomplishments of African-American artists existed. Both of these books were written by Alain LeRoy Locke, a professor at the university where Porter also taught. While these earlier studies by Locke are interesting for being the first to survey the field, neither addressed the critical issue of African precursors; Porter's book addressed this issue, painstakingly integrating the history of African-American art into the larger history of art in the Americas without separating it from those qualities that gave it its unique ties to African artisanship. Porter may have been especially attuned to these ties because of his conscious effort to maintain them in his own paintings, many of which combine the style of the genre portrait with evidence of an extensive knowledge of the cultural history of various African peoples.

In his later years, Porter wrote additional chapters for later editions of his book, constantly revising and correcting his findings, some of which had been based of necessity on fragmentary evidence. Among his later achievements were his definitive reckoning of the birth year of the painter Patrick Reason, long a point of scholarly uncertainty, and his identification of an unmarked grave in San Francisco as that of the sculptor Edmonia Lewis. At his death, Porter left extensive notes for an unfinished project aimed at exploring the influence of African art on the art of the Western world generally, a body of research whose riches scholars still have not exhausted.

8. Which one of the following most accurately states the main idea of the passage?

(A) Because the connections between African-American art and other art in the Americas had been established by earlier scholars, Porter's work focused on showing African-American art's connections to African artisanship.

(B) In addition to showing the connections between African-American art and African artisanship, Porter's most important achievement was illustrating the links between African-American art and other art in the Americas.

(C) Despite the fact that his last book remains unfinished, Porter's work was the first to devote its attention exclusively to the accomplishments of African-American artists.

(D) Although showing the connections between African-American art and African artisanship, Porter's work concentrated primarily on placing African-American art in the context of Western art in general.

(E) While not the first body of scholarship to treat the subject of African-American art, Porter's work was the first to show the connections between African-American art and African artisanship.

9. The discussion of Locke's books is intended primarily to

(A) argue that Porter's book depended upon Locke's pioneering scholarship

(B) highlight an important way in which Porter's work differed from previous work in his field

(C) suggest an explanation for why Porter's book was little known outside academic circles

(D) support the claim that Porter was not the first to notice African influences in African-American art

(E) argue that Locke's example was a major influence on Porter's decision to publish his findings.

10. The passage states which one of the following about the 1943 edition of Porter's book on African-American art?

(A) It received little scholarly attention at first.

(B) It was revised and improved upon in later editions.

(C) It took issue with several of Locke's conclusions.

(D) It is considered the definitive versions of Porter's work.

(E) It explored the influence of African art on Western art in general.

11. Given the information in the passage, Porter's identification of the ancestry of Duncanson and Johnston provides conclusive evidence for which one of the following statements?

(A) Some of the characteristics defining the Hudson River school are iconographically linked to West African artisanship.
(B) Some of the works of Duncanson and Johnston are not in the style of the Hudson River school.
(C) Some of the work of Euro-American painters displays similarities to African-American crafts of the eighteenth and nineteenth centuries.
(D) Some of the works of the Hudson River school were done by African-American painters.
(E) Some of the works of Duncanson and Johnston were influenced by West African artifacts.

12. Which one of the following can most reasonably be inferred from the passage about the study that Porter left unfinished at his death?

(A) If completed, it would have contradicted some of the conclusions contained in his earlier book.
(B) If completed, it would have amended some of the conclusions contained in his earlier book.
(C) If completed, it would have brought up to date the comprehensive history of African-American art begun in his earlier book.
(D) If completed, it would have expanded upon the project of his earlier book by broadening the scope of inquiry found in the earlier book.
(E) If completed, it would have supported some of the theories put forth by Porter's contemporaries since the publication of his earlier book.

13. Which one of the following hypothetical observations is most closely analogous to the discoveries Porter made about African-American crafts of the eighteenth and nineteenth centuries?

(A) Contemporary Haitian social customs have a unique character dependent on but different from both their African and French origins.
(B) Popular music in the United States, some of which is based on African musical traditions, often influences music being composed on the African continent.
(C) Many novels written in Canada by Chinese immigrants exhibit narrative themes very similar to those found in Chinese folktales.
(D) Extensive Indian immigration to England has made traditional Indian foods nearly as popular there as the traditional English foods that had been popular there before Indian immigration.
(E) Some Mexican muralists of the early twentieth century consciously imitated the art of native peoples as a response to the Spanish influences that had predominated in Mexican art.

14. The passage most strongly supports which one of the following inferences about Porter's own paintings?

(A) They often contained figures or images derived from the work of African artisans.
(B) They fueled his interest in pursuing a career in art history.
(C) They were used in Porter's book to show the extent of African influence on African-American art.
(D) They were a deliberate attempt to prove his theories about art history.
(E) They were done after all of his academic work had been completed.

15. Based on the passage, which one of the following, if true, would have been most relevant to the project Porter was working on at the time of his death?

(A) African-American crafts of the eighteenth and nineteenth centuries have certain resemblances to European folk crafts of earlier periods.
(B) The paintings of some twentieth-century European artists prefigured certain stylistic developments in North American graphic art.
(C) The designs of many of the quilts made by African-American women in the nineteenth century reflect designs of European trade goods.
(D) After the movement of large numbers of African Americans to cities, the African influences in the work of many African-American painters increased.
(E) Several portraits by certain twentieth-century European painters were modeled after examples of Central African ceremonial masks.

*Humanities Practice Passages Explanations

1. (24/1 #21) ~ C

Organization. This is a slightly unusual stem for an organization question. The introduction begins by discussing the broad concerns of Fake? The Art of Deception and the passage goes on to explore the ranges of "fakes." The passage explores the complex question of what "original" actually means.

2. (24/1 #22) ~ D

Main Point. The author deals with the complexity of the issue of originality and the main point that it is tough to say whether something is actually a fake. This is supported by the examples of various peoples and cultures discussed that have different views on originality. With a subtle topic such as this one, look for a main point that reflects the complexity of the passage.

3. (24/1 #23) ~ C

Detail. Lines 1-2 state that a fake is artwork that is intended to deceive. Sometimes it is difficult to recall specific details that occurred at the beginning of the passage because you read them first. Here, thinking about how the whole passage is devoted to the concept of fakes in art should point you towards the beginning of the passage where the concept would be defined.

4. (24/1 #24) ~ E

Detail. The correct answer will be an example that is not provided by the author. Not surprisingly, we have to work each choice on this Except question to find that E is correct (many Except questions feature the correct answer as D or E forcing you to work all or most of the choices). The author never gave an example of contemporary artists whose works have inspired fakes. There were examples given of older artists whose works have inspired fakes, such as Michelangelo, but not contemporary artists.

5. (24/1 #25) ~ C

Detail. Lines 2-3 state that the merit of the object is a separate issue from whether it is a fake, which means that a fake may or may not have artistic merit. The fact that it is a fake does not matter one way or the other.

6. (24/1 #26) ~ E

Match. Lines 38-40 state that in African art authenticity depends on function. Line 50 states that the crown with pegs is authentic because it is tied to the form's original function. So if something is designed for a specific function and can fulfill it, then it is authentic. Otherwise, it is a fake. Choice E works because the altarpiece is designed to serve its traditional role. That is the information that we need in order to deem it authentic with this standard.

Choice D is incorrect because we are never told that the crown is designed to fulfill the role of the original.

7. (24/1 #27) ~ D

Role. The last paragraph gives an interesting example about how some cultures do not even have the concept of authenticity. This is a refinement on the distinction between authentic and real that is discussed throughout the passage. The previous paragraph talked about how fakes have existed throughout history, and how the line between fake and authentic varies from place to place. The idea that some cultures do not even understand the concept of authentic is an expansion of this discussion. The term "another facet" in the answer choice should stand out because the discussion in the final paragraph brings in a new viewpoint.

(C) is incorrect because the passage is not trying to prove an argument, it is exploring concepts.

8. (26/4 #6) ~ E

Main Point. The first sentence of the passage summarizes the main idea: Porter was the first to connect African American art with its forbearers. Line 26 mentions that he was not the first to address African American art.

9. (26/4 #7) ~ B

Role. Lines 26-34 discuss Locke's books. They are mentioned as the only books devoted exclusively to the accomplishments of African American artists before Porter's. The author mentions that they did not address the concept of African precursors. Therefore, mentioning these books helps to establish Porter's books as the first to cover his specific topic.

10. (26/4 #8) ~ B

Detail. Lines 44-46 tell that Porter revised and improved upon his book in later additions. The final paragraph is devoted to this idea, so it should be easy to remember it.

11. (26/4 #9) ~ D

Detail. Lines 18-24 tell us that some of the works of the Hudson River school were done by African-American painters.

12. (26/4 #10) ~ D

Deduction. The study that Porter left unfinished was analyzing the influence of African art on the Western World generally (lines 52-55). His earlier work was analyzing the influence of African Art on visual art in the Americas. So, his new study was an expansion on his previous work.

13. (26/4 #11) ~ C

Match. Porter discovered that African-American art was closely tied to West African influence (Lines 8-12). Choice C works: it is an example of immigrants being influenced by art from their native country.

14. (26/4 #12) ~ A

Deduction. Lines 38-43 talk about Porter's paintings. Porter consciously maintained these ties to African artisanship, so it is likely that his paintings contained images or figures derived from the work of African artisans.

15. (26/4 #13) ~ E

Deduction. At the time of his death, Porter was exploring the influence of African art on the art of the Western world (lines 52-55). E would be relevant: it shows the influence of African art (ceremonial masks) on western art (20th century European painters). Evaluate every choice on Beyond questions so that you do not miss the best one.

More Common Types

Now that you have learned about the most common types of RC question, you can build on that knowledge. The following types are also common, although less frequent than the previous set.

Agree

Agree questions ask you which statement the author or a speaker would agree with. These are closely related to Deduction questions because choosing which statement the author would agree requires inferring their opinion from clues in the passage. The inference does not need to be based on an opinion. Anything written in the passage that is not attributed to a speaker is supported by the author. For example, a passage tells you that an environmental book is aimed at an audience over 50 in P1, and later the author disapproves of the fact that the book is written in conversational style that turns off older readers. In that situation, the author would agree with this choice:

(A) The book could more effectively reach its target audience if it had a more formal tone.

This inference is supported by the two points we mentioned. The correct choice on an Agree question will often pull together information from disparate parts of the passage. You can think of Agree answers as big inferences. Of course, sometimes agreement inferences will be on a smaller scale, summing up information from one paragraph instead of two or three, almost indistinguishable from a Deduction inference. While Agree questions have some important differences from Deductions questions, they both ask you to understand the implication of information in the passage.

Query, References and Frequency

Agree queries usually contain the word "agree" or "view:"

The author of the passage would be most likely to ***agree*** with which one of the following statements?

The passage provides the strongest support for inferring that the author holds which one of the following ***views***?

Mandelbrot would be most likely to ***agree*** with which of the following statements about cyanide?

The information in the passage suggest that the author would be most likely to ***agree*** with which one of the following statements regarding training in statutory law?

These queries ask for a statement that a specific person would agree with. That person is usually the author, but sometimes it is a prominent person.

About 75% of Agree questions are global, the rest have a topic reference, like the last two example queries above. The fact that most are global makes sense because a lot of the inferences are broad; they pull information that is spread out in the passage. Agree questions are quite common: you will see about three on your official LSAT.

Approach

You are looking for a choice that is proven by the passage; never forget this. You are not asked to **guess** what the author or person would agree with. Instead, understand what that party said in the passage and find the choice that is supported by that information. Just like with Deduction questions, you must **interpret** the passage to find which choice is logically accurate. One difference is that you are limited to the information given by a specific person. Of course, if that person is the author, then most of the passage is a viable source of information.

Big Deductions

About half of the time, the correct choice will encapsulate ideas developed over many paragraphs. This stands in contrast to Deduction questions where you are either tested on a concept that is developed in a single paragraph, or you are asked to rephrase/summarize several sentences from a single paragraph. The correct statement on an Agree question can easily draw support from two or more paragraphs, ones that are not necessarily sequential. For instance, a passage about a painter's career may imply **throughout** that exploring challenging questions in art was more important to the painter than honing a specific style of painting. This is a big inference. The evidence that supports it could come in many different sentences:

> She then transitioned to abstract painting instead of continuing to develop her skills on portraits.
>
> How best to portray light through coloration was one of her many concerns.
>
> Never one to be pigeon-holed, Agatha constantly explored the deep questions underlying the art of painting.

Big inferences are also generally more **abstract** than more narrow ones. They are encapsulating ideas and they say something more complex than smaller inferences. To help you understand this distinction, compare these two inferences:

> Agatha focused her career on answering the hard questions in painting rather than learning how to master a specific style.
>
> Agatha used colors more aggressively than her contemporaries in art school.

The first, bigger inference above contains ideas of a larger scale and would need an entire passage to develop. This is partly due to the fact that describing an artist's career takes more time than describing how that same artist used color in art school. The second inference could be supported by a couple of sentences:

> At RISD (Rhode Island School of Design) Agatha sometimes received below average grades in painting classes. Teachers often deducted points on her works for using color in unconventional, unproven ways. Unlike her fellow students, Agatha always chose to experiment with color, even in areas of a painting where she knew the "appropriate" use.

Many students find these large scale inferences to be more challenging to spot than smaller ones. This is understandable: big deductions force you to integrate more information and to draw connections between less closely spaced ideas. Knowing that you may be looking for such an inference will help you work the choices on global Agree questions. These inferences are usually closely related to the main point.

Normal Deductions

Not all Agree questions contain big deductions. Many contain normal-sized inferences that resemble the correct answer on a Deduction question. These inferences are more likely to occur when the person in question is not the author, because a speaker (a person or group with a viewpoint) generally gets less time to convey ideas. Normal inferences also show up with topic references, as these narrow the scope of information that can go into creating the inference.

Note the Viewpoints

Circles around speakers and "A's" next to the author's viewpoints can help you on Agree questions because viewpoints will be involved in the answer. For instance, one of the more obvious author viewpoints could be combined with another fact in the passage to create the statement that she would agree with. Also, if you need to refer back to the passage on a global Agree question, you might be able to use your viewpoint markings to help you eliminate or support an answer choice.

Incorrect Choices

Like Deduction questions, Agree questions often feature new information choices. If the information in a choice is not supported by the passage, then it is incorrect. The author cannot agree with information that features a topic never mentioned.

Likewise, many false choices are tempting because they rehash *some* information directly from the passage. The rest of the choice will then contradict how the passage treated that information. For instance, a passage that analyzes the effectiveness of a trade treaty might imply that the author thinks the development of the treaty was an arduous process between two countries and involved many rounds of revisions. The passage stated that the author believed there was **only one** round of revisions.

Example Agree Questions

This Agree question is from the passage about cytologists and biochemists:

> 15. Which one of the following statements about cells is most compatible with the views of late nineteenth-century biochemists as those views are described in the passage?

"Most compatible with the views" tells us that we are dealing with an Agree question. Specifically: which statement would late nineteenth-century biochemists agree with regarding cells? The topic reference is easy to find because only one part of the passage talks about biochemists opinions in the late 19th century. Here are the lines we need:

> ...Many biochemists, on the other hand, remained skeptical of the idea that so much structure existed, arguing that the chemical reactions that occur in cytological preparations might create the appearance of such structures. Also, they stood apart from the debate then raging over whether protoplasm, the complex of living material within a cell, is homogeneous, network like, granular, or foam like. Their interest lay in the more "fundamental" issues of the chemical nature of protoplasm, especially the newly formulated enzyme theory of life.
>
> In general, biochemists judged cytologists to be too ignorant of chemistry to grasp the basic processes...

Actually, we do not need the final sentence above because it describes the biochemists' views on cytologists and we are only interested in how biochemists view cells. We included it here to show this distinction. When referring back to the passage, you would stop reading at the beginning of P3 because it is irrelevant to the question. So, we focus on the first three sentences excerpted above. There is a lot there about what biochemists think about cells. Do not try to memorize this information or envision. Instead, simply refresh your memory of the biochemists' views and then work the choices.

(A) The secret of cell function resides in the structure of the cell.

(A) is not supported in the part of the passage we read, the only relevant part of the passage. Further, it seems like we would remember such bold statements as "the secret." This is a new choice and it is incorrect.

(B) Only by discovering the chemical composition of protoplasm can the processes of the cell be understood.

19th century biochemists were said to be interested in "the chemical nature of protoplasm." The choice is a strong statement because of the use of "only." However, it is valid because the passage says that biochemists of this era thought discovering the chemical composition of protoplasm was a fundamental issue. This choice is correct.

(C) Scientific knowledge about the chemical composition of the cell can help to explain behavioral patterns in organisms.

"Behavioral patterns in organisms"? That type of information is never mentioned in the entire passage, and therefore this choice is incorrect. "Chemical composition of the cell" sounds like it would fit in an answer for this question, but the end of the choice is clearly incorrect. Do not be fooled by half right/half wrong choices.

(D) The most important issue to be resolved with regard to the cell is determining the physical characteristics of protoplasm.

We are never given support for this idea. The **physical characteristics** of protoplasm are not of interest to biochemists: "they stood apart from the debate then ranging over whether protoplasm… is homogeneous, network like, granular or foam like." Biochemists are interested in the **chemical** nature of protoplasm. This is a false choice.

(E) The methods of chemistry must be supplemented before a full account of the cell's structures can be made.

This information is not supported. The beginning of P3 tells that biochemists think that cytologists need to know more chemistry to understand the processes in a cell, but that is a different concept. This is a sounds similar choice.

Example Agree Question 2

Now work (read and mark) this passage to set yourself up for the next Agree example question. Marked passage on the next page:

(2.4) The Constitution of the United States does not explicitly define the extent of the President's authority to involve United States troops in conflicts with other nations in the absence of a declaration of war. Instead, the question of the President's authority in this matter falls in the hazy area of concurrent power, where authority is not expressly allocated to either the President or the Congress. The Constitution gives Congress the basic power to declare war, as well as the authority to raise and support armies and a navy, enact regulations for the control of the military, and provide for the common defense. The President, on the other hand, in addition to being obligated to execute the laws of the land, including commitments negotiated by defense treaties, is named commander in chief of the armed forces and is empowered to appoint envoys and make treaties with the consent of the Senate. Although this allocation of powers does not expressly address the use of armed forces short of a declared war, the spirit of the Constitution at least requires that Congress should be involved in the decision to deploy troops, and in passing the War Powers Resolution of 1973, Congress has at last reclaimed a role in such decisions.

Historically, United States Presidents have not waited for the approval of Congress before involving United States troops in conflicts in which a state of war was not declared. One scholar has identified 199 military engagements that occurred without the consent of Congress, ranging from Jefferson's conflict with the Barbary pirates to Nixon's invasion of Cambodia during the Vietnam conflict, which President Nixon argued was justified because his role as commander in chief allowed him almost unlimited discretion over the deployment of troops. However, the Vietnam conflict, never a declared war, represented a turning point in Congress's tolerance of presidential discretion in the deployment of troops in undeclared wars. Galvanized by the human and monetary cost of those hostilities and showing a new determination to fulfill its proper role, Congress enacted the War Powers Resolution of 1973, a statute designed to ensure that the collective judgment of both Congress and the President would be applied to the involvement of United States troops in foreign conflicts.

The resolution required the President, in the absence of a declaration of war, to consult with Congress "in every possible instance" before introducing forces and to report to Congress within 48 hours after the forces have actual ly been deployed. Most important, the resolution allows Congress to veto the involvement once it begins, and requires the President, in most cases, to end the involvement within 60 days unless Congress specifically authorizes the military operation to continue. In its final section, by declaring that the resolution is not intended to alter the constitutional authority of either Congress or the President, the resolution asserts that congressional involvement in decisions to use armed force is in accord with the intent and spirit of the Constitution.

(2.4) The Constitution of the United States does not explicitly define the extent of the President's authority to involve United States troops in conflicts with other nations in the absence of a declaration of war. Instead, the question of the President's authority in this matter falls in the hazy area of concurrent power, where authority is not expressly allocated to either the President or the Congress. The Constitution gives Congress the basic power to declare war, as well as the authority to raise and support armies and a navy, enact regulations for the control of the military, and provide for the common defense. The President, on the other hand, in addition to being obligated to execute the laws of the land, including commitments negotiated by defense treaties, is named commander in chief of the armed forces and is empowered to appoint envoys and make treaties with the consent of the Senate. Although this allocation of powers does not expressly address the use of armed forces short of a declared war, the spirit of the Constitution at least requires that Congress should be involved in the decision to deploy troops, and in passing the War Powers Resolution of 1973, Congress has at last reclaimed a role in such decisions.

Historically, United States Presidents have not waited for the approval of Congress before involving United States troops in conflicts in which a state of war was not declared. One scholar has identified 199 military engagements that occurred without the consent of Congress, ranging from Jefferson's conflict with the Barbary pirates to Nixon's invasion of Cambodia during the Vietnam conflict, which President Nixon argued was justified because his role as commander in chief allowed him almost unlimited discretion over the deployment of troops. However, the Vietnam conflict, never a declared war, represented a turning point in Congress's tolerance of presidential discretion in the deployment of troops in undeclared wars. Galvanized by the human and monetary cost of those hostilities and showing a new determination to fulfill its proper role, Congress enacted the War Powers Resolution of 1973, a statute designed to ensure that the collective judgment of both Congress and the President would be applied to the involvement of United States troops in foreign conflicts.

The resolution required the President, in the absence of a declaration of war, to consult with Congress "in every possible instance" before introducing forces and to report to Congress within 48 hours after the forces have actually been deployed. Most important, the resolution allows Congress to veto the involvement once it begins, and requires the President, in most cases, to end the involvement within 60 days unless Congress specifically authorizes the military operation to continue. In its final section, by declaring that the resolution is not intended to alter the constitutional authority of either Congress or the President, the resolution asserts that congressional involvement in decisions to use armed force is in accord with the intent and spirit of the Constitution. MP

This is a straightforward passage: the author explores the origin of the War Powers Resolution. Note the authors opinion on the necessity of the resolution in the final sentence of P1. The author uses the phrase "at last." That indicates that such a shift of power in declaring war was overdue; the author approves of it. Other notable markings include the list of examples in the second paragraph and the MPD at the end of the final paragraph. The idea that the Resolution realigned reality with the **intentions of the constitution** is the author's conclusion.

Now tackle this Agree question. Explanation on the following page:

26. It can be inferred from the passage that the author believes that the War Powers Resolution of 1973

(A) is not in accord with the explicit roles of the President and Congress as defined in the Constitution

(B) interferes with the role of the President as commander in chief of the armed forces

(C) signals Congress's commitment to fulfill a role intended for it by the Constitution

(D) fails explicitly to address the use of armed forces in the absence of a declaration of war

(E) confirms the role historically assumed by Presidents

26. It can be inferred from the passage that the author believes that the War Powers Resolution of 1973

Although we are given a topic reference, the War Powers Resolution is the subject of the passage, so this is similar to a global question. But we know the author expressed an opinion at the end of P1, so we reread that:

> ...the spirit of the Constitution at least requires that Congress should be involved in the decision to deploy troops, and in passing the War Powers Resolution of 1973, Congress has at last reclaimed a role in such decisions.

That is all the research we can do with such a broad topic. We move to the choices, looking for a statement that the author would support regarding the Resolution:

(A) is not in accord with the explicit roles of the President and Congress as defined in the Constitution

This is a false choice. The author stresses that the Resolution **restores the roles** of the President and Congress in declaring war as defined in the constitution. This is the conclusion we marked at the end of the passage.

(B) interferes with the role of the President as commander in chief of the armed forces

This choice not supported. Congress having a stronger say in the involvement of troops in foreign conflicts does not necessarily limit the control the President has as commander in chief of the armed forces.

(C) signals Congress's commitment to fulfill a role intended for it by the Constitution

This matches the opinion we reread during our research phase. The author repeatedly states that the Resolution honors the Constitution. This fits the idea of concurrent power where Congress and the president share control over declaring war. This is a rephrasing deduction.

(D) fails explicitly to address the use of armed forces in the absence of a declaration of war

This is a false choice. The beginning of P3 tells that the Resolution addresses the use of the armed forces in the absence of a declaration of war. The repeating of key terms from that paragraph makes this a similar sounding incorrect choice.

(E) confirms the role historically assumed by Presidents

The passage lists multiple examples of the president taking greater control of armed forces than provided by the Resolution, so **historically**, Presidents have not followed the limitations introduced. Another false choice.

Role

Role questions ask you to identify **why** the author mentions a topic or sentence, or what role a paragraph plays in the overall passage. No matter the size of the part of the text you are asked about, your job is to understand how that piece fits in. This requires rereading; it is very challenging to remember the answers to Role questions from your initial reading.

While Deduction and Agree questions ask you to understand concepts and combine parts of the passage, Role questions ask you to single out an individual part and determine why it is there. Identifying and articulating a role is not a skill that comes naturally to many students, but with guidance and practice, you will have no trouble with Role questions.

Query, References and Frequency

Purpose queries ask what the author is "seeking to do" with a part or what the "purpose" of that part is. There are more possible phrasings for these queries than normal:

> In discussing the philosopher Wallace, the author of the passage ***seeks*** primarily to…
>
> The author most probably quotes directly from the charter (lines 20-22) for ***which one of the following reasons***?
>
> In the first paragraph, the author ***refers*** to a the reputed critic's opinion primarily in order to…
>
> The main ***purpose*** of the third paragraph is to…
>
> Which one of the following most accurately describes the ***function*** of the first two sentences of the second paragraph?

Take a moment and reread those queries.

Sometimes a query will ask the "reason" the author writes something. Although these queries come in a variety of forms, they center on the role of a specific part.

Almost all recent Role questions have an exact reference: they tell you where in the passage to find the part they ask the role of. Most ask the role of a topic from the passage, but they give an exact reference when they do so. Look at this query:

> The author mentions Maria's cell phone (lines 54-59) primarily in order to…

It is easy to refer to the passage with exact references. When you are given a Role of a Paragraph question, that too is an exact reference. There is only one P2 in a passage.

Role questions are common, you will see 2 or 3 on your official LSAT.

Approach

There is a bit of variety with Role questions based on the nature of the part you are asked to identify the role of. Subtypes include: phrases, sentences, topics and paragraphs.

Find and Read the Part

This is a difficult type, but there is no challenge in locating the right area of the passage to refer to. Use the exact reference and start reading a sentence or two before the part and read through the part. If you have not found the answer, read past the part until you do. Sometimes the author will reference a topic that only gets fully incorporated into the discussion a few sentences **after** it was first introduced. You might need to start reading earlier than a sentence or two before the part. You will likely know this as you are reading.

Use your Memory

Regardless of the subtype, when you reread the relevant part of the passage, that may be all the "research" you need to do on the question. This occurs when the reread refreshes your memory of why the author used that part. When you reread, think back to your first reading, and link the part to the meaning of a larger part of the passage. If the part is a phrase, try to remember the main point of the paragraph it is in. If the part is a paragraph, think about the main point of the entire passage. Reach back into your more general knowledge of the passage; this will give you context. Thinking about the part in a vacuum does you no good. Tougher Role questions force you to articulate a role that connects to parts of the passage **far away** from the one you are asked about. You can answer these effectively only by appreciating the larger context.

Find the Context

After referring to the passage and thinking about the larger context surrounding the part, you must articulate the role. This is something of an art, because every part has a unique purpose. The key idea here is find exactly why the author wrote that phrase or brought in that topic. How does it tie into what came **before** and **after** it? The choices demand a clear view of the role. Use the passage until you are confident in the role. Do not spend an inordinate amount of time rereading the passage to articulate the role, but realize that the choices may not help you much if you cannot figure out the role using the passage.

Follow the author's flow of ideas around the part. Does the author need an example to illustrate a point? Does the sentence help introduce an idea developed later? Whatever it may be, the role is intricately tied to expressing the author's ideas. Thinking of the general structure of the passage can be helpful as well. For instance, if the author is exploring two different views on roadway congestion, going back and forth between the two, then the part must work with that structure. Realize that articulating the role takes practice; be patient with yourself on this question type.

Subtype Advice

On recent RC sections, most questions have asked the role of a topic. On older LSATs, Role of a Paragraph questions were much more common. For your official LSAT, get ready to analyze the role of topics and maybe a word, phrase or paragraph.

The smaller the part of the passage you are asked about, the less of the passage you need to reread and analyze. If you are asked why the author used a specific **word**, you should read the sentence before the word and the one it is in. Perhaps you will need to read the sentence after the one with the word. Maybe you will only need to read the one sentence that has the word. When figuring out the role of a topic, you might need to understand what the author said **two sentences** before or after it. Understanding the role of a paragraph usually requires reading the final sentence of the paragraph before, skimming the paragraph and perhaps reading a bit into the next paragraph. Of course, you might take one look at the paragraph and remember its exact role from your first reading. That is ideal.

Envision

Express the role in your own words as specifically as you can. It can be tough to articulate what the role is because the correct choice will be narrow, but the process of *trying* is helpful. Even stating what other topic of the passage the part connects to is useful. Often, you will roughly understand what that part does, but not be able to state it. Keeping your envisioning concrete. If an author brings up a viewpoint supporting communism and then immediately argues against communism, you can say that the role of the viewpoint is "backing an idea later refuted." Taking those extra 10 seconds to put into words what the role is will help you work the choices because it gives you something to critique them against. It makes their complicated language less confusing, because you can see if their general meaning is accurate without getting tied up trying to understand **exactly** what they mean.

The Answer Choices

The answer choices center on the **nouns** they use. Although they start with a verb, those actions are usually interchangeable and do not add much to the meaning of the choice. Look at these example choices:

(A) ***describe*** an interpretation of animal communication that the author believes rests on a logical error

(B) ***suggest*** by illustration that there is conscious intention underlying the communicative signs employed by certain animals

(C) ***present*** an argument in support of the view that animal communication systems are spontaneous and creative

"Describe," "suggest" and "present" all basically mean to communicate. Sure, suggesting means making a proposal, while describing is to give an account of a thing. Those differences are subtle compared to the variation in the nouns of the choices. With (A), does the part asked about connect to a theory of animal communication that the author disagrees with? With (C), does the part support the idea that animal communication systems are spontaneous? Do take the choices as a whole, but focus on the way they describe the part with nouns.

Incorrect Choices

Most incorrect choices on Role questions describe an irrelevant role or one that does not match the meaning of the passage. These choices might sound good because they reference topics related to the part (similar sounding choices), but they often confuse the ideas. Or, an incorrect choice may simply describe a role that does not relate to the passage at all. Stay focused on your envisioned answer, or what you know about the role, and analyze the **meaning** of each choice.

Be especially wary of choices that describe roles that are played by **other** parts of the passage. These are tempting answers because they ring true with your knowledge of how the passage works.

Example Role Questions

This Role question is from the scientific disciplines passage and asks about the role of a Topic:

13. The author quotes Fruton (lines 62-64) primarily in order to

The phrase "in order to" is a sign that this is a Role question. The topic is the quotation from Fruton. Here is the paragraph that contains the lines:

> This interaction between paired disciplines can have important results. In the case of late nineteenth-century cell research, progress was fueled by competition among the various attitudes and issues derived from cell biology and biochemistry. Joseph Fruton, a biochemist, has suggested that such competition and the resulting tensions among researchers are a principal source of vitality and "are likely to lead to unexpected and exciting novelties in the future, as they have in the past."

We start rereading at a logical point: the beginning of the paragraph. The first two sentences, you should recall, are the author's opinion that competition between sister disciplines is beneficial. We marked this earlier. It is important to be clear on what is said directly before the part. Next, we read the specific part. Fruton supports the author's idea. He says that competition between researchers will likely lead to future advances. We can sum up this role as "supporting the authors conclusion about paired disciplines." That envisioned answer will help use work the choices:

(A) restate the author's own conclusions

(A) matches. The author uses Fruton to back her main point in this paragraph. With a match this good, select and move on.

(B) provide new evidence about the relationship of cytology to biochemistry

New evidence? No, what Fruton says cannot be considered evidence. That would involve data, not his beliefs. What he says also does not deal with the specific fields of cytology and biochemistry. He talks about competition among all scientific researchers. This choice does not match the role.

(C) summarize the position of the biochemists described in the passage

Fruton does not summarize the position of the biochemists. That would involve talking about their specific beliefs (fascination with the chemical nature of protoplasm, etc.).

(D) illustrate the difficulties encountered in the synthesis of disciplines

Fruton does not talk about difficulties; his tone is quite positive. This is a false choice because Fruton talks about the **benefits** of the competition of disciplines.

(E) emphasize the ascendancy of the theories of biochemists over those of cytologists

Like choice (B), this mistakenly states that these disciplines are discussed. There is no comparison made between these two scientific fields, so the quote cannot play this role.

Example Role Question 2

This Role question comes from the medical profession passage:

> 28. Which one of the following best describes the author's purpose in lines 18-42 of the passage?

The word "purpose" stands out in the query. Your job: identify why the author wrote lines 18 – 42. Those lines, spanning three paragraphs, are reproduced below. Because they are so long, there is no need to begin rereading earlier. If you cannot determine the role from these lines alone, you can read before or after this part.

> ..."To profess" preserves the meaning of its Latin source, "to declare publicly; to announce, affirm, avow." A profession is an activity or occupation to which its practitioner publicly professes, that is, confesses, devotion. But public announcement seems insufficient; publicly declaring devotion to plumbing or auto repair would not turn these trades into professions.
>
> Some believe that learning and knowledge are the diagnostic signs of a profession. For reasons probably linked to the medieval university, the term "profession" has been applied to the so-called learned professions-medicine, law, and theology-the practices of which are founded upon inquiry and knowledge rather than mere "knowhow." Yet it is not only the pursuit and acquisition of knowledge that makes one a professional. The knowledge involved makes the profession one of the learned variety, but its professional quality is rooted in something else.
>
> Some mistakenly seek to locate that something else in the prestige and honor accorded professionals by society, evidenced in their special titles and the special deference and privileges they receive. But externalities do not constitute medicine a profession.

There is a lot contained in these lines. They center on exploring what a profession is, first explaining the devotion aspect of it and then moving into the fact that devotion is not sufficient. A profession also requires the pursuit and acquisition of knowledge, but that too is not enough to deem one a professional: there is another quality required. Some seek to identify that quality in the honor accorded professionals, but that is *not* the missing quality.

We can summarize the role as "exploring the key qualities that make a job a profession, while hinting at a third quality." That envisioned answer will help us work the choices:

> (A) The author locates the "something else" that truly constitutes a profession.

At the end of the part, the author says that the "something else" is **not** the honor given the profession. The author does locate that something else **after** these lines. Further, this choice misses the qualities of devotion and knowledge that are discussed in this section of the passage.

(B) The author dismisses efforts to redefine the meaning of the term "profession."

This choice does not fit our envisioned answer. Early on, the passage talks about why medicine should not be renamed a trade instead of a profession. Nowhere in the passage does the author dismiss efforts to redefine the meaning of the term profession. This is a similar sounding choice.

(C) The author considers, and largely criticizes, several definitions of what constitutes a profession.

(C) matches our envisioned answer. The lines explore possible definitions of a profession and reject several of them. A profession is more than a job that someone publicly devotes themselves to, nor is a profession solely defined by the quest for knowledge associated with it. Even though our envisioned answer does not line up **precisely** with this choice, our envisioning helped a great deal. We knew that the lines deal with exploring the qualities of a profession, even if we did not focus on the fact that the author is rejecting narrower definitions of a profession. Select this choice and move on.

(D) The author clarifies the meaning of the term "profession" by advocating a return to its linguistic and historical roots.

This is a false choice. The first two paragraphs of the excerpt reject both the linguistic root (it is not just devotion that makes a profession) and the historical root of the term. Because the author does explore and *reject* the roots of the term, this can be a tempting choice. Our envisioned answer helps enormously in not falling for this choice.

(E) The author distinguishes trades such as plumbing and auto repair from professions such as medicine, law, and theology.

The author does do this when she talks about the learned professions, but (E) does not describe the role of the lines. The lines do much more than (E) describes. Avoid answers that state a unimportant fraction of what the piece does.

Match

Match questions ask you to understand a concept or situation from the passage and then to match its form or nature with an answer choice. These are also called Analogy questions. Those Match questions that ask you to match a **situation** are similar to LR Parallel Structure questions, only less complex. Other Match questions ask you to understand a **concept** from the passage and then choose an example that fits with that concept.

Match questions are more abstract and ask you to move further from the content of the passage than any others. You take an idea from the passage and then match it to a situation that is totally separate from the passage. These questions are often challenging and time consuming. Improving your match skills can help you get those last few points on the RC section and build your confidence in conquering the more difficult RC questions.

Query, References, Frequency

As just touched on, there are two different subtypes of Match questions: Situation and Concept. Situation Match questions ask you to find a situation in the choices that is analogous to a situation described in the passage. Their queries often contain the word "analogous" and often the word "scenarios." Example Situation queries:

> Which one of the following is ***most analogous*** to the role that custom made sculptures play in the fine homes?
>
> The reaction described in which one of the following scenarios is ***most analogous*** to the reaction of the art critics mentioned in line 13?
>
> As it is presented in the passage, the approach to history taken by mainstream U.S. historians of the late nineteenth and early twentieth centuries is ***most similar to*** the approach exemplified in which one of the following?

Situation questions always ask you to compare two similar situations. That idea of relating two things that are analogous makes these queries easy to identify, regardless of the different phrasings you might see.

The other subtype are Concept questions. These ask you to grasp how a concept in the passage works and then to illustrate that knowledge by finding the example that is consistent with the concept. These queries often use the word "example" or "exemplified" or sometimes "applicable." Example Concept queries:

> Suppose that a group of independent journalists has uncovered evidence of human rights abuses being perpetrated by a security agency of a UN member state upon a group of political dissidents. Which one of the following approaches to the situation would most likely be advocated by present-day delegates who share the views of the delegates and representatives mentioned in lines 11-14?
>
> As it is described in the passage, the transnational approach employed by African American historians working in the late nineteenth and early twentieth centuries would be best exemplified by a historical study that
>
> Given the information in the passage, to which one of the following would taxonomy be most applicable?

Most Match questions give you a topic reference, the reference being the situation or concept you must match. Sometimes, you are given an exact reference. This question type is common: you will likely see 2 or 3 on your official LSAT.

Approach

Regardless of the subtype you are dealing with, the main challenge is understanding the concept or situation that you are asked to match. Unless you remember **all** the features of the situation, or understand the concept completely from your first reading, you will need to reference the passage. To locate the right part of the passage, use the topic reference fully.

Sometimes, the topic you are dealing with is discussed in multiple places. In that case, reference where it is **first** discussed, as that is where the author will often explain its important aspects. Usually, those references are the easiest to locate. After that step, if you still need to learn more about the topic, look at one or two more places where it is discussed and reread the appropriate lines.

As you are rereading the passage, mentally compile the specific features of that concept or situation. Figure out exactly what the core aspects are; you use those features to work the choices. Here is an example Match question, Situation subtype. It comes from the Wheatley passage:

> 2. The approach to poetry taken by a modern-day Italian immigrant in America would be most analogous to Phillis Wheatley's approach, as it is described in the passage, if the immigrant

Our topic reference is Wheatley's approach to poetry. We need to understand the main aspects of that in order to work the choices. This is a main topic, but it is dealt with explicitly in P4:

> The standards of eighteenth-century English poetry, which itself reflected little of the American language, led Wheatley to develop a notion of poetry as a closed system, derived from imitation of earlier written works. No place existed for the rough-and-ready Americanized English she heard in the streets, for the English spoken by Black people, or for Africanisms. The conventions of eighteenth-century neoclassical poetry ruled out casual talk; her voice and feelings had to be generalized according to rules of poetic diction and characterization; the particulars of her African past, if they were to be dealt with at all, had to be subordinated to the reigning conventions....Wheatley adopted a foreign language and a foreign literary tradition; they were not extensions of her past experience, but replacements.

That last sentence is especially telling. Wheatley adopted the rules of English poetry and allowed them to supplant her history and voice. When evaluating the choices, keep in mind this idea of **the new culture replacing the old**. That was the key aspect of the situation we took away. Here is the correct answer choice:

> (E) adopted the language and forms of modern American poetry

The Italian immigrant adopts the characteristics of American poetry, just like Wheatley did.

Clearly understanding the concept or situation you must match is absolutely crucial. Work with the passage until you feel confident you understand the key aspects. Do not rush to the choices. Think of stating the feature(s) as the envisioning step for match questions. Because the choices can contain any number of possibilities, you should not waste any time trying to articulate an actual answer.

Situation Subtype

Recently, Situation Match questions have been the more common subtype. Situation questions can be challenging if you do not approach them in a structured way. Other than referring back to the passage and understanding the aspects of the situation, you should also describe the situation **in general terms**. This forces you to get at the underlying ideas of the situation. This is similar to the approach on LR Parallel Structure questions. For instance, to describe Wheatley's approach to poetry in general terms, we would say something like: "a foreigner fully embraces the rules and traditions of a specific written art." This description does not mention Wheatley or Eighteenth century English poetry, and it should not. The approach as we described it could describe many individuals, and that is why it is useful for working the choices. It helps us see the choices in a new light. You may be able to effectively work every answer choice evaluating it against the general description. If you are having trouble, then try describing each **choice** in general terms. This tells you if the aspects and features that you need to match are present. With practice, you may unconsciously work the choices in this way.

Be less aggressive when working the choices. It can be hard to know conclusively that you have the right features, so take your time. Analyze every choice, even those after a strong hit. On the more abstract and demanding question types, it never hurts to be sure. If you are down to two hits and you cannot determine which is correct, analyze the specific elements in each choice. Look for differences that help you match one choice more successfully to the situation. For instance, on the Wheatley question above, you might think that both of these are strong choices:

(A) translated Italian literary forms into the American idiom

(E) adopted the language and forms of modern American poetry

(A) involves **translation**, something that Wheatley was not mentioned doing. She never translated any African songs into English poetry, for instance. That specific feature of choice (A) helps you eliminate it.

In general, Situation Match questions are more time consuming than other question types. This is because you have to interpret the choices because they are each a scenario. Also, referring back to the passage for these questions can take a while. For these reasons, lower scoring students may wish to make an educated guess on Situation Match questions to save time. Higher scoring students may wish to do the same when running low on time.

Concept Subtype

The Concept subtype asks you to either remember or relocate the major characteristics of the concept in the passage. They are similar to Agree RC questions, except you are looking for the choice that fits with an idea, instead of a group. The concepts can be a strategy, rule or a definition of a term. For example, a passage could describe a technique for figuring out how old a tree is and then ask you for a situation where that technique would be applicable. If the technique requires that the tree be in an area with plenty of water, that is a feature you could match with a choice that says "measuring the age of an oak alongside a river." Just like on Situation Match questions, be sure that you use the passage thoroughly and have a clear understanding of the concept you are asked to match before you move to the choices. Use the features of the concept to support or eliminate choices.

Concepts are not any less complicated (have less features) than situations, but their choices are generally easier to work through. This is because the choices involve less interpretation. Instead of analyzing situations in the choices and trying to think of them abstractly, you will be given specific information which you can rapidly compare against your understanding of the concept. Therefore, you can work the choices more quickly and be more confident when you find a hit than with Situation Match questions.

Incorrect Choices

On both types of Match questions avoid choices that repeat or summarize parts of the passage, but do not provide the features needed. These wrong part choices are tempting because they rehash familiar parts of the passage. Stick with the core features of what you are trying to match and you cannot go wrong.

On Situation questions, watch out for choices that match the subject matter of the passage, but not the attributes of the situation. These choices can be tempting for students who get excited to see a match in the choices, even if the match is superficial. You are looking for an analogous situation, with certain features, not for an analogous subject.

Example Match Question

Please read and mark this passage. Marked passage with explanation is on the next page:

Three basic adaptive responses - regulatory, acclimatory, and developmental - may occur in organisms as they react to changing environmental conditions. In all three, adjustment of biological features (morphological adjustment) or of their use (functional adjustment) may occur. Regulatory responses involve rapid changes in the organism's use of its physiological apparatus-increasing or decreasing the rates of various processes, for example. Acclimation involves morphological change-thickening of fur or red blood cell proliferation-which alters physiology itself. Such structural changes require more time than regulatory response changes. Regulatory and acclimatory responses are both reversible.

Developmental responses, however, are usually permanent and irreversible; they become fixed in the course of the individual's development in response to environmental conditions at the time the response occurs. One such response occurs in many kinds of water bugs. Most water-bug species inhabiting small lakes and ponds have two generations per year. The first hatches during the spring, reproduces during the summer, then dies. The eggs laid in the summer hatch and develop into adults in late summer. They live over the winter before breeding in early spring. Individuals in the second (overwintering) generation have fully developed wings and leave the water in autumn to overwinter in forests, returning in spring to small bodies of water to lay eggs. Their wings are absolutely necessary for this seasonal dispersal. The summer (early) generation, in contrast, is usually dimorphic-some individuals have normal functional (macropterous) wings; others have much-reduced (micropterous) wings of no use for flight. The summer generation's dimorphism is a compromise strategy, for these individuals usually do not leave the ponds and thus generally have no use for fully developed wings. But small ponds occasionally dry up during the summer, forcing the water bugs to search for new habitats, an eventuality that macropterous individuals are well adapted to meet.

The dimorphism of micropterous and macropterous individuals in the summer generation expresses developmental flexibility; it is not genetically determined. The individual's wing form is environmentally determined by the temperature to which developing eggs are exposed prior to their being laid. Eggs maintained in a warm environment always produce bugs with normal wings, but exposure to cold produces micropterous individuals. Eggs producing the overwintering brood are all formed during the late summer's warm temperatures. Hence, all individuals in the overwintering brood have normal wings. Eggs laid by the overwintering adults in the spring, which develop into the summer generation of adults, are formed in early autumn and early spring. Those eggs formed in autumn are exposed to cold winter temperatures, and thus produce micropterous adults in the summer generation. Those formed during the spring are never exposed to cold temperatures, and thus yield individuals with normal wings. Adult water bugs of the overwintering generation, brought into the laboratory during the cold months and kept warm, produce only macropterous offspring.

Three basic <u>adaptive responses</u> - regulatory, acclimatory, and developmental - may occur in organisms as they react to changing environmental conditions. In all three, adjustment of biological features (morphological adjustment) or of their use (functional adjustment) may occur. <u>Regulatory responses</u> involve rapid changes in the organism's use of its physiological apparatus-increasing or decreasing the rates of various processes, for example. <u>Acclimation</u> involves morphological change - thickening of fur or red blood cell proliferation - which alters physiology itself. Such structural changes require more time than regulatory response changes. Regulatory and acclimatory responses are both reversible.

<u>Developmental responses</u>, however, are usually permanent and irreversible; they become fixed in the course of the individual's development in response to environmental conditions at the time the response occurs. One such response occurs in many kinds of <u>water bugs</u>. Most water-bug species inhabiting small lakes and ponds have two generations per year. The first hatches during the spring, reproduces during the summer, then dies. The eggs laid in the summer hatch and develop into adults in late summer. They live over the winter before breeding in early spring. | Individuals in the second (<u>overwintering</u>) generation have fully developed wings and leave the water in autumn to overwinter in forests, returning in spring to small bodies of water to lay eggs. Their wings are absolutely necessary for this seasonal dispersal. The <u>summer</u> (early) generation, in contrast, is usually <u>dimorphic</u>-some individuals have normal functional (macropterous) wings; others have much-reduced (micropterous) wings of no use for flight. The summer generation's dimorphism is a compromise strategy, for these individuals usually do not leave the ponds and thus generally have no use for fully developed wings. But small ponds occasionally dry up during the summer, forcing the water bugs to search for new habitats, an eventuality that macropterous individuals are well adapted to meet.

The dimorphism of micropterous and macropterous individuals in the summer generation expresses <u>developmental flexibility</u>; it is not genetically determined. The individual's wing form is environmentally determined by the <u>temperature</u> to which developing eggs are exposed prior to their being laid. Eggs maintained in a warm environment always produce bugs with normal wings, but exposure to cold produces micropterous individuals. Eggs producing the overwintering brood are all formed during the late summer's warm temperatures. Hence, all individuals in the overwintering brood have normal wings. Eggs laid by the overwintering adults in the spring, which develop into the summer generation of adults, are formed in early autumn and early spring. Those eggs formed in autumn are exposed to cold winter temperatures, and thus produce micropterous adults in the summer generation. Those formed during the spring are never exposed to cold temperatures, and thus yield individuals with normal wings. Adult water bugs of the overwintering generation, brought into the laboratory during the cold months and kept warm, produce only macropterous offspring.

LSAT students often dislike heavy science passages. With them, learn the important terms, especially those defined by the passage. When you begin reading a natural science passage, accept the fact that the first couple of paragraphs will introduce many **new terms**. In this first paragraph, we learn the three types of adaptive responses. Realizing that they will likely be developed as we read further, we do not have to underline them all at once. Understanding the two types of adjustment of biological features from this paragraph is also helpful, but not crucial as those ideas are developed throughout.

In P2, which we have split into two parts on line 26, the concept of a developmental response is explained through the discussion on water bugs. We also get some more terms here: macropterous and micropterous, along with the two types of water bugs (overwintering and summer).

Read slowly and carefully and make sure you underline and understand the main topics. One good thing about natural science passages is that they are not subtle: few analogies, little is implied, etc. Your job is to follow the facts. This passage does end with an experiment that has an **implication** that should be obvious. When bugs that would normally produce dimorphic offspring are kept warm, all their offspring have normal wings and the dimorphic trait is stamped out. This result supports the idea in the final paragraph that temperature is the key determinant of wing form.

Now, an example Concept Match question:

15. The passage supplies information to suggest that which one of the following would happen if a pond inhabited by water bugs were to dry up in June?

It is not always easy to spot Concept queries. This one is identifiable by the fact that it asks us for a **hypothetical** situation based on information from the passage. The topic reference here involves water bugs in a drying pond in June. The information we need comes from the end of P3:

> But small ponds occasionally dry up during the summer, forcing the water bugs to search for new habitats, an eventuality that macropterous individuals are well adapted to meet.

Recall that macropterous individuals are those with functional wings. This information implies that in a situation where the pond dried up, **some** of the water-bugs would be able to relocate to a better habitat. That is all we need to envision before moving to the choices.

(A) The number of developmental responses among the water-bug population would decrease.

You may have noticed that the concept this question centers upon is not particularly complicated. Because of this, the test-makers have added difficulty with more complex answer choices. (A), for instance, uses a term from the passage, "developmental responses." Recall that these responses are changes to individuals that are permanent, and they occur during development due to environmental conditions. With that understanding, we see this choice is incorrect. We do not have much information on the type of permanent changes that could occur in water-bugs should their pond dry up. It also seems unlikely that the number of developmental responses would decrease in the event that the bugs habitat changes drastically; they would probably increase. Definite dud.

(B) Both micropterous and macropterous water bugs would show an acclimatory response.

Continuing the trend of demanding choices, (B) references an **acclimatory response**. Here is the info on that type of response, from P1:

> Acclimation involves morphological change - thickening of fur or red blood cell proliferation - which alters physiology itself. Such structural changes require more time than regulatory response changes.

Because this type of response takes time and there is little a bug could do to deal with a drying pond, this response seems unlikely. This choice also does not match our envisioned answer.

(C) The generation of water bugs to be hatched during the subsequent spring would contain an unusually large number of macropterous individuals.

(C) deals with the next generation of bugs. But we know that the number of macropterous individuals born is tied to the temperature when the bugs are born; this was a big idea in the passage. This choice does not make sense because we are dealing with a pond drying up. Dud.

(D) The dimorphism of the summer generation would enable some individuals to survive.

(D) matches our envisioned answer. The dimorphism means that some of the bugs can fly, and those bugs would probably survive by moving to a new pond. We had to do a little translating with this choice, but it is obviously on point. Select and move on.

(E) The dimorphism of the summer generation would be genetically transferred to the next spring generation.

The spring generations are typically not dimorphic and we have no reason to believe that a pond drying up would change that. This choice is unsupported by the passage.

*More Common Types Review

Agree

- "The author of the passage would be most likely to **agree** with which one of the following statements?"
- Identify the statement the author or a person from the passage would agree with.
- These require inferring the opinion from clues in the passage; they are mostly global questions.
- Approach
    - Find the proven choice, you never need to guess.
    - Often the correct choice will encapsulate ideas developed over many paragraphs.
    - Use the viewpoint markings – "A" and speakers.

Role

- The author quotes directly from the charter (lines 20-22) for **which one of the following reasons**?
- Identify **why** the author mentions a topic or sentence, or what role a paragraph plays in the overall passage
- Almost all Role questions feature exact references.
- Approach
    - Find and read the part.
        - References make this step easy.
    - Find the context.
        - Start reading before the part and read through it if necessary.
    - Envision as specifically as you can.
    - When working the choices, focus on the nouns (topics and ideas covered) over the verbs.
- Incorrect choices often describe the role played by another part of the passage (wrong part choices).

Match

- "Which one of the following is analogous to the role that custom made sculptures play in the fine homes?"
- Understand a concept or situation from the passage and then to **match** it.
- Most give you a topic reference. If the concept is discussed in multiple places, reference where it is first discussed.
- Be sure you understand the concept or situation.
- Situation subtype
    - Describe a situation that matches the one in the passage.
    - After research, state the situation in general terms.
    - Be cautious when working the choices.
    - Watch out for choices that match the subject matter but not the attributes of the situation.
- Concept subtype
    - Remember or relocate the characteristics of a concept (could be a definition, rule or strategy).
    - Research the features of the concept and then match those in the choices.

*Law Practice Passages

In England before 1660, a husband controlled his wife's property. In the late seventeenth and eighteenth centuries, with the shift from land-based to commercial wealth, marriage began to incorporate certain features of a contract. Historians have traditionally argued that this trend represented a gain for women, one that reflects changing views about democracy and property following the English Restoration in 1660. Susan Staves contests this view; she argues that whatever gains marriage contracts may briefly have represented for women were undermined by judicial decisions about women's contractual rights.

Sifting through the tangled details of court cases, Staves demonstrates that, despite surface changes, a rhetoric of equality, and occasional decisions supporting women's financial power, definitions of men's and women's property remained inconsistent – generally to women's detriment. For example, dower lands (property inherited by wives after their husbands' deaths) could not be sold, but "curtesy" property (inherited by husbands from their wives) could be sold. Furthermore, comparatively new concepts that developed in conjunction with the marriage contract, such as jointure, pin money, and separate maintenance, were compromised by peculiar rules. For instance, if a woman spent her pin money (money paid by the husband according to the marriage contract for the wife's personal items) on possessions other than clothes she could not sell them; in effect they belonged to her husband. In addition, a wife could sue for pin money only up to a year in arrears-which rendered a suit impractical. Similarly, separate maintenance allowances (stated sums of money for the wife's support if husband and wife agreed to live apart) were complicated by the fact that if a couple tried to agree in a marriage contract on an amount, they were admitting that a supposedly indissoluble bond could be dissolved, an assumption courts could not recognize. Eighteenth-century historians underplayed these inconsistencies, calling them "little contrarieties" that would soon vanish. Staves shows, however, that as judges gained power over decisions on marriage contracts, they tended to fall back on pre-1660 assumptions about property.

Staves' work on women's property has general implications for other studies about women in eighteenth-century England. Staves revises her previous claim that separate maintenance allowances proved the weakening of patriarchy; she now finds that an oversimplification. She also challenges the contention by historians Jeanne and Lawrence Stone that in the late eighteenth century wealthy men married widows less often than before because couples began marrying for love rather than for financial reasons. Staves does not completely undermine their contention, but she does counter their assumption that widows had more money than never-married women. She points out that jointure property (a widow's lifetime use of an amount of money specified in the marriage contract) was often lost on remarriage.

1. Which one of the following best expresses the main idea of the passage?

   (A) As notions of property and democracy changed in late seventeenth- and eighteenth-century England, marriage settlements began to incorporate contractual features designed to protect women's property rights.

   (B) Traditional historians have incorrectly identified the contractual features that were incorporated into marriage contracts in late seventeenth- and eighteenth-century England.

   (C) The incorporation of contractual features into marriage settlements in late seventeenth- and eighteenth-century England did not represent a significant gain for women.

   (D) An examination of late seventeenth- and eighteenth-century English court cases indicates that most marriage settlements did not incorporate contractual features designed to protect women's property rights.

   (E) Before marriage settlements incorporated contractual features protecting women's property rights, women were unable to gain any financial power in England.

2. Which one of the following best describes the function of the last paragraph in the context of the passage as a whole?

   (A) It suggests that Staves' recent work has caused significant revision of theories about the rights of women in eighteenth-century England.

   (B) It discusses research that may qualify Staves' work on women's property in eighteenth-century England.

   (C) It provides further support for Staves' argument by describing more recent research on women's property in eighteenth-century England.

   (D) It asserts that Staves' recent work has provided support for two other hypotheses developed by historians of eighteenth-century England.

   (E) It suggests the implications Staves' recent research has for other theories about women in eighteenth-century England.

3. The primary purpose of the passage is to

(A) compare two explanations for the same phenomenon
(B) summarize research that refutes an argument
(C) resolve a long-standing controversy
(D) suggest that a recent hypothesis should be reevaluated
(E) provide support for a traditional theory

4. According to the passage, Staves' research has which one of the following effects on the Stones' contention about marriage in late eighteenth-century England?

(A) Staves' research undermines one of the Stones' assumptions but does not effectively invalidate their contention.
(B) Staves' research refutes the Stones' contention by providing additional data overlooked by the Stones.
(C) Staves' research shows that the Stones' contention cannot be correct, and that a number of their assumptions are mistaken.
(D) Staves' research indicates that the Stones' contention is incorrect because it is based on contradictory data.
(E) Staves' research qualifies the Stones' contention by indicating that it is based on accurate but incomplete data.

5. According to the passage, Staves indicates that which one of the following was true of judicial decisions on contractual rights?

(A) Judges frequently misunderstood and misapplied laws regarding married women's property.
(B) Judges were aware of inconsistencies in laws concerning women's contractual rights but claimed that such inconsistencies would soon vanish.
(C) Judges' decisions about marriage contracts tended to reflect assumptions about property that had been common before 1660.
(D) Judges had little influence on the development and application of laws concerning married women's property.
(E) Judges recognized the patriarchal assumptions underlying laws concerning married women's property and tried to interpret the laws in ways that would protect women.

6. The passage suggests that the historians mentioned in line 5 would be most likely to agree with which one of the following statements?

(A) The shift from land-based to commercial wealth changed views about property but did not significantly benefit married women until the late eighteenth century.
(B) Despite initial judicial resistance to women's contractual rights, marriage contracts represented a significant gain for married women.
(C) Although marriage contracts incorporated a series of surface changes and a rhetoric of equality, they did not ultimately benefit married women.
(D) Changing views about property and democracy in post-Restoration England had an effect on property laws that was beneficial to women.
(E) Although contractual rights protecting women's property represented a small gain for married women, most laws continued to be more beneficial for men than for women.

In recent years, scholars have begun to use social science tools to analyze court opinions. These scholars have justifiably criticized traditional legal research for its focus on a few cases that may not be representative and its fascination with arcane matters that do not affect real people with real legal problems. Zirkel and Schoenfeld, for example, have championed the application of social science tools to the analysis of case law surrounding discrimination against women in higher education employment. Their studies have demonstrated how these social science tools may be used to serve the interests of scholars, lawyers, and prospective plaintiffs as well. However, their enthusiasm for the "outcomes analysis" technique seems misguided.

Of fundamental concern is the outcomes analysts' assumption that simply counting the number of successful and unsuccessful plaintiffs will be useful to prospective plaintiffs. Although the odds are clearly against the plaintiff in sex discrimination cases, plaintiffs who believe that their cause is just and that they will prevail are not swayed by such evidence. In addition, because lawsuits are so different in the details of the case, in the quality of the evidence the plaintiff presents, and in the attitude of the judge toward academic plaintiffs, giving prospective plaintiffs statistics about overall outcomes without analyzing the reason for these outcomes is of marginal assistance. Outcomes analysis, for example, ignores the fact that in certain academic sex discrimination cases-those involving serious procedural violations or incriminating evidence in the form of written admissions of discriminatory practices-plaintiffs are much more likely to prevail.

Two different approaches offer more useful applications of social science tools in analyzing sex discrimination cases. One is a process called "policy capturing," in which the researcher reads each opinion; identifies variables discussed in the opinion, such as the regularity of employer evaluations of the plaintiff's performance, training of evaluators, and the kind of evaluation instrument used; and then uses multivariate analysis to determine whether these variables predict the outcome of the lawsuit. The advantage of policy-capturing research is that it attempts to explain the reason for the outcome, rather than simply reporting the outcome, and identifies factors that contribute to a plaintiff's success or failure. Taking a slightly different approach, other scholars have adopted a technique that requires reading complete transcripts of all sex discrimination cases litigated during a certain time period to identify variables such as the nature of the allegedly illegal conduct, the consequences for employers, and the nature of the remedy, as well as the factors that contributed to the verdict and the kind of evidence necessary for the plaintiff to prevail. While the findings of these studies are limited to the period covered, they assist potential plaintiffs and defendants in assessing their cases.

7. Which one of the following best expresses the main idea of the passage?

(A) The analysis of a limited number of atypical discrimination suits is of little value to potential plaintiffs.
(B) When the number of factors analyzed in a sex discrimination suit is increased, the validity of the conclusions drawn becomes suspect.
(C) Scholars who are critical of traditional legal research frequently offer alternative approaches that are also seriously flawed.
(D) Outcomes analysis has less predictive value in sex discrimination cases than do certain other social science techniques.
(E) Given adequate information, it is possible to predict with considerable certainty whether a plaintiff will be successful in a discrimination suit.

8. It can be inferred from the author's discussion of traditional legal research that the author is

(A) frustrated because traditional legal research has not achieved its full potential
(B) critical because traditional legal research has little relevance to those actually involved in cases
(C) appreciative of the role traditional legal research played in developing later, more efficient approaches
(D) derisive because traditional legal research has outlasted its previously significant role
(E) grateful for the ability of traditional legal research to develop unique types of evidence

9. Which one of the following statements about Zirkel and Schoenfeld can be inferred from the passage?

(A) They were the first scholars to use social science tools in analyzing legal cases.
(B) They confined their studies to the outcomes analysis technique.
(C) They saw no value in the analysis provided by traditional legal research.
(D) They rejected policy capturing as being too limited in scope.
(E) They believed that the information generated by outcomes analysis would be relevant for plaintiffs.

10. The author's characterization of traditional legal research in the first paragraph is intended to

(A) provide background information for the subsequent discussion
(B) summarize an opponent's position
(C) argue against the use of social science tools in the analysis of sex discrimination cases
(D) emphasize the fact that legal researchers act to the detriment of potential plaintiffs
(E) reconcile traditional legal researchers to the use of social science tools

11. The information in the passage suggests that plaintiffs who pursue sex discrimination cases despite the statistics provided by outcomes analysis can best be likened to

(A) athletes who continue to employ training techniques despite their knowledge of statistical evidence indicating that these techniques are unlikely to be effective
(B) lawyers who handle lawsuits for a large number of clients in the hope that some percentage will be successful
(C) candidates for public office who are more interested in making a political statement than in winning an election
(D) supporters of a cause who recruit individuals sympathetic to it in the belief that large numbers of supporters will lend the cause legitimacy
(D) purchasers of a charity's raffle tickets who consider the purchase a contribution because the likelihood of winning is remote

12. The policy-capturing approach differs from the approach described in lines 48-59 in that the latter approach

(A) makes use of detailed information on a greater number of cases
(B) focuses more directly on issues of concern to litigants
(C) analyzes information that is more recent and therefore reflects current trends
(D) allows assessment of aspects of a case that are not specifically mentioned in a judge's opinion
(E) eliminates any distortion due to personal bias on the part of the researcher

13. Which one of the following best describes the organization of the passage?

(A) A technique is introduced, its shortcomings are summarized, and alternatives are described.
(B) A debate is introduced, evidence is presented, and a compromise is reached.
(C) A theory is presented, clarification is provided, and a plan of further evaluation is suggested.
(D) Standards are established, hypothetical examples are analyzed, and the criteria are amended.
(E) A position is challenged, its shortcomings are categorized, and the challenge is revised.

*Law Practice Passages Explanations

1. (26/4 #22) ~ C

Main Point. P1 introduces the fact that Staves disagrees with the view that women benefited from marriage having contractual features. P2 gives the evidence for her view: definitions of property were to women's detriment. P3 discusses how Stave's work has implications for other studies about women in 18th century England and gives the example of wealthy men marrying widows research. The main idea is that women did not benefit from the shift to contractual features in marriage settlements. The author uses Stave's research to support the main idea of the passage.

2. (26/4 #23) ~ E

Role. The first sentence of the paragraph points to choice E. Rereading the first and last lines of a paragraph usually helps to zero in on its role in the passage. Also, final paragraphs that talk about an author's work usually expand their work to a broader context: here the implications for other studies on women in 18th century England.

3. (26/4 #24) ~ B

Primary Purpose. Choice B is fairly obvious because of how dominant P2 is in the passage. Summarizing Stave's research is a main concern of the author.

4. (26/4 – 25) ~ A

Detail. Rereading lines 55–57 makes A obviously correct. Your mental map hopefully pointed to the section where Stave's work was referenced with that of others so that you could quickly get this information.

5. (26/4 #26) ~ C

Detail. Lines 41-44 point to Choice C. Judge's decisions tended to reflect the earlier mindsets about property.

6. (26/4 #27) ~ D

Deduction. Read before and after line 5. The first line of the passage talks about how a husband controlled a wife's property before 1660, but this changed. The historians believed that the shift to marriage being a contract benefitted women and reflected changing views about property and democracy. The fact that the new views had an impact on property laws is the key mental step that you must take to reach the correct answer.

7. (24/1 #14) ~ D

Main Point. The passage starts off talking about how social science tools have begun to be used in court cases, but how there are limitations to "outcome analysis" (P1). Next, the argument progresses to the issues with outcome analysis (it just says who won the case) and how this is not very useful for plaintiffs in sex discrimination cases (P2). P3 discusses the policy capturing and complete transcript reading approaches that are "more useful applications of social science in analyzing sex discrimination cases." Choice D gets at the heart of what P 2 and 3 are stating. P1 is really a setup for the rest of the discussion. Lines 35-37 serve as a good Main point sentence.

8. (24/1 #15) ~ B

Deduction. Identify something about the author based on her discussion of traditional legal research. Lines 2-6 discuss traditional legal research: you may recall that this was the introduction to the passage. In those lines, the author says "justifiably criticized" meaning that she agrees with their stance that this research focuses on a few unrepresentative cases and does not connect well to reality. Choice B is perfect: the author is critical of traditional legal research because it is "fascinated with arcane matters that do not affect real people."

9. (24/1 #16) ~ E

Deduction. Zirkel and Schoenfeld are mentioned in lines 6-13. They champion the application of these tools to cases involving women involved in discrimination cases and the "for example" on line 7 implies that they do care about real people with real problems, unlike traditional legal research. That fits well with E: they likely thought outcome analysis would be relevant for plaintiffs.

10. (24/1 #17) ~ A

Role. The author talks about traditional legal research to set up the entire passage. Outcome Analysis is a response to traditional legal research and the author wants to discuss that and its superior alternatives. Traditional legal research is the background to the newest theories in the legal research field that she discusses at length in P2 and P3.

11. (24/1 #18) ~ A

Match. The sentence starting on line 20 gives context to these plaintiffs: they think they will prevail despite the statistics. Athletes who keep using training techniques despite statistics against those techniques are similar to the plaintiffs: they ignore the overall statistical evidence because they believe the techniques will work for **them**.

12. (24/1 #19) ~ D

Detail. The policy-capturing approach (line 37) involves finding which variables predict the outcome; the other approach involves identifying variables among all cases in a certain time frame by reading **complete transcripts**, not just the judge's opinion. Differences can be small in Fact questions that ask you to distinguish two things.

13. (24/1 #20) ~ A

Organization. The technique of outcomes analysis is described in P1, critiqued in P2 and its alternatives are discussed in P3. Simply thinking about the subject of each paragraph of the passage makes choice A the obvious correct answer.

Other Types

The types you have learned about – Main Point, Detail, Deduction, Agree, Role and Match - make up about 70 percent of the RC questions. The less common types will we now discuss are often somewhat similar to a common type, making it easier to learn their methods.

Meaning

Meaning questions ask you to identify the meaning of a small piece of the passage: usually a word, sometimes a phrase. In determining the author's meaning, use the context around the piece, much as you do on Role questions. On both these types, you need to refer to the passage, analyze the piece thoroughly and spend a lot of time envisioning because the choices are challenging. The approach to a Meaning question has a lot in common with that of Role questions. One major difference is that Meaning questions are more specific: they ask you about very small pieces of the passage.

Query, References, Frequency

Meaning queries ask you what the author meant by a specific piece. The author's **intention** is often asked for, or the query may directly ask you for the **meaning** or **sense** of the word. Meaning queries always have line references: a great signal of the type. Example queries:

> By referring to the declaration as "sumptuous" (line 39) the author most likely intends to emphasize...
>
> The phrase "gaining disproportionally from awards of damage" (lines 20-21) is most likely intended by the author to mean
>
> Which one of the following phrases most accurately conveys the sense of the word "pragmatic" as it is used in line 22?
>
> In saying that romantic fiction was based on a conception of fiction as part of a "sequence" (line 40), the author probably means which of the following?

Because Meaning queries always feature exact references, it is simple to find the word or phrase you are asked about. Understanding the meaning of that piece in the context of the passage is more challenging.

Expect to see about two Meaning questions on your RC section.

Approach

Get Context

Meaning questions tell you exactly where in the passage to refer back, so do so. When you first read the query, fix the exact word or phrase in your mind. Then, move to the lines indicated and begin reading a sentence before those lines and read through the sentence containing the piece. The goal of the rereading is to refresh your memory on what that piece means.

The test-makers quiz you on pieces that have a deep meaning. For example, if an author uses the word "immediacy" in describing a play, think about what that word means in relation to the ideas before it. If the sentences before that line talk about how the actors are playing roles that they can relate to, then that helps you understand the meaning. There, "immediacy" means being able to express the roles **vividly** to the audience. This is certainly not the classical or most common definition of the word. That definition would be: "lack of an intervening or mediating agency." But here, immediacy takes on a fuller, more specific meaning due to its context. Words with multiple meanings are often chosen, as are words that are being used in a unique way (not their typical definition).

Watch the ideas right before the sentence with the piece and see how those ideas relate to the piece. Even though you are analyzing a small piece, try to think about the meaning of that entire paragraph. Think on the level of **medium sized** ideas, as the meaning is likely related to one of those.

Envision Meaning

After you find the meaning of the piece in its specific context, think of a **few key words** that express that meaning. Or, failing that, think of a few key ideas/topics in the passage that the piece connects to. Try to think about nouns. Be as specific as you can and think about the full meaning implied by that piece. For example, in envisioning a good meaning for "immediacy," the words "expressive" and "direct" might come to mind. Hopefully, you would think about these in relation to the audience and how well they are absorbing the performance. As you practice on Meaning questions, force yourself to envision specific words that help you express the meaning.

Read the Choices Carefully

Meaning questions are made challenging by choices that are hard to interpret, so read them carefully. Focus on the **meaning** of the choices instead of how they are worded. Figure out what ideas in the passage the choice refers to, and how well those ideas match the ones you envisioned. Keep an open mind as you read each choice. Sometimes the test-makers can phrase a choice in such a way that it sounds incorrect even if it is not. Read the entirety of each choice to grasp its meaning.

Compare Two Meanings (Subtype)

Some Meaning questions ask you to compare the meanings of two different pieces of the passage. These questions can be a lot of work because you must understand the context of two pieces instead of one. If you are strapped for time, these are good questions to skip. The key idea here is that you are forced to relate the two pieces. If the pieces are close together spatially, read the text **in between** them. That will help you understand what ideas the author puts forth after the first piece, and knowing those can be helpful. If they are far apart, learn the meaning of both through rereading.

Incorrect Choices

Do not fall for a choice that talks about the **most common** definition of the word or phrase, if it is not relevant in this situation. Also, beware choices that only describe a part of the meaning of the piece. You are looking for a full definition, not a partial one. Although these choices sound good because they match part of what you have envisioned, they are not correct.

Most incorrect choices will center around the ideas of that part of the passage, but use them incorrectly. For instance, in the "immediacy" example we have been using, an incorrect choice might be: "the actor's speak their lines directly to the audience." This choice deals with how the audience relates to the actors performances, but it misses the crucial idea of the roles being vivid for the audience. Another incorrect choice might talk about how close the actors worked with the director to build their skills. This relates to ideas in the right part of the passage, but confuses the meaning of "immediacy" here for one of its more common meanings. Realize that the incorrect choices will often have the right ideas and topics and also potentially incorporate correct meanings of the word or phrase.

Example Meaning Question

This Meaning question comes from the Wheatley passage:

4. By a "closed system" of poetry (lines 34-35), the author most probably means poetry that...

The words "the author... means" are a clear signal that this is a Meaning question. With that in mind, reference the passage to understand how Wheatley uses the phrase "closed system." Here is the paragraph that phrase is used in:

> But this was a potential that her poetry unfortunately did not exploit. The standards of eighteenth-century English poetry, which itself reflected little of the American language, led Wheatley to develop a notion of poetry as a closed system, derived from imitation of earlier written works. No place existed for the rough-and-ready Americanized English she heard in the streets, for the English spoken by Black people, or for Africanisms. The conventions of eighteenth-century neoclassical poetry ruled out casual talk; her voice and feelings had to be generalized according to rules of poetic diction and characterization; the particulars of her African past, if they were to be dealt with at all, had to be subordinated to the reigning conventions.

A logical place to begin reading is the beginning of the paragraph, because the reference comes in the second sentence. The definition of the phrase occurs immediately after it: "derived from imitation of earlier written works." This implies that "closed system" means that new input was not accepted. The next sentence reinforces this idea by saying that there was no place for different forms of English that Wheatley was familiar with.

We can envision a few words that are synonymous with how the phrase is used: "restricted and formal." Wheatley could not bring in other forms of English, which is a major theme of the passage and is a focus of the final paragraph. That last part can be summed up as "limiting to new forms of English." With this research done, we work the choices.

(A) cannot be written by those who are not raised knowing its conventions

(A) is a false choice: Wheatley **learned** the conventions and wrote poetry with this system. It contradicts the passage to say that the closed system meant that outsiders could not learn the rules as an adult.

(B) has little influence on the way language is actually spoken

This choice sounds good because it is a reasonable definition for "closed system," but it does not capture the idea of the poetry limiting Wheatley's expression of different forms of English. The idea of the poetry influencing English is **backwards**. The passage says that the English of the streets could not make its way into the poetry, not the poetry could not influence the English of the streets.

(C) substitutes its own conventions for the aesthetic principles of the past

This is a new information choice: nothing in the passage supports the idea that eighteenth century poetry is sacrificing its own rules for ideals of writing from the past. The paragraph clearly makes the point that the poetry follows its **own conventions**. This choice is phrased in a convoluted way, but our envisioning helps us to eliminate it.

(D) does not admit the use of street language and casual talk

This choice matches our envisioned ideas. The poetry is closed to the English of Wheatley's day. This matches the sentence after the reference perfectly: "No place existed for the rough-and-ready Americanized English she heard in the streets, for the English spoken by Black people, or for Africanisms." This is why you should read both **before and after** the piece until you have a good grasp of its meaning. You never know what part of the passage will help you see the specific meaning.

(E) is ultimately rejected because its conventions leave little room for further development

This is a false choice; Wheatley **embraced** the rules of eighteenth century English poetry.

Primary Purpose

Primary Purpose (or simply Purpose) questions are closely related to Main Point questions. While Main Point questions ask what the author's core conclusion is, Purpose questions ask **why** the author wrote the passage, what she was trying to accomplish with the passage. The correct answer to a Purpose question will tell the author's motivation for discussing the subject of the passage. The Purpose transcends the Main Point; it is a more general description of what the passage does. For example, the main point of a passage could be that climate change is real, and will soon affect billions of people around the world. There, the purpose is to educate people about climate change. The correct answer to the Purpose question might be "to explain the impacts of climate change." Or, because some Purpose choices feature abstract wording, the correct choice could be "to educate readers on a relevant scientific subject." Both of these answers tell how the author approaches the subject of the passage, climate change. The author addresses that subject by teaching about its impacts.

Query, References and Frequency

Purpose queries generally feature the word "purpose" or "reason." And they usually include the word "primary," although sometimes "main" is used in its place. Example queries:

> Which one of the following accurately expresses the primary reason the author wrote the passage?
>
> The passage as a whole functions primarily as…
>
> Which one of the following most accurately states the main function of the passage?
>
> The author's primary purpose in the passage is to…

Sometimes, a question will feature a very different sounding query, while still asking roughly why the author wrote the passage. These questions should be considered Purpose questions, although they often have some unique features. Example query of this type:

> The passage was written primarily in order to answer which one of the following questions?

Although the query looks different, it does mention the word "primarily" and asks about the author's motivation when writing the passage. An author's purpose can be thought of as answering a specific question. Another unique query:

> The passage most strongly suggests that it is targeting an audience that is interested in which one of the following?

This query is harder to interpret. The key is that it asks what the passage is trying to convey to the audience by asking "What is the target audience interested in?" That is the same as asking "What is the subject of the passage?" The author's purpose is centered on the subject, so analyzing what the author is attempting to accomplish with the subject helps us answer this question.

References and Frequency

Purpose questions ask about the passage as a whole, so they have no references. Like most global questions, you will answer them based on your first reading. This question type is somewhat uncommon: you will probably see one, or at most two, on your official LSAT.

Approach

To effectively answer a Purpose question, you need to analyze the choices quite carefully.

Know the Subject

Purpose answer choices are usually short and feature a verb and a subject (one or more nouns). Here are example choices:

(C) Provide causal explanations for a type of environmental pollution

(B) Describe the general composition and properties of drilling muds

(A)'s verb is "provide." The subject of (A) is "causal explanations" and these are explained as explanations provided for a type of environmental pollution. We call your attention to these aspects of the choices because the subject in the correct choice will be the main subject of the passage. If you are clear on the subject, you can effectively work the choices.

Unfortunately, finding the subject of the passage in one of the choices may be a little easier said than done. Some incorrect choices feature nouns that are closely related to the subject, but not quite a match. For instance, a correct choice may have a narrow subject of "the properties of drilling muds," while an incorrect choice has the more general subject "drilling muds." This slight distinction makes all the difference.

From your initial reading of the passage, you will know the subject, so state it in your own words *before* you look at the choices. Then, as you analyze each choice, compare its subject with the passage's subject and eliminate choices that do not match. For instance, if the passage is focused on the impacts of climate change, a choice that centers on environmental pollution will be incorrect. A choice that discusses the plausibility of climate change is also incorrect, because that is different from the expected **impacts** of climate change.

Analyze the Verbs

Along with the subjects, you should also analyze the **verbs** in the choices. The verb in a choice tells the action the author takes regarding the subject, how she or he approaches it. Look at the verb in this choice:

(B) ***describe*** the general composition and properties of drilling muds

"Describe" indicates that the author gives a lot of information about the subject. If this answer is correct, the passage must be descriptive in nature, full of facts and details about the composition of drilling muds.

Now look at this answer choice:

(D) ***explain*** why oil-well drilling requires the use of drilling muds

This choice obviously features a different subject than (B) above: why oil-wells require drilling muds. But this choice also features a different verb: "explain" is a different action than "describe." Explaining means either answering a question, or making a complex idea more understandable. "Describing" involves giving an account of something. These two verbs, although similar, are different enough that you can use them to evaluate each choice. If the passage is more descriptive than explanatory, then you would lean more towards (B). If there is a central question that the passage answers, then (D) might be a better choice.

Read the Choices Carefully

Paying special attention to the subjects and verbs forces you to read the choices critically, which is very important on Purpose questions. You cannot reference on this type, so other than stating the subject, there is no preliminary work you can do. Much of the difficulty comes in sorting through the answer choices.

Evaluate them as a whole, even as you compare their individual parts (subjects and verbs) to your knowledge of the passage. The verbs and subjects interact in a way that gives further meaning. It makes more sense to describe the **properties** of drilling muds then it does to explain them. On the other hand, it is logical to **explain** why a drilling process requires drilling muds, while it would sound strange to **describe** why that process requires them. Verbs are chosen carefully to match the subjects. The fact that the subjects are easier to distinguish from one another than the verbs means that it is easier to evaluate choices using their subjects.

In summary, you should analyze each choice as a whole first and then rely on the subject. Those are the best ways to evaluate a choice on a Purpose question. If you find yourself stuck however, you might be able to differentiate the choices based on the verbs used.

Use the Main Point

Purpose questions often occur in a passage set that also includes a Main Point question. Usually, the Purpose question comes second. This works to your advantage, because the answer to a Purpose question is similar to the answer to a Main Point question. The difference between the two is usually one of scope. Purpose questions have a larger scope, while Main Point questions are more focused. For instance, assume the main point of a passage is: "the type of emotion experienced by a sports viewer is based on the level to which her expectations are satisfied." The purpose could be "to explore the impact of sports viewing on human emotional states." This purpose is a broader description of the subject. The main point is more detailed: it explains what the author says about the subject of the passage. The purpose explains how and why the author discusses the subject.

When facing a Purpose question, check to see if you have already answered a Main Point question. If you are confident in that answer, it can help you on the Purpose question. This process can also work in reverse, although usually the questions are not presented this way.

Abstract Wording

About one fourth of Purpose questions feature abstract wording in the choices. This usually means that the **specific** subject is not mentioned. Abstract choices were also featured in Argument Structure LR questions. For instance:

> describe the general composition and properties of drilling muds

could be phrased in a general way:

> describe the properties of a substance used in a specific industry

"Substance" is an abstract way to say "drilling muds," and "a specific industry" refers to oil drilling. Here is a question with abstract choice wording:

8. The primary purpose of the passage is to

(A) clarify an ambiguous assertion
(B) provide evidence in support of a commonly held view
(C) analyze an unresolved question and propose an answer
(D) offer an alternative to a flawed interpretation
(E) describe and categorize opposing viewpoints

When the choices are phrased abstractly, you must mentally translate them to see if they match the author's purpose. It is usually easiest to translate the subject of a choice to see if it could reasonably fit the subject of the passage. For instance, "technology" or "concoction" would also be acceptable words for drilling muds. But "guide" or "instructions" would not as those words have a different meaning.

Incorrect Choices

Identifying incorrect choices also involves a careful analysis of the subject and verb of the choices.

Similar Sounding

Avoid choices that feature a closely related, but different, subject than that in the passage. These choices are appealing because you are familiar with the subject they focus on. When evaluating **multiple** choices that seem to have correct subjects, carefully reread the subjects and make sure you are interpreting them correctly. Subtle differences can be important. Next, look to verbs in the choices. The verb in one choice will fit the author's actions better than the others. And always try to see the big picture of a choice, how its verb and subject work together. All these techniques will help you distinguish between choices with similar sounding subjects.

Overly Strong Verbs

Some choices feature extreme verbs like "prove" or "reject" that may not fit how the author discusses the subject. Such verbs can appear in correct choices, but usually more moderate verbs are correct: "argue, identify, demonstrate," etc. Strong verbs can often create an extreme choice, and you know those are incorrect. Be wary of verbs that sound overly decisive, unless the passage is equally one sided. If you have trouble figuring out whether a verb is too strong, use the subject in the choice as another evaluating point.

Example Purpose Question

Please read and mark this passage:

(7.2) Critics have long been puzzled by the inner contradictions of major characters in John Webster's tragedies. In his *The Duchess of Malfi,* for instance, the Duchess is "good" in demonstrating the obvious tenderness and sincerity of her love for Antonio, but "bad" in ignoring the wishes and welfare of her family and in making religion a "cloak" hiding worldly self-indulgence. Bosola is "bad" in serving Ferdinand, "good" in turning the Duchess' thoughts toward heaven and in planning to avenge her murder. The ancient Greek philosopher Aristotle implied that such contradictions are virtually essential to the tragic personality, and yet critics keep coming back to this element of inconsistency as though it were an eccentric feature of Webster's own tragic vision.

The problem is that, as an Elizabethan playwright, Webster has become a prisoner of our critical presuppositions. We have, in recent years, been dazzled by the way the earlier Renaissance and medieval theater, particularly the morality play, illuminates Elizabethan drama. We now understand how the habit of mind that saw the world as a battleground between good and evil produced the morality play. Morality plays allegorized that conflict by presenting characters whose actions were defined as the embodiment of good or evil. This model of reality lived on, overlaid by different conventions, in the more sophisticated Elizabethan works of the following age. Yet Webster seems not to have been as heavily influenced by the morality play's model of reality as were his Elizabethan contemporaries; he was apparently more sensitive to the more morally complicated Italian drama than to these English sources. Consequently, his characters cannot be evaluated according to reductive formulas of good and evil, which is precisely what modern critics have tried to do. They choose what seem to be the most promising of the contradictory values that are dramatized in the play, and treat those values as if they were the only basis for analyzing the moral development of the play's major characters, attributing the inconsistencies in a character's behavior to artistic incompetence on Webster's part. The lack of consistency in Webster's characters can be better understood if we recognize that the ambiguity at the heart of his tragic vision lies not in the external world but in the duality of human nature. Webster establishes tension in his plays by setting up conflicting systems of value that appear immoral only when one value system is viewed exclusively from the perspective of the other. He presents us not only with characters that we condemn intellectually or ethically and at the same time impulsively approve of, but also with judgments we must accept as logically sound and yet find emotionally repulsive. The dilemma is not only dramatic: it is tragic, because the conflict is irreconcilable, and because it is ours as much as that of the characters.

(7.2) Critics have long been puzzled by the inner contradictions of major characters in John Webster's tragedies. In his *The Duchess of Malfi,* for instance, the Duchess is "good" in demonstrating the obvious tenderness and sincerity of her love for Antonio, but "bad" in ignoring the wishes and welfare of her family and in making religion a "cloak" hiding worldly self-indulgence. Bosola is "bad" in serving Ferdinand, "good" in turning the Duchess' thoughts toward heaven and in planning to avenge her murder. The ancient Greek philosopher Aristotle implied that such contradictions are virtually essential to the tragic personality, and yet critics keep coming back to this element of inconsistency as though it were an eccentric feature of Webster's own tragic vision.

The problem is that, as an Elizabethan playwright, Webster has become a prisoner of our critical presuppositions. We have, in recent years, been dazzled by the way the earlier Renaissance and medieval theater, particularly the morality play, illuminates Elizabethan drama. We now understand how the habit of mind that saw the world as a battleground between good and evil produced the morality play. Morality plays allegorized that conflict by presenting characters whose actions were defined as the embodiment of good or evil. This model of reality lived on, overlaid by different conventions, in the more sophisticated Elizabethan works of the following age. Yet Webster seems not to have been as heavily influenced by the morality play's model of reality as were his Elizabethan contemporaries; he was apparently more sensitive to the more morally complicated Italian drama than to these English sources. Consequently, his characters cannot be evaluated according to reductive formulas of good and evil, which is precisely what modern critics have tried to do. They choose what seem to be the most promising of the contradictory values that are dramatized in the play, and treat those values as if they were the only basis for analyzing the moral development of the play's major characters, attributing the inconsistencies in a character's behavior to artistic incompetence on Webster's part. The lack of consistency in Webster's characters can be better understood if we recognize that the ambiguity at the heart of his tragic vision lies not in the external world but in the duality of human nature. Webster establishes tension in his plays by setting up conflicting systems of value that appear immoral only when one value system is viewed exclusively from the perspective of the other. He presents us not only with characters that we condemn intellectually or ethically and at the same time impulsively approve of, but also with judgments we must accept as logically sound and yet find emotionally repulsive. The dilemma is not only dramatic: it is tragic, because the conflict is irreconcilable, and because it is ours as much as that of the characters.

MP

This passage deals with abstract topics. The first paragraph introduces the subject: the complex characters in Webster's plays. Through several examples, we learn that the moral judgment of characters in his plays appears to be contradictory, and critics see this feature as unique to Webster's works.

P2 is extremely long, and as expected, contains two different main ideas. The first half of the paragraph gives the author's view that critics have assumed that Webster modeled his works after morality plays. The second main idea is that Webster was more influenced by the morally complicated Italian dramas. This leads his plays to explore the duality of human nature and force the audience to face some jarring questions. This helps to explain the features of his plays described in P1.

This passage is full of opinions: we have circled several speakers in P1 and also noted the author's views in P2. Lines 35 – 38 serve as a MPD.

Now, the Purpose question from this passage set:

8. The primary purpose of the passage is to

(A) clarify an ambiguous assertion
(B) provide evidence in support of a commonly held view
(C) analyze an unresolved question and propose an answer
(D) offer an alternative to a flawed interpretation
(E) describe and categorize opposing viewpoints

The query is a typical Purpose question, so we know we will have to work the choices quite carefully, looking for the one that accurately describes how the author discusses the subject. Before moving to the choices, we state the subject in our own words: "interpretation of the moral contradictions of Webster's characters." Anything similar is fine – as long as it deals with Webster's characters and how they are viewed. The correct choice must feature this subject. And the purpose could be stated as: "providing a new interpretation of these contradictions." That crucial preliminary step completed, we evaluate each choice:

(A) clarify an ambiguous assertion

This is an abstract choice because it does not mention a specific subject. An "ambiguous assertion" could refer to many different things. With abstract choices, it can be more helpful to analyze the verb and the choice as a whole than to focus on the subject. With choices that are worded abstractly, the subject often plays a less important role than the verb.

With this choice, however, we can tell that the subject is not a match. In the passage, the author **does not** explain an ambiguous statement. Instead, she explores an **idea** that critics have proposed regarding Webster's work.

(B) provide evidence in support of a commonly held view

The author **refutes** the view (perhaps commonly held) of critics that Webster has inconsistent characters. The author does not support that opinion by providing evidence. This choice is incorrect; the author's provides a new view on how critics see Webster's work and this choice does not describe that.

(C) analyze an unresolved question and propose an answer

What would the "unresolved question" be? Perhaps: "Why do Webster's characters feature contradictions?" The passage never poses this question, and this choice is not a good fit. Passages that provide answers to unresolved questions tend to pose the question directly somewhere in the passage. Further, in this passage, the author does not propose an **answer** to the situation. Instead, she provides her opinion. This choice does not fit well, due to both of its subjects: "unresolved question" and "answer."

(D) offer an alternative to a flawed interpretation

This choice is a match. The author interprets Webster as dealing with the duality of human nature in his characters. This is an **alternative** to the critics view that Webster was modeling his work after morality plays. The author sees that view as flawed, and argues against it towards the end of P2.

When taking a full section, this choice is such a good fit that we would select it and move on. The next choice is explained for teaching purposes.

(E) describe and categorize opposing viewpoints

The passage is opinionated, so the verbs "describe" and "categorize" are not a match. Those would fit the actions of an author who wrote an unbiased, explorative passage. Further, the choice implies that the author analyzes at least two existing viewpoints, and she does not. She explains one viewpoint and then argues against it.

Attitude

Attitude questions usually ask you about the author's feelings towards a topic; rarely, they ask you for the attitude of another group. This type requires less interpretation of the passage than Agreement questions. Instead of inferring a correct statement, you need to **translate** signal words into a description of an attitude. You will work with the passage in a more literal way. Find the specific phrasing used to describe the topic and draw from that a description of how the author (or another party) feels about that topic.

Query, References and Frequency

Most Attitude queries contain the word "attitude" but some say "stance" instead. Example queries:

> The author's ***attitude*** toward the testimony of medical experts in personal injury cases is most accurately described as

> The author's ***stance*** toward the Universal Declaration of Human Rights can best be described as

Attitude queries always feature topic references, so use the reference before moving to the choices. This question type is not particularly common on the recent RC sections: you will likely see one on your official LSAT.

Approach

The topic asked about can play a small or large role in the passage. Unless you are clear on the attitude from your first reading, refer back to the passage. Usually, you will be looking for the author's attitude, and this is told through the author's **word choices** when describing the topic. Each of the words below can be a signal word for how the author feels:

- well-reasoned; unreasonable
- clearly
- obviously
- likely, unlikely
- probable, improbable
- correct, incorrect
- valid, invalid
- appropriate, inappropriate
- supported, unsupported

There are many other possible signal words the author may use. Keep in mind that due to the academic nature of the passages, the author will be somewhat restrained in her word choice. Do not expect to see strong, bold words:

> The singer did a ***horrible*** job with the piece he was given.

> The treaty was ***perfect*** and without flaws.

Instead, learn to derive meaning from **moderate** words that convey the author's attitude. Further, realize that the author will likely have a complex view of the topic, one not easily summed up with a single word. "Reserved optimism" is a great example of an attitude you will see because it is positive, but indicates that the author has reservations and is not 100% positive.

Other example attitudes have been:

> Convinced that Tutuola's works should be viewed within the context of the African oral tradition...
>
> Both authors consider the problems that the Roma face in relation to international law to be anomalous and special.
>
> They were well-meaning attempts to do as much as was feasible at the time.

Notice that the attitudes also include a close description of other topics involved in the passage.

Use Your Viewpoint Markings

The "A's" next to an author opinion and the circles around speakers will highlight the obvious attitudes in the passage. That simple act of marking such attitudes helps you remember and, if necessary, relocate the attitudes. When you face an Attitude question, use the reference and your markings to find the topic.

Short, Challenging Choices

The choices are often hard to decipher because they have words with complex meanings. Look at this example Attitude question, especially the choices:

> 8. Which one of the following most accurately characterizes the author's attitude with respect to Phillis Wheatley's literary accomplishments?
>
> (A) enthusiastic advocacy
> (B) qualified admiration
> (C) dispassionate impartiality
> (D) detached ambivalence
> (E) perfunctory dismissal

Each has an adjective and a noun. Some of these adjectives are tough to understand in reference to their nouns. Dispassionate means "unaffected by strong emotion or prejudice," so "dispassionate impartiality" is being **utterly** impartial, weighing both sides equally. That phrase is redundant and does not need the adjective. The test-makers use tricky phrases to make Attitude questions more difficult. Moving to another choice, "perfunctory dismissal" has a different meaning than "dismissal." A perfunctory one is a hasty, unthinking dismissal; this means that the author rejects Wheatley's literary accomplishments without taking them seriously.

If you cannot understand a choice, analyze only its noun. For instance, if you do not know what "qualified" means (in this situation it means **restricted**), just focus on "admiration." Of course, the adjective does modify the noun and change the meaning, but understanding **part** of a choice is better than not understanding it at all. Because the choices are dense, take your time reading them. Be clear on which ones you understand or which parts of them you understand.

Envision, Envision, Envision

Because the choices in Attitude questions are designed to confuse you, it is vitally important that you envision a good answer before you move to the choices. After using the topic reference and reading the relevant part of the text, you should know the attitude. State it in your own words. Attitudes will be either positive, negative or neutral; figuring that out is a good place to begin. However, you want to be as descriptive as possible when envisioning a good answer. Look at these example sentences:

> Richter rightly refused to conform to the traditions of his time. Although the homes he designed were not aesthetically pleasing from the outside, he refined the art of comfort and room flow within. By designing specifically for a wonderful inside living experience, Richter broke new ground at an important time in architecture history.

The word "rightly" in the first sentence is approving, as are the phrases "refined the art of comfort" and "broke new ground." We might sum up this attitude as "strongly approving." If you were to only think of the attitude as "positive" then you would have trouble working the choices that are variations of "positive." Be as specific as possible during envisioning and you will find the choices easier to deal with.

Overlapping Viewpoints

Attitude questions sometimes ask you which topic the author and a speaker share an attitude about; we call this variation <u>Overlapping Viewpoints</u>. Example query:

> Based on the passage, it can be concluded that the author and Franklin hold the same attitude toward...

These require a different approach than normal Attitude questions. Ideally, you can find the **overlap** between the two parties in the passage. The author can express her opinion anywhere, so find where the other party expresses a viewpoint. Read that opinion carefully. Often, the speaker will only have one viewpoint. When you pinpoint it, you need only confirm that the author shares that viewpoint. You may need to **infer** the author's attitude on the topic from subtle signal words.

If the speaker expresses an attitude on multiple topics, then find the author's attitude that is most likely to interact with one of those attitudes. As you search, use the underlined topics to guide you. After all, the correct answer on Overlapping Viewpoint questions is a **topic**, not a description of an attitude.

Incorrect Choices

The most common incorrect type on Attitude questions is extreme. These choices exaggerate the attitude in either direction, positively or negatively. For instance, if the author's attitude towards a declaration is "qualified approval," an extreme choice could be any of these three:

> (A) Unbridled enthusiasm
> (B) Absolute neutrality
> (C) Strong hostility

"Unbridled enthusiasm" is too positive. The author approves of the declaration, but still has specific qualifications. "Unbridled" signals that the author can barely contain her enthusiasm and has no qualifications. Authors are rarely **that** enthusiastic. "Absolute neutrality" is too strong in the other direction. The author approves of the declaration, so she is not neutral (having no opinion). Finally, "Strong hostility" is even more negative. This signals that the author is **against** the declaration, and this is not the case, no matter how big her qualifications may be.

Zero in on exactly how the author feels about the topic during envisioning. Once you do that, working the choices requires eliminating those that are too strong in one direction or another, while looking for a match for the envisioned attitude.

Example Attitude Question

Let us work the Attitude question introduced earlier:

> 8. Which one of the following most accurately characterizes the author's attitude with respect to Phillis Wheatley's literary accomplishments?

Clearly an Attitude query. The specific topic: Wheatley's literary accomplishments, the subject of the passage. Noticing a theme here? The subject of the passage is often the topic asked about for the author's attitude.

The author gives a summary of her beliefs in the final paragraph. When dealing with the subject of the passage, look to the end for the author's summarized opinion. Here are the lines we need:

> Thus limited by the eighteenth-century English literary code, Wheatley's poetry contributed little to the development of a distinctive African American literary language. Yet by the standards of the literary conventions in which she chose to work, Wheatley's poetry is undeniably accomplished, and she is justly celebrated as the first Black American poet.

This paragraph starts with a **negative** aspect of Wheatley's literary accomplishments: she did not contribute to the development of a unique African American literary language. Then, the author shifts gears and is positive for the rest of the paragraph. "Undeniably accomplished" is strong praise from an RC author, as is "justly celebrated as the first Black American poet." To sum up this attitude in our own words, we can say something like "mostly positive and supportive, but with a reservation." That envisioned answer is specific enough to help us deal with the challenging wording in the choices:

> (A) enthusiastic advocacy

Always on the lookout for choices that are extreme, we thinks this one raises a red flag. While the author is positive regarding Wheatley's literary accomplishments, she is not quite an *enthusiastic* advocate. Advocacy is not necessarily wrong, but enthusiastic makes this choice too positive. It leaves out the reservation that starts the final paragraph, and that is an important part of her view.

> (B) qualified admiration

This is a good fit. The author does admire Wheatley's accomplishments, but qualifies that admiration because Wheatley did not help develop a distinctly African American written language. Because this matches our envisioned answer so well, we confidently select it.

(C) dispassionate impartiality

This choice is incorrect because the author is not impartial; she views Wheatley's work in a positive light. Dispassionate impartiality would demand that the author express no attitude at all towards this topic. The final paragraph of the passage is fairly opinionated, and proves this choice wrong.

(D) detached ambivalence

(D) would require the author to not care about the Wheatley's work. The author does have solid views about Wheatley's accomplishments.

(E) perfunctory dismissal

This choice says that the author dismisses Wheatley's accomplishments without analyzing them. This choice is far too negative and also quite false: the author spends a lot of passage time analyzing the topic.

Weaken/Strengthen

Weaken and Strengthen questions show up on the RC section as well as the LR section, although much less frequently. You already know the basic approach for these question types from your LR work. If you have not read the LR chapters that cover these types, or if you want a quick refresher on those methods, we recommend reading them before proceeding. Turn to page **

Query, References, Frequency

Example Weaken queries:

> Which one of the following would, if true, most weaken the author's argument as expressed in the passage?
>
> Which one of the following, if true, would most weaken the position that the passage attributes to critics of the New Urbanists?
>
> Which one of the following would, if true, most weaken the author's position in the passage?
>
> Which one of the following, if true, most seriously undermines the author's criticism of the LRCWA's recommendations concerning contingency-fee agreements?

Example Strengthen queries:

> In the context of the passage, the author would be most likely to consider the explanation in the third paragraph more favorably if it were shown that
>
> Which one of the following, if true, would most strengthen Lessing's contention that a painting can display aesthetic excellence without possessing an equally high degree of artistic value?
>
> Which one of the following, if true, would provide the most support for Emeagwali's prediction mentioned in lines 55-58?

These are easy to identify; almost all begin with the phrase "Which of the following, if true..." The choices for these types bring in outside information that you must consider to be true, just like their LR brothers. The queries will contain the word "strengthen" or "weaken."

The references for these types vary. On recent tests, Weaken questions generally have topic references, although sometimes they are global. That version asks you weaken the author's **whole argument.** Strengthen questions contain mostly exact references; they give you a specific part of the passage to strengthen.

Weaken/Strengthen questions are somewhat rare: you will see one or two on your official LSAT.

General Approach

Your job is to hurt or help the argument in some way. The argument will not be a perfect (proven) one, otherwise you could not affect it much. You are not asked to obliterate or conclusively prove the argument. Weakening or strengthening the conclusion, even to a small degree, is sufficient. The arguments you will be asked to affect will usually be less complex than those found in LR blurbs. Often, they will not even have evidence: your job is to simply know the conclusion stated by the author or a speaker.

If applicable, use the reference to reread the right part passage to understand the argument. Know the conclusion and evidence for the claim. Otherwise, you cannot interpret in the choices in light of how they affect the conclusion.

New Information

New information (not featured anywhere in the passage) is often **required** to answer these questions. On most RC questions, you can reject a choice that is not supported in the passage, but that is not the case here.

Do not Envision

Only envision an answer if you understand the argument's lacking and believe you effectively address it in a specific way. Otherwise, keep the conclusion and evidence in mind as you move to the choices and evaluate them carefully. In general, we do not recommend envisioning answers to this type of question because the correct answer can often come from left field.

Strengthen

To strengthen an argument, look for a weakness or gap in the argument as you read it. Filling in that the gap is an easy way to strengthen an argument and you can work each choice asking yourself if it serves that purpose. Look for assumptions the argument makes: stating those explicitly strengthens an argument.

On some questions, you must understand the **evidence** in order to strengthen the conclusion. There, the correct choice will bolster the evidence. Be aware of this possibility.

Incorrect choices

There are two common varieties of incorrect choices for Strengthen and Weaken questions: opposite answers and wrong part answers. Opposite answers affect the argument in the wrong direction. For instance, on a Strengthen question, you might be tempted by a choice that **weakens** the argument if it gets at a flaw in the argument that you thought needed addressing. You might remember the flaw and think, ok this choice relates to that. Opposite answers are easy to avoid if you are aware of them. Do not confuse your purpose on the question.

Wrong part choices are tempting as well. Recall that these do not directly affect the argument, but they sound familiar because they reference information that you remember from the passage. Stay zeroed in on affecting the **conclusion** and you will be able to eliminate wrong part choices.

Weaken

Now some general advice for Weaken questions. Attack the conclusion, try to make it less plausible, just like you do on LR questions. When you reread the passage - which you should do when given a reference, which is most of the time - look for flaws in the conclusion. Focus mainly on being clear on the conclusion, but realize that thinking about weaknesses before you work the choices can be helpful. Think of this as **educated** research instead of envisioning. Thinking generally about the conclusion's flaws is more efficient than trying to think of a specific answer; there are simply too many possibilities there.

Simple Conclusion

On some Weaken questions, you are given a simple conclusion with no evidence for it. Your job becomes simple: find the choice that directly refutes the conclusion. The difficulty on these questions comes in finding the claim in the passage and being clear on what it is. After that, analyze each choice and ask whether it goes against the conclusion. Some incorrect choices will weaken other ideas from the passage.

Global Weaken Questions

Global Weaken questions demand a unique strategy. You will be weakening the author's main point, so if you recall that, then there is no need to do any referencing. Otherwise, to refresh your memory, reread a MPD in the passage or reread your answer to a Main Point question. One of those will likely be present.

Because the entire passage supports the main point, there are many ways to attack the evidence used. Most correct answers are direct: they attacking the author's conclusion head on. For instance, if the main point is that college basketball coaches should teach their players how to deal with the demands of the NBA press, either of these choices would weaken that conclusion, **without dealing with the evidence:**

> A vast, vast majority of college basketball players never play in the NBA.
>
> Most rookie NBA players quickly and easily learn how to interact with the Press.

Example Questions

This Weaken question comes from the Wheatley Passage:

> 6. Which one of the following, if true, would most weaken the author's argument concerning the role that Wheatley played in the evolution of an African American literary language?

The query starts with the classic beginning of "Which one of the following..." and it also asks us which would most weaken the argument. We are given a topic reference: the argument the author makes about Wheatley's participation in the evolution of an African American literary language. One of the author's main points is that Wheatley did not contribute to this evolution. Here are the relevant lines:

> Thus limited by the eighteenth-century English literary code, Wheatley's poetry contributed little to the development of a distinctive African American literary language.

The conclusion we must weaken is clear, so we can move to the choices.

> (A) Wheatley's poetry was admired in England for its faithfulness to the conventions of neoclassical poetry.

(A) does not argue against the idea that Wheatley did not contribute to the evolution. There is no mention of neoclassical poetry in the passage; this choice does not affect the argument either way.

> (B) Wheatley compiled a history in English of her family's experiences in Africa and America.

This is a tempting incorrect choice. It mentions Wheatley writing about her past in English, but the passage stated that she did not do so with her poetry. We need support that she helped to create a unique African American **literary style**. Writing a family history in English is not enough.

> (C) The language barriers that Wheatley overcame were eventually transcended by all who were brought from Africa as slaves.

This information does not relate at all to our conclusion. Yes, all those brought over from Africa learned to speak English, but that information is not helpful. We are concerned with a written language. This choice does rehash information from the passage, making it a wrong part choice.

> (D) Several modern African American poets acknowledge the importance of Wheatley's poetry to American literature.

This information is irrelevant. American literature is not a new African American literary language. If anything, this **strengthens** the argument by implying that Wheatley's **only** contribution was to the existing body of American literature. This can be considered an opposite answer.

> (E) Scholars trace themes and expressions in African American poetry back to the poetry of Wheatley.

(E) directly shows that Wheatley contributed to a uniquely African American literary language. Themes and expressions are crucial elements of a written language, and Wheatley influenced those in African American poetry.

Example Strengthen Question

This Strengthen question comes from a passage you have not yet worked. We will give you the part of the passage you would reference.

27. Which one of the following, if true, would most strengthen the author's argument regarding the true motivation for the passage of the Dawes Act?

The typical beginning ("Which one of...") and the word "strengthen" tell us the type we are dealing with. The Topic: the author's argument regarding the true motivation for the Dawes Act. To learn that conclusion, read the following excerpt from the passage:

> While neither Native Americans nor the potential non-Native American purchasers benefited from the restraint on alienation contained in the Dawes Act, one clearly defined group did benefit: the BIA bureaucrats. It has been convincingly demonstrated that bureaucrats seek to maximize the size of their staffs and their budgets in order to compensate for the lack of other sources of fulfillment, such as power and prestige. Additionally, politicians tend to favor the growth of governmental bureaucracy because such growth provides increased opportunity for the exercise of political patronage. The restraint on alienation vastly increased the amount of work, and hence the budgets, necessary to implement the statute.

The conclusion is that the Act was passed **to benefit the BIA bureaucrats** who wanted to expand their staffs and budgets. There is no obvious weakness to shore up, so work each choice, looking for one that supports the conclusion:

(A) The legislators who voted in favor of the Dawes Act owned land adjacent to Native American reservations.

(A) weakens the conclusion, making it an opposite choice. It shows that there was a different motivation for those passing the Dawes Act; they wanted to influence how the land next to their own land was managed. Information that affects the conclusion strongly, but in the wrong direction, is incorrect.

(B) The majority of Native Americans who were granted fee patents did not sell their land back to their tribes.

(B) is irrelevant to the conclusion that focuses on the motivation of the BIA bureaucrats. It is an attempt to trick you if you are unclear on the conclusion you are trying to strengthen.

(C) Native Americans managed to preserve their traditional culture even when they were geographically dispersed.

Native American culture does not have anything to do with the BIA bureaucrats. We can eliminate (C) because it is completely off topic.

(D) The legislators who voted in favor of the Dawes Act were heavily influenced by BIA bureaucrats.

(D) is correct. It supports the argument by telling that the BIA did have influence on the voting process, thus backing the idea that their motivations were what helped get the Act passed.

(E) Non-Native Americans who purchased the majority of Native American lands consolidated them into larger farm holdings.

This is an opposite choice: it slightly supports the idea that those who wanted the Native American lands - perhaps farmers or real estate moguls - were the ones who benefited from the Act. This implies that they were the ones pushing for the Act to be passed, not the BIA. Beware of choices that strengthen the wrong conclusion.

*More Types Chapter Review

Meaning

- "Which one of the following phrases conveys the sense of the word "pragmatic" as it is used in line 22?"
- Identify the meaning of a small piece of the passage: usually a word, sometimes a phrase.
- Approach
    - Refer to the passage and gain context for the piece.
    - Envision clearly.
        - Think of a few key words to describe the piece.
    - The choices are hard to interpret, so read them carefully.
- Incorrect choices
    - Avoid the most common meaning of the word if it is not a good match.
    - Watch out for similar sounding choices that confuse two parts of the passage.

Primary Purpose

- "Which one of the following accurately expresses the primary reason the author wrote the passage?"
- **Why** the author wrote the passage, what she was trying to accomplish with the passage.
- These questions are always global.
- Primary Purpose questions are very good for envisioning.
- Approach
    - Envision first.
        - Can use the answer to a main point question if there is one.
    - Match the subject of the passage carefully to the choices.
    - Avoid overly strong verbs such as "prove" or "reject."

Attitude

- "The author's stance toward the Universal Declaration of Human Rights can best be described as…"
- Attitude questions ask you about the author's or another group's feelings towards a topic.
- All of these have topic references.
- Use the references to find signal words that give away the attitude.
- Approach
    - Use your viewpoint markings.
    - Envision thoroughly because the choices are challenging.
    - Avoid choices that exaggerate the opinion in either direction.

Weaken/Strengthen

- "Which one of the following would, if true, most weaken the author's argument as expressed in the passage?"
- Weaken questions give topic references, while Strengthen give exact references.
    - Use the passage when possible.
- Correct choices are often outside information, so do not envision on these types.
- Weaken
    - If it is a simple conclusion with no evidence, directly refute it.
    - If it is a global weaken question, weaken the author's main point.
- Strengthen
    - Boost the argument in some way.
    - One way is to make an assumption explicit.
- Incorrect Choices
    - Opposite answers – these choices weaken when they are supposed to strengthen and vice versa.
    - Wrong part choices reference information from the passage that does not affect the correct argument.

*Social Sciences Practice Passages

Recently, a new school of economics called steady-state economics has seriously challenged neoclassical economics, the reigning school in Western economic decision making. According to the neoclassical model, an economy is a closed system involving only the circular flow of exchange value between producers and consumers. Therefore, no noneconomic constraints impinge upon the economy and growth has no limits. Indeed, some neoclassical economists argue that growth itself is crucial, because, they claim, the solutions to problems often associated with growth (income inequities, for example) can be found only in the capital that further growth creates.

Steady-state economists believe the neoclassical model to be unrealistic and hold that the economy is dependent on nature. Resources, they argue, enter the economy as raw material and exit as consumed products or waste; the greater the resources, the greater the size of the economy. According to these economists, nature's limited capacity to regenerate raw material and absorb waste suggests that there is an optimal size for the economy, and that growth beyond this ideal point would increase the cost to the environment at a faster rate than the benefit to producers and consumers, generating cycles that . impoverish rather than enrich. Steady-state economists thus believe that the concept of an ever growing economy is dangerous, and that the only alternative is to maintain a state in which the economy remains in equilibrium with nature. Neoclassical economists, on the other hand, consider nature to be just one element of the economy rather than an outside constraint, believing that natural resources, if depleted, can be replaced with other elements-i.e., human-made resources-that will allow the economy to continue with its process of unlimited growth.

Some steady-state economists, pointing to the widening disparity between indices of actual growth (which simply count the total monetary value of goods and services) and the index of environmentally sustainable growth (which is based on personal consumption, factoring in depletion of raw materials and production costs), believe that Western economies have already exceeded their optimal size. In response to the warnings from neoclassical economists that checking economic growth only leads to economic stagnation, they argue that there are alternatives to growth that still accomplish what is required of an economy: the satisfaction of human wants. One of these alternatives is conservation. Conservation-for example, increasing the efficiency of resource use through means such as recycling-differs from growth in that it is qualitative, not quantitative, requiring improvement in resource management rather than an increase in the amount of resources. One measure of the success of a steady-state economy would be the degree to which it could implement alternatives to growth, such as conservation, without sacrificing the ability to satisfy the wants of producers and consumers.

1. Which one of the following most completely and accurately expresses the main point of the passage?

   (A) Neoclassical economists, who, unlike steady-state economists, hold that economic growth is not subject to outside constraints, believe that nature is just one element of the economy and that if natural resources in Western economies are depleted they can be replaced with human-made resources.

   (B) Some neoclassical economists, who, unlike steady-state economists, hold that growth is crucial to the health of economies, believe that the solutions to certain problems in Western economies can thus be found in the additional capital generated by unlimited growth.

   (C) Some steady-state economists, who, unlike neoclassical economists, hold that unlimited growth is neither possible nor desirable, believe that Western economies should limit economic growth by adopting conservation strategies, even if such strategies lead temporarily to economic stagnation.

   (D) Some steady-state economists, who, unlike neoclassical economists, hold that the optimal sizes of economies are limited by the availability of natural resources, believe that Western economies should limit economic growth and that, with alternatives like conservation, satisfaction of human wants need not be sacrificed.

   (E) Steady-state and neoclassical economists, who both hold that economies involve the circular flow of exchange value between producers and consumers, nevertheless differ over the most effective way of guaranteeing that a steady increase in this exchange value continues unimpeded in Western economies.

2. Based on the passage, neoclassical economists would likely hold that steady-state economists are wrong to believe each of the following EXCEPT:

   (A) The environment's ability to yield raw material is limited.

   (B) Natural resources are an external constraint on economies.

   (C) The concept of unlimited economic growth is dangerous.

   (D) Western economies have exceeded their optimal size.

   (E) Economies have certain optimal sizes.

3. According to the passage, steady-state economists believe that unlimited economic growth is dangerous because it

   (A) may deplete natural resources faster than other natural resources are discovered to replace them
   (B) may convert natural resources into products faster than more efficient resource use can compensate for
   (C) may proliferate goods and services faster than it generates new markets for them
   (D) may create income inequities faster than it creates the capital needed to redress them
   (E) may increase the cost to the environment faster than it increases benefits to producers and consumers

4. A steady-state economist would be LEAST likely to endorse which one of the following as a means of helping a steady-state economy reduce growth without compromising its ability to satisfy human wants?

   (A) a manufacturer's commitment to recycle its product packaging
   (B) a manufacturer's decision to use a less expensive fuel in its production process
   (C) a manufacturer's implementation of a quality-control process to reduce the output of defective products
   (D) a manufacturer's conversion from one type of production process to another with greater fuel efficiency
   (E) a manufacturer's reduction of output in order to eliminate an overproduction problem

5. Based on the passage, a steady-state economist is most likely to claim that a successful economy is one that satisfies which one of the following principles?

   (A) A successful economy uses human-made resources in addition to natural resources.
   (B) A successful economy satisfies human wants faster than it creates new ones.
   (C) A successful economy maintains an equilibrium with nature while still satisfying human wants.
   (D) A successful economy implements every possible means to prevent growth.
   (E) A successful economy satisfies the wants of producers and consumers by using resources to spur growth.

6. In the view of steady-state economists, which one of the following is a noneconomic constraint as referred to in line 7?

   (A) the total amount of human wants
   (B) the index of environmentally sustainable growth
   (C) the capacity of nature to absorb waste
   (D) the problems associated with economic growth
   (E) the possibility of economic stagnation

7. Which one of the following most accurately describes what the last paragraph does in the passage?

   (A) It contradicts the ways in which the two economic schools interpret certain data and gives a criterion for judging between them based on the basic goals of an economy.
   (B) It gives an example that illustrates the weakness of the new economic school and recommends an economic policy based on the basic goals of the prevailing economic school.
   (C) It introduces an objection to the new economic school and argues that the policies of the new economic school would be less successful than growth-oriented economic policies at achieving the basic goal an economy must meet.
   (D) It notes an objection to implementing the policies of the new economic school and identifies an additional policy that can help avoid that objection and still meet the goal an economy must meet.
   (E) It contrasts the policy of the prevailing economic school with the recommendation mentioned earlier of the new economic school and shows that they are based on differing views on the basic goal an economy must meet.

8. The passage suggests which one of the following about neoclassical economists?

   (A) They assume that natural resources are infinitely available.
   (B) They assume that human-made resources are infinitely available.
   (C) They assume that availability of resources places an upper limit on growth.
   (D) They assume that efficient management of resources is necessary to growth.
   (E) They assume that human-made resources are preferable to natural resources.

Personal names are generally regarded by European thinkers in two major ways, both of which deny that names have any significant semantic content. In philosophy and linguistics, John Stuart Mill's formulation that "proper names are meaningless marks set upon ... persons to distinguish them from one another" retains currency; in anthropology, Claude Levi-Strauss's characterization of names as being primarily instruments of social classification has been very influential. Consequently, interpretation of personal names in societies where names have other functions and meanings has been neglected. Among the Hopi of the southwestern United States, names often refer to historical or ritual events in order both to place individuals within society and to confer an identity upon them. Furthermore, the images used to evoke these events suggest that Hopi names can be seen as a type of poetic composition.

Throughout life, Hopis receive several names in a sequence of ritual initiations. Birth, entry into one of the ritual societies during childhood, and puberty are among the name-giving occasions. Names are conferred by an adult member of a clan other than the child's clan, and names refer to that name giver's clan, sometimes combining characteristics of the clan's totem animal with the child's characteristics. Thus, a name might translate to something as simple as "little rabbit," which reflects both the child's size and the representative animal.

More often, though, the name giver has in mind a specific event that is not apparent in a name's literal translation. One Lizard clan member from the village of Oraibi is named Lomayayva, "beautifully ascended." This translation, however, tells nothing about either the event referred to-who or what ascended-or the name giver's clan. The name giver in this case is from Badger clan. Badger clan is responsible for an annual ceremony featuring a procession in which masked representations of spirits climb the mesa on which Oraibi sits. Combining the name giver's clan association with the receiver's home village, "beautifully ascended" refers to the splendid colors and movements of the procession up the mesa. The condensed image this name evokes-a typical feature of Hopi personal names---displays the same quality of Western Apache place names that led one commentator to call them "tiny imagist poems."

Hopi personal names do several things simultaneously. They indicate social relationships-but only indirectly-and they individuate persons. Equally important, though, is their poetic quality; in a sense they can be understood as oral texts that produce aesthetic delight. This view of Hopi names is thus opposed not only to Mill's claim that personal names are without inherent meaning but also to Levi-Strauss's purely functional characterization. Interpreters must understand Hopi clan structures and linguistic practices in order to discern the beauty and significance of Hopi names.

9. Which one of the following statements most accurately summarizes the passage's main point?

(A) Unlike European names, which are used exclusively for identification or exclusively for social classification, Hopi names perform both these functions simultaneously.

(B) Unlike European names, Hopi names tend to neglect the functions of identification and social classification in favor of a concentration on compression and poetic effects.

(C) Lacking knowledge of the intricacies of Hopi linguistic and tribal structures, European thinkers have so far been unable to discern the deeper significance of Hopi names.

(D) Although some Hopi names may seem difficult to interpret, they all conform to a formula whereby a reference to the name giver's clan is combined with a reference to the person named.

(E) While performing the functions ascribed to names by European thinkers, Hopi names also possess a significant aesthetic quality that these thinkers have not adequately recognized.

10. The author most likely refers to Western Apache place names (line 46) in order to

(A) offer an example of how names can contain references not evident in their literal translations

(B) apply a commentator's characterization of Western Apache place names to Hopi personal names

(C) contrast Western Apache naming practices with Hopi naming practices

(D) demonstrate that other names besides Hopi names may have some semantic content

(E) explain how a specific Hopi name refers subtly to a particular Western Apache site

11. Which one of the following statements describes an example of the function accorded to personal names under Lévi-Strauss's view?

(A) Some parents select their children's names from impersonal sources such as books.

(B) Some parents wait to give a child a name in order to choose one that reflects the child's looks or personality.

(C) Some parents name their children in honor of friends or famous people.

(D) Some family members have no parts of their names in common.

(E) Some family names originated as identifications of their bearers' occupations.

12. The primary function of the second paragraph is to

    (A) present reasons why Hopi personal names can be treated as poetic compositions
    (B) support the claim that Hopi personal names make reference to events in the recipient's life
    (C) argue that the fact that Hopis receive many names throughout life refutes European theories about naming
    (D) illustrate ways in which Hopi personal names may have semantic content
    (E) demonstrate that the literal translation of Hopi personal names often obscures their true meaning

13. Based on the passage, with which one of the following statements about Mill's view would the author of the passage be most likely to agree?

    (A) Its characterization of the function of names is too narrow to be universally applicable.
    (B) It would be correct if it recognized the use of names as instruments of social classification.
    (C) Its influence single-handedly led scholars to neglect how names are used outside Europe.
    (D) It is more accurate than Lévi-Strauss's characterization of the purpose of names.
    (E) It is less relevant than Lévi-Strauss's characterization in understanding Hopi naming practices.

14. It can be inferred from the passage that each of the following features of Hopi personal names contributes to their poetic quality EXCEPT:

    (A) their ability to be understood as oral texts
    (B) their use of condensed imagery to evoke events
    (C) their capacity to produce aesthetic delight
    (D) their ability to confer identity upon individuals
    (E) their ability to subtly convey meaning

15. The author's primary purpose in writing the passage it to

    (A) present an anthropological study of Hopi names
    (B) propose a new theory about the origin of name
    (C) describe several competing theories of names
    (D) criticize two influential views of names
    (E) explain the cultural origins of names

*Social Sciences Practice Passages Explanations

1. (28/4 #14) ~ D

Main Point. P1 introduces steady-state economics by first telling how neoclassical economics views growth. P2 explains how steady-states economics views the neo classical model and how this relates to neoclassical economics. P3 states that steady-state economists believe that Western economies have already exceeded optimal size, but how alternatives, like conservation, can fulfill people's wants without the negative effects of normal growth. The passage builds up to its main point and Choice D, which is a summary of the final paragraph, works well.

2. (28/4 #15) ~ A

Detail. Look for an area where neoclassical economists would not disagree with steady–state economists. The neoclassical view is given in lines 4–8, while the rest of the passage discusses steady-state economists. Working the choices carefully is your best option. A is correct: both steady–state economists (line 20) and neoclassical economists (line 33) believe that the environment's ability to yield raw material is limited.

3. (28/4 #16) ~ E

Detail. Lines 19-26 point to Choice E. You may recall that P2 is where the two different economic schools are talked about together, so it is a likely place for a point about why steady-state disagrees with neoclassical on the benefits of unlimited growth.

4. (28/4 #17) ~ B

Agree. A steady-state economist would be unlikely to endorse a method of reducing growth without compromising ability to satisfy human wants if it was unsuccessful at doing so. Using a less expensive fuel in a production processes does not necessarily reduce growth. This is simply a substitution of one input for another. The rest of the choices involve conservation in some way.

5. (28/4 #18) ~ C

Logical Reasoning – Identify Principle. A steady-state economist would agree with a balance between taking from nature and allowing nature to regenerate, while still satisfying human wants. This is also the final sentence of the passage.

6. (28/4 #19) ~ C

Detail. Lines 19-26 state that steady-state economists believe that nature's capacity to absorb waste is a noneconomic constraint, because it puts a limit on growth.

7. (28/4 #20) ~ D

Role. The final paragraph discusses the belief that many steady–state economists hold: western economies have already exceeded their optimal size. It then discusses a remedy for this and analyses those in terms of neoclassical ideas. D states this well. The objection is that checking growth leads to stagnation and the alternative policy is conservation. Rereading the paragraph's first and last lines is helpful if you do not have time to reread the entire paragraph.

8. (28/4 #21) ~ B

Detail. Lines 30-36 tell that neoclassical economists believe that human made resources will allow the economy to continue with unlimited growth. This means that those resources must be unlimited.

9. (27/3 #8) ~ E

Main Point. P1 introduces two schools of thought on names, Mills and Strauss's viewpoints, then discusses the Hopi as a society where names work differently. P2 gives some details on Hopi name practices and, P3 talks about how Hopi names often contain condensed information and imagery. P4 states that Hopi names do what the two European viewpoints mentioned in P1 do, and more: they have a poetic quality. P4 effectively states the main point that the passage builds up to.

10. (27/3 #9) ~ B

Role. The passage discusses Hopi names in depth and the detail here is used to tie in information about Western Apache place names to the Hopi personal names. Note the words "same quality" used in drawing the connection.

11. (27/3 #10) ~ E

Match. Strauss says that names are instruments of social classification. Choice E reflects this: family names that originated as IDs of their bearers jobs would certainly be social classification because they would identify where in the social hierarchy that family fit.

12. (27/3 #11) ~ D

Role. P2 fleshes out the idea that Hopi names can be seen as a type of poetic composition because it describes when they receive their names and why. It mentions that they can say something about the child's characteristics. "Semantic content" tells that the names have meaning.

13. (27/3 #12) ~ A

Agree. Mills states that names are arbitrary ways to make individuals distinctive from one another. The author would argue that that view is only applicable in some societies and certainly not in Hopi society, where names are not arbitrary and have deeper meaning.

14. (27/3 #13) ~ D

Deduction. This question requires that you read the stem carefully and consider everything the passage said about the names being poetic. Working the choices, D should stand out as not being something that contributes to the name's poetic quality. Conferring identity is more pragmatic and less poetic than evoking events or conveying meaning. Lines 49-51 also point to D, as individuating persons is set in contrast to poetic qualities.

15. (27/3 #14) ~ D

Primary Purpose. The first and last paragraphs point to the author's purpose being a critique of the two theories of names presented. P2 and P3 illustrate the Hopi counter example to the other two theories. Lines 53 – 56 point to this focus of the passage as well.

*Natural Sciences Practice Passages

Scientists typically advocate the analytic method of studying complex systems: systems are divided into component parts that are investigated separately. But nineteenth-century critics of this method claimed that when a system's parts are isolated its complexity tends to be lost. To address the perceived weaknesses of the analytic method these critics put forward a concept called organicism, which posited that the whole determines the nature of its parts and that the parts of a whole are interdependent.

Organicism depended upon the theory of internal relations, which states that relations between entities are possible only within some whole that embraces them, and that entities are altered by the relationships into which they enter. If an entity stands in a relationship with another entity, it has some property as a consequence. Without this relationship, and hence without the property, the entity would be different - and so would be another entity. Thus, the property is one of the entity's defining characteristics. Each of an entity's relationships likewise determines a defining characteristic of the entity.

One problem with the theory of internal relations is that not all properties of an entity are defining characteristics: numerous properties are accompanying characteristics-even if they are always present, their presence does not influence the entity's identity. Thus, even if it is admitted that every relationship into which an entity enters determines some characteristic of the entity, it is not necessarily true that such characteristics will define the entity; it is possible for the entity to enter into a relationship yet remain essentially unchanged.

The ultimate difficulty with the theory of internal relations is that it renders the acquisition of knowledge impossible. To truly know an entity, we must know all of its relationships; but because the entity is related to everything in each whole of which it is a part, these wholes must be known completely before the entity can be known. This seems to be a prerequisite impossible to satisfy.

Organicists' criticism of the analytic method arose from their failure to fully comprehend the method. In rejecting the analytic method, organicists overlooked the fact that before the proponents of the method analyzed the component parts of a system, they first determined both the laws applicable to the whole system and the initial conditions of the system; . proponents of the method thus did not study parts of a system in full isolation from the system as a whole. Since organicists failed to recognize this, they never advanced any argument to show that laws and initial conditions of complex systems cannot be discovered. Hence, organicists offered no valid reason for rejecting the analytic method or for adopting organicism as a replacement for it.

1. Which one of the following most completely and accurately summarizes the argument of the passage?

   (A) By calling into question the possibility that complex systems can be studied in their entirety, organicists offered an alternative to the analytic method favored by nineteenth-century scientists.

   (B) Organicists did not offer a useful method of studying complex systems because they did not acknowledge that there are relationships into which an entity may enter that do not alter the entity's identity.

   (C) Organicism is flawed because it relies on a theory that both ignores the fact that not all characteristics of entities are defining and ultimately makes the acquisition of knowledge impossible.

   (D) Organicism does not offer a valid challenge to the analytic method both because it relies on faulty theory and because it is based on a misrepresentation of the analytic method.

   (E) In criticizing the analytic method, organicists neglected to disprove that scientists who employ the method are able to discover the laws and initial conditions of the systems they study.

2. According to the passage, organicists' chief objection to the analytic method was that the method

   (A) oversimplified systems by isolating their components

   (B) assumed that a system can be divided into component parts

   (C) ignored the laws applicable to the system as a whole

   (D) claimed that the parts of a system are more important than the system as a whole

   (E) denied the claim that entities enter into relationships

3. The passage offers information to help answer each of the following questions EXCEPT:

   (A) Why does the theory of internal relations appear to make the acquisition of knowledge impossible?
   (B) Why did the organicists propose replacing the analytic method?
   (C) What is the difference between a defining characteristic and an accompanying characteristic?
   (D) What did organicists claim are the effects of an entity's entering into a relationship with another entity?
   (E) What are some of the advantages of separating out the parts of a system for study?

4. The passage most strongly supports the ascription of which one of the following views to scientists who use the analytic method?

   (A) A complex system is best understood by studying its component parts in full isolation from the system as a whole.
   (B) The parts of a system should be studied with an awareness of the laws and initial conditions that govern the system.
   (C) It is not possible to determine the laws governing a system until the system's parts are separated from one another.
   (D) Because the parts of a system are interdependent, they cannot be studied separately without destroying the system's complexity.
   (E) Studying the parts of a system individually eliminates the need to determine which characteristics of the parts are defining characteristics.

5. Which one of the following is a principle upon which the author bases an argument against the theory of internal relations?

   (A) An adequate theory of complex systems must define the entities of which the system is composed.
   (B) An acceptable theory cannot have consequences that contradict its basic purpose.
   (C) An adequate method of study of complex systems should reveal the actual complexity of the systems it studies.
   (D) An acceptable theory must describe the laws and initial conditions of a complex system.
   (E) An acceptable method of studying complex systems should not study parts of the system in isolation from the system as a whole.

What it means to "explain" something in science often comes down to the application of mathematics. Some thinkers hold that mathematics is a kind of language-a systematic contrivance of signs, the criteria for the authority of which are internal coherence, elegance, and depth. The application of such a highly artificial system to the physical world, they claim, results in the creation of a kind of statement about the world. Accordingly, what matters in the sciences is finding a mathematical concept that attempts, as other language does, to accurately describe the functioning of some aspect of the world.

At the center of the issue of scientific knowledge can thus be found questions about the relationship between language and what it refers to. A discussion about the role played by language in the pursuit of knowledge has been going on among linguists for several decades. The debate centers around whether language corresponds in some essential way to objects and behaviors, making knowledge a solid and reliable commodity; or, on the other hand, whether the relationship between language and things is purely a matter of agreed-upon conventions, making knowledge tenuous, relative, and inexact.

Lately the latter theory has been gaining wider acceptance. According to linguists who support this theory, the way language is used varies depending upon changes in accepted practices and theories among those who work in a particular discipline. These linguists argue that, in the pursuit of knowledge, a statement is true only when there are no promising alternatives that might lead one to question it. Certainly this characterization would seem to be applicable to the sciences. In science, a mathematical statement may be taken to account for every aspect of a phenomenon it is applied to, but, some would argue, there is nothing inherent in mathematical language that guarantees such a correspondence. Under this view, acceptance of a mathematical statement by the scientific community-by virtue of the statement's predictive power or methodological efficiency-transforms what is basically an analogy or metaphor into an explanation of the physical process in question, to be held as true until another, more compelling analogy takes its place.

In pursuing the implications of this theory, linguists have reached the point at which they must ask: If words or sentences do not correspond in an essential way to life or to our ideas about life, then just what are they capable of telling us about the world? In science and mathematics, then, it would seem equally necessary to ask: If models of electrolytes or E == mc", say, do not correspond essentially to the physical world, then just what functions do they perform in the acquisition of scientific knowledge? But this question has yet to be significantly addressed in the sciences.

6. Which one of the following statements most accurately expresses the passage's main point?

(A) Although scientists must rely on both language and mathematics in their pursuit of scientific knowledge, each is an imperfect tool for perceiving and interpreting aspects of the physical world.

(B) The acquisition of scientific knowledge depends on an agreement among scientists to accept some mathematical statements as more precise than others while acknowledging that all mathematics is inexact.

(C) If science is truly to progress, scientists must temporarily abandon the pursuit of new knowledge in favor of a systematic analysis of how the knowledge they already possess came to be accepted as true.

(D) In order to better understand the acquisition of scientific knowledge, scientists must investigate mathematical statements' relationship to the world just as linguists study language's relationship to the world.

(E) Without the debates among linguists that preceded them, it is unlikely that scientists would ever have begun to explore the essential role played by mathematics in the acquisition of scientific knowledge.

7. Which one of the following statements, if true, lends the most support to the view that language has an essential correspondence to the things it describes?

(A) The categories of physical objects employed by one language correspond remarkably to the categories employed by another language that developed independently of the first.

(B) The categories of physical objects employed by one language correspond remarkably to the categories employed by another language that derives from the first.

(C) The categories of physical objects employed by speakers of a language correspond remarkably to the categories employed by other speakers of the same language.

(D) The sentence structures of languages in scientifically sophisticated societies vary little from language to language.

(E) Native speakers of many languages believe that the categories of physical objects employed by their language correspond to natural categories of objects in the world.

8. According to the passage, mathematics can be considered a language because it

   (A) conveys meaning in the same way that metaphors do
   (B) constitutes a systematic collection of signs
   (C) corresponds exactly to aspects of physical phenomena
   (D) confers explanatory power on scientific theories
   (E) relies on previously agreed-upon conventions

9. The primary purpose of the third paragraph is to

   (A) offer support for the view of linguists who believe that language has an essential correspondence to things
   (B) elaborate the position of linguists who believe that truth is merely a matter of convention
   (C) illustrate the differences between the essentialist and conventionalist positions in the linguists' debate
   (D) demonstrate the similarity of the linguists' debate to a current debate among scientists about the nature of explanation
   (E) explain the theory that mathematical statements are a kind of language

10. Based on the passage, linguists who subscribe to the theory described in lines 21 24 would hold that the statement "The ball is red" is true because

    (A) speakers of English have accepted that "The ball is red" applies to the particular physical relationship being described
    (B) speakers of English do not accept that synonyms for "ball" and "red" express these concepts as elegantly
    (C) "The ball is red" corresponds essentially to every aspect of the particular physical relationship being described
    (D) "ball" and "red" actually refer to an entity and a property respectively
    (E) "ball" and "red" are mathematical concepts that attempt to accurately describe some particular physical relationship in the world

*Natural Sciences Practice Passages Explanations

1. (25/1 #22) ~ D

Main Point. The final line of the paragraph describes much of the main point. The author also shows in P4 that Organicism is based on a faulty theory. The passage as a whole introduces and then debunks this theory.

2. (25/1 #23) ~ A

Detail. This information is given in the sentence that begins on line 3: "when a system's parts are isolated its complexity tends to be lost." The passage first gives the background of the theory, and part of that background includes why the theory came into being.

3. (25/1 #24) ~ E

Detail. Work each choice to see which question cannot be answered based on the information in the passage. Like many Except Fact questions, the correct answer is far down the choices. The passage never discusses the advantages of separating out the parts of a system for study. This choice is a reference to the analytic method, which is discussed only in context with organicism. The merits of its methods are never touched on.

4. (25/1 #25) ~ B

Agree. "Strongly supports" and "view" tip that this is an agreement question. Only the first and final paragraphs mention the Analytic method and give hints as to what scientists who follow it would agree with. Choice A is tempting because the method does involve studying individual parts, but lines 43 – 50 tell how this is choice incorrect. Scientists who follow this method would support B: parts should be studied with an awareness of aspects of the greater system.

5. (25/1 #26) ~ B

Detail. The argument against the theory of internal relations is in P4. The thrust of the argument is that the theory renders knowledge impossible which is ironic because it sets out to help others gain knowledge. The basic premise of gaining knowledge is contradicted by building blocks of the theory itself.

6. (22/1 #22) ~ D

Main Point. The passage slowly builds up to its main point, which is stated in the final paragraph. Lines 13-15 serve as the introduction to this idea that the passage develops. Lines 49-54 state: it is necessary to ask what role models play if they do not correspond essentially to the physical world. Linguists ask the same sort of question about language.

7. (22/1 #23) ~ A

Strengthen. This is a rare RC question where you can use only the stem and the choices to answer the question. The passage never really comes into play. If language has an innate connection to the things it describes than Choice A would be true. The fact that two languages that developed independently both have categories for physical objects that correspond closely implies that each language is tied to the objects themselves and not just a product of human creation that is separate from the objects.

8. (22/1 #24) ~ B

Detail. This is in the first sentence of the passage. "...language - a systematic contrivance of signs..."

9. (22/1 #25) ~ B

Role. P3 expands upon a theory presented in the previous paragraph. That theory is articulated in the final part of the last sentence of P2 – "the relationship between language and things is purely a matter of agreed-upon conventions, making knowledge tenuous, relative and inexact." This paragraph has tough language, and keeping an eye on what came immediately before it is helpful.

10. (22/1 #26) ~ A

Detail. If someone believes that the relationship between language and things is only a matter of convention, and that knowledge is relative and inexact, then they would say the statement is true because that is what speakers of English have agreed upon. The "ball is red" expresses what it does because that relative relationship is a matter of convention.

*Humanities and Law Problem Sets

Average (28)

19 / 3 # **1** Ⓐ Ⓑ Ⓒ Ⓓ Ⓔ
19 / 3 # **2** Ⓐ Ⓑ Ⓒ Ⓓ Ⓔ
19 / 3 # **3** Ⓐ Ⓑ Ⓒ Ⓓ Ⓔ
19 / 3 # **4** Ⓐ Ⓑ Ⓒ Ⓓ Ⓔ
19 / 3 # **5** Ⓐ Ⓑ Ⓒ Ⓓ Ⓔ
19 / 3 # **6** Ⓐ Ⓑ Ⓒ Ⓓ Ⓔ
19 / 3 # **7** Ⓐ Ⓑ Ⓒ Ⓓ Ⓔ
19 / 3 # **8** Ⓐ Ⓑ Ⓒ Ⓓ Ⓔ
22 / 1 # **1** Ⓐ Ⓑ Ⓒ Ⓓ Ⓔ
22 / 1 # **2** Ⓐ Ⓑ Ⓒ Ⓓ Ⓔ
22 / 1 # **3** Ⓐ Ⓑ Ⓒ Ⓓ Ⓔ
22 / 1 # **4** Ⓐ Ⓑ Ⓒ Ⓓ Ⓔ
22 / 1 # **5** Ⓐ Ⓑ Ⓒ Ⓓ Ⓔ
22 / 1 # **6** Ⓐ Ⓑ Ⓒ Ⓓ Ⓔ
22 / 1 # **7** Ⓐ Ⓑ Ⓒ Ⓓ Ⓔ
22 / 1 # **8** Ⓐ Ⓑ Ⓒ Ⓓ Ⓔ

---

27 / 3 # **1** Ⓐ Ⓑ Ⓒ Ⓓ Ⓔ
27 / 3 # **2** Ⓐ Ⓑ Ⓒ Ⓓ Ⓔ
27 / 3 # **3** Ⓐ Ⓑ Ⓒ Ⓓ Ⓔ
27 / 3 # **4** Ⓐ Ⓑ Ⓒ Ⓓ Ⓔ
27 / 3 # **5** Ⓐ Ⓑ Ⓒ Ⓓ Ⓔ
27 / 3 # **6** Ⓐ Ⓑ Ⓒ Ⓓ Ⓔ
27 / 3 # **7** Ⓐ Ⓑ Ⓒ Ⓓ Ⓔ
28 / 4 # **22** Ⓐ Ⓑ Ⓒ Ⓓ Ⓔ
28 / 4 # **23** Ⓐ Ⓑ Ⓒ Ⓓ Ⓔ
28 / 4 # **24** Ⓐ Ⓑ Ⓒ Ⓓ Ⓔ
28 / 4 # **25** Ⓐ Ⓑ Ⓒ Ⓓ Ⓔ
28 / 4 # **26** Ⓐ Ⓑ Ⓒ Ⓓ Ⓔ

Difficult (14)

21 / 4 # **9** Ⓐ Ⓑ Ⓒ Ⓓ Ⓔ
21 / 4 # **10** Ⓐ Ⓑ Ⓒ Ⓓ Ⓔ
21 / 4 # **11** Ⓐ Ⓑ Ⓒ Ⓓ Ⓔ
21 / 4 # **12** Ⓐ Ⓑ Ⓒ Ⓓ Ⓔ
21 / 4 # **13** Ⓐ Ⓑ Ⓒ Ⓓ Ⓔ
21 / 4 # **14** Ⓐ Ⓑ Ⓒ Ⓓ Ⓔ
21 / 4 # **15** Ⓐ Ⓑ Ⓒ Ⓓ Ⓔ
21 / 4 # **16** Ⓐ Ⓑ Ⓒ Ⓓ Ⓔ
25 / 1 # **8** Ⓐ Ⓑ Ⓒ Ⓓ Ⓔ
25 / 1 # **9** Ⓐ Ⓑ Ⓒ Ⓓ Ⓔ
25 / 1 # **10** Ⓐ Ⓑ Ⓒ Ⓓ Ⓔ
25 / 1 # **11** Ⓐ Ⓑ Ⓒ Ⓓ Ⓔ
25 / 1 # **12** Ⓐ Ⓑ Ⓒ Ⓓ Ⓔ
25 / 1 # **13** Ⓐ Ⓑ Ⓒ Ⓓ Ⓔ

Grueling (22)

19 / 3 # **9** Ⓐ Ⓑ Ⓒ Ⓓ Ⓔ
19 / 3 # **10** Ⓐ Ⓑ Ⓒ Ⓓ Ⓔ
19 / 3 # **11** Ⓐ Ⓑ Ⓒ Ⓓ Ⓔ
19 / 3 # **12** Ⓐ Ⓑ Ⓒ Ⓓ Ⓔ
19 / 3 # **13** Ⓐ Ⓑ Ⓒ Ⓓ Ⓔ
19 / 3 # **14** Ⓐ Ⓑ Ⓒ Ⓓ Ⓔ
20 / 2 # **7** Ⓐ Ⓑ Ⓒ Ⓓ Ⓔ
20 / 2 # **8** Ⓐ Ⓑ Ⓒ Ⓓ Ⓔ
20 / 2 # **9** Ⓐ Ⓑ Ⓒ Ⓓ Ⓔ
20 / 2 # **10** Ⓐ Ⓑ Ⓒ Ⓓ Ⓔ
20 / 2 # **11** Ⓐ Ⓑ Ⓒ Ⓓ Ⓔ
20 / 2 # **12** Ⓐ Ⓑ Ⓒ Ⓓ Ⓔ
20 / 2 # **13** Ⓐ Ⓑ Ⓒ Ⓓ Ⓔ
20 / 2 # **14** Ⓐ Ⓑ Ⓒ Ⓓ Ⓔ
21 / 4 # **1** Ⓐ Ⓑ Ⓒ Ⓓ Ⓔ
21 / 4 # **2** Ⓐ Ⓑ Ⓒ Ⓓ Ⓔ
21 / 4 # **3** Ⓐ Ⓑ Ⓒ Ⓓ Ⓔ
21 / 4 # **4** Ⓐ Ⓑ Ⓒ Ⓓ Ⓔ
21 / 4 # **5** Ⓐ Ⓑ Ⓒ Ⓓ Ⓔ
21 / 4 # **6** Ⓐ Ⓑ Ⓒ Ⓓ Ⓔ
21 / 4 # **7** Ⓐ Ⓑ Ⓒ Ⓓ Ⓔ
21 / 4 # **8** Ⓐ Ⓑ Ⓒ Ⓓ Ⓔ

*Humanities and Law Problem Sets ~ Answers

Average

19 / 3 # **1** A
19 / 3 # **2** E
19 / 3 # **3** B
19 / 3 # **4** E
19 / 3 # **5** A
19 / 3 # **6** D
19 / 3 # **7** D
19 / 3 # **8** C
22 / 1 # **1** C
22 / 1 # **2** B
22 / 1 # **3** A
22 / 1 # **4** B
22 / 1 # **5** C
22 / 1 # **6** E
22 / 1 # **7** C
22 / 1 # **8** D
27 / 3 # **1** E
27 / 3 # **2** A
27 / 3 # **3** B
27 / 3 # **4** C
27 / 3 # **5** C
27 / 3 # **6** B
27 / 3 # **7** E
28 / 4 # **22** A
28 / 4 # **23** C
28 / 4 # **24** D
28 / 4 # **25** B
28 / 4 # **26** D

Difficult

21 / 4 # **9** A
21 / 4 # **10** B
21 / 4 # **11** B
21 / 4 # **12** D
21 / 4 # **13** E
21 / 4 # **14** D
21 / 4 # **15** C
21 / 4 # **16** A
25 / 1 # **8** C
25 / 1 # **9** B
25 / 1 # **10** A
25 / 1 # **11** C
25 / 1 # **12** D
25 / 1 # **13** A

Grueling

19 / 3 # **9** C
19 / 3 # **10** E
19 / 3 # **11** D
19 / 3 # **12** B
19 / 3 # **13** A
19 / 3 # **14** D
20 / 2 # **7** C
20 / 2 # **8** A
20 / 2 # **9** B
20 / 2 # **10** C
20 / 2 # **11** A
20 / 2 # **12** B
20 / 2 # **13** B
20 / 2 # **14** C
21 / 4 # **1** B
21 / 4 # **2** E
21 / 4 # **3** D
21 / 4 # **4** A
21 / 4 # **5** B
21 / 4 # **6** B
21 / 4 # **7** E
21 / 4 # **8** B

*Science Problem Sets

Average

Test / Section	#	Question	Answer
20 / 2	#	**22**	Ⓐ Ⓑ Ⓒ Ⓓ Ⓔ
20 / 2	#	**23**	Ⓐ Ⓑ Ⓒ Ⓓ Ⓔ
20 / 2	#	**24**	Ⓐ Ⓑ Ⓒ Ⓓ Ⓔ
20 / 2	#	**25**	Ⓐ Ⓑ Ⓒ Ⓓ Ⓔ
20 / 2	#	**26**	Ⓐ Ⓑ Ⓒ Ⓓ Ⓔ
21 / 4	#	**17**	Ⓐ Ⓑ Ⓒ Ⓓ Ⓔ
21 / 4	#	**18**	Ⓐ Ⓑ Ⓒ Ⓓ Ⓔ
21 / 4	#	**19**	Ⓐ Ⓑ Ⓒ Ⓓ Ⓔ
21 / 4	#	**20**	Ⓐ Ⓑ Ⓒ Ⓓ Ⓔ
21 / 4	#	**21**	Ⓐ Ⓑ Ⓒ Ⓓ Ⓔ
23 / 4	#	**14**	Ⓐ Ⓑ Ⓒ Ⓓ Ⓔ
23 / 4	#	**15**	Ⓐ Ⓑ Ⓒ Ⓓ Ⓔ
23 / 4	#	**16**	Ⓐ Ⓑ Ⓒ Ⓓ Ⓔ
23 / 4	#	**17**	Ⓐ Ⓑ Ⓒ Ⓓ Ⓔ
23 / 4	#	**18**	Ⓐ Ⓑ Ⓒ Ⓓ Ⓔ

Test / Section	#	Question	Answer
25 / 1	#	**14**	Ⓐ Ⓑ Ⓒ Ⓓ Ⓔ
25 / 1	#	**15**	Ⓐ Ⓑ Ⓒ Ⓓ Ⓔ
25 / 1	#	**16**	Ⓐ Ⓑ Ⓒ Ⓓ Ⓔ
25 / 1	#	**17**	Ⓐ Ⓑ Ⓒ Ⓓ Ⓔ
25 / 1	#	**18**	Ⓐ Ⓑ Ⓒ Ⓓ Ⓔ
25 / 1	#	**19**	Ⓐ Ⓑ Ⓒ Ⓓ Ⓔ
25 / 1	#	**20**	Ⓐ Ⓑ Ⓒ Ⓓ Ⓔ
25 / 1	#	**21**	Ⓐ Ⓑ Ⓒ Ⓓ Ⓔ
26 / 4	#	**1**	Ⓐ Ⓑ Ⓒ Ⓓ Ⓔ
26 / 4	#	**2**	Ⓐ Ⓑ Ⓒ Ⓓ Ⓔ
26 / 4	#	**3**	Ⓐ Ⓑ Ⓒ Ⓓ Ⓔ
26 / 4	#	**4**	Ⓐ Ⓑ Ⓒ Ⓓ Ⓔ
26 / 4	#	**5**	Ⓐ Ⓑ Ⓒ Ⓓ Ⓔ

Difficult

Test / Section	#	Question	Answer
20 / 2	#	**15**	Ⓐ Ⓑ Ⓒ Ⓓ Ⓔ
20 / 2	#	**16**	Ⓐ Ⓑ Ⓒ Ⓓ Ⓔ
20 / 2	#	**17**	Ⓐ Ⓑ Ⓒ Ⓓ Ⓔ
20 / 2	#	**18**	Ⓐ Ⓑ Ⓒ Ⓓ Ⓔ
20 / 2	#	**19**	Ⓐ Ⓑ Ⓒ Ⓓ Ⓔ
20 / 2	#	**20**	Ⓐ Ⓑ Ⓒ Ⓓ Ⓔ
20 / 2	#	**21**	Ⓐ Ⓑ Ⓒ Ⓓ Ⓔ
21 / 4	#	**22**	Ⓐ Ⓑ Ⓒ Ⓓ Ⓔ
21 / 4	#	**23**	Ⓐ Ⓑ Ⓒ Ⓓ Ⓔ
21 / 4	#	**24**	Ⓐ Ⓑ Ⓒ Ⓓ Ⓔ
21 / 4	#	**25**	Ⓐ Ⓑ Ⓒ Ⓓ Ⓔ
21 / 4	#	**26**	Ⓐ Ⓑ Ⓒ Ⓓ Ⓔ
21 / 4	#	**27**	Ⓐ Ⓑ Ⓒ Ⓓ Ⓔ

Test / Section	#	Question	Answer
23 / 4	#	**19**	Ⓐ Ⓑ Ⓒ Ⓓ Ⓔ
23 / 4	#	**20**	Ⓐ Ⓑ Ⓒ Ⓓ Ⓔ
23 / 4	#	**21**	Ⓐ Ⓑ Ⓒ Ⓓ Ⓔ
23 / 4	#	**22**	Ⓐ Ⓑ Ⓒ Ⓓ Ⓔ
23 / 4	#	**23**	Ⓐ Ⓑ Ⓒ Ⓓ Ⓔ
23 / 4	#	**24**	Ⓐ Ⓑ Ⓒ Ⓓ Ⓔ
23 / 4	#	**25**	Ⓐ Ⓑ Ⓒ Ⓓ Ⓔ
23 / 4	#	**26**	Ⓐ Ⓑ Ⓒ Ⓓ Ⓔ
26 / 4	#	**14**	Ⓐ Ⓑ Ⓒ Ⓓ Ⓔ
26 / 4	#	**15**	Ⓐ Ⓑ Ⓒ Ⓓ Ⓔ
26 / 4	#	**16**	Ⓐ Ⓑ Ⓒ Ⓓ Ⓔ
26 / 4	#	**17**	Ⓐ Ⓑ Ⓒ Ⓓ Ⓔ
26 / 4	#	**18**	Ⓐ Ⓑ Ⓒ Ⓓ Ⓔ
26 / 4	#	**19**	Ⓐ Ⓑ Ⓒ Ⓓ Ⓔ
26 / 4	#	**20**	Ⓐ Ⓑ Ⓒ Ⓓ Ⓔ
26 / 4	#	**21**	Ⓐ Ⓑ Ⓒ Ⓓ Ⓔ

Grueling

19 / 3	#	**15**	Ⓐ Ⓑ Ⓒ Ⓓ Ⓔ
19 / 3	#	**16**	Ⓐ Ⓑ Ⓒ Ⓓ Ⓔ
19 / 3	#	**17**	Ⓐ Ⓑ Ⓒ Ⓓ Ⓔ
19 / 3	#	**18**	Ⓐ Ⓑ Ⓒ Ⓓ Ⓔ
19 / 3	#	**19**	Ⓐ Ⓑ Ⓒ Ⓓ Ⓔ
19 / 3	#	**20**	Ⓐ Ⓑ Ⓒ Ⓓ Ⓔ
19 / 3	#	**21**	Ⓐ Ⓑ Ⓒ Ⓓ Ⓔ
19 / 3	#	**22**	Ⓐ Ⓑ Ⓒ Ⓓ Ⓔ
19 / 3	#	**23**	Ⓐ Ⓑ Ⓒ Ⓓ Ⓔ
19 / 3	#	**24**	Ⓐ Ⓑ Ⓒ Ⓓ Ⓔ
19 / 3	#	**25**	Ⓐ Ⓑ Ⓒ Ⓓ Ⓔ
19 / 3	#	**26**	Ⓐ Ⓑ Ⓒ Ⓓ Ⓔ
19 / 3	#	**27**	Ⓐ Ⓑ Ⓒ Ⓓ Ⓔ
28 / 4	#	**6**	Ⓐ Ⓑ Ⓒ Ⓓ Ⓔ
28 / 4	#	**7**	Ⓐ Ⓑ Ⓒ Ⓓ Ⓔ
28 / 4	#	**8**	Ⓐ Ⓑ Ⓒ Ⓓ Ⓔ
28 / 4	#	**9**	Ⓐ Ⓑ Ⓒ Ⓓ Ⓔ
28 / 4	#	**10**	Ⓐ Ⓑ Ⓒ Ⓓ Ⓔ
28 / 4	#	**11**	Ⓐ Ⓑ Ⓒ Ⓓ Ⓔ
28 / 4	#	**12**	Ⓐ Ⓑ Ⓒ Ⓓ Ⓔ
28 / 4	#	**13**	Ⓐ Ⓑ Ⓒ Ⓓ Ⓔ

*Science Problem Sets ~ Answers

Average

Test / Section	#	Question	Answer
20 / 2	#	**22**	D
20 / 2	#	**23**	E
20 / 2	#	**24**	E
20 / 2	#	**25**	B
20 / 2	#	**26**	E
21 / 4	#	**17**	D
21 / 4	#	**18**	B
21 / 4	#	**19**	A
21 / 4	#	**20**	B
21 / 4	#	**21**	C
23 / 4	#	**14**	D
23 / 4	#	**15**	A
23 / 4	#	**16**	E
23 / 4	#	**17**	C
23 / 4	#	**18**	D
25 / 1	#	**14**	C
25 / 1	#	**15**	A
25 / 1	#	**16**	A
25 / 1	#	**17**	E
25 / 1	#	**18**	E
25 / 1	#	**19**	C
25 / 1	#	**20**	B
25 / 1	#	**21**	C
26 / 4	#	**1**	E
26 / 4	#	**2**	A
26 / 4	#	**3**	A
26 / 4	#	**4**	E
26 / 4	#	**5**	B

Difficult

Test / Section	#	Question	Answer
20 / 2	#	**15**	B
20 / 2	#	**16**	A
20 / 2	#	**17**	B
20 / 2	#	**18**	A
20 / 2	#	**19**	E
20 / 2	#	**20**	D
20 / 2	#	**21**	B
21 / 4	#	**22**	C
21 / 4	#	**23**	B
21 / 4	#	**24**	B
21 / 4	#	**25**	A
21 / 4	#	**26**	A
21 / 4	#	**27**	B
23 / 4	#	**19**	C
23 / 4	#	**20**	E
23 / 4	#	**21**	C
23 / 4	#	**22**	D
23 / 4	#	**23**	B
23 / 4	#	**24**	C
23 / 4	#	**25**	A
23 / 4	#	**26**	B
26 / 4	#	**14**	D
26 / 4	#	**15**	E
26 / 4	#	**16**	A
26 / 4	#	**17**	A
26 / 4	#	**18**	E
26 / 4	#	**19**	E
26 / 4	#	**20**	C
26 / 4	#	**21**	D

Grueling

19 / 3	#	**15**	C
19 / 3	#	**16**	E
19 / 3	#	**17**	A
19 / 3	#	**18**	E
19 / 3	#	**19**	D
19 / 3	#	**20**	B
19 / 3	#	**21**	B
19 / 3	#	**22**	A
19 / 3	#	**23**	D
19 / 3	#	**24**	C
19 / 3	#	**25**	B
19 / 3	#	**26**	A
19 / 3	#	**27**	C
28 / 4	#	**6**	D
28 / 4	#	**7**	E
28 / 4	#	**8**	D
28 / 4	#	**9**	D
28 / 4	#	**10**	A
28 / 4	#	**11**	C
28 / 4	#	**12**	C
28 / 4	#	**13**	C

Games

Introduction

The Games section, also called the Analytical Reasoning section by those who like big words, makes up 23% of your total LSAT score. With practice, you can dramatically improve your score on this section. Although the skills the section tests are very foreign at first, they can be acquired more easily than those on the other two sections on the test.

4 Games, 23 Questions

The LSAT has a single scored Games section, composed of four scenarios or "games." Each game is followed by a set of 5 to 8 questions. The average games section has 23 questions, but sometimes a section will have 22 or 24 questions. Like all the sections on the LSAT, you have 35 minutes to complete the Games section. Therefore, if you complete all four games, you have an average of 8.5 minutes per game. However, how long each game will take you varies due to the length (number of questions) and difficulty of that particular game. For most students, the easiest games take 5-7 minutes, while the harder ones take 9-11 minutes.

Proven Answers

Games questions have a single correct answer, which can be proven using the logic of the setup, the information given to you by the game. In this way, Games questions are like math questions: only one answer will work, and there is no ambiguity on why that answer is correct. The concrete nature of the questions can make them more satisfying to answer than Reading Comprehension or Logical Reasoning questions, which tend to have less clear cut answers. With Games, you know conclusively when you have the right answer.

Variables, Inferences and Diagrams

The Games section features concepts that you have probably not dealt with before. This section tests your ability to understand a set of relationships between variables, the players in the game. For instance, in a game that asks you to order runners in the lanes on a track, the runners are the variables. Inferences are new, valid information that is derived from the given relationships between the variables. You will need to draw inferences in almost every game you face. The Games section is also very visual. Diagrams are pictures that represent the relationships between variables. Diagrams help you understand the game and that helps you draw inferences. Learning how to effectively draw diagrams is a big part of what you will learn in this guide.

Official Directions

Become familiar with the directions for the section by reading them twice:

> Each group of questions in this section is based on a set of conditions. In answering some of the questions, it ***may be useful*** to draw a rough diagram. Choose the response that most accurately and completely answers each question and blacken the corresponding space on your answer sheet.

These directions are misleading. Diagrams, drawings that represent information in the game in a visual form, are **extremely** important. You should draw a few diagrams when answering every game. We will talk about the most effective diagrams to draw for different situations at length.

Game Structure

Each game has three basic parts: the setup, the rules and the questions. This snapshot of the upper left hand corner of a game shows them:

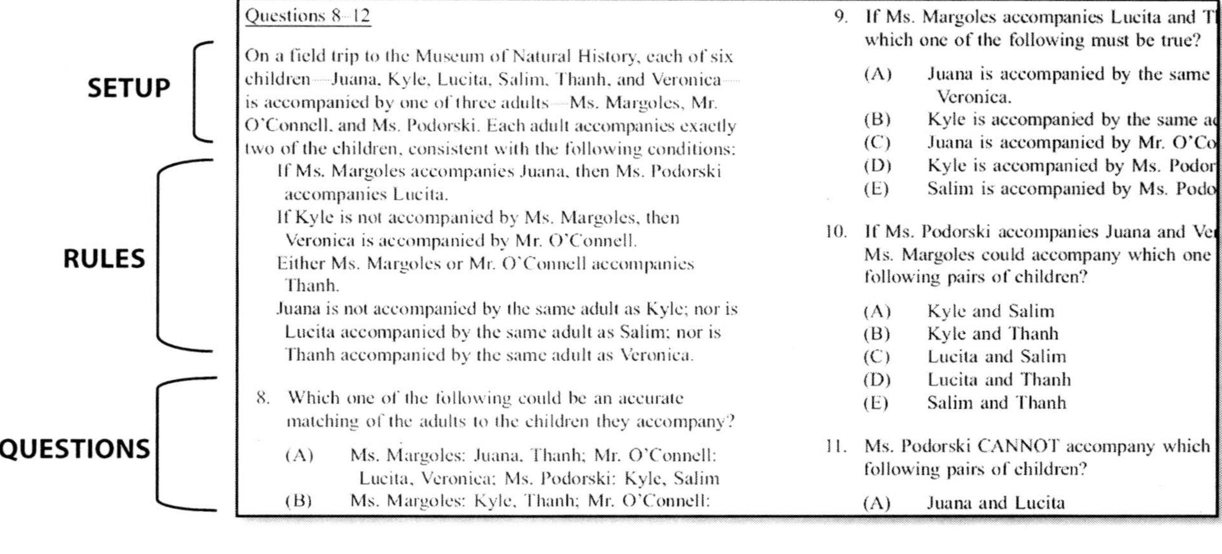

Questions 8–12

On a field trip to the Museum of Natural History, each of six children—Juana, Kyle, Lucita, Salim, Thanh, and Veronica—is accompanied by one of three adults—Ms. Margoles, Mr. O'Connell, and Ms. Podorski. Each adult accompanies exactly two of the children, consistent with the following conditions:

If Ms. Margoles accompanies Juana, then Ms. Podorski accompanies Lucita.
If Kyle is not accompanied by Ms. Margoles, then Veronica is accompanied by Mr. O'Connell.
Either Ms. Margoles or Mr. O'Connell accompanies Thanh.
Juana is not accompanied by the same adult as Kyle; nor is Lucita accompanied by the same adult as Salim; nor is Thanh accompanied by the same adult as Veronica.

8. Which one of the following could be an accurate matching of the adults to the children they accompany?
   (A) Ms. Margoles: Juana, Thanh; Mr. O'Connell: Lucita, Veronica; Ms. Podorski: Kyle, Salim
   (B) Ms. Margoles: Kyle, Thanh; Mr. O'Connell:

9. If Ms. Margoles accompanies Lucita and T which one of the following must be true?
   (A) Juana is accompanied by the same Veronica.
   (B) Kyle is accompanied by the same a
   (C) Juana is accompanied by Mr. O'Co
   (D) Kyle is accompanied by Ms. Podor
   (E) Salim is accompanied by Ms. Podo

10. If Ms. Podorski accompanies Juana and Ve Ms. Margoles could accompany which one following pairs of children?
   (A) Kyle and Salim
   (B) Kyle and Thanh
   (C) Lucita and Salim
   (D) Lucita and Thanh
   (E) Salim and Thanh

11. Ms. Podorski CANNOT accompany which following pairs of children?
   (A) Juana and Lucita

The setup introduces the variables involved in the game. The variables are the moving pieces: people, things, events, places, etc. The variables are involved in some kind of exercise or activity: lining up to run a race, sorting into boats, being selected for teams, etc. The setup tells you how the game works, how the variables will be involved in the activity. The setup may give specific information that helps you in working through the game, but it primarily provides the foundation for understanding what the variables will be doing. Here is an example setup:

> Four runners - Jason, Megan, Ryan and Crystal – are running a race at a high school track meet. There are four lanes on the track, numbered 1 through 4. Each runner has his or her own lane.

The runners - Jason, Megan, Ryan and Crystal – are the variables. The action is **ordering** the runners on the track, so naturally, the Questions test your understanding of how the runners can be ordered on the track.

We have a special name for the role played by the track in this setup: the base. The variables need something stable to interact with, and that is the base. Here, the track is the base because we are sorting the runners onto the lanes of the track. The lanes are set; they have a specific order and placement, 1 through 4. What is unknown is how the runners will be ordered within those lanes. That is the key characteristic of the base: variables can interact with it in many ways. For most games, it will be easy to determine the base and this is one of the first steps you take as you read the setup.

The Rules

After the setup, is the rules, a group of statements that dictate how the variables can interact with one another and the base. The rules add structure to the setup. For instance, after reading the setup above, we know only that we are lining up the runners on the track. From that alone, we could put them in any order: Jason could be first or last, etc. The rules give us specific restrictions and guidance on how we can sequence the runners.

Example set of rules:

> Jason cannot be in lane 4.
> If Ryan is in lane 2, then Crystal is in lane 4.
> Megan is in lane 3.

The rules apply to all questions in the game, unless a specific question suspends a rule for that question alone. Questions featuring rule suspensions will only appear towards the end of a game, and are rare. A vast majority of the time, every rule is in play for the entire game.

With the rules in place, how the runners can be ordered is confined to fewer scenarios. For instance, Megan is always going to be in lane 3. We can never put Jason in lane 4. That is a specific restriction on how that variable can interact with a part of the base. Understanding the rules, their implications, and how they relate to one another is crucial for working the questions.

The Questions

The rules are followed by five to eight questions. <u>The questions</u> test your understanding of how the game works: what the setup and rules dictate as possible and the relationships between the variables and the base. The questions are where you score the points in the section, but they are answered using the setup and rules. Example question:

> 1. If Ryan is in lane 2, which of the following cannot be true?

This question gives new information about the game that is applicable **for that question alone**. The fact that Ryan is in lane 3. We call information given in a question a <u>local rule</u>. These pieces of new information only apply to the question at hand. Questions that contain local rules are called <u>local questions</u>.

To answer this question, we need to reference the rules. Rule 2 is quite applicable: when R is in 2, then C must be in 4. Therefore, a correct answer to this question could be this choice:

> (A) C is in lane 3

The statement above cannot be true because when R is in 2, C is in 4, not in 3. Therefore, this choice correctly answers the question; it tells us what cannot be true. More on the different question type to come.

The Initial Work is Crucial

A great deal of preparation goes into understanding and diagramming the setup and rules. That preparation allows you to effectively answer the questions. Working carefully with the setup and rules makes the questions doable. Otherwise they would be difficult and time consuming.

Think of each game as a public speech. The preparation time writing and editing the speech and rehearsing it in front of the mirror is what makes it successful, yet people only hear the message of the speech when it is given. In the same way, you get no credit for the work you do on a game **before** you answer the questions, but it is that work that will help you succeed on the questions for which you get the credit.

Approaching a Game

When you begin a game, first read through the setup carefully to identify the type of game and the action involved with the variables. There are a limited number of game types and you will soon know them all. The game type dictates how to approach and diagram the game.

Read the entire setup before writing anything (except for the variable list which we will discuss momentarily). Next, read the rules. Understanding the rules demands more attention because they are more complicated than the setup. Take your time working the rules. We recommend that you diagram many rules **as you read them** to help you see their concepts visually. Certain rules are hard to understand without a diagram. Of course, not every rule should be diagrammed right away. Here is the process for reading the rules:

1) Read Carefully

Read slowly enough to understand the rules and to fix many of them in your memory. The more familiar you are with them, the easier it will be to diagram them. You will also refer back to the rule diagrams less when you answer the questions, which saves time and effort. Pause after reading each rule and check that you understood it.

Reading the rules **too quickly** can cost you time later if you must refer back to the rules too much. It can also hinder your ability to effectively diagram and draw inferences from the rules. However, you do not have time to memorize all of them, so do not read *too* slowly. Experience will help you find a good balance there.

2) Find Interactions Between Rules

Keep an eye out for how the rules interact with and affect one another. This allows you to draw inferences, new information from the interaction between two or more rules. Inferences are **required** to solve almost every game.

3) Analyze Importance

As you read, analyze which rules are the most important. Some rules give more structure to a game than others; they contain more limits on how the variables can interact. These rules often deal with two or more variables. Note the rules that seem the most important as those will be the crucial rules to understand as you work the game.

Diagramming

Your first reading of the setup and rules will tell you how to diagram the game as a whole, how to represent the base and variables in a visual way that expresses a lot of information. Diagrams are information stored in a picture. Creating good diagrams allows you to understand the game more fully and to draw connections between its different parts. In a diagram, everything is laid out in a logical way. You can just *see* the information instead of trying to mentally translate what you are reading.

You are not given scratch paper for the LSAT, so all your diagramming must be done on the page that holds the game. Your diagrams must convey a great deal of information in a small amount of space. Much attention will be given to drawing effective, condensed diagrams. Write **neatly** when diagramming; you need to be able to easily read what you write.

Understanding the best way to diagram and approach each game type allows you to work games quickly. Games are all about speed; beating the clock is one of your main priorities on the games section. So, master diagramming and your Games section score will benefit greatly.

Variable List

After reading the variables' names in the setup, write a list of all the variables in the empty space at the top of the page, above the setup. Each variable should be represented in an abbreviated form, with a single letter. Use the first letter of the variable's name as its symbol. For instance, "Ryan" is abbreviated with an "R." Using a single letter for each variable is space efficient. The LSAT-writers are kind enough to never repeat the first letter of the variables; you will not have two A's in a single game.

Capitalize the letter for each variable because capitals are easier to read than lowercase letters. Your variable list will give you a feel for all the players in the game, which can be very helpful. Many inferences in games come from asking "who is left?" and "where do they go?" Your variable list will help you answer those questions.

After you work the rules, **circle** in your variable list any variable that is not mentioned in a rule. These variables are more flexible than the others, as the rules do not dictate where they are placed. These leftovers are often placed after the other variables are on the base. Or, they are placed in slots where no other variable can go.

Main Diagram

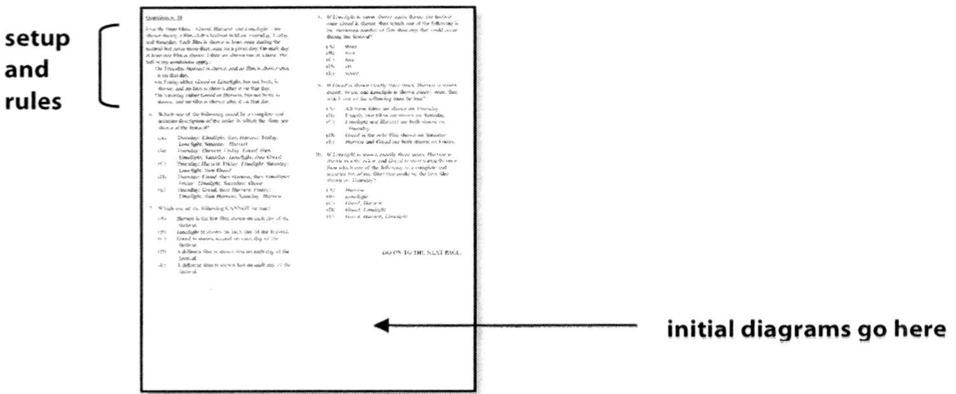

Draw your initial diagrams, diagrams for the setup and rules, at the bottom of the page, where there is blank space after the final question in each column:

The most important of your initial diagrams is your main diagram (or MD). Your MD represents the entire game and incorporates much of the information from the rules. You will also create individual rule diagrams. How you diagram rules is based on the layout of your MD. This is because the rule diagrams are often incorporated, at least mentally, into the MD. Your main diagram pulls all the details of the setup and rules into one drawing and you will refer to it throughout the game. It is important that you create an effective MD.

You will also draw diagrams for individual questions, and these are called mini diagrams. Mini diagrams are created as needed as you work through the questions and are placed next to the question itself. Mini diagrams are distinct from the initial diagramming. Your initial diagrams are based only on the setup and rules and contain no information from the questions. You should not even look at the questions before creating your initial diagrams.

Rule Diagrams

Rule diagrams describe the information in each rule visually. These are a separate group of diagrams written **above** your MD at the bottom of the page. Here is an example rule:

> Crystal is directly after Megan.

And here is the rule diagram we would draw for it:

MC

Do not worry about understanding this diagram; just keep in mind that how you diagram the rules must fit with your MD and its representation of the game.

Any inferences from the setup and rules will be written among your rule diagrams or built into the MD. Inferences are essentially new rules that you have uncovered.

Example Diagrams

Here are the setup and rules from the game discussed earlier:

> Four runners - Jason, Megan, Ryan and Crystal – are running a race at a high school track meet. There are four lanes on the track, numbered 1 through 4. Each runner has his or her own lane.
>
> Jason cannot be in lane 4.
> If Ryan is in lane 2, then Crystal is in lane 4. ⟶ Rules
> Megan is in lane 3.

Here are the diagrams we would draw:

J M R C ⟶ **variable list (written above the setup)**

R2 → C4 ⟶ **rule diagram for rule 2** (Rules 1 and 3 are represented in the Md)

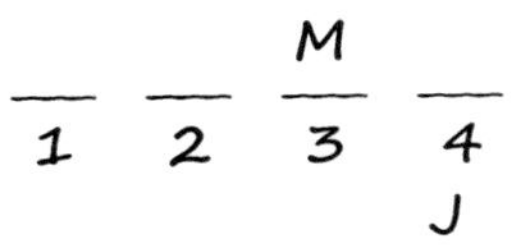

```
         M
__  __  __  __
1   2   3   4
            J
```
⟶ **main diagram**

How to effectively create the MD and the rule diagrams will be discussed in much more detail shortly.

Possibility Placement

In your MD, you can distinguish between where variables can and cannot be placed by using the numbers or symbols (usually lines or slots) of the base as the dividing line. The variables placed **below** the slots are not possibilities. Variables placed **above** the numbers are possibilities. This concept is best explained with another example game:

> Four runners - William, Tiffany, Crystal and Michelle – are running a race at a high school track meet. There are four lanes on the track, numbered 1 through 4 and each runner has his or her own lane.
>
> William is in lane 3 or 4.
>
> Crystal cannot be in lane 1.

main diagram

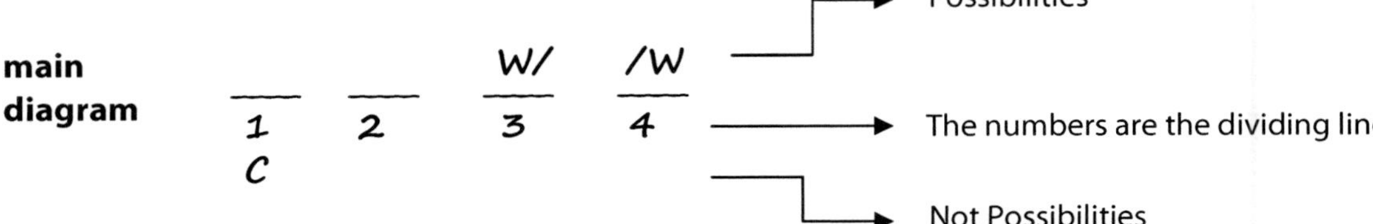

We see from the /Ws that William can be placed in lanes 3 or 4. These are the two possible lanes where he can go. Likewise, the MD tells us that Crystal **cannot** be in lane 1, because her variable abbreviation, *C*, is beneath lane 1.

That sequencing game was represented horizontally, but some sequencing games are best represented vertically. In a MD for one of these games, everything to the **left** of the numbers is not possible, while everything to the **right** of the numbers is a possibility.

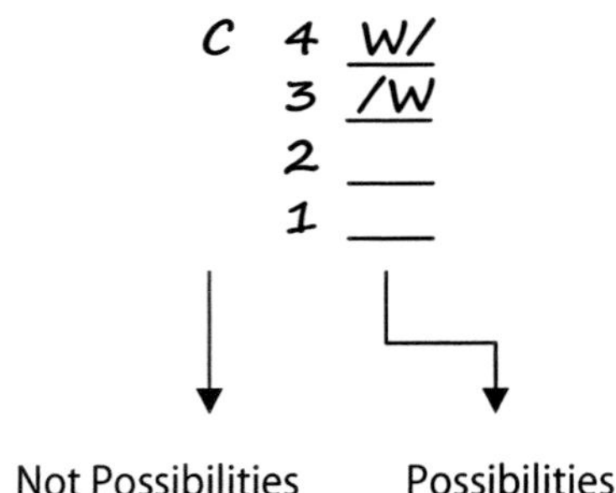

The easy way to remember where the possibilities are is that they are on the side of the MD with the slots, the lines that can hold variables. In this game, each lane has a slot. The possible slots where W can be are placed, lanes 3 and 4, are shown.

Rules & The Main Diagram

How well you diagram the rules and build their information into your MD determines to a large extent how well you do on the game. The setup only gets you started on the game; the rules provide the details. Your rule diagrams help you find inferences in the rules, a crucial step on any game. There are two different ways to diagram a rule:

1. Diagram the rule itself by creating a rule diagram.
2. Build the rule or its implications into the MD.

Rules vary in how they should be diagrammed. Some rules need both their own diagram and to be built into the MD. Other rules lend themselves to representation in only one of those ways. The following example rules illustrate these concepts:

> Michelle comes before Crystal.

You should diagram this rule and build its implications into the MD. Rule diagram:

M · C

Next, we build the implications of the rule into the MD:

```
___  ___  ___  ___
 1    2    3    4
 C              M
```

Michelle cannot be in lane 4 because that would leave no room for Crystal to come **after** Michelle. We show this by placing an M **under** lane 4. We call the fact that Michelle cannot be in lane 4 a not rule. Likewise, C cannot be in lane 1, because Michelle must come before her. So, we place C under lane 1, to show that is not a possibility.

Other rules should be diagrammed but cannot be built into the MD:

> If Tiffany is in lane 1, then Brian is not in lane 2.

Rule Diagram:

T1 → -B2

You will learn how to diagram conditional rules like this one later. The important point here is that there is no way to build this rule or any of its implications into the MD. We are told only what happens *if* Tiffany is in lane 1, and we do not know that she is in lane 1 from this rule alone. Therefore, whether Brian is not in lane 2 is up in the air.

The third type of rule is **fully** represented in the MD, and therefore does not need a rule diagram:

> Michelle is in lane 3 or 4.

We build this possibility right into the MD:

```
          M/   /M
___  ___  ___  ___
 1    2    3    4
```

There is no need to diagram this rule separately: all its information is evidence in the MD.

Mini Diagrams

Leave your MD alone once you move to the questions. That way, it will stand as a clean guide to the game, and will not be interfered with by local rules that only apply to one question. When you need to do extra diagramming for a question draw a mini diagram next to a question. Your mini diagrams do not need to have all the details of the MD, they only need to contain the information relevant to that question. And, you do not need to write the numbers on the base. Skipping that step can save time.

Example game setup from earlier:

> Four runners - Jason, Megan, Ryan and Crystal – are running a race at a high school track meet. There are four lanes on the track, numbered 1 through 4. Each runner has his or her own lane.
>
> Jason cannot be in lane 4.
>
> If Ryan is in lane 2, then Crystal is in lane 4.
>
> Megan is in lane 3.

Here is a local question:

1. If Ryan is in lane 2, which of the following cannot be true?

In our mini diagram next to the question, we place R in lane 2 and M in lane 3:

__ R M __

We have skipped writing out the numbers beneath the slots. Slots are quicker to draw and it is easy to identify their number at a glance. Because both lanes 2 and 3 are filled, and rule 1 states that J cannot be in 4, (we see this by glancing at our MD), J must be placed in lane 1:

J R M __

The only runner left, Crystal, must be in lane 4 because there are no other open lanes.

Notice that the mini diagram is simple, only a representation of the base. There is no need to copy not rules or possibilities into your mini diagrams. You can glance down at your MD at the bottom of the page for that information.

Mini diagrams next to individual questions are valuable beyond the question at hand. They can help you on other questions that feature some of the same aspects of the game because a mini diagram expands your knowledge of the possibilities of the game. Therefore, **do not erase** your mini diagrams; leave them for future use.

Again, it might be tempting to just do all work on your MD, but using mini diagrams is the most effective way to work the games.

The Questions

Each question on the games section is worth the same amount, so do not get stuck on one. If you are having a lot of difficulty or taking an inordinate amount of time, move on to the next. Often, answering later questions in the section will help you with earlier, perhaps more difficult, ones. When we cover the different question types, you will learn about a few question types that you may want to always skip and leave for the end of the game.

Global vs Local Questions

The global/local distinction refers to where the information comes from to answer the question. Global questions require you to draw your information **only** from the setup and rules. They test your knowledge of the game without giving you any new information. Example global question:

> Which of the following lists all the runners that can run in lane 3?

For question 1, we use our understanding, MD and rule diagrams to tackle the question.

As mentioned earlier, local questions provide new information about the game called a local rule. Local rules are only applicable for the question at hand. The words "if," "when," and "suppose" are often used to introduce these rules. Example local question:

> If Jason is in lane 2, which of the following must be false?

To answer this question effectively, look for **inferences** based on the local rule. Think about the local information in terms of what you already know about the game. A mini diagram is often helpful in visualizing the impact of the local rule. A good visual understanding often leads to inferences.

Question Types

There are many different types of questions on the Games section; we will discuss these in detail after introducing Sequencing games. Once you know a bit about that game category, we can use it to explain various question types that apply to all game categories.

Early Recommendations

Here are some tips to keep in mind as you work through the rest of this guide:

Focus on what must be **true** and what must be **false** as you do the initial work in the game: reading the setup and rules, creating the MD, and diagramming the rules. Information about what has to be true and what cannot be true is generally more useful than what **can** be true. This advice will make more sense after you have worked through several games. One exception to this idea is figuring out how the most important rules impact the game. Drawing a few hypothetical diagrams next to your MD to explore how these rules work can be quite useful.

Finally, do your best to enjoy the games. They become much easier with practice.

*Introduction Review

- There are four games in each section and how long each game will take varies based on the difficulty of the game.
- The correct answers to Games questions are unambiguous.
    - Each is proven by the information in the game.
- Diagrams are drawings that represent information in a visual format.
    - Creating effective diagrams is crucial on this section.

Game Structure

- The setup introduces the variables involved in the game and tells you generally how the game works.
- The variables are the moving pieces of the game that are involved in an exercise or activity.
    - Example: runners at a track race.
- The base is the stable foundation that the variables interact with in various ways.
    - Example: the track that runners are lined up on.
- The rules tell you how the variables can interact with one another and the base.
    - The rules apply to all questions in the game unless a question specifically suspends a rule.
- The questions test your understanding of how the game works.
    - Questions sometimes introduce a new rule relevant only to that question called a local rule.

Approaching a Game

- Read the setup carefully and identify the game type.
    - Do not write anything during this stage.
- Read the rules and diagram those that are easy to diagram.
    - Try to fix many of the rules in your memory.
    - As you are reading and after you finish reading the rules, find inferences
        - Inferences are connections between the rules.
    - Analyze the importance of the rules.
        - The most important rules tend to involve several variables.

Diagramming

- Diagrams express a lot of information in a visual way and help you to understand a game.
- Write neatly because there is not much extra space on the page that holds each game.
- Variable list – a list of all the variables given in the setup.
- Abbreviate the names of variables with their first letter.
    - Use capital letters as they are easy to read.
- After you work the rules, circle any leftovers, variables not mentioned by any rules.
- Main diagram (or MD) – a drawing that represents the entire game and holds lots of info from the rules.
    - Your rule diagrams are based on the layout of your MD.
    - Draw your MD at the bottom of the page.
    - Once your MD is created, do not modify it.
        - Use mini diagrams next to a question to deal with local rules and to try out situations.
    - Possibility placements indicate where variables can be placed in the MD.
    - On games with a horizontal layout, variables placed above the slots are possibilities.
        - Those placed below the slots are not possibilities, otherwise known as not rules.
    - On vertical games, variables to the right of the slots are possibilities, and those to the left are not.
    - Use a slash (/) to signify "or."
        - To show two possible placements for a variable, place it in each possible slot on the MD with a slash after it.
- A rule diagram shows a rule visually.
    - Write your rule diagrams at the bottom of the page, above your MD.
    - Inferences are valid new rules that are unstated.
        - Write them next to or within your rule diagrams.
    - Some rules can be completely built into the MD. Others need to be represented in the MD and separately among the rule diagrams.
- Mini diagrams
    - Mini diagrams help you see the implications of local rules or try out scenarios in the game.
    - Create mini diagrams next to the question.
    - Draw in only enough detail to understand the scenario.
        - There is no need to write numbers under the slots, etc.
    - Do not erase your mini diagrams, as they can be helpful on future questions.

Introduction to the Questions

- Do not get stuck on a question that is taking too long.
- Global vs Local is a key distinction in the question type.
    - Global questions test your knowledge of the game without giving you any new information.
    - Local questions provide new information about the game with a local rule.
        - Always look for inferences based on the local rule before working the choices on this question type.

Early Recommendations

- Focus on what must be true and what must be false as you work through a game.
- Enjoy the games. They are entertaining and fun once you get comfortable with them.

Sequencing Games

We will now cover specific types of games, starting with Sequencing games. In a Sequencing game, you are asked to **order** the variables onto a linear base. The base is made up of slots in a line that the variables can be placed in. In a Sequencing game that involves ordering runners into six lanes on a track, the six lanes are the base. Because you are sequencing the variables, the rules will give you information on their ordering (Tom is in a lane before Sally) and also information on the specific **slots** of the base (Bill cannot be in lane 3).

The base of a sequencing game can be either horizontal, like the days of the week, or vertical, like the floors of a building. Most games give you obvious direction on which orientation you should lay out the variables, but sometimes you can use your discretion. You want everything to visually make sense in your MD, so whatever comes to mind first for the layout of the base is probably the orientation you should use.

Rules in Sequencing Games

In order to conquer Sequencing games, you must be comfortable diagramming and drawing inferences from the rules. There are many types of rules and a great deal of subtlety in how you should think about and diagram them.

Placement Rules

The simplest rules will tell you exactly where a variable is in the base:

Jim is in lane 1.

Build these rules directly into your MD:

```
 J
___ ___ ___ ___
 1   2   3   4
```

You should have a good idea on how to draw your MD after reading the setup. That means that when you read a rule that should be built directly into the MD, you can create the MD then and there and build the rule in. That is what we have done above.

Not Rules

Some placement rules will tell you where a variable cannot be placed. We will call these not rules. To build a not rule into the MD, place the variables abbreviation **below** the slot where that variable cannot be placed. Example:

Sarah cannot be in lane 2 on the track.

Show this on the MD:

```
___ ___ ___ ___
 1   2   3   4
     S
```

S cannot go in the slot for the second lane. Always build not rules directly into MD; there no need to diagram them separately.

Links

Links are a type of rule that tells you how two or more variables relate to each other. They crop up in many game types. In Sequencing games, a link is two or more variables that have a specific **spatial connection**. For instance, a rule could tell you which variable is ordered before another variable, or how many spaces there are between two variables.

The easiest way to diagram links in Sequencing games is to draw the symbols for the variables in the specific spatial relationship they have, as that relationship fits the MD. We will illustrate this concept with many examples:

Simple Links

The most basic links are those rules which tell you that one variable is sequenced before or after another variable. Example:

John is in the lane directly before Mark's lane on the track.

To diagram this rule, place the abbreviation/symbol for John (*J*) directly in front of the one for Mark (*M*):

JM

"Before" means in a lower lane number (1 is before 2). It is easiest to draw your MDs with the first lane on the left side and the numbers **ascending** to the right. As mentioned earlier, how you represent your rules is based on how you draw your MD.

With that rule diagram drawn, you can picture placing this link on the MD in three different ways:

J	M		
1	2	3	4

or

	J	M	
1	2	3	4

or

		J	M
1	2	3	4

That is the core idea of diagramming a rule - helping your visualize how it can interact with the MD.

Another example simple link:

Phil is in the lane after Jessica's lane.

Diagram:

JP

"After" refers to a higher ranked lane, one further to the right. Our diagram illustrates that.

Links with Spaces

Many links tell you which of two variables comes first and that there are spaces between the variables. There are two ways links with spaces are described. The first is when the rule tells you the number of spaces between the two variables and which variable is first:

Claire comes before Burch and there is one lane between them.

Being told the number of spaces, this is fairly simple to diagram:

C _ B

Another example:

Michael comes after Ben and there are two spaces separating them.

B _ _ M

The second way that links with spaces are described involves the rule stating one variable's location in relation to the other variable. Example:

Bill is four lanes ahead of Jane.

With this description, you have to do a little translating. Start by figuring out which variable is first. "Ahead" or "before" indicates the first variable. "After" or "behind" indicates the later variable. Because we read left to right, it makes sense to think that "ahead" and "before" mean to the left of and "after" and "behind" mean to the right of.

The next translating step is to take the number gap given (here four lanes) and subtract one. This tells you how many **empty spaces** to put in between the two variables. Example:

Bill is four lanes ahead of Jane.

Bill comes first because he is "ahead" of Jane. If he is four lanes ahead, then there are three lanes in between these two variables (4 -1 = 3). Diagram:

B _ _ _ J

Another example of a link with spaces described in this way:

Michael is two lanes behind Heather.

Michael is the later variable because he is "behind" Heather. There is one empty lane between the two (2 – 1 = 1). Diagram:

H_M

No Ordering Information

Sometimes when you are dealing with a link with spaces, you are not told the ordering of the variables (which of them comes first); you are only told the number of spaces between them. We have a special symbol to use in these situations that means "or." This is that symbol: /. So,

S/Y

means either Sam **or** Yolanda. We can use the or symbol to diagram links with spaces where we do not know the ordering of the variables. Example Rule:

There are two lanes separating Sam and Yolanda.

Diagram:

S/Y _ _ S/Y

This diagram is a smart way to represent the rule. An alternative is to draw this diagram:

S _ _ Y / Y _ _ S

This one is clear, but it takes up a lot of space. We recommend the condensed diagram.

Adjacency Links

An adjacency link occurs when a rule tells you that two variables are **next to each other** without telling you which one comes first. Use the / for this situation.

Joshua and Tiffany are next to each other on the track.

Diagram:

JT/TJ

Joshua and Tiffany are adjacent; they are next to each other and either can come first.

You can also diagram Adjacency links like this:

The circle indicates the adjacency. This diagram takes up less space; if you like it better, use it.

Adjacency links do not have readily identifiable inferences for the MD, unless they interact with other rules. For instance, if we know that Joshua and Tiffany are adjacent and we are told that Joshua is in lane 2, then Tiffany must be in lane 1 or lane 3. We can diagram that in the MD:

```
/T   J   /T
__   __  __   __
1    2   3    4
```

Tiffany can only be in lanes 1 or 3. She cannot be in lane 4, but we do not need to indicate that on the diagram, because it is implied by the two possibilities in 1 and 3.

Variables that are Not Adjacent

Sometimes a rule states that two variables are **not next** to one another. This is called a not link, because it tells you a way that two variables are not related spatially.

Richard and Kelly are never in adjacent lanes.

Simply write a negative sign (-) before the normal diagram for an Adjacency link:

- RK / KR

or

It can be challenging to build this type of rule into the MD. That is only possible when the rule interacts with other information. Links tend to give you more information than not links.

Link Representation in Vertical Games

The orientation of the Sequencing game (horizontal or vertical) changes how you represent links. A vast majority of the time, you will work games that are best diagrammed horizontally. In those games, placing the letter abbreviation for two variables next to one another indicates that those two will be adjacent: PT. This is what you have just learned.

However, in a game that is represented with a vertical MD, to show a link like that, the variables would be aligned vertically. If P comes immediately before T, then we would diagram that link like this:

```
T
P
```

We could stick the above link right into this MD:

```
4 __
3 __
2 __
1 __
```

Just by looking at the vertical link representation, we can see not rules that derive from it. Assuming that all variables must be given a slot, P cannot be in 4, because that would push T off the MD. For the same reason, T cannot be in 1, because that would push P off the top of the MD.

We can diagram those not rules this way in the MD:

```
P  4 __
   3 __
   2 __
T  1 __
```

On the other hand, if we are working on a game that is represented **horizontally**, this diagram:

```
T
P
```

would mean that both P and T go in the same slot, for instance, slot 1:

```
 P
 T
___ ___ ___ ___
 1   2   3   4
```

In a vertical game, we could show that two variables are in the **same** slot by putting them adjacent to each other:

```
SY
```

And we could then know that they could go in the MD, like so:

```
4 SY
3 __
2 __
1 __
```

As you practice the games, you will become more comfortable representing links and other rules in a way that matches how the MD works.

Relative Links

You will often be told information about the ordering of two or more variables that is not **exact.** This relative information will tell you only which variable comes first; it will not tell their exact spatial relationship. For instance, look at this rule:

> Bill is interviewed before Ted.

You cannot represent this with the diagrams you have already learned for links. For relative links, you should use a dot (•).

The dot indicates that the ordering is relative, that you do not know how far apart the two variables are. We can diagram this rule in that way:

```
B · T
```

We place the B for Bill before the T, because our to be interviewed first, B must be to the left of T. With the diagram above, it could be the case that Bill and Ted are **adjacent** or they could be separated by three slots. We only know that Bill comes first out of these two variables.

We can derive new not rules from this relative link between B and T. We know that B cannot be last, because then there would be no slot for T to go into. Along the same lines, T cannot come first, because that would leave no room for B to come before it:

1	2	3	4
T			B

You will often face rules that tell you the relative ordering of several variables. Example rule:

> Jim comes before Valerie but after Xavier.

We use this diagram:

X · J · V

We can start writing with J and then put V after him. Then, we know that J comes after X, so we put X to the left of J. Here are the inferences we can derive from this rule:

1	2	3	4
V	V	X	X
J			J

Because X and J both come before V, we know that V cannot be in slot 1 or slot 2. Same thing with X: he cannot be in slots 3 or 4 because J and V have to come after him. Three variables in a relative link will always create six <u>not inferences (not rules that are inferred, not directly stated in the rules)</u>.

Layered Links

Sometimes, you will be told a relative relationship between variables that requires using **layers** to diagram the rule effectively:

> Agatha comes before Caroline and Karden.

The rule does not specify when (how many slots) Agatha comes before Caroline or Karden, so this is a relative link. This is also a <u>layered link</u>, because we do not know which one of Caroline and Karden comes first. We only know that Agatha comes before both of them. We could diagram the rule by splitting it into two links:

A · C
A · K

But that is not as efficient as this representation of a Layered link:

A < C
    K

This diagram tells us that Agatha comes before Caroline and Karden, and we do not know which of Caroline and Karden comes first after her. The slanted lines branching off of Agatha tell us that Karden and Caroline are each on their own **layer**. Think of a slanted line as a dot (·) that tells you that the variable it leads to is a distinct layer. The slanted line indicates a relative link; we do not know exactly when Caroline comes after Agatha.

Here are the Inferences we can draw from this layered links diagram:

1	2	3	4
C		A	A
K			

Agatha cannot be third or fourth because Caroline and Karden must come after her. Likewise, neither Caroline or Karden can come first, because Agatha must come before *both* of them. Either Caroline or Karden could be second.

A layered representation is an efficient way to represent both links (A · C and A · K) at once, partly because it takes up less space on the page and space is a premium on the pages of the Games section. More importantly, this layered diagram allows us to incorporate information from other rules. For instance, if we are told

John is after Caroline.

Diagrammed:

C · J

We can build that information directly into the diagram that includes Agatha, Caroline and Karden:

```
     C · J
A &lt;
     K
```

From the diagram above, we see that A must come before C, K **and J**. These are the three variables after the relative link symbol following A. The diagram gives us that information easily in a visual format, and that is what is so powerful about diagrams.

Notice that we use the normal relative link symbol (the dot) in between C and J. We do this because they are on the same layer. You can think of the diagram above as containing two **chains**:

A · C · J
A · K

The slanted lines off of A that lead to C and K lead you along each chain.

You might face a layered link with three variables:

Darrel comes before Ethan, Thomas and Lexi.

We know only that Darrel is before these three; we do not know the order among Ethan, Thomas and Lexi. So, they each get their own layer in the diagram:

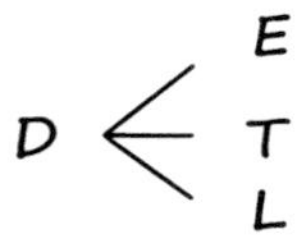

```
     E
D <  T
     L
```

Combining Different Types of Links

A Normal link can easily be combined with a Relative link. Take a look at this rule:

Christine comes immediately after Peter and sometime before Whitney.

The first part is a normal, absolute link: Christine comes immediately after Peter. The second part is a relative link, Christine comes **sometime** before Whitney. This diagram combines both the links:

PC · W

Here are the not rule inferences we can derive from this rule Diagram:

1	2	3	4
W	W	P	P
C			C

Whitney cannot be placed earlier than slot 3, because both Peter and Christine must come **after** her. Christine cannot be in slot 1, because Peter must come before her. Nor can Christine be fourth because Whitney must come **after** her. Finally, Peter cannot be in slot 3 or 4 because both Christine and Whitney are after him.

Variable Possibilities

You may have noticed in the MD above that there are only a few slots where each of the variables can go. Whitney cannot be first or second, so she must be in slot 3 or 4, the only ones left on the base. We can diagram these possibilities using the or symbol, "/"

		W/	/W
1	2	3	4

Whitney will be in 3 *or* she will be in slot 4. Placing the variables right in the slots makes it easy to see that these are possible placements.

The example above shows a possibility, one that we inferred based on our understanding of the MD and two not rules.

Here is another possibility, this time given to us by a rule:

Tara will be placed either second or third.

This rule is diagramed directly on the MD:

```
       T/    /T
____  ____  ____  ____
 1     2     3     4
```

No need to represent the possibility with its own rule diagram.

Slot Possibilities

A rule may state the possibilities for a single slot of the base:

Either Donnie or Samantha will be seen last.

Like other possibilities, build a slot possibility right into your MD; that is the easiest way to represent it:

```
                   D/S
____  ____  ____  ____
 1     2     3     4
```

Here, the D or S possibility fills up the last slot, making it clear that **only** D or S can be last. No other variable can go in that slot. Whichever variable not placed in lane 4 (D or S) will be elsewhere on the track. The possibility indicated here is only for that one slot.

It is possible to have a triple slot possibility, where you are told that one of three variables will fill a specific slot:

Wendy, Alyson or Oliver must be judged during the first hour.

We show the three possibilities for that first slot on the MD using two slashes:

```
W/A/O
____  ____  ____  ____
 1     2     3     4
```

Conditional Rules

Conditionals (if/then statements, also known as formal logic) crop up in the Games section, just like in the Logical Reasoning section. Example conditional:

> If it is sunny today, Jim will go for a walk.

Diagram: *Sunny* → *Walk*
indicator requirement

Recall from the LR Methods that the indicator tells when the requirement occurs. If we are told that it is sunny today, then we know that Jim will go for a walk.

The requirement is **necessary** for the indicator to occur. If Jim went for a walk, then that means it was **possible** that it was sunny out. If Jim did not go for a walk, then that means it was not sunny out; the requirement was not met, so the indicator cannot be true. More on this idea of the requirement not being met when we discuss the contrapositive.

Representing Slots

In Sequencing games, the indicator and requirement will often involve a variable being in a specific slot of the base. Just like you learned for the LR section, use an arrow to diagram these statements. Simply place the number of the slot after the variable. For instance, if the indicator of a conditional rules says

> If Charles is second…

The diagram looks like this:

C2 →

Let us work through diagramming a full conditional rule.

> If Charles is second, then Paige is first.

C2 → *P1*

Whenever the indicator is true (whenever Charles is second), we know that Paige will be first (the requirement). So, if a local rule on a question tells us that Charles is second (*C2*), we can also fill P in 1:

P	C		
1	2	3	4

The Contrapositive

Conditionals are powerful rules because you can draw inferences from them by taking their contrapositive. Recall that taking the contrapositive of a conditional involves **negating** both sides of the conditional and then **reversing** them. Here is how we would create the contrapositive of the rule just discussed:

C2 → P1 The original diagram of the rule.

-C2 → -P1 Negate both the indicator and the requirement.

-P1 → -C2 Reverse the indicator and the requirement. You are left with the contrapositive.

Now we have new information, or information that is easier to see: when P is not in 1 (the indicator of the contrapositive), then C cannot be in 2. So if a local rule told us -P1, then our mini diagram would look like this:

1	2	3	4
P	C		

Taking the contrapositive is not always helpful in a game, but often it is.

As you become more comfortable with conditionals through practice, you may easily understand the information of the contrapositive just from diagramming the normal form of the conditional. In that case, there is no need to diagram the contrapositive; you can save time by skipping that step.

Conditionals and Absolute Links

Conditional rules can incorporate links:

If Noah is not third, then Zoey is immediately before Lucas.

Here is how we diagram the indicator, "If Noah is not third"

-N3 →

Remember to use the dash in front of the link to indicate that he is not third. The requirement, Zoey is immediately before Lucas, has this diagram:

ZL

Putting it all together:

-N3 → ZL

This diagram tells us that if N is not in the third slot, then Z and L are an absolute link with Z coming first.

Taking the contrapositive of this diagram requires negating one side of a conditional that is already negative. Recall that negating a variable that is already negative makes that variable **positive**:

-N3 negated, becomes... N3

Think of the two negations as canceling each other out.

Here are the steps for creating the contrapositive of the rule:

-N3 → ZL Original diagram

N3 → -ZL Negate both the indicator and the requirement.

-ZL → N3 Reverse the indicator and the requirement, and you are left with the contrapositive.

This tells us that if Z is *not* immediately before L, N must be in 3. The contrapositive gives us new information on the game. You will not find any easier inferences on the games section. Further, your new rules that you derive from taking the contrapositive may interact with other rules to give you inferences.

Phrasing of Conditionals

Conditional rules in Sequencing games often feature unique phrasing:

John will be last only if Sarah does not run first.

The words "only if" in this example signal the requirement. "Sarah does not run first" is the requirement, and "John will be last" is the indicator. Let us assume we know that the final slot of the base is the fourth lane. That means John is in lane 4 if he runs last. Here is the diagram for the conditional rule:

J4 → -S1

And the contrapositive:

S1 → -J4

Using the contrapositive, we infer that if Sarah runs first, John cannot be in lane four.

Keep in mind that if J is not in 4, that does not mean that S is not in 1. S *can* be in one in that situation, or S can be in a different lane. When the requirement is true, that does not tell us that the indicator must be true. If you make this type of error, the LSAT-Writers are ready for you. There will be an appealing, but incorrect, answer choice that matches the error.

Conditionals and Relative Links

There are a lot of different combinations of rules you may face on the games section. This rule features both conditionality and a relative link:

Michael is second only if Jennifer is in a higher ranked lane than Chris.

The indicator is easy, we diagram it M2 →. The requirement is a bit tougher. "A higher ranked lane than" means **after**. So the relative link for the requirement is C · J. The fully diagrammed rule:

M2 → C · J

To take the contrapositive of this conditional, we need to negate a relative link. In Sequencing games where each slot can only hold one variable, there is a good way to negate relative links - reverse the order of the variables:

J · C

If C is not before J, then C is after J, because they cannot share the same slot. This way of negating tells us more information than this diagram:

no C · J

This diagram is accurate but it is harder to interpret because it tells you what is not true. You need to move quickly during games, so you want your diagrams to be easily interpretable. The full contrapositive diagram for the rule:

M2 → C · J	Original Diagram
J · C → -M2	contrapositive

If J is before C, then M is not in 2.

A Tricky Conditional

Sometimes the LSAT-Writers can disguise a conditional in wording that sounds like a link. The rule below is given in a game where people work shifts during a week and each worker can work **more than one** shift:

Joey always works the shift immediately after Lena.

You might want to diagram this rule like this:

LJ

That would be a mistake. We are told that Joey always works right after Lena works, but we are not told that Lena always works before Joey. This rule only tells us what happens **when Lena works**. This is not a normal link; it is a conditional rule. You can diagram this link using the conditional diagram form:

L → LJ

When Lena works, Joey works immediately after her. It is possible for Joey to work when she does not.

Inferences

If you want to do well on the Games section, you must become proficient at drawing inferences. Recall that inferences are new rules that you can derive from the information in the game. Inferences are valid rules, they are simply **unstated**. It will help to see some examples of Sequencing inferences to get a feel for exactly what it means to derive new information from the setup and rules. The insight required to find inferences comes more easily to some students than others, but everyone can learn to recognize patterns and locate these crucial missing pieces. The LSAT-writers are counting on you finding these inferences; most games take too long or are very difficult to complete without them.

For some students, it is helpful to read all the rules first, before diagramming anything, because this allows you to have a context for drawing inferences. Also, many inferences allow you to diagram rules more efficiently, for instance, often you can connect two rules to create a more powerful single rule. That saves you time and space. Experiment with this tactic, as other students find that diagramming some of the rules as they read them is preferable.

Connection Inferences

There are two broad categories of inferences: connections and limits. Connections are easier inferences to find; they require you to find a variable that is in two different rules. Once you identify the common variable, you need to understand if and how those two rules can be connected to create new information. You can also think of connection inferences as combining two diagrams into one.

Basic Connection Inference

Look at these two rules:

> Matthew is immediately before Ashley on the track.
> Ashley is in a lower ranked lane than Josh.

Diagrams:

```
MA
A · J
```

Ashley is in both rules; she is our common variable. Because of the way the diagrams line up, we can connect them and create a single diagram:

```
    MA
+    A · J
----------
=   MA · J
```

Josh must come sometime after the MA link, because he is after Ashley. This diagram represents two rules.

We have shown this addition-style drawing to help you visualize why the rules can be combined. The rules give us sequencing information regarding either side of Ashley. Matthew is directly in front of her (to the left) and Josh is somewhere after her (to the right). Because of this, we can combine both types of information easily into the same diagram. The connection inference allows us to save time by only writing out one rule diagram instead of two.

The inference also helps us understand the game more fully. For instance, we can draw more not rules based on it than either of the two rules alone:

1	2	3	4
J	J	M	M
A			A

By connecting J to the MA link, it is clear that J cannot be in lane 2. Without this inference, we would only know that J could not be in lane 1, because A comes before it. Both M and A must come before J.

Connection Inference w/ a Second New Layer

If the rules were a little different, then we would not be able to represent both of the rules on a single layer. Look at this subtle change to the first rule:

> Matthew is after Ashley on the track.
> Ashley is in a lower ranked lane than Josh.

Diagrams:

```
A · M
A · J
```

Now, both rules give us information about variables that come *after* Ashley. Because the second rule gives a relative link, we cannot relate that to the relative link in the first rule on a single layer. We need to use a second layer in order to combine the diagrams:

```
A · M
 \
  J
```

Matthew comes after Ashley, and Josh too comes sometime after Ashley. Josh could be two slots after her, or he could be five, we do not know. Recall that the slanted line is a relative link that creates another layer. Note that the combined diagram above is a connection inference, just one that is not as easily created as the previous one.

Conditional Connection Inference

Take a look at these two rules:

> If Amanda is third, then Sarah is second.
> If Sarah is not fourth, then David is in lane one.

Diagrams:

```
A3  →  S2
-S4 →  D1
```

The key to making this inference is realizing that -S4 is logically equal to S2.

If Sarah is in 2 then she is **not** in 4. So, we can infer that when Amanda is third, Sarah is second and David is first:

A3 → S2 → D1

You can think of this connection like this:

```
    A3  →  S2
+         -S4  →  D1
-------------------
=   A3  →  S2  →  D1
```

This inference allows us to add more information to rule 1, but it **cannot replace** rule 2. We still need the diagram for rule 2 because it tells us that whenever Sarah is not in 4, David is in 1. Our inference chain does not give us that information; it only tells us more about what is the case when Sarah is in lane 2. If Sarah is in lane 1 or 3, we still want to have the rule 2 diagram so that we see that David is in lane 1. Also, it is possible that you can link information from other rules to that rule diagram, allowing you to draw more inferences. So, draw rule 1 with the addition of information from rule 2, and also draw rule 2:

A3 → S2 → D1

-S4 → D1

Limit Inferences

The second category of inference is a limit inference. Instead of seeing how two rules interact like you do with connection Inferences, limit inferences involve finding an interaction with one or more rules and **other aspects of the game**. To find these inferences in Sequencing games, look for areas on the MD where there are limited ways one or more variables can be placed on the base. Those limitations can help you to infer new information. Look for areas on the MD with many not rules.

Also, be aware of the various links in the game and how they can be placed. Links can create limit inferences because they set restrictions on the placement of specific variables.

Link Placement Inference

Here is a situation where a limit inference can be drawn:

Rule 1: James is in lane 1.

No need to diagram this rule individually; build it directly into your MD:

J			
1	2	3	4

The next rule:

Rule 2: Daniel is two lanes after Stephanie.

Diagram for this split link: *S _ D*

Rules 1 and 2 interact with the limits of the base, which only has four slots. There is only one way to place the Stephanie-Daniel link because of J's placement - in lanes 2 and 4.

J	S		D
1	2	3	4

This is a simple example, but the idea is applicable to more complex situations. After working the rules, analyze the MD to see how the links in the game can be placed.

Slot Possibility Inference

The next limit Inference is in a game with four runners - Robert, Nicole, John and Melissa – and four lanes on a track:

Rule 1: Robert is in a higher lane than Nicole.

Diagram for this relative link:

N · R

Rule 2: John is lane 3.

MD, with the not rule for the first slot built in and J placed in lane 3:

		J	
1	2	3	4
R			

The limit Inference is drawn by looking at the only slot with a not rule, lane 1. Robert cannot be in lane 1, because Nicole must come before him; we see this in the not rule. John cannot be in lane 1 because he is already placed in lane 3. Because the game only has four runners, either Nicole or Melissa **must** be in lane 1. We show that slot possibility:

N/M		J	
1	2	3	4
R			

Recall that positive information is generally more useful than negative information. Knowing that either Nicole or Melissa must be first is more powerful than knowing that Robert and John cannot be first. For example, if a rule tells us that Melissa is second, then we quickly see on the MD that Nicole must be first. And Robert must be fourth:

N	M	J	R
1	2	3	4

You could also tease out this situation by analyzing the NR link and seeing that R must be fourth to come after N. The diagram would look like this:

	M	J	R
1	2	3	4

However, the possibilities shown in lane 1 save you time, and working the games effectively requires making your diagrams as user friendly as possible.

Variable Fit

So far we have discussed Sequencing games that have the same number of variables as slots in the base. For example, a game with seven lanes on a track will have seven runners. This creates a perfect variable fit because when all the variables are placed, all the slots are filled. But not all Sequencing games are like this. Often, Sequencing games will have more or less variables than slots. Imperfect variable fit adds complexity to a game. Variable fit, as you can infer, relates to how the variables fit into the number of the slots in the base. The setup gives the information regarding variable fit.

Too Few Variables

Rarely, Sequencing games will feature too few variables for the slots. For instance, a track game could have only three runners to order within four lanes. Assuming that each runner only gets one lane, the track will have an empty lane. To deal with this situation, you could create a variable to represent the empty lane, *E*. Or if there is already a variable with that first letter, you could use X. This way, you can place the empty lane in a slot, which can make the game easier to handle.

Or, in that same game, you might be told in the setup that one of the three runners will be given two consecutive lanes. You would need to keep your eye on the fact that one variable will occupy two lanes. You can think of whichever variable that is as being a link of two adjacent slots. If A is given two lanes, then you can represent that variable like this: AA.

In a different Sequencing game, perhaps one dealing with ordering different types of chocolates, you might have too few variables for the slots, but you are told in the setup that you can **reuse** one or more variables. This might mean that a raspberry filled truffle is placed in slots 1 and 5. This would not make sense on a track because you cannot have a runner occupy non-adjacent lanes, but it is logical with chocolates because you can have two different chocolates that are the same kind. Here is another example of a game with two few variables for the slots. This one deals with scheduling meetings:

> Four attorneys – Justin, Amy, Brandon and Rachel - are scheduled to meet with the senior partner during a work week, Monday through Friday. The senior partner of the firm will meet with one attorney each day. One of the attorneys will meet with the senior partner twice.

The base of the MD is the five days of the work week, Monday through Friday. We will schedule one attorney **twice** and there will be no open slots in the base.

There are often inferences based on one variable being placed twice. For instance, assume we know that Justin is placed twice and that Amy cannot be on a day adjacent to when Justin is scheduled. These two rules limit where Justin can be placed. Even if we do not know where Amy is placed, we know that this scheduling for Justin's two meetings will not work:

	J		J	
M	T	W	T	F

In the scenario above, there is no day of the week that is not adjacent to Justin, so Amy cannot be placed anywhere. This scenario might provide the answer to the following question:

1. On which two days of the week can Justin not be interviewed?

Too Many Variables

Sequencing games can also feature more variables than the number of slots on the base. Unless one or more variables are not placed, which is highly uncommon in Sequencing games, the base will have **room** for each variable, just not in the sense that each variable gets a part of the base (a part of the base being a lane on the track or one day of the week, a slot). The extra placement will arise from doubling up variables on a slot of the base. For instance, in the attorney meeting game discussed above, if the setup is changed slightly, we have a game with too many variables instead of too few:

> Six attorneys – Justin, Amy, Brandon, Rachel, William and Danielle - are scheduled to meet with the senior partner during a work week, Monday through Friday. The senior partner of the firm will meet with at least one attorney at each day. On one day she will meet with two attorneys in consecutive meetings.

The base only has five natural parts: the five days of the week. On one day, two attorneys will met with the partner. This means that one of the days of the week will have two slots. Here is an example of diagramming this:

	W			
R	J	A	D	B
M	T	W	T	F

Both Justin and William are scheduled for Tuesday, shown by adding another level to the diagram. This representation helps us diagram the rules. For instance, this rule:

> William and Justin have meetings scheduled for the same day, with Justin's coming first.

...can be diagrammed like this:

W
J

Show that William's meeting is second by placing it on top. You should not diagram the rule like this:

JW

The diagram above is how we would indicate that Justin's meeting is immediately before William's meeting. Do not use a rule diagram for two different situations in the same game type. Confusion leads to trouble on the games section.

Games with too many variables for the slots are generally harder than those with too few variables because they can force you to change how you think about the base or how you diagram one or more of the rules. It is important to know which slots get more than one variable and **how** the extra variable is accounted for; keep this in mind as you work games like this.

Sequencing Example Setups

The following example Games setups tie together what you have learned thus far about Sequencing games. Follow the setups carefully and make sure each step makes sense to you before you move on.

Example Game 1

> Five swimmers – Zachary, Vanessa, Kenneth, Courtney, and Tyler – are swimming in a relay together. Each swimmer will swim exactly one leg of the relay. The ordering of the swimmers will follow these conditions:
>
> Courtney swims before Tyler and there are two swimmers in between them.
>
> Zachary does not swim immediately before or after Courtney.

Variable list: Z (V K) C T

Both V and K are not mentioned by the rules, so they are leftovers. Circle them to remind yourself of this fact. Now onto diagramming the rules:

Rule 1 needs its own rule diagram and its implications to be built in the MD. Rule diagram:

C _ _ T

We could draw all the not rules in the MD based on this rule:

1	2	3	4	5
T	T	T		
		C	C	C

However, if we think about the link for a moment in regards to the MD, we realize that there are only two ways that it can be placed:

1	2	3	4	5
C			T	

1	2	3	4	5
	C			T

We can build both of these possible placements into our MD like this:

C/	/C		T/	/T
1	2	3	4	5

C will be placed in slot 1 or 2 and T will be placed in slot 4 or 5.

Rule 2 also needs its own diagram and its implications to be built into the MD. The rule diagram:

- (ZC)

Z and C are never adjacent. Now we need to think about how that rule might interact with the MD. Normally, a not adjacent link cannot be built into the MD unless it interacts specifically with other rules. This not adjacent link does interact with the possibilities we have on the MD.

Because C must be in either slot 1 or 2, Z can never be in those slots, because it cannot be adjacent to C:

/C	/C		/T	/T
1	2	3	4	5
Z	Z			

Z can be the third swimmer if C is in slot 1. Diagramming is powerful because it helps you see relationships that you might otherwise miss, like this one.

Here are all the diagrams for the game, laid out for your viewing pleasure:

Variable list (written above the setup, immediately after you read the variables):

Z V K C T

Rule list:

C _ _ T

no ZC/CZ

Main diagram:

/C	/C		/T	/T
1	2	3	4	5
Z	Z			

Example Game 2

Six parakeets of different colors – blue, red, purple, yellow, orange and green – are being placed into six cages lined up in a row. The birds must be ordered according to the following conditions:

The blue parakeet is in the third cage.
The green parakeet is in the next cage after the red parakeet.
The yellow parakeet is not in the second cage.
The red parakeet is two cages in front of the orange parakeet.

Variable list: B R (P) Y O G

Build rule 1 directly into the MD. No need to diagram that rule separately:

___	___	B	___	___	___
1	2	3	4	5	6

During your initial read through of the rules, you might have noticed that the red parakeet appears in both rules 2 and 4. Here are those rule diagrams, if they are created separately:

RG + R_O

But, we can easily **combine** those two links:

RGO

The combined link is powerful because there is only one place on the MD that this three-variable link will fit - cages 4, 5 and 6:

___	___	B	R	G	O
1	2	3	4	5	6

The last rule we need to address is rule 3. Build this not rule into the MD:

___	___	B	R	G	O
1	2	3	4	5	6
	Y				

Taking another moment to look at our MD, we see that Y must go in 1; it is the only spot left for it. That means P must be in the last open slot, 2:

Y	P	B	R	G	O
1	2	3	4	5	6

Official games will not be this simple; they will not allow you to figure out the one solution to the game from the rules alone. A solution is when you have placed all the variables without violating any rules or the setup. No Sequencing games have only one solution.

The idea with this example game is to show you how important it is to combine rules when possible. Always have your eye on how each rule interacts with what you already have on the MD.

Example Game 3

Seven books by great, living American authors – McCarthy, Roth, DeLillo, Bujold, Cunningham, Stephenson, and Irving – will be stacked on a desk, not necessarily in that order.

The DeLillo book is directly underneath the Stephenson book.

The McCarthy book is fourth in the stack.

The Roth book rests on top of the Cunningham book.

If the Bujold book is 1st in the stack, then the Roth book is 7th.

Variable list: M R D B C S (I)

This game is best represented vertically, so our MD will be a vertical one. It is intuitive to have the book closest to the desk be book 1 (the first book), as we generally think of stacks of things in this way: floors in a building, shelves, etc.

Rule 1 is easily represented with just a rule diagram:

S
D

We know that D comes immediately before (ie, is under) S. We build two not rules into the MD at this point: D cannot be 7th and S cannot be 1st:

```
D  7 __
   6 __
   5 __
   4 __
   3 __
   2 __
S  1 __
```

Build rule 2 directly into the MD:

```
D  7 __
   6 __
   5 __
   4 M
   3 __
   2 __
S  1 __
```

Rule 3 is another absolute link:

R
C

This is the second two-variable link and both deal with different variables. Recall that links give games structure. Here, we have four variables tied up in links. Looking at the MD, we see that M effectively splits the base in half and each half only has **three** open slots. That means that the two links must be split onto each side of M, one on each side.

Here is how you can think about this situation:

```
DC  7 __        / S
    6 __       /  R
    5 __
    4 M
    3 __        / S
    2 __       /  R
SR  1 __
```

The possibilities to the **right** of the base show that either the SD link will be placed somewhere in slots 5, 6, 7 or the RC link will be. We have the same situation with slots 1, 2, 3. You do not need to draw these possibilities. Once you have a realization like this in the game, you will likely remember it. The advantage of drawing them is that it helps you visualize the situation more clearly.

There is a concrete inference we can take away from how these two links have to be placed. Neither B nor I, the two variables that are not part of the links, can be in slots 2 or 6. This is because one of the variables from each of the links must always be in that spot. The middle spot of the three slots available above and below M is reserved for a variable in a link. Here are the not rules:

```
DC  7 __
BI  6 __
    5 __
    4 M
    3 __
BI  2 __
SR  1 __
```

Recall that variables placed to the left of the base in vertical games are not possibilities. Now is a good time to build in the not rules that involve M and the two links. For instance, S cannot be in 5, because that would force D to be in 4 and M is already occupying that slot. There are three more:

```
DC  7 __
BI  6 __
SR  5 __
    4 M
DC  3 __
BI  2 __
SR  1 __
```

Notice the symmetry here: D and C always form not rules on the same slots, 3 and 7. This is because these variables are both at the top of their link respective links. S and R form not rules on the same slots, 5 and 1, for this reason as well.

Now the final rule: If B is 1st, then R is 7th. This is a conditional rule involving variables in specific slots:

B1 → R7

There are no inferences from this rule. We do not know anything unless B *is* in 1, in which case we know that R is in 7. From the setup and rules, B can be in 1, but it can also be in 3, 5 or 7. The contrapositive of the rule:

-R7 → -B1

R can also be in 1, 3, 5 or 7, so knowing this information above does not help much.

*Sequencing Games Review

- Sequencing games ask you to order variables onto a linear base.
- The base is made up of slots in a line.
- Depending on the game, the base will be represented vertically or horizontally.
- Horizontally bases:
  - Draw your MDs with the "first" slot on the left side and the numbers ascending to the right.
- The rules give you information about how variables can be ordered and about the slots on the base.

Rule Diagrams

- Placement Rules tell you exactly where a variable is on the base.
  - Example rule: "Jim is in lane 1."

    J
    __ __ __ __
    1 2 3 4
  - "Sarah cannot be in lane 2."

    __ __ __ __
    1 2 3 4
    S
- Links tell you how two or more variables relate to each other.
  - In Sequencing games, a link will tell you how two variables are ordered relative to one another.
  - "John is in the lane directly before Mark's lane on the track."

    JM
  - "Michael is two lanes behind Heather."

    H_M
  - "There are two lanes separating Sam and Yolanda."
    - With no ordering information, we need to use the slash for "or":

      S/Y_ _S/Y
- Adjacency
  - "Joshua and Tiffany are next to each other on the track." A circle indicates adjacency:

  - "Richard and Kelly are never in adjacent lanes."

- Relative Links
  - Use a dot in between variables when you do not know how many spaces there are.
  - "Bill is interviewed before Ted."

    B · T

- Layered Links
    - "Agatha comes before Caroline and Karden."

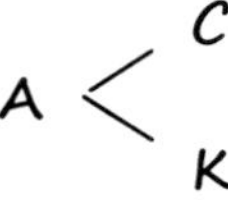

- Possibilities
    - "Tara will be placed either second or third."

	T/	/T	
1	2	3	4

    - "Either Donnie or Samantha will be seen last."

			D/S
1	2	3	4

- Conditional Rules
    - "If Charles is second, then Paige is first."

$C2 \rightarrow P1$
$-P1 \rightarrow -C2$ (the contrapositive)

        - Take the contrapositive of conditional rules when it seems like an important rule.

    - "Michael is second only if Jennifer is in a higher ranked lane than Chris."

$M2 \rightarrow C \cdot J$

Inferences

- Inferring new information from the rules is required to effectively solve games.
- A connection Inference involves combining two rules.
    - "Matthew is immediately before Ashley on the track."
    - "Ashley is in a lower ranked lane than Josh."

$$\begin{array}{ll} & MA \\ + & \quad A \cdot J \\ \hline = & MA \cdot J \end{array}$$

    - "If Amanda is third, then Sarah is second. If Sarah is second, then David is in lane one."

$$\begin{array}{lccccc} & A3 & \rightarrow & S2 & & \\ + & & & S2 & \rightarrow & D1 \\ \hline = & A3 & \rightarrow & S2 & \rightarrow & D1 \end{array}$$

- A limit inference involves finding an interaction with one or more rules and other aspects of the game.
    - For instance, a link can only go in one group of slots on the base when other slots are occupied.

Variable Fit

- <u>Variable fit</u> refers to how the number of variables matches the number of slots on the base.
- Perfect variable fit is when all the slots are filled with no variables left over.
- Imperfect variable fit is when the game has more or less variables than the number of slots.
    - Imperfect variable fit makes games more challenging.
    - Too few variables for the slots
        - Create a variable to represent the empty slot such as an "X" or the letter "E."
        - Sometimes, the game will tell you to reuse a variable to account for that extra slot.
    - Too many variables
        - One or more slots will hold two variables.

Question Types

Now that you have an understanding of Sequencing games, we can cover the different types of questions and use Sequencing games examples to illustrate them. You are already familiar with the global/local distinction that applies to all question types. Within this broad division, there are specific types of questions. Each question will be either global or local **and** a specific type. To illustrate the question types and how to approach them, we will work through this sequencing game (7/2 #1-7):

> Seven consecutive time slots for a broadcast, numbered in chronological order 1 through 7, will be filled by six song tapes - G, H, L, O, P, S - and exactly one news tape. Each tape is to be assigned to a different time slot, and no tape is longer than any other tape. The broadcast is subject to the following restrictions:
> L must be played immediately before O.
> The news tape must be played at some time after L.
> There must be exactly two time slots between G and P, regardless of whether G comes before P or whether G comes after P.

Variable list:

G (H) L O P (S) N

We represent the news tape with an "N." Both H and S are not mentioned by any rules, so we circle them to indicate that they are leftovers. Remember that variables not limited by any rules can usually fill in slots that no other variables can. They are more adaptable and therefore it is good to keep your eye on them. For instance, if both H and S are placed, then we know that we have no leftovers to fill slots; that might be an important thing to be aware of in that situation.

Rule diagrams:

LO · N (rules 1 and 2 are easily combined)

G/P _ _ G/P

Main diagram:

___	___	___	___	___	___	___
1	2	3	4	5	6	7
N	N				L	L
O						O

Many not rules flow from the LON link. Much of the structure of the game will be given by rule 3. Now that the game is set up, we can use it to explain the nature of the various question types.

Could Be True

Could be True questions ask you to locate the choice that contains information that works in at least one solution of the game. For instance, this is one solution to the game above:

G	L	O	P	H	N	S
1	2	3	4	5	6	7

No rules are violated by this ordering of the variables, so it is a successful solution. A correct answer to a global (no local rule is given) Could be True question could be:

A) O is played third.

This matches the information in the solution we showed, so it is correct. It **could be true** that O is played third. At least one solution does feature O in the third slot. It could also be the case that O is not played third. Here is a solution that does not feature O in the third slot:

H	G	L	O	P	N	S
1	2	3	4	5	6	7

Queries

Could be True questions are local questions about 80% of the time, so get ready to make some mini diagrams. Could be True are the most common question type on the Games section, so get ready to see many of them.

Example query for a local Could be True question:

If John is met with earlier than Phil, then which one of the following could be true?

Note the words "could be true." These are the signal that you are dealing with a Could be True question. The "If" at the beginning of the question is a sign that you are dealing with a local question.

Example query for a global Could be True question:

Which one of the following could be true?

This features no local information; it is a global question. Use only the setup and rules to answer the question.

Correct Answer

The correct answer to a Could be True question will be the choice that is possible, the choice that works at least some of the time. When you setup the game, you can create a solution where the information in that choice holds. If there is a local rule given in the question, then the correct choice will work in at least one scenario **with the local rule in play**. The correct choice is not necessarily always true, but it can be true in all solutions.

Incorrect Answers

In contrast, all the incorrect answers to a Could Be True question are not possible; they provide information that makes it so that **no solution** to the game can be created. Taking into account the local rule, if there is one, the information in those choices can never be the case in a solution. This is useful: you can eliminate any choice that you know violates a rule or does not yield any solutions.

Plan of Attack

Local questions give you information that gives more structure to the game. Your job is to use that information given, draw **inferences** from it and think about its implications, and then find the correct choice. With a majority of Could be True questions, that is all you have to do: analyze the local rule and find inferences based upon it. Draw a mini diagram next to the question if that will help. Then, work each choice looking for one that can be true based on your work with the local rule. If you can create a solution with the information in the choice, then that choice is correct. All it takes is a single solution. Eliminate any choice that violates a rule or otherwise goes against the setup.

On a **global** Could be True Question, you must work through the each choice, checking whether that choice is possible. If you find a choice that works with all the rules given in the game, then that choice is correct. Select it and move on. All four incorrect choices will feature information that contradicts a rule.

Example Could be True Question (Local)

1. If H and S are to be scheduled as far from each other as possible, then the first, the second, and the third time slots could be filled, respectively, by

   (A) G, H, and L
   (B) S, G, and the news
   (C) H, G, and L
   (D) H, L, and O
   (E) L, O, and S

We know that this is a Could be True question because it says "**could be** filled." The local rule is that H and S (our two leftovers) must be as far apart as possible. So, after separating H and S by as many slots as possible, we look for the three variables that can fill slots 1, 2 and 3.

To obey the local rule, we need to place our two links so that there is space on either side of the links for H and S, because that will give us maximum space between H and S. Drawing a mini diagram helps. This is the only way to place the GP link and the LON link with open slots on either side:

	G/P	L	O	G/P	N	
1	2	3	4	5	6	7

We have chosen to write the numbers for the slots instead of drawing the slots because a mini diagram only needs to be understandable, you do not have to have every detail represented from the MD. You could just draw the slots, but with **seven** slots and no numbers labeling them it might be tricky to tell which slot is which. This is up to you.

Now that we have the other five variables set, we can place H and S five spaces apart, the most possible given that the MD has only seven slots. This is the only arrangement where we can place all the other variables in the middle of the base. This means that the correct choice must feature either G or P in slot 2 and L in 3. There is no other way to separate H and S by five slots. Let us now look at the choices using our mini diagram:

(A) G, H, and L

This choice does not work because we know that slot 2 must be either G or P.

(B) S, G, and the news

Slot three must be L, not N.

(C) H, G, and L

(C) works. We needed to find the one choice that worked with the partial solution we diagrammed. Here is the full solution given the information in (C):

H	G	L	O	P	N	S
1	2	3	4	5	6	7

During an actual game, you would select this choice and move on. Confidently picking the correct choice and then moving without working through the rest of the choices will save you time on the games section. For teaching purposes, we will work through the final two choices:

(D) H, L, and O

We know that L and O must come in 3 and 4, not 2 and 3, so this choice is incorrect.

(E) L, O, and S

Again, this does not match the partial solution in our mini diagram, which we know to be the only way that H and S can be separated by as many slots as possible.

Must Be True

Our next question type, Must be True questions, ask you to find the choice that contains information that **always** works, is present in every solution. These questions make up ~20% of all questions on the Games section. Must be True are local questions only 65% of the time, which contrasts with Could be True questions. Here is an example Must be True question:

> If P is played fifth, L must be played…

Note the words "must be." These are an obvious indicator that you are dealing with a Must be True question. The "if" followed by new information (P is played fifth) tells you that this is a local question. This question asks you where L must be played when we know that P is 5th.

Correct Answer

The correct answer to this type will be the choice that is always true, the choice that works all the time given the local rule. If there is no local rule, then the correct choice is always the case based on the initial rules and setup. The correct answer is present in every possible solution to the game.

Incorrect Answers

The incorrect choices are not true **all the time**. They can be false, information that is never true. Or they can be true only some of the time: true in some solutions but not others.

It is impossible to setup a solution that does not feature the information in the correct choice. If you can set up a solution where the information in the choice is not true, then that choice is incorrect. This is a powerful way to eliminate incorrect choices to Must be True questions: set up a solution that contradicts the choice. For instance, on the example question above, if this was one of the choices:

A) 2nd

You can disprove it by creating a working solution where L is not played 2nd. Here is an example solution from earlier that features L in *3*:

H	G	L	O	P	N	S
1	2	3	4	5	6	7

Because L is played 3rd, L is obviously not only played second. Choice (A) is incorrect.

Plan of Attack

With **local** Must be True questions, use the local rule as fully as possible – find inferences based upon it. Draw a mini diagram or make a mental diagram of the local information. The process of analyzing the local rule is identical to what you do for a Could be True question. However, when you work the choices, you are looking for a different kind of information – information that is always true.

On a **global** Must be True question, check each choice against your knowledge of the game and any inferences you found based on the initial rules. If you are having difficulty figuring out whether a choice must always be true, try to disprove it. If you can create a solution where the information of the choice is not true, then that choice is incorrect. Cross it off and move on to the next choice.

Example Must be True Question (Local)

2. If G is played second, which one of the following tapes must be played third?

(A) the news
(B) H
(C) L
(D) O
(E) S

"G is played second" is the local rule. Use that information to figure out which variable must come third. Let us use a mini diagram to see the impact of the local rule. The first thing we notice is that the G/P split link must go in slots 2 and 5:

```
    G           P
1   2   3   4   5   6   7
```

Next, we look to the LON link. The LO part of it must go in slots 3 and 4, because N must come after it and those are the only **two open slots in a row** that can have a variable (here, N) follow after them:

```
    G   L   O   P
1   2   3   4   5   6   7
```

We know that L must be in 3 and that is all we need to solve the question. (C) is correct. Move to the next question.

Example Must be True Question (Global)

3. Which one of the following must be true?

(A) H is played first
(B) G is played before P
(C) L is played before the fourth song.
(D) O is played before N
(E) S is fifth

On a global Must be True Question, analyze each choice to see how it relates to the starting rules of the game. Look to see if based on the way the game works, the information in the choice is always true, in every single solution.

(A) H is played first

Because we have no rules that deal with H, it is very unlikely that there is only a single slot that this variable can fit. Also, H and S are **interchangeable** because they are both leftovers. Therefore, there is no one spot that is the only spot that H can be placed in, because whatever spot H can be placed in, so can S. So, this choice must be incorrect.

We can also disprove this choice with a scenario where G or P is in the first slot, because it shows that H is not always in that slot:

G/P	S	H	G/P	L	O	N
1	2	3	4	5	6	7

(B) G is played before P

Because of the G/P link, we know that these two variables are interchangeable. G can easily come after P, because they can switch places. This choice is incorrect.

(C) L is played before the fourth song.

In the scenario we used to eliminate (A), L is placed fifth without a problem. O and N come after it and the G/P link comes before it, with S and H in the middle of the GP link. So, L does not have to be played before the fourth song.

(D) O is played before N

This must be true. Our combination of rules 1 and 2 tells us that in the LON link, O comes before N. That combination inference points directly to (D) being correct. On an actual games section you would select this choice and move on to the next question. We will disprove (E) for teaching purposes:

(E) S is fifth

This must be incorrect for the same reason that (A) was incorrect: S and H are interchangeable, so neither can only be in one slot.

S **can** be fifth...

G/P	L	O	G/P	S	H	N
1	2	3	4	5	6	7

...but it certainly is not always fifth. In the solution above, we could simply switch the locations of S and H. That makes S sixth. Answers that only **can** be true are incorrect on Must be True questions.

Cannot Be True

Cannot be True questions ask you to locate the choice that contains information that is never true, information that does not fit the game globally or when the local rule is taken into account. Cannot be True questions are common: they make up 10% of the games questions. These questions are local questions about half of the time. Here is an example local Cannot be True query:

> If G is played fourth, which of the following cannot be true?

Note the words "cannot be." These are an obvious signal that you are dealing with a Cannot be True question. Cannot be True questions can also feature the word "EXCEPT" in the query:

> The news tape can be played in any one of the following time slots EXCEPT the...

This would be a query for a Could be True question, if it were not for the "EXCEPT" at the end. To answer this question, find the time slot that the news tape **cannot** be played in.

Correct & Incorrect Answers

The correct answer to a Cannot be True question features information that never works in any solution or in any solution when the local rule is taken into account.

The four incorrect answers always work at least some of the time, and an incorrect choice can work all the time. The **logical** opposite of information that cannot be true is information that is true or is sometimes true. If you create a solution where the information in the choice works, then you can eliminate that choice. This is counterintuitive. You are looking for the choice that does not work in any solutions, which feels a little strange at first.

Plan of Attack

As you can guess, on local Cannot be True questions, work through the local rule and its implications before you tackle the choices. When you move to the choices, look for information that you know must never be true.

With global Cannot be True questions, focus on negative information (what cannot be true) inferences from your rules and setup and then scan the choices to see if there is a match. That can be a very helpful shortcut on all types of global questions.

Example Cannot be True Question (Global)

4. The news tape can be played in any one of the following time slots EXCEPT the

   (A) second
   (B) third
   (C) fourth
   (D) fifth
   (E) sixth

We are focusing on a specific variable, N, so think about the not rules that deal with N. N can *never* be first or second, because that would push either L or **L and O** off the base. Look at the choices to see if either of those slots are listed. Yes, the second slot is listed. (A) must be correct because N **cannot** be placed second. Select this choice and move on. For teaching purposes, all the other choices are possible:

N 3rd:

L	O	N	G/P	H/S	H/S	G/P
1	2	3	4	5	6	7

N 4th:

L	O	G/P	N	H/S	G/P	H/S
1	2	3	4	5	6	7

N 5th:

G/P	L	O	G/P	N	H/S	H/S
1	2	3	4	5	6	7

N 6th:

G/P	L	O	G/P	H/S	N	H/S
1	2	3	4	5	6	7

There is no need to prove that the other choices are **possible** during a game. Select the choice that you know cannot be true and move on.

List Questions

List questions are common (just under 20% of Games questions) and often easy if you know how to approach them. They typically ask you which of the choices is a working solution to the game. Example query:

> Which one of the following could be the order, from first to seventh, in which the songs are played?

The choices for this question in this game will list all seven variables in different orderings, and only one of those is a working solution. List questions are often the **first question** in the game. Almost all List questions are global.

Correct & Incorrect Answers

The correct answer is the only solution that does not violate any rules or aspects of the setup. When you find a solution that violates no rules, select it and move on. All four incorrect answers will violate a rule of the game. This relates to the most effective way to solve these questions.

Approach

The fastest way to solve List questions is to use process of elimination to eliminate the four incorrect choices. Because each incorrect choice will violate at least one rule, use the rules as your tools of elimination. Start by picking a rule that is visually easy to recognize when violated. Generally, the simpler rules with fewer variables are faster to use. Take a rule and work through each choice, checking to see if the choice violates that rule. Cross off any choices that do. Then move on to the next rule and use the same process. Eventually, you will find yourself left with only one choice, the correct choice.

Example List Question

5. Which one of the following could be the order, from first to seventh, in which the songs are played?

   (A) P, L, O, N, G, H, S
   (B) N, G, L, O, P, H, S
   (C) G, L, O, P, N, S, H
   (D) H, S, G, O, L, P, N
   (E) H, L, O, P, N, G, S

Let us start with rule 1. There is no need to use our more complex, combined rule of 1 and 2 for this process of elimination, we will just use the LO link. We can eliminate choice (D) based on this rule, because O comes before L there. Next, use rule 2, that N is after L, to eliminate (B). Finally, rule 3, that there are two spaces in between G and P, eliminates choices (A) and (E). We are left with choice (C) which is a working solution and must be correct through process of elimination.

This method of using the rules to eliminate the incorrect choices is much easier and quicker than taking each choice one at a time to analyze whether it obeys **all** the rules. With one rule in mind, you can quickly check each choice to see if it matches and then move onto the next rule. It is a much faster process.

Slot List Questions

Sometimes List questions will ask you all the **variables** that can be placed in a specific slot. Example query:

> Which one of the following is a complete and accurate list of the songs any one of which can be played second?

This query asks you for the full list of which variables could be played second in various **different** solutions of the game. If a choice is:

> A) P, N, G, H

Then, this means that P can be played second in one solution, N can be played second in a different solution, etc.

You can narrow the choices down by using the not rules for the slot. Eliminate any choices that feature those variables. You can also quickly check the rules and see if they dictate that certain variables cannot be placed in that slot if you feel you may have missed some in your not rules.

Next, work the remaining choices. You are searching for a complete and accurate list, so anything less will not do. Start with the choice with the **most variables**. Check each variable listed by that choice. If they all work in different solutions, then it must be the correct answer, because it has at least as many variables as the other choices. If the variables in that choice do not all work in a solution, then that choice is incorrect. Move on to the choice with the next highest number of variables. Continue the process until you find a choice with the full list of working variables.

Variable List Questions

Sometimes List questions will ask you all the **slots** that a specific variable can be placed in. Example query:

> Which one of the following is a complete and accurate list of the time slots in which the O song tape can be played?

These typically appear later in a game and are uncommon. The process for this type is similar to that for Slot List questions.

First analyze any rules relating to that variable. Then, use process of elimination to get rid of choices that feature the variable in slots where it obviously cannot be placed. After those eliminations, work the choice with the most slots and see if all of them work. If so, select that answer. If not, move on to the choice with the next highest number of slots. Continue with this process until you find a choice that lists every possible slot that the variable can be placed in.

Structure Questions

Structure questions come in two flavors: Full Scenario and Rule Replacement. The sub-types are distinct but both ask you to understand the underlying interactions between the rules to get at the very nature/structure of the game. For this reason, Structure questions are often quite difficult.

Full Solution

A Full Solution Structure question asks you to identify the choice that forces a full solution for the game where every variable is placed in a specific slot. Example query:

> There is exactly one possible order for the songs if which one of the following is true?

The correct choice will give you some placement information that will be enough to know exactly where the rest of the variables are. Example Full Solution choice:

> A) S is played first, G is played second and N is played after H.

We are told the placement of S, which is crucial for this game because S and H are interchangeable. So the correct choice must tell us where one of them is, otherwise, we will not know the full placement of all variables. Also, placing G second forces the GP and OLN blocks into specific arrangements, which is also crucial. This choice gives us a full solution. Here are a series of mini diagrams that show how:

We start off by placing P in slot 5 according to the GP link:

S	G			P		
1	2	3	4	5	6	7

Now we must place L and O in slots 3 and 4 because those two must come before N:

S	G	L	O	P		
1	2	3	4	5	6	7

That leaves us with only H and N to place. The choice tells us that H comes first out of those two, so those two must be in slots 6 and 7 respectively:

S	G	L	O	P	H	N
1	2	3	4	5	6	7

That is a full solution, all structured by the information in choice (A).

When working Full Solution questions, look for choices that provide the placement of **key variables**. Here, putting G in 2 allowed us to specifically place P, L and O. Find the choices that place important variables and then work them out mentally or with a mini diagram to see if every variable is forced into a single slot. If so, that choice is correct. If you can move variables around, finding more than a single solution, eliminate the choice.

Rule Replacement

A Rule Replacement question, the second type of Structure question, asks you to substitute information for a rule in such a way that the new information gives the same structure to the game that the rule it is replacing provided. Full Solution questions require that you understand which variables are the most important. Rule Replacement questions require that you understand the **role** a rule plays in the game as a whole. Both types of understanding are fairly complex and get at the heart of how the game works, which is why these types are named Structure questions.

Example Rule Replacement query (from a different game):

> Which one of the following, if substituted for the condition that *Hibiscus* must be hung somewhere before *Katydid* but cannot be the first photograph, would have the same effect in determining the arrangement of the photographs?

Note the words "the same effect." Those indicate that the new rule must have the same impact on the game; it must give the same structure.

On rule Replacement questions, focus on the impact of the rule being replaced in relation to the rest of the game. Take a few moments to do so. Exactly what part does that rule play? Which variables does it affect? What inferences did you make off of it? With that role in mind, look to the choices for a new rule that can affect the other variables or the game in the same way. Also, you can look for your inferences from that rule being stated explicitly in a choice. That is an easy answer to this question type.

Rule Replacement questions can be challenging and time consuming. Leave them until last in the game, when you will have a better feel for all the relationships involved.

Local Choices Questions

Local Choices are a rare subset of Must be True questions. They give you **five local rules**, one in each answer choice, and ask you which one must be true. This question type is recognizable by its answer choices, instead of its query. The query appears to be a normal Must be True question:

14. Which one of the following must be true?

    A) If G is in 2, P is in 4.
    B) If H is in 1, N is in 6.
    C) If O is in 2, L is in 3.
    Etc.

Local Choices questions can take a long time because you often have to work each choice and deal with a unique situation in each. Sometimes you can scan the choices looking for a local rule in the first part of the choice that you recognize. That is an effective way to save time on this question type.

In general, just like Structure questions, leave local choice questions until the end of the game when you have worked the other questions and have a great understanding of the game. This may allow you to sift through the choices more quickly. Working this type last will mean that if the question takes you a long time, you have already gotten all the quicker, likely easier, points from the other questions. If you are crunched for time on the section as a whole, make an educated guess on this question and move on.

Slot Questions

Slot questions ask you about a specific slot on the base. The general strategy for a question of this type is to focus your energy on that slot on the MD and also any rules relating to it before working the choices.

Cannot be True Slot Questions

Cannot be True Slot questions ask you which variable cannot be placed in a slot or which pair of variables cannot be placed in two slots. These are generally global questions, which is intuitive because they are asking you about an inherent limit of the game regarding that slot or slots. Example global Cannot be True Slot query:

> Which one of the following songs CANNOT be played second?

The quickest way to answer a global Cannot be True Slot question is to see a not rule in your MD that lines up with one of the choices. For question 1 above, we know that N cannot be played second, because of the LON link (L would be pushed off the base). If N is a choice, then you should select it and move on.

If using the not rules is not an option (it rarely will not be) you can work each choice by placing the variable in the slot in question and then seeing if you can create a solution around it. But that can be time consuming and require a lot of mini diagrams or mental work. Another, better option is to analyze what you know about the variables with an eye on the slot in question. You may come up with a few variables that you suspect will not work in that slot. Scan the choices for those, and then test one or more to confirm that they cannot go in that slot. A little preemptive work can help you more actively attack the choices.

Here is an example query for a local Cannot be True Slot question:

> If S is played second, which one of the following songs CANNOT be played sixth?

For the local Cannot be True Slot questions, use a mini diagram or mental diagram and see the implications of the local rule for the spot in question. For instance, on the question above, we can plug S into slot 2:

	S					
1	2	3	4	5	6	7

Recall that S and H are our leftovers and tend to be placed last because we have no restrictions on them. In this situation, one of our leftovers is already placed and that may limit how we can place other variables. We want to know which variable cannot be played sixth. Look at the GP link, as it has a lot of impact on where the LON link can be placed. The GP link can go in 3 and 6:

	S	G/P			G/P	
1	2	3	4	5	6	7

From here, we can place LO in 4 and 5 and N in 7. If we place the GP link in 1 and 4, its only other possible placement given the local rule, then we can get O in 6:

G/P	S		G/P	L	O	N
1	2	3	4	5	6	7

We can never place N or L in 6, because the GP link can only fit in two ways (given the local rule), and each of them limits the LON link to either 5, 6, 7 or 4, 5, 7. Either N or L could be the correct answer to this question.

Slot Max Questions

Other Slot questions ask you the **maximum** number of variables that can go in a specific slot. Example query:

> What is the maximum number of songs that can be played in the seventh slot?

On Slot Max questions, you need to be more active than on Slot List questions. Your job is to analyze the rules and not rules related to that slot and then figure out exactly how many different variables can go there. Create various solutions to get as many different variables in that slot as possible. As you are doing so, it might be helpful to write out the possible variables next to the question. Once you have created the maximum number of possibilities, count them and find that number among the choices.

Here is how we would work the question above. Start with the GP link as that gives a lot of structure. That link can be in the seventh slot (you might do this placement mentally):

			G/P			G/P
1	2	3	4	5	6	7

We can place the LON link in various slots with H and S filling in around them. So, this means **both** G and P can be in the 7th slot. We know that H and S can be in that slot, because they are be anywhere. And N can be in the slot too. But neither L nor O can be in the seventh slot because they must both come before N. So here is the complete list of variables that can be in the 7th slot: G, P, H, S, N. That is **five** and here is the correct answer to that question:

> B) Five.

It required analysis, but we discovered exactly how many variables could be in that slot. This is much more effective than trying to work each choice and asking yourself, can four variables be in that slot? No? How about five? Etc. Slot Max questions are generally solvable without looking at the choices. You only need the rules and setup and perhaps a mini diagram or two.

These questions can be time consuming: you may wish to leave them for last in a game or skip them if you are running out of time on a section.

*Question Types Review

- Each question is either global or local, depending on whether it gives additional information to the game.
- Further, each question is a specific type.

Could be True

- "If John is met with earlier than Phil, then which one of the following **could be true**?"
- Could be True questions ask you to find the choice that works in at least one solution to the game.
- The correct choice is not necessarily true in every solution to the game, but it can be.
- Incorrect choices are <u>false</u>, they do not work in a single solution.
- These questions are often local.
    - Use the local rule as much as possible to draw inferences before working the choices.

Must be True

- "If P is played fifth, L must be played…"
- Find the choice that **always** works; information that is present in every solution.
- Incorrect choices are false or only true some of the time.
    - If you can setup a solution where the choice is not accurate, then that choice is incorrect.

Cannot be True

- "If G is played fourth, which of the following cannot be true?"
- Locate the choice that contains information that is never true.
    - The choice either does not fit the game globally or does not fit the game when the local rule is taken into account.
- Incorrect answers work in at one solution, and sometimes, in all solutions.

List Questions

- "Which one of the following could be the order, from first to seventh, in which the songs are played?"
- List questions ask you which choice is an accurate solution.
- These are often the first question in a game.
- Use the rules for process of elimination.
    - First, narrow the choices down using any not rules – it is easy to see when these are violated.
    - Then, work the choices using one rule at a time to check each choice.
    - The choice remaining is the correct one.
- Variations
    - Slot List questions ask you all the possible variables that can be placed in one slot on the base.
    - Variable List questions ask you all the slots that one variable can be placed in.
        - Analyze all the rules relating to the variable to find slots it cannot go in.
        - Then work the choices, starting with those with the most slots listed.

Structure Questions

- "There is exactly one possible order for the songs if which one of the following is true?"
- Full Solution Structure questions
    - Find the choice with placement information that forces a full solution to the game.
    - Look for choices that provide the placement of **key variables** and evaluate those first.
- Rule Replacement questions
    - Substitute information for a rule so that the new information gives the same structure to the game that the rule it replaces provided.
    - Focus on the impact of the rule being replaced in relation to the rest of the game.
        - Try to state it in your own words before working the choices.

Slot Questions

- Slot questions can be time consuming, so you may wish to leave them until last in a game.
- Cannot be True Slot questions ask you which variable cannot be placed in a slot.
    - "Which one of the following songs CANNOT be played second?"
    - Analyze what you know about the variables with an eye on the slot in question.
    - You may come up with variables that you suspect will not work in that slot.
        - Scan the choices for those variables and then test them.
- Slot Max questions ask you the maximum number of variables that can go in a specific slot.
    - "What is the maximum number of songs that can be played in the seventh slot?"
    - Analyze the rules and not rules related to that slot.
    - Next, figure out how many different variables can go there.
        - Create different solutions to get as many different variables in that slot as possible.

Example Sequencing Games

Now that you are familiar with both Sequencing games and the different question types, you can join that knowledge by walking through these example sequencing games. Pay special attention to the specific way that the different question types are approached.

28/2 #1-5

Six racehorses—K, L, M, N, O, and P—will be assigned to six positions arranged in a straight line and numbered consecutively 1 through 6. The horses are assigned to the positions, one horse per position, according to the following conditions:

K and L must be assigned to positions that are separated from each other by exactly one position.
K and N cannot be assigned to positions that are next to each other.
N must be assigned to a higher-numbered position than M.
P must be assigned to position 3.

We begin with an easy sequencing game. After reading the setup, it is clear that the six positions for the horses are the base of the MD. We have perfect variable fit: one horse for each slot on the base. Conveniently, the variables are already given in symbol format, so there is no need to deal with names of horses. We are only given **letters** to identify them.

Variable list:

K L M (N) O P

O is a leftover because it is not mentioned by any rules.

Rule List:

K/L _ K/L (A link that tells separation but not ordering)
no (KN) (A non adjacency link)
M · N (A relative link)

We build the fourth rule, that P is third, directly into the MD. We also add the various not rules:

M/O		P	K/L		
NKL				KL	M

We gain a lot from the not rules on the MD. Because K and L are one space apart, neither can be in 1 because that would put the other variable in 3 and P is already occupying that slot. The same is true of slot 5. Also, N cannot be in 1 because M comes before it. With three not rules on the first slot and only two variables that can go there, it makes sense to show the M/O possibility.

We also have a **major** inference involving the KL link: it can only go in 2, 4 or 4, 6. With 1 and 3 accounted for, there is nowhere else it fits. We show the possibility in 4: it must be either K or L. After you make one inference on the MD (here that K/L cannot go in 1), check the rules again, especially the important links, to see if you can draw further inferences. New knowledge of the game can help you gain more new knowledge.

We are now ready to work the questions:

1. Which one of the following lists an acceptable assignment of horses to positions 1 though 6, respectively?

(A) K, L, P, M, N, O
(B) M, K, P, L, N, O
(C) M, N, K, P, L, O
(D) N, O, P, K, M, L
(E) O, M, P, L, N, K

This is a List question and it is, unsurprisingly, the first question for the game. Recall that the fastest way to answer this question type is to pick a rule, use it to eliminate as many choices as possible, then pick the next rule and use it to eliminate choices, and so on. The simplest rule we have is rule 4 because it only involves P. We start with it and eliminate (C) because P is in 3, not 4. Next, we use rule 2 (K and N are not adjacent), because it is easy to see when two variables are touching in the lists that appear in the choices. We eliminate choice (E) with rule 2. Next, use rule 1 to eliminate (A). Finally, use rule 3 (N is after M) to eliminate Choice (D). We are left with (B), which must be the correct choice by process of elimination. Select it and move on.

2. Which one of the following is a complete and accurate list of the positions any one of which can be the position to which K is assigned?

(A) 1, 2
(B) 2, 3
(C) 2, 4
(D) 2, 4, 5
(E) 2, 4, 6

Another list question, but this one is a Variable List question: it asks us to list all the slots that the variable K can be assigned to. Fortunately, our inferences tell us exactly where the KL link can go: in 2, 4 or 4, 6. K and L are interchangeable as long as we obey rule 2, that K cannot be next to N. N can go in slots 2, 5 or 6, so it is easy to satisfy that rule as we move K around. So, K can be in spots 2, 4 and 6 and (E) is correct.

On a Variable List question, you need to focus on your MD and your knowledge of the variable. Here, that was all we had to do to figure out the three slots where K can be. On more challenging variable list questions, you may need to do some added analysis and work the choices, starting with the one with the **most** slots and working down the choices in order of the number of slots listed. Next question:

3. Which one of the following CANNOT be true?

This is a global Cannot be True question. Find the choice that puts a variable in a position where it can never be based on the initial rules. Quickly, check each choice against the MD and see if any are obviously not possible. You can work through all the choices rapidly this way, and may find the correct choice.

(A) K is assigned to position 2.

(A) is possible; we just talked about how K can be in slot two on the previous question. Here is a mini-diagram featuring this scenario:

M K P L O N

You would not want to take the time to draw this diagram out on the test. You can complete analysis like this mentally and save a great deal of time and drawing space.

(B) L is assigned to position 2.

K and L are interchangeable, so if (A) is possible, then so is (B). L can be in position 2 and this choice is incorrect.

(C) M is assigned to position 1.

Our MD has either M or O filling slot 1, so this is a possibility. (C) is incorrect.

(D) M is assigned to position 5.

We know that M must come before N, so if M is in 5, then N is in 6. That forces KL to be in 2, 4 (because 6 is occupied, and means that O is in 1:

O K P L M N

This is a solution, so this choice is incorrect. Again, you may not need this mini diagram; you could probably work off of the MD.

(E) O is assigned to position 2.

The first four choices were all possible, so (E) must be correct. Let us analyze what happens when we place O in 2. That means that M must be in 1 (because 1 is either M or O) and KL must be in 4, 6.

M	O	P	K/L		K/L
1	2	3	4	5	6

We need to place N and the only spot left is in 5 and that is next to K, regardless of whether K is in 4 or 6, and that violates rule 2. Therefore, (E) cannot be true and that choice is *correct*.

On tougher global Cannot be True questions, you might work through every choice and not find one that is obviously correct, in which case you would have to analyze the choices again more carefully. Try to avoid this happening by finding a good balance between moving smoothly through the choices, while also giving each enough time to rule out whether the information in it is possible. Next question:

4. Which one of the following must be true?

This is a global Must be True question. Here, much like the previous global question, we rely on our MD to work the choices efficiently, looking for information that must be true in every solution.

(A) Either K or else L is assigned to position 2.

This is not on our MD as something that **must** be the case. It is possible that this is true, but this question type demands that the correct choice be true all the time. The KL link can also be in 4, 6. Here is a solution that does not feature K or L in 2:

M	N	P	K/L	O	K/L
1	2	3	4	5	6

(A) is incorrect.

(B) Either K or else L is assigned to position 4.

(B) is an inference built into our MD. Because of P's placement in 3, the KL link must be in either 2,4 or 4,6. (B) is the correct answer. We work the next three choices for teaching purposes:

(C) Either M or else N is assigned to position 2.

(C) does not have to be the case. We can put K or L in 2 and N in 6, to satisfy rule 2:

	K/L	P	K/L		N
1	2	3	4	5	6

M and O are interchangeable in slots 1 and 5 above.

(D) Either M or else N is assigned to position 5.

In the mini diagram used for (C), O is in 5, so (D) is not always true. (D) is incorrect.

(E) Either M or else O is assigned to position 6.

The mini diagram also shows that N can be in 6. We have few limitations on slot 6 other than that M cannot be there. Therefore, (E) is incorrect. Next question:

5. Which one of the following CANNOT be true?

Another global Cannot be True question. Work at a moderate pace through the choices, looking for variables assigned to positions that will not yield *any* solutions. Eliminate a choice if you can create a single solution.

(A) L and N are assigned to positions that are next to each other.

This seems plausible: just place O late in the game. We know N could be in 2, 5 or 6 and L is fairly flexible as well (2, 4 or 6), so it seems easy to put L and N side by side without breaking any rules. A mini diagram shows how it can work:

M	K	P	L	N	O
1	2	3	4	5	6

(A) is incorrect, because we are looking for information that **cannot** be true.

(B) M and K are assigned to positions that are next to each other.

The mini diagram above shows M adjacent to K, so (B) is clearly possible and therefore incorrect.

(C) M and O are assigned to positions that are next to each other.

(C) seems promising because M and O are far apart from each other in the solutions we have seen so far. Either M or O must be in 1, so to place them next to each other, the other has to be in 2. It does not matter which we put first, because neither has any rules dictating how it interacts with P, the only variable one of them will touch:

M	O	P			
1	2	3	4	5	6

There is not a solution to the game from this point because we have K, L and N to place. N must go in between the other two and that violates rule 2. (C) is correct. For teaching purposes:

(D) L and N are assigned to positions that are separated from each other by exactly one position.

To have L and N separated by a slot, we can place N in 6 and L in 4:

	K	P	L		N
1	2	3	4	5	6

M and O are interchangeable in the other two slots. (D) is incorrect.

(E) M and P are assigned to positions that are separated from each other by exactly one position.

Our MD shows that either M or O must be in 1 and P is in 3, so this arrangement can clearly work and therefore the choice is incorrect.

27/2 #20-24

Our next example Sequencing game is more difficult and features repeated variables:

> Six cars are to be arranged in a straight line, and will be numbered 1 through 6, in order, from the front of the line to the back of the line. Each car is exactly one color: two are green, two are orange, and two are purple. The arrangement of cars is restricted as follows:
>
> No car can be the same color as any car next to it in line.
> Either car 5 or car 6 must be purple.
> Car 1 cannot be orange.
> 4 cannot be green.

The setup tells that the variables are the colors of the cars. We have three distinct colors – green, orange and purple - and two of each of them. Variable list:

G G O O P P

This is the first time we have seen variables that are not individuals, people, horses, etc., but instead a *quality*. For this reason, they are easily repeated. The fact that there are two of each color means that you need to be careful not to get confused. The two greens are interchangeable. Use the variable list as a resource for thinking about what colors are left to place. For instance, if two Gs, one O, and two Ps have been placed, then the final variable is the second O.

Rule diagrams:

No same colors adjacent

Certain rules that do not lend themselves to a visual representation, like rule 1, are best written out in your **own words**. This will help you remember them. rule 1 gives the game a great deal of structure, so keep it in mind.

Build rules 2, 3 and 4 directly into the MD. There are only three colors, so when we get not rules about a single color (like we do in rules 3 and 4) we can use those to show the possibilities on the MD. If slot 1 is not an O, then it must be a P or G. We show that possibility to make this clear. This is an effective choice, especially regarding slots 4, 5 and 6:

G/P			O/P	P/	/P
1	2	3	4	5	6

We see that **if** 5 is P, then neither 4 or 6 can be P. This means that 4 must be O, because it cannot be G.

Note that if 5 is P that does not mean that 1 must be P. Just because 4 and 6 are not purple does not mean that the other P must be in 1. It could be, or it could be in 2 or 4. It is important to be clear on what the possibilities mean. *P/G* means that particular slot will be either P or G. It must be one or the other. With slots 5 and 6, the */P* means that P will be in **one** of those two spots, but not both. So / can be used in two related but different ways depending on if more than one variable is with the / in the slot. This is important to keep in mind when analyzing the MD of this game.

We do not have a lot of structure going forward. That likely means the questions will probably have plenty of local rules because those give guidance to how the solutions for that question can be crafted.

The first question:

20. The cars in which one of the following pairs CANNOT be the same color as each other?

(A) cars 1 and 4
(B) cars 1 and 5
(C) cars 3 and 5
(D) cars 3 and 6
(E) cars 4 and 6

We start off with a global Cannot be True question. Let us work through the choices at a moderate pace, looking for ones with information that seems implausible. We will explore those choices in more depth.

(A) cars 1 and 4

1 and 4 are slots that are somewhat limited because they both have not rules on them. Limited slots are more likely to not be able to have the same variable, so we will take a close look at this choice. We know that 1 and 4 cannot both be purple because either 5 or 6 must be purple. Therefore, we cannot use both P's and have none left for 5 or 6. P is the only color those two slots have in common for their possibilities. Therefore, this choice is correct: it cannot be the case that 1 and 4 have the same color cars. All the other choices feature cars that can be the same color. Next question:

21. If car 2 is the same color as car 4, then which one of the following statements must be true?

(A) Car 1 is purple.
(B) Car 2 is orange.
(C) Car 3 is green.
(D) Car 5 is purple.
(E) Car 6 is green

A local Must be True question. First analyze the impact of the local rule. Our MD tells that car 4 can be either P or O. If car 2 is the same color as car 4, then that means neither car is P, because of rule 2 (either 5 or 6 is P). So cars 2 and 4 must be O:

G/P	O		O	/P	/P
1	2	3	4	5	6

There is not much else we can infer here. Where the two P's and G's are placed is fairly open. So, move to the choices and see if the insight that both 2 and 4 must be O yields the answer.

(A) Car 1 is purple.

This is not on our mini diagram. We can easily see a solution where car 1 is G, which eliminates this choice. Recall that on Must be True questions, if you can create **a single solution** that does not feature the information in the choice, then that choice is incorrect. Mini-diagram:

G	O	P	O	P	G
1	2	3	4	5	6

(B) Car 2 is orange.

This was our inference from the local rule and must be true. (B) is correct.

22. If car 4 is purple, which one of the following must be true?

(A) Car 1 is orange.
(B) Car 2 is green.
(C) Car 3 is orange.
(D) Car 5 is green.
(E) Car 6 is purple.

Another local Must be True question, so check the implications of the local rule. If car 4 is P, then that means that of cars 5 and 6, 6 has to be the P because of rule 1 (no same colors adjacent). Here is our mini diagram:

G			P		P
1	2	3	4	5	6

Draw one or two inferences from a local rule and then quickly scan the choices to see if you have enough information for the answer. If not, continue working with your mini diagram. On this question, it is easy to spot that (E) is correct. The "scan for our inferences" technique saved time. For teaching purposes, here are the rest of the inferences possible from the local rule:

Because both P's are placed, 1 must be G. And because 1 is G, 2 must be O, because it cannot be P or G.

G	O		P		P
1	2	3	4	5	6

That makes 3 G, because orange and purple are on either side of it. And the final O is placed in 5:

G	O	G	P	O	P
1	2	3	4	5	6

We were able to create a full solution from the local rule. Next question:

23. Which one of the following statements must be false?

(A) Car 2 is green.
(B) Car 4 is orange.
(C) Car 5 is purple.
(D) Car 6 is orange.
(E) Car 6 is green.

This is a global Cannot be True question. "Must be False" means "Cannot be True." Work each choice at a moderate pace with an eye on the MD, looking for what cannot be the case:

(A) Car 2 is green.

None of our previous mini diagrams show G in 2, so let us see if we can create a solution with this. If we can, then the choice is incorrect, as Cannot be True choices create no solutions. With G in 2, slot 1 must be P. Because P is in 1 and also in either 5 or 6, 3 cannot be P, so it must be O (because we cannot have two G's in a row):

P G O
1 2 3 4 5 6

This situation will **not** lead to a solution, because 4 must be either O or P and it cannot be either. It cannot be O, because car 3 is O, and it cannot be P because we already placed our **floating P** (the other P is locked down in 5 or 6). (A) is correct. It must be false that 2 is G. Next question:

24. If one of the two orange cars is replaced by a third green car, and if the arrangement of cars in line must conform to the same restrictions as before, then which one of the following is a complete and accurate list of the cars each of which must be green?

(A) car 1
(B) car 3
(C) car 5
(D) car 1, car 3
(E) car l, car 3, car 5

This is an interesting final question to the game. It is a variable list question asking where G must be placed, but there is a twist. The entire setup has been changed: we are now ordering these variables: GGGPPO. The rules are still in play and therefore our MD still works; the fact that there are three Gs and one less O does not change any of our possibilities. Leave questions that change part of the setup or rules until last in a game as they are often quite challenging and/or time consuming. Working the other questions first will give you a stronger understanding of the game that will help on these trickier questions. Fortunately, this question is already last.

The key to this question is that the Gs cannot be placed next to one another. With three of them, this is a stricter requirement than when there were only two. We know that 4 cannot be G, and that is very important. We *can* place one G in 5 or 6. That means that the other two Gs must be in 1 and 3. There is no other way to place two Gs in slots 1, 2 and 3 and keep them separated:

	G		G		
1	2	3	4	5	6

This inference in hand, we check the choices and see that (D) is correct. Fully analyzing how the Gs can be placed takes a little time, but it leads us directly to the correct answer.

For teaching purposes, we will work through the possible solutions. If the third G is in 5, then 6 is purple and the final P and O are interchangeable in 2, 4:

G	P/O	G	P/O	G	P
1	2	3	4	5	6

If the third G is in 6, then 5 is P and 4 must be O:

G	P	G	O	P	G
1	2	3	4	5	6

*Sequencing Practice Games

Game 1, Questions 1-7

A college offers one course in each of three subjects - mathematics, nutrition, and oceanography - in the fall and again in the spring. Students' book orders for these course offerings are kept in six folders, numbered 1 through 6, from which labels identifying the folders' contents are missing. The following is known:

Each folder contains only the orders for one of the six course offerings.

Folder 1 contains orders for the same subject as folder 2 does.

The orders in folder 3 are for a different subject than are the orders in folder 4.

The fall mathematics orders are in folder 1 or else folder 4.

The spring oceanography orders are in folder 1 or else folder 4.

The spring nutrition orders are not in folder 5.

1. Which one of the following could be the list of the contents of the folders, in order from folder I to folder 6 ?

    (A) fall mathematics, spring mathematics, fall oceanography, fall nutrition, spring nutrition, spring oceanography
    (B) fall oceanography, spring nutrition, fall nutrition, fall mathematics, spring mathematics, spring oceanography
    (C) spring mathematics, fall mathematics, spring nutrition, fall oceanography, fall nutrition, spring oceanography
    (D) spring oceanography, fall oceanography, fall nutrition, fall mathematics, spring mathematics, spring nutrition
    (E) spring oceanography, fall oceanography, spring mathematics, fall mathematics, fall nutrition, spring nutrition

2. Which one of the following statements must be false?

    (A) The spring mathematics orders are in folder 3.
    (B) The fall nutrition orders are in folder 3.
    (C) The spring oceanography orders are in folder 1.
    (D) The spring nutrition orders are in folder 6.
    (E) The fall oceanography orders are in folder 5.

3. If the fall oceanography orders are in folder 2, then which one of the following statements could be true?

    (A) The spring mathematics orders are in folder 4.
    (B) The spring mathematics orders are in folder 6.
    (C) The fall nutrition orders are in folder 1.
    (D) The spring nutrition orders are in neither folder 3 nor folder 6.
    (E) Neither the spring nor the fall nutrition orders are in folder 3.

4. Which one of the following statements could be true?

    (A) The spring mathematics orders are in folder 1.
    (B) The fall oceanography orders are in folder 1.
    (C) The fall nutrition orders are in folder 4, and the fall oceanography orders are in folder 6.
    (D) The fall oceanography orders are in folder 2, and the spring oceanography orders are in folder 1.
    (E) The spring oceanography orders are in folder 1, and neither the spring nor the fall nutrition orders are in folder 3.

5. If the fall oceanography orders are in folder 2, then for exactly how many of the remaining five folders can it be deduced which course offering's orders are in that folder?

    (A) one
    (B) two
    (C) three
    (D) four
    (E) five

6. Which one of the following lists a pair of folders that must together contain orders for two different

    subjects?

    (A) 3 and 5
    (B) 4 and 5
    (C) 3 and 6
    (D) 4 and 6
    (E) 5 and 6

7. Which one of the following could be true?

    (A) The fall mathematics and spring oceanography orders are in folders with consecutive numbers.
    (B) Folder 5 contains the orders for a spring course in a subject other than mathematics.
    (C) Folder 6 contains the orders for a subject other than nutrition.
    (D) The mathematics orders are in folders I and 4.
    (E) The orders for the fall courses are in folders 1, 3, and 6.

Game 2, Questions 8-12

Five people--Harry, Iris, Kate, Nancy, and Victor--are to be scheduled as contestants on a television show, one contestant per day, for five consecutive days from Monday through Friday. The following restrictions governing the scheduling of contestants must be observed:

Nancy is not scheduled for Monday.

If Harry is scheduled for Monday, Nancy is scheduled for Friday.

If Nancy is scheduled for Tuesday, Iris is scheduled for Monday.

Kate is scheduled for the next day after the day for which Victor is scheduled.

8. Victor can be scheduled for any day EXCEPT

(A) Monday
(B) Tuesday
(C) Wednesday
(D) Thursday
(E) Friday

9. If Iris is scheduled for the next day after Harry, which one of the following lists all those days any one of which could be the day for which Harry is scheduled?

(A) Monday, Tuesday
(B) Monday, Wednesday
(C) Monday, Thursday
(D) Monday, Tuesday, Wednesday
(E) Monday, Wednesday, Thursday

10. If Kate is scheduled for Wednesday, which one of the following could be true?

(A) Iris is scheduled for Friday.
(B) Nancy is scheduled for Tuesday.
(C) Nancy is scheduled for an earlier day than the day for which Harry is scheduled.
(D) Nancy is scheduled for an earlier day than the day for which Iris is scheduled.
(E) Nancy is scheduled for an earlier day than the day for which Kate is scheduled.

11. If Kate is scheduled for Friday, which one of the following must be true?

(A) Harry is scheduled for Tuesday.
(B) Harry is scheduled for Wednesday.
(C) Iris is scheduled for Monday.
(D) Iris is scheduled for Wednesday.
(E) Nancy is scheduled for Wednesday.

12. If Iris is scheduled for Wednesday, which one of the following must be true?

(A) Harry is scheduled for an earlier day than the day for which Nancy is scheduled.
(B) Harry is scheduled for an earlier day than the day for which Kate is scheduled.
(C) Kate is scheduled for an earlier day than the day for which Harry is scheduled.
(D) Nancy is scheduled for an earlier day than the day for which Kate is scheduled.
(E) Nancy is scheduled for an earlier day than the day for which Iris is scheduled.

Game 3, Questions 13-18

John receives one grade for each of the following six courses: economics, geology, history, Italian, physics, and Russian. From highest to lowest, the possible grades are A, B, C, D, and E. E is the only failing grade. Two letter grades are consecutive if and only if they are adjacent in the alphabet.

John's grades in geology and physics are consecutive.
His grades in Italian and Russian are consecutive.
He receives a higher grade in economics than in history.
He receives a higher grade in geology than in physics.

13. If John receives the same grade in economics and Italian, and if he fails Russian, which one of the following must be true?

(A) John's geology grade is a B.
(B) John's history grade is a D.
(C) John's history grade is an E.
(D) John's physics grade is a B.
(E) John's physics grade is a C.

14. If John passes all his courses and receives a higher grade in geology than in either language, which one of the following must be true?

(A) He receives exactly one A.
(B) He receives exactly one B.
(C) He receives exactly two Bs.
(D) He receives at least one B and at least one C.
(E) He receives at least one C and at least one D.

15. If John receives a higher grade in physics than in economics and receives a higher grade in economics than in either language, which one of the following allows all six of his grades to be determined?

(A) His grade in history is D.
(B) His grade in Italian is D.
(C) His grades in history and Italian are identical.
(D) His grades in history and Russian are identical.
(E) His grade in history is higher than his grade in Russian.

16. If John receives a higher grade in physics than in economics and receives a higher grade in history than in Italian, exactly how many of his grades can be determined?

(A) 2
(B) 3
(C) 4
(D) 5
(E) 6

17. Assume that John's grade in physics is higher than his grade in Italian and consecutive with it and that his grades in Russian and physics differ. Which one of the following must be true?

(A) John receives both an A and a B.
(B) John receives both an A and a C.
(C) John receives both a B and a D.
(D) John receives both a B and an E.
(E) John receives both a D and an E.

18. Assume that John receives a lower grade in economics than in physics. He must have failed at least one course if which one of the following is also true?

(A) He receives a lower grade in Italian than in economics.
(B) He receives a lower grade in Italian than in physics.
(C) He receives a lower grade in physics than in Italian.
(D) He receives a lower grade in Russian than in economics.
(E) He receives a lower grade in Russian than in history.

*Sequencing Games Explanations

Game 1 (18/1 #7 – 13)

Variable Lists

Course: fM, fN, fO, sM, sN, sO
We use a lowercase f to signal fall courses and a lowercase s to signal spring courses.

Rule List

Rule 1: **Each folder contains one course.**

Rule 2: **1 and 2 are the same subject.**

Rule 3: **3 and 4 are different subjects.**

Rule 4: fM_1 or fM_4

Rule 5: sO_1 or sO_4
We know the two possibilities for folders 1 and 4.

Rule 6: ~~sN_5~~

Main Diagram

Because we know that 1 and 2 are the same subject, we know that subject is either M or O. Likewise, 3 and 4 are not the same subject, so 3 must be subject N because 1 and 2 will be either M,M or O,O. Either way, 4 will be the other and therefore 3, cannot be either M or O. Either 5 or 6 must also be subject N.

QUESTIONS

1. Global, Could be True, List

Use Rule 6 (it is easy to spot) to eliminate A. Next use Rule 2 to eliminate B. Rule 3 eliminates E. Finally, Rule 4 eliminates C. **D** is correct.

2. Global, Cannot be True

Work each choice using the central diagram.

A) This is not possible – folder 3 must contain N.

3. Local, Could be True

sO	fO		fM		
1	2	3	4	5	6

1 and 2 have the same subject, we fill in sO in 1. That forces fM to 4.

A) Not possible, fM must be in 4.
B) This is possible. Nutrition courses would be in 3 and 5.

4. Global, Could be True

A) Not possible, due to Rules 4 and 5.

B) Not possible, due to Rules 4 and 5

C) Not possible, due to Rules 4 and 5

D) This matches the scenario in the question above.

5. Global, Could be True

This matches the scenario from Question 9. **B** is correct – you know where sO and fM must be placed.

6. Global, Must be True

We check each choice to see which pair must contain different subjects.

A) 3,5 can both be N.

B) 4,5 can both be M.

C) 3,6 can both be N.

D) 4,6 can both be M.

E) Must contain different subjects. Only one can be N, the other must be M or O.

7. Global, Could be True

A) Not possible – this pair is split to 1,4.

B) sN cannot be fifth, nor can sO so this is not true.

C) This is possible.

Game 2 (13/1 # 7 – 11)

Variable List

Contestants: H, I, K, N, V

Rule List

Rule 1: ~~N_M~~

Rule 2: $H_M \rightarrow N_F$

Contrapositive:

~~N_F~~ $\rightarrow$ ~~H_M~~

Rule 3: $N_T \rightarrow I_M$

Contrapositive:

~~I_M~~ $\rightarrow$ ~~N_T~~

Rule 4: VK

Initial Central Diagram

—	—	—	—	—
M	T	W	Th	F
~~N~~				~~V~~
~~K~~				

Not much to go on in the Central Diagram. Keep in mind that the two Contrapositives from conditional rules will be useful.

QUESTIONS

8. Global, Cannot be True

V cannot be scheduled for Friday, because K comes after him. **E** is correct.

9. Local, List

The local rule is HI and there are two blocks. H cannot be placed on Friday. H cannot be on Tuesday because that forces the VK block to Thursday, Friday and N to Monday, which doesn't work with Rule 1. **E** is correct: H can go on Monday, Wed. or Fri.

10. Local, Could be True

	V	K	N/	/N
M	T	W	Th	F

N must go on Thurs. or Fri. We check the choices one by one.

A) Doesn't work because N must go on Thursday and H on Monday, which conflicts with rule 2.

B) This is not possible.

C) H could be scheduled on Friday, and I on Monday, with N on Thursday.

11. Local, Must be True

I			V	K
M	T	W	Th	F
~~N~~				
~~H~~				

With VK on Thursday/Friday, H cannot be on Monday, because due to Rule 2, that would put N on Friday. Therefore, only I can be on Monday. **C** is correct.

12. Local, Must be True

V	K	I	N/H	N/H
M	T	W	Th	F
~~N~~	~~N~~			~~V~~
~~K~~				

With I on Wednesday, N cannot be on Tuesday thanks to the Contrapositive of Rule 3. Therefore N must be on Thursday or Friday and VK goes on Monday, Tuesday. H therefore must also go on Thursday or Friday. **C** is correct.

Game 3 (5/2 # 1-6)

Reading the setup, this looks like a fairly unique sequencing game. We have the six courses: *e g h i p r* and the five potential grades: *A D C D E*. We use lowercase letters for the classes to distinguish between economics and a grade "e." The best way to think of this game is sorting the classes into their appropriate grades. So the base will be the grades. E is a failing grade – that fact will probably be tested in the questions. The final sentence of the setup sounds a little strange, but it only means that consecutive grades are those right next to each other: A is consecutive to B, but A is not consecutive to C. Note that we are not told that every grade is represented and multiple classes can receive the same grade. So, before working the rules, it would be possible to have four A's and one E, for example.

Onto the rules:

Rule 1 tells us that g and p are consecutive. Represent that adjacency in one of these two ways, whichever you prefer:

gp/gp or (*gp*)

This means that g and p do not get the same grade. g might get an "A" and P might get a "B," or vice versa. We do not know if the grades are actually adjacent to each other That is an important aspect of the game.

Rule 2 is also adjacency information:

ir/ri

i and r also do not get the same grade.

Rule 3 finally gives us some sequencing information: he gets a higher grade in economics than history:

e · h

We know that h cannot be an "A" and e cannot be an "E". We can build this into our MD when we finish working the rules.

Rule 4 tells us that g is one grade higher than p, because they are consecutive (Rule 1) and g comes first:

gp

For our MD, we start with the five grades as the base. We have chosen to represent them horizontally, but vertically is fine too:

A B C D E

We build in the Not Rules based on Rules 3 and 4:

A	B	C	D	E
hp				*eg*

h and p cannot have an "A" grade and e and g cannot have an "E" (failing) grade.

Right now, we have two blocks: gp and ir/ri. e and h are a relative link and will fit in around those blocks. Not a whole lot of structure to the game right now, so we expect the questions to give us structure with local rules.

13.

We start out with a Local Must be True question. We are told that John fails r, which means he gets an "E" in that class and, because i and r are adjacent (Rule 2), he gets a "D" in i. Also, e is a "D" as well, thanks to the fact that it is the same grade as i. Mini-diagram:

			ei	*r*
A	B	C	D	E

Further, we know that e gets a higher grade than h, so h must be an "E." We work the choices and see that (C) is correct.

14.

Local Must be True, making two in a row. We are told that no class receives a E and that g is a higher grade than i and r (the two languages). This means that g must be at least a B, because it comes before the i/r block and the earliest that can come is in C/D:

	g	*i/r*	*i/r*	
A	B	C	D	E

Of course, g could also be an A and then everything switches over:

g	*i/r*	*i/r*		
A	B	C	D	E

Either way, (D) must be correct.

15.

This is a Full Solution Structure question, and it begins with a local rule. We are told that John receives a higher grade in p than e, so we have this link, which combines rules 3 and 4:

gp · e · h

Also, he gets a higher grade in e than in i or r:

gp · e · h
 \ ir/ri

So, we know quite a bit. Because i and r must each take up a grade, each grade will have at least one class, and gpe must go in ABC:

g	p	e		
A	B	C	D	E

So, to have a full placement, we need to place h and figure out which of i and r comes first. So, information about just one of those groups does not help us. We can eliminate (A), (B). (C) and (D) don't work either, because we do not know what grade h and i or h and r share. (E) by process of elimination is correct. If h is a higher grade than r, than it must be a D and i is also a D:

g	p	e	h i	r
A	B	C	D	E

16.

Surprise! Another local rule. Didn't we say that because the game had so little structure there would be a lot of these? If p is before e, and h is before i, then we have this link:

gp · e · h · i

Notice that this is all five letter grades taken up. r must be with h in D:

g	p	e	hr	i
A	B	C	D	E

A very similar situation to the previous question. All six grades are determined and (E) is correct.

17.

Local Rules:

gp · ir

Because i and r are adjacent, if p and r are not the same grade, then r must come **after** i. e and h can be placed anywhere. pp and ir do not overlap, which could be important. That is as far as we can go with the local rules, so we work the choices to see what must be true:

(A) Nope, there does not have to be an A. We can place g in B and then fill the other subjects in lower than A.

(B) This is even more specific than (A). There does not have to be an A grade.

(C) B and D are right in the middle of the base:

A (B) C (D) E

Because gp and ir do not overlap there is no way to place our two blocks without hitting both B and D. Simply put, to avoid them, we would have to place everything on ACE and we have at least four different grades. (C) is correct.

18.

If e is lower than p, then we have this link:

gp · e · h

In order to fail at least one course, we need proof that either i or r must be **before** g (pushes h into E) or **after** h (meaning i or r is in E). (E) gives us what we need:

g	p	e	h	r
A	B	C	D	E

i must be a D.

Relative Sequencing Games

Relative Sequencing games ask you to order variables, but all the rules are relative. You are only told information about each variable **in relation** to another variable, never in relation to the base. The variables are sequenced, but they are never "attached" to a base. For instance, you are never told that Tim is in lane three. That is direct information that connects Tim to the base. To be successful on Relative Sequencings Games, you need to work without that type of information. The rules will tell you that Tim is ahead of Ryan, information that compares variables to one another.

Relative Sequencing games make up 13% of the recent games questions. You run about a 50% chance of seeing one on your official LSAT, so it is worth your time to learn their unique methods.

No Main Diagram

A Relative Sequencing game might feature a comparison of house sizes as its central activity. You may be told that Jim has a larger house than Sam, but you will never be told that Jim's house is 3000 square feet or how much bigger Jim's house is than Sam's. You will not even be told the scale for houses that you are working with (what the size range is). You will only know that certain people have larger or smaller houses than other people. Usually, all the rules can be combined into a single rule diagram that will serve as your MD.

Approach

Do not assume that because you are comfortable with Sequencing games that you can easily handle Relative Sequencing games. They are another beast. The key is to treat them as such, while still employing some of the Sequencing rule diagrams.

Pick the Direction of Your Scale

On Relative Sequencing games, you will need to represent objects on a directional scale. In the house game above, we might decide that to the left are the small houses and to the right are the big ones:

Small → Big

On this scale, a house that is to the left of another is smaller than the one that is to its right.

You must be clear on the direction of your scale so that your rule Diagram is consistent. Without a MD with a base to look at, it is important to give yourself a scale for the diagrams you are using. Once you have your scale down for the game, you can easily represent rules. Example rule:

Pat's house is smaller than Jenny's.

Because we know that smaller houses are to the left of larger ones, we can easily create a diagram for the rule:

P · J

Here is another example:

Kate's house is larger than Bill's but smaller than Reid's.

Diagram:

B · K · R

We recommend representing the "smaller" part of the scale on the left. In a game that deals with numbers, the left side would be the smaller numbers and the right side the larger ones. Because we read from left to right, most students are comfortable with having the scale "grow" as it progresses to the right.

Link Rules When Possible

To setup the rules effectively on Relative Sequencing games, you will need to link many different rules. You learned how to do this with Sequencing games.

Pat's house is smaller than Jenny's.
Pat's house is bigger than Ryan's.

Individual Diagrams and how we link them:

```
      P · J
+   R · P
-----------
=   R · P · J
```

If you can see how to connect the rules as you read them, do not bother with individual rule diagrams. Instead, diagram one rule and then link the next rule right into it. In the example above, we would draw this diagram:

P · J

And then we would add "R ·" to the front of the diagram to link in the second rule:

R · P · J

On Relative Sequencing games, it is fine to diagram the rules as you read them. An initial read through of the rules before diagramming is less necessary on this type.

Layers

Recall that layers are a way to condense information from relative links. Being comfortable with layers is crucial on Relative Sequencing games.

Normal Layers

Here is a rule that should be diagrammed using layers:

> Kate's house is smaller than Bill's and Reid's.

We do not know who out of Bill and Reid has the bigger house. We show that Kate's house is smaller than (to the left of) both of the other houses:

```
    B
K <
    R
```

In a layer diagram, we can only compare variables connected through the slanted lines. We can compare K and B, and see that K has a smaller house. We cannot compare B to R because they are on separate layers and are not connected. Here is another example:

> John's and Phil's houses are smaller than Kate's house.

Put John and Phil on their own layers and show that both have smaller houses than Kate does:

```
J
  >  K
P
```

We can connect these two layered diagrams because the diagrams have Kate as a common variable:

```
J          B
  >  K  <
P          R
```

This combined diagram tells us more than using each part. For instance, if there are only five variables in the game, we know that Kate is third. That is because J and P come before her and B and R come after her:

J/P J/P K B/R B/R

We do not know who comes first with J and P or B and R, but we know the relative ordering of the variables due to our combined diagram.

Here is another pair of rules that you need to use layers to diagram:

Sam's house is smaller than Yvette's and Agatha's.
Agatha's house is smaller than Tim's.

Diagramming the first rule is easy:

```
   Y
S <
   A
```

Diagramming the second rule requires adding a relative link to a variable that is in a layer. To do so, use the relative link symbol and add the variable after it:

```
   Y
S <
   A · T
```

This diagram tells us that **both A and T** come after S and that T comes after A. Y also comes after S. We do not know how Y and A or Y and T relate because they are on separate layers. Each layer is its own path, its own set of relative links. Here, we have these two paths:

S · Y
S · A · T

The layers allow you to show both paths on the same diagram and to draw information from that combination. For instance, we know that S comes before three variables – Y, A and T. This information is obvious on the combined diagram.

Advanced Layers

Sometimes, you will need to add a link to a variable that is already on a layer. Or you may need to link to a variable that is in a long chain. In these situations, draw another slanted line to that variable to create a new layer. We call these advanced layers. Look at these rules:

Sam's house is smaller than Yvette's and Agatha's.
Agatha's house is bigger than Jack's.

These rules are similar to those in the previous example, but the second rule is harder to incorporate. Rule 1 Diagram:

```
   Y
S <
   A
```

How do we show that Jack's house is smaller than Agatha's?

We cannot draw this diagram:

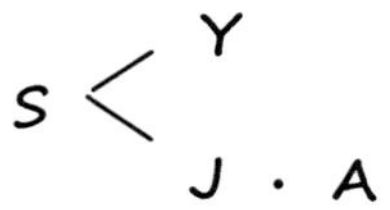

```
      Y
S <
      J · A
```

The above diagram tells us that Jack's house is bigger than Sam's house, and we do not know that. We only know that Jack comes before Agatha and that Agatha comes after Sam. Therefore, we need another layer in the diagram that links J to A. Add another layer off of A to the left, because J has a smaller house than A:

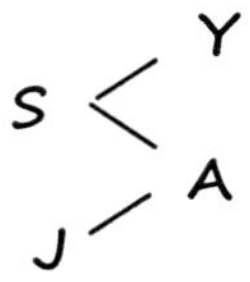

```
      Y
S <
      A
J /
```

The three paths that this diagram represents are:

S · Y
S · A
J · A

The combined diagram tells you more than these separate rules. For instance, that both S and J have smaller houses than A.

Here is another set of rules that is challenging to diagram without using an additional slanted line to create another layer:

> Mark's house is smaller than Kyle's and bigger than Paul's.
> Nicole's house is bigger than Kyle's.
> Richard's house is bigger than Mark's house.

We diagram the first rule with a relative chain:

P · M · K

Then, to represent rule 2, add N to the end of the chain:

P · M · K · N

To build in the final rule, connect R to the chain using an additional layer:

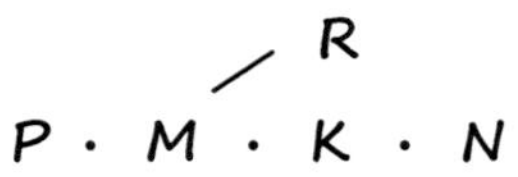

```
         R
       /
P · M · K · N
```

We have two paths:

P · M · R
P · M · K · N

As we see on the first path, R can be compared to P and M (R has a larger house than both). R is not on a path with K or N, so we cannot compare it to those variables. R could have a larger or smaller house than N.

New Concepts

Relative Sequencing games test concepts that you have never seen before. Learn these well so they do not catch you by surprise on test day:

Equality

It is possible for variables **to be equal** in Relative Sequencing games. A rule can tell you that one variable is not ahead of or not behind another variable:

Kate's house is not smaller than Phil's.

We know that Kate's house is equal to or larger than Phil's. Use the relative link dot and a line underneath it to signal that these variables may be equal. Diagram:

K $\underline{\cdot}$ P

The line underneath the dot indicates the potential for equality and is crucial. A question may hinge on the fact that these two variables are equivalent.

Mutually Exclusive Rules

Watch out for rules that introduce two possibilities that cannot exist at the same time. We call these mutually exclusive rules. They change the nature of the game and how you diagram the rules. Mutually exclusive rule:

James has a smaller house than Sara, or Sara has a smaller house than James.

Diagram both possibilities and work off of each chain when incorporating the rest of the rules:

J · S
S · J

Imagine that the next rule in the game is this one:

Bryan has a bigger house than Sara.

You need to build the above rule into both of the chains that you created for the mutually exclusive rule. Here are both chains:

J · S · B

S < J, B

The second diagram above shows that Sarah has a smaller house than both Brian and James. One rule with two meanings can create extra work. Be ready for this rare situation and accept the fact that you need two rule chains for the game.

One Variable Rules

You may be given a rule about a variable that is difficult to show in your rule chain. When that happens, circle the variable as a reminder of the rule. Then, diagram the rule separately, away from the rule chain. For this example rule, assume that Karen is part of a rule chain:

> Karen cannot be fourth.

Here is the rule chain with K circled:

```
             R
P · M  <
             Ⓚ · N
```

Below is the individual rule diagram:

- K4

If you had a MD with slots, then you could build in a not rule. However, Relative Sequencing games are not conducive to MDs. The circle is an easy way to remember that a specific rule applies to K.

Check the Limits of the Game

After diagramming the rules but before starting the questions, figure out who can be first and who can be last in the game. This information gives you context by thinking who can be on either extreme, and it may help you answer a question or eliminate incorrect choices. Look at this rule chain:

```
P           R
  > M  <
Q           K · N
```

How can we tell who can be first? Look at the variables that **begin each path**, those furthest to the left. P starts one path and Q another, so only those two variables can come first. To see who can come last, check the variables that are furthest to the right on any path. Only R and N can come last; they end their respective paths.

Information about the extremes can be helpful, so remember to derive it before you turn to the questions.

*Relative Sequencing Games Review

- Relative Sequencing games ask you to order variables like a normal sequencing game, but all the rules are relative.
    - The rules do not give you information on how the variables connect to the base.
- Generally, all the rules can be combined into a single **rule diagram** that will serve as your MD.

Approach

- Pick the direction of your scale. All rules will be represented with that scale in mind.
    - Example in a game where you are ordering houses by size:

      Small → Big

- Diagram the rules as you read them.
- Link rules when possible.
- Be ready to use layers:
    - "John's house and Phil's house are smaller than Kate's house."

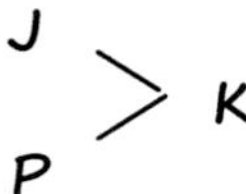

    - You can connect a variable to a chain by adding a new layer with a line.
    - "Ryan has a smaller house than Michael."

      R
      /
      P · M · K · N

New Concepts

- Equality - two variables can be equal in Relative Sequencing games.
    - "Kate's house is not smaller than Phil's."

      K $\underline{\cdot}$ P

    - The line underneath the dot indicates the potential for equality
- Mutually exclusive rules - rules that introduce two possibilities that cannot exist at the same time.
    - "James has a smaller house than Sara, or Sara has a smaller house than James."
    - Diagram both possibilities and work off of each chain when incorporating the rest of the rules.
        - This takes a lot of time, but is necessary.
- One Variable rules – rules that only affect a single variable. These are hard to show in your rule chain.
    - Circle the variable in the chain as a reminder of the rule.
    - Then, diagram the rule separately, away from the chain.
- Check the <u>limits</u> of the game.
    - After diagramming the rules but before starting the questions, figure out which variables can be first and which can be last in the game.
    - To tell who can be first, look at the variables that begin each path, those furthest to the left.
    - To tell who can be last, look at the variables that are at the end of each path, those on the right.

55/4 #13-18

Example Relative Sequencing game:

> Mercotek carried out a study to compare the productivity of its night shift with that of its day shift. Every week the company's six crews - F, G, H, R, S, and T - were ranked from first (most productive) to sixth (least productive). There were no ties. For any given week, either G and T were the two night-shift crews or else S and H were; the four other crews were the day-shift crews for that week. The following relationships held for every week of the study:
>
> F is more productive than G.
> R is more productive than S.
> R is more productive than T.
> S is more productive than H.
> G is more productive than T.

This is a Relative Sequencing game because the study includes multiple iterations: every week the variables are reordered. In normal Sequencing games the variables are ordered once. Every rule is relative: there is no discussion of slots in the rules. No rule says that a variable is 2nd or that a variable cannot be last. Get ready for a Relative Sequencing game with a single, complicated rule diagram.

At this point, we are not sure how the night shift versus the day shift aspect will play out. Note who can work the night shifts:

Night: GT or SH

Now onto the rules. We first establish our scale:

More productive → Less Productive

We use this scale even though it is somewhat counter intuitive. The setup gives us this scale when it says that the first shift is the most productive, so we have little choice. Diagram rule 1 using the scale:

F · G

Diagram rules 2-4 on a different chain, building in each new part of the chain as you read the rule. Rules 2 and 3 need to be diagrammed simultaneously (built into one layered link). Here is the big chain:

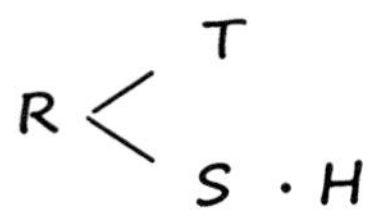

```
    T
R <
    S · H
```

Rule 5 allows you to build rule 1 into the big chain because it links G and T:

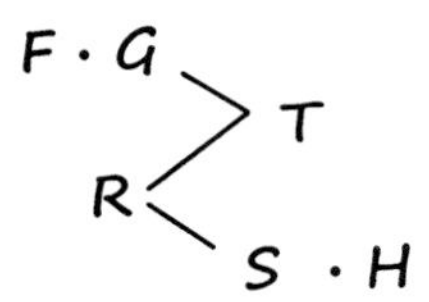

```
F · G
      > T
  R <
      S · H
```

Keep in mind that you can only compare variables that are linked through dots and lines. For instance, we know that F and G are more productive than T. But, we cannot say that F or G is more productive than S.

This solution is possible:

R S H F G T

Even though our diagram looks like F and G would be more productive than S because they are further to the left, this is not what the links in the diagram say. Always follow the links (either dots or lines) and you will not go wrong.

With our central diagram set up, check the extremes. Use the rule chain to identify who can be first by looking at those on the left side of the two paths. F or R must be first (the most productive). Now look at the right side of the paths to identify who can be last. T or H must be last. Onto the questions:

13. Which one of the following could be an accurate ranking of all the crews, in order from first to sixth, for a given week of the study?

(A) F, G, T, R, S, H
(B) F, R, G, T, H, S
(C) G, R, T, S, H, F
(D) R, F, G, S, H, T
(E) R, S, H, T, F, G

This is a List question. Because we know who can be first and last, we can use that information to eliminate any choices that feature other variables in those locations. F or R must be first, so eliminate (C), which features G first. Next, we use the fact that T or H must be last to eliminate (B) and (E). We are left with (A) and (D). (A) is eliminated by looking at our rule diagram: R must be before T. (D) is correct.

14. If F is ranked third for a given week of the study, then which one of the following could also be true of that week?

(A) G ranks second.
(B) H ranks fourth.
(C) R ranks second.
(D) S ranks fourth.
(E) T ranks fourth.

This is a local Could be True question, one that benefits from a mini diagram. If F is ranked 3rd, then exactly two variables come before it. R must be first because F is not. S must be second, because no other variable can be before F other than S. Diagram:

R S F __ __ __

G, T and H must come in the last three slots, but we do not know the order, except that G is before T. With a solid mini diagram like this, working the choices is simple. (B) is possible, all the rest are not.

15. Which one of the following CANNOT be the crew ranked fifth for any given week of the study?

(A) G
(B) H
(C) R
(D) S
(E) T

This is a global Cannot be True question. We are asked who cannot be fifth. Start by looking for variables that are far to the left because it is unlikely that they can be ranked fifth. R and F are on the left sides of their respective chains. (C) must be correct. The lowest that R can be ranked is 3rd: only F and G can be ahead of R. S, T and H all come after R.

16. For any given week of the study, the ranking of all the crews is completely determined if which one of the following is true?

(A) F ranks second that week.
(B) G ranks fifth that week.
(C) H ranks third that week.
(D) R ranks third that week.
(E) S ranks third that week.

This is a Structure question, a Full Solution one. Analyze the choices while looking for a **single variable placement** that will force all the other variables into specific spots. We know we are looking for one variable that will determine a full solution, because all the choices feature a single variable. Looking at our rule chain, we need to know who comes first out of S and T, because they are on different layers. Any choice that does not force S and T into a specific ordering cannot be correct.

(A) If F ranks second, then R ranks first. We do not know who comes first out of S and T and this choice is incorrect.

(B) If G is fifth, then T must be sixth. But we do not know who is first between R and F. This is incorrect.

(C) If H is 3rd, then R and S must be first and second because they are ahead of H on that path. The other path in the rule chain, FGT, must be in 4- 6, their order in their path:

R S H F G T
__ __ __ __ __ __

By setting one path before the other path, every variable is given a slot and a full solution is determined. (C) is correct. For teaching purposes:

(D) If R is third, then F and G both come before it. They are the only variables that can because every other variable comes after R. But we do not know who comes first between T and S. This does not provide a full solution.

(E) If S is third, then H and T must come after it and R before it, but we do not know much else. This is incorrect. Next:

17. If the night-shift crews rank fifth and sixth for a given week of the study, then which one of the following could also be true of that week?

(A) G ranks fourth.
(B) H ranks fifth.
(C) R ranks third.
(D) S ranks fourth.
(E) T ranks fifth.

This is a local Could be True question. The information about the night crews comes into play: they are either S and H or G and T. Notice that these are the two variables at the ends of their respective chains. Work each choice:

(A) G ranks fourth.

If G is fourth, that means G and T are not the night crew, so S and H are the night crew, and they are located 5th and 6th. This cannot work because T must come after G and the last three slots are already filled.

(B) H ranks fifth.

This is not possible, because H is part of the SH night crew and S must come before H. So either S and H are in 5, 6 respectively or G and T are in 5, 6. Given the local rule, H cannot be 5th.

(C) R ranks third.

If R is 3rd, then F and G must be 1st and 2nd because they are the only crews that can be ranked higher than R. This means that T must be 4th and S and H are 5th and 6th:

F G R T S H

The SH night crew is placed and the rest of the variables fit. (C) is correct. The final question:

18. Which one of the following is a complete and accurate list of the crews that CANNOT be ranked third for any given week of the study?

(A) G, H, S
(B) R, T
(C) F, T
(D) G, T
(E) T

This is a Slot List question, a Cannot be True one. Identify all crews that cannot be third. Look at the rule chain and analyze which crews must have more than two variables before them. Any crew with three or more shifts in front of it cannot be third.

Only one variable fits the bill: T. T has three variables that come before it, RFG, so T can never be third. Every other variable in the game can be third. (E) is correct.

*Relative Sequencing Practice Games

Game 1, Questions 1–5

On the basis of an examination, nine students—Fred, Glen, Hilary, Ida, Jan, Kathy, Laura, Mike, and Nick—are each placed in one of three classes. The three highest scorers are placed in the level 1 class; the three lowest scorers are placed in the level 3 class. The remaining three are placed in the level 2 class. Each class has exactly three students.

Ida scores higher than Glen.
Glen scores higher than both Jan and Kathy.
Jan scores higher than Mike.
Mike scores higher than Hilary.
Hilary scores higher than Nick.
Kathy scores higher than both Fred and Laura.

1. How many different combinations of students could form the level 1 class?

(A) one
(B) two
(C) three
(D) four
(E) six

2. Which one of the following students could be in the level 2 class but cannot be in the level 3 class?

(A) Fred
(B) Glen
(C) Jan
(D) Kathy
(E) Nick

3. Which one of the following students could be placed in any one of the three classes?

(A) Fred
(B) Jan
(C) Kathy
(D) Laura
(E) Mike

4. The composition of each class can be completely determined if which one of the following pairs of students is known to be in the level 2 class?

(A) Fred and Kathy
(B) Fred and Mike
(C) Hilary and Jan
(D) Kathy and Laura
(E) Laura and Mike

5. Which one of the following pairs of students cannot be in the same class as Fred?

(A) Hilary and Nick
(B) Jan and Laura
(C) Kathy and Laura
(D) Jan and Mike
(E) Laura and Mike

Game 2, Questions 7-12

A farmer harvests eight separate fields—G, H, J, K, L, M, P, and T. Each field is harvested exactly once, and no two fields are harvested simultaneously. Once the harvesting of a field begins, no other fields are harvested until the harvesting of that field is complete. The farmer harvests the fields in an order consistent with the following conditions:

Both P and G are harvested at some time before K.
Both H and L are harvested at some time before J.
K is harvested at some time before M but after L.
T is harvested at some time before M.

6. Which one of the following could be true?

(A) J is the first field harvested.
(B) K is the second field harvested.
(C) M is the sixth field harvested.
(D) G is the seventh field harvested.
(E) T is the eighth field harvested.

7. If M is the seventh field harvested, then any one of the following could be the fifth field harvested EXCEPT:

(A) H
(B) J
(C) K
(D) L
(E) P

8. Which one of the following CANNOT be the field that is harvested fifth?

(A) G
(B) J
(C) M
(D) P
(E) T

9. If J is the third field harvested, then which one of the following must be true?

(A) L is the first field harvested.
(B) H is the second field harvested.
(C) T is the fourth field harvested.
(D) K is the seventh field harvested.
(E) M is the eighth field harvested.

10. If H is the sixth field harvested, then which one of the following must be true?

(A) G is harvested at some time before T.
(B) H is harvested at some time before K.
(C) J is harvested at some time before M.
(D) K is harvested at some time before J.
(E) T is harvested at some time before K.

11. If L is the fifth field harvested, then which one of the following could be true?

(A) J is harvested at some time before G.
(B) J is harvested at some time before T.
(C) K is harvested at some time before T.
(D) M is harvested at some time before H.
(E) M is harvested at some time before J.

*Relative Sequencing Practice Games Explanations

Game 1 (10/2 # 1 – 5)

Variable Lists

Students: F, G, H, I, J, K, L, M, N

Rule List

Combine the rules as you write them down because they add up easily.

Rules 1 and 2: I • G • J/K (J above K, divided by a dashed line)

We do not know who scores higher out of J and K, so place them vertically and divide them with a dashed line.

Rules 3, 4, 5: J • M • H • N

And we combine this group with rules 1 and 2:

I • G • J • M • H • N / K (J • M • H • N above K, divided by a dashed line)

Rule 6: K • F/L (F above L, divided by a dashed line)

Combined with the larger group:

I • G • J • M • H • N / K • F/L (J • M • H • N above, dashed line, K • F/L below)

Initial Central Diagram

1 I G J/K
2
3

I and G must be in the first group, because they score higher than all the other students.

Only J and K can also be in that group because there is only space for one more student and those two are at the top of their respective chains. Draw a line under J/K to show that one of those two will take a single spot.

QUESTIONS

1. Global, Must be True

There are only two possible combinations from the central diagram. **B** is correct.

2. Global, Must be True

Looking at the big block, J cannot be in Level 3, because three students scored lower than her. But J can be in the level 2 class, if K is in the level 1 class. **C** is correct.

3. Global, Must be True

Who can go in all three of the classes? It must be either J or K, because they are the only two who can be in 1 or elsewhere (I and G must be in 1). The previous question showed that J cannot be in 3, so K must be the answer. **C** is correct.

4. Global, Must be True

Try each pair in level 2 to see which dictates the placement of the rest of the students.

A) If F and K are in 2, then we do not know if L is placed in 2 or 3.
B) If F and M are in 2, then we do not know whether K or J is in 1.
C) If H and J are in 2, then K must be in 1 (because J is not). Also, M must be in 2, because it comes before H. Therefore, N, F and L must be in 3. **C** works.

5. Global, Must be True

Who cannot be with F? I and G cannot be so we check the choices. Those options are not present. Work the choices.

A) H, N and F can all be in level 3.
B) J, L and F can all be in level 2, with K in 1.
C) K, F and L can all be in level 3, with J in 1.
D) J, M and F can be in level 2.
E must be correct, because all the other pairs could be with F.

This question was long because we had to work through four choices to see that the fifth was correct. There is no way around this.

Game 2 (48/ 2 # 7-12)

Variable List: G H J K L M P T

The setup tells us that each field is harvested once and only one at a time. This is standard sequencing information, yet we do not know whether it is a normal or relative sequencing game. Because the setup has no information about multiple fields being harvested on a given day, we can rule out this being an advanced sequencing game.

Rule 1: P and G are harvested at some point before K.

As we read this rule and quickly glance over the rest of them, we see no specific slot information, so we know this is a relative sequencing game. That means we want to end up with a complete MD (main diagram) that incorporates every variable and we might need to do some tricky linking to get there. Let us get the first rule diagrammed:

```
P
  > K
G
```

We use this scale with all our diagrams: earlier harvest -> later harvest. So, K is to the right of both P and G. We do not know which comes first of P and G.

Rule 2: H and L are harvested at some time before J.

```
H
  > J
L
```

We are not sure how this diagram will interact with the one from Rule 1 yet.

Rule 3: K is harvested before M but after L.

This rule gives us a connection between K and L, and a way to combine the two diagrams from rules 1 and 2. We can combine them like this, using L as the variable in common:

```
P
G > K · M
L
  > J
H
```

To create this more integrated diagram, we show three variables before K. One of those variables is L, which also comes before J, so we connect L to J. And we know that H comes before J as well, as is shown above in much the same way it was shown for Rule 1. Finally, we show that M comes after K, the final part of Rule 3.

Rule 4: T comes at sometime before M.

Build off of the large diagram:

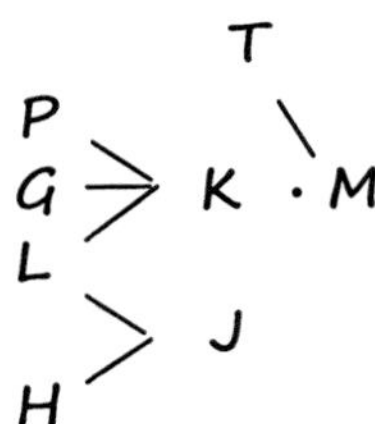

Now that we have a comprehensive MD that lets us see the relative positions of each variable, we can think about who can go first and who can go last. T, P, G, L and H can all go first, because they have no variables to the left of them on our diagram. Not very much can be derived from this fact because there are five of them. However, only two variables can go last: M and J. We know this fact because these variables have no variables to the right of them in the MD. So, we know if either of those two is NOT last, then the other must be. For instance, if M is in 7, then J must be in 8.

Now, with this solid foundation, we move to the questions:

7. A global Could be True question. Work each choice, using the MD with an eye towards elimination:

(A) J cannot be first because L and H come before it.

(B) K cannot be second because P, G and L all come before it. The earliest K can be is 4th.

(C) M 6th? We see no reason this cannot be the case. Keep the choice and work the rest.

(D) G cannot be 7th because both K and M come after it. The latest G could be is 6th.

(E) Recall that only M and J can be the final field harvested.

Only (C) can work.

8. A local question that asks us who cannot be 5th if M is 7th. Think about the local rule before working the choices. Recall our insight that if either M or J is NOT 8th, then the other of the two must be. Here, we are told that M is 7th (this is the same as NOT 8th). So, J must be 8th, which means J cannot be 5th. (B) is correct.

Here, analyzing the local rule thoroughly before working the choices was quite helpful.

9. A global question asking which variable cannot be 5th. Let's take a moment with our MD to see who must either be quite early or quite late in the ordering. Not many need to come quite early (ie have a lot of variables after them – at most L must have three variables come after it (K, M and J), but that means that it could still be 5th. M fits the bill for having to come quite late, because 5 variables come before it. (C) is correct.

Notice that M played a prominent role in this and the previous question. M and J will turn out to be key variables in this game.

10. A local Must be True question. If J is 3rd, then we know that M must be last. That inference about the possibilities for who can be last is really coming in handy. (E) is correct. Again, M played a key role in this question. The extreme variables on relative sequencing games give the game a lot of structure.

11. Let's look at the implications of the local rule. If H is sixth, then we know that J must come after it and be either 7th or 8th. From here, we look at the rest of the variables, this diagram:

T

P

G > K · M

L

We see that M has to come after these five other variables. That means that M must be 7th or 8th. Knowing that, we work the choices. (D) must be true.

12. A local Could be True question. Let's see the implications of the local rule. If L is 5th, then K, M and J must all come after it. The other variables, P, G, L, H can be anywhere in slots 1-4. Working the choices, we can eliminate A through D. (E) must be correct: M could come before J. These two have tended to be interchangeable except when we are told otherwise, so this makes sense.

Advanced Sequencing Games

Now that you understand Sequencing games, you can learn the next game type: Advanced Sequencing Games. These are more complex than normal sequencing games because they involve multiple levels on top of the base. Look at this setup:

> Six brothers – Tim, Jeff, Rob, Bill, Zack and Alex – are building a fence and working in shifts. One brother will work each shift and the shifts are morning and night, from a Monday through a Thursday. Two brothers will each work two shifts during the building process. The ordering of the shifts conforms to the following rules:
>
> Rob works on Monday morning.
> Alex only works one shift and it is after both of Bill's.
> Zack does not work any morning.
> Tim does not work in the afternoon on the first two work days.
> Bill works Tuesday afternoon.

The base is the days of the week. To represent this game, our MD needs to account for the fact that there are two shifts each day, so each day of the base needs two slots, with one on top of the other:

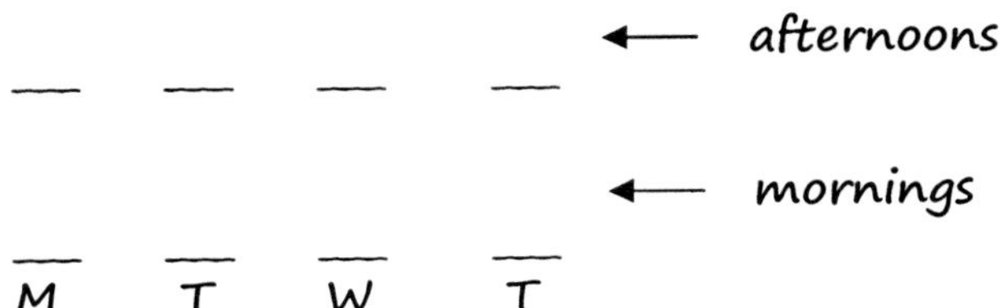

The mornings are the first level stacked on top of the base, which should be intuitive; the afternoons are the second. Each level will hold variables in its slots. For instance, rule 1 - Rob works on Monday morning – is built directly into the MD:

```
___   ___   ___   ___

 R
___   ___   ___   ___
 M     T     W     T
```

We build rule 5 – Bill works Tuesday afternoon - directly into the MD as well:

```
       B
___   ___   ___   ___

 R
___   ___   ___   ___
 M     T     W     T
```

Do not confuse **levels** in an Advanced Sequencing game with **layers** used in rule diagrams in a normal sequencing game. A normal Sequencing game has no levels, so the layers used have a different meaning: they indicate another chain or variable.

Draw the Slots

With the game above, we have drawn the slots for each level of the base. Slots are important here because you are working with at least two levels and without the slots your diagram can get confusing, especially when diagramming not rules. For your mini diagrams on Advanced Sequencing games, you have the option of not drawing the slots to save time.

You can write the name of each level next to it on one side of the diagram as we have or, if you can keep them straight in your mind, you can skip that step. With afternoons and mornings, it is pretty easy to remember which level is which. It can be more complicated when dealing with three levels or when you have levels that have no inherent structure.

Open vs Locked

There are two kinds of Advanced Sequencing games: open and locked. The fence building game just discussed is an <u>open game</u> because, in general, any variable can go on any level. Jeff can work a morning shift or a night shift; he can be on either the morning or afternoon level. Your job with that game is to figure out which level each variable should be placed on.

In a <u>locked</u> Advanced Sequencing game, each variable set has a specific level that it can be placed on and any variable from that set cannot be placed on a different level. Each variable set is "locked" on its level. Example locked Advanced Sequencing game:

> Nicaro has six songs for his demo cd – *All I See, Karambolage, Otherside, Resurrection, Trade Skins*, and *What Came First*. Four of the songs he considers great; the other two he thinks are only average. The six songs will be ordered on a cd with the following conditions:
>
> Resurrection will be played last.
> He considers the second song to be great.

The songs in this game have a trait **of quality**: they are either average or great. The songs themselves and the traits are separate variable sets. The trait variable set will go on a second level above the base, with the songs placed on the first level. Each variable set has its own level and the two do not mix: you will never place a song on the quality level or a quality on the song level. Here is the MD for this game with the two rules built in:

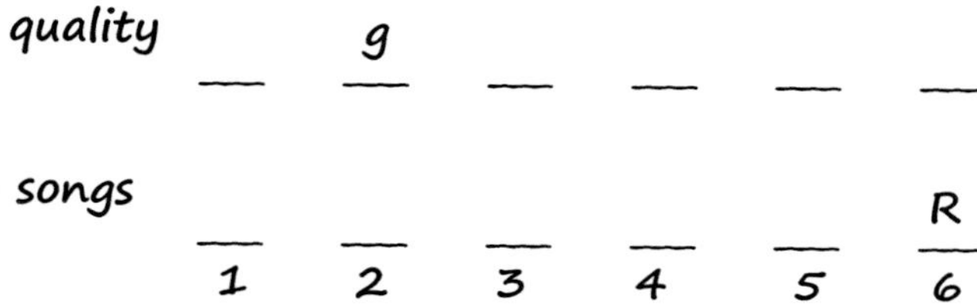

This is different from the fence building game where a single variable set was placed onto both levels of the game. We represent the quality variable set with **lowercase letters** to help us distinguish the two sets:

Quality: g g g g a a

Songs: A K O R T W

We need a differentiating feature for the **A** for "All I See" from the song variable set and the **a** for "average" from the quality set. The difference in capitalization is quite helpful as we work the game.

Forced Overlap in Locked Games

Locked games often repeat variables on a level, like the game above which features four gs and two as. Locked games with repeated variables often have a quality we call forced overlap. This is where a variable from one set must overlap with a variable from a different set. This concept is challenging to explain so bear with us. This locked game illustrates forced overlap:

> There are five mailboxes on a street. Three of the mail boxes are blue, one is red and one is green. The mail boxes are either cement or wooden, and there are three wooden mail boxes.

We have two variable sets related to the qualities of the mailboxes: color and material.

Color: B B B R G

Material: W W W C C

The first letters of the variables are all unique, so write both sets of symbols in uppercase, which is easier to read than lowercase.

Forced overlap tells you that there will be a specific overlap between the variables from the two sets because of the total numbers of those variables relative to the number of parts of the base (here the parts is five: the number of mailboxes). In this game, forced overlap tells us that there must be a wooden mailbox that is **blue**. This is because there are three blue mailboxes and three wooden mailboxes. Because there are only five **total** mailboxes, one of the five must be both blue and wooden:

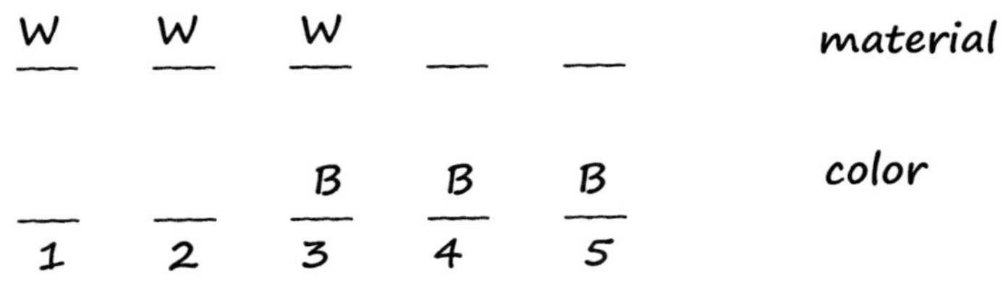

W	W	W	___	___	*material*
___	___	B	B	B	*color*
1	2	3	4	5	

Whenever you add up the number of a repeated variable from two different variables sets and that number totals more than the number of parts of the base, then you will have forced overlap. In this example, there are 3 wooden mailboxes and 3 blue mail boxes; those are the repeated variables. That total is 6, and there are only 5 parts of the base, 5 mailboxes. Because 6 is more than 5, we have forced overlap. There must be at least one blue, wooden mailbox. Whenever forced overlap occurs, games will usually test your knowledge of it.

Rule Diagrams

Here is an example rule we might see in the song game:

Otherside is not a great song.

Each song is either great or average, so Otherside must be average. We diagram the rule like this:

```
a
O
```

This is a **two-level link** that features one variable from each set. O is linked to a: they always come together. Knowing this, we know that O cannot be 2, because the second song is g, not a.

Here is a rule for the game that, at first, seems tough to diagram:

All I See is two songs before an average song.

As always, our rule diagrams need to match our MD. If this were a normal sequencing game with a one-level base, we would represent this rule like this:

```
A _ a
```

The problem is that we are dealing with a two-level MD for this game. Therefore, the rule diagram above would represent two levels of variables in a single level. The vertical information in the rule is lost. This diagram is much more useful:

```
   _ a
A _
```

It is not necessary to draw the empty slot above the A or below the a. Those slots are obvious due to the two middle slots that A is on the lower level and a is on the upper level. The diagram is quite readable as is.

You must be clear on how your variable sets interact with the MD, so you do not accidently put a on the song level or A on the quality level. This is one of the challenges of Advanced Sequencing games, knowing which level is which. If you find yourself having trouble with this, label the levels on your MD.

This two-level rule Diagram above does take up more space, but it helps us by showing how the rule will look when applied to the MD. For instance, if we are told by a rule that the third song is g, then we can visualize that A cannot be in 1 because the a it is attached to by the link already has a g in its slot:

```
 __   g    g   __   __   __

                         R
 __   __   __  __   __   __
 1    2    3   4    5    6
```

When we look at our rule diagram, it is clear that the a cannot go in the quality level slot of the third song, so we build in the not rule for the A:

```
__   g    g   __   __   __
    __   __

                         R
__   __   __   __   __   __
1    2    3    4    5    6
A
```

We just illustrated how powerful two-level rule diagrams are in **locked games**. In open Advanced Sequencing games, we **must** use two-level rule diagrams because there is only one variable set. There is no way to know that one variable in the rule Diagram should be on one level and the other variable on another level, because any variable can be on any level. For instance, in the building a fence game, to show this rule:

Rob works the afternoon on the day before Tim works the morning shift.

We must use two layers:

```
R
__  __
    T
```

This diagram makes the nature of the rule clear. Drawing the slots is recommended because they take very little time and make the diagram more organized.

There are some situations in open Advanced Sequencing games where you are better off with a one-level rule diagram. Example rule:

Rob works before Tim.

We can use a one level rule diagram because we are not told any level information. We know only *relative* ordering information:

R · T

This is how we would diagram this rule in a normal Sequencing game. Mornings come before afternoons, so R could be before T on the **same day**. This is what a mini-diagram illustrating this situation could look like:

```
T
R
__   __   __   __
```

Relative Links with Levels Information

Of course, sometimes relative links, like the one just covered, also feature level information. Returning to the Advanced Sequencing game dealing with songs, here is a more challenging rule to diagram:

> There is exactly one average song played before Trade Skins.

This is a relative link dealing with variables from two levels. We diagram it like this:

a · T

We use the relative symbol to show that we do not know exactly when the a comes before T. Another rule:

> There are three great songs played before What Came First.

This rule is challenging to represent. We use commas to show that the three g's are not necessarily consecutive:

g, g, g · W

Drawing the slots to make the separate levels clear is up to your discretion. If you feel more comfortable, instead of representing this rule visually, you can simply write it out in your own words:

Three g's before W

Do not be afraid to write out a rule that you are not comfortable diagramming.

Use a Rectangle to Represent A Part of the Base

Sometimes you will want to represent all the levels for one part of the base. This is most useful on **open games**, where any variable can go into any spot. For instance, look at this rule:

> Jeff works the day after Alex.

Use a <u>rectangle</u> to represent a day. Recall that a day is one complete part of the base; in this fence building game there are four days, each has two slots. Here is the diagram we would draw:

Stick the rectangles right next to each other to indicate that the days are consecutive. This diagram indicates that we do not know what level the variables will be on. The rectangle is a useful tool, because there are **four** different possibilities for the placement of variables on consecutive days here, so having a representation for an entire part of the base is vital.

All of these situations fit the bill (they are in mini diagram format):

```
A
       J
___    ___    ___    ___
```

```
 A      J
___    ___    ___    ___
```

```
        J
 A
___    ___    ___    ___
```

```
 A      J

___    ___    ___    ___
```

In other situations, you can use a rectangle to represent two variables occurring on the same part, when you do not know the order:

Rob works the same day as Jeff.

Diagram:

```
┌─┐
│R│
│J│
└─┘
```

Using the rectangle makes sense here because we do not know who is in the morning and who is in the afternoon. We just know they both work on that day. If we did know who was on what level, we would not use the rectangle. For instance:

Rob works in the morning on the day Jeff works in the afternoon.

Diagram:

```
J
R
```

Stick the two variables on top of one another in the correct order. No need to use a rectangle.

Not Links

To deal with not links, represent the rule as you would if it were positive and then add a "no" before the diagram.

Alex is never the day after Zack.

Use a couple of rectangles to diagram the situation of Alex being the day after Zack and then put "no" before it:

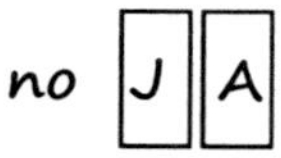

no [J][A]

To show that two variables are never on the same day, use no in front of a single rectangle with both variables in it.

Tim is never on the same day as Rob.

no [R / T]

Recall that we do not know which level which variable is on, and the rectangle indicates that. We are saying that Rob and Tim cannot share a part of the base. This diagram does not indicate that Rob cannot work on the afternoon on a day Tim works the morning. This diagram would indicate that:

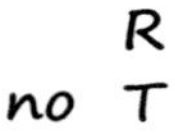

R
no T

Not Rules on the MD

On open Advanced Sequencing games, leave sufficient space under the upper levels of your MD (levels two and three) to draw not rules. Because any variable can go on any level, you may discover not rules for specific levels.

This is extra space is not important on locked games, because you can represent all not rules under the base of the MD. This is because you know exactly which level each variable can be placed on, so there is no confusion.

Open Games

Look at this rule from the fence game, which is an open game:

Tim does not work in the morning on Thursday.

Place Tim's variable abbreviation under Thursday as you would on a Sequencing game:

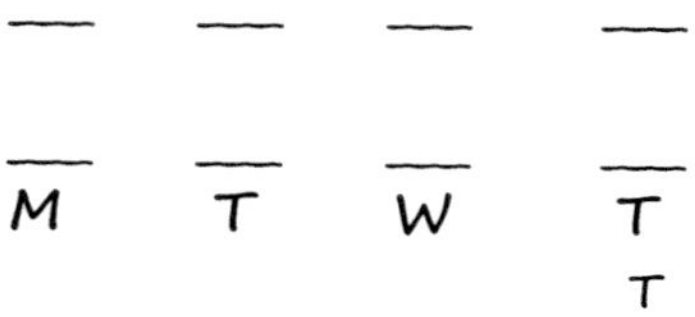

___	___	___	___
___	___	___	___
M	T	W	T
			T

Making the T for Tim smaller than the T for Thursday helps keep the meaning of MD clear.

Now look at this rule, which involves the second level:

Tim does not work in the afternoon on the first two work days.

We cannot use this diagram:

```
___   ___   ___   ___

___   ___   ___   ___
 M     T     W     T
 T     T
```

The diagram above implies that Tim cannot work on the **mornings** of Monday or Tuesday. This interpretation makes sense because the not rules are directly underneath the morning level, but of course, it is not what the rule says. Here is how you should diagram the two not rules:

```
___   ___   ___   ___
 T     T

___   ___   ___   ___
 M     T     W     T
```

This MD makes it clear that Tim cannot be in the **afternoon** on Monday or Tuesday. Just like with Sequencing games, the variables are placed underneath the slots they cannot be placed in. Draw the not rules a little smaller than the labels for the days of the week to help distinguish the different parts of the MD and to have room to fill in possibilities for the first level. On open games, leave plenty of space between your levels so that you can fit in not rules and still have space for the possibilities on the slots below any not rules.

A Part of the Base

To diagram a not rule that applies to an entire part of the base, you can either put the not rule under the slot for each level, or you can draw an arrow next to the variable abbreviation and place that diagram it underneath the part of the base. The arrow method avoids clutter in your MD. Example rule:

Tim does not work on Wednesday.

Diagram:

```
___   ___   ___   ___

___   ___   ___   ___
 M     T     W     T
             T↑
```

Based on this MD, we know that Tim cannot work in the morning *or* afternoon on Wednesday.

An Entire Level

If you are given a rule that says that a variable cannot be placed on an entire level of the MD, represent that by placing the variable to the left of the level with a negation sign (–) before it. The negation sign is helpful for this type of not rule because possibilities are generally in line with the slots, and we want to be clear that this is *not* a possibility. Example rule:

Bill does not work any morning shifts.

Diagram:

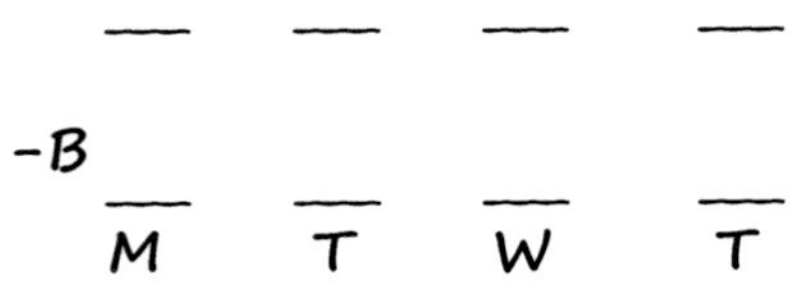

```
      ___   ___   ___   ___

-B
      ___   ___   ___   ___
       M     T     W     T
```

The diagram above indicates that Bill cannot be placed in **any of the shifts** on the first level. Here is how you would represent that Bill cannot be placed on the second level, the afternoon shifts:

Bill does not work any afternoon shifts.

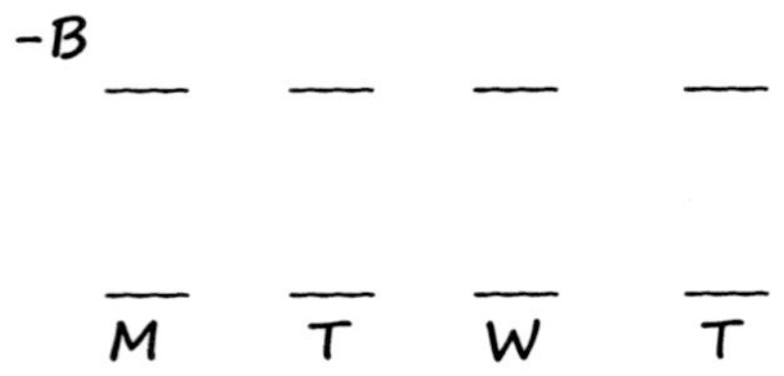

```
-B
      ___   ___   ___   ___


      ___   ___   ___   ___
       M     T     W     T
```

Repeating Variable Sets

Sometimes, an Advanced Sequencing game will ask you to order one set of variables in two different ways. This means you are repeating an entire variable set. Look at this example game setup:

> Five runners – Dustin, Brittany, Travis, April and Sean - will each be competing in two races, the 400m dash and the 800m dash.

We have a single variable set that will be used twice, on two separate levels. Each level will contain five runners:

```
___   ___   ___   ___   ___        → D B T A S

___   ___   ___   ___   ___        → D B T A S
 1     2     3     4     5
```

You would not need to write out all the variables on the side of each level; we have done so to help you visualize how repeating variable sets work in Advanced Sequencing games. The 8 and 4 to the left of each level indicate which race is on that level.

Let's practice the skills you have been learning by diagramming the rules for this game:

> Rule1: In both races, Dustin finishes after April.

We show the relative links on both levels:

```
A · D
A · D
```

Stacking the levels close to one another helps show that this is a single rule diagram. The implications for the MD are standard not rules: D cannot be first in either race, and A cannot be last in either race.

```
___   ___   ___   ___   ___

___   ___   ___   ___   ___
 1     2     3     4     5
D↑                      A↑
```

> Rule 2: Sean finishes last in the 800m dash.

This is an easy rule to build into the MD; just put Sean in the final slot for the 800m race:

```
                         S
___   ___   ___   ___   ___

___   ___   ___   ___   ___
 1     2     3     4     5
D↑                      A↑
```

Rule 3: Whoever wins the 400m dash takes second in the 800m.

This is a special kind of rule that can only occur when a variable set is reused. We use a star in the two slots to indicate that they are the same runner:

—	*	—	—	S
*	—	—	—	—
1	2	3	4	5
D↑				A↑

Whoever occupies the star slot in one race will occupy it in the other. Next rule:

Rule 4: Brittany does not finish better than fourth place in either race.

B must be either 4 or 5 in both races. Because S is already 5 in the 800m, B must be 4 there. We show the possibilities for B in the 400m:

—	*	—	B	S
*	—	—	B/	/B
1	2	3	4	5
D↑				A↑

Having worked all the rules, we can now look for inference. We have limited possibilities for who can be 1 in the 400m and 2 in the 800m, so focus we focus attention there. We know that D cannot win the 400m because A beats him in both races. Likewise, S cannot be the runner in the star positions because we already know that S is 5 in the 800m, not 2. And B is either 4 or 5. That only leaves T and A as possibilities in those slots, so we show those on the MD:

—	A/T	—	B	S
A/T	—	—	B/	/B
1	2	3	4	5
D↑				A↑

Also, D must be 3 in the 800m because he cannot be 1 or 2.

*Advanced Sequencing Games Review

- Advanced Sequencing games are more complex than Sequencing games.
  - They involve two or three levels on top of the base.
  - Writing labels for the different levels above the base can be helpful.
- Example Setup:
  - "Six brothers – Tim, Jeff, Rob, Bill, Zack and Alex – are building a fence and working in shifts. One brother will work each shift. The shifts are morning and night, Monday through Thursday. Two of the brothers will work two shifts during the building process."
    - Each day of the base has two slots: one that represents the mornings, another that represents the afternoons.
- Open vs Locked Games
  - In open games, any variable can go on any level of the base.
  - In locked games, each variable set has a specific level that it must be placed on.
  - Forced overlap is when a variable from one set must overlap with a variable from a different set. For instance, if you have a variable set of colors and cars, one truck must be blue.

Rule Diagrams

- Two level links feature two variables from different sets.
  - "Otherside is an average song."

    a
O

  - "Otherside is two songs before an average song."

    _ a
O _

- Use a rectangle to represent a complete part of the base and slots on all levels, for instance an entire day.
  - "Jeff works the day after Alex."

    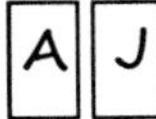

Not Rules

- On open games, leave space to draw not rules under each level of your MD.
  - "Tim does not work in the afternoon on the first two work days."

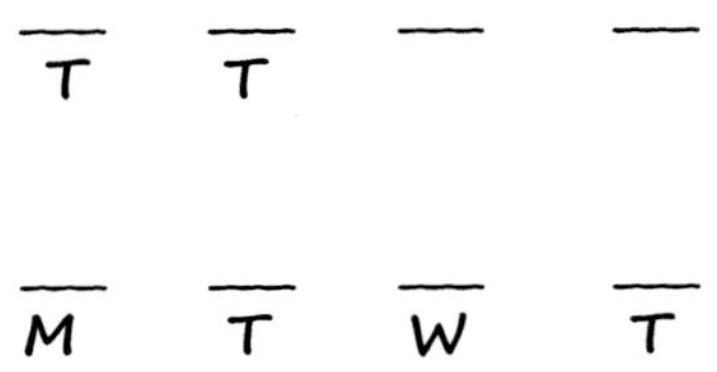

```
___   ___   ___   ___
 T     T


___   ___   ___   ___
 M     T     W     T
```

  - "Tim does not work on Wednesday."
  - Use an arrow to signify a not rule applies to multiple levels.

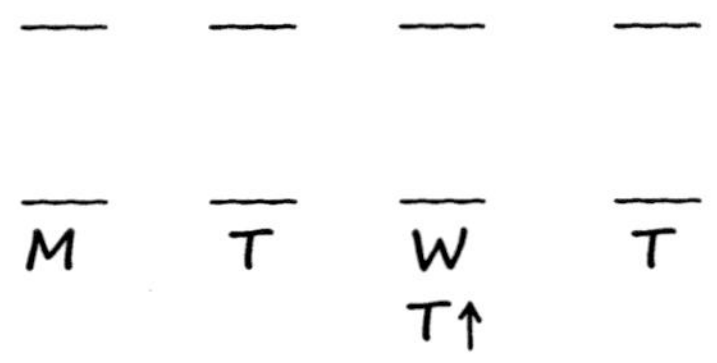

```
___   ___   ___   ___


___   ___   ___   ___
 M     T     W     T
             T↑
```

  - "Bill does not work any morning shifts."

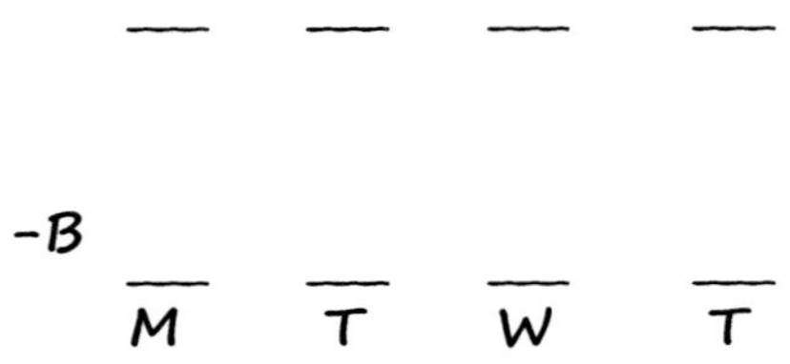

```
      ___   ___   ___   ___


-B
      ___   ___   ___   ___
       M     T     W     T
```

Repeating Variable Sets

- Advanced Sequencing games with repeated variable sets ask you to order one set of variables in two different ways.
- Example setup:
  - "Five runners – Dustin, Brittany, Travis, April and Sean - will each be competing in two races, the 400m dash and the 800m dash."
  - Here, each runner is used twice, once on each level.
- Use a * to indicate that two slots have the same variable and you are not sure which variable that is.

Example Advanced Sequencing Games

Now that you have a solid foundation for diagramming Advanced Sequencing games, let us work through a couple example games:

26/1 #1-7

> Eight physics students - four majors: Frank, Gwen, Henry, and Joan; and four non-majors: Victor, Wanda, Xavier, and Yvette - are being assigned to four laboratory benches, numbered 1 through 4. Each student is assigned to exactly one bench, and exactly two students are assigned to each bench. Assignments of students to benches must conform to the following conditions:
>
> Exactly one major is assigned to each bench.
> Frank and Joan are assigned to consecutively numbered benches, with Frank assigned to the lower-numbered bench.
> Frank is assigned to the same bench as Victor.
> Gwen is not assigned to the same bench as Wanda.

In this Advanced Sequencing game, we are asked to deal with two variables sets: majors and non-majors. We will use a two level MD to sequence these variable sets onto the four benches. We do so because of the following game aspects: the setup tells us that we will have two people per bench and the first rule states that one major is assigned to each bench. The other spot on each bench must be filled by a non-major, and therefore one level dedicated to each variable set works well.

This is a locked game because each variable set has its own level. This means we need less space between the levels on our MD because we can show not rules under the base, instead of needing to show them under the specific slots of each level.

Variable lists:

Majors: F G H J
Non-Majors: v w x y

We use lowercase letters for the non majors to help us visually distinguish between the two groups. With Advanced Sequencing games, we recommend writing out your variable lists next to the MD as a way to reinforce who can go on which level, instead of at the top of the page. This is built into the MD below. Onto the rules:

> Exactly one major is assigned to each bench.

We do not need to diagram the first rule because we have built it into the MD. Onto rules 2 and 3:

> Frank and Joan are assigned to consecutively numbered benches, with Frank assigned to the lower-numbered bench.
> Frank is assigned to the same bench as Victor.

Combined diagram, a link that spans two levels:

```
v __
F J
```

This three-variable link will come in quite handy.

We are dealing with only four variables for each level and we have already been told that v sits with F. That means that v cannot be with G. Because rule 4 tells us that G is not with w, G can only sit with x or y:

x/y
G

We show what can be instead of what cannot be. For instance, with this diagram in place, we know that if y sits with a major who is not G, then G must sit with x. We could show the not link for rule 4 instead, but it is much less informative than the possibility diagram. Here is what that not link would look like:

w
no G

Here is our MD at this point, with the not rules for the vFJ link built in:

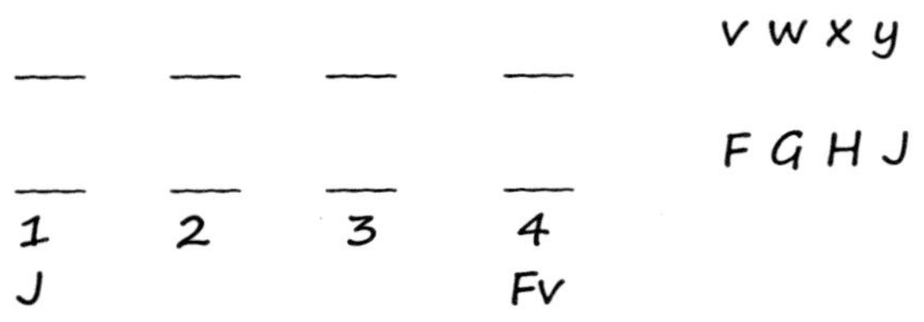

___	___	___	___	v w x y
___	___	___	___	F G H J
1	2	3	4	
J			Fv	

Because this is a locked game (each variable set has its own level) we can put the not rules underneath the slots in the MD, instead of underneath the specific level they apply to. This makes the MD more condensed because we do not need to put extra space under the second level.

There are no major inferences from the rules, but our MD is powerful. Onto the questions:

1. Which one of the following could be the assignment of students to benches?

(A) 1: Frank, Victor; 2: Joan, Gwen; 3: Henry, Wanda; 4: Xavier, Yvette
(B) 1: Gwen, Yvette; 2: Frank, Xavier; 3: Joan, Wanda; 4: Henry, Victor
(C) 1: Henry, Wanda; 2: Gwen, Xavier; 3: Frank, Victor; 4: Joan, Yvette
(D) 1: Henry, Xavier; 2: Joan, Wanda; 3: Frank, Victor; 4: Gwen, Yvette
(E) 1: Henry, Yvette; 2: Gwen, Wanda; 3: Frank, Victor, 4: Joan, Xavier

This is a List question so we will use the rules to eliminate choices until we are left with the correct one. rule 4 is a good rule to use initially because we can easily locate G and see who is with her. We eliminate choices (A) and (E) because we know that G can only be with x or y. Next use the vF link to eliminate (B) and then use the FJ link to eliminate (D). Choice (C) is correct.

2. If Victor is assigned to bench 2 and Wanda is assigned to bench 4, which one of the following must be true?

(A) Frank is assigned to bench 1.
(B) Gwen is assigned to bench 1.
(C) Henry is assigned to bench 3.
(D) Xavier is assigned to bench 1.
(E) Yvette is assigned to bench 3.

A local Must be True question. As with all local questions, we ponder whether it will be useful to draw a mini diagram. It seems like it will be.

You do not need to write the draw the slots for the second level:

```
      v          w
      F     J
___  ___   ___  ___
```

We place the vFJ link and w. From here, we see that G must go in 1, because she cannot be in 4 with w.

```
      v          w
 G    F     J
___  ___   ___  ___
```

We scan the choices at this point to see if we understand the scenario enough to find the answer. We do, (B) is correct. Select it and move on to the next question:

3. If Gwen and Henry are not assigned to consecutively numbered benches, which one of the following must be true?

   (A) Victor is assigned to bench 2.
   (B) Victor is assigned to bench 3.
   (C) Wanda is assigned to bench 1.
   (D) Wanda is assigned to bench 3.
   (E) Wanda is assigned to bench 4.

This is a local Must be True question. We can use the scenario from the previous question to eliminate a few choices because in that mini diagram G and H were not consecutive, so it applies to this question. We eliminate (B), (C) and (D). The information in those choices was not present in that scenario we created for question 2, so they are incorrect. To be the correct answer to a Must be True question, the information must be true **all the time**.

From here, we can eliminate (E) by moving w over to 3 with J in the scenario from question 2. That does not cause any problems. That means that it does not have to be the case that w is in 4 when G and H are not consecutive. We are left only with (A), the correct answer. This question demonstrates how helpful using scenarios from previous questions can be.

A more direct, but not necessarily faster, way to solve this question is to analyze the impacts of the local rule. If G and H are not consecutive, that means that they must be on either side of the FJ link:

```
G/H   F    J   G/H
___  ___  ___  ___
```

There is no other way to have G and H not be side by side. We see in the diagram above that the FJ link has to be in the middle of the benches, with F and v in 2 and therefore v in 2 as well. (A) must be true. Next question:

4. If Henry and Yvette are both assigned to bench 1, which one of the following could be true?

(A) Gwen is assigned to bench 3.
(B) Joan is assigned to bench 2.
(C) Wanda is assigned to bench 2.
(D) Wanda is assigned to bench 3.
(E) Xavier is assigned to bench 3.

A local Could be True question. The local rule tells us that y sits with H in 1. According to our understanding of rule 4, that means the x must sit with G. That leaves w (the last non-major) to be with J. Here is a mini diagram that helps us visualize the impact of the local rule and see the big link:

y
H
___ ___ ___ ___

v w
F J (the vFJ link with our local info that w is with J)

We have to place the vFwJ link in 2 and 3 or 3 and 4, so x and G will be together in either 2 or 4.

We work the choices, looking for one that is possible. (A) is not possible because there is no space to place the vFwJ link; x and G cannot be in 3. (B) is not possible because F comes before J. (C) is not possible because w is with J and, just like with (B), J cannot be on bench 2. (D) is possible:

y v w
H F J
___ ___ ___ ___

x and G fill in 4 in the mini diagram above. When you see a choice that can create a working solution on a Could be True question, you have found the correct answer and should move on to the next question.

For teaching purposes, (E) does not work, because the xG link cannot be in 3. That placement splits the remaining spots and prevents us placing the vFwJ link. This is the same reason (A) cannot be correct.

5. If Gwen is assigned to bench 4 and Xavier is assigned to bench 3, then any one of the following could be true EXCEPT:

(A) Gwen is assigned to the same bench as Yvette.
(B) Henry is assigned to the same bench as Wanda.
(C) Henry is assigned to the same bench as Xavier.
(D) Joan is assigned to the same bench as Xavier.
(E) Joan is assigned to the same bench as Yvette.

A local Cannot be True question. Here is the mini diagram, with the fact that G must sit with y (because she is not with x) built in:

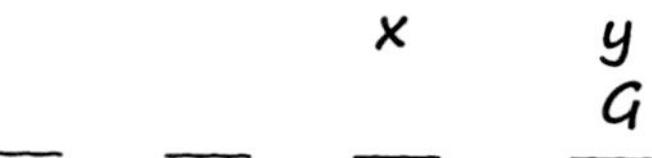

Work the choices, looking for one that cannot be true. (A) this is our main inference from the local rule. (B) this can work: Hw can be in 1 with the vFJ link in 2, 3. (C) is a working scenario too, with H in 3, the link must be in 1, 2. (D) is possible: the VFJ link can be in 2, 3 when J sits with x in 3. We have eliminated the other four choices so (E) must be correct. J cannot be with y, because G is with y, so (E) cannot be true. This is a correct choice based on our inference from the local rule, but we had to work through the other four choices to get to it. Scanning the choices more quickly looking for one of our inferences would have been a good choice because it would have saved time in working the question.

6. If Wanda is assigned to a lower-numbered bench than is Joan, then Henry must be assigned to a

(A) lower-numbered bench than is Frank
(B) lower-numbered bench than is Gwen
(C) lower-numbered bench than is Xavier
(D) higher-numbered bench than is Victor
(E) higher-numbered bench than is Yvette

This is a local Must be True question. The local rule tells us that w comes before J and therefore before the vFJ link. We can diagram this situation:

```
w  .  v __
      F J
```

The question asks us about H, so we focus our attention there. We know that H must be with w, because if H is not with w, then the only major left, G, must be with w and that breaks rule 4. We have this large link on our hands:

```
w  .  v __
H     F J
```

It is easy to work the choices and see that (A) must be true. H is assigned to a lower numbered bench than F. Next question:

7. Which one of the following could be the assignments for bench 2 and bench 4?

(A) 2: Gwen, Xavier
4: Henry, Yvette
(B) 2: Henry, Yvette
4: Joan, Xavier
(C) 2: Joan, Victor
4: Gwen, Xavier
(D) 2: Joan, Wanda
4: Gwen, Xavier
(E) 2: Joan, Xavier
4: Henry, Yvette

This is a global Could be True question involving benches 2 and 4. Check each choice carefully, eliminating those that are not possible. Keep the vFJ link in mind because that gives the game a lot of structure. (A) cannot work because there is no place to put the FJ link. G and H are the majors in 2 and 4 and they have effectively divided up the board to where no two majors can be placed in a row. (B) cannot work because both y and x are assigned to majors that are not G and we know that G sits with either x or y. (C) places v with J, which is incorrect. v is with F, not J. (D) looks promising. Here is a mini-diagram that shows the vFJ link:

```
 v     w           x
 F     J           G
___   ___   ___   ___
```

No reason why H and y, the remaining variables, cannot be on 3. (C) is correct, so select it. For teaching purposes: (E) does the same thing as (B). Both x and y are assigned to other majors; G has no one to sit with.

19/1 #8-12

The second example Advanced Sequencing game:

> In a theater company, four two-day workshops - Lighting, Production, Rehearsals, and Staging - are conducted over the course of five days, Monday through Friday. The workshops are conducted in a manner consistent with the following constraints:
>
> The two days on which a given workshop is in session are consecutive.
>
> On each of the five days, at least one, but no more than two, of the workshops are in session.
>
> The workshops on Production and Rehearsals begin no earlier than the day immediately following the second day of the workshop on Lighting.

After reading through the setup and rules, we see that this is an Advanced Sequencing game because we are sequencing workshops and we can have two workshops in a single day. Each workshop is two days long, and our base has five days: Monday through Friday. This game is open because any variable can go on any level.

Variable list: *LL PP RR SS*

We only have four workshops, but each runs for two consecutive days (according to rule 1) and we will be placing them on the MD in pairs. Think of each of the two day workshops as a two variable link.

Two workshops can be going on simultaneously on any day. Our two levels on our MD can be thought of as different conference rooms, instead of afternoon and morning (as we would often think of for a game with days as the base and two levels). There is no need to label the levels because this is an open game; any workshop can be in either conference room on a given day.

Rule 2 tells us that on any day, there will be either one or two workshops in session. We have a total of 10 slots on the base (5 days x 2 slots each day = 10 slots). Only *8* slots will be filled by the workshops. This means that two slots will be empty. Make a note:

2 empty slots

Rule 3 is our only sequencing rule. It tells us that the first day of P **and** the first day of R start later than the last day of L. This is a classic layered link, because we do not know when the first day of P is in relation to the first day of R, we only know they both start after the last day of L. rule diagram:

LL · PP / RR (PP over RR)

We draw both the days for each workshop to make things very clear. Remember, each workshop is a link of two days. Thinking about how we can place these three workshops can tell us a great deal. This is a necessary mental exercise because rule 3 is the only rule that gives us any information about individual variables.

We need space for RR and PP to come after the second L, and we only have two levels. Therefore, the latest that LL can be placed is Tuesday, Wednesday and the earliest is Monday, Tuesday. So, one L must be on Tuesday. Likewise, the earliest that PP can be placed is Wednesday, Thursday (assuming that LL is Monday, Tuesday) and the latest that PP can be placed is Thursday, Friday because those are the last days. So one P must be on Thursday. RR has the same characteristics as PP, so one R must be conducted on Thursday.

The MD with these implications built in:

__	__	__	R	__
__	L	__	P	__
M	T	W	T	F

It does not matter which level we put the variables on because the levels have no specific connection to the variables. We just need to show the placements because they take up space and give structure.

Looking at our MD and thinking about SS, the variable we know little about, we realize that one S must be on Tuesday. This is because the SS link must be placed sometime between Monday and Wednesday, just like the LL link. It cannot be later because there is no way to have consecutive days for SS after Wednesday while also placing RR and PP. Even if RR and PP are Wednesday, Thursday, we cannot have SS fit on Friday; it needs two days. We build that knowledge about S on Tuesday into the MD:

__	S	__	R	__
__	L	__	P	__
M	T	W	T	F

Our analysis of where the different links can be placed is incredibly helpful: we now understand roughly where the links can go. Here are mini diagrams that show possible variations based on our current understanding and keeping in mind that **at least one conference must be shown each day:**

S	S		R	R
	L	L	P	P

	S	S	R	R
L	L		P	P

	S	S	R	R
L	L	P	P	

It is not necessarily the case that S and R are on the same level; R and P are interchangeable in this diagrams. The levels do not matter much. The days and ordering of RR and PP in relation to the LLs are much more important. note that one workshop must be held on each day. This means that either L or S will be on Monday because R and P cannot be. Likewise, either R or P must be on Friday. With no more inferences to draw, we move to the questions:

8. Which one of the following could be true?

(A) Only one workshop is in session on Thursday.
(B) Only one workshop is in session on Friday.
(C) The workshop on Rehearsals is in session on Tuesday.
(D) The workshop on Staging is in session on Thursday.
(E) The workshops in Rehearsals and Production are both in session on Wednesday.

A global Could be True question: work each choice to see which is possible. (A) is not possible. We know that both R and P are on Thursday. (B) is possible: either P or R can have their second session on Friday and the other can have their first session on Wednesday. This is an example solution involving that:

	S		R	R
L	L	P	P	

The second S can be on either Monday or Wednesday. Select (B) and move on.

For teaching purposes we show why (C), (D) and (E) are not possible. (C) is incorrect because the earliest a R can be is Wednesday. For (D), the latest an S can be is Wednesday. (E) breaks rule 2 which says that at least one workshop is in session on each day. If RR and PP are both placed Wednesday, Thursday, then no one can be on Friday.

9. Which one of the following could be true?

(A) The workshop on Lighting is in session on Wednesday, and the workshop on Rehearsals is in session on Tuesday.
(B) The workshop on Lighting is in session on Wednesday, and the only workshop in session on Thursday is the workshop on Rehearsals.
(C) The workshop on Lighting is in session on Wednesday, and the only workshop in session on Monday is the workshop on Staging.
(D) The workshop on Lighting is in session on Monday, and the only workshop in session on Thursday is the workshop on Staging.
(E) The workshops on Lighting and Production are both in session on Wednesday.

Another global Could be True question. Work the choices for one that is possible. (A) does not work because we know that R cannot be on Tuesday. (B) is incorrect because both R and P are on Thursday. (C) can work, if RR and PP are both on Thursday, Friday. Here is that solution:

S	S		R	R
	L	L	P	P

Choose (C) and move on to the next question.

10. If the workshop on Production is in session on Wednesday, which one of the following must be true?

(A) The workshop on Lighting is in session on Monday.
(B) The workshop on Rehearsals is in session on Wednesday.
(C) The workshop on Staging is in session on Thursday .
(D) The workshop on Staging is in session on Monday.
(E) The workshop on Staging is in session on Wednesday.

This is a local Must be True question. After two global Could be True questions in a row, it is refreshing to have a local rule to draw inferences from. The first P being on Wednesday gives us this mini diagram:

	S		R	R
L	L	P	P	___

We know from rule 3 that the first L must be on Monday because both Ls are before the first P. And the second R must be on Friday because either P or R must be on that day and . We scan the choices looking for one of our inferences and find it in (A). This information must be true, so you can confidently move on to question 11.

11. If the workshop on production is the only workshop in session on Friday, which one of the following must be false?

(A) The workshop on Lighting is in session both on Tuesday and on Wednesday.
(B) The workshop on Rehearsals is in session both on Wednesday and on Thursday.
(C) The workshop on Staging is in session both on Monday and on Tuesday.
(D) The workshop on Lighting is in session on the same two days as is the workshop on Staging.
(E) The workshop on Rehearsals is in session on a day when the workshop on Staging is also in session.

A local Cannot be True question. If P is the only workshop on Friday, then one R must be on Wednesday because it is not on Friday. R on Wednesday forces the first L to be on Monday:

	S	R	R	
L	L	___	P	P

The other S can be on either Monday or Wednesday. Work the choices, looking for what cannot be true. (A) must be false. The workshop on Lighting is on Monday and Tuesday, not Tuesday and Wednesday.

Next question:

12. If the workshop on Lighting is the only workshop in session on Monday, which one of the following could be true?

(A) The workshops on Rehearsals and Staging are both in session on Tuesday.
(B) The workshop on Rehearsals is the only workshop in session on Wednesday.
(C) The workshop on Staging is the only workshop in session on Wednesday.
(D) The workshops on Staging and Rehearsals are both in session on Wednesday and on Thursday.
(E) The workshops on Staging and Production are both in session on Thursday.

This is a local Could be True question; find the choice that creates are least one solution. The local rule tells that L is the only workshop on Monday, which means that SS must be on Tuesday, Wednesday:

	S	S	R	
L	L		P	
___	___	___	___	___

Note here that the other R could be on Wednesday. Just because we placed it on the second level does not mean it cannot also be on the first level (i.e. a different conference room). Work the choices, looking for information that is possible. (A) does not work: R and P can never be earlier than Wednesday. (B) is false because S is in session on Wednesday.

(C) is possible; the second R and P can be on Friday:

	S	S	R	R
L	L		P	P
___	___	___	___	___

For teaching purposes:

(D) is incorrect because S can never be **later** than Wednesday.

(E) - P can never be earlier than Wednesday.

*Advanced Sequencing Practice Games

Game 1, Questions 1-5

Doctor Yamata works only on Mondays, Tuesdays, Wednesdays, Fridays, and Saturdays. She performs four different activities - lecturing, operating, treating patients, and conducting research. Each working day she performs exactly one activity in the morning and exactly one activity in the afternoon. During each week her work schedule must satisfy the following restrictions:

She performs operations on exactly three mornings.

If she operates on Monday, she does not operate on Tuesday.

She lectures in the afternoon on exactly two consecutive calendar days.

She treats patients on exactly one morning and exactly three afternoons.

She conducts research on exactly one morning.

On Saturday she neither lectures nor performs operations.

1. Which one of the following must be a day on which Doctor Yamata lectures?

(A) Monday
(B) Tuesday
(C) Wednesday
(D) Friday
(E) Saturday

2. On Wednesday Doctor Yamata could be scheduled to

(A) conduct research in the morning and operate in the *afternoon*
(B) lecture in the morning and treat patients in the afternoon
(C) operate in the morning and lecture in the afternoon
(D) operate in the morning and conduct research in the afternoon
(E) treat patients in the morning and treat patients in the afternoon

3. Which one of the following statements must be true?

(A) There is one day on which the doctor treats patients both in the morning and in the afternoon.
(B) The doctor conducts research on one of the days on which she lectures.
(C) The doctor conducts research on one of the days on which she treats patients.
(D) The doctor lectures on one of the days on which she treats patients.
(E) The doctor lectures on one of the days on which she operates.

4. If Doctor Yamata operates on Tuesday, then her schedule for treating patients could be

(A) Monday morning, Monday afternoon, Friday morning, Friday afternoon
(B) Monday morning, Friday afternoon, Saturday morning, Saturday afternoon
(C) Monday afternoon, Wednesday morning, Wednesday afternoon, Saturday afternoon
(D) Wednesday morning, Wednesday afternoon, Friday afternoon, Saturday afternoon
(E) Wednesday afternoon, Friday afternoon, Saturday morning, Saturday afternoon

5. Which one of the following is a pair of days on both of which Doctor Yamata must treat patients?

(A) Monday and Tuesday
(B) Monday and Saturday
(C) Tuesday and Friday
(D) Tuesday and Saturday
(E) Friday and Saturday

Game 2, Questions 6-12

During a four-week period, each of seven previously unadvertised products – G, H, J, K, L, M, and O – will be advertised. A different pair of these products will be advertised each week. Exactly one of the products will be a member of two of these four pairs. The following constraints must be observed:

J is not advertised during a given week unless H is advertised during the immediately preceding week.

The product that is advertised during two of the weeks is advertised during week 4 but is not advertised during week 3.

G is not advertised during a given week unless either J or else O is also advertised that week.

K is advertised during one of the first two weeks.

O is one of the products advertised during week 3.

6. Which one of the following could be the schedule of advertisements?

(A) week 1: G, J; week 2: K, L; week 3: O, M; week 4: H, L
(B) week l: H, K; week 2: J, G; week 3: O, L; week 4: M, K
(C) week 1: H, K; week 2: J, M; week 3: O, L; week 4: G, M
(D) week 1: H, L; week 2: J, M; week 3: O, G; week 4: K, L
(E) week 1: K, M; week 2: H, J; week 3: O, G; week 4: L, M

7. Which one of the following is a pair of products that CANNOT be advertised during the same week as each other?

(A) H and K
(B) H and M
(C) J and O
(D) K and L
(E) L and M

8. Which one of the following must be advertised during week 2?

(A) G
(B) J
(C) K
(D) L
(E) M

9. Which one of the following CANNOT be the product that is advertised during two of the weeks?

(A) G
(B) H
(C) K
(D) L
(E) M

10. If L is the product that is advertised during two of the weeks, which one of the following is a product that must be advertised during one of the weeks in which L is advertised?

(A) G
(B) H
(C) J
(D) K
(E) M

11. Which one of the following is a product that could be advertised in any of the four weeks?

(A) H
(B) J
(C) K
(D) L
(E) O

12. Which one of the following is a pair of products that could be advertised during the same week as each other?

(A) G and H
(B) H and J
(C) H and O
(D) K and O
(E) M and O

*Advanced Sequencing Practice Games Explanations

Game 1 (7/2 # 8 – 12)

Variable Lists

Activities: L, O, P, R
P is the abbreviation for treating patients and R is used for conducting research.

Rule List

Rule 1: **Operations on 3 Mornings**
We show this on the central diagram with 3 o's next to the morning.

Rule 2: $O_M \rightarrow \not{O}_T$
The small letters indicate days of the week.
Contrapositive:

$O_T \rightarrow \not{O}_M$

Rule 3: Exactly LL in the Afternoon
Notice the importance of "calendar days" here. Wednesday, Friday do not count because they are no consecutive days.

Rule 4: **P on 1 Morning and 3 Afternoons**

Rule 5: **R on one Morning.**

Rule 6: $\not{L}_S$ $\not{O}_S$
Combined with Rule 3, it becomes clear that afternoon lectures must come on MT or TW. They cannot be F, S.

Main Diagram

L/P	L	L/P	P	P	PPPLL
O/	/O	O	O	R/P	OOORP
M	T	W	F	S	

Saturday Morning must be R or P, because it cannot be O, and R and P are the only other activities done in the morning. O must be either Monday or Tuesday morning but not both, and both Wednesday and Friday mornings.

Friday and Saturday afternoons must both be P because the two LL's are M,T or T, W.

QUESTIONS

1. Global, Must be True
Tuesday must be a day that Dr. Yamata lectures. **B** is correct.

2. Global, Could be True
Check the central diagram. L and P are options in the afternoon and Dr. operates in the morning. **C** is possible.

3. Global, Must be True
Scan the choices using the Central Diagram.

A) Saturday could have this, but not necessarily.

B) Not necessarily true, R can be on Saturday.

C) Again, not necessarily true. R could be on Tuesday Morning.

D) Not possible.

E) Must be true, due to process of elimination.

4. Local, Could be True

L/P	L	L/P	P	P
R/P	O	O	O	R/P

Use the mini diagram to see which choice can work.

A) Friday morning is O.

B) P cannot be on both Monday Morning and Saturday Morning.

C) Wednesday morning is O.

D) Same issue as above.

E) Must be possible.

5. Global, Must be True
The Central Diagram shows that Friday and Saturday must be P in the afternoon. **E** is correct.

Game 2 (21/1 # 18 – 24)

Variable Lists

Products: G, H, J, K, L, M, O

Rule List

Rule 1: **HJ**

Each of the products must be shown at least once, so J must be shown and must be shown the week after H is shown. J cannot be in 1 because then H cannot be before it. But H can be in 4, because it could be the second of two Hs.

J can only be shown twice if it is shown twice in the same week. Otherwise, we would need two Hs as well as two Js.

Rule 2: **T4 T3**

We refer to the product advertised twice as T.

Rule 3: **G/J / G/O** (G stacked above J, or G stacked above O)

We stack products shown in the same week vertically.

We know that G cannot be shown twice because it would have to be paired once with O and J and O is in 3 and any product in 3 will not be shown twice.

Also J and O cannot be together, because one would have to be with G elsewhere. O cannot be doubled and J can only be doubled with itself. This means J cannot be in 3. Notice how much we can infer from this one rule.

Rule 4: **K1 / K2**

Rule 5: **O3**

O cannot be T.

Main Diagram

K/T	K/T		
H	J	O	T
1	2	3	4

We check to see where J can go because it is limited. It can go in 2 with H in 1. But it cannot go in 4 because then H would have to be in 3 with O and there would be no place to put G (Rule 2: G and J cannot be shown twice and T must be in 4). J must go in 2 and H in 1. H cannot go in 3 because that would be doubling up in the wrong weeks.

QUESTIONS

6. Global, Could be True, List

We use Rule 1 to eliminate A and E, Rule 3 to eliminate C and Rule 4 to eliminate D. **B** is correct.

7. Global, Cannot be True

One of our inferences from Rule 3 is that J and O cannot be together. **C** is correct.

8. Global, Must be True

We know from our inference on our central diagram that J must be shown in week 2.

9. Global, Cannot be True

Our inference from Rule 3 tells us that the answer is **A**.

10. Local, Must be True

If L is shown twice then it must be in week 4 and in 1 or 2. Because it takes up a spot in 1 or 2, K must be in the other. That leaves G and M to go in 3 and 4. So L must be with M in 4. **E** is correct.

11. Global, Could be True

We know that O, J and H can only be shown in certain weeks. Likewise, K cannot be shown in 3, because it is tied to 1 or 2 as well. That means L must be able to be shown in any week. **D** is correct.

12. Global, Could be True

We work these one by one.

A) G and H cannot be shown together (Rule 3).

B) This is not possible according to Rule 1.

C) H cannot be doubled up in 3.

D) Same problem as above. K is definitely in 1 or 2 so cannot be doubled in 3.

E) This pair must be possible.

Notes

Working hard on the Rules and inferences really paid off in terms of making the questions much easier and quicker.

*Sequencing Problem Sets

Average (22)

Test / Section	#	Question	Answer
19 / 1	#	1	Ⓐ Ⓑ Ⓒ Ⓓ Ⓔ
19 / 1	#	2	Ⓐ Ⓑ Ⓒ Ⓓ Ⓔ
19 / 1	#	3	Ⓐ Ⓑ Ⓒ Ⓓ Ⓔ
19 / 1	#	4	Ⓐ Ⓑ Ⓒ Ⓓ Ⓔ
19 / 1	#	5	Ⓐ Ⓑ Ⓒ Ⓓ Ⓔ
19 / 1	#	6	Ⓐ Ⓑ Ⓒ Ⓓ Ⓔ
19 / 1	#	7	Ⓐ Ⓑ Ⓒ Ⓓ Ⓔ
23 / 1	#	1	Ⓐ Ⓑ Ⓒ Ⓓ Ⓔ
23 / 1	#	2	Ⓐ Ⓑ Ⓒ Ⓓ Ⓔ
23 / 1	#	3	Ⓐ Ⓑ Ⓒ Ⓓ Ⓔ
23 / 1	#	4	Ⓐ Ⓑ Ⓒ Ⓓ Ⓔ
23 / 1	#	5	Ⓐ Ⓑ Ⓒ Ⓓ Ⓔ
24 / 4	#	6	Ⓐ Ⓑ Ⓒ Ⓓ Ⓔ
24 / 4	#	7	Ⓐ Ⓑ Ⓒ Ⓓ Ⓔ
24 / 4	#	8	Ⓐ Ⓑ Ⓒ Ⓓ Ⓔ
24 / 4	#	9	Ⓐ Ⓑ Ⓒ Ⓓ Ⓔ
24 / 4	#	10	Ⓐ Ⓑ Ⓒ Ⓓ Ⓔ
26 / 1	#	8	Ⓐ Ⓑ Ⓒ Ⓓ Ⓔ
26 / 1	#	9	Ⓐ Ⓑ Ⓒ Ⓓ Ⓔ
26 / 1	#	10	Ⓐ Ⓑ Ⓒ Ⓓ Ⓔ
26 / 1	#	11	Ⓐ Ⓑ Ⓒ Ⓓ Ⓔ
26 / 1	#	12	Ⓐ Ⓑ Ⓒ Ⓓ Ⓔ

Difficult (28)

Test / Section	#	Question	Answer
20 / 3	#	1	Ⓐ Ⓑ Ⓒ Ⓓ Ⓔ
20 / 3	#	2	Ⓐ Ⓑ Ⓒ Ⓓ Ⓔ
20 / 3	#	3	Ⓐ Ⓑ Ⓒ Ⓓ Ⓔ
20 / 3	#	4	Ⓐ Ⓑ Ⓒ Ⓓ Ⓔ
20 / 3	#	5	Ⓐ Ⓑ Ⓒ Ⓓ Ⓔ
20 / 3	#	13	Ⓐ Ⓑ Ⓒ Ⓓ Ⓔ
20 / 3	#	14	Ⓐ Ⓑ Ⓒ Ⓓ Ⓔ
20 / 3	#	15	Ⓐ Ⓑ Ⓒ Ⓓ Ⓔ
20 / 3	#	16	Ⓐ Ⓑ Ⓒ Ⓓ Ⓔ
20 / 3	#	17	Ⓐ Ⓑ Ⓒ Ⓓ Ⓔ
20 / 3	#	18	Ⓐ Ⓑ Ⓒ Ⓓ Ⓔ
25 / 3	#	19	Ⓐ Ⓑ Ⓒ Ⓓ Ⓔ
25 / 3	#	20	Ⓐ Ⓑ Ⓒ Ⓓ Ⓔ
25 / 3	#	21	Ⓐ Ⓑ Ⓒ Ⓓ Ⓔ
25 / 3	#	22	Ⓐ Ⓑ Ⓒ Ⓓ Ⓔ
25 / 3	#	23	Ⓐ Ⓑ Ⓒ Ⓓ Ⓔ
25 / 3	#	24	Ⓐ Ⓑ Ⓒ Ⓓ Ⓔ
27 / 2	#	1	Ⓐ Ⓑ Ⓒ Ⓓ Ⓔ
27 / 2	#	2	Ⓐ Ⓑ Ⓒ Ⓓ Ⓔ
27 / 2	#	3	Ⓐ Ⓑ Ⓒ Ⓓ Ⓔ
27 / 2	#	4	Ⓐ Ⓑ Ⓒ Ⓓ Ⓔ
27 / 2	#	5	Ⓐ Ⓑ Ⓒ Ⓓ Ⓔ
27 / 2	#	6	Ⓐ Ⓑ Ⓒ Ⓓ Ⓔ
28 / 2	#	19	Ⓐ Ⓑ Ⓒ Ⓓ Ⓔ
28 / 2	#	20	Ⓐ Ⓑ Ⓒ Ⓓ Ⓔ
28 / 2	#	21	Ⓐ Ⓑ Ⓒ Ⓓ Ⓔ
28 / 2	#	22	Ⓐ Ⓑ Ⓒ Ⓓ Ⓔ
28 / 2	#	23	Ⓐ Ⓑ Ⓒ Ⓓ Ⓔ

Grueling (26)

Test / Section	#	Question	Answer
21 / 1	#	12	Ⓐ Ⓑ Ⓒ Ⓓ Ⓔ
21 / 1	#	13	Ⓐ Ⓑ Ⓒ Ⓓ Ⓔ
21 / 1	#	14	Ⓐ Ⓑ Ⓒ Ⓓ Ⓔ
21 / 1	#	15	Ⓐ Ⓑ Ⓒ Ⓓ Ⓔ
21 / 1	#	16	Ⓐ Ⓑ Ⓒ Ⓓ Ⓔ
21 / 1	#	17	Ⓐ Ⓑ Ⓒ Ⓓ Ⓔ
22 / 3	#	8	Ⓐ Ⓑ Ⓒ Ⓓ Ⓔ
22 / 3	#	9	Ⓐ Ⓑ Ⓒ Ⓓ Ⓔ
22 / 3	#	10	Ⓐ Ⓑ Ⓒ Ⓓ Ⓔ
22 / 3	#	11	Ⓐ Ⓑ Ⓒ Ⓓ Ⓔ
22 / 3	#	12	Ⓐ Ⓑ Ⓒ Ⓓ Ⓔ
22 / 3	#	13	Ⓐ Ⓑ Ⓒ Ⓓ Ⓔ
22 / 3	#	14	Ⓐ Ⓑ Ⓒ Ⓓ Ⓔ
24 / 4	#	11	Ⓐ Ⓑ Ⓒ Ⓓ Ⓔ
24 / 4	#	12	Ⓐ Ⓑ Ⓒ Ⓓ Ⓔ
24 / 4	#	13	Ⓐ Ⓑ Ⓒ Ⓓ Ⓔ
24 / 4	#	14	Ⓐ Ⓑ Ⓒ Ⓓ Ⓔ
24 / 4	#	15	Ⓐ Ⓑ Ⓒ Ⓓ Ⓔ
24 / 4	#	16	Ⓐ Ⓑ Ⓒ Ⓓ Ⓔ
24 / 4	#	17	Ⓐ Ⓑ Ⓒ Ⓓ Ⓔ
28 / 2	#	13	Ⓐ Ⓑ Ⓒ Ⓓ Ⓔ
28 / 2	#	14	Ⓐ Ⓑ Ⓒ Ⓓ Ⓔ
28 / 2	#	15	Ⓐ Ⓑ Ⓒ Ⓓ Ⓔ
28 / 2	#	16	Ⓐ Ⓑ Ⓒ Ⓓ Ⓔ
28 / 2	#	17	Ⓐ Ⓑ Ⓒ Ⓓ Ⓔ
28 / 2	#	18	Ⓐ Ⓑ Ⓒ Ⓓ Ⓔ

*Sequencing Problem Sets ~ Answers

Average

19 / 1 # **1** B
19 / 1 # **2** E
19 / 1 # **3** C
19 / 1 # **4** E
19 / 1 # **5** D
19 / 1 # **6** D
19 / 1 # **7** C
23 / 1 # **1** B
23 / 1 # **2** D
23 / 1 # **3** B
23 / 1 # **4** C
23 / 1 # **5** D

---

24 / 4 # **6** A
24 / 4 # **7** B
24 / 4 # **8** C
24 / 4 # **9** E
24 / 4 # **10** A
26 / 1 # **8** C
26 / 1 # **9** E
26 / 1 # **10** A
26 / 1 # **11** C
26 / 1 # **12** A

Difficult

20 / 3 # **1** A
20 / 3 # **2** A
20 / 3 # **3** D
20 / 3 # **4** A
20 / 3 # **5** B
20 / 3 # **13** C
20 / 3 # **14** D
20 / 3 # **15** C
20 / 3 # **16** E
20 / 3 # **17** E
20 / 3 # **18** D
25 / 3 # **19** E
25 / 3 # **20** D
25 / 3 # **21** A
25 / 3 # **22** A
25 / 3 # **23** A
25 / 3 # **24** D
27 / 2 # **1** E
27 / 2 # **2** E
27 / 2 # **3** C
27 / 2 # **4** C
27 / 2 # **5** D
27 / 2 # **6** B
28 / 2 # **19** D
28 / 2 # **20** E
28 / 2 # **21** A
28 / 2 # **22** C
28 / 2 # **23** E

Grueling

21 / 1 # **12** D
21 / 1 # **13** D
21 / 1 # **14** B
21 / 1 # **15** E
21 / 1 # **16** E
21 / 1 # **17** A
22 / 3 # **8** B
22 / 3 # **9** B
22 / 3 # **10** D
22 / 3 # **11** B
22 / 3 # **12** B
22 / 3 # **13** A
22 / 3 # **14** A
24 / 4 # **11** B
24 / 4 # **12** A
24 / 4 # **13** D
24 / 4 # **14** B
24 / 4 # **15** E
24 / 4 # **16** A
24 / 4 # **17** D
28 / 2 # **13** D
28 / 2 # **14** C
28 / 2 # **15** B
28 / 2 # **16** B
28 / 2 # **17** D
28 / 2 # **18** D

Sort Games

You now know about Sequencing games and their siblings, Relative and Advanced Sequencing Games. The second major game type involves grouping variables. In a Grouping Game the relationships between the variables are not based on order. Instead, the rules deal with who is, or is not, grouped with who and who can, or cannot, be in a certain group. In this way, Grouping Games are more about how the variables interact with one another than how the variables interact with the base. This distinction changes the character of the rules.

Sort & Select

There are two sub-categories of Grouping games: Sort games and Select games. Sort games are the most common game type on the games section: they made up 33% of the games in tests 59-64. Select games only made up 4%; they will be discussed at the end of the Games methods. Your focus needs to be on Sort games.

Sort Games ask you to organize variables into two or more groups. In almost all Sort games, no variables are left out; every variable is sorted into a group. Example Sort setup:

> A group of college friends – P, L, R, Q, M, and T - are at a lake house. They decide to take two 3-person kayaks out onto the lake.

In this game, you would divide the friends up into two kayaks, the two groups. For instance, one possible way to divide the groups would be PRT in one kayak and LQM in the other.

The Base

In Sort games, the base is made up of the different groups. Sort games must inherently deal with two or more groups, so we represent the slots **vertically** to be space efficient and to help us quickly compare groups. Here is a MD for the kayaking game, where there are two groups of three people. The kayaks, each of which are a part of the base, are labeled 1 and 2:

___ ___

___ ___ ← *Sorted variables and possibilities*

___ ___

1 2 ← *Not rules*

You can easily compare one kayak to the other because the slots are lined up next to one another. Notice that this MD in resembles that of an Advanced Sequencing game. Be sure to keep these MDs distinct in your mind. The key way to distinguish them is that Advanced Sequencing bases tend to be longer and have less levels on top of the base.

If this game instead had nine variables and three 3-person kayaks, we would draw the base like this:

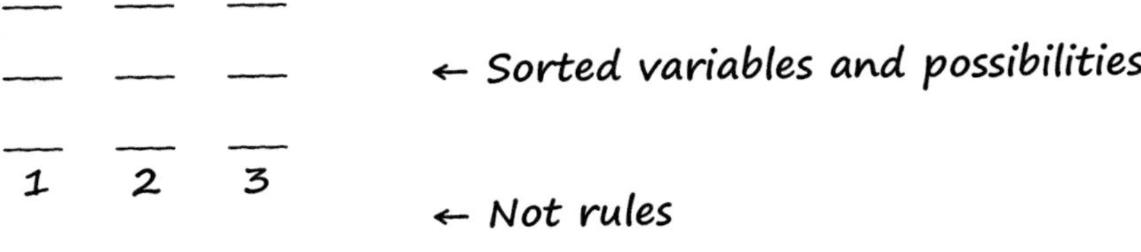

How Many Slots?

With Sequencing games, you typically know the number of slots on the base. You are either told exactly how many slots ("there are six lanes on the track") or you can determine the number of slots using the number of variables. This is not always the case with Sort games. Sometimes, you know how many variables are being sorted, but not how many go in each specific group. Look at this game setup:

> At a restaurant, a party of six – Jim, Linda, Chris, Susan, Tommy, and Maria – is seated at two tables. At least two people sit at each table.

We do not know if we are dealing with two tables of three people, or one table of two people and one table of four people. We can draw the game this way, with certain slots drawn less darkly:

```
___
___   ___
___   ___
___   ___
 1     2
```

One table will have at least **three** people, and the other table will have at least **two** people, regardless of the division. In either possible scenario, the 4/2 split or 3/3 split, one of the lighter colored slots will not be used.

Multiple Variable Sets

Sometimes, Sort games ask you to sort more than one variable set. You have run into this situation in Sequencing and Advanced Sequencing games. It is important to distinguish between the variable sets and the **groups** of the base, which are what you are sorting the variables into. The variable sets are introduced in the setup and will be clearly named.

Two Sets

When dealing with **two** variable sets, use lowercase letters for one set and uppercase for the other. Example Sort game with two variable sets:

> Two different relays of four swimmers will be chosen from the JV swimmers – Agatha, Sarah, Megan – and the varsity swimmers – Christine, Elspeth, Lauren and Kate.

JV swimmers variable list: a s m

Varsity swimmers variable list: C E L K

It is easy to tell the two variable sets apart due to the difference in the letters.

We make the JV swimmers the lowercase set because that is a younger group. Tie the variable abbreviations to properties that you associate with the group whenever possible. Use this tactic when dealing with adults and children: make the children lowercase.

Three Sets

When you have three variable sets, you need to distinguish all three groups from one another. We suggest using a superscript, a small dash at the top right of the letter of one group. Look at this game:

> Four Boy Scouts – T, M, P, L – their fathers – A, G, X, R – and their mothers – S, Y, Q, E – will be divided into three groups for a hike.

Boy Scouts: t m p l

Fathers: A G X R

Mothers: S' Y' Q' E'

It is not absolutely necessary to distinguish the two capitalized groups with a visual reminder like the superscript shown here, but we recommend it. The rules and questions will deal with the three groups differently, and seeing at a glance exactly which group a variable belongs to can be helpful. For instance, if this pair is in a group:

E' A

We know immediately that both a mother and a father are in the group. Without the superscript to identify E as a mother, we would have to check back to the variable lists or try and remember that information. Using superscripts saves you time.

It is not likely that you will have to deal with four variable sets on a game.

Rule Diagrams

Because Sort games have a fundamentally different action than Sequencing games, you will be given new types of rules. These require new diagrams. So, mentally switch gears. Sometimes, you will use rule diagrams from Sequencing games that take on a different **meaning** in the context of a Sort game.

You will face many not links and negative information in Sort games. For instance, you might be told that Jim cannot be in the same group as Rachel. In Sort games, unlike in Sequencing games, negative information is generally as useful as positive. This is because which variables cannot be selected together tells you a great deal. Keep this in mind when you evaluate the importance of the rules in Grouping games.

Links

Links in Sort games address how variables interact with one another, who can or cannot, be in a group with who. Here is a common rule type in Sort games:

Bill and Ted are in the same group.

Diagram the fact that two variables are together by sticking the two abbreviations next to each other:

BT

Bill and Ted are in the same group, so the rule makes sense visually. If we are told that Bill is in group 1, then Ted must be in group 1 as well.

The above diagram used in a Sequencing game would tell us that Bill was sequenced immediately before Ted; this is what we mean by switching gears mentally. Here is another link rule:

Will, Jim and Chevy are in the same group.

Diagram this link in the same way, by sticking all three of the variables together:

WJC

We know that If Will is in a group, then Jim and Chevy are also in that group.

Not Links in Sort Games

Here is another common rule in Sort games:

Jim and Ted are **not** in the same group.

To diagram this rule, we use a special symbol, a vertical bar (|). Place the bar in between the two variables that cannot be together:

J | T

Extend the bar far enough down to distinguish it from a variable that is represented with an "I." The bar is a dividing line. This diagram means that the two variables will not be placed in the **same group**. A not link still allows for both of the variables to be placed in **a** group. In almost every Sort game, all the variables are placed in a group.

In some Sort games, you are told that **three variables** cannot be in the same group. You have to diagram this situation differently. Look at this rule:

> Will, Ted and Bill cannot all be in the same group.

Here is our favorite way to diagram this rule:

- WTB

Placing the negative sign in front of the WTB link indicates that these variables cannot all be in the same group. Any **two** of the variables could be in the same group. This rule only tells us that **all three** cannot be placed together. Some students prefer writing "no" in front of the link instead:

no WTB

Not Links and Possibility Fills

Here is an example Sort game setup and rule:

> Four Boy Scouts – T, M, P, and L – their fathers – A, G, X, and R – and their mothers – S, Y, Q, and E – will be divided into two groups for a hike. All hikers will be in a group.
>
> T and X do not go on the same hike.

Not link rule:

t | X

T will not be in the same group as X.

Because this game only has two groups and all hikers are placed in a group, this is a special situation. We call these Either/Or games, because a variable is either in one group or it is in the other. If t is in group 1, then we know that X must be in group 2, and vice versa. We can show this fact with a possibility fill:

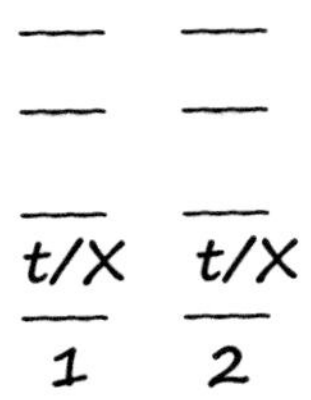

1	2
___	___
___	___
___	___
t/X	t/X

We do not know which group t or X will be in, but we do know they will both be in a group and not the same one. So, we reserve a slot in each group for one of the pair. This technique of filling in the possibilities is a powerful move on Either/Or Sort Games.

Conditional Rules

Grouping games feature more conditional rules than Sequencing games, and more complex ones. However, we represent them in the same way: using an arrow in between the indicator and the requirement.

Conditionals that Create Not Links

Conditional rules in Sort games look different because they tell you that if one variable is in group X, then another variable cannot be in group X:

> If A is in group 1, then B is not in group 1.

Diagram:

A1 → -B1

Contrapositive:

B1 → -A1

A and B cannot be together in group 1. You can represent the not link like this:

A1 | B1

The addition of the group numbers allows you to use the dividing line with group-specific conditionals.

Another example:

> Seven Frisbees of different colors – red, orange, yellow, green, blue, indigo, and violet - will be thrown into three baskets.
>
> If the red frisbee is thrown into the first basket, then so is the green frisbee.

Diagram:

R1 → G1

If R is in 1, then G is in 1 too. Here is the contrapositive of the rule:

-G1 → -R1

If G is not in 1, then R is not in 1. Stated another way, if G is in group 2 or 3, then R must be in 2 or 3. If this game only had two groups, if it was an Either/Or game, then we could express the contrapositive of the rule in a positive way:

G2 → R2

When a Frisbee is not in 1, it must be in 2. So, if G is not in 1, then G must be in 2. "not in 1" would mean "In 2" for R as well. Either/Or games have some readily exploitable characteristics; be on the lookout for these games.

Inferences

Sort games are no different than Sequencing games regarding inferences: you must find them to succeed. Further, the same ideas for finding inferences apply: look for information beyond what is directly expressed in the rules and setup. Such information is usually found by drawing connections between two rules or between a rule and the MD. Sometimes, you can connect information from a rule or the MD with **another inference** you have made; your inferences can build on one another.

Combinations

The rules in Grouping games are often ripe for combining. For instance, you can join links:

> Terry must be in the same boat as Sam.
> Sam and Jenny are in the same boat.

Because T is with S and S is with J, you can connect these two links. All three variables must be in the same boat. Diagram these two rules as a single, combined diagram:

TSJ

Now, you have a link with three variables, instead of two links with two variables. Combining the rules saved space and time. Even more importantly, you know that T is in the same group as J, the inference.

You can also sometimes join a link that tells you that two variables cannot be together, with a link that tells you that two variables are together:

> Amber is not in the same boat as Barry.
> Barry and Yvette are in the same boat.

You could diagram these two rules separately like this:

A | B
BY

However, you can learn more by combining them. Combined diagram:

A | BY

This diagram tells you that neither Barry nor Yvette is in the boat with Amber, **and** that B and Y are in the same boat. The dividing line divides the BY link from A. This makes sense because if A and B cannot be in the same boat, and Y is with B, then Y also cannot be in the same boat as A. Now, look at these two rules:

> Claudia is not in the same boat as Zach.
> Elisa cannot be in a boat with Zach.

Individual rule diagrams:

C | Z
E | Z

We cannot combine the two diagrams into this diagram:

Z | CE

This diagram implies that C and E are a link, and we do not know that they are. Sometimes two not links cannot be combined, even if they have a variable in common.

Group Size

Pay attention to the size of the groups you are sorting the variables into. Often, one or two groups will be smaller than the others. Focusing on that group can help you draw inferences, because the smaller groups fill up more quickly with variables than the other(s). Example setup and rules:

> Terry, Sam, Jenny, Barry, Amber, and Yvette will be splitting up into two boats, one of four people and one of two. The division into the boats will follow these guidelines:
>
> Terry must be in the same boat as Sam.
>
> Sam and Jenny are in the same boat.

We saw earlier that these two rules combine to form a three-variable link: *TSJ*. When we analyze the two boats, we see that this link cannot fit in the smaller boat, because it does not have slots for three variables. Therefore, these three must be placed in the big boat:

```
__
J
__
S
__    __
T
__    __
```

Looking at the smaller group paid off because it showed us where the link had to be placed.

Sometimes a game will dictate that certain slots are occupied in a group, making that group a "small group." This happens when one or more variables are placed in a group or when there are other restrictions on the group. In the game above, there is now only one slot open in the larger boat, while there are two slots open in the smaller boat. Therefore, the larger boat has become the "small group." At this point, if we have a two-variable link, it can only go in the other boat, because it has two slots open:

> Barry and Amber are in the same boat.

Rule Diagram:

BA

We still draw this horizontally, even though the MD has slots oriented vertically. It is easy enough to read the rule, and it is helpful to keep the diagramming for Sort rules consistent. The BA link must be placed in the two person boat because the four person boat does not have room for two.

Be aware of these "created" small groups that spring up as slots get filled. Look not only at the group size given in the initial setup but also at available slots within each group as you work the questions and the situation changes.

Either/Or Games and Reverse Swaps

Recall that Sort games with only two groups where all variables are placed are called Either/Or games. These games have specific inferences that hinge on the fact that if you know a variable is not in one group then it must be in the other group. Let us return to the previous example with the two boats. Look at this rule:

If Barry is in the larger Boat, then Yvette is not.

Because there are only two boats, if Yvette is not in the large boat, she must be in the small boat. So, we diagram the rule in a positive way, showing that Yvette is in the small boat:

$B_L \rightarrow Y_S$

We use subscripts to indicate the boat. If you do not like using subscripts, you could also number the larger boat 1 and the smaller boat 2 and diagram that rule like this:

$B1 \rightarrow Y2$

Either diagram works. Note that because S is a variable in the game, you should **not** diagram that rule like this:

$Bl \rightarrow Ys$

Even with a lowercase s, it would be easy to get confused between the variable S and the small boat.Now that we have diagrammed the rule, we can take the contrapositive:

Original diagram: $B_L \rightarrow Y_S$

Contrapositive: $-Y_S \rightarrow -B_L$

Remember that when a variable is not in one group, it is in the other. When Y is not in the small boat, it is in the large boat. So we can diagram the contrapositive this way, which is more informative:

$Y_L \rightarrow B_S$

We call this a reverse swap. In an Either/Or game, when you are dealing with a conditional that has group placement, you can use the reverse swap method to take the contrapositive of the rule. Here are the steps:

1. **Reverse** the order of the variables in the conditional (the indicator variable becomes the requirement and vice versa).
2. **Switch** the group associated with each variable instead of negating the variables. Due to the nature of the game, switching the group is exactly the same as negating the first group.

Here is another reverse swap example. Starting conditional:

$A_S \rightarrow Y_S$

If Amber is in the small boat, so is Yvette.

To take the contrapositive, reverse the order of the variables and then swap each group to the other. Because the group here for each variable is the small boat, we swap those to the large boat:

$$Y_L \rightarrow A_L$$

When Yvette is in the large boat, so is Amber. This makes sense, because if Amber was not in the large boat, she would be in the small boat. And when that is the case, Yvette is in the small boat too, according to the normal form of the conditional.

This is an advanced way of taking the contrapositive in a specific situation: Either/Or Sort games. If not every variable in the Sort game is placed, then this shortcut does not work. For instance, in the above example, we say that when Yvette is in the large boat Amber must be too. But if there is a chance that Amber is not placed period, the fact that she is not in the small boat does not mean that she is in the large boat.

This trick also does not work when the game has more than two groups. For example, in a three group Sort game, if Amber is not in the small boat, she could be in either the large boat or the medium boat (the third boat). In that situation, we do not know where she will be placed so we cannot say she is in the large boat.

Possibility Fill Inferences

As you have seen, showing possibilities on the MD in Grouping games is very helpful. When you know that certain variables will take up slots, show those possibilities in the MD, even if you do not know exactly which variable will be in which group. Example game:

> Seven puppies – Bobbie, Jackie, Karen, Stella, Freddie, Aaron and Trusty - are being divided into two cardboard boxes. One of the boxes holds three pups, the other holds four.
>
> Bobbie and Aaron are not in the same box.
> Trusty is not in the same box as Karen.
> Stella and Freddie are in the same box.

We can show the first two rules directly on the MD with possibility fills. Because Bobbie and Aaron are not in the same box, but they are each in **a** box, we fill a slot in each box for one of them. We do the same for Trusty and Karen:

___	
___	___
T/K	T/K
B/A	B/A

Now we see that the smaller box only has one slot open. Because Stella and Freddie are a link, they cannot go in the smaller box; they must be in the bigger box. That inference comes from keeping an eye on the available slots. Finally, Jackie must be in the only slot left in the smaller box:

S	
F	J
T/K	T/K
B/A	B/A

We would not have known nearly as much as we do about the game without the use of possibility fills. They gave us the insight we needed to place S, F and J in specific groups.

After an Inference, Check Back

Often, when you draw an inference it allows you to draw further inferences from earlier parts of the rules or setup. So, every time you learn something new, quickly check back with the earlier parts of the game to see if that new piece you found affects anything else. This is one example of how taking your time when working the rules really pays off. Sometimes a single inference sets off a chain of greater understanding regarding the game, but if you do not check back, you will never reap those benefits.

*Sort Games Review

- The rules for Grouping Games deal with who is grouped with who, instead of who comes before who.
- Grouping games are more about how the variables interact with one another than how the variables interact with the base.
- Sort games are currently the most common type of Grouping game.
- Sort games ask you to organize variables into two or more groups.
    - No variables are left out.
    - Example setup: "A group of college friends – P, L, R, Q, M, and T - are at a lake house. They decide to take two kayaks out onto the lake."
- Represent the slots of each base vertically to save space and to allow you to more easily compare the groups:

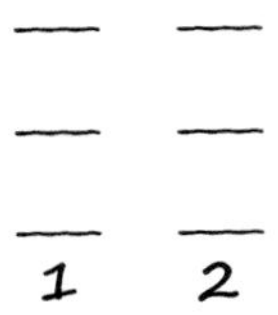

    ___ ___

    ___ ___

    ___ ___

    1 2

    - Numbering the groups is not crucial

Multiple Variable Sets

- Distinguish between several variable sets in a game that you are sorting:
    - 2 variable sets - capitalize the letters of one set and leave the other set lowercase.
    - 3 variable sets - use an a superscript (A^|^) to distinguish the third set.

Links

- You will sometimes use rule diagrams from Sequencing games that take on a different meaning in the context of a Grouping game.
    - Links are a good example of this.
- "Bill and Ted are in the same group."

    BT

- "Jim and Ted are not in the same group."

    J | T

- "Will, Ted and Bill cannot all be in the same group."

    - WTB

Possibility Fills

- Use possibility fills to show how not links work in two-group Sort games:
- "T and X do not go on the same hike."

```
___   ___

___   ___
t/X   t/X
___   ___
 1     2
```

Conditional Rules

- "If the red frisbee is thrown into the first basket, then so is the green frisbee."

  R1 → G1

Inferences

- Combinations:
  - "Terry is in the same boat as Sam."
  - "Sam and Jenny are in the same boat."

    TSJ
  - "Amber is not in the same boat as Barry."
  - "Barry and Yvette are in the same boat."

    A | BY
- Reverse swaps occur in Either/Or Sort games.
  - "If Barry is in the larger Boat, then Yvette is not."
  - Yvette must be in the smaller boat when she is not in the larger one, because there are only two boats:

    $B_L \rightarrow Y_S$

Example Sort Games

21/1 #1-6

> Seven students – fourth-year students Kim and Lee; third-year students Pat and Robin; and second-year students Sandy, Terry, and Val – and only those seven, are being assigned to rooms of equal size in a dormitory. Each room assigned must have either one, or two, or three students assigned to it, and will accordingly be called either a single, or a double, or a triple. The seven students are assigned to rooms in accordance with the following conditions:

The setup tells that this is a Sort grouping game, especially the words "assigned to rooms." After reading the setup, we have little idea how many **groups** there are, so we will likely get more information from the rules about that. We do know that each group can be from one to three students. So, at this stage, that means that we can have as few as three groups or as many as seven.

There are three variable sets, which you should diagram immediately after reading to help you remember them:

4th: K' L'

3rd: P R

2nd: s t v

Use a superscript dash to distinguish between 3rd and 4th year students. Represent 2nd year students with lower case letters. Because there are three variable sets, the game will likely hinge on differences between these sets. Onto the rules:

> No fourth-year student can be assigned to a triple.
> No second-year student can be assigned to a single.
> Lee and Robin must not share the same room.
> Kim and Pat must share the same room.

Be sure to read all the rules before diagramming anything. We will now analyze them individually:

> No fourth-year student can be assigned to a triple.

K and L, the 4th years, cannot be in a triple. They can only be in singles or doubles. There is no quick way to diagram that rule, so write it out in your own words:

K' L' *no triple*

We cannot add anything into our MD, because we do not know how to draw our MD. We still have little idea how many groups there are. The fact that K and L cannot be in triples does not tell us much. Rule 2:

> No second-year student can be assigned to a single.

Write it out in your own words, listing all the 2nd year students:

s t v *no single*

We know that s, t and v will each have at least one roommate: they are in doubles or triples. This rule limits how many groups there can be. Before, it was possible that every student was in a single. Now we know that there must be at least two doubles. Next rule:

> Lee and Robin must not share the same room.

The not link Diagram:

L' | R

This creates two specific rooms: one with L and one with R. We know that L cannot be in a triple, but R can be. The final rule:

> Kim and Pat must share the same room.

This is a normal link:

K'P

Because of rule 1, which tells that K cannot be in a triple, the KP link must constitute **a complete room**. No other students will be in this room.

Now that we have worked all the rules, we can start to create the MD. Rules 3 and 4 give us a lot of information. KP makes up one room, and L and R are separated into two other rooms. Here is what this situation looks like:

P	___	___
K'	L'	R

Place only one slot above L because L is a 4th year and cannot be in a triple. The three 2nd year students – s, t and v – are left to place and none of them can be in a room by themselves. That means that at most there can be only one more room, because we cannot form *two* new doubles with **three** students. This is **one** grouping arrangement with four rooms:

P	___	2nd	2nd
K'	L'	R	2nd

Alternatively, we could have only three rooms. In this arrangement, we put two 2nd year students in a triple with R and the final 2nd year with L:

		2nd
P	2nd	2nd
K'	L'	R

Because there are multiple possible group arrangements, we are dealing with partially unknown slots. In a Sort game like this, we strongly recommend drawing out quick sketches of basic arrangements that are possible for the groups.

Here we can have either three or four groups. The placement of the three 2nd year students will determine how many rooms we have and who is in each room. They are the variables that can move: P, K, L and R are stuck. The second years are interchangeable in the diagrams above. Their important quality is that they are 2nd years; we have no rules that deal specifically with any one of them. This is the official MD for when we move to the questions:

t s v

P	___	___
K'	L'	R

Not all of these slots will be filled, and another group can be created by the 2nd years. We show the 2nd years off to the side of the MD to remind us of the exact variables that will be sorted. With a solid understanding of the game, we move to the questions.

1. Which one of the following is a combination of rooms to which the seven students could be assigned?

This is a Grouping game version of a List question; we are being asked for a solution to the game. However, we should approach it differently because the choices only tell us the **size of the rooms**, not the variables that fill them. Therefore, it is more difficult to use the rules and process of elimination. We have a good feel for the possible groups, so simply work each choice to see if that room arrangement is possible:

(A) two triples and one single

We can have at most one triple in the game, either with R and two 2nd years or with all three of the 2nd years. Therefore this arrangement cannot work and (A) is incorrect.

(B) one triple and four singles

It is possible to have at most two singles if we leave L and R in their own rooms and put the 2nd years in a triple. The fact that P and K are together in a double means that more than two singles is impossible. Eliminate (B).

(C) three doubles and a single

During our analysis of the game, we saw that this is possible. Place two of the 2nd years together in a fourth room and then place the final 2nd year with either L or R. Here the "floating" 2nd year is with R:

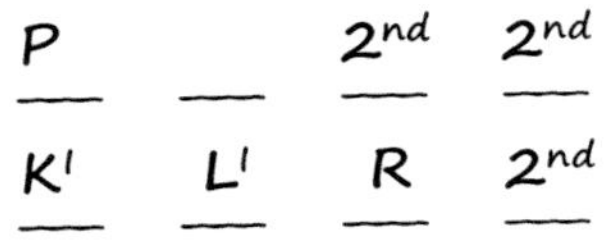

P	___	2nd	2nd
K'	L'	R	2nd

On a real games section, you would move on to the next question because you have found a choice that works on a Could be True question. For teaching purposes we will work through (D) and (E).

(D) two doubles and three singles

Recall from (B) that we can have at most two singles.

(E) one double and five singles

(E) does not work for the same reason as (B) and (D). Rule 2 eliminated a lot of the choices here.

You can work this question successfully by quickly checking the numbers of triples and singles. These are limiting factors in the game: there can be at most one triple and at most two singles. Eliminating choices based on the way the variables can be distributed is an advanced technique. Be aware of it on similar questions on Sort games.

2. If the room assigned to Robin is a single, which one of the following could be true?

This is a local Could be True question. If R is in a single then we have two possible group arrangements: either all the 2nd years are in a triple, or one of the 2nd years is with L and the other two 2nd years are in a double. Here are the mini diagrams:

			2nd
P			2nd
K'	L'	R	2nd

P	2nd		2nd
K'	L'	R	2nd

You do not need to draw these mini-diagrams unless you have trouble visualizing them. Diagrams take more time but are worth it if you are more comfortable with them than mental ones. Work each choice, seeing which can be true based on this local rule:

(A) There is exactly one double that has a second-year student assigned to it.

This is a somewhat strangely phrased choice. It says that there is a solution where there is only one double that contains a 2nd year. This is never possible in the game. Either there are no doubles with 2nd years, as in our first mini-diagram for this question, or there are **two** doubles with 2nd years, as seen in our second mini-diagram. There is no way that there is only **one** double with a 2nd year.

(B) Lee is assigned to a single.

This is possible. In fact it is our first scenario above. The three 2nd years are assigned to a triple. Choose (B) and move on. For teaching purposes:

(C) Sandy, Pat and one other student are assigned to a triple together.

We know that Pat and Kim's room cannot be a triple because K is a 4th year.

(D) Exactly three of the rooms assigned to the students are singles.

This is never possible. As discussed during the analysis of the first question, we can have at most two singles in the game.

(E) Exactly two of the rooms assigned to the students are doubles.

This is never possible. There are either three doubles (second scenario) or only one (first scenario).

3. Which one of the following must be true?

A global Must be True question. Work each choice:

(A) Lee is assigned to a single.

This does not have to be true. There are solutions where Lee is in a double with a 2nd year.

(B) Pat shares a double with another student.

This has to be true, as we learned early on when analyzing the rules. Select this choice and move on. For teaching purposes:

(C) Robin shares a double with another student.

It is possible for Robin to be in a single, so this does not have to be true.

(D) Two of the second-year students share a double with each other.

This does not have to be the case. We can have all three 2nd years in a triple.

(E) Neither of the third-year students is assigned to a single.

We can assign R, the only free 3rd year, to a single. That proves this choice incorrect. Next question:

4. If Robin is assigned to a triple, which one of the following must be true?

A local Must be True question. The local rule states that R is assigned to a triple, and the only way to do so is to put two 2nd years with R and the final 2nd year with L. That final 2nd year must be with L because he or she cannot be in a single. Mini-diagram:

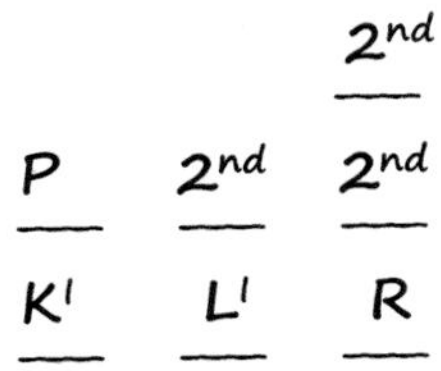

		2nd
P	2nd	2nd
K'	L'	R

This solution was one of the initial game sketches, so it would be available on the page you are working; there is no need to rewrite it. We know the implications of the local rule, so we now work the choices. The correct answer cannot deal with the specific placement of one of the 2nd years, because they are interchangeable.

(A) Lee is assigned to a single.
(B) Two second-year students share a double with each other.

Both of these choices are not possible.

(C) None of the rooms assigned to the students is a single.

(C) is correct: we have two doubles and a triple. Select this choice with confidence and move on.

5. If Terry and Val are assigned to different doubles from each other, then it must be true of the students' rooms that exactly

Another local Must be True question. This one asks about the room layout if t and v (two of the 2nd years) are in different doubles. We need two of the 2nd years in one double and the third (t or v) in a double with either L or R. Here is an example solution:

P	t		v
K'	L'	R	s

And a corresponding answer choice:

(A) one is a single

This is correct. Either L or R will be in a single, and that will be the only single in the solution. Knowing that (A) is correct is great because you skip working the other choices.

6. Which one of the following could be true?

A global Could be True question. Eliminate any choice that is not possible and select a choice if it can work with a single solution to the game.

(A) The two fourth-year students are assigned to singles.

This is never possible because K is always in a double.

(B) The two fourth-year students share a double with each other.

Again, the KP link tells us that this is impossible.

(C) Lee shares a room with a second-year student.

(C) works. The other two 2nd years can either be in a double by themselves, or they can be in a triple with R. Select this choice and move on.

27/2 #13-19

> Exactly seven film buffs - Ginnie, Ian, Lianna, Marcos, Reveka, Viktor, and Yow - attend a showing of classic films. Three films are shown, one directed by Fellini, one by Hitchcock, and one by Kurosawa. Each of the film buffs sees exactly one of the three films. The films are shown only once, one film at a time. The following restrictions must apply:
>
> Exactly twice as many of the film buffs see the Hitchcock film as see the Fellini film.
> Ginnie and Reveka do not see the same film as each other.
> Ian and Marcos do not see the same film as each other.
> Viktor and Yow see the same film as each other.
> Lianna sees the Hitchcock film.
> Ginnie sees either the Fellini film or the Kurosawa film.

This is another Sort game, as we will be dividing the film buffs among the three films. There is only one variable set, the buffs: G I L M R V Y

Before we draw the MD, we need to work the rules to determine the size of the three groups. When dealing with partially unknown slots, work several rules to gain information about the game before you create the MD. This stands in contrast to Sequencing games where the MD can usually be drawn immediately after reading the setup, allowing you to build in the rules as you read them. The first rule:

> Exactly twice as many of the film buffs see the Hitchcock film as see the Fellini film.

We have 7 buffs to distribute, so it is possible that 1 person sees the Fellini film and 2 people see the Hitchcock film. Or, 2 people see the Fellini and 4 see the Hitchcock. To derive those possibilities, start with 1 for the Fellini film and increase the number of people that see it, until you end up with too many buffs in the Fellini and Hitchcock films. For instance, it cannot be the case that 3 people see the Fellini film, because then 6 would see the Hitchcock film, requiring 9 film buffs. We only have 7 total buffs.

This rule does not talk about how many people see the Kurosawa film, but we can figure that out by subtracting the total that see the other two films from 7. For instance, if a total of 3 film buffs see the Fellini and Hitchcock films, then 4 buffs see the Kurosawa (7 - 3 = 4).

We have these two possibilities for the distribution of film watchers:

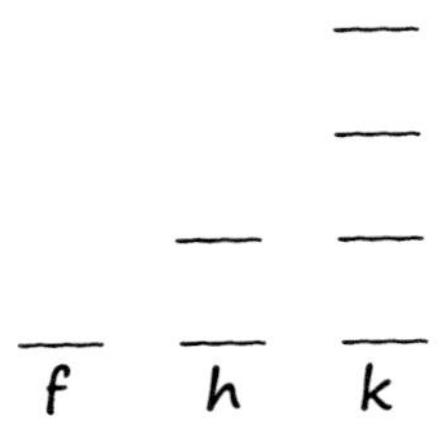

```
          ___
          ___
     ___  ___
___  ___  ___
 f    h    k
```

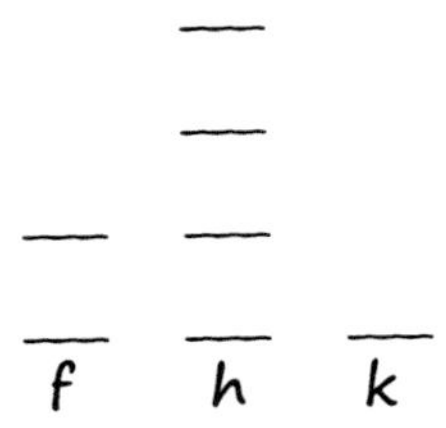

```
     ___
     ___
___  ___
___  ___  ___
 f    h    k
```

No need to draw those diagrams out when working the game. If you must draw something, then these diagrams would be more space efficient when trying to visualize the impacts of Rule 1:

```
1   2   4          2   4   1
f   h   k          f   h   k
```

The key idea here is that we will have a 1-2-4 variable split, regardless of which films have which number of buffs. This realization will prove very important in working the game. Next rule:

> Ginnie and Reveka do not see the same film as each other.

This is a classic not link. Diagram: G | R

The third rule:

> Ian and Marcos do not see the same film as each other.

Another not link: I | M

We now have two different pairs of variables that need to be separated. Without more context, we cannot derive any inferences from these not links because there are three groups the variables will be sorted into. No possibility fills can be created at this time. Onto the next rule:

> Viktor and Yow see the same film as each other.

Link Diagram: VY

With the two not links, the VY link must go in the film with four buffs. If it goes in the film with two buffs, then there will not be a way to split up the variables in the not links. This is because with VY taking up the group of two, we will be left groups of 1 and 4. There is no way to separate two not links when one of the groups only has *one* slot. In this example, I and M are in the same group, violating Rule 3:

```
      I/M
      I/M
G/R   G/R
```

Because VY is in the group with four buffs, that pair can never be in the Fellini group which can have at most two buffs. Here is what the VY not rule looks like in our early MD:

```
     ___
___  ___  ___
 f    h    k
VY
```

Show not rules by placing the variables under the group they cannot be in, just as we did with slots in Sequencing games. The MD only shows the slots that *must* be in each group. The Hitchcock film must have at least two buffs – it either has two or four. Both the Fellini and the Kurosawa have a minimum of one.

Next rule:

Lianna sees the Hitchcock film.

Build this placement rule into the MD:

```
          L
___  ___  ___
 f    h    k
VY
```

Next rule:

Ginnie sees either the Fellini film or the Kurosawa film.

This means that G cannot see the Hitchcock film. Build that not rule into the MD:

```
      L
___  ___  ___
 f    h    k
VY    G
```

There are no inferences we can draw from the fact that G does not see the Hitchcock film.

Taking an overview of our current knowledge: we know that the VY link will go in the group with 4 buffs, L sees the Hitchcock and the variables from the links (I/M and G/R) will fill in the remaining slots. On to the questions:

13. Which one of the following could be an accurate matching of film buffs to films?

(A) Ginnie: the Hitchcock film; Ian: the Kurosawa film; Marcos: the Hitchcock film
(B) Ginnie: the Kurosawa film; Ian: the Fellini film; Viktor: the Fellini film
(C) Ian: the Hitchcock film; Reveka: the Kurosawa film; Viktor: the Fellini film
(D) Marcos: the Kurosawa film; Reveka: the Kurosawa film; Viktor: the Kurosawa film
(E) Marcos: the Hitchcock film; Reveka: the Hitchcock film; Yow: the Hitchcock film

This is a variation of a List question. We are not given full solutions, so it is a bit difficult to use process of elimination. Take the choices one by one, looking for one that is a working solution:

(A) We know that G cannot see the Hitchcock film, so this choice cannot work.

(B) This places I and V in the Fellini film and with V comes Y. That means there are three buffs in that film and the Fellini film can have at most two buffs.

(C) We know that VY cannot be in the Fellini film, so this choice is incorrect.

(D) We have four buffs in the Kurosawa film so G must be in the Fellini film:

```
           R
           M
           Y
 G    L    V
___  ___  ___
 f    h    k
```

This leaves I to go in the Hitchcock. (D) works.

14. Each of the following must be false EXCEPT:

This is a global Could be True question, but is phrased in a difficult way. If something is not false, then it could be true. Work each choice to find one that is possible, while eliminating those choices that are false.

(A) Reveka is the only film buff to see the Fellini film.

If only one buff sees the Fellini, then two see the Hitchcock and four see the Kurosawa film. VY see Kurosawa because it is the group of four. G must see Kurosawa too because she does not see the Hitchcock and the Fellini is full. That leaves I and M to place, and they can be split between Hitchcock and Kurosawa. (A) is possible; R can be the only buff to see the Fellini film. mini diagram:

		I/M
		Y
	I/M	V
R	L	G
f	h	k

15. Which one of the following could be a complete and accurate list of the film buffs who do NOT see the Hitchcock film?

(A) Ginnie, Marcos
(B) Ginnie Reveka
(C) Ginnie, Ian, Reveka
(D) Ginnie, Marcos, Yow
(E) Ginnie, Viktor, Yow

This is a List question dealing with who is *not* part of a specific group. Let us try process of elimination. We know that at most there can be four buffs who see the Hitchcock film, so that means that at **least three** do not see it. So, we can eliminate choices (A) and (B) right away because two variables cannot be a complete list.

The remaining choices all have three variables, meaning that four buffs do see the Hitchcock film. Therefore, the VY link sees the Hitchcock because those two always see the film with four buffs. Eliminate any choice that features V or Y because we know that neither can be in the list of those who do not see the film. That eliminates (D) and (E) and tells us that (C) is correct. Process of elimination is powerful on all varieties of List questions.

16. If exactly one film buff sees the Kurosawa film, then which one of the following must be true?

(A) Viktor sees the Hitchcock film.
(B) Ginnie sees the Fellini film.
(C) Marcos sees the Fellini film.
(D) Ian sees the Fellini film.
(E) Reveka sees the Hitchcock film.

A local Must be True question. The local rule tells us that only one buff sees the Kurosawa film. That means that two see the Fellini and four see the Hitchcock film, including V and Y. We start working the choices and immediately see that (A) is correct. The inference that VY must be in the film seen by four buffs is quite valuable here.

17. Which one of the following must be true?

(A) Ginnie sees a different film than Ian does.
(B) Ian sees a different film than Lianna does.
(C) Ian sees a different film than Viktor does.
(D) Ian, Lianna, and Viktor do not all see the same film.
(E) Ginnie, Lianna, and Marcos do not all see the same film.

A global Must be True question. The first three choices deal with only a couple of variables and ones that are not easy to pin down. More complex choices will be easier to analyze, because they are less likely to be true. Skip to (D) and (E) which deal with more variables, and work them first:

(D) Ian, Lianna, and Viktor do not all see the same film.

These three can all see the Hitchcock film (which we know L sees), so this choice is incorrect. To have all three see the Hitchcock, we keep G and R apart, so they cannot both be in the Fellini film.

(E) Ginnie, Lianna, and Marcos do not all see the same film.

(E) must be true. L sees the Hitchcock and G cannot. So G and L cannot see the same film. That means that G, L and M do not all see the same film.

18. If Viktor sees the same film as Ginnie does, then which one of the following could be true?

A local Could be True question. If VY see the same film as G, then those three must see the Kurosawa because three variables is too many for Fellini and G cannot see the Hitchcock film (rule 6). Use a mini-diagram and then work the choices:

```
        Y
        V
    L   G
__  __  __
f   h   k
```

Onto the choices:

(A) Ginnie sees the Fellini film.

(A) cannot be true. As mentioned in the analysis of the local rule, GVY cannot see the Fellini.

(B) Ian sees the Hitchcock film.

(B) is possible. We separate R and G by putting R in Fellini and then M sees the Kurosawa. Here is the mini-diagram, which is a good idea to draw:

```
        M
        Y
    I   V
R   L   G
__  __  __
f   h   k
```

Choose (B) and move on to the next question. For teaching purposes:

(C) Reveka sees the Kurosawa film.

This cannot work because that would put G and R together in the Kurosawa film.

(D) Viktor sees the Hitchcock film.
(E) Yow sees the Fellini film.

The VY link sees the Kurosawa.

19. Each of the following could be complete and accurate list of the film buffs who see the Fellini film EXCEPT:

(A) Ginnie, Ian
(B) Ginnie, Marcos
(C) Ian, Reveka
(D) Marcos, Reveka
(E) Viktor, Yow

This is a Cannot be True List question regarding the Fellini group. You know that it is this type because you are asked which cannot be a complete list. Let us check our MD to see who cannot see the Fellini. VY cannot see the Fellini film; (E) is correct. That was an easy question to work using our inference.

For teaching purposes, the rest of the choices are discussed. We are looking at **pairs** who see the Fellini film. That means that 4 buffs see the Hitchcock and 1 sees the Kurosawa.

(A) Ginnie, Ian

G and I can be the only two variables to see the Fellini; (A) can work. We have separated G from R and I from M.

(B) Ginnie, Marcos

This works too, the not links are separated. Ditto for (C) and (D).

*Sort Practice Games

Game 1, Questions 1-6

Exactly eight consumers--F, G, H, J, K, L, M, and N--will be interviewed by market researchers. The eight will be divided into exactly two 4 person groups--group 1 and group 2--before interviews begin. Each person is assigned to exactly one of the two groups according to the following conditions:

F must be in the same group as J.
G must be in a different group from M.
If H is in group 1, then L must be in group 1.
If N is in group 2, then G must be in group 1.

1. Group 1 could consist of

(A) F, G, H, and J
(B) F, H, L, and M
(C) F, J, K, and L
(D) G, H, L, and N
(E) G, K, M, and N

2. If K is in the same group as N, which one of the following must be true?

(A) G is in group 1.
(B) H is in group 2.
(C) J is in group 1.
(D) K is in group 2.
(E) M is in group 1.

3. If F is in the same group as H, which one of the following must be true?

(A) G is in group 2.
(B) J is in group 1.
(C) K is in group 1.
(D) L is in group 2.
(E) M is in group 2.

4. If L and M are in group 2, then a person who could be assigned either to group 1 or, alternatively, to group 2 is

(A) F
(B) G
(C) H
(D) J
(E) K

5. Each of the following is a pair of people who could be in group 1 together EXCEPT

(A) F and G
(B) F and H
(C) F and L
(D) H and G
(E) H and N

6. If L is in group 2, then each of the following is a pair of people who could be in group 1 together EXCEPT

(A) F and M
(B) G and N
(C) J and N
(D) K and M
(E) M and N

Game 2, Questions 7-12

A newly formed company has five employees F, G, H, K, and L. Each employee holds exactly one of the following positions: president, manager, or technician. Only the president is not supervised. Other employees are each supervised by exactly one employee, who is either the president or a manager. Each supervised employee holds a different position than his or her supervisor. The following conditions apply:

There is exactly one president.

At least one of the employees whom the president supervises is a manager.

Each manager supervises at least one employee.

F does not supervise any employee.

G supervises exactly two employees.

7. Which one of the following is an acceptable assignment of employees to the positions?

	President	Manager	Technician
(A)	G	H, K, L	F
(B)	G	H	F, K, L
(C)	H	F, G	K, L
(D)	H, K	G	F, L
(E)	K	F, G, H, L	–

8. Which one of the following must be true?

(A) There are at most three technicians.
(B) There is exactly one technician.
(C) There are at least two managers.
(D) There are exactly two managers.
(E) There are exactly two employees who supervise no one

9. Which one of the following is a pair of employees who could serve as managers together?

(A) F, H
(B) F, L
(C) G, K
(D) G, L
(E) K, L

10. Which one of the following could be true?

(A) There is exactly one technician.
(B) There are exactly two managers.
(C) There are exactly two employees who are not supervised.
(D) There are more managers than technicians.
(E) The president supervises all of the other employees.

11. If F is supervised by the president, which one of the following must be true?

(A) G is the president.
(B) H is the president.
(C) L is a technician.
(D) There is exactly one manager.
(E) There are exactly two technicians.

12. If K supervises exactly two employees, which one of the following must be true?

(A) F is supervised by K.
(B) G is a manager.
(C) L is supervised.
(D) There are exactly two managers.
(E) There are exactly two technicians.

Game 3, Questions 13-18

Each of seven judges voted for or else against granting Datalog Corporation's petition. Each judge is categorized as conservative, moderate, or liberal, and no judge is assigned more than one of those labels. Two judges are conservatives, two are moderates, and three are liberals. The following is known about how the judges voted:

If the two conservatives and at least one liberal voted the same way as each other, then both moderates voted that way.

If the three liberals voted the same way as each other, then no conservative voted that way.

At least two of the judges voted for Datalog, and at least two voted against Datalog.

At least one conservative voted against Datalog.

13. If the two moderates did not vote the same way as each other, then which one of the following could be true?

(A) No conservative and exactly two liberals voted for Datalog.
(B) Exactly one conservative and exactly one liberal voted for Datalog.
(C) Exactly one conservative and all three liberals voted for Datalog.
(D) Exactly two conservatives and exactly one liberal voted for Datalog.
(E) Exactly two conservatives and exactly two liberals voted for Datalog.

14. Which one of the following must be true?

(A) At least one conservative voted for Datalog.
(B) At least one liberal voted against Datalog.
(C) At least one liberal voted for Datalog.
(D) At least one moderate voted against Datalog.
(E) At least one moderate voted for Datalog.

15. If the three liberals all voted the same way as each other, which one of the following must be true?

(A) Both moderates voted for Datalog.
(B) Both moderates voted against Datalog.
(C) One conservative voted for Datalog and one conservative voted against Datalog.
(D) One moderate voted for Datalog and one moderate voted against Datalog.
(E) All three liberals voted for Datalog.

16. If exactly two judges voted against Datalog, then which one of the following must be true?

(A) Both moderates voted for Datalog.
(B) Exactly one conservative voted for Datalog.
(C) No conservative voted for Datalog.
(D) Exactly two liberals voted for Datalog.
(E) Exactly three liberals voted for Datalog.

17. Each of the following could be a complete and accurate list of those judges who voted for Datalog EXCEPT

(A) two liberals
(B) one conservative, one liberal
(C) two moderates, three liberals
(D) one conservative, two moderates, two liberals
(E) one conservative, two moderates, three liberals

18. If the two conservatives voted the same way as each other, but the liberals did not all vote the same way as each other, then each of the following must be true EXCEPT:

(A) Both conservatives voted against Datalog.
(B) Both moderates voted for Datalog.
(C) At least one liberal voted against Datalog.
(D) Exactly two liberals voted for Datalog.
(E) Exactly five of the judges voted against Datalog.

*Sort Practice Games Explanations

Game 1 (13/1 #1 – 6)

Variable Lists

Consumers: F, G, H, J, K, L, M, N
Divide the consumers into two 4-person groups.

Rule List

Rule 1: **FJ**
This block will be helpful to keep in mind.

Rule 2: **G | M**

Rule 3: $H_1 \rightarrow L_1$
Contrapositive:
$L_2 \rightarrow H_2$
This is written based on the fact that if L is not in 1, then it must be in 2.

If HL are together in either 1 or 2, then the FJ block must be in the other group, because G/M takes a spot in each group.

$H_1 \rightarrow L_1\ FJ_2$
and
$L_2 \rightarrow H_2\ FJ_1$
H and L can only be separated when H_2 and L_1.

Rule 4: $N_2 \rightarrow G_1 M_2$

Contrapositive:
$G_2 \rightarrow N_1 M_1$
Rule 2 is built into these.

Never GN_2
These two cannot be together in 2.

Main Diagram

G/M /FG	G/M /FG
1	2
	~~GN~~

K is never mentioned by the rules so it will fill in the spot needed.

1. Global, Could be True
Rule 1 eliminates B. Use Rule 2 to eliminate C and E. Rule 3 eliminates A. **D** is correct.

2. Local, Must be True
If K is with N, we have a second block along with FJ. That means that L and H cannot be paired together: there cannot be 3 blocks because of G and M always needing to be split up. So H is in 2 and L is in 1 (scenarios that do not start the chains in Rule 3 where H and L are forced together). **B** is correct. The blocks in the game give it an enormous amount of structure.

3. Local, Must be True
If FH, then H and L cannot be a block, because that would put FJHL all in one group. So H must be in 2 and L is in 1.

G/M L	HFJ G/M
1	2

This makes group 2 full, so K must be in 1.

4. Local, Must be True
If L and M are in 2 then the Contrapositive of Rule 3 is in action:

FJM	LHG
1	2

N and K are left and N cannot be with G in 2. K can go in either group.

5. Global, Cannot be True
Scan the rules to see any pairs that cannot go together in 1. The inference on Rule 3 shows that H and F cannot both be in 1. **B** is correct.

6. Local, Cannot be True
If L is in 2 then:

FJ	LH
1	2
	~~GN~~

K and M cannot be together in 1, because that would force G and N to be together in 2, which is not possible (inference of Rule 4). **D** is correct.

Game 2 (14/1 #1 – 6)

Variable Lists

Employees: F, G, H, K, L

Rule List

Rule 1: **One P.**

The one president must supervise all the manager(s), because each supervised employee holds a different position than her supervisor and the technicians do not supervise.

Rule 2: **P supervises at least one M.**

There is at least one M.

Rule 3: **Each M supervises at least one employee.**

This means that there can never be more managers than Employees (because the scenario states that each employee is only supervised by one person), and because there is one president there can be no more than two managers.

Rule 4: **F doesn't not supervise.**

This means F must be a T, because of rules 2 and 3.

Rule 5: **G supervises 2.**

G must either be the president or a manager. If G is the president then there are only 2 Managers. If G is a manager than there must be two technicians for him to supervise.

Main Diagram

G/	/G		F
P	M		T

We show the possibilities for G and place F with the technicians. We also show only two blanks for managers because that is the maximum possible.

QUESTIONS

7. Global, Could be True, List

Use Rule 1 to eliminate D, Rule 4 to eliminate C and E. Use the Central Diagram to eliminate A (too many Ms). **B** is correct.

8. Global, Must be True

Work each choice to see which must be true.

A) This is true because of Rule 2.

9. Global, Could be True

Check these pairs out one by one.

A) F is a T.

B) Same problem with A.

C) This cannot work, because of Rule 5. G supervises 2, and with K as another manager there would only be two employees for both of them.

D) Same problem with C.

E) Must be correct due to process of elimination.

10. Global, Could be True

We check to see which can work.

A) There are at least two Ts.

B) This can work if G is P.

11. Local, Must be True

The implication of F being supervised by the P is that there can only be one M. If there were two, then there would not be enough Ts for the Ms to supervise, because the P is supervising one. In the situation where there are two M, each manages one of the Ts. Find this insight in choice **D**.

12. Local, Must be True

G supervises two employees as well. This means that no one else supervises anyone (there are only four total employees that get supervised because the P does not). Either K or G is P and the other is the only M. We scan the choices and see that **C** must be true – L is supervised as is F and H.

Game 3 (7/2 # 13 – 18)

Variable Lists

Judges: CC, MM, LLL

Group the judges into either For or Against.

Rule List

Rule 1: **CCL → CCLMM**

Contrapositive:

~~CCLMM~~ → ~~CCL~~

If the moderates are split up then CCL cannot be together.

Rule 2: **LLL → LLL | CC**

Contrapositive:

~~LLL | CC~~ → ~~LLL~~

If the C's are split up or if a L votes with a C, then the L's cannot all vote the same way.

Rule 3: **At least 2 For and 2 Against.**

Combine with Rule 1:

CCL → CCLMM | LL

If there are five on one side, then the final two must be on the other side.

Rule 4: **At least one** C_A.

Combine with Rule 2:

LLL → LLL | CC_A

Based on this, all three L's cannot be Against, because at least one C is Against and when the Ls are together, the Cs are not with them (Rule 2). So, one L must be For.

Main Diagram

L	C
FOR	AGAINST

13. Local, Could be True

The Contrapositive of Rule 1 tells that if the M's are split then CCL cannot all be against. It is tough to draw any further inferences, so work the choices.

A) This sets up CCL in Against, which we know cannot be the case.

B) This puts MCL in For and CM in Against. The other two L's can be split into each:

MCL L	CML
FOR	AGAINST

14. Global, Must be True

Work the choices. C must be true based on the inference from Rule 4.

15. Local, Must be True

If the Ls are together, they must all be For. Based on Rule 2, the other C must be Against:

LLL	CC

The two Ms can vote either way. Scan the choices to see that E must be true.

16. Local, Must be True

If only two judges voted Against, then one must be a C . Because of Rule 2, the other Against must be an L or the other C. This is the case, because if the Ls are together it must be the other C (Rule2). Likewise, if the other spot is not a C, then the Ls cannot be together (Contrapositive of Rule 2), so one must be Against. Therefore, Choice A is the case: both Ms voted For because neither filled the second spot in Against.

17. Global, List

Locate a list of those who couldn't all vote For. E is impossible because it is six judges (Rule 1).

18. Local, Could be False

If the Cs vote together and the Ls do not then at least one L must vote Against (Inference of Rule 2):

L	CCL
FOR	AGAINST

This brings up the scenario in Rule 1 and means both Ms vote Against and the other L votes For. B is correct.

Select Games

Select Grouping games ask you to choose variables from one or more variable sets to form single group. The variables selected make up the group; the other variables are left out. Example Select game setup:

> Seven baseball players – Michael, Jennifer, Chris, Ashley, Sarah, David, and Nicole - are competing for five spots in a league.

In this Select game, five baseball players are selected from the total variable set of seven players. Two players will not make the league.

Select Bases

In Select games, the base consists of the variables that are selected. Draw Select bases **horizontally**, with the number of slots matching the number of variables selected, assuming you know that information. In the baseball setup above, there are five players who will make the league, so the base has five slots. Diagram:

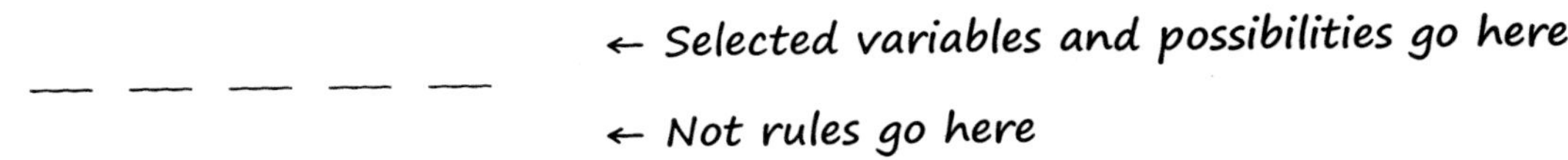

Never number the slots; the order of the variables does not matter. It only matters which variables are given a slot and which are left out.

How Many Slots?

In Select games, you sometimes do not know how many variables are chosen and how many slots to draw on the base.

Unknown Slots

Rarely, and **only in Select Games**, you will have no idea how many slots there should be on the MD. You are not told any information about how many variables will be chosen. That is the case in this game:

> Artists will be chosen from a group of eight finalists – A, B, C, D, E, F, G, H – to paint a mural in downtown Manhattan.

As few as two or as many as seven artists could be chosen. All eight cannot be chosen, because then no selection has occurred. We initially do not know how many slots to draw for the base. Sort games that feature unknown slots are generally difficult. In these games, derive as much information as you can from the rules and be ready to deal with a lot of local questions that give the game more structure.

Unknown slots only occur in Select games, because Sort games do not leave any variables out of the sorting; the number of slots in Sort games corresponds to the number of variables.

Partially Unknown Slots

Some grouping games tell you the **maximum or minimum number** of variables selected, but they do not tell you exactly how many variables will be. These games have partially unknown slots. Such games give you some structure to work with. This modification to the Select game setup above gives it partially unknown slots:

> At least four artists will be chosen from a group of eight finalists – A, B, C, D, E, F, G, H. The artists will paint a mural in downtown Manhattan.

Here, we are given a minimum number selected: four. We do not know exactly how many slots to build on the base, but we know there will be at least four and at most seven slots. So, we can draw the base like this:

___ ___ ___ ___ ___ ___ ___

The last three slots are drawn more lightly to signify that we do not know if any of them will be filled. When diagramming, actively make some slots darker and the rest lighter, creating a contrast.

Known Slots

Finally, many Sort games will tell you exactly how many slots you should draw, making the game, and drawing the base, simpler. Also, in these situations, you can often find more inferences to the game because you know more about its limits. In this Select game, we know exactly how many slots to draw:

> Five artists will be chosen from a group of eight finalists – A, B, C, D, E, F, G, H.

Five artists will be chosen, so we draw the base with confidence:

___ ___ ___ ___ ___

Knowing how many slots can help you draw inferences in various ways. For instance, if we know that four slots are filled in a certain situation and one of the rules states that the variable **A** is always chosen, then we also know that **A** is the fifth artist selected. Any variable not selected at that point is left out. If we did not know whether more variables were selected, then we could not say that **A** was the last to be selected.

Basic Rule Diagrams

Here are quite common rules that you will face in Select games.

Not Links

In general, you will use many diagrams that you have seen in Sort games, but in Select games they have slightly different meanings. Look at this rule:

Pete and Jill are not both chosen.

Diagram:

P | J

Recall that the vertical bar **does not mean** "or." It indicates separation. The diagram above tells that P and J cannot both be selected. So, if we are told by a local rule that P is selected, then we know that J is not. The diagram does not mean that one of the variables **is** chosen; it is possible that neither are. It only tells us that the variables are not selected together.

Onto a similar rule:

Will, Ted and Bryan cannot all be selected.

Diagram:

-WTB

W,T and B cannot all be selected. Recall that the negative sign (-) means "no." You will be using that sign a great deal in Select games. The diagram above allows for the possibility that W and T can be selected at the same time, or W and B or just T, etc.

Possibility Fills

Look at this rule:

Either Ross or Simone will be selected, but not both.

Only one of R and S will be chosen. Build this into the MD using the possibility symbol you are familiar with, the slash (/):

R/S __ __ __ __

In all Grouping games, the order of the slots does not matter. So, this diagram on the MD **does not mean** that either Ross or Simone will be in that first slot and the other variable could be in another slot. The possibility fill means that one out of the two variables will be chosen. If Ross is chosen, then he fills that slot and Simone is not selected at all.

Here are more rules that allow for possibility fills:

> Andy and Tyler cannot be selected together.
> Gene and Louise cannot be selected together.

Assume we know that exactly two variables are left out of this Select game. That means that one of Andy and Tyler will be left out and one of Gene and Louise will be left out:

___ A/T G/L ___ ___

We fill in the possibilities because we know that we need one variable from each of those pairs to be selected in order to have enough variables to fill all the slots.

Possibility Rectangles

Here is an interesting rule variation that you will see in Select games:

> Out of Frank, Nancy and Tabitha, exactly two will be chosen.

There are three different arrangements for the pair that will be chosen from the three variables: FN, FT, and NT. The possibilities do not matter for our diagramming; the point is that two variables will be chosen from that group of three. To show this situation on the MD, draw a rectangle over the number of slots the variables will take up and fill it with the variables who could be chosen:

[F N T] ___ ___ ___

Out of F, N and T, two will be chosen, so the rectangle is over **two slots**. One of the variables in the rectangle will not be chosen. Here is another example:

> One person will not be selected out of Phil, Russell, Britney and Claudia.

This time we need to show that three out of these four variables will be chosen. The rectangle extends over three slots and the four variables are placed within it:

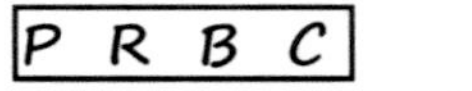

Three slots will be occupied up by a subset of the group PRBC.

Conditional Rules

Select games feature more conditional rules than Sequencing games, and more complex ones. However, we represent them in the same way: using an arrow in between the indicator and the requirement. Conditional rules in Select games can give the game structure by telling you that if one variable is selected then another variable is also selected:

> A relay of four swimmers will be chosen from the JV swimmers – Sarah, Agatha, Megan – and the varsity swimmers – Christine, Elspeth, Lauren and Kate.
>
> If Sarah is chosen for the relay, then Kate will be as well.

Rule diagram:

S → K

If S (Sarah is chosen) then K (Kate is chosen). In Select games, when a variable abbreviation is shown, it means that variable **is selected**. To show that Kate makes the relay team, we write a "K." The contrapositive:

-K → -S

If Kate is not chosen then Sarah is not chosen. Just as showing a variable means it is selected, showing a variable with a negative sign before it means that the variable is **not selected**.

Not Links

Another example rule:

> If Sarah is chosen for the relay, then Lauren will not be.

S → -L

If Sarah is selected then Lauren is not selected. The negative sign before the L indicates that Lauren is left out when Sarah is selected. Here is the contrapositive:

L → -S

If Lauren is selected, then Sarah is not. There is something important to notice here: Sarah and Lauren can never **both** be selected. Looking at the two conditional forms, we see that if one is selected, then the other is not. So, we have a not link created by a conditional. Because we know that Sarah and Lauren can never be selected together, we can diagram the rule as a not link:

S | L

There are three possible scenarios stemming from this rule:

1. S is chosen and L is not.
2. L is chosen and S is not.
3. Neither S nor L is chosen.

Drawing out the not link is faster than writing out the conditional **and** its contrapositive. You can use this trick on Select games whenever you see a conditional rule that tells you that if one variable is selected, then another variable is not. The form:

Selected → Not Selected

Now look at this rule:

If Agatha is chosen, Elspeth is not.

To diagram this rule, do not bother with the conditionals. Just write out the not link:

A | E

A **big** caveat: do not create not links with compound conditionals, conditionals that have "and" or "or." Look at this rule:

If Agatha and Kate are chosen, Christine is not.

This diagram is **incorrect**:

AK | C

It implies that neither A nor K can be chosen with C, and that is not the case. Either A **or** K can be selected with C as long as one of AK is left out. Do not try to create not links with compound conditionals. Just write them out:

AK → -C

If both A and K (represented by sticking them together) are chosen, then C is not.

Contrapositive:

C → -AK

If C is chosen then both A and K cannot be chosen. Either one can be.

At Least One Rules

At Least one is a unique rule type that you will see in some Select games. These rules tell you that if one variable is not selected then another variable is selected.

If Sarah is not chosen for the relay, then Christine will be.

Let us first work through the rule in a traditional way. Diagram:

-S → C

We can take the contrapositive:

-C → S

If Christine is not selected then Sarah will be. Looking at both of the forms of the rule tells us that **at least one** of the two girls will be chosen. This is clear when you look at the requirements of each conditional: they are both positive variables. This means that if one is not selected, then the other must be.

It is also possible that **both girls** are chosen. The rule tells us that the only scenario not possible involving these two variables is that neither is chosen. Write out the possibilities regarding the two variables:

S/C or SC

At least one (S/C) or both (SC). Whenever you see this form for a rule:

Not Selected → Selected

Write it out as an at least one rule. Another example:

If Megan is not chosen for the relay, then Lauren will be.

Diagram:

M/L or ML

Conditionals with Double Negation

Sometimes, you will be faced with a rule where both the indicator and the requirement are in negated form:

If Kate is not chosen for the relay, then Megan is also not chosen.

Diagram:

-K → -M

It is challenging to interpret what that diagram means.

When we take the contrapositive, the diagram is clearer:

M → K

When Megan is chosen, Kate is also chosen. Taking the different form of the rule makes it more useful. So, **automatically** take the contrapositive of any rules that feature double negatives. For example:

If Christine is not selected, then Agatha is also not selected.

Reverse the terms and negate them for your conditional diagram:

A → C

Combining Conditionals

Combining conditional rules can help you draw inferences and understand a game more deeply. **Select Grouping games** are often ripe for linking conditionals. **Sort games** are usually less conducive because their conditionals tend to deal with different groups and are of a more diverse variety, giving you less variables in common to connect.

Look at these rules from a Select game:

> If Sarah is chosen for the relay, then Kate will be as well.
> If Kate is selected then Megan is also selected.

Diagrams:

$$S \rightarrow K$$
$$K \rightarrow M$$

To link two conditionals, you need to have a term in common, a variable the two conditionals share. You must also have the arrow in one conditional **pointing into** that common term and the arrow in the other conditional **pointing away** from the term. We can link these two conditionals:

$$\begin{array}{lccccc} & S & \rightarrow & K & & \\ + & & & K & \rightarrow & M \\ \hline = & S & \rightarrow & K & \rightarrow & M \end{array}$$

In the combined diagram, we see that when Sarah is selected, Kate is selected, which means that Megan is also selected. Think of the selection of Sarah as starting a chain reaction, where events occur in the direction of the arrows. When you look at the chain above and see that Kate is chosen, we start the reaction in the **middle** of the chain. That means that we only know that Megan is chosen; we do not have any information about Sarah. We cannot work backwards from Kate being selected and say that Sarah is selected.

Back to the nature of combining conditionals, we cannot connect these two conditional rules:

$$S \rightarrow K$$
$$L \rightarrow K$$

Here, both conditionals feature K, so we have a variable in common, but we need one arrow leading into K and another leading out of it. Because both arrows lead into K, no chain can be set up here. We can, however, combine the contrapositives of these two rules:

$$-K \rightarrow -S$$
$$-K \rightarrow -L$$

Becomes:

$$-K \rightarrow -L + -S$$

Combining a Conditional with a Not Link

In order to combine a conditional with a not link, you need a variable in common and the arrow in the conditional to be **pointing into the not link**. Example conditional that creates a not link:

> If Kate is chosen, Elspeth is not chosen.

K and E can never be chosen together. Diagram the conditional as a not link:

K | E

We can link the rule above to the rule that Kate is chosen if Sarah is.

```
   S → K
+      K | E
  ___________
=  S → K | E
```

From the diagram above, we learn this:

S | E

Sarah and Elspeth can never be selected together. If Sarah is selected, then Kate is selected. And Kate and Elspeth can never be selected together, so in that situation Elspeth is not selected. Therefore, Sarah and Elspeth are never both selected.

This is a common combining inference that you can make when you have a not link and a conditional rule. Lookout for it. Note that this combination of diagrams only works when the arrow **points into** the variable in common between the two rules. The arrow above points into the not link because it points to Kate.

We cannot combine these rules:

S | A
S → K

Here, Sarah is the variable in common, and the arrow in the conditional **points away** from Sarah. Therefore, it is not the case that Kate and Agatha can never be chosen together. This would be confusing what the arrow means. Just because Sarah and Agatha cannot be together does not mean that Kate and Agatha can never be chosen together. Kate can be selected **when Sarah is not**.

Compound Conditionals

Some rules feature advanced conditionals that contain several logical parts in either the indicator or the requirement. For instance, this rule features a **compound** requirement:

If the orange frisbee is selected, then the red one is selected and the indigo one is not.

Diagram the above rule using a plus sign to indicate "and" in between r and i. We recommend using two layers if you think that you can link other rules to the conditional:

```
            R
O    →      +
            -I
```

The plus sign tells that both occur: R is selected and I is not. You do not have to use layers for compound conditional parts, as we have done above. However, doing so allows you to create chains of logic off of each layer, which can be useful. For instance, if we have this diagram from another rule:

-I → P

Then we can easily link it to the compound rule diagram:

```
          R
O    →    +
          -I  →  P
```

When O is selected, I is not and P is. Here is an alternative rule diagram for the original compound conditional. It iseasier to draw if you know that you cannot link any other rules to it:

O → R + -I

Taking the contrapositive of compound rules is not complicated. The key is changing the "and" to an "or."

-R or I → -O

If the R is not selected **or** if I is selected, then O is not. Either of these possibilities occurring sets off the conditional and means that O is not selected. Here is another compound conditional. This one features a compound indicator:

If the green frisbee and the blue frisbee are selected, then the yellow one is not.

G + B → -Y

Contrapositive (change the "and" to an "or"): Y → -G or -B

If Y is selected, then G is not selected or B is not selected. And, they can both be not selected. That is also a logical possibility when you are dealing with "or." It sounds strange, but "or" leaves open the possibility of "and." Either G is not selected, or B is not selected, or G **and** B are not selected. The requirement only tells us that **both variables cannot be selected** when Y is selected.

*Select Games Review

- Select games ask you to choose variables from one or more variable sets to form a single group.
  - Variables not chosen are left out.
  - "Seven baseball players – Michael, Jennifer, Chris, Ashley, Sarah, David, and Nicole - are competing for five spots in a league."
- In Select games, the base is the variables that are selected.
  - Represent the slots horizontally:

    ___ ___ ___ ___ ___

  - Do not number them; the order does not matter.

The Number of Slots

- In Select games you will sometimes not know many slots should be on the MD.
  - In these games, derive as much information as you can from the rules.
  - Be ready to deal with a lot of local questions that give the game more structure.
- Some Select games tell you the maximum or minimum number of variables selected, but they do not tell you exactly how many variables.
  - For your MD, draw what you do know about the base.
    - For instance, if there must be at least four slots, draw those slots.

Possibility Fills

- "Either Ross or Simone, but not both, will be selected."

  R/S
  ___ ___ ___ ___ ___

- "Out of Frank, Nancy and Tabitha, exactly two will be chosen."

  [F N T]
  ___ ___ ___ ___ ___

Conditional Rules

- "If Sarah is chosen for the relay, then Kate will be as well."

  $S \rightarrow K$

- Created Not Links
  - "If Sarah is chosen for the relay, then Lauren will not be."

    S | L

- At Least One
  - "If Sarah is not chosen for the relay, then Christine will be."
  - At least one of the variables, and perhaps both, will be selected.

    S/C or SC

- Created links
  - "Agatha is selected if, and only if, Lauren is selected."
  - The two become a link.

    AL

9/3 #8-13

Example Select game:

> From a group of seven people — J, K, L, M, N, P, and Q — exactly four will be selected to attend a diplomat's retirement dinner. Selection must conform to the following conditions:
>
> Either J or K must be selected, but J and K cannot both be selected.
> Either N or P must be selected, but N and P cannot both be selected.
> N cannot be selected unless L is selected.
> Q cannot be selected unless K is selected.

This is a Select Grouping game. The setup tells us that we are selecting four variables from the set of seven. **Three** people will not be selected to attend the dinner. Variable list:

J K L M N P Q

The rules for this game are challenging. The first two rules are "only one" rules. These are best built into the MD with possibility fills:

Either J or K will be selected but not both of them. We show this by taking up a slot with both variables surrounded by a rectangle. N and P are in the same situation and we diagram it the same way. Three variables will not be chosen in the game and two of them will come from J, K, N and P. That means that exactly one of L M Q will be left out. Build in the Possibility Rectangle for those three:

[J K] [N P] [L M Q]
___ ___ ___ ___

Two of the slots will be filled with a pair from L, M and Q.

Moving on to the final two rules. Rule 3 is a conditional rule.

> N cannot be selected unless L is selected.

"Unless" is tricky to deal with. Recall that the condition that follows "unless" is the requirement and the **negated form** of the other conditional is the indicator. So, "L is selected" is the requirement. The negated form of "N cannot be selected" is "N is selected" and that is the indicator. Here is the rule diagram:

N → L

If N is selected, then L is also selected. Because N also appears in rule 2, it is a good idea to take the contrapositive:

-L → -N

Because of rule 2, we know that when N is **not selected**, P must be selected. We can substitute in "P" for the "-N"

-L → P

Rule 4:

Q cannot be selected unless K is selected.

Diagram using the same methods as rule 3. Make the condition after "unless" the requirement, and then negate the other condition and place it as the indicator:

Q → K

When Q is chosen, so is K. Again, take the contrapositive:

-K → -Q

Substitute in J for the –K, because we know that when K is not selected, J must be:

J → -Q

When J is chosen, Q is not chosen.

Whoever is chosen in the "only one" rules will dictate to some extent who out of L, M and Q is chosen. For instance, if J is chosen, then Q is not. Based on our possibility fill of L, M and Q for the last two slots, we know that when Q is **not** chosen, L and M are. Alternatively, when N is chosen, L must be as well. This interaction between the possibilities in rules 1 and 2 and the conditionals in rules 3 and 4 will play a large role in the game.

No rules deal with M, so it is a leftover: circle it in the variable list. Here are the diagrams we will use to work the game:

J K (L) M N P Q

N → L
-L → P
Q → K
J → -Q

[J K] [N P] [L M Q]
___ ___ ___ ___

Onto the questions:

8. Which one of the following could be the four people selected to attend the retirement dinner?

(A) J, K, M, P
(B) J, L, N, Q
(C) J, M, N, Q
(D) K, M, P, Q
(E) L, M, N, P

We start off with a List question. Use rule 1 to eliminate (A) because both J and K are chosen in that solution, which is not possible. Rule 1 also eliminates (E) because **neither J nor K** are chosen there. rule 2 does not eliminate any choices. Rule 3 eliminates (C) because N is chosen and L is not. Rule 4 eliminates (B) because Q is chosen and K is not. (D), the choice left standing, is correct.

9. Among the people selected to attend the retirement dinner there must be

(A) K or Q or both
(B) L or M or both
(C) N or M or both
(D) N or Q or both
(E) P or Q or both

This global Must be True question asks us to find the choice that features at least one variable that must be selected. We worked thoroughly with possibility fills on our MD, so analyzing each choice should not take long.

(A) K and Q do not share a rectangle, so it is possible that neither is selected. Therefore, this choice is incorrect.

(B) is correct. Either L *or* M must be selected because those two variables, along with Q, must fill two slots on the MD. The final three choices feature variables from different possibility fills on our MD, meaning that it is possible to create solutions where **none** of those variables are selected. These solutions prove the choices incorrect:

(C) K P L Q

(D) K P L M

(E) K N L M

Next question:

10. Which one of the following is a pair of people who CANNOT both be selected to attend the retirement dinner?

(A) J and N
(B) J and Q
(C) K and L
(D) K and N
(E) N and Q

This is a global Cannot be True question. Find the pair of variables that cannot be selected together. The easiest way to spot such a pair is to look at our conditional rules and locate any that show that when one variable is chosen, another variable cannot be. There is only one conditional like that, the contrapositive of rule 4. When J is chosen, Q is not. Scanning the choices, we find this situation in (B). Thoroughly analyzing conditional rules pays off when working the questions.

11. If M is not selected to attend the retirement dinner, the four people selected to attend must include which one of the following pairs of people?

(A) J and Q
(B) K and L
(C) K and P
(D) L and P
(E) N and Q

A local Must be True question. Which pair must be selected given the local rule that M is not selected? The rule means that **both L and Q must be chosen**: we see this clearly in our possibility fill for the final two slots. And if Q is chosen, then so is K according to rule 4. So, L, Q and K are chosen. Scan the choices looking for a pair out of these two. (B) is correct: Both K and L must be chosen.

We analyzed the local rule and then saw how it interacted with the other rules (specifically rule 4) before working the choices. That extra effort gave us all the information we needed to quickly answer the question.

12. If P is not selected to attend the retirement dinner, then exactly how many different groups of four are there each of which would be an acceptable selection?

(A) one
(B) two
(C) three
(D) four
(E) five

This unique question asks us how many possible solutions there are to the game when P is not selected. We know that N is selected when P is not and, when N is selected, so is L (rule 3). Here is a mini diagram of the possible solutions we will have moving forward:

J/K N L M/Q

Either J or K and either M or Q must be selected. Q is the only variable out of these four that is limited by a conditional rule. If Q is selected, so is K. This is the *only* solution when Q is selected:

K N L Q

When M is selected either J or K can be selected because M is not limited by **any** rules. So, here are two more solutions:

J/K N L M

There are **three** possible solutions given the local rule: two when M is selected, one when Q is. (C) is correct.

13. There is only one acceptable group of four that can be selected to attend the retirement dinner if which one of the following pairs of people is selected?

(A) J and L
(B) K and M
(C) L and N
(D) L and Q
(E) M and Q

This is a Full Solution Structure question. We need to know which two people, when selected, dictate the other two people that must be selected.

In order to have a full solution, we must figure out which two are selected from LMQ. There are few different ways to do that, but the simplest is to find a choice that chooses two of those variables. Then we will know the third variable is left out. Scan the choices to see if any do that.

(D) does; L and Q are selected, which means that M is left out. Because Q is selected, we know that K must be as well. But, we do not know which out of N or P is selected. According to rule 3, L being selected **makes it possible** for N to be selected, but it **does not indicate** that N is selected. The requirement of that conditional occurs, but that does not mean that the indicator (Q being selected) occurs too. (D) is incorrect because it does not provide a full solution.

(E) also features two variables out of L, M and Q. M and Q are selected, so we know that L is left out. Because Q is selected, we know that K is also selected. And, regarding the N/P possibility, we know that N cannot be chosen, because L is not chosen (contrapositive of rule 3). Therefore, we have a full solution and (E) is correct:

K P M Q

Narrowing down which choices to work through by analyzing the LMQ variables saved a great deal of time. If you did not have that insight, you would need to work the choices one by one:

(A) J and L

With (A), we do not know who is selected out of the N/P possibility. N can be chosen because L is, and P also can be chosen. We do know that Q cannot be chosen because K is not. There is no need to draw a mini diagram to prove this choice incorrect when it is easy to analyze mentally, but here is what it looks like:

J N/P L M

Onto (B):

(B) K and M

This choice gives very little structure to the game, as we do not know who is chosen out of either N/P or Q/L. (B) is incorrect.

(C) L and N

With (C), we do not know who is chosen out of J/K and M/Q.

Select Practice Games

Questions 1-6

In each of two years exactly two of four lawmakers - Feld, Gibson, Hsu, and Ivins - and exactly two of three scientists - Vega, Young, and Zapora - will serve as members of a four-person panel. In each year, one of the members will be chairperson. The chairperson in the first year cannot serve on the panel in the second year. The chairperson in the second year must have served on the panel in the first year. Service on the panel must obey the following conditions:

Gibson and Vega do not serve on the panel in the same year as each other.

Hsu and Young do not serve on the panel in the same year as each other.

Each year, either Ivins or Vega, but not both, serves on the panel.

1. Which one of the following could be the list of the people who serve on the panel in the first year?

(A) Feld, Gibson, Vega, Zapora
(B) Feld, Hsu, Vega, Zapora
(C) Feld, Ivins, Vega, Zapora
(D) Gibson, Hsu, Ivins, Zapora
(E) Hsu, Ivins, Young, Zapora

2. If Vega is the chairperson in the first year, which one of the following is a pair of people who must serve on the panel in the second year?

(A) Gibson and Young
(B) Gibson and Zapora
(C) Hsu and Ivins
(D) Ivins and Young
(E) Vega and Young

3. If Hsu is the chairperson in the first year, which one of the following could be the chairperson in the second year?

(A) Feld
(B) Gibson
(C) Hsu
(D) Ivins
(E) Young

4. If Feld serves on the panel in a given year, any one of the following could serve on the panel that year EXCEPT:

(A) Gibson
(B) Hsu
(C) Ivins
(D) Vega
(E) Young

5. If Ivins is the chairperson in the first year, which one of the following could be the chairperson in the second year?

(A) Feld
(B) Gibson
(C) Hsu
(D) Vega
(E) Young

6. Which one of the following must be true?

(A) Feld is on the panel in the second year.
(B) Hsu is on the panel in the first year.
(C) Ivins is on the panel in both years.
(D) Young is on the panel in both years.
(E) Zapora is on the panel in the second year.

Game 1 (26/1 #19–24)

Lawmakers: F, G, H, I
Scientists: V, Y, Z

Rule List

We get information about the chairperson in the scenario that we must build into our rules:

First chairperson doesn't serve in second year

Second Chairperson served in the First year

Rule 1: ~~GV~~

In a game with groups as small as these (3 scientists, 4 lawmakers), it pays to see who must go together based on who cannot go together. G must be with Y and Z because it cannot be with V

G → YZ contrapositive: **~~YZ~~ → ~~G~~**

Rule 2: ~~HY~~

H must be with V and Z because it cannot be with Y:

H → VZ

We could take the contrapositive of this rule now, but during our initial reading we noticed that V appeared in two rules. We wait to see if we have inferences relating to V.

Rule 3: **always I / V**

V cannot be with G or I, so V must be with F and H:

V → FH

Inferences:

Combine rule 3 with **H → VZ** (rule 2) to get:

H → VZF & **V → FHZ**

Contrapositives: **~~VZF~~ → ~~H~~** & **~~FHZ~~ → ~~V~~**

Because G cannot be with V, G must be with I:

G → I Contrapositive: **~~I~~ → ~~G~~**

Z is always on the panel, because V with Y eliminates G, H and I and we need two lawmakers.

Main Diagram

```
            Z
2 __ __ __ __
   L     S
            Z
1 __ __ __ __
   L     S
```

1. Global, Could be True

We use our inference, **V → FHZ**, to eliminate A, and then see that **B** is possible – it fits this scenario.

2. Local, Must be True

If V is the chairperson in the first year then V cannot serve in the second year. That means that I must serve that year (rule 3). There are only three scientists, so both Y and Z serve in V's absence. So we know that IYZ and must serve. We choose **D.**

3. Local, Could be True

A mini -diagram is very helpful for this one, because we need to see who can be chairperson in the second year based on who served in the first year.

```
  (H)  F   V   Z
1 __  __  __  __
     L       S
```

We simply plugged **H → VZF** into year 1. Based on the rules governing the chairperson given in the scenario, we know that H cannot serve in year 2. V cannot serve either - **~~FHZ~~ → ~~V~~**. So F and Z are the only two possible candidates for chairperson in the second year. Choice **A** is correct.

4. Local, Cannot be True

Who cannot serve with F? We know who can – V, H, Z. We eliminate B and D. We check the rest to see which one does not work. Choice **A** is correct because G goes with I and no other lawmaker.

5. Local, Could be True

```
   I  G/F  Y   Z
1 __  __  __  __
     L       S
```

I cannot serve with V so Y and Z serve. Because Y serves H cannot so either G or F do. I cannot serve the second year so V does and that gives us H, F, V and Z in the second year. F and Z are in both years so either can be chairperson in 2. Choice **A** is right.

6. Global, Must be True

Our final inference is that Z is always on the panel. So E must be true. If we did not have this inference when working through the rules, we would have had to take the choice one by one, attempting to eliminate them based on scenarios – a lengthy process. This question shows how spending time figuring out who must be chosen pays off.

*Grouping Problem Sets

Average (16)

Set	#	Problem	Answer
21 / 1	#	**1**	Ⓐ Ⓑ Ⓒ Ⓓ Ⓔ
21 / 1	#	**2**	Ⓐ Ⓑ Ⓒ Ⓓ Ⓔ
21 / 1	#	**3**	Ⓐ Ⓑ Ⓒ Ⓓ Ⓔ
21 / 1	#	**4**	Ⓐ Ⓑ Ⓒ Ⓓ Ⓔ
21 / 1	#	**5**	Ⓐ Ⓑ Ⓒ Ⓓ Ⓔ
21 / 1	#	**6**	Ⓐ Ⓑ Ⓒ Ⓓ Ⓔ
24 / 4	#	**1**	Ⓐ Ⓑ Ⓒ Ⓓ Ⓔ
24 / 4	#	**2**	Ⓐ Ⓑ Ⓒ Ⓓ Ⓔ
24 / 4	#	**3**	Ⓐ Ⓑ Ⓒ Ⓓ Ⓔ
24 / 4	#	**4**	Ⓐ Ⓑ Ⓒ Ⓓ Ⓔ
24 / 4	#	**5**	Ⓐ Ⓑ Ⓒ Ⓓ Ⓔ
25 / 3	#	**1**	Ⓐ Ⓑ Ⓒ Ⓓ Ⓔ
25 / 3	#	**2**	Ⓐ Ⓑ Ⓒ Ⓓ Ⓔ
25 / 3	#	**3**	Ⓐ Ⓑ Ⓒ Ⓓ Ⓔ
25 / 3	#	**4**	Ⓐ Ⓑ Ⓒ Ⓓ Ⓔ
25 / 3	#	**5**	Ⓐ Ⓑ Ⓒ Ⓓ Ⓔ

Grueling (19)

Set	#	Problem	Answer
23 / 1	#	**6**	Ⓐ Ⓑ Ⓒ Ⓓ Ⓔ
23 / 1	#	**7**	Ⓐ Ⓑ Ⓒ Ⓓ Ⓔ
23 / 1	#	**8**	Ⓐ Ⓑ Ⓒ Ⓓ Ⓔ
23 / 1	#	**9**	Ⓐ Ⓑ Ⓒ Ⓓ Ⓔ
23 / 1	#	**10**	Ⓐ Ⓑ Ⓒ Ⓓ Ⓔ
23 / 1	#	**11**	Ⓐ Ⓑ Ⓒ Ⓓ Ⓔ
24 / 4	#	**18**	Ⓐ Ⓑ Ⓒ Ⓓ Ⓔ
24 / 4	#	**19**	Ⓐ Ⓑ Ⓒ Ⓓ Ⓔ
24 / 4	#	**20**	Ⓐ Ⓑ Ⓒ Ⓓ Ⓔ
24 / 4	#	**21**	Ⓐ Ⓑ Ⓒ Ⓓ Ⓔ
24 / 4	#	**22**	Ⓐ Ⓑ Ⓒ Ⓓ Ⓔ
24 / 4	#	**23**	Ⓐ Ⓑ Ⓒ Ⓓ Ⓔ
28 / 2	#	**6**	Ⓐ Ⓑ Ⓒ Ⓓ Ⓔ
28 / 2	#	**7**	Ⓐ Ⓑ Ⓒ Ⓓ Ⓔ
28 / 2	#	**8**	Ⓐ Ⓑ Ⓒ Ⓓ Ⓔ
28 / 2	#	**9**	Ⓐ Ⓑ Ⓒ Ⓓ Ⓔ
28 / 2	#	**10**	Ⓐ Ⓑ Ⓒ Ⓓ Ⓔ
28 / 2	#	**11**	Ⓐ Ⓑ Ⓒ Ⓓ Ⓔ
28 / 2	#	**12**	Ⓐ Ⓑ Ⓒ Ⓓ Ⓔ

Difficult (32)

Set	#	Problem	Answer
19 / 1	#	**13**	Ⓐ Ⓑ Ⓒ Ⓓ Ⓔ
19 / 1	#	**14**	Ⓐ Ⓑ Ⓒ Ⓓ Ⓔ
19 / 1	#	**15**	Ⓐ Ⓑ Ⓒ Ⓓ Ⓔ
19 / 1	#	**16**	Ⓐ Ⓑ Ⓒ Ⓓ Ⓔ
19 / 1	#	**17**	Ⓐ Ⓑ Ⓒ Ⓓ Ⓔ
19 / 1	#	**18**	Ⓐ Ⓑ Ⓒ Ⓓ Ⓔ
19 / 1	#	**19**	Ⓐ Ⓑ Ⓒ Ⓓ Ⓔ
19 / 1	#	**20**	Ⓐ Ⓑ Ⓒ Ⓓ Ⓔ
19 / 1	#	**21**	Ⓐ Ⓑ Ⓒ Ⓓ Ⓔ
19 / 1	#	**22**	Ⓐ Ⓑ Ⓒ Ⓓ Ⓔ
19 / 1	#	**23**	Ⓐ Ⓑ Ⓒ Ⓓ Ⓔ
19 / 1	#	**24**	Ⓐ Ⓑ Ⓒ Ⓓ Ⓔ
20 / 3	#	**6**	Ⓐ Ⓑ Ⓒ Ⓓ Ⓔ
20 / 3	#	**7**	Ⓐ Ⓑ Ⓒ Ⓓ Ⓔ
20 / 3	#	**8**	Ⓐ Ⓑ Ⓒ Ⓓ Ⓔ
20 / 3	#	**9**	Ⓐ Ⓑ Ⓒ Ⓓ Ⓔ
20 / 3	#	**10**	Ⓐ Ⓑ Ⓒ Ⓓ Ⓔ
20 / 3	#	**11**	Ⓐ Ⓑ Ⓒ Ⓓ Ⓔ
20 / 3	#	**12**	Ⓐ Ⓑ Ⓒ Ⓓ Ⓔ
25 / 3	#	**6**	Ⓐ Ⓑ Ⓒ Ⓓ Ⓔ
25 / 3	#	**7**	Ⓐ Ⓑ Ⓒ Ⓓ Ⓔ
25 / 3	#	**8**	Ⓐ Ⓑ Ⓒ Ⓓ Ⓔ
25 / 3	#	**9**	Ⓐ Ⓑ Ⓒ Ⓓ Ⓔ
25 / 3	#	**10**	Ⓐ Ⓑ Ⓒ Ⓓ Ⓔ
25 / 3	#	**11**	Ⓐ Ⓑ Ⓒ Ⓓ Ⓔ
25 / 3	#	**12**	Ⓐ Ⓑ Ⓒ Ⓓ Ⓔ
26 / 1	#	**13**	Ⓐ Ⓑ Ⓒ Ⓓ Ⓔ
26 / 1	#	**14**	Ⓐ Ⓑ Ⓒ Ⓓ Ⓔ
26 / 1	#	**15**	Ⓐ Ⓑ Ⓒ Ⓓ Ⓔ
26 / 1	#	**16**	Ⓐ Ⓑ Ⓒ Ⓓ Ⓔ
26 / 1	#	**17**	Ⓐ Ⓑ Ⓒ Ⓓ Ⓔ
26 / 1	#	**18**	Ⓐ Ⓑ Ⓒ Ⓓ Ⓔ

*Grouping Problem Sets

Average

21 / 1 # **1** C
21 / 1 # **2** B
21 / 1 # **3** B
21 / 1 # **4** C
21 / 1 # **5** A
21 / 1 # **6** C
24 / 4 # **1** D
24 / 4 # **2** A
24 / 4 # **3** A
24 / 4 # **4** B
24 / 4 # **5** C
25 / 3 # **1** B
25 / 3 # **2** B
25 / 3 # **3** D
25 / 3 # **4** E
25 / 3 # **5** D

Very Difficult

23 / 1 # **6** C
23 / 1 # **7** E
23 / 1 # **8** E
23 / 1 # **9** E
23 / 1 # **10** B
23 / 1 # **11** B
24 / 4 # **18** E
24 / 4 # **19** E
24 / 4 # **20** E
24 / 4 # **21** E
24 / 4 # **22** D
24 / 4 # **23** C
28 / 2 # **6** D
28 / 2 # **7** B
28 / 2 # **8** C
28 / 2 # **9** C
28 / 2 # **10** A
28 / 2 # **11** B
28 / 2 # **12** D

Difficult

19 / 1 # **13** C
19 / 1 # **14** E
19 / 1 # **15** C
19 / 1 # **16** A
19 / 1 # **17** B
19 / 1 # **18** A
19 / 1 # **19** B
19 / 1 # **20** E
19 / 1 # **21** A
19 / 1 # **22** C
19 / 1 # **23** D
19 / 1 # **24** A
20 / 3 # **6** A
20 / 3 # **7** E
20 / 3 # **8** B
20 / 3 # **9** A
20 / 3 # **10** A
20 / 3 # **11** C
20 / 3 # **12** E
25 / 3 # **6** C
25 / 3 # **7** A
25 / 3 # **8** B
25 / 3 # **9** E
25 / 3 # **10** B
25 / 3 # **11** E
25 / 3 # **12** E
26 / 1 # **13** D
26 / 1 # **14** D
26 / 1 # **15** B
26 / 1 # **16** B
26 / 1 # **17** E
26 / 1 # **18** C

Combination Games

Grouping and Sequencing are the core skills of the games section. 84% of recent games (Tests #50 and higher) are straightforward Sequencing, Advanced Sequencing or Grouping games. However, a small percentage of games test your ability to both sequence and group in the same game; these are Combination games. The skills you have learned on Sequencing and Grouping games will help enormously on this hybrid game type.

Group then Order

The core strategy in Combination games is to focus first on grouping and then on sequencing the variables. This should be intuitive, because you have to know the contents of a group in order to sequence it. For instance, if you are in charge of a swim meet, you cannot assign lanes for a race until you know the names of the swimmers in the race.

Prioritizing the grouping aspect of combination games gives you a general plan of attack for the game, which can be helpful in dealing with a game you are not quite sure how to approach. Due to the dual nature of these games, they often seem strange at first. Keep in mind that Combination games only test skills you already know, albeit in slightly new ways.

"Select then Order" Example Game Setup

Combination games often ask you to select a group of variables and then order the variables you have selected. Here is an example game setup:

> Charlie is having friends over to watch a basketball game. He will invite six out of eight friends - Todd, Marshall, Aaron, Will, Pete, Greg, Bert and Frank. Charlie has a line of six chairs in his living room and will assign his friends specific seats for watching the game.

Select six of the eight friends and then sequence them in the chairs in the living room. Some of the game rules will give you grouping information:

> Todd and Will are not both invited.

Diagram: T | W

Some of the rules will give you sequencing information:

> Bert sits in a higher numbered chair than Greg.

Diagram: G · B

Your job is to understand both types of rules and see how they interact when creating inferences and solving the questions.

Grouping Elements

Both when setting up a Combination game and primarily when working each individual question, first pay attention to grouping rules and elements. Watch the impact of variables being selected or left out. For instance, in the example game above, if you are told that Todd is invited, then you will know that Will is not. Because only two variables are left out, you know that one more variable will not be selected to watch the game. On each question you face, first think about who is selected. Deal with the impacts of local rules in that way before you do anything else.

Pay attention to the important grouping variables, those variables that have the most impact on who is or is not selected. These variables will likely be in multiple rules or in one very important rule. Keep your eye on them at all times during the game. You should actively do this with the most important rules and variables on any game, but especially on Combination games.

Sequencing

You will likely need to find some sequencing inferences. After you have considered the grouping aspects of the setup or question, sequence the variables. Look for inferences or simply sequence as much as you can.

An Example Game Will Help

The approach to Combination games probably seems vague right now. That is partly because you already have the skills to approach these games, so there is not a much new material to cover. Also, the strategy of grouping before sequencing is, by its very nature, general. The example game that follows will flesh out some of these strategies.

*Combination Games Review

- A small percentage of games test your ability to sequence and group variables in the same game.
- Focus first on grouping and then on sequencing the variables.
    - Watch the impact of variables being selected or left out.
    - Pay attention to the grouping variables that have the most impact on who is or is not selected.
- After you have considered the grouping aspects of the game or question, sequence the variables.

13/1 #12-17

Here is the setup for an example Combination game:

> An art teacher will schedule exactly six of eight lectures - fresco, history, lithography, naturalism, oils, pastels, sculpture, and watercolors - for three days - 1, 2, and 3. There will be exactly two lectures each day - morning and afternoon. Scheduling is governed by the following conditions:

We select six of these eight lecturers: F H L N O P S W.

Two lecturers will be left out. We will sequence the six selected on an two level MD. This game is a combination of a Select Grouping game and an Advanced Sequencing game (because a variable can be on either level of the MD). Onto the rules:

> Day 2 is the only day for which oils can be scheduled.

We do not know whether O will be selected, but if it is, it will be on Day 2. Show the O possibility for both slots on day 2:

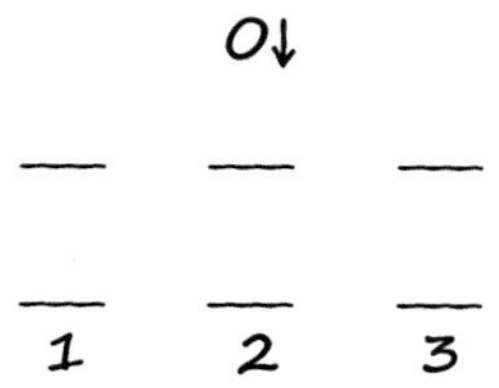

```
      O↓

___  ___  ___

___  ___  ___
 1    2    3
```

As always, show possibilities above the slots and not rules below the slots. The arrow next to O tells that the possibility applies to both slots of that day. Because O can only be on day 2, we will know that O is not selected if both slots for this day are filled. Next rule:

> Neither sculpture nor watercolors can be scheduled for the afternoon.

This is another sequencing rule. Note that you should analyze the rules in the order they appear; do not skip around looking for the grouping ones. That is not what we mean by prioritize grouping elements over sequencing ones. That advice refers more to creating mini diagrams and working the questions.

Build rule 2 directly into the MD, by showing the possibilities for S and W in the morning, which is logically represented on the first level:

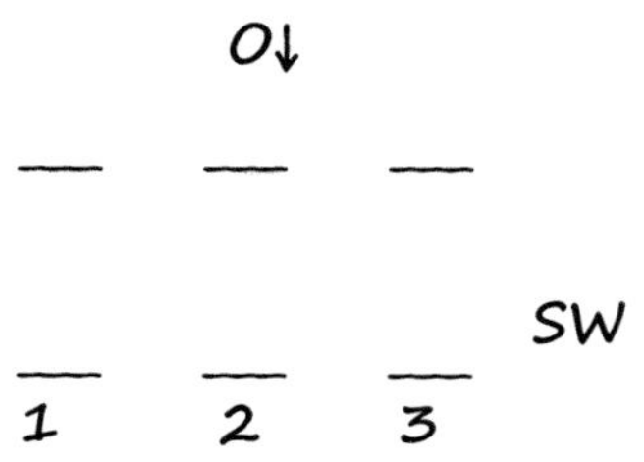

```
      O↓

___  ___  ___

               SW
___  ___  ___
 1    2    3
```

Keep in mind that rules 1 and 2 indicate where the variables can be placed, not where they **are placed**. We do not know which variables are selected at this point.

If it helps you understand the MD, you can show the not rule versions of the rules:

-SW ___ ___ ___

___ ___ ___
1 2 3
O↑ O↑

We prefer the positive version, but to use it effectively, you must keep in mind that these are only where the variables can be placed. On to the next rule:

> Neither oils nor pastels can be scheduled for the same day as lithography.

We represent this sequencing rule by showing the not links:

no [O/L] no [P/L]

Recall that the vertical rectangle around O and L symbolizes the entire day (the slots on both levels), so which variable is on top is not important. The first diagram shows that L cannot be with O on a given day, *not* that L cannot be in the morning on a day when O is in the afternoon. Notice that two rules mention O, so O is an important variable. The fourth rule:

> If pastels is scheduled for day 1 or day 2, then the lectures scheduled for the day immediately following pastels must be fresco and history, not necessarily in that order.

This is a complex conditional rule to diagram. Here is how we choose represent it (there are other effective ways):

$P_{1/2}$ → P [H/F]

If P is on day 1 or 2, then H and F will be scheduled for the next day H. Again, we used the vertical rectangle to encapsulate H; we do not know which slots they are in on that day.

If you had a lot of trouble diagramming this rule, you could simply write it out in your own words:

P 1 or 2 → day after P is F and H

This rule has a lot of impact on the game. For instance, looking at the interaction between this rule and rule 1, we see that when P is scheduled for day 1, O is not scheduled at all. This is because H and F will take up both slots on day 2, the only day that O can be seen.

Likewise, if P is scheduled in the morning on days 1 or 2, then either S or W will not be scheduled. This is because in this situation, P takes up one of the mornings and then either H or F takes up the morning of the next day. There will be only one morning left for both S and W, so at least one of those two will not be selected. These thought processes are recommended when first setting up a game, because they force you to analyze how the game works.

The contrapositive:

no $P\boxed{\begin{matrix}H\\F\end{matrix}} \rightarrow -P_{1/2}$

When H and F are not on the day following P, P cannot be on day one or day two. You do not need to diagram the contrapositive, but you should be aware of its meaning. Anytime H and F are not on the same day, or when they are on day 1, you know that P is not on day 1 or 2.

Before moving to the questions, notice that P, like O, is mentioned in several rules. Much of the game will center on those variables. No rules mention N so it can fill in slots that other variables cannot because it has no limitations. Circle it because it is a leftover:

F H L (N) O P S W

We do not have any ground breaking inferences, but some games are like that. Diagrams:

O↓

___ ___ ___

___ ___ ___ SW

1 2 3

no $\boxed{\begin{matrix}O\\L\end{matrix}}$ no $\boxed{\begin{matrix}P\\L\end{matrix}}$

$P_{1/2} \rightarrow P\boxed{\begin{matrix}H\\F\end{matrix}}$

12. Which one of the following is an acceptable schedule of lectures for days 1, 2, and 3, respectively?

(A) Morning: lithography, history, sculpture
Afternoon: pastels, fresco, naturalism

(B) Morning: naturalism, oils, fresco
Afternoon: lithography, pastels, history

(C) Morning: oils, history, naturalism
Afternoon: pastels, fresco, lithography

(D) Morning: sculpture, lithography, naturalism
Afternoon: watercolors, fresco, pastels

(E) Morning: sculpture, pastels, fresco
Afternoon: lithography, history, naturalism

This is a List question, so use the rules to eliminate the incorrect choices. Start with rule 1, because it is easy to see if O is scheduled on any day other than 2. This eliminates (C). Next, use rule 2 because you need only check the afternoon line of each choice with that rule. This eliminates (D) because W cannot be in the afternoon. Rule 3 eliminates (A). Finally, rule 4 eliminates (E) because P is on day 2 so H and F should be on day three. (B) is correct.

13. If lithography and fresco are scheduled for the afternoons of day 2 and day 3, respectively, which one of the following is a lecture that could be scheduled for the afternoon of day 1

This is a local Could be True question, one ripe for a mini diagram:

```
      L     F

___  ___   ___
```

L cannot be with O or P. This means that O is not placed, because L is on its only possible day. Also, P cannot be placed on day 2 because L is there. P also cannot be on day 1, because, according to the final rule, that would mean F and H were on day 2. F is actually on day 3. There is not much more we can derive from this mini-diagram. See which variable in the choices can be scheduled for the afternoon of day 1.

(A) history

This choice looks like it can work because we have no rules dealing with H other than rule 4, which is not in play here. Try filling in the rest of the mini-diagram by putting S and W in the mornings:

```
 H    L     F
 S    W
___  ___   ___
```

Our Leftover, N, can go on in the morning on day 3. This choice is correct, so select it and move on. For teaching purposes:

(B) oils

Rule 1 tells that O is limited to day 2 and it cannot be on the same day as L. (B) is not possible.

(C) pastels

When we first set up the mini-diagram, we realized that putting P in the afternoon of day 1 is not possible because it sets off the conditional in rule 4 and L and F are on the wrong days.

(D) sculpture
(E) watercolors

Neither S nor W can be in the afternoon (rule 2).

14. If lithography and history are scheduled for the mornings of day 2 and day 3, respectively, which one of the following lectures could be scheduled for the morning of day 1?

(A) fresco
(B) naturalism
(C) oils
(D) pastels
(E) sculpture

Local questions are common when there is not much structure given by the rules, because the local questions give you new, temporary rules that provide structure. This is a local Could be True question dealing with who can be in the morning of day 1.

Mini-diagram:

```
__    L    H
      __   __
```

Once again, L limits our placement of both O and P. O is not selected because L is on its only possible day, and P cannot be on days 1 or 2 because of L's placement.

Because the question asks about the morning of the first day, analyze that slot. Two of the three mornings are occupied due to the local rule, which means that only one of S or W will be placed. O is already left out of this solution, and we can only have two variables not placed. Therefore, one of S or W must be placed in the morning of the first day or we will not have enough variables to fill all six slots. Quickly scan the choices to find the one with S or W:

(E) sculpture

(E) is correct. If you did not have this realization about either S or W being placed based on the local rule, you would need to work all the choices. You can eliminate (C) and (D) immediately, for reasons already discussed. Now work (A). Let us try a mini or mental diagram with F in the morning on day 1:

```
F    L    H
__   __   __
```

From here, we can place P on day 3 and N on an evening:

```
     N    P
F    L    H
__   __   __
```

But S, W and O cannot be placed, meaning we are one lecture short. At this point, you should realize that F and N need to be in the afternoon and **one** of S or W must be in that morning slot. Next question:

15. If oils and lithography are scheduled for the mornings of day 2 and day 3, respectively, which one of the following CANNOT be scheduled for any day?

    (A) fresco
    (B) history
    (C) naturalism
    (D) pastels
    (E) sculpture

This local Cannot be True question asks us which lecture is not scheduled for any day. Here is a mini diagram based on the local rules:

```
__    O    L
      __   __
```

There is only one morning slot left, so either S or W will be left out, but we do not know which one. They are interchangeable, so neither can be the correct answer because **neither one must be left out**. Let us take a look at P because it is such a central variable. P cannot be in 1 or 2 because the slots for F and H are not free on the day after days 1 or 2. P also cannot be on day 3 because it cannot be with L. Therefore, P cannot be placed and

Choice (D) is correct. Spending time with your mini diagrams and local rules can help you solve some questions without more than a glance at the choices, especially questions that are as specific as "who is left out?"

16. If neither fresco nor naturalism is scheduled for any day, which one of the following must be scheduled for day 1?

    (A) history
    (B) lithography
    (C) oils
    (D) pastels
    (E) sculpture

This is a local Must be True question. Which lecture must be on day 1 given that neither F nor N is scheduled? F and N are flexible lectures, filling in slots that other lectures cannot. N has no rules that deal with it, so it can be placed anywhere and F is only limited when P is in 1 or 2, which has not occurred in a solution yet. So, we must place all the other variables: S W O P H L.

We know that P must be on day 3 because F is not placed, so we cannot set off the conditional in rule 4. Also, O is placed on day 2, its only possible day. This means that L must be in day 1, because L cannot be with either P or O. Choice (B) is correct.

Notice how the same variables – L, O and P – are the focus of most questions. O and P are in multiple rules, and in a game with little structure, you must focus on what you know.

17. If the lectures scheduled for the mornings are fresco, history, and lithography, not necessarily in that order, which one of the following could be true?

    (A) Lithography is scheduled for day 3.
    (B) Naturalism is scheduled for day 2.
    (C) Fresco is scheduled for the same day as naturalism.
    (D) History is scheduled for the same day as naturalism.
    (E) History is scheduled for the same day as oils.

This is a local Could be True question. The local rule tells which variables fill the morning slots. If F and H are both in the morning and therefore not on the same day, then P cannot be on day 1 or 2. Also, all the morning slots are taken, so both S and W are not placed. Therefore, all the other variables – O, N and P - are placed in the afternoon. P must be on day 3, O on day 2 and N on day 1:

```
N    O    P
L   F/H  F/H
—    —    —
```

We know that L must be on day 1 because it cannot be on the same day as O or P. F and H are interchangeable on days 2 and 3. We are close to a complete solution to the game, so it is easy to work the choices. Only (E) is possible.

*Combination Practice Game

Questions 19–24

A soloist will play six different guitar concertos, exactly one each Sunday for six consecutive weeks. Two concertos will be selected from among three concertos by Giuliani — H, J, and K; two from among four concertos by Rodrigo — M, N, O, and P; and two from among three concertos by Vivaldi — X, Y, and Z. The following conditions apply without exception:

If N is selected, then J is also selected.

If M is selected, then neither J nor O can be selected.

If X is selected, then neither Z nor P can be selected.

If both J and O are selected, then J is played at some time before O.

X cannot be played on the fifth Sunday unless one of Rodrigo's concertos is played on the first Sunday.

1. Which one of the following is an acceptable selection of concertos that the soloist could play on the first through the sixth Sunday?

	1	2	3	4	5	6
(A)	H	Z	M	N	Y	K
(B)	K	J	Y	O	Z	N
(C)	K	Y	P	J	Z	M
(D)	P	Y	J	H	X	O
(E)	X	N	K	O	J	Z

2. If the six concertos to be played are J, K, N, O, Y, and Z and if N is to be played on the first Sunday, then which one of the following concertos CANNOT be played on the second Sunday?

(A) J
(B) K
(C) O
(D) Y
(E) Z

3. If J, O, and Y are the first three concertos to be played, not necessarily in the order given, which one of the following is a concerto that CANNOT be played on the fifth Sunday?

(A) H
(B) K
(C) N
(D) P
(E) X

4. If O is selected for the first Sunday, which one of the following is a concerto that must also be selected?

(A) J
(B) K
(C) M
(D) N
(E) X

5. Which one of the following is a concerto that must be selected?

(A) J
(B) K
(C) O
(D) Y
(E) Z

6. Which one of the following is a concerto that CANNOT be selected together with N?

(A) M
(B) O
(C) P
(D) X
(E) Z

*Combination Practice Game Explanation

Game 1 (10/2 #19–24)

Variable Lists

Giuliani: H, J, K

Rodrigo: m, n, o, p

Vivaldi: X, Y, Z

Select two concertos from each composer and sequence them. With G and V concerto, if the one possibility is eliminated, then the other two must be chosen. The same is true for R with 2 eliminations.

Rule List

Rule 1: **n → J**

Contrapositive:

~~J~~ → ~~n~~

Rule 2: **m | Jo**

m will never be selected with J or o. It is most efficient to show this in this way as opposed to an if/then arrow because this format immediately implies the Contrapositive. Combining this with Rule 1 (n always goes with J), we see that m cannot be with n either:

m | Jon

M must be chosen with p (because it cannot be chosen with o or n) and H and K (because J is not chosen):

m → pHK

Rule 3: **X | Zpm**

Because m always brings p (inference of Rule 2), m can never go with x either. Notice that X and Z are never together, which means **Y must always be chosen.** Because X cannot be with p or m, it must be with n and o and n brings J.

X → noJ

Rule 4: **Jo → J... o**

Contrapositive: **o1 → ~~J~~ ~~n~~**

This is combined with the contrapositive of Rule 1.

le 5: **X5 → mnop1**

trapositive: **~~mnop1~~ → ~~X5~~**

Initial Central Diagram

There is not much to draw as an initial diagram: this game is all about understanding the rules and their implications.

1. Global, List

Use Rule 1 to eliminate A. Rule 2, C. Rule 3, D and E. B is correct.

2. Local, Cannot be True

Rule 4 states that J must come before o when they are both played, so o cannot be second.

3. Local, Cannot be True

Rule 5 says something about the 5th spot. If J, o and Y are the first three to be played, then o cannot be first and either J or Y must be first, so X cannot be played 5th. **E** is correct.

4. Local, Must be True

The Contrapositive of Rule 4 tells us that when o is 1, then J is not selected, meaning H and K must be. **B** is correct.

5. Global, Must be True

This is an inference from Rule 3. Y must always be selected.

6. Global, Could be True

We see this from our analysis of Rule 2: m cannot go with n.

Notes

Taking time with the rules and their inferences really paid off here and made the questions quick to work through.

can be obtained at www.ICGtesting.com

?2B/1317/P

9 780984 456925